An Important Message to Our Readers

This product provides information and general advice about the law. But laws and
procedures change frequently, and they can be interpreted differently by different
people. For specific advice geared to your specific situation, consult an expert. No
book, software or other published material is a substitute for personalized advice
from a knowledgable lawyer licensed to practice law in your state.

2nd Edition

E V E R Y

TENANT'S
LEGAL GUIDE

By Attorney Janet Portman & Marcia Stewart

Edited by Attorneys Ralph Warner & Mary Randolph

nolo.com
LAW FOR ALL

Keeping Up to Date

To keep its books up to date, Nolo issues new printings and new editions periodically. New printings reflect minor legal changes and technical corrections. New editions contain major legal changes, major text additions or major reorganizations. To find out if a later printing or edition of any Nolo book is available, call Nolo at 510-549-1976 or check our website: www.nolo.com.

To stay current, follow the "Update" service at our website: www.nolo.com. In another effort to help you use Nolo's latest materials, we offer a 35% discount off the purchase of the new edition of your Nolo book when you turn in the cover of an earlier edition. (See the "Special Upgrade Offer" in the back of the book.)
This book was last revised in **October 1999**.

First Edition	OCTOBER 1999
Illustrations	LINDA ALLISON
Cover Design	TONI IHARA
Layout Design	TERRI HEARSH
Production	LORI PACHECO
Index	THÉRÈSE SHERE
Proofreading	JOE SADUSKY
Printing	CONSOLIDATED PRINTERS, INC.

Portman, Janet.
    Every tenant's legal guide / by attorney Janet Portman & Marcia
Stewart. -- 2nd ed.
      p.   cm.
    Includes index.
    ISBN 0-87337-492-4
    1. Landlord and tenant--United States--Popular works.
 I. Stewart, Marcia. II. Title.
KF590.Z9P67 1999
346.7304'34--dc21

                              98-25916
                                CIP

For information on bulk purchases or corporate premium sales, please contact the Special Sales Department. For academic sales or textbook adoptions, ask for Academic Sales. Call 800-955-4775 or write to Nolo.com, Inc., 950 Parker Street, Berkeley, CA 94710.

Acknowledgments

Jake Warner deserves much of the credit for this book—so much, that we consider him more co-author than editor. Jake's creative ideas, boundless energy and enthusiasm inspired and sustained us.

Mary Randolph, a great friend and editor, worked her usual magic with her purple pen. Mary's writing and editing skills are unmatched.

Terri Hearsh, a long-time Nolo book designer, is always a delight to work with. She turned our manuscript into stylish, readable pages—and made it look so easy.

Several other Nolo friends and colleagues generously helped with this book:

Stephanie Harolde skillfully prepared the manuscript—draft, after draft, after draft—and offered many useful suggestions along the way.

Stan Jacobsen provided research assistance and cheerfully took on any task.

Naomi Starkman and Erica Etelson found and analyzed countless statutes, leaving no page unturned.

Barbara Kate Repa contributed many useful ideas on a wide variety of subjects including discrimination and privacy issues.

Robin Leonard shared her expertise on consumer credit and bankruptcy.

Toni Ihara designed the beautiful cover.

Jackie Mancusco gave lots of useful advice on renting in New York City.

We're also very thankful to people who provided their expertise on various aspects of landlord-tenant law, including the staff and members of the National Apartment Association and the Joint Legislative Committee of the NAA and the Multi-Housing Council; Mike Mansel of Insurance Associates of Walnut Creek, California; cable TV experts Carolyn Perkins and C.J. Hirschfield; and Volunteer Legal Services of the San Francisco Bar Association.

Finally, thanks to Linda Allison for her clever illustrations.

Table of Contents

4 Security Deposits

5 Discrimination

6 Inspecting the Rental Unit and Moving In

7 Roommates

8 Major Repairs and Maintenance

9 Minor Repairs and Maintenance

10 Making Improvements and Alterations

11 Your Right to Privacy

12 Injuries on the Premises

13 Environmental Hazards

14 Crime on the Premises

15 How Tenancies End or Change

16 Moving Out and Getting Your Security Deposit Back

17 Termination Notices Based on Nonpayment of Rent and Other Illegal Acts

18 Evictions: An Overview

Appendix I

State Laws and Agencies

Appendix II

Tear-Out Forms

Index

Introduction

Dealing with your landlord or property manager can be challenging, to say the least. Doing it successfully requires not only knowing the basics of landlord-tenant law, but also coping with your landlord's business policies and idiosyncrasies and keeping your cool at the same time you protect your rights.

This book is based on the view that your life will be much easier if you are both a responsible tenant and legally knowledgeable—that is, if you pay the rent on time and comply with your lease rules. If you are also savvy enough to send written requests when repairs are needed, your landlord is far more likely to make repairs quickly than if you're late with the rent or throw noisy parties that disturb other tenants.

That's why this book spends a good deal of space suggesting ways you can do business with your landlord, even a difficult one. If you know both the law and how the landlord business works, you can probably come up with problem-solving strategies that are in the landlord's best interest as well as yours. For example, if your landlord refuses your request to move in a roommate, first read about the legal occupancy limits that apply in your situation (Chapter 5). You may find that your unit is large enough for two, meaning that an absolute rule prohibiting roommates is illegal. Your next step might be to not only explain the legal realities to your landlord, but also to demonstrate that the person you want to bring in is creditworthy and meets or exceeds your landlord's criteria for selecting tenants.

But let's face it—even a conscientious and knowledgeable tenant can't always get good results. Some landlords are avaricious, petty and obnoxious, bent on extracting the last dollar from their tenants at the least possible cost to themselves. Trying to deal with them reasonably just doesn't work. If that sounds like your landlord, this book may become a combat manual, something you study closely to discover legal weapons to protect your rights. You'll probably find there is much you can do to fight back.

Be warned, however, that an attractive legal solution to every problem may not be possible. Even though the law is far friendlier to tenants than it was 25 years ago, the legal playing field in most states is still tilted in the landlord's direction. Landlords have powerful organizations that lobby state and federal lawmakers; the efforts of individuals or a few tenants' organizations are no match for them. And if you and your landlord become involved in a legal joust, the landlord, not you, is more likely to be able to afford an experienced lawyer.

Even if the law is 110% on your side, there are times when it won't make sense to do battle with your landlord. When dealing with difficult, unhappy people, avoiding conflict is often wiser than engaging in a drawn-out, costly and risky legal dispute. In the context of rental housing, you may simply want to find a new place to live, although it is often unpalatable to let a law-violating landlord call the shots.

We hope that by reading this book, you'll find the information you need to make an intelligent decision about whether to stay or go—and even better, that you'll learn strategies that will help you avoid these conflicts in the first place.

Icons Used in This Book

 Books or organizations that give more information about the issue discussed in the text.

 Related topics covered in this book.

 Slow down and consider potential problems.

 A tear-out copy of the form discussed in the text is in the Appendix.

 A practical tip or good idea.

 A rent control ordinance may address the issue discussed in the text.

Finding a Place to Rent

t goes almost without saying that choosing a place to live is an extremely important decision. A good apartment or house should provide more than shelter, warmth and a place to lay your head; it should be a true home. Yet many people make bad choices—spending too much money, picking the wrong location, landlord or neighbors, or settling on a place that's too small, dreary, noisy, unsafe or in bad shape. Sure, if you're in a tight rental market, such as those in New York City, San Francisco or Chicago, you can have an especially difficult time finding a good place to live at a reasonable price, but it's still possible to find decent housing.

Finding a good place to live is rarely a lucky accident. Whether rental housing is plentiful or scarce, there are specific steps you can take to find an apartment or house that meets your needs and budget. Most important, you need to take your time. One of the worst—and most costly—mistakes you can make is to sign a lease or put down a hefty deposit at the end of a long, frustrating day of apartment-hunting, only to realize later that the place is completely unsuitable. Even if it means staying with friends for a few weeks, finding a short-term rental or house-sitting arrangement, or (horrors) moving back in with your parents temporarily, it may be well worth it.

Whether you're looking for your first or tenth rental, living by yourself or with others, this chapter shows you how to find a good place to live within your price range, by:

- setting clear priorities before you start looking for a place to rent
- using a variety of resources to tap into available rentals, and
- beating the competition by pulling together the information landlords want to see—good references and credit information—before you visit prospective rentals.

This chapter also explains your legal rights and responsibilities regarding the rental application process, credit reports, credit-check fees and holding deposits.

If you're moving from one rental to another, be sure you understand all the legal and practical rules for ending a tenancy, getting your deposit returned and moving out. See Chapters 15 and 16 for details.

Check Your Credit Rating Before You Start Your Housing Search

Your credit report contains a wealth of information that landlords use to choose (or reject) tenants—for example, whether or not you have ever paid rent or bills late or been involved in a lawsuit. To make sure your credit report is clean—or to give yourself time to clean it up if there are problems or errors—get a copy of your report before you start looking. Section D provides complete details.

A. Setting Your Rental Priorities

While most people start their housing search with some general idea of how much they can afford to pay, where they want to live and how big a place they need, that doesn't guarantee good results. The best way to find an excellent rental home is to set specific guidelines in advance, being realistic, of course, both as to your budget and what's available for rent.

Here's our approach to finding a house or apartment you can afford and will enjoy living in:

Step 1: Firmly establish your priorities—such as maximum rent, desired location and number of bedrooms—before you start looking. The list of Rental Priorities, below, will help you do this.

If you're renting with one or more other people, review the Rental Priorities list together and make sure you agree on the basics. Always consider each person's strong likes and dislikes when you're choosing a rental. For example, you might care most about a modern kitchen and a sunny deck or patio. If so, you'll surely be miserable if you allow your spouse or partner to talk you into renting an older apartment with its original 1940s kitchen because it has a great view (but no deck).

Step 2: Once you've set your priorities, you'll want to see how prospective rental units measure up. To make this simple, we've prepared a Rental Priorities Worksheet, shown below. There's space for you to write down your mandatory ("must have") priorities, as well as secondary ("it would be nice, but aren't crucial") priorities and your absolute "no ways." Try to limit your mandatory priorities to those features your rental unit must have, such as "less than $750 a month rent," "two or more bedrooms," and "near the bus line to work." Take time developing your list of "no ways." Avoiding things you hate—for example, a high-crime area or noisy neighborhood—may be just as important as finding a place that meets all your mandatory priorities.

 A tear-out copy of the Rental Priorities Worksheet is in Appendix II.

Step 3: Once you complete the priorities section of the Worksheet, make several copies for use when looking at apartments or rental houses.

Step 4: Complete a Worksheet for each rental unit you're seriously considering, as follows:

- Enter the address, contact person, phone number, rent, deposit, term (month-to-month or year lease) and other key information on the top of the form.
- As you walk around the rental unit and talk with the landlord or manager, indicate the pluses and minuses and the mandatory and secondary priorities (as well as "no ways") that apply.
- Make notes next to a particular feature that can be changed to meet your needs—for example, "Rent is high, but space is fine for an extra roommate."
- Jot down additional features in the section for Other Comments, such as "Neighbors seem very friendly" or "Tiny yard for kids to play, but great park is just a block away."

Step 5: If at all possible (but it may not be, especially in tight rental markets), insist that any apartment or house meets at least your most important priorities.

Check Out All Important Conditions of the Tenancy

Leases and rental agreements cover many issues, such as the amount of rent and deposits, length of the tenancy, number of tenants and pets. In addition, some rental agreements may include provisions that you find unacceptable—for example, restrictions on guests, design alterations or the use of an apartment as a home office. Ask for a copy of the lease or rental agreement early on, so you are not reading it for the first time with a pen in your hand. Be sure to read Chapter 2 for details on leases and rental agreements and how to negotiate terms before you sign on the dotted line.

Rental Priorities

When you're making your list of priorities, consider these issues:

Rent

Figure out the maximum you can afford to pay. Be sure to include utilities and any additional charges such as for parking. As a broad generalization, you probably don't want to spend more than 25% to 35% of your monthly take-home pay on rent, but this will obviously depend on your expenses. Be careful about overspending—you don't want to live in a penthouse if it means you need to eat popcorn for dinner every night.

Deposits

Depending on state law and landlord practices, you may need to pay as much as two months' rent as a security deposit. (Chapter 4 covers security deposits.) If you have limited cash to pay deposits and other up-front fees, include the maximum you can pay in the Priorities list on your worksheet.

Location and Neighborhood

Where you live is often more important than the size and amenities of the unit you rent. If you know the exact area you want, list it. If you don't, think of the features that are important. If living in a low-crime area or being able to walk to bookstores, restaurants, athletic facilities or a kid-friendly park is important, don't end up renting a nicer apartment in a neighborhood with none of these features.

Schools

If you have school-age children, the proximity and quality of local schools are very important considerations. If you're new to the area, start by contacting your state department of education. It should be able to provide data for individual schools and districts, including academic test scores, enrollment figures, racial and ethnic information and even dropout rates. Your next step is to call and visit local schools and school districts to learn about class size, class offerings, instructional practices and services. Finally, check out resources, such as newspaper articles on the local school board or PTA at public libraries and online sites.

Work or School Commute

If you're looking at a potentially long commute, note the maximum times or distance you're willing to travel to and from work or school.

Ability to Work From Home

If you're planning to work from home, make sure local law or landlord policies don't prohibit your home-based business. See Chapter 2, Section D, for more information on this topic.

Public Transit

Do you need to be close to a bus line, subway, train or airport? Write it down.

Pets

If you have a dog, cat or other pet, you'll need to make sure the landlord allows pets. (See Chapter 2, Section D, for suggestions on how to negotiate with landlords who don't normally allow pets.)

Number of Tenants

If you want to live with an unusually high number of people, given the size of the rental you can afford, you must make sure the landlord will allow it. (Chapter 5 discusses occupancy standards many landlords set, limiting the number of tenants in a particular rental unit.)

Rental Term

Do you want the flexibility of a short-term rental agreement, or the security of a long-term lease? (Chapter 2 discusses the pros and cons of leases and rental agreements. Also, Chapter 15 discusses sublets, which may be a short-term rental option.)

Move-In Date

If you need a place immediately, write "Must be available now" in your priority list. But don't be too quick to pass up a great place that's not available for several weeks. It might be worth your while. (Remember the importance of patience.) Also, if a fantastic apartment is available now, but you have to give 30 days' notice on your current place, it might be worth paying double rent for a while, rather than give up a terrific apartment.

Rental Priorities (continued)

Number and Type of Rooms

How many bedrooms, baths or other rooms do you need? Do you need suitable space for your home office? Is a finished basement important—for your pottery studio or band practice or kids' playroom? Is a modern kitchen with lots of counter space and good light ideal? How about a large living room for entertaining? List what you can't live without.

Furnishings

If you want something completely furnished, make this a priority. Remember, however, you can always rent furniture yourself if you can't find a furnished apartment—in fact, it might be cheaper. A few calls to local furniture rental places will quickly give you the information you need.

Other Interior Needs

Other priorities may include good space separation for roommates, a fireplace, lots of closets, air conditioning or laundry facilities in the building. For some people, an ISDN or T-1 line for fast Internet access, or the right to have a dish for satellite TV are important. (Chapter 10 explains the limits your landlord may impose on installing satellite dishes.) If you need multiple phone lines for your fax and modem, make sure your building (and budget) can accommodate them. If you are disabled and have special needs, such as wheelchair accessibility, mark these as priorities. (For more on rights of the disabled, see Chapter 5.)

Type and Style of Building and Rental Unit

Do you have a clear idea of the type of place you want to live in? One-family house, duplex, six-to-ten-unit apartment building, high-rise or gated community? If you have your heart set on a flat in a Victorian house, a loft, a small cottage or a modern apartment with lots of windows and a great view, note that, too.

Security

For many people, a top-notch security system for the building and rental unit is important—for example, bars on all windows, a doorman or a front gate security system with intercom that allows you to screen visitors before they actually get to the front door of your apartment.

Quiet

If you can't stand the idea of living on a busy street with lots of traffic or in an apartment with paper-thin walls, make this a priority.

Yard and Outdoor Space

If you have a large dog or want room for a garden or for kids to play, a fenced-in yard will be important. Or maybe a deck, patio or balcony ranks high on your wish list.

Parking

Parking can be a critical consideration, especially if you live in an urban area. Write down how many vehicles you have and whether you need garage parking or easy street parking with no restrictions.

Other Tenants

While we'd all like quiet, considerate neighbors, you may prefer a building with certain types of tenants—for example, mainly seniors, college students, gays or families with children. While your landlord cannot deliberately choose tenants because they belong to these groups (and exclude others) without courting a lawsuit, sometimes renters tend to choose, on their own, certain properties. For example, affordable housing near a college will be filled with students, and pricey buildings in spruced-up business or financial areas are likely to be peopled with older, professional types.

Landlord and Manager

Maybe you don't want to share a duplex house with the landlord. Or you want a place with an on-site manager who's always available to make repairs.

Purchase Potential

If you want to move into a rental you can eventually buy, such as condo, co-op or lease-option-to-buy house, investigate this from the start. This book does not cover these options, so you'll need to check the real estate section of your bookstore or library (or online sites) for advice on the subject.

Rental Priorities Worksheet

Address: ___178 West 81st St., #4F___

Contact: ___Emily Greenwood (Broker)___   Phone #: ___(212) 555-1212___

Rent: ___$2,000/month___   Deposit: ___$2,000___   Other fees: ___$2,000 (broker's fee)___

Term: ___one year lease___   Date seen: ___February 15, 200X___ Date available: ___March 1, 200X___

Brief description of rental unit and building: ___Sunny two-bedroom apt. in four-story___
___brownstone. Small kitchen & bath. Lots of charm. Great location!___
___

Mandatory Priorities:

☒ _Upper West Side_

☐ _Maximum $1,800 rent_ (over our limit, but it's worth the price)

☐ _View of park_

☒ _Lots of light_

☒ _Two+ bedrooms_

☐ _Easy street parking_ (No—but inexpensive garage parking nearby)

☐ _____

Secondary Priorities:

☒ _Hardwood floors_

☒ _Small building_

☐ _Doorman_

☐ _Fireplace_

☐ _____

☐ _____

Absolute No Ways:

☐ _High-crime area_

☐ _Run-down area_

☐ _____

☐ _____

☐ _____

☐ _____

Other Comments: ___Neighbors seem very friendly. Noisy dog next door. Subway stop a___
___block away. Last vacancy was two years ago.___
___
___
___

B. How to Find an Apartment or House for Rent

In Section A, above, you did an important part of the job of finding a place to live by creating your list of Rental Priorities. Now you need a plan to find a place that matches it as closely as possible. Focus on your time and financial constraints and consider how they will influence your search. For example, the housing search of a well-paid single person with money in the bank who wants to move to a bigger apartment sometime in the next six months should differ tremendously from that of a graduate student on a limited budget with a small child who only has a few weeks to find a place before school starts.

What type of search will work best for you will also depend on a number of factors, most importantly where you want to live and whether you want a lease for a year or more or prefer a month-to-month rental agreement. In some cities, classified ads are your best resource. In others, you may want to work with a real estate broker or homefinders' agency. In all areas, it always makes sense to assertively and creatively use your own personal contacts and networks. Of course, the tighter the rental market you face, the more important it will be to pursue as many search options as possible. Here's a rundown of your choices.

1. Personal Contacts

If you know people who live or work near where you want to live, ask them for leads. Using personal contacts as housing scouts can be quite effective, because when people plan to move, friends, neighbors and business associates almost always know about it before a for-rent sign goes up. Prepare a brief description of exactly what you want (your rental priorities). Send this to friends, co-workers and fairly close acquaintances, including local business people with whom you have a friendly relationship—doctors, shopkeepers, lawyers and insurance brokers are all good bets. If your company has an employee grapevine (possibly part of your internal e-mail system), get the word out this way. Let as many people know of your housing search as possible. You never know who may come through with the perfect apartment—it might be the woman with the flower stand down the block or your dental hygienist.

See the sample Apartment-Hunting Note, below, for a good way to describe your housing needs and priorities.

Sample Apartment-Hunting Note

Dear Friends:

We're in the market for a new apartment and hope you can help. We're looking for a one- or two-bedroom place on the Upper West Side (close to the park would be terrific!). We can afford up to $1,800 per month. We'd like to move within the next few months, but definitely by April 1 when Hannah starts her new job.

It is important that the apartment be light and airy, in good condition and in a secure building (doorman preferred). Hardwood floors and a fireplace would be great. We eat out more than in, so a gourmet kitchen is not necessary. We don't have any pets but are thinking of getting a cat in the future, so we'd like a place that allows pets.

We have always been good tenants and can provide excellent references and credit.

If you hear about a rental unit that seems likely, please phone us at 609-555-3789 (home). Here are our work numbers:

Dennis: phone 609-555-2345; e-mail Dennis@work.com

Hannah: phone 609-555-4567; e-mail Hannah @work.com

Thanks so much for your help!

Regards,
Dennis Olson and Hannah Silver

2. Pound the Pavement

In addition to enlisting the help of friends, you can do much looking on your own. In some neighborhoods, landlords simply post "Apartment For Rent" signs in front of the building or in one of the windows. Others put notices on neighborhood bulletin boards, such as the local laundromat or coffee shop.

Many tenants find great apartments or houses to rent by posting their own "Apartment Wanted" signs (sometimes offering a finder's fee) in local stores or businesses, such as a dance studio, health club, or even an auto repair shop. You might also consider buying a classified ad in the daily paper or putting a notice in the newsletter of a community organization. Some enterprising tenants go so far as to track down the owners of houses that have been for sale for a long time, hoping to work out a rental arrangement.

If you want to live in a particular apartment building or complex, but there's no sign listed, stop by anyway and talk to the manager or doorman. (A generous tip might just do the job!) Also, try to talk with some of the other tenants. You might just get a good lead on someone who's planning to move soon. Spend a lot of time walking around the neighborhood you want to live in—this will give you a chance to meet local people who may know about available rentals before they're advertised.

Looking for a pet-friendly rental? Go to a local park or veterinarian's office and talk to people with animals. They may have some good leads.

3. Classified Ads

Many landlords advertise their rental units in the newspaper real estate classified ads. The largest section usually runs in the Sunday paper. The classifieds are usually organized by city or neighborhood and include basic information such as rent, location, number of bedrooms and baths and any special features such as a fireplace or view.

Get early editions of papers (for example, Sunday papers are available late Friday night in some areas) and start calling as soon as possible to get a jump on the competition. Better yet, go online. Many papers post their classifieds before the information hits the streets.

Classified ads run by landlords should never mention sex, race, religion, disability or age (unless the rental is really legally sanctioned senior citizens housing). Chapter 5 discusses the topic of discriminatory advertising.

4. Apartment-Finding Services

Many landlords list their rental property with a home-finders' service that provides a centralized listing of rental units for a particular geographic area. This can be a very efficient way to find listings, especially in big cities. Rather than call landlords one-by-one in response to classified ads, you can zero in on listings that meet your particular specifications. And apartment-finding services usually provide a lot more detail on rental units than classified ads.

Prices of apartment-finding services vary, but typically you'll pay a flat fee, such as $50 to $100 for a one-month membership. In some cases, you may need to actually visit the company's office to check out listings, but many services will fax or e-mail you daily updates of available rental units or provide you information over the phone.

Check newspaper ads or look in the Yellow Pages under "Apartment Finding and Rental Service." Many of the larger agencies have online sites.

Many homefinding services do a good job of helping people to find a place to rent, but some are sloppy and a few are actually crooked. For example, to get prospective tenants to fork over a hefty fee, several homefinding services have been caught running ads about imaginary apartments in good locations at low rents. When the new customers ask to see the unit, the answer is "So sorry, we just rented that apartment, but here's another one you will really like" (it just so happens to be a crummy place at a higher rent). Other problems include companies that sell outdated rental lists (most or all of the apartments have already been rented), or that have lists no different from what you could find in the newspaper.

So do a little investigating first. Talk with other home-seekers or check with the Better Business Bureau before you pay anyone a substantial sum to help you find a home. If you feel an apartment locator service has seriously misrepresented its service, ask for your money back and file a complaint with the consumer fraud division of your local district attorney's office.

Before you sign up with an apartment-finding service, be sure it's reputable and worth the money. The Apartment-Finding Service Checklist shown below, is one good way to organize and collect the information you need.

A tear-out copy of the Apartment-Finding Service Checklist is in Appendix II.

5. Real Estate Brokers

Some local real estate offices, especially in large cities, also handle rental properties, often exclusively for a property owner. If you're moving into a new area, especially someplace like New York City, or have limited time to apartment-hunt, real estate brokers can be very useful. A good broker should do lots of leg work for you. The more prepared you are (by setting priorities as we discuss in Section A, above), the more helpful a broker can be.

As with apartment-finding services, choose your broker carefully:

- **Get full information about all fees, which can be quite hefty.** In New York City, for example, real estate brokers often charge either a fee that is tied to the rent (for example, 15% of the first year's rent) or a flat fee of $1,000 or more for a rental. Sometimes, the property owner covers the real estate broker's fee, but typically the tenant pays.

Avoid brokers who try to pressure you into paying their fee before you sign a lease or rental agreement. Don't pay until the deal is final.

- **Ask about the type and exclusivity of the broker's listings**. Why pay a hefty fee if you can find the same place through a newspaper ad, or for a lower price through an apartment-finding service? And don't waste your time with a broker whose properties don't meet your needs as to neighborhood, type of unit or budget.
- **Choose a broker with lots of experience and a good reputation.** The best way to do this is through recommendations from people who have used the particular broker in the last few years and whose judgment you trust. Interview a few brokers and ask a lot of questions about their services, how long they've been in business and their knowledge of the area. Be sure to check if any complaints are on file with a local consumer agency or Better Business Bureau.

6. Management Companies

Property management companies often contract with landlords to rent units and manage all aspects of the rental property. In many areas, a handful of management companies control a significant number of rental properties. You can find the names of the bigger companies just by driving around and looking at signs posted outside apartment buildings. Or, check the phone book Yellow Pages under "Real Estate Management."

Apartment-Finding Service Checklist

Name of Company: __City Rentals__

Address: ___549 Main St., San Francisco___

Phone Number: __415-555-4477__

Hours: __Mon.-Fri., 9-7; Sat., 9-5; Sun., 11-4.__

Date: __March 17, 200X__

1. Description of listings:

   - geographic areas covered ___San Francisco___
   - type of rentals ___all kinds and price ranges___
   - total number of listings ___hundreds at any one time___
   - number of new listings/day ___20-50___
   - exclusivity ___often___
   - type of information available/listing ___50 different pieces of information/rental unit, including rent, deposits, number of bedrooms, parking, pet policies and neighborhood map.___

2. Type of access to listings, cost and duration of service:

   - ☐ phone _____
   - ☒ fax ___$95 for 40 days___
   - ☒ e-mail ___$95 for 40 days___
   - ☐ pager _____
   - ☒ books available in-office ___$65 for 40 days___

3. Free phone available in office for members' use?   ☒ Yes   ☐ No

4. Other services and costs:

   - ☐ roommate referrals _____
   - ☒ credit screening ___$25/credit report___
   - ☐ other _____

5. Percentage of members who find a rental unit through service: ___Don't know___

6. Refund if rental not found through company: ___$40 after 40 days___

7. Length of time in business: ___18 years___

8. Other comments: _____

You can usually approach management companies directly. When choosing a property management company, follow our advice on real estate brokers (discussed above).

💡 **Beat the competition by getting on a waiting list.** If you want to rent in a particular big complex and you have a little time, you may be able to prequalify and get on a waiting list for the next available rental unit. To convince the landlord to screen you now (and to allay his fears that he would be wasting his time because you'll probably end up living elsewhere before he has a vacancy), assure him that you are in no hurry and are not considering other properties.

7. University, Alumni and Corporate Housing Offices

College housing offices can be an excellent source of rentals, especially services geared to faculty members. If you want a short-term rental, you can often find places that never appear in the newspaper—for example, the home of a professor who's going on sabbatical for six months. If you're not affiliated with a university, try to find someone who is. The same holds true for housing offices available to employees of local corporations. And don't forget to check out your college alumni association. It may also provide information on rentals in the area (or you can contact fellow alumni for leads).

8. Online Rental Services

Computer-savvy renters may find their dream apartment online, by posting an "Apartment Wanted" notice in a local online bulletin board.

Also, there are many online rental services, which are especially useful if you are moving to a new area. One of the biggest online services is Rent.Net (www.rent.net), which represents nearly one million apartment units in the United States and Canada. Rent.Net's site includes details and photos on available rental properties, local maps, and relocation books on different areas.

Many regional apartment hunting services are also available for specific metropolitan areas.

9. Apartment Rental Guides or Magazines

Depending on where you're looking, publications such as *For Rent Magazine*, available at supermarkets and online, may provide useful information on local rentals, including photographs of the building and rental units.

Renting a Place When You're New in Town

If you're completely unfamiliar with the area you're moving to, you're at an obvious and serious disadvantage—you simply don't have the basic information normally considered essential to locating a good place in a congenial location at a fair price. Your personnel office at work or college housing office are good places to start. Also, check the local library or bookstore for area guidebooks. But there's no substitute for your own legwork. Ask your friends and colleagues, walk and drive around neighborhoods, talk to local residents and shop owners, read local newspapers, check the library's community resources file, visit the local planning department and chamber of commerce and do whatever else will help you get a better sense of a neighborhood or city. You can get a wealth of information on different geographic areas on the Internet and commercial online services. Also, a good real estate broker can be invaluable.

If you're in a hurry to move, one sensible alternative is to leave your furniture in storage and stay in a hotel or take a short-term furnished rental. Sure, this means moving twice, but it's far better than settling on an apartment or area that's not to your taste.

How to Find a Roommate

You may want to find a rental where current tenants need a roommate, or you may be looking for a roommate to share a rental you've found. Either way, there are lots of sources for finding roommates, including local newspaper ads and university housing offices. You may want to check out the roommate referral services often provided by apartment-finding services, or check the Yellow Pages under Roommate Assistance or Referral Services. For a fee (typically $50 or less), you can gain access to roommate-wanted listings tailored to your specifications. Many agencies will screen and match compatible roommates, based on detailed questionnaires you fill out; some serve primarily gay and lesbian tenants. Some groups—senior or religious organizations, for example—may keep lists or help you to find a compatible person. Section G, below, provides advice on choosing roommates.

C. Visiting Prospective Rentals

Everyone needs a home-hunting strategy—whether you make an appointment to see an apartment by yourself or attend an open house with dozens of others. Here are some basic tips:

Take your time. If you're looking at lots of apartments, schedule your appointments liberally, so that you give yourself enough time to see one place and move on to the next. You don't want to give prospective landlords or managers a bad impression by showing up late. Consider taking some time off from work so you can visit rentals as soon as they come on the market.

Be prepared. Come equipped with your own handy-dandy apartment-hunter's kit. Include a street map, notebook, pen or pencil, pocket calculator, tape measure (to make sure the living room is big enough for your carpet), graph paper and camera. (You may want to take pictures if it's okay with the landlord.) Most important, bring your list of Rental Priorities and complete the Worksheet as discussed in Section A, above. Don't forget your checkbook. (You may fall in love with a place and need to leave a holding deposit while the landlord checks out your credit history and references. Section F discusses holding deposits.)

Impress the landlord by showing up with everything you need to fill out a rental application, including references and credit information. (See Section D for more on these issues.)

Be on your best "good tenant" behavior. Clearly understand that while you're looking at a rental unit, the landlord or manager will be looking at and evaluating you. This means showing up on time, dressing neatly, and presenting yourself as being both conscientious and agreeable. (This also means keeping your love of drums to yourself.) Realize that landlords live in fear of overly demanding and fussy tenants who will give them constant headaches by ceaselessly complaining about trivial things. So while we recommend checking out the rental unit's condition (see below), and making sure significant defects are being remedied, it's usually a mistake to ask for a long list of upgrades and repairs before you're even offered the place. Better to save your requests until the landlord makes you an offer. But make sure you do your essential negotiating before you sign a lease or rental agreement.

Look around carefully for tell-tale signs of problems in the rental unit and building. While you don't want to come across as a nit-picking housing inspector with white gloves, do keep your eyes open. Don't broadcast your concerns (subtlety is a strong point here), but try to check as many of the following things as possible:

- Look for obvious damage, such as loose steps, torn carpet or shaky handrails.
- Check for dirt, mildew and signs of insects or rodents. (But try to overlook the sloppiness of a current tenant. Piles of dishes in the sink and mounds of clothes on the floor are only temporary.)
- Flush the toilet and run water in the shower and sinks. Check the water temperature and pressure.

- Make sure the windows and doors are in good shape, open and close easily and have secure locks.
- Walk around the building, checking out any elevators and common areas such as stairs, laundry rooms and lobbies as well as the parking area, garage and yard. Again, check for general cleanliness and repair. Good lighting is especially important in common areas.

At this point, you're just trying to get a general sense of the place. Ask yourself: Does this feel safe and comfortable? Clean and in good repair? If you decide you want the rental unit, and before you actually sign a lease or rental agreement, you will want to do a more detailed inventory of the condition of the rental unit, completing the Landlord-Tenant Checklist we recommend in Chapter 6. (You want your landlord to acknowledge any existing defects so he or she can't blame you later for causing them.)

If there are some minor problems, or improvements you want—for example, a new coat of paint in the living room—you may be able to negotiate with the landlord on this before you move in. (Chapter 2, Section B, shows how.) Major problems, such as lack of heat, may be the landlord's legal responsibility to fix. (For details on housing standards and landlords' responsibility to provide habitable housing, see Chapter 8.) Also, see Chapter 2 for information on disclosures landlords must tell prospective tenants, such as the presence of lead-based paint in the rental unit.

Think of creative ways to use space. You may need to compromise on the number and type of rooms in exchange for a great location or lower rent. Use your imagination or check out home design books and magazines for ideas on how to make the most of your living space. For example, you might be able to carve out a study at the end of an extra-large living room, using bookcases or screens to divide the space. Rolling carts with butcher block tops can add instant space to a kitchen with limited counters.

Find out about other tenants and the landlord and manager. Your prospective landlord will probably check you out pretty thoroughly (asking for references and getting credit reports); turn-around is not only fair play, but a good way to find out what it's like to live in your landlord's building. Visit the building after work and ask residents, especially the person whose unit you're considering, about pluses and minuses of living in the building. Inquire about security and noise in the building or neighborhood and if there are any problems regarding repairs and basic services such as heat and hot water. See if you can get a sense of the landlord's personality and style of operating. An excellent indicator of whether you can expect smooth sailing is to find out how often there are vacancies in the building and, in particular, how often your prospective landlord has had to evict tenants. A low rate of turnovers and evictions suggests that tenants like living there and that the landlord has chosen considerate, law-abiding renters who will be good neighbors.

Walk around the neighborhood. If you're not familiar with the area, check out restaurants, shops, local businesses and schools and bus, subway and train stops.

Report Bait-and-Switch Operations

If a rental unit is unavailable, inferior or higher priced than advertised, contact the consumer fraud division of the local district attorney's office. Such bait-and-switch advertising is clearly illegal, and many property owners have been prosecuted for such practices.

D. Rental Applications and Credit Reports

Once you find a place you like, you're part, but not all of the way home. First, you will probably be asked to fill out a rental application. Landlords use rental applications to screen potential tenants and select those who are likely to pay the rent on time, keep the rental in good condition and not cause problems. Conscientious landlords will insist on checking your references and credit history before signing a lease or rental agreement. You should be happy they do so. You'll probably have fewer problems with other tenants in the building if the landlord is strict about screening. Who wants to move into a great building where one tenant is dealing drugs, holding midnight rehearsals for her rock band or otherwise causing trouble that the landlord could have averted by proper screening?

1. Rental Applications

On a written rental application, you must provide information on your employment, income, credit history (including any bankruptcies), rental housing history (including evictions) and any criminal convictions. If you are self-employed, the landlord may require the last few years' tax returns and other documentation of income. It's legal to ask for your Social Security and driver's license numbers. Landlords may also ask for proof of eligibility to work under U.S. immigration laws; many landlords use Form I-9 of the Immigration and Naturalization Service. Under federal fair housing laws, landlords who ask for such immigration information must ask all

tenants, not just those whom they suspect may be in the country illegally. It is, however, illegal to discriminate on the basis of national origin. (See Chapter 5, Section A.)

A sample Rental Application is shown below, so that you can get an idea of the information you will need. It may be a good idea to complete this rental application and take it with you when you see a potential rental unit. This type of information is sure to impress a landlord.

 A tear-out copy of the Rental Application is in Appendix II.

Fill out applications only when you're truly interested. Don't waste your time (or money, if the landlord charges a credit-check fee) filling out a rental application unless you really want a place. If you are interested, but still want to keep your options open, go ahead and fill out an application. Don't worry that this will lock you into taking a place—only signing a lease or rental agreement does so.

How to Impress Prospective Landlords

Bringing the following information when you first meet prospective landlords will give you a competitive edge over other applicants:

- A completed rental application
- Written references from landlords, employers, friends and colleagues
- Current copy of your credit report.

a. Landlord References

Landlords usually want references from your current and previous landlords, and details on your rental history. In talking with your past landlord or manager, prospective landlords will ask the following types of questions:

Rental Application

Separate application required from each applicant age 18 or older.

THIS SECTION TO BE COMPLETED BY LANDLORD

Address of Property to Be Rented: ___178 West 81st St., Apt. 4F___

Rental Term: ☐ month-to-month ☒ lease from ___March 1, 200X___ to ___February 28, 200X___

Amounts Due Prior to Occupancy

First month's rent .... $___1,500___

Security deposit .... $___1,500___

Credit check fee .... $___30___

Other (specify): ___Broker's fee___ $___1,500___

TOTAL .... $___4,530___

Applicant

Full Name—include all names you use(d): ___Hannah Silver___

Home Phone: (609) 555-3789   Work Phone: (609) 555-4567

Social Security Number: 123-000-4567   Driver's License Number/State: NJD123456

Vehicle Make: Toyota   Model: Tercel   Color: White   Year: 1994

License Plate Number/State: NJ1234567

Additional Occupants

List everyone, including children, who will live with you:

Full Name	Relationship to Applicant
Dennis Olson	Husband

Rental History

Current Address: ___39 Maple St., Princeton, NJ, 08540___

Dates Lived at Address: May 1996–date   Reason for Leaving: New job in NYC

Landlord/Manager: Jane Tucker   Landlord/Manager's Phone: (609) 555-7523

Previous Address: ___1215 Middlebrook Lane, Princeton, NJ, 08540___

Dates Lived at Address: June 1990-May 1996   Reason for Leaving: Better apartment

Landlord/Manager: Ed Palermo   Landlord/Manager's Phone: (609) 555-3711

Previous Address: 1527 Highland Dr., New Brunswick, NJ, 08444

Dates Lived at Address: Jan. 1986–June 1990   Reason for Leaving: Wanted to live closer to work

Landlord/Manager: Millie & Joe Lewis   Landlord/Manager's Phone: (609 555-9999

Employment History

Name and Address of Current Employer: Argonworks, 54 Nassau St., Princeton, NJ

Phone: (609 555-2333

Name of Supervisor: Tom Schmidt   Supervisor's Phone: (609 555-2333

Dates Employed at This Job: 1983–date   Position or Title: Marketing Director

Name and Address of Previous Employer: Princeton Times

13 Junction Rd., Princeton, NJ   Phone: (609) 555-1111

Name of Supervisor: Dory Krossber   Supervisor's Phone: (609 555-2366

Dates Employed at This Job: June 1982–Feb. 1983   Position or Title: Marketing Assistant

Income

1. Your gross monthly employment income (before deductions): $ 6,000

2. Average monthly amounts of other income (specify sources): $

Note: This does not include my husband's income. See his application.

TOTAL: $ 6,000

Credit and Financial Information

Bank/Financial Accounts	Account Number	Bank/Institution	Branch
Savings Account:	1222345	N.J. Federal	Trenton, N.J.
Checking Account:	789101	Princeton S&L	Princeton, N.J.
Money Market or Similar Account:	234789	City Bank	Princeton, N.J.

Credit Accounts & Loans	Type of Account (Auto loan, Visa, etc.)	Account Number	Name of Creditor	Amount Owed	Monthly Payment
Major Credit Card:	Visa	123456	City Bank	$1,000	$500
Major Credit Card:	Dept. Store	45789	Macy	$500	$500
Loan (mortgage, car, student loan, etc.):					
Other Major Obligation:					

Miscellaneous

Describe the number and type of pets you want to have in the rental property: None now, but

we might want to get a cat some time

Describe water-filled furniture you want to have in the rental property:

Do you smoke? ☐ yes ☒ no

Have you ever: Filed for bankruptcy? ☐ yes ☒ no   Been sued? ☐ yes ☒ no

Been evicted? ☐ yes ☒ no   Been convicted of a crime? ☐ yes ☒ no

Explain any "yes" listed above:

References and Emergency Contact

Personal Reference: Joan Stanley   Relationship: Friend, co-worker

Address: 785 Spruce St., Princeton, NJ, 08540

Phone: (609) 555-4578

Personal Reference: Marnie Swatt   Relationship: Friend

Address: 82 East 59th St., #12B, NYC

Phone: (212) 555-8765

Contact in Emergency: Connie & Martin Silver   Relationship: Parents

Address: 7852 Pierce St., Somerset, NJ, 08321

Phone: (609) 555-7878

I certify that all the information given above is true and correct and understand that my lease or rental agreement may be terminated if I have made any false or incomplete statement in this application. I authorize verification of the information provided in this application from my credit sources, current and previous landlords and employers, and personal references.

February 15, 200X   *Hannah Silver*

Date   Applicant

Notes (Landlord/Manager):

- Did you pay rent on time?
- Were you considerate of neighbors (no loud parties; you cleaned up after your dog)?
- Did you make any unreasonable demands or complaints?
- Did you take good care of the rental property?
- In general, were you a good (ideally, great) tenant?

Extra-picky landlords may actually want to visit your current rental to see how it looks. If your place usually looks like a cyclone just hit it, either clean up or forget it.

b. Employer References

Conscientious landlords will usually want to speak with your current employer to verify your income and length of employment and to get a better sense of your character—for example, to see if you're a responsible person.

Before talking with a prospective landlord, your employer may require your written permission. Rental applications often include this type of authorization—see, for example, the bottom of the rental application included here.

c. Character References

Some landlords also want character references from people (non-relatives) who know you well. Here's an example of the type of letter that will help you beat the competition.

 Alert references. Make sure that all of your references know to expect a call from a potential landlord. Even better, get written references first. And obviously, only give out the names of people who know you well and who have positive things to say about you—anticipate the crafty landlord who asks for four references and calls only the fourth one on the list. If you had a horrible manager (in fact, that's the reason you're moving out), be prepared to explain the situation. Provide other character references to help bolster your case.

⚠ Complete all rental applications truthfully. Prospective landlords will be able to verify much of the information you give by ordering a credit report. Nothing will hurt your chances of getting a place more than lying.

2. The Importance of Your Credit History

Many landlords find it essential to check a prospective tenant's credit history with at least one credit reporting agency to see how responsible you are at managing money and whether you will be a reliable tenant who pays rent on time. This credit check can be the most important part of the rental application process.

A landlord can find out your credit history over the past seven years, including whether you have ever been:

- late or delinquent in paying rent or bills, including student or car loans
- convicted of a crime, or, in many states, even arrested
- evicted, or
- involved in another type of lawsuit, such as a personal injury claim.

A credit report will also state whether or not you have filed for bankruptcy in the past ten years.

If a landlord does not rent to you because of negative information in your credit report, or charges you a higher rent because of such information, he is legally required (under the federal Fair Credit Reporting Act, 15 U.S. Code §§ 1681 and following) to give you the name and address of the agency that reported the negative information. Landlords must tell you that you have a right to obtain a free copy of your file from the agency that reported the negative information. You must request it within 60 days of being rejected by the landlord. Landlords must also tell you that the credit reporting agency did not make the rejection decision and cannot explain it; and that if you dispute the information in the report, you can provide a consumer statement setting forth your position.

Sample Character Reference

February, 200X

To Whom It May Concern:

I am writing to recommend Hannah Silver for the rental unit you have available. I have known Hannah for ten years and I cannot recommend her too highly. You won't find a better tenant.

I know Hannah both as a close personal friend and a colleague. We first met in 1985 when I started work as a technical writer at Argonworks in Princeton. Hannah has been the marketing director at Argonworks since 1983.

Hannah is extremely reliable and responsible. She's not the type of person who will pay her rent late (or come up with excuses why she needs a few extra days), bother you about small things, annoy other tenants with loud music or generally cause you problems. I have been to her house many times and she is a meticulous housekeeper and very organized. She will take excellent care of your rental property.

Hannah is trustworthy, and she keeps her commitments. She has always worked 100% plus on marketing Argonworks products, consistently meets her deadlines and gives her best. She is a wonderful person to work with, a talented businesswoman and cooperative team player. I am confident that Hannah will be one of your best tenants.

All in all, Hannah is a fantastic person who will be greatly missed when she moves to New York City. My husband and I are both from New York City so we know how much she'll love living there.

I will be happy to provide further information about Hannah. If you have any questions, please feel free to call me at work (609-555-1232) or home (609-555-4578)

Sincerely,

Joan Stanley

Joan Stanley
785 Spruce St.
Princeton, NJ, 08540

How Far Can Credit Reporting Agencies Go?

Some landlords—especially those who rent luxury units or insist on long-term leases—may go beyond a routine credit report and ask a credit bureau to pull together detailed information about your character, general reputation, personal characteristics or mode of living. Credit bureaus may interview your neighbors, friends and associates to prepare this type of report.

Almost all such checks are considered "investigative consumer reports" under federal law (15 U.S. Code §§ 1681 and following). Legally, a landlord who requests a background check on a prospective tenant must:

- tell you within three days of requesting the report that the report may be made and that it will concern your character, personal characteristics and criminal history, and
- tell you that more information about the nature and scope of the report will be provided upon your written request. The landlord must provide this added information within five days of your request.

If you are turned down wholly or in part on information contained in the investigative report, the landlord must tell you this and give you the name and address of the agency that prepared the report.

a. Credit-Check Fees

It is legal in most states for a prospective landlord to charge you a fee for the cost of the credit report itself and the landlord's time and trouble. Any credit-check fee should be reasonably related to the cost of the credit check—$20 or $30 is common. If you think you're being charged too high a fee, call your city or district attorney's office for advice.

Be sure you understand the purpose of any fee you are charged and whether or not it it's any kind of guarantee that you will get the rental unit, such as a holding deposit.

Watch out for fraudulent credit-check fees. Some landlords have been known to take credit-check fees from several prospective tenants and never run the credit checks, pocketing the money instead. You can easily find this out by contacting a credit reporting agency as soon as you've been rejected by a landlord. As discussed above, you're entitled to a free copy of your credit report which should indicate who's requested your report recently. It is illegal for a landlord to charge a credit-check fee and not use it for the stated purpose. Problems can also develop if the landlord takes a long time to check a tenant's credit and the tenant, not knowing whether the rental will be approved, rents another place. To avoid these and other possible areas of dispute, it is wise to sign a brief agreement with a landlord, clarifying the purpose of any up-front fee and whether or not it will be refunded if you don't get the place. (See the discussion of holding deposits in Section F.) If you have any problems, contact your city or district attorney's office or a tenants' rights group for advice.

b. Check Your Credit Rating and Clean Up Your File

Because your credit report is so important, you should always check it before you start your housing search. This will give you the opportunity to correct or clear up any mistakes, such as out-of-date or just plain wrong information. It's all too common for credit bureaus to confuse names, addresses, Social Security numbers or employers. Especially if you have a common name (say John Brown), chances are good you'll find information in your credit file on other John Browns, or even John Brownes or Jon Browns. Obviously, you don't want this incorrect information given to prospective landlords, especially if the person you're being confused with is in worse financial shape than you are.

The three largest credit bureaus, with offices throughout the United States, are Experian (formerly TRW), Equifax and Trans Union. As mentioned above, you are entitled to a free copy of your report if you were denied credit (including a place to live) because of information in your credit report. If you live in Colorado, Georgia, Maryland, Massachusetts, New Jersey or Vermont, you are entitled to a free copy of your credit report once a year. In most states, however, you will have to pay a fee of up to $10.

There are certain circumstances that do entitle you to one free copy of your credit report. If you

- receive public assistance
- are unemployed and will be applying for a job in the next 60 days, or
- believe your file contains errors due to fraud, contact any one of the credit bureaus: Experian at 888-397-3742, www.experian.com; Trans Union at 800-888-4213, www.tuc.com; or Equifax at 800-685-1111, www.equifax.com.

Once you get your report, if you find errors, check your files at the other two agencies. You have the right to insist that the credit bureau verify anything that's wrong, inaccurate or out-of-date. Information that can't be verified must be removed.

If the credit reporting agency fails to remove inaccurate or outdated information, lists a debt you refused to pay because of a legitimate dispute with the creditor or reports a bogus lawsuit against you that was abandoned, you have the right to place a 100-word statement in your file, giving your version of the situation. Do so immediately.

If the credit bureau fails to cooperate, and the information is really wrong, contact the creditor that reported the information for help in getting it out. If that doesn't work, you have several options:

- Contact the Federal Trade Commission (FTC) for advice. Check the government section of your phone book or call the national office at 202-326-2222.
- Threaten to sue the credit reporting agency in small claims court. (Chapter 19 discusses small claims suits.)
- Complain to your Congressional representative, who might be able to put pressure on the FTC to fix your problem.

c. How to Deal With Problems in Your Credit Report

If your credit file shows negative but accurate information, or you have no credit history because you're a first-time renter and have never borrowed money or used a credit card, there are steps you can take to look better to prospective landlords:

- Get a creditworthy person to co-sign the lease or rental agreement. (See Chapter 2, Section F, for details on cosigners.)
- Pay a large deposit, or offer to prepay rent for several months. (Chapter 4 discusses security deposits and state limits.)
- Show proof of steps you've taken to improve bad credit—for example, your enrollment in a debt counseling group, your recent history of making and paying for purchases on credit and maintaining a checking or savings account.
- Get more positive references from friends, colleagues, employers and previous landlords.

For more information on obtaining your credit file, getting out of debt and rebuilding your credit, see *Money Troubles: Legal Strategies to Cope With Your Debts*, and *Credit Repair*, both by Robin Leonard (Nolo). Or contact Debt Counselors of America, reached at 800-680-3328.

E. How Landlords Reject Tenants

Federal and state antidiscrimination laws limit what landlords can say and do in the tenant selection process. (See Chapter 5.) Basically, a landlord is legally free to choose among prospective tenants as long as all tenants are treated more or less equally. For example, a landlord can probably refuse to rent to a smoker, as long as this no smoking policy applies to all tenants.

1. Permissible Reasons for Rejecting Tenants

A landlord is entitled to reject you for any of the following reasons:

- poor credit history, which leads the landlord to believe that you will be unable to pay rent
- income that the landlord reasonably regards as insufficient to pay the rent
- negative references from previous landlords indicating problems—such as property damage or consistent late rent payments
- previous eviction lawsuits
- convictions for criminal offenses, unless the conviction was for past drug use. (See Chapter 5 for a discussion of illegal discrimination on the basis of disability.)
- current illegal behavior, such as dealing drugs
- your inability to meet terms of the lease or rental agreement—for example, if you want to keep a pet and the landlord's policy is no pets
- more people than the landlord wants to live in the unit—assuming that the limit on the number of tenants is clearly tied to health and safety or legitimate business needs. (Chapter 5 discusses occupancy limits.)
- untruthful responses on the rental application.

2. Illegal Discrimination

Antidiscrimination laws specify clearly illegal reasons to refuse to rent to a tenant. The federal Fair Housing Acts (42 U.S. Code §§ 3601-3619) prohibit discrimination on the basis of race, color, religion, national origin, gender, age, familial status (children), physical or mental disability (including alcoholism and past drug addiction). Many states and cities also prohibit discrimination based on marital status or sexual orientation. (Chapter 5 discusses illegal discrimination and how to file a complaint with a fair housing agency.)

Also, landlords risk violating the law if they screen certain categories of applicants more stringently than others—for example, requiring credit reports or a higher income level only from racial minorities.

F. Finder's Fees and Holding Deposits

Almost every landlord requires tenants to give a substantial security deposit. The laws concerning how much can be charged and when deposits must be returned are discussed in Chapters 4 and 16. Here we discuss some other fees and deposits that are occasionally required.

1. Finder's Fees

Real estate brokers and apartment-finding services may legitimately charge a fee for their services. And there's nothing wrong with a landlord charging you for the actual cost of performing a credit check.

Less legitimate, however, is the practice of some landlords, especially in cities with a tight rental market, of collecting "finder's fees" just for renting the place to a tenant. Unlike brokers or services, which actually do some work for their money, a finder's fee charged by a landlord just for the privilege of being offered a rental is nothing short of a rip-off. You should suspect this ploy if you're told to pay a finder's fee directly to the landlord or management company to get a particular unit. You should also be suspicious if you're directed to pay a finder's fee to an apartment locator "service" set up by the landlord as a front to collect the fee (as opposed to really being in the business of locating apartments).

What can you do about this blatant nonsense? If the rental is a good one and the fee something you can afford without too much pain, perhaps it's in your best interests to shut up and pay up. However, if you want to challenge this "pay me for nothing" fee, consider the following avenues:

Read your state's security deposit statutes and the cases that have interpreted them. (The citations are found in "Citations for State Laws on Security Deposits" in Appendix I; Chapter 20 explains how to find cases that explain statutes.) If your state prohibits nonrefundable security deposits (security deposits are explained at length in Chapter 4), look

for a case where the judge ruled that the term "security deposit" includes a finder's fee. Since the fee is kept by the landlord, a landlord who collects a finder's fee violates the statute. This theory was used successfully by a group of tenants in California. (*People v. Sangiacomo,* 129 Cal. App. 3d 364 (1982).)

Sue in small claims court. You might argue that you're being forced to pay for a nonexistent service —in legalese, it's a case of fraud. You could also point out that it's a matter of bait-and-switch: Charging a finder's fee is the same as charging a higher rent for the first month, which your landlord probably has not made clear in ads for the place. (Chapter 19 gives advice on using small claims court.)

Contact your city attorney or district attorney's office (consumer fraud unit) for advice, or your local rent control board. Especially in areas with rent control, finder's fees may be illegal by statute or court decision.

2. Holding Deposits

Sometimes, if you make a deal with a landlord but don't actually sign a lease or rental agreement, she will want some type of cash deposit, then and there, to hold the rental unit. This might happen when the landlord wants time to do a credit check or call your references. Or it can happen if you need to borrow money (or wait for a paycheck) to come up with enough to cover the rent and security deposit. For example, a landlord might ask for $500 cash to hold the place for you until you bring your first month's rent and any deposits you agreed on, pending the results of a credit check.

If you give a landlord a holding deposit and later decide not to take the place, there is a good chance you won't get most or all of your deposit back. So be sure you really want the place before making this kind of deposit. The laws of most states are unclear as to what portion of a holding deposit a landlord can keep if a would-be tenant changes his mind about renting the property or doesn't come up with the remaining rent and deposit money, or if

Receipt and Holding Deposit Agreement

This will acknowledge receipt of the sum of $__500__ by __Jim Chow__

_____ (Landlord) from __Hannah Silver__

_____ (Applicant) as a holding deposit to

hold vacant the rental property at __178 West 81st St., #4F, New York City__

_____,

until __February 20, 200X__ at __5 P.M.__. The property will be rented to Applicant

on a __one-year__ basis at a rent of $__2,000__ per month, if Applicant

signs Landlord's written __lease__ and pays Landlord the

first month's rent and a $__$1,500__ security deposit on or before that date, in which

event the holding deposit will be applied to the first month's rent.

This Agreement depends upon Landlord receiving a satisfactory report of Applicant's
references and credit history. Landlord and Applicant agree that if Applicant fails to sign
the Agreement and pay the remaining rent and security deposit, Landlord may retain of
this holding deposit a sum equal to the pro-rated daily rent of $__67__ per day
plus a $__35__ charge to compensate Landlord for the inconvenience.

__February 16, 200X__   _Hannah Silver_ _____
Date   Applicant

__February 16, 200X__   _Jim Chow_ _____
Date   Landlord

your credit doesn't check out to the landlord's satisfaction. And even if the law does limit the landlord to keeping a "reasonable" amount (often based on how long the unit was kept off the market), you may have to go to small claims court to force the landlord to actually return your money.

In California, for example, the basic rule is that a landlord can keep an amount that bears a "reasonable" relation to the landlord's costs—for example, for more advertising and for prorated rent during the time the property was held vacant. A California landlord who keeps a larger amount may be sued for breach of contract. A few states, such as Washington, require landlords to provide a receipt for any holding deposit and a written statement of the conditions under which the fee or deposit is refundable.

Most states, however, do not have specific laws on holding deposits. So, whatever you and a landlord agree on, such as your right to get half of the holding deposit back if you decide not to take the place within a certain number of days, be sure to write your agreement down. Include:

- the amount of the deposit
- the dates the landlord will hold the rental property vacant
- the conditions for returning the deposit or applying it to the security deposit.

Also, be sure you and the landlord understand what is to happen to the deposit when you take the place. Usually, it will be applied to the first month's rent. To make this clear, have the landlord give you a receipt for the deposit and have her write on the receipt what is to happen to the deposit when you come back with the rent.

A sample Receipt and Holding Deposit Agreement which you might want to adapt to your own situation is shown above.

 Appendix II includes a tear-out copy of the Receipt and Holding Deposit Agreement.

G. Choosing Roommates

The greatest place in the world won't make up for an obnoxious, inconsiderate or financially irresponsible roommate. Whoever you live with, make sure you're compatible, particularly with respect to issues such as neatness and privacy needs.

The Odd Couple: It Works in the Movies, Not in Life

While it may seem obvious that you should take time and care in choosing a person to live with, the number of roommate spats (and advertisements for replacements) proves that many people don't put this wisdom into practice. To keep the peace, make sure you're in synch on the following issues:

- neatness
- financial responsibility
- privacy
- noise
- amount of entertaining, including overnight guests
- pets
- food tastes and sharing
- political preferences or strong personal beliefs
- children
- smoking.

Whether you're filling out an application with an agency that matches roommates, or responding to a "Roommate Wanted" notice on a campus bulletin board, be honest and try to make sure you're getting clear answers from prospective roommates. It might sound excessive, but checking references is usually a good idea. (If you don't think so, rent the movie *Single, White Female* some night.) Talk to former landlords and other roommates, following our advice in Section D on how landlords screen tenants.

Before you move in with roommates, it's always a good idea to make a written agreement of important issues, including rent, cleaning, food sharing and overnight guests. No, this isn't overkill—after all, you routinely sign an agreement with the landlord, whom you won't see a fraction as often as a roommate. Roommate referral services often have form agreements or you can use the sample co-tenant agreement in Chapter 7.

 Always know your legal status when you move into an existing rental with roommates. Are you a full-fledged co-tenant (having signed the lease or rental agreement) or a subtenant (responsible to the other tenant, not the landlord)? You have very different legal rights and responsibilities depending on your status. (See the detailed discussion of roommates in Chapter 7.) ■

Leases and Rental Agreements

The lease or rental agreement you and your landlord sign defines your legal relationship. It is a contract in which:

- you agree to pay rent and abide by other terms (such as no pets and no additional roommates), and
- your landlord agrees to provide you with a place to live, often with a number of listed amenities.

If you don't pay rent, or you violate another contract provision, the landlord will have grounds to end your tenancy. If your landlord violates a lease or rental agreement term, you also have certain rights. Depending on the situation, you may have the right to break the lease or sue the landlord for damages.

Because it is so important, you should never sign a lease or rental agreement until you understand what's in it. Also remember that, unlike a tax return, there is no one officially blessed form, so you can negotiate terms with your landlord.

This chapter discusses the key provisions typically included in leases and rental agreements, and explains the differences between these two documents. We highlight terms that are unfair to tenants and show how to bargain for better provisions when you start a tenancy, and know when to turn down an agreement altogether.

A. How Written Leases and Rental Agreements Differ

Leases and rental agreements usually look so much alike they can be hard to tell apart. Both cover nitty-gritty issues, such as the amount of rent and deposits you must pay and the number of people who can live in the rental unit. The primary difference between the two is the length of the tenancy. A rental agreement lasts only from one month to the next, while a lease almost always covers a longer, fixed term. It's crucial that you understand this difference because it affects not only how long you can stay, but, even more important, the strength of your bargaining position if you and your landlord get into a dispute.

1. Month-to-Month Rental Agreement

A written rental agreement provides for a tenancy for a short period of time, usually one month. The law refers to these agreements as periodic or month-to-month tenancies, although it is usually legal for landlords to base rental agreements on other time periods—for example, if the rent were due every two weeks.

A month-to-month rental agreement is automatically renewed each month unless you or your landlord gives the other the proper amount of written notice (typically 30 days) to terminate the agreement. A landlord can also raise the rent or change other terms of the month-to-month rental agreement with proper written notice. (Chapter 15 discusses these changes.)

If you live in an urban area with a tight rental market, where new tenants are easy to find, you may be offered a rental agreement. Landlords sometimes prefer to use a rental agreement because it:

- gives them the right to raise the rent as often as they wish (unless there is a local rent control ordinance), and
- usually allows them to easily get rid of problem tenants without the need to give a reason, because in most states, rental agreements can be terminated for no reason.

But of course, not all landlords think this way. Some wisely prefer to find and keep good long-term tenants, and avoid the hassles of new tenants coming and going—even if it means less flexibility in terms of increasing rent or terminating the tenancy.

2. Fixed-Term Lease

A lease is a contract that obligates both you and the landlord for a set period of time, usually a year. With a lease, your landlord can't raise the rent or change other terms of the tenancy until the lease runs out, unless the lease itself provides for an increase.

Many landlords prefer the stability of renting to long-term tenants. As a result, landlords who use leases will probably take an extra measure of care when choosing tenants who will be around for a while. Sometimes external factors influence the landlord's choice. If you live in an area with a high vacancy rate or where it is difficult to find tenants for a particular season of the year—for example, a college town, where most students are gone during the summer, or a resort town, where residents leave for part of the year—many landlords insist on a fixed-term lease, usually for one year. Single-family houses are likely to come with leases, since the landlord will want to minimize the number of times it must be prepared for new tenants. Preparing an apartment, by contrast, is not as big a job.

A lease has a definite beginning and ending date. Your landlord can't force you to move out before the lease term expires unless you fail to pay the rent or violate another significant term of the lease or state law, such as repeatedly making too much noise, damaging the rental unit or selling drugs on your property. (Chapter 18 discusses evictions for lease violations.)

What happens when a lease expires? At the end of the lease term, your landlord may decline to renew the lease, or may opt to negotiate with you to sign a new lease with the same or different terms. If you stay and keep paying monthly rent, most states will consider you a month-to-month tenant renting under an oral lease. (Chapter 15 discusses what happens at the end of a lease period.)

3. Lease or Rental Agreement: What's Better for You?

You may not have the bargaining power to insist on one arrangement (lease or rental agreement) over the other. But you'll want to recognize situations in which a rental agreement or lease is a clear necessity or a definite problem.

For example, if you may want to move soon, you'll prefer the flexibility of a rental agreement. But if you plan to stay put for the foreseeable future, it's often better to have a lease, because of the security it provides. There is the enormous practical advantage to having the right to occupy your rental unit for an extended time. If you ask for needed repairs or protest unreasonable landlord conduct (for example, entering your home without notice when there isn't an emergency), the landlord can't respond by giving you a 30-day notice to move—something that's generally allowed if you have a month-to-month tenancy. (If your state protects you against landlord retaliation, you can fight a spiteful landlord, but it will cost you time and money.) Even if your landlord decides to sell the property halfway into the lease, the new owner usually must honor existing leases.

Should you feel nervous about seeing your future (or at least one year of it) set in concrete by virtue of a lease, you can relax. Most leases don't lock you in nearly as much as you might think. If you need to break your lease before the term ends, you can often avoid or substantially limit your financial obligation. In most states, the landlord must try to find another suitable tenant as soon as is reasonably possible in order to "mitigate" (minimize) the loss suffered as a result of a broken lease. If the landlord re-rents the unit fairly quickly, your financial exposure may not be that great.

Chapter 15 discusses state laws prohibiting retaliation, the impact of a rental property sale on tenants and how to break a lease as painlessly as possible.

Rent control gives you many of the protections of a lease. If your unit is covered by a local rent control ordinance that limits the landlord's ability to raise rent or terminate the tenancy without a good reason, your need for the protection a lease provides is lessened. On the other hand, many rent control ordinances do allow some rent increases—for example, if the landlord's operating costs, such as taxes and bonds, have risen. Also, rent control ordinances usually allow a landlord to evict a tenant in order to move himself or a relative in or to make certain repairs. A lease normally protects you against these dangers. (Chapter 3 discusses rent control.)

Lease With Option to Purchase

If you want to buy a single-family rental, especially in a rising market, and you expect to stay in the area and have more money soon, consider a lease-option. It's a possibility if your landlord wants to sell you the rental house, and you're in general agreement about the price and terms, but can't come up with the necessary financing now. Here are the basics.

Under a lease-option contract, you lease a house for a set period of time—usually from one to five years—and get the right (option) to buy the house for a price established in advance.

The rent you pay may increase during the contract term. In addition to rent, you pay some money for the option: a lump sum payment at the start of the contract, or in the form of higher-than-market rent.

You may pay only a few dollars—or thousands—for tying up the property with the option. You are not entitled to a refund of your option fee or any refund in rent if you do not exercise the option.

Depending on the terms of the contract, you can exercise the option to buy the property:

- at any time during the lease period
- at a date specified in the contract, or
- when another prospective buyer makes an offer on the house. The owner must give you a chance to match the offered price.

Nolo's Tenant-Friendly Forms

Nolo has developed standard lease and rental agreement forms that are clearly written and fair to both landlords and tenants. If your landlord does not give you a written lease or rental agreement, or hands you one that is clearly unfair, you might suggest using Nolo's forms.

Our forms (on paper and disk) are available in *Every Landlord's Legal Guide*, by Marcia Stewart, Ralph Warner and Janet Portman. Also, Nolo's small book, *Quick and Legal Leases and Rental Agreements*, by Marcia Stewart and Ralph Warner, has tear-out forms. *LeaseWriter*, Nolo's interactive software, lets you write a lease or rental agreement that complies with the legal requirements of your state. (An order form is in the back of this book.)

B. Oral Leases and Rental Agreements

Oral leases or rental agreements are perfectly legal for month-to-month tenancies and, in most states, for leases of a year or less. If you have an oral lease for a term exceeding one year, it becomes an oral month-to-month agreement after the first year is up.

Under an oral understanding, the period between rent payments typically determines how much notice your landlord must give you before increasing the rent or terminating your tenancy. For example, if you pay monthly, you are entitled to 30 days' notice.

1. Should You Use an Oral Rental Agreement?

While an oral agreement is legal and enforceable, it's usually unwise to rely on one. You don't necessarily need a full-blown complicated legal document, especially if you know and trust your landlord, but you should at least get the basic terms in writing. If you want long-term security from rent increases and termination of tenancy, you'll most certainly prefer a fixed-term lease of one year or more. And even with month-to-month rental agreements, you'll want the clarity of having everything written down.

Oral agreements often lead to disputes. As time passes, people's memories (even yours) have a funny habit of becoming unreliable. And you can almost count on your landlord forgetting key agreements—for example, an oral promise that there would be no rent increase the first six months or that your unit would be completely repainted within 60 days. And with oral agreements, other important issues—for example, your landlord's policies on returning security deposits—probably won't be discussed at all. If you and your landlord disagree about a particular policy or procedure, you will not be able to settle it by referring to your written agreement. Instead, you are likely to end up in court arguing over who said what to whom, when and in what context.

2. How to Make Oral Understandings Binding

An effective way to lock in your landlord's oral promises is to write a letter of understanding, in which you relate your understanding of what was discussed and agreed to, and invite the landlord to respond if he feels that you have misrepresented the conversation and conclusion. Whether you hand-deliver the letter to the landlord, mail it return-receipt requested or mail it first class, the laws in most states will presume that your landlord received the letter and agrees with your version unless you promptly hear otherwise. If you hear nothing back, and the landlord fails to make good on his promise and you end up in court, your letter should help you prove your version of the facts. It's almost as good as getting the promise into a lease or rental agreement. (See the sample Letter of Understanding in Section C, below.)

C. Typical Provisions in Leases and Rental Agreements

Here are the most important provisions found in most leases and rental agreements. Unfortunately, these are often dressed up with legal frills and froufrous (like calling the landlord the "party of the first part") or buried in paragraph-long sentences. Hang in there and follow along with the lease your prospective new landlord has given you. We'll strip pretentious phrases and verbose clauses down to their usually simple legal meanings.

If you run across terms or whole clauses not discussed here, get more information before you sign. Tenants' rights groups, which exist in many areas, will be able to answer your questions. Or, if you're signing a long-term lease for a valuable property, you may even want to see a lawyer. (See Chapter 20 for how to find and work with an attorney and do your own legal research, including online resources.)

If you are protected by rent control, there will be additional information in your lease or rental agreement, such as the name and address of the rent control board, a citation to the ordinance itself and sometimes basic information on how to enforce your rights under the ordinance. (Chapter 3 provides details on rent control.)

1. Identification of Landlord and Tenant

Every lease or rental agreement must identify the tenant and the landlord or the property owner—often called the "parties" to the agreement. The tenant may be referred to as the "lessee" and the landlord as the "lessor."

Any competent adult—at least 18 years of age—may be a party to a lease or rental agreement. A teenager who is under 18 may also be a party to a lease in most states if she has achieved legal adult status through a court order (called emancipation), military service or marriage.

Landlords typically want all adults who will live in the premises, including both members of a couple, to sign the lease or rental agreement. Doing this makes everyone who signs responsible for all terms, including the full amount of the rent.

To remind tenants of this rule, many leases and rental agreements state that all tenants are "jointly and severally" liable for paying rent and abiding by terms of the agreement. This bit of legalese means that each tenant is legally responsible for the whole rent, and that the misdeeds of one tenant—for example, keeping a pet in violation of a no-pets clause—will allow the landlord to evict all of you.

Chapter 7 provides complete details on tenants and co-tenants, including the concept of joint and several liability, what to do if your co-tenant disappears or is asked to leave by the landlord and tips on how to present a new, prospective co-tenant to your landlord.

2. Identification of the Premises

Your lease or rental agreement will state the address of the property being rented (often called "the premises") and should provide details on any furnishings, parking space, storage areas or other extras. In addition, your landlord may require you to sign a separate inventory of the rental furnishings, as discussed in Chapter 6.

Some lease or rental agreements also specify that you will use the premises as your "primary residence." This condition would exclude, for example, the tenant who lives primarily with his girlfriend but wants some private space now and then, or the businessperson who travels to the same city a few times a month and needs a regular home away from home. From a landlord's point of view, the primary residence requirement makes sense because landlords worry that:

- You won't pay the rent on time if you are responsible for rent or house payments elsewhere.
- A home that is infrequently occupied will not be kept up with the same care as you would give a steady residence, and

- A vacant unit will be an easy mark for a burglary.

If in fact your rented home will *not* be your primary residence, you'll need to think about how to deal with this issue. If the landlord lives at a distance and you are sure that you can always pay the rent on time, you might decide to take a chance and remain mum. But if your landlord or manager lives nearby or is often on-site, your absence will be noticed. As long as you always pay rent on time, every time, your tenancy probably won't be terminated—especially if you let the landlord know when you will be out of town for extended periods of time. In fact, this type of notification might even be a lease requirement or a state law. (See subsection 17, below.)

Suppose now that your landlord lets you stay, knowing full well that you're in violation of the "primary residence" provision. If the landlord decides to terminate your tenancy on this ground many months down the line, it may be too late. If you fight an eviction action you may be able to convince a judge that since your landlord knowingly let you stay, she waived her right to enforce that provision.

3. Restrictions on Home Businesses

If you are one of the over 20 million Americans who run a business from your house or apartment, make sure your lease or rental agreement doesn't specify that the premises are "for residential purposes only." If you're working alone or your job primarily consists of making phone calls or using your computer, you've probably got nothing to worry about. But if clients or deliveries will be coming on a regular basis, you'll want to discuss the issue with your landlord. Obviously, you don't want to print stationery or business cards listing your new address only to be given notice to move based on your violation of your agreement.

Your landlord's concern will rise especially if neighboring tenants will be inconvenienced. Where will your visitors park, for example? Will your piano students disturb the neighbors?

A landlord who does allow you to run a business from your rental unit may require that you maintain certain types of liability insurance. That way, the landlord won't wind up paying if someone gets hurt on the rental property—for example, a business customer who trips and falls on the front steps. Also, be aware that if you use your residence as a commercial site, the property may need to meet the accessibility requirements of the federal Americans with Disabilities Act (ADA). For more information on the ADA, contact the Department of Justice, Office on the Americans with Disabilities Act, Civil Rights Division, 1425 New York Avenue N.W., Suite 4039, Washington, DC 20005; 202-307-2227; 800-514-0383; FAX 202-307-1198.

Finally, even if it's okay with your landlord, your home-based business may violate local zoning laws restricting the type of businesses allowed (if any) in your residential neighborhood. The ordinances are often vague as to the type of business you can operate—for example, many allow "traditional home-based businesses," whatever they are. They are usually tighter when it comes to:

- restricting the amount of car and truck traffic the business can generate
- barring outside signs
- prohibiting employees or at least limiting their number, and
- setting a limit on the percentage of the floor space that can be devoted to the business.

In Los Angeles, for example, dentists, physicians (except for psychiatrists) and unlicensed massage therapists may not operate home offices. In addition, photo labs and recording studios are banned.

4. Limits on Occupants

You probably encountered your landlord's occupancy policy (the limit on the number of occupants for your unit) when you visited the rental. Many landlords limit occupants in the lease or rental agreement to remind tenants that they may not bring in additional roommates without permission.

Occupancy limits are legal as long as they are tied to health and safety needs, such as the size and number of bedrooms, or the landlord's legitimate business needs, such as limitations of the plumbing or electrical systems. They are not legal if based on the age or sex of the occupant or the whim of the landlord. For example, restricting a spacious two-bedroom flat to one occupant would be illegal under federal law if it were imposed because the landlord simply preferred to have fewer people living on the property.

Landlords cannot use overcrowding as an excuse for refusing to rent to tenants with children. Discrimination against families with children is illegal, except in housing reserved for senior citizens only. (Chapter 5 discusses antidiscrimination laws.)

 Occupancy policies are explained in detail in Chapter 5.

5. Guest Policies

Most landlords do not want people living in their building unless they are full-fledged tenants who have been screened and approved, and who have signed the lease or rental agreement. There are several reasons for this:

- More people cause more wear and tear; if there are more permanent residents living in the unit, landlords want to increase the rent.
- It's harder for landlords to get unauthorized occupants to pay for rent or repairs.
- Unapproved residents can create legal hassles in the event of an eviction.

To deal with these potential problems, some landlords go so far as to set a time limit for guest stays, such as no more than ten days in any six-month period, with written approval required for longer stays. This type of provision can be annoying because it allows your landlord to nose into your private affairs.

If you plan on having regular guests—for example, your college roommate stays with you two weekends a month when she's in town on business, or your boyfriend sleeps over a few nights a week—you'll need to think about how to handle this issue. If your landlord lives far away and doesn't have a resident manager, you may decide to take a chance that you'll never be found out. You might get away with it if you're always current with the rent and have no hassles with other tenants. (Be assured that the first words out of a disgruntled neighbor's mouth will be a description of your boyfriend's overnight stays, even if they have nothing to do with your problem with the neighbor.) But if the landlord lives downstairs, ask her to revise this clause. If she resists, consider looking for another rental.

6. Term of the Tenancy

Your agreement will state whether it's a month-to-month tenancy or a fixed-term lease. Section A, above, discusses the differences between these two approaches to renting.

a. Lease Provision

A lease obligates both you and the landlord for a specific term, typically one year. It sets a definite date for the beginning and expiration of the lease. It may also cover

- what happens at the end of the lease—for example, there may be a built-in option to extend the lease at the same or a higher rent.
- monetary consequences if you "hold over," or fail to leave, after the lease ends—for example, the monthly rent may increase if you stay without permission. These clauses are not always legal. (See the discussion on penalties for holding over in Chapter 15.)
- periodic rent increases, perhaps tied to a consumer price index or the landlord's operating expenses. Without this type of built-in rent

increase, your landlord can't increase the rent until the lease ends. Landlords in rent control cities may build in the rent board's annual allowable increase.

- financial penalties if you break the lease. Most of these penalties (called liquidated damages) are illegal. See "Watch Out for Liquidated Damages Provisions," below.

Watch Out for Liquidated Damages Provisions

Occasionally, a lease includes what lawyers quaintly call a "liquidated damages" clause. This means if you move out before the lease expires, you are supposed to pay the landlord a predetermined amount of money (damages) for the losses caused by your early departure. Usually landlords set the amount of liquidated damages at the entire amount of the security deposit or many hundreds, or even thousands, of dollars.

Unless the amount of liquidated damages is low, this approach is unfair and likely to be ruled illegal. If you move out before your lease expires, under the law of most states you are legally responsible to pay the landlord only for the actual losses you cause. If you provide a suitable new tenant to move in immediately, this may be little or nothing. (And in most states, the landlord is legally obligated to minimize his losses by trying to find a new tenant to replace you as soon as possible.) In short, why should a landlord—who didn't lose any money when you moved out—get a liquidated damages windfall?

The answer is, he often can't. Courts don't look kindly on liquidated damages clauses, especially if the amount far exceeds the amount the landlord really lost. Of course, should the issue ever come up, it takes time and trouble to go to court and get a judge to throw out a liquidated damages clause. If possible, try to get a clause like this deleted before you sign a lease or rental agreement.

b. Rental Agreement Provision

Rental agreements usually provide for a month-to-month tenancy. They also specify how much written notice your landlord must give to change or end the tenancy—most commonly, 30 days. See Chapter 15 for details.

7. Rent, Late Fees and Grace Periods

Your lease or rental agreement will specify the amount of rent, when it's due (typically, the first of the month) and where it's to be paid (via mail to the landlord's office or home is common). Your agreement may also include details on how rent is to be paid, such as personal check or money order. Many landlords spell out their policies on late fees (if rent is not paid on time) and charges if your rent check bounces. In most states, there are legal limits on the amount that can be charged for late fees. (See Chapter 3.) The agreement may list any extra items that are included in the rent, such as parking, cable TV hookup or water.

A grace period is a promise by the landlord that he won't terminate the tenancy until you are a certain number of days late with the rent. Except for a few states that impose mandatory grace periods, you'll almost never encounter a grace period spelled out in a rental agreement. You may see something like a "late fee after five days" clause, but this is not the same thing as a grace period—that is, your landlord can take steps to terminate your tenancy if you don't pay rent on the due date.

Check Chapter 3 to see if your landlord's lease or rental agreement violates your state's law on rent, including rent control rules, grace periods and late fees.

8. Deposits and Fees

All states allow landlords to collect a deposit when a tenant moves in and hold it until the tenant leaves. This may be called a security deposit, cleaning deposit or last month's rent. The general purpose of a deposit is insurance: It's a financial cushion for the landlord should you fail to pay the rent when it is due or leave the rental unit filthy or in poor repair.

State laws typically control the amount landlords can charge, how deposits may be used, when they must be returned and what type of itemization a landlord must provide to a tenant when deductions are made. In addition, some states allow landlords to charge a nonrefundable fee such as for cleaning or pets, while others specifically prohibit nonrefundable fees. Several cities and states require landlords to put deposits in a separate bank account and pay tenants interest on them.

If your lease or rental agreement is a good one, it may provide lots of helpful details on deposits—for example, where they will be held, interest payments and the conditions under which the security deposit will be returned or withheld. A few states require specific information like this to be included in leases and rental agreements, but most don't, so most agreements simply state the dollar amount of the deposit.

The use and return of security deposits is a frequent source of disputes between landlords and tenants. To avoid confusion and legal hassles, be sure you get all the information you need on security deposits before you sign a lease or rental agreement, especially as to what deductions are allowed, how the landlord expects you to clean the rental unit when you leave, when the deposit must be returned and whether or not the deposit can be used for last month's rent. If this information isn't spelled out in the lease or rental agreement, ask your landlord to add it.

 Chapters 4 and 16 provide details on the use and return of security deposits.

Watch out for automatic lien provisions. Your lease may have a clause that gives the landlord an "automatic lien" on your possessions if you fail to pay the rent or damage the unit. The purpose of this clause is to give your landlord the right to seize and sell your property without first going to court to prove the debt and give you a chance to hang on to certain property that is protected by state law. If you are presented with a lease that has an automatic lien provision, you don't need to worry too much, since it's unlikely that a court would enforce it. Still, you're better off without this type of clause.

9. Utilities

Your lease or rental agreement may specify who pays for the utilities. Normally, landlords pay for garbage, and sometimes for water, if there is a yard. Tenants usually pay for other services, such as phone, gas and electricity.

Make sure you're not paying anyone else's utility bills. Some older buildings and some duplexes and triplexes do not have separate gas and electric meters for each unit. In other situations, your meter also measures gas or electricity used in areas outside of your unit—such as a water heater that serves several apartments or lighting in a common area. Whenever you'll be required to pay for utilities that are not 100% under your control, your landlord should disclose this in your lease or rental agreement. (This type of disclosure is required by law in some states. See subsection 21, below.) To avoid hassles later on with neighbors who are wasteful of energy, your best approach is to ask the landlord to install a separate meter for all areas served outside your unit. Alternatively, your landlord should place the particular utility in his name and pay the bill.

10. Assignment and Subletting

Most leases and rental agreements include a clause forbidding sublets—for example, if you want someone to stay in your place and pay rent while you're gone for an extended period of time—without the prior written consent of your landlord. Also common is a prohibition against "assignments," a legal term that means you transfer your entire tenancy to someone else. Landlords include these clauses to prevent you from bringing in tenants whom they haven't approved, and to preserve their occupancy policies.

Even if your lease or rental agreement prohibits sublets and assignments without consent, however, state law usually prohibits your landlord from arbitrarily withholding consent to your request to sublet or assign your lease to someone else.

If your lease or rental agreement doesn't specifically prohibit sublets or assignments, you can do so without your landlord's consent (except in Texas). Nevertheless, it's always wise to get the landlord's permission first, since most landlords will want to know to whom they're renting.

 Chapter 7 discusses all the issues involving sublets and assignments in detail.

11. Condition of the Rental Unit and Landlord's Responsibilities

Many leases and rental agreements include a clause in which you agree that the premises are in habitable (livable) condition. Before you sign off on a clause like this, we strongly recommend that you inspect the rental unit and note any problems, using the Landlord-Tenant Checklist in Chapter 6. Doing so will help you identify problems that need fixing before you move in, and help you avoid losing your security deposit over something that was not your fault. It's best to insist that this Checklist be made a part of your lease or rental agreement. You can add a clause like this:

"Tenant has examined the premises, including appliances, fixtures, carpets, drapes and paint, and has found them to be in good, safe and clean condition and repair, except as noted in the Landlord-Tenant Checklist."

If the landlord won't do this, at least include the landlord's specific promises in the lease or rental agreement. If the landlord promises to fix the oven or install security bars on the ground floor windows, for example, write this into the lease or rental agreement, and set a deadline for work to be completed (ideally, before you move in). (Chapter 6 includes sample agreements regarding repairs.) You could also use a letter of understanding, as explained below in subsection 25.

Some states require landlords to notify tenants in writing, usually in the lease or rental agreement, of procedures for making complaints and repair requests and to alert landlords to defective or dangerous conditions. Even where it is not required, good leases and rental agreements include this information.

Know your rights to live in a habitable rental unit—and don't give them up. As a general rule, landlords are legally required to offer livable premises when a tenant originally rents a rental unit and to maintain the premises throughout the rental term. Your lease or rental agreement will probably provide very few details on the landlord's exact repair and maintenance responsibilities. And you'll probably never see a clause that describes your options, such as withholding rent, if the landlord fails to provide habitable premises. To protect your rights, it is crucial you know the laws on these issues.

Also, in most states, language a landlord sticks in a lease or rental agreement saying a tenant gives up his right to habitable housing won't be effective. By law, the landlord has to come through with habitable housing, no matter what the agreement says. And even if your state law allows such clauses, as is true in Maine and Texas, you'll want to avoid any landlord who operates this way.

For complete details on landlord's repair and maintenance responsibilities and how to enforce your rights, see Chapters 8 and 9.

Many leases and rental agreements outline the landlord's responsibilities if the rental property is damaged or destroyed by a natural disaster, such as an earthquake or flood. For example, the landlord might have the right to declare the lease terminated if the premises are totally destroyed, or the option to simply suspend the lease and begin repairs reasonably quickly. If your lease has no provision regarding destruction, it's likely that state law has something to say on the subject. See Chapter 8.

12. Tenant's Repair and Maintenance Responsibilities

Most leases and rental agreements state that you are responsible for keeping the rental premises clean, sanitary and in good condition, and that you must reimburse the landlord for the cost of repairing damage caused by your abuse or neglect. Some clauses go beyond a general statement and actually detail tenants' responsibility for problems like broken windows, clogged drains or snow removal. And a few landlords go so far as to delegate some of their own repair and maintenance responsibilities to tenants. This is most common, and most practical, for single-family houses or duplexes, because owners of these properties seldom have on-site managers or maintenance people.

Your lease or rental agreement will probably also tell what you what you *can't* do in the way of repairs. Typically, it will prohibit you from making alterations or repairs, such as painting or nailing holes in the walls, installing cable TV or fixing the broken heater, without your landlord's consent. In addition, your lease or rental agreement may specify that if you add any "fixtures"—a legal term that means any addition that is attached to the structure, such as a bolted-on bookcase or built-in dishwasher—will become the landlord's property and may not be removed without permission. And because your landlord has the legal right to enter your unit in an emergency, there may be a clause specifically forbidding you from adding or re-keying locks or installing a burglar alarm system without your landlord's consent.

Regardless of what the lease or rental agreement says, tenants have certain limited rights to alter or repair the premises. For example:

- In most states, tenants have the right to repair defects or damage that make the premises uninhabitable.
- Texas law specifically allows tenants to install security devices without the landlord's prior consent. (Texas Security Devices Act, Texas Property Code §§ 92.151-170.)
- Disabled tenants have certain rights to modify rental living space under the Federal Fair Housing Act. (42 U.S. Code §§ 3601-3619.)
- Federal law gives tenants limited rights to install wireless antennas and small satellite dishes. See Chapter 10, Section C for details.

Chapters 8, 9 and 10 provide details on your rights and responsibilities regarding repair and maintenance, and tenant improvements and alterations.

Who's Responsible for Appliance Repair?

Most state laws do not require landlords to provide major appliances such as refrigerators or stoves, although many landlords do. So, if you see a refrigerator or stove in a rental unit, you would naturally expect it comes with the deal, and that if an appliance breaks through no fault of your own, it's the landlord's job to repair it. Think again. Some landlords, trying to save a buck, include a clause in the lease or rental agreement stating that the appliances are there for the tenant's use but are not part of the rent. The clause goes on to say that if you use the appliances, you are responsible for their repair and maintenance.

This kind of clause is a clear sign that you're dealing with a cheap landlord who's almost certain to do a poor job in the repairs and maintenance department. If the apartment is otherwise terrific and the appliances in pretty good shape, you might decide to put up with this nonsense, but it probably makes more sense not to rent from someone who pinches pennies this hard. (Chapter 9 gives advice on how to pry appliance repairs out of a reluctant landlord.)

damage or injury to other people. Landlords with exclusive properties are especially likely to require periodic proof of renters' insurance.

But even if your landlord does not require renters' insurance, buying it can be a good idea if you can afford it. Renters' insurance typically costs about $350 a year for a $50,000 policy. It covers the following:

- loss due to theft, including some losses that occur away from home
- negligent destruction of your property (for example, you start a fire that destroys your kitchen)
- liability for injuries to others (a guest slips and breaks her leg on your freshly-washed kitchen floor, or you leave the water on, ruining the downstairs tenant's computer), and
- natural disasters or damage caused by other people (the creek rises, flooding the building, or your neighbor starts a fire that damages your unit).

13. Renters' Insurance

Your lease or rental agreement may include a clause alerting you to the fact that your landlord's insurance does not cover any liability that may result from your negligence. This means that the landlord's policy won't cover you if your carelessness causes:

- damage to the rental unit or other tenants' property
- loss of or damage to your belongings, or
- injuries to yourself or others.

You may also see a clause requiring you to obtain renters' insurance that covers losses to your belongings as a result of fire or theft, and also provides coverage if your negligence causes property

How to Choose Renters' Insurance

When considering renters' insurance, follow these steps:

Take a property inventory. In order to choose a policy limit, you'll need to know the value of the items that you'll insure. (The smallest amount of coverage is usually $16,000.) You will be surprised at how fast the totals will mount up, given our ever-expanding inventory of modern necessities—computers, VCRs, bicycles, cameras, clothing, stereos, even pets. Also, taking an inventory will make it easier to make a claim, should you need to do so. Make a copy of your inventory and keep it in a safe place *away* from home. Consider using Nolo's *Personal RecordKeeper,* an interactive software program that will generate a full inventory of your assets. (See the order form at the end of this book.)

Shop around. Find an agent or company representative you trust—possibly your automobile insurance agent, or one recommended by friends or relatives. Keep your inventory handy so that you can compare premiums.

Check what's covered. Ask about things not covered by the policy or where dollar limits are low. Cash is usually not covered and jewelry, computers and table silver coverage typically is limited, but you may be able to buy additional coverage (called a "floater" policy). Bicycles are usually covered (but not cars, vans, boats or trucks). If you run a home business, you may need to purchase additional coverage for office equipment.

Determine whether the policy is for replacement value. If you suffer a loss, your renters' policy can cover your belongings in one of two ways. It can reimburse you for the actual cash value (what your three-year-old computer would sell for today on the open market) or pay replacement value (what you would have to spend today to get a comparable computer). Obviously, a replacement value policy is preferable but is likely to cost more.

Check the deductibles amount. The typical range of deductibles is $250 to $500 for property loss claims (the higher the deductible, the lower the premium). There are no deductibles for liability claims against the policy.

If you aren't worried about your property, get a high deductible. If your landlord requires renters' insurance to cover any damage you cause to his property, but you really aren't worried about the theft or loss of your own goods (maybe they aren't worth much, or you live in an extremely safe area), you can save a bundle by getting the highest deductible the insurance company offers.

Read your policy. Don't assume that the fine print exactly mirrors what you and the insurance agent discussed. Unless you check the important points (and complain, if there are any discrepancies), you'll be stuck.

You can get more information on renters' insurance by contacting the Independent Insurance Agents of America, 127 South Peyton Street, Alexandria, VA 22314; 800-221-7917; 703-683-4422; FAX 703-683-7556; email info@iiaa.org. The Insurance Information Institute can also give you information; 1750 K Street N.W., Washington, DC 20006; 202-833-1580; www.iii.org/individuals/home/renters.html.

Watch Out for Hold Harmless and Exculpatory Clauses

Many form leases include illegal provisions that attempt to absolve the landlord in advance from responsibility for all damages, injuries or losses, including those caused by the landlord's misdeeds. These clauses come in two varieties:

- Exculpatory: "If there's a problem, you won't hold me responsible," and
- Hold-harmless: "If there's a problem traceable to me, you're responsible."

For example, the lease generated by one popular legal software package contains an exculpatory provision so broad that it states that your landlord is not responsible for injuries to tenants and guests—for instance, if you fall down broken stairs and break your leg (even, apparently, if the landlord personally littered the stairs with banana peels).

Such pro-landlord language is blatantly illegal. If your landlord assaults you, or you're injured because of a dangerous or defective condition the landlord failed to fix for several months, no boilerplate lease provision will protect your landlord from civil and possibly even criminal charges. To this end, most states have laws that declare that exculpatory clauses in residential leases and rental agreements are void. This means that a judge will not enforce them.

14. Violating Laws and Causing Disturbances

Most form leases and rental agreements contain a clause forbidding you from using the premises or adjacent areas, such as the sidewalk in front of the building, in such a way as to:

- violate any law or ordinance, including laws prohibiting the use, possession or sale of illegal drugs,

- seriously damage the property (sometimes called "committing waste" in legalese), or
- create a nuisance by annoying or disturbing other tenants or nearby residents—for example, by continuous loud noise.

You may also see reference to tenants' right to "quiet enjoyment" of the premises. This bit of legal jargon amounts to a promise that your landlord will not act (or fail to act) in a way that seriously interferes with your ability to use the rented premises—for example, by allowing garbage to pile up, tolerating a major rodent infestation or failing to control (or evict) a neighboring tenant whose constant loud music makes it impossible for tenants to sleep (or even think). Fortunately, you have the right to quiet enjoyment even if your lease or rental agreement doesn't mention it.

Many landlords also include specific rules—for example, no loud music played after midnight—in a separate set of rules and regulations. As discussed in subsection 19, as long as these rules are fairly reasonable—and sometimes even if they are not—your landlord can enforce them.

 Chapter 8 explains your right to quiet enjoyment. Chapter 14 covers legal nuisances.

15. Pets

Your landlord has the right to prohibit all pets, or restrict the types allowed—for example, no dogs or cats, but birds are okay. However, a landlord may not prohibit trained animals used by blind, deaf or physically or mentally disabled people, as provided by the federal Fair Housing Amendments Act, discussed in Chapter 5.

Many landlords spell out pet rules—for example, that the tenants will keep the yard free of all animal waste, or that dogs will always be on leash—in a separate set of rules and regulations (see subsection 19, below).

Some landlords allow pets but require tenants to pay a separate deposit to cover any damage that may be caused by the pet. The laws of a few states specifically allow separate, nonrefundable pet deposits. In others, charging a designated pet deposit is legal only if the total amount your landlord charges for deposits does not exceed the state maximum for all deposits. Also, it is illegal to charge an extra pet deposit for people with trained guide dogs, signal dogs or service dogs.

 See Chapter 4 for details on security deposit limits and uses.

Opening Landlords' Doors to Pets

Several humane societies across the country offer help to both landlords and tenants, in hopes that pet-owning tenants won't be shut out of the rental market. For example, Project Open Door, an ambitious program of the San Francisco Society for the Prevention of Cruelty to Animals (SPCA), offers pet-owning tenants helpful materials on how to negotiate with a landlord who doesn't normally allow tenants to keep a pet. The SPCA also offers
- checklists to help landlords screen pet-owning tenants
- pet policies that can be incorporated into a lease or rental agreement, and
- free mediation if landlords and tenants have pet-related problems after moving in.

For more information, contact the San Francisco SPCA at 2500 16th St., San Francisco, CA 94103, 415-554-3000.

Also, *Dog Law,* by Mary Randolph (Nolo), includes a chapter on how to negotiate a lease and other issues of interest to pet-owning tenants. (See order form at the back of this book.)

16. Landlord's Right of Access

Some leases and rental agreements spell out rules covering the landlord's right to enter your rental unit, including circumstances allowing access and the minimum amount of notice the landlord must provide. Others are silent on the subject. Even if the lease tries to restrict your right to privacy, however, most states with laws guaranteeing a tenant's privacy prohibit a landlord from enforcing unreasonably strict rules.

Nearly every state clearly recognizes the right of a landlord to enter rented premises while a tenant is still in residence, under certain narrow circumstances, such as to deal with a genuine emergency (for example, a fire or broken pipe) and when the tenant gives permission. Many states have access laws specifying the other circumstances under which landlords may legally enter rented premises—for example, to make repairs and inspect the property and to show property to prospective tenants or buyers. State access laws often require the landlord to give the tenant at least 24 hours' notice for non-emergency entries. A few states simply require the landlord to provide "reasonable" notice, often presumed to be 24 hours. Many states have no statutes covering landlord's access.

To protect your privacy, particularly if your state does not set specific rules on landlords' entry, be sure your lease or rental agreement covers the subject. Here's an example of the kind of lease clause you should get your landlord to write into your lease or rental agreement:

"Landlord or his agent will not enter tenant's home except to deal with an emergency; to make necessary or agreed repairs; to supply necessary or agreed services or to show the unit to potential purchasers, tenants or repair persons. Unless there is an emergency, or it is impractical to do so, Landlord will give tenant at least 24 hours' written notice of the date, time and purpose of the intended entry."

 Chapter 11 covers the topic of the landlord's right to enter rental property and tenant privacy rights in detail.

17. Extended Absences by Tenant

Some leases and rental agreements require you to notify the landlord in advance if you will be away from the premises for a certain number of consecutive days (often seven or more). Such clauses may give the landlord the right to enter the rental unit during your absence to maintain the property as necessary and to inspect for damage and needed repairs. You'll most often see this type of clause if you live in a cold-weather place where, in case of extreme cold weather, landlords want to check the pipes in rental units to make sure they haven't burst. By state law in Alaska, a rental agreement or lease must say that you need to inform the landlord of any planned absences over seven days (Alaska Stat. § 34.03.150).

 Chapter 11 discusses the landlord's entry during a tenant's extended absence.

18. Possession of the Premises

Many leases and rental agreements include a clause explaining what happens if you choose not to move in after signing the lease or rental agreement. Generally, you will still be required to pay rent and satisfy other conditions of the agreement. This does not mean, however, that your landlord can sit back and expect to collect rent for the entire lease or rental agreement term. Instead, as we explain in Chapter 15, landlords in most states must take reasonably prompt steps to re-rent the premises, and must credit the rent they collect against your rent obligation under the lease.

Most leases and rental agreements also cover situations when the landlord is unable to turn over possession of the unit to the tenant on time after having signed the agreement or lease. This clause is included in case fire destroys the building, contracted repairs aren't done on time or a prior tenant illegally fails to leave as expected. In the absence of a clause like this, the law would usually consider the landlord's failure to allow you to move in on time to

mean that the lease was breached, justifying your walking away and looking for another place. But landlords hate to lose a new tenant just because the old one failed to leave or the contractor didn't get the refurbishing done on time. So they typically insert a clause that states that the lease will be considered breached only if *the landlord* says it is. Usually, they give themselves ten to 30 days to make up their minds. In the meantime, you are obligated to honor the lease—even though you can't move in! You may be able to sue the landlord for reasonable costs of temporary housing, although some particularly nasty leases attempt to eliminate that remedy, too.

Another common approach to the "not ready" apartment is to allow the new tenant to walk away—in other words, to acknowledge that the lease has been breached—but to try to limit the landlord's liability for failing to have the unit ready on move-in day. This is done with a clause that limits the landlord's financial liability to new tenants to the return of any prepaid rent and security deposits (the "sums previously paid" is the language common in this type of clause). If you have a limiting clause like this in your lease, you won't be able to sue the landlord for temporary housing while you wait for repairs or for the prior tenant to move out. You could, however, file a small claims court case and sue the hold-over tenant himself or the person who caused the delay for your inconvenience and expenses, although your chances of winning are slight.

19. Tenant Rules and Regulations

Many landlords don't worry about detailed rules and regulations, especially when they rent single-family homes or duplexes. However, in large multi-tenant buildings, landlords usually set out rules to control the use of common areas and equipment and to protect the rental property from damage. Rules and regulations also help avoid confusion and misunderstandings about day-to-day issues such as garbage disposal and use of recreation areas.

Many landlords spell out their rules and regulations right in their lease or rental agreement.

However, if the rules and regulations are lengthy, a clause in the agreement usually refers to them as a separate document (lawyers call this "incorporating by reference").

Tenant rules and regulations can have a significant impact on your daily life and enjoyment of the rental premises. Be sure to read them carefully.

What's Covered in Tenant Rules and Regulations

Tenant rules and regulations typically cover issues such as:

- elevator safety and use
- pool rules
- garbage disposal and recycling
- vehicles and parking regulations—for example, restrictions on repairs on the premises or types of vehicles (such as no RVs), or where guests can park
- lock-out and lost key charges
- pet rules
- security system use
- no smoking in common areas
- specific details on what's considered excessive noise, (for example, playing loud music after 10 p.m.)
- dangerous materials—nothing flammable or explosive should be on the premises
- storage of bikes, baby strollers and other equipment in halls, stairways and other common areas
- specific landlord and tenant maintenance responsibilities (such as stopped-up toilets or garbage disposal or lawn and yard maintenance)
- use of the grounds
- maintenance of balconies and decks—for instance, no drying clothes on balconies
- display of signs in windows
- laundry room rules
- waterbeds
- no business (or very limited types).

20. Attorney Fees in a Lawsuit

People who sign contracts, including leases and rental agreements, sometimes end up in a legal dispute involving lawyers and courts. Usually, each side pays for his or her own attorney and court costs, unless a judge orders the losing side to pay the winner's expenses. This happens only rarely, and only when the conduct of the loser was particularly outrageous—for example, filing a totally frivolous lawsuit. If your lease or rental agreement has no "attorney fees" clause in it, then you'll be playing by the general rule if you end up in a court spat with your landlord.

But parties to a contract can decide in advance that they would like the rules to be otherwise. Many leases and rental agreements specify who will pay the costs of a lawsuit, by including one of two types of attorney fee clauses:

- **The "Loser Pays" Attorney Fees Clause.** A common and even-handed attorney fees clause requires the losing side in a landlord-tenant dispute to pay attorney fees and court costs (filing fees, service of process charges, deposition costs and so on) to the winning ("prevailing") party in a lawsuit. With an attorney fees clause of this type, if you hire a lawyer to sue your landlord (for example, over the security deposit) and win, the judge will order your landlord to pay your costs and attorney fees. A "loser pays" clause is attractive if you're confident that you will be a law-abiding and conscientious tenant—in other words, if you expect to be in the right.

On the other hand, if you qualify for legal aid or just feel confident about representing yourself in most situations, you may prefer not to have an attorney fees clause, reasoning that your landlord may be more willing to compromise any dispute if he can't sue you and recover his attorney fees.

- **"Losing Tenant" Pays.** Some landlords aren't content to make the loser (possibly themselves, after all) pay for lawyers' fees. Instead, they write a clause that obligates the tenant to pay the landlord's fees and costs if the landlord wins. But if the landlord loses, the clause says the landlord isn't obligated to pay the tenant's expenses.

This is a pretty shifty arrangement, and it hasn't gone down well. By law in California, New York and a number of other states, any attorney fees clause in a lease or a rental agreement must work both ways, even if it's not written that way. That is, even if the lease states that only your landlord is entitled to attorney fees for winning a lawsuit, you will be entitled to collect your attorney fees from your landlord if you prevail. Your landlord would be ordered to pay whatever amount the judge decides is reasonable.

Assuming you have any choice in the matter (you often won't), is it a good idea to include an attorney fees clause in your lease? It depends. The presence of an attorney fees clause will make it far easier for you to find a willing lawyer to take a case that does not have the potential for a hefty money judgment. For example, if you successfully defend against an eviction, you're likely to get the right to stay, but you probably won't be entitled to any money from the landlord. If your lease has a clause providing that the winner pays the loser, your attorney will get paid by the landlord. Knowing this, a lawyer will be more likely to take your case. Similarly, if your case has the potential for only a small

monetary award but will involve a lot of work, a lawyer will be more willing to take it knowing that the fees will come from the landlord and not from your modest winnings.

⚠ Attorney fee clauses don't cover all legal disputes. They cover fees only for lawsuits that concern the meaning or implementation of a rental agreement or lease—for example, a dispute about rent, security deposits or the landlord's right to access (assuming that the rental document includes these subjects). The clause would not apply in a personal injury or discrimination lawsuit.

Be Careful—Attorney Fees Often Go Only to the Winner, Not the Compromiser

In some states, a one-sided attorney fees clause (a winning landlord gets attorney fees but a winning tenant doesn't) will be read as a two-way, or loser pays, clause only if you *win* the lawsuit. If a case is dismissed or settled, your state law may consider that there is no "winner," in which case a one-sided attorney fees clause will operate as written and not be read to pay your fees. Say, for example, you have a one-way attorney fees clause in your lease, and your landlord files an eviction lawsuit against you for nonpayment of rent. Then the landlord dismisses the case before trial when you come up with good evidence that the unit is uninhabitable. You may think that you won the case (after all, you were not evicted). Unfortunately, in this situation, the law doesn't see you as a "prevailing party." This means you won't be entitled to attorney fees from your landlord unless you can get the landlord to sign a statement as part of the landlord's dismissal of the eviction lawsuit that names you as the prevailing party. If you're in this situation, ask your lawyer, or follow the legal research tips in Chapter 20 to find out your state's law.

Chapter 20 discusses how to find and work with a lawyer.

21. Disclosures

Federal, state or local laws may require your landlord to make certain disclosures before you sign a lease or rental agreement or move in. Some disclosures that may be required include:

- the name of the owner and the person authorized to receive legal papers such as a property manager (see subsection 22)
- any known lead-based paint hazards in the rental premises (discussed in Chapter 13)
- hidden (not obvious) defects of the rental property that could cause injury or substantially interfere with your safe enjoyment and use of the dwelling—for example, a warning that the building walls contains asbestos insulation, which could be dangerous if anyone made a hole in the wall
- the name and address of the bank where security deposits are held, and the rate of interest and its payment to the tenant (see Chapter 4), and
- planned condominium conversions (discussed in Chapter 15).

Here are specific disclosures required by some state laws:

- property located near former military ordnance (Cal. Civ. Code §1940.7)
- tenant's gas or electric meter serves areas outside of the rental unit (Cal. Civ. Code § 1940.9)
- existence of a statewide database listing violent sexual offenders and those convicted of sexual offenses against minors (Cal. Civ. Code § 2079.10a)
- availability of fire protection in building over three stories high (Fla. Statutes Annotated § 83.50)
- rental unit has been flooded within the past five years (Ga. Code Ann. § 44-7-20; Okla. Stat. tit. 41.§ 113a)

- landlord's excise tax number, so that tenants may file for a low-income tax credit (Haw. Rev. Stat. § 521-43)
- outstanding inspection orders, condemnation orders or declarations that the property is unfit. Citations for violations that do not involve threats to tenant health or safety must be summarized and posted in an obvious place, and the original must be available for review by the tenant. (Minn. Stat. §§ 504.246(a), (b)).

Rent control ordinances typically include additional disclosures, such as the name and address of the government agency or elected board that administers the ordinance and special rules governing sublets and assignments.

22. Authority to Receive Legal Papers

It's the law in many states, and a good idea in all, to know to whom you should send legal papers. For example, you may need to send a notice that you are ending the tenancy, or you may even need to sue the landlord one day. Leases and rental agreements typically include the name and address of the landlord or whoever is authorized to receive notices and legal papers on the landlord's behalf, such as a property manager.

23. Grounds for Termination of Tenancy

There is usually a clause stating that any violation of the lease or rental agreement by you, or by your guests, is grounds for terminating the tenancy, according to the procedures established by state or local laws.

 Chapters 17 and 18 discuss grounds and procedures for terminating tenancies.

24. Mediation

Some landlords have wisely learned that disputes which can't be worked out between the landlord and tenant are often best resolved without lawyers, but with the help of a skilled, professional mediator. You may see a clause obligating you to go through mediation "in good faith" if a dispute arises over the meaning or implementation of your lease or rental agreement. All this means is that you agree that you won't rush off and sue until you have met with the landlord and a mediator and have genuinely tried to work out a solution to your dispute. This is an excellent requirement from your point of view, since it also gives you a way to get help with your grievance. Mediation is not binding—if you don't come to an agreement, you can assert your rights in court.

 Mediation is explained in more detail in Chapter 19.

 A mediation clause covers only lease and rental agreement disputes. A provision requiring good faith mediation requires you to mediate disputes that arise from the lease or rental agreement itself. For example, if you intend to sue your landlord for discriminating against you in violation of federal or state fair housing laws, you need not mediate first, because that behavior is not connected with the meaning or implementation of the lease or rental agreement.

25. Additional Provisions

Some form lease and rental agreements include a blank space for any other agreement you and your landlord wish to make. For example, your landlord may want to add a provision that prohibits smoking in your apartment or in the common areas.

Write down any agreement that's important to you, such as a landlord's promise to paint the unit before you move in or replace the deck within two months. If you don't, and the promised improvement is put off or not done as promised, you'll be left with little more than your word against the landlord's.

If there is no place on the form to add your own clause, you can modify the lease as shown below in Section E.

If you don't get everything added to the agreement you sign, be sure to send your landlord a letter of understanding. See the discussion in Section C, above, and the sample Letter of Understanding, below.

Sample Letter of Understanding

777 Walnut Street
San Gimo, Arizona 00000

January 20, 200X

Manny Money
125 Capitol Mall
San Gimo, Arizona

Dear Mr. Money,

Thank you for showing me Apartment #3 today at your apartment complex, Willow Run. As you doubtless remember, we discussed the poor condition of the living room carpet, which you said you were planning to replace within two months. Since I was very pleased with every other aspect of the apartment and the building, I signed a lease, based on your promise that the carpet would in fact be replaced within two months of my starting date of February 1, 199X.

Please let me know immediately if your understanding of your promise regarding the living room rug differs from mine. I would not want to live with that stained carpet for more than two months, and would consider the lease to be breached if the carpet were not replaced by April 1, 200X. I have every hope that you will attend to the matter as promised and that I will fully enjoy my tenancy at Willow Run.

Yours truly,

Sally Smart

Sally Smart

26. Validity of Each Part

Leases and rental agreements commonly include what lawyers call a "savings" clause, which means that, in the event that one of the other clauses in the lease or rental agreement is found to be invalid by a court, the remainder of the agreement will remain in force. Given the number of blatantly illegal clauses that lots of landlords stick in their agreements, it's not hard to see why they need this one.

27. Entire Agreement

Somewhere in the fine print, usually at the end, most leases have a provision which says that the agreement, and any attachments such as rules and regulations, is the entire agreement of the parties. That means that if the landlord (or you) made any promises which weren't in or attached to the lease or rental agreement, then they don't count and can't be enforced.

Does this clause mean that your landlord's oral promises ("Of *course* I'll fix the ice maker before you move in!") will never be enforced? Probably not, but if the landlord claims he never promised you anything, it will make it harder for you to convince a judge that he did. For this reason, we counsel you again to get all promises from the landlord in writing and part of or attached to the lease. (Section E, below, discusses how to modify signed rental agreements and leases.)

D. Negotiating With the Landlord

Your lease or rental agreement is probably loaded with clauses written to maximize the landlord's rights and minimize yours. That's because these rental documents are typically written by lawyers hired by landlords or their trade associations.

Don't assume, however, that every clause is written in stone. Armed with a little legal knowledge, you'll be able to figure out whether the terms and conditions of your lease or rental agreement—its clauses—are legal or illegal, subject to negotiation or not. Here's how to do it.

Knowing *when* to negotiate is as important as knowing *how*. Don't start bargaining the minute you see a promising rental. Take some time to establish a rapport with the landlord and give him reason to want to choose you over other applicants. Even seemingly implacable rules, especially no-pets restrictions, may melt away if the landlord likes and wants you as a tenant.

1. Four Types of Lease Clauses

Every rental clause falls into one of four categories, depending on the issue's connection to any federal, state or local laws on that subject. As we explain below, determining how (or whether) to negotiate with your landlord over a rental clause will depend on which category the issue fits into.

Category 1: A Restatement of Your Guaranteed Legal Rights

Many states have passed tenant-friendly laws covering key areas such as landlords' access to rental property, the amount and use of security deposits and your right to a livable home. In addition, you may have important legal rights under federal law (particularly in the area of discrimination) and local law (especially if your community has rent control). *Your landlord cannot legally diminish these rights and cannot ask you to waive them.* This book explains which important tenant rights belong in this category, and Subsection D.2, below, provides further clarification.

Your landlord is obliged to comply with these tenant rights, but is not usually required to inform you of them in your lease or rental agreement. A conscientious and knowledgeable landlord may relay information on tenant rights in a lease clause as a way of educating you as to how things are done.

You don't have to bargain for legal rights that are guaranteed under local, state or federal law. If your landlord spells out guaranteed tenant rights in your rental document, fine, but you've got them regardless. So is there any reason to bring them up and ask your landlord to explicitly include your guaranteed rights in your lease or rental agreement? This might make sense if you feel you're dealing with an ignorant or shifty landlord. If he's merely unaware of the law, you've educated him. And if he was hoping to pull the wool over your eyes, you've disabused him of that plan.

There is, however, a risk in correcting or educating your prospective landlord. He may regard you as a troublemaker and may concoct some reason to turn you down. Since these tenant rights are yours anyway, it may not be worth the risk of instant alienation. On the other hand, you'll learn a lot about the landlord (and whether you want to do business with him) if he reacts in horror when you mention your right to heat, hot water and a leak-proof roof.

Please, Sir, I Want Some More

Even if your guaranteed rights are specified in your lease or rental agreement, there's nothing stopping you from asking for *more*—for example, if your state sets a security deposit limit at two months' rent, you can always ask for a lower figure. Similarly, if your state guarantees you thirty days' notice before the rent can be raised, you and your landlord can agree that he'll give you sixty days instead.

Should you bargain for more favorable terms? In general, you should save your negotiating strength for the most important issues. If there is something important about your tenancy that is not even partly guaranteed under state law (such as a parking spot, which falls within Category 4, see below), save your breath for that one.

Category 2: A Variation of a Negotiable State or Local Law

Not all tenant-protection laws are off-limits to landlord tinkering, as are the ones in Category 1, above. For example, in some states a landlord and tenant may agree that the statutory notice periods for changing or ending a tenancy may be shortened if *both* agree. In California, for instance, landlords and tenants may agree to shorten the normal 30-day notice period to as little as seven days. If the rental document doesn't mention the issue, however, state law prevails.

If you see a clause that restricts rights that are given you by a state or local statute, you'll obviously need to know whether this restriction is allowed in your state—in other words, whether the subject instead fits within Category 1, above. To find out, follow the suggestions for placing your clause in the right category as explained in subsection 2, below.

If your state or local law allows the landlord some wiggle room on a tenant-friendly proce-

dure, he's allowed to take advantage of that liberty. You can't force him back to the original law. If he's stubborn, you must be prepared to offer reasons why the variation is either not necessary or not fair. You may be able to work out a compromise or offer a concession of your own in exchange for your full rights under the law. Ultimately, however, if a landlord won't budge and you feel very strongly about the issue, you'll have to look elsewhere.

Category 3: Illegal Clauses

Landlords cannot diminish certain tenant-protection laws, such as your rights to a habitable rental unit and to be free from illegal discrimination. These are the rights that fit within Category 1, above. Nonetheless, many landlords attempt to circumvent the law by rewriting it. The best example of this is when landlords try to limit their responsibility to provide habitable housing, despite the laws that exist in the vast majority of states to the contrary. Incredible though it may seem, you'll see rental clauses in which the landlord states that the premises are not warranted as fit, safe, secure or in good repair. Most states will not uphold these clauses (Texas is a notable exception). This means that even if you sign a lease or rental agreement that contains a clause absolving the landlord of the duty to offer and maintain fit housing, you can still complain (or use a tenant remedy such as repair and deduct, explained in Chapter 8) and a court will not hold you to your "waiver."

A misstatement of a guaranteed tenant right isn't the only kind of illegal clause you may encounter. Some clauses are illegal because they violate an important public policy. For example, many landlords use a lease clause that states that the tenant will not hold the landlord responsible for injuries the tenant may suffer as a result of the landlord's negligence or carelessness. Most courts will not enforce these clauses because our society expects that, for the most part, people should be held accountable for their screw-ups.

Remember that we are dealing here with tenant rights that can't be waived or diminished—in other words, they are *non-negotiable*. If your landlord nevertheless attempts to avoid his responsibilities, it means that he is either unaware of your rights or deliberately violating the law. Your approach will depend on your reading of the landlord.

- **The landlord doesn't know the law.** If you think the landlord has made an honest mistake, and especially if your options as to other rentals are narrow, you may decide that it's worth pointing out to the landlord that his clause is invalid. Doing so lets him know that he's not dealing with a dummy or a pushover, and hopefully he'll be more careful in the future. There is a risk, however: You may discover that he'll do everything possible to get rid of you, preferring to rent to people who don't know their rights.
- **The landlord is deliberately violating the law.** If every sign suggests that the landlord has deliberately circumvented the law, the wise course is clear: Move on. If you don't, you can count on problems ahead.

⚠ Keep quiet and lie in the weeds. If you really need or want this rental, there is an alternate but risky approach to a shifty landlord. Knowing that the clause is illegal anyway, you may want to be silent and raise your objections when and if the issue comes up. The drawback of this tactic is that making your point after the fact can be a long and tedious process. For example, suppose you sign a lease with a clause that gives the landlord permission to throw you and your possessions onto the street if you're late with the rent (called a "self-help" eviction, such a clause is invalid in virtually every state). If you're late and come home to find your belongings on the sidewalk, you may ultimately get your tenancy back and some money damages out of the landlord to boot; but the emotional toll (and the time you spend in court) will not be worth it.

⚠ Go along with the deal at your peril. If you're really desparate for this rental and you think you can live with the landlord's illegal clause, you might consider keeping quiet *and* doing what the landlord has asked. For example, you may agree to pay a higher-than-legal security deposit or an exorbitant late fee. But be forewarned: Agreeing to go along with an illegal scheme has its drawbacks—your landlord may expect that you'll again roll over when he tries another legal short cut.

Category 4: A Policy or Rule Not Covered by State or Local Law

Finally, you'll see lots of lease clauses that are not regulated in the slightest by your local or state laws or court decisions. Examples include provisions for parking spaces, amount of rent (rent control excepted), rent due date, move-in date, rules regarding common area use and procedures for registering complaints and repair requests. Some of these issues are written as clauses in the lease or rental agreement itself, but many are covered in "house rules," which landlords attach to leases.

But minor, day-to-day issues aren't the only ones that may be untethered to a federal, state or local law. In some states, extremely important issues, such as security deposit limits or rules governing landlords' access to rental property, are not governed by law. For example, New York and Texas do not limit the amount of security a landlord may demand. Clearly, before sounding off with a haughty demand to reform an "illegal" clause, you'll need to know whether your state law does, in fact, regulate the issue. Subsection 2, below, suggests ways to correctly place your clause.

Issues that aren't governed by law are the truly negotiable ones. Here you are both free to bargain, restrained only by the strength of your position. If it's a renters' market and the landlord's property is littered with "Vacancy" signs, you can expect more cooperation than if there are 17 professional couples lined up waiting to take the unit with no demands. Rather than push now for a better deal, it sometimes makes sense to get the rental and then, after you have established yourself as a stable, desirable tenant, ask the landlord to revisit the issue and possibly change that lease clause (changing rental agreements and leases is covered in Chapter 15).

2. Placing a Clause in the Right Category

It's one thing to understand that lease clauses run the gamut from correct restatements of guaranteed legal rights (Category 1) to permissible variations on tenant rights (Category 2) to downright illegal provisions (Category 3) and, finally, to issues that aren't governed by law (Category 4). But before you can plan a negotiation strategy, you need to understand where a *particular* clause belongs. For example, suppose a clause of your lease states that the tenant agrees to allow the landlord to enter the rental property with no notice. Are there any laws that protect rental privacy in your state? If not, it's a Category 4 issue and there's nothing you can do but bargain for a more considerate arrangement. But maybe your state does regulate the times and manner in which a landlord may enter and doesn't allow the landlord to deviate from this scheme. If so, this clause may belong in Category 3. Yet again, if the landlord and tenant *are* allowed to bargain over this issue, it's a Category 2 matter.

In order to find out where a particular clause falls, you'll need to read about the issue first, by turning to the appropriate chapter in this book. To continue with our privacy example, you'd turn to Chapter 11, Your Right to Privacy, to learn about the ways that states do (and don't) protect tenants' privacy. Then, you'd turn to the chart in the Appendix, "State Laws on Landlords' Access to Rental Property," to see whether your state has a law (statute) on the subject. If it does, you'd be well advised to read that statute (in Chapter 20, we show you how to access your state statutes online).

We don't pretend, however, that it's always easy to find out where your clause belongs in our four-part scheme. A lot of landlord-tenant law isn't in statutes at all, but instead in law that is made in court cases and written down by judges in court opinions. And even when there is a statute on the subject, you may have to read court decisions to find out whether it's OK for landlords to vary the rules (Category 2).

Besides doing your own research, a useful aid to properly categorizing a lease clause is to contact your local tenants' rights group or state consumer protection agency. A good rule of thumb is that the more important the issue, such as habitability, the more likely it is to be an ironclad, Category 1 matter. When crafting tenant-friendly statutes, many times lawmakers want to make sure that the law is understood as Category 1—no variations allowed—and say so right in their statute. Less important matters, such as amount of notice to change or end a tenancy, are more apt to be open to bargaining (Category 2). And there are several big-ticket issues, such as discrimination, avoiding responsibility for injuries and physically evicting you without first going to court, that are downright illegal (Category 3) in virtually every state. Finally, "housekeeping" issues such as parking and facilities use rules aren't likely to be subjects of legislation or court cases, meaning that they're wholly negotiable.

3. Concluding Your Negotiations

Negotiation with your landlord should always end with a written version of what the two of you agreed to. Never, ever walk away from a negotiation session without reducing your deal to writing, either by changing the rental document or adding to it. Follow our instructions for changing a lease or rental agreement in Section E, below.

E. Changing a Lease or Rental Agreement

If you and your landlord agree to make changes to your lease or rental agreement, the process is simple.

1. Deleting Language

You may be able to convince your landlord that a particular clause need not be in your lease—for example, perhaps you have successfully shown that your four-legged pal is friendlier and better behaved than most of the existing tenants, so that your landlord is willing to delete the no pets clause. Never rely on the landlord's sincere promise that he won't enforce that part of the lease (he may change his mind or sell the building). To protect yourself, all you do is cross out the unwanted portion, write in desired changes (if any), and have everyone who is going to sign the document initial and date the changes. If your landlord has the lease in a computer, he will probably want to print out a clean copy to sign.

2. Adding Language

You or your landlord may write or type in minor changes to your lease or rental agreement, as explained above. If the proposed changes are fairly lengthy, however, your landlord will either need to enter the changes in the lease-generating software program or one of you will need to prepare an amendment page (lawyers use the word "addendum") to the original document.

Appendix II includes a blank, tear-out Amendment to Lease or Rental Agreement form which you can tear out, copy and use to make changes or insert additions before you sign a lease or rental agreement. A sample is shown in Chapter 15.

To use the amendment form, follow these steps:

Step 1: On the original document, at the end of the rental provisions and before your signature, add the sentence "See Amendment A for additional provisions." That way, if the attachment gets lost (or the landlord removes it), the fact that it ought to be there will be recorded on the lease, and the landlord cannot claim that it never existed.

Step 2: Tear out and copy the Amendment form in the Appendix. If it is the only addition, label it "A" in the space provided in the title and set out the additional lease provision in the space below. (If you later add more provisions, label them "B," "C" and so on, and refer to them on your copy at least of the original lease or rental agreement.) See the sample in Chapter 15. Include a date by which the landlord is to accomplish the promise, if appropriate.

Step 3: Consider what you want to happen if the landlord fails to follow through. If the amendment is absolutely essential to you—for example, you simply must have a parking space within three months—and you want to be able to legally move out if the landlord doesn't follow through, add this sentence: "Failure of the Landlord to comply with the terms and conditions of this Amendment constitutes a material breach of the Lease/Rental Agreement." This means that the landlord's breach excuses your obligations to stay and pay rent. On the other hand, if noncompliance would not be so devastating to your ability to stay and enjoy your home, specify another consequence, such as that your rent will be reduced a certain amount per day or week until the provision is complied with.

Step 4: Sign and date the amendment. Since it's part of your lease or rental agreement, store it carefully with the other important documents relating to your tenancy, as suggested in Chapter 6.

Chapter 15 provides details on notice and procedures for changing a lease or rental agreement after you have begun your tenancy.

F. Signing a Lease or Rental Agreement

At the end of the lease or rental agreement, there will be space to include your landlord's signature, street address and phone number, or that of the person she authorizes to receive legal papers, such as a property manager. There's also space for your and other tenants' signatures and phone numbers, as well as any cosigner. (Cosigners are discussed below.)

If your landlord has altered a preprinted form by writing or typing in changes, be sure that you and the landlord initial and date the changes when you sign the document.

Make sure you sign the lease or rental agreement at the same time as the landlord and that you get a copy then and there. This assures both sides that no changes can be made after only one party has signed.

About Cosigners

Some landlords require cosigners on rental agreements and leases, especially when renting to students who depend on parents for much of their income. The cosigner signs either the rental agreement or lease, or a separate agreement under which he agrees to cover any rent or damage-repair costs the tenant fails to pay.

Your landlord may require your cosigner to fill out a separate rental application and agree to a credit check to make sure he has the financial resources, should you default on the rent or damage the rental property, to pay the bill.

Basic Rent Rules

This chapter shows how to get accurate answers to important questions about rent, including the following:

- How much rent can my landlord charge?
- Am I allowed a grace period to pay rent?
- What happens if I can't pay on time?
- Are there any limits to late fees a landlord charges?
- How much notice must my landlord give before increasing my rent?
- What are my options if I think the rent increase is unfair?

Normally, you'll need to look at your lease or rental agreement, refer to your state's law (you'll find handy charts in Appendix I), and consider your landlord's unwritten business practices.

Paying rent on time is the most important thing you can do to establish a good relationship with your landlord. By paying your rent in full on time every month, you meet the legal requirements of your lease or rental agreement. But you do something else that can be almost as important: You establish yourself in your landlord's mind as a conscientious, reliable person. Put another way, you identify yourself as one of your landlord's best customers. Although this reputation is only occasionally of legal importance, it is likely to be of great practical help when you make a repair request or ask for a favor such as a little extra time to pay the rent one month.

 Related topics covered in this book include:

- Paying first and last month's rent: Chapter 4.
- Negotiating a late rent payment and eviction for nonpayment of rent: Chapter 17.

A. How Much Can Your Landlord Charge?

Except for the cities and counties with rent control ordinances, landlords are free to charge as much rent as they like. (Rent control is discussed in Section B.) Most landlords monitor the rental market and price their rental units accordingly. To make sure you're not overpaying, you should do the same thing: Check ads and visit a few similar-sounding places to make sure your rent isn't out of line. Real estate offices and apartment-finding services are also good sources of information on area rents. (See Chapter 1 for a discussion of how to find an apartment or house.) In addition, local tenants' associations can be a terrific resource. (To find out whether there is a tenants' group in your area, check the phone book under "Tenants" or ask local real estate offices that handle rentals. If there's a landlords' association in your area, they'll know the answer for sure.)

If the rent seems low, find out why. When you're apartment-hunting, keep in mind that a lower rent does not always reflect less value. Many wise landlords charge a little less than the going rate as part of a policy designed to find and keep excellent tenants. On the other hand, if you find an attractive unit at an unbelievably low rent, be sure to ask the landlord when the rent last went up. If it's been more than 18 months since rent was raised, you can bet an increase will happen soon. For reassurance, you might want to ask the landlord for a lease of a year or more at the existing rent.

Public Housing

Many tenants with low incomes qualify for federally subsidized housing assistance. The most common is the Section 8 program of the federal Department of Housing and Urban Development (HUD). ("Section 8" refers to Section 8 of the United States Housing Act of 1937, 42 U.S.C. § 1437f.) That program determines a "market rent" for each rental property and then pays a percentage of the rent directly to the landlord, with the tenant paying the rest. The local housing authority, the landlord and the tenant enter into a one-year agreement, using a written lease supplied by the county housing authority.

Section 8 housing can often be a good deal, since "market rent" for a unit is often set at a fairly low rate and, of course, part of this amount is subsidized. In addition, Section 8 tenants cannot be evicted except for nonpayment of rent or other serious breaches of the lease. Landlords are not required to participate in Section 8 rentals, however, and most choose not to.

If you think you may be eligible for Section 8 assistance, contact your local HUD office. (You can reach your regional office by calling HUD's Fair Housing Information Clearinghouse at 800-343-3442.)

"rent stabilization" or "maximum rent regulation") are now in effect in some of the country's largest cities, including New York City, Washington, D.C., Los Angeles, San Francisco, Newark, San Jose and Oakland. The important details of these cities' rent control laws are set out in Appendix I.

Rent control ordinances vary widely. Some, like the ones in New York, have real teeth, while others (in San Jose and Oakland, for example) are practically useless. And rent control is increasingly unpopular politically—so any changes to existing ordinances are likely to be pro-landlord. State law often restricts local rent control rules or bans them altogether; over 30 states have laws prohibiting local rent control ordinances.

The Rent Control Board

In most cities, the administration of rent control rests in the hands of a rent control board of five to ten people. Board members often decide important issues, such as the maximum amount a landlord can charge for rental units. (In many areas, the law itself limits how and when the rent can be raised.) Depending on the city, rent control board members are elected by voters or appointed by the mayor or city council. Because rent control boards interpret the provisions of the law, they usually have significant power over landlords and tenants.

B. Rent Control

➡️ Unless you live in California, the District of Columbia, Maryland, New Jersey or New York, you aren't affected by rent control. You can skip ahead to Section C.

Some cities and counties in California, Maryland, New Jersey, New York and Washington, D.C., have laws that limit the amount of rent landlords may charge. Local rent control ordinances (also called

Rent control laws commonly regulate much more than rent—for example, they may limit the circumstances under which landlords may evict tenants. Because local ordinances are complicated, vary widely and change often, this book cannot provide fine details on each city's program. Instead, we give a good general description of what rent control ordinances cover and an outline of seven big-city ordinances. (See "Selected Rent Control Ordinances" in Appendix I.)

Where to Get Information About Rent Control

If you are protected by a rent control ordinance, use these resources to get straight information:

- **Your city rent control board.** It can supply you with a copy of the current local ordinance, and possibly also with a brochure explaining the main features of the ordinance. The table "Selected Rent Control Ordinances" in Appendix I gives the addresses and phone numbers for the boards of seven major cities.
- **Your local tenants' organization.** Virtually every city with a rent control ordinance has an active and vocal tenants' group. (In many cases, the pressure from these groups is why the city has rent control in the first place.) These organizations typically are vigorous watchdogs of the rent board and monitor court decisions and any political goings-on (such as proposed ballot amendments) that affect the ordinance. Most importantly, tenant organizations can usually provide a written explanation of the ordinance and how it works, and many have volunteer staff available to explain ambiguous or complex facets of the ordinance.
- **Local attorneys who specialize in landlord/ tenant law.** Chapter 20 discusses how to find and work with a lawyer.

1. Property Subject to Rent Control

Not all rental housing within a rent-controlled city is subject to rent control. Commonly, ordinances exempt:

- new buildings
- owner-occupied buildings with no more than three or four units
- single-family houses and luxury units that rent for more than a certain amount.

For example, in Los Angeles a one-bedroom apartment that rents for over a specified rent per month is not subject to rent control; in San Francisco, tenants (lodgers) in a landlord-occupied single-family home are not covered by the ordinance's protections; and rentals of single-family homes in Los Angeles and San Jose are exempt from rent control.

2. Limits on Rent

Rent control comes in two basic styles: one that protects only the present tenant, and one that regulates rent over the long term, regardless of turnover. In rent control jargon, these varieties are known as "vacancy decontrol" and "vacancy control" statutes. Here's how they work.

a. Vacancy Decontrol Statutes: Protecting Current Tenants

In most rent control areas, landlords may raise rent —either as much as they want or by a specified percentage—when one tenant moves out and a new one moves in. This feature, called "vacancy decontrol" or "vacancy rent ceiling adjustment," means that rent control applies to a particular rental unit only as long as a particular tenant (or tenants) stays there. If a tenant voluntarily leaves or, in some cities, is evicted for a legal or "just" cause (discussed below), the rental unit is not subject to rent control again until the new (and presumably higher) rent is established.

Some ordinances automatically allow a specific percentage rent increase each year for existing tenants. This may be set by the rent control board, as a fixed percentage of the rent or a percentage tied to a local or national consumer price index.

In addition to built-in annual increases, some rent control boards allow landlords to petition for a rent hike based on an increase in costs, such as taxes or capital improvements.

EXAMPLE: Marla has lived in Edward's apartment building for seven years. During that time, Edward has been allowed to raise the rent only by the modest amount authorized by the local rent board each year. Meanwhile, the market value of the apartment has gone up significantly.

When Marla finally moves out, Edward is free to charge the next tenant the market rate. But once set, that tenant's rent will also be subject to the rent control rules, and Edward will again be limited to small annual increases as approved by the rent control board.

b. Vacancy Control Statutes: Protecting Future Tenants

These rent control ordinances set a base rent for each rental unit. (The brute forces of the market have no place here.) The base rent usually takes into account several factors, including the rent that was charged before rent control took effect, the landlord's operating and maintenance expenses, inflation and housing supply and demand. The base rent may be raised during the tenancy under certain circumstances, such as an increase in inflation. When the tenant moves out, a landlord cannot raise the rent to market level. Rent stays controlled, subject to the formula of the rent control ordinance.

EXAMPLE: Sergei has been a tenant in Rudolph's apartment complex for two years. Every year on January 1, Rudolph raises the rent according to the rate set by the rent control board. When Sergei moves out on June 1 and Sasha moves in, Rudolph must charge her the same rent as Sergei paid during that year. He cannot raise her rent until the following January 1.

Slumlords can't raise the rent. Even if your landlord is entitled to raise the rent under the terms of your rent control ordinance, the rent board may deny permission if the landlord hasn't adequately repaired and maintained the rental property. Read your ordinance carefully to see if you have the right to protest a rent increase based on a pattern of substandard conditions in your building or unit. If your landlord doesn't keep the premises habitable, you probably have other, independent remedies—for example, you may be able to withhold rent—independent of the rent control ordinance. (Chapter 8 discusses your options.)

3. Evictions in Rent Control Areas

For rent control to work—especially if the ordinance allows rents to rise when a tenant leaves—it must place some restrictions on eviction. Otherwise, landlords have an incentive to create a vacancy by throwing out existing tenants. Recognizing this, many local ordinances require landlords to have a "just cause"—that is, a good reason—to evict.

Rent control ordinances specify a limited number of reasons that justify eviction, including:

- You violate a significant term of the lease or rental agreement—for example, by failing to pay rent, causing substantial damage to the premises or allowing unauthorized people to live in the rental unit. However, in many situations, state law requires that a landlord must first give you a chance to correct the problem. (See Chapter 17.)
- The landlord wants to move into the rental unit or give it to an immediate family member.

"Relative move-ins" are often bogus. Unscrupulous landlords often cite the need for a relative (or personal) move-in as the reason for evicting a tenant. Then, after a ridiculously short tenancy (or none at all), the relative or landlord moves out. In areas with vacancy control, this enables the landlord to raise the rent to market rate for the next tenant.

If you suspect an illegitimate relative move-in, investigate further. See if you can find out whether the landlord or a real relative actually moved in and, if so, for how long. If the tenancy is patently short or the "relation" isn't one at all, consider seeing a lawyer or suing in small claims court to recoup your moving costs and higher new rent. Some rent control ordinances presume that the move-in is fraudulent if the landlord or relative stays less than a prescribed amount of time. In San Francisco and New York City, for example, the period is three years.

- The landlord wants to substantially remodel the property, which requires you to move out. Under some ordinances, a landlord who rents a number of units (for example, in a good-sized apartment building) must make available to you another similar unit or give you first chance to move back in after the remodeling. In some cases, the landlord may raise the rent based on the improvements.
- You create a serious nuisance—for example, by repeatedly disturbing other tenants or engaging in illegal activity, such as drug-dealing or prostitution, on the premises.

Rent control ordinances affect renewals as well as evictions. Rent control ordinances typically protect you not only from an eviction in the middle of a tenancy, but from a landlord's decision to not renew your lease. Unless the landlord can point to a "just cause" for tossing you out, you are entitled to renew under the same terms and conditions, including the length of the rental term.

Landlords often refer to this aspect of a rent control ordinance as "the endless lease."

Your Landlord's Right to Go Out of Business

It's not uncommon for landlords in rent-controlled cities to decide to get out of the residential rental business entirely. To do so, however, they must evict tenants, who will protest that the eviction violates the rent control ordinance.

A rent control ordinance cannot force an unwilling landlord to stay in business, though an ordinance may attempt to restrict the number of condominium conversions (the number one reason most landlords withdraw from the rental market). However, a landlord who withdraws rental units from the market must usually have plenty of evidence that his motive is not to evade the rent control ordinance: Rent control boards do not want landlords to use going out of business as a ruse for evicting long-term tenants, only to start up again with a fresh batch of tenants whose rents will be substantially higher.

If your landlord files an eviction lawsuit because he is going out of business, check your ordinance carefully. It may require the landlord to offer you relocation assistance, and may impose a minimum time period during which the landlord may not resume business. A landlord who owns multiple units may be prohibited from withdrawing only a portion of the units; and if the premises are torn down and new units constructed, the ordinance may insist that the landlord offer former tenants a right of first refusal. State law may also address these issues. Contact your local tenants' group or rent control board for details.

4. Interest Payments on Security Deposits

Local rent control ordinances sometimes impose rules regarding security deposits that supplement those set out by state law. For example, San Francisco landlords are required to put security deposits in interest-bearing bank accounts, something not required under California law. Check your ordinance to see whether similar protections apply to you. (Chapter 4 discusses interest payments on security deposits.)

5. Special Notice Requirements

State laws typically require landlords to give a specified amount of notice when it comes to raising the rent or terminating the tenancy. (Notice requirements are explained in Chapter 15.) In rent control situations, however, the notice requirements are often tighter in two respects:

- **Raising the rent.** State law typically requires a 30-day notice for a rent increase. A local rent control law might also require the notice to tell the tenant that the rent control board can verify that the new rental amount is legal under the ordinance.
- **Terminating the tenancy.** Most rent control ordinances forbid the landlord from terminating (or refusing to renew) a tenancy without a "just cause," as explained above. And even where the landlord does have a just cause, the termination or non-renewal period is longer than that required under general state law.

C. When Is Your Rent Due?

Most leases and rental agreements call for rent to be paid monthly, in advance, on the first day of the month. However, landlords are normally legally free to establish a different monthly payment date—or even to require that rent be paid weekly or bi-

weekly. Some landlords make the rent payable each month on the date the tenant first moved in. Most find it easier, however, to pro-rate rent for a short first month and thereafter collect rent on the first of the month.

A twice-a-month schedule is the most common variation on the standard monthly payment arrangement. This is often imposed by landlords on tenants who have relatively low-paying jobs and get paid twice a month. Some landlords assume that a tenant can't be trusted to save the needed portion of the mid-month check until the first of the month. Can your landlord require bi-monthly checks from you, yet let a wealthier tenant pay once a month? Under certain circumstances, yes; in others, this would be an act of illegal discrimination. (Chapter 5 discusses discrimination in detail.)

Special provisions for public assistance recipients. If you receive public assistance in Hawaii, for example, you may choose to establish a due date for your rent that is on or before the third day after the day you usually receive your public assistance check. (For more information, check your state's rent rules. Citations are listed in "State Rent Rules," in Appendix I.)

1. When a Lease or Rental Agreement Doesn't Specify a Rent Due Date

In rare circumstances, a lease or rental agreement may not specify a due date—in which case, the law of your state will probably fill the breach.

In most states, for month-to-month rental agreements, rent is due at the beginning of the month, unless otherwise agreed. In a few states, however, including California, Indiana and Michigan, rent is not due until the end of the term unless the lease or rental agreement says otherwise. No landlord would deliberately allow a tenant who moved in on the first day of the month to wait until the 31st to pay rent. But a careless landlord might inadvertently allow it.

When Rent Is Due

If the lease doesn't specify otherwise, state law makes the rent due on these days:

1st of the month, in advance		Last day of the month
Alaska	Nebraska	California
Arizona	Nevada	Indiana
Connecticut	New Mexico	Michigan
Delaware	Oklahoma	North Dakota
Florida	Oregon	South Dakota
Hawaii	Rhode Island	
Iowa	South Carolina	
Kansas	Tennessee	
Kentucky	Virginia	
Montana		

Citations for these state laws are listed in "State Rent Rules" in Appendix I. States that are not listed here have no statute on the subject.

2. When Rent Is Due Under an Oral Lease

Oral leases, though never a good idea, are legal for tenancies of up to one year. If you have an oral lease and you and your landlord have not discussed when the rent is due, how do you know when to pay?

The safest route is to raise the issue immediately with the landlord. (And, in the process, get a written lease!) Failing that, consider the due date to be the same as it would be if you did, in fact, have a written lease that was silent on the issue (see "When Rent Is Due," above). For example, a tenant with an oral lease in Oregon (and the majority of states) would have to pay at the beginning of the term, but a tenant in California would consider rent to be due at the end. But if you live in a state where rent is due at the end of the rental period, unless otherwise arranged, heed this word of advice: Your landlord

probably doesn't know the law, and probably expects rent at the start of the term.

If you live in a state that has no law on the subject, we suggest paying at the start of the term.

3. When the Due Date Falls on a Weekend or Holiday

Most lease and rental agreements state that when the rent due date falls on a weekend day or legal holiday, the tenant must pay rent by the next business day. This sensible practice is legally required in some states and is the general practice in most. If your landlord insists on receiving the rent check by the first of the month (or other due date), even if mail is not delivered on that day, you may want to check your written agreement. If you get no help there, take a look at the law in your state; you may find that your landlord is violating it. If not, you may have to bite the bullet and get your rent in early.

D. Grace Periods for Late Rent

Lots of tenants are absolutely convinced that if rent is due on the 1st, they actually have until the 5th (or sometimes the 7th or even the 10th) of the month to pay, because they are within a legal grace period. Sorry, but this is not true. Rent is legally due on the date specified in your agreement or on the next business day, if your state's law contains that rule.

Landlords May Wink at Late Rent— For a While

Many landlords do not get upset about late rent or impose a late fee (discussed in Section F) until the rent is a few days past due. And most states actually require the landlord to give you a written notice granting you a few days (typically three to ten) in which to pay the rent or move out before beginning eviction procedures. But even if you believe nothing will happen if you pay rent a few days late, this does not mean that it's a good idea. You're far better off consistently paying the rent on time. If, on rare occasions, you can't do so, follow our suggestions for promptly and courteously informing your landlord of your money troubles. (See Section H.) This will keep you straight with the law and help avoid spats with your landlord about late fees.

A landlord who must repeatedly deliver pay-the-rent-or-leave notices may simply decide to end your tenancy—even if you always come up with the rent within the notice period.

See Chapter 17 for details on tenancy terminations for nonpayment of rent.

E. Where and How Rent Is Due

Your lease or rental agreement probably states where you should pay the rent and how it should be paid—for example, by check or money order only.

1. Where Rent Must Be Paid

Many, if not most, leases and rental agreements specify where you are to pay the rent, such as:

By mail to the landlord's business address. This is the most common method of rent payment. If you mail your rent check, make sure that it arrives on or before the date the rent is due—it is not sufficient to post your check on that date. Given the sluggishness of the U.S. mail, you should obviously allow at least three days for a local delivery. If your rent check will be in the mail on a Sunday or holiday, give yourself an extra day. If the due date is a Sunday or holiday, usually the following business day will suffice—but check your lease or rental agreement and your landlord's policy on this.

At your home. Your landlord may send someone to each unit every month to pick up the rent. This old-fashioned way of collecting the rent isn't well-suited to modern life, since in most households it's hard to find someone at home during the day. On the other hand, it's a tried-and-true method to pressure a tenant who is chronically late with the rent.

At your landlord's—or manager's—office. This option is practical only for those owners with on-site offices. Often, there is a drop box or mail slot; but if the office is open when you come by with the rent, spend a few minutes talking with your landlord or manager. It's a perfect time to raise any concerns, suggest improvements or thank the landlord for attention to previous requests. A conscientious landlord will appreciate the feedback and the opportunity to discuss little problems before they become big ones. Of course, don't make every visit a gripe session, or your landlord will come to dread your visits.

2. Form of Rent Payment

Most leases and rental agreements also specify how rent must be paid. Cash, check and money order are most common, but many landlords now allow payment by credit card or automatic debit. Tenants often feel that the form of payment should be up to them but, just like restaurants and shops, landlords are usually legally free to insist on a particular form of payment (exceptions involve government-subsidized rent payments).

New Ways to Pay the Rent

More and more owners, especially those with large numbers of rental units, are looking for ways to ensure that rent payments are quick and reliable. There are two common methods:

Credit card. Some landlords offer tenants the option of using credit cards. Some may even insist on an automatic billing to your credit account at the same time every month, which means you do not have to show up at the rental office with your card. This is an extremely convenient arrangement assuming your credit card can support it. It is obviously not a good idea if you are regularly over your credit limit or if you consistently pay interest on your balance.

Automatic debit. At the time you move in, your landlord may ask your permission—or even require you—to have rent payments debited automatically each month from your bank account and transferred into the landlord's account. This is also convenient but, like the automatic use of your credit card, should not be used by tenants whose checking accounts are thin or often overdrawn. (If your account cannot honor the automatic debit, it's just like having written a bad check.)

For most landlords, personal checks are the norm—but, folk wisdom to the contrary, your landlord does *not* have to accept your personal checks. If you don't have a checking account (or if you have bounced a few checks), your landlord may legally require a certified check or money order. (Section E3, below, explains landlords' rights to change the method of rent payment.)

There is no legal requirement that a landlord accept post-dated checks, and most won't, because there's absolutely no assurance that necessary funds will ever be deposited in the account. If you are short on funds, far better to handle it in a straight-forward manner. See Section H for advice on paying late rent.

⚠ Don't pay rent in cash unless you have no choice. These days, few landlords will accept rent in cash—they are justifiably wary of the risks of keeping large amounts of cash on hand. Your safety, too, will be imperiled if the word gets out that you regularly make a trip to the manager's office carrying several hundred dollars in cash. If you must pay in cash, be sure to get a written, dated receipt stating your name and the amount paid. It's your only proof that you did, indeed, pay the rent.

3. The Landlord's Right to Change Where and How Rent Is Due

If you've bounced a check or two, chronically pay rent late or have lost your job, can your landlord suddenly refuse personal checks and accept only certified checks or money orders? Or, if you've been paying by mail, as specified in your lease or rental agreement, can your landlord now require you to bring your rent to the manager's office?

Legally the answer is usually no. Your landlord may not unilaterally change terms in the lease or rental agreement. This means that if you have a year's lease, the payment arrangement is in force for a year; and if you rent month to month, most states require your landlord to give at least 30 days' written notice before changing a rental agreement clause.

If your lease or rental agreement doesn't say where and how rent is to be paid, your landlord's past practice is more likely to legally control how rent is paid. For example, a landlord who has always asked for your rent check on the first of the month, has established a due date that you must honor until the landlord formally changes the system with proper notice (in most states, 30 days).

How Landlords May Change Lease or Rental Agreement Terms

To change the terms and conditions of your lease or rental agreement—such as how and where you pay the rent, pet policies or late rent policies—your landlord must give you proper notice. Here are the basics, which are explained in detail in Chapter 15, Section A:

Type of tenancy	Amount of notice
Rental Agreement	Typically 30 days, although some states require as much as 45 or 60 days
Lease	Lease provisions cannot be changed until the lease runs out and a new tenancy begins

Don't be too quick to assert your rights. It may be a mistake to point out to your landlord that the rent payment clause cannot be changed without proper notice, or at all if you have a lease. Especially if you have been habitually late paying rent or have broken some other significant provision for which you could be evicted (for example, your boyfriend has moved in, violating your lease's restrictions on occupants), you may end up winning the battle but losing the war. In short, if the landlord has a legal ground for eviction (or may be considering giving you a 30-day notice to end a month-to-month tenancy), it is probably far better to go along with the rent payment change than to stand on your rights and invite the end of your tenancy. Similarly, if, after several bounced checks, a landlord demands a certified check or money order, it can make sense to go along for a few months. When you have paid on time for several months and hopefully things have calmed down, your landlord may once again be willing to accept your personal check.

If, however, the proposed change is both inconvenient to you and not motivated by your violation of a lease clause (but perhaps by the landlord's fear that because you lost your job you are or may become insolvent), you are within your rights to just

say no. As long as you have a lease, the landlord can't evict you because you've done nothing wrong. But if you have a month-to-month agreement, you may as well go along with the new system; the landlord can change it easily, anyway, by giving you proper notice.

A landlord who has been allowing you to pay rent in a different way than is required by the lease or rental agreement can probably start enforcing the written policy at any time. For example, suppose your lease or rental agreement specifies that rent be paid by certified check, but your landlord regularly and happily accepts your personal checks. Can the landlord suddenly decide to enforce the clause, even if your checks have not bounced? There is no clear answer. If such a dispute ended up in court, it would depend on whether the judge concluded that regular acceptance of your personal checks constituted a valid oral amendment of the written lease or rental agreement. Since your ability to prevail in court is unpredictable, unless you are very seriously inconvenienced by the change, it's probably best to accept your landlord's insistence that the written agreement be followed.

F. Late Charges and Discounts for Early Payments

Rare is the tenant who's never had a problem paying rent on time. If you are a conscientious and honest tenant who is temporarily short on funds, most landlords won't evict you for paying rent a little late one month. However, landlords are wary of sending a message that late payments are okay, and often impose a late fee when rent is even a few days late. But the size of the late fee is subject to legal limits, and in some situations it's not legal to impose one at all.

1. Are Late Fees Legal?

If your lease or rental agreement says nothing about late fees, your landlord may not impose one, no matter how reasonable it is. For example, if you hand your rent check to the landlord two days late and he tells you he will accept it only if you pay an additional $10, you may refuse unless your lease or rental agreement includes a late fee clause. But don't be too hasty to assert your rights if you live in a state that allows landlords to refuse late rent and begin eviction proceedings as soon as the rent is even one day late. (Chapter 17 explains your land-lord's legal options when you are late with the rent.)

2. Limits on Late Fees

Some states put dollar limits on late fees. (See "State Law Restrictions on Late Fees," below.) But even if your state doesn't, general legal principles still pro-hibit unreasonably high fees. Courts in a number of states have ruled that contracts that provide for un-reasonably high late charges are not enforceable. In other words, if you refuse to pay an outlandish late fee and your landlord attempts to evict you because of it, you should survive the eviction.

Rent control protections. Some rent control ordinances also regulate late fees. If you are covered by rent control, check the ordinance.

Of course, the crucial question in any court fight is: How big a fee is "unreasonable?" To make that determination, many courts use these guidelines:

- **The fee shouldn't begin immediately.** Nor-mally, a late fee should not apply until at least three days after the rent due date.
- **The fee must be within a certain percentage of your rent.** Your landlord is always on shaky ground if the late charge exceeds 5% of the rent. That's $38 on a $750-per-month rental. And a few states, including Maine, set lower limits. Even in the majority of states with no statutory limits, a higher late charge, such as 10%, might not be upheld in court, unless the rent was extremely late—at least ten days.
- **The fee should not increase without limit.** Late fees that increase a little bit each day the

rent is late are likely to be upheld only if the increase is moderate and there is an upper limit to the total charge. For example, $5 per day for the first four days the rent is late, and $10 for each subsequent day up to a $50 limit on a rent of $1,000 would amount to a maximum fee of 5% and would probably be accepted by a court. However, a late charge that increases fast and has no limit is likely to be considered too high.

If you evaluate your late fee in light of these guidelines and conclude that it is clearly too high, communicate your reasons in writing to your land-lord. If you decide not to pay it, be prepared to be asked to move at the first legal opportunity—with proper notice if you rent with a rental agreement, or by the landlord refusing to renew your lease when it expires. A sufficiently annoyed landlord might even initiate eviction proceedings against a tenant with substantial time remaining on the lease. To avoid the risk of eviction, it may make more sense to pay the fee and challenge it in small claims court, where the worst-case scenario is losing your time, court filing fee and the offer of a renewal when the lease is up.

3. Late Fees Disguised as Early Payment Discounts

Some landlords try to disguise excessive late charges by giving a so-called "discount" for on-time rent payment. Here's how this dodge is often structured: A landlord who knows that he can't get away with charging a $50 late charge on a $425 monthly rent payment will set the rent at $475 and offer a $50 discount if the rent is no more than three days late. Fortunately, this bit of landlord subterfuge is un-likely to stand up in court unless the discount for on-time payment is modest. Giving a discount of more than 4% to 5% is in effect the same as charg-ing an excessive late fee, and a judge is likely to see it as such.

Of course, if you are always prompt with the rent, a "discount" for prompt payment may not be a problem—after all, if you argue the point with the landlord when you sign the lease or rental agree-ment, you might end up with a reasonable late fee but a higher rent. And you can still complain about paying an overly high fee if, unfortunately, you *are* late with the rent a time or two. Most courts will still invalidate an unreasonable late fee although you may have in a sense benefited from its prompt payment "discount" by paying rent on time, or even if you have paid the late fee once or twice before complaining.

4. Avoiding Late Fees

Obviously, the surest way to avoid a late fee is to pay your rent on time. But if you cannot do this, don't automatically assume that there's nothing you can do about the penalty. Negotiation is often the tenant's best friend.

You should handle the late fee in the same manner that you handle the late rent payment itself: If you know that you will not be able to make the rent due date, notify your landlord in advance, explain the situation, suggest a payment schedule and get it in writing. (Section H explains this process in detail.) As part of your negotiations, ask

State Law Restrictions on Late Fees	
California	Pre-set late fees are invalid.
Connecticut	Landlords may not charge late fee until nine days after rent is due.
Delaware	To charge a late fee, landlord must maintain an office in the county where the rental unit is located at which tenants can pay rent. If a landlord doesn't have a local office for this purpose, ten-ant has three extra days (beyond the due date) to pay rent before the landlord can charge a late fee. Late fee cannot exceed 5% of rent and cannot be imposed until the rent is more than five days late.
Maine	Late fees cannot exceed 4% of the amount due for 30 days. Landlord must notify tenants, in writing, of any late fee at the start of the tenancy, and cannot impose it until rent is 15 days late
Maryland	Late fees can't exceed 5% of the rent due.
Massachusetts	Late fees, including interest on late rent, may not be imposed un-til the rent is 30 days late.
New Jersey	Landlord must wait five days be-fore charging a late fee.
New Mexico	Late fee may not exceed 10% of the rent specified per rental pe-riod. Landlord must notify the ten-ant of the charge no later than the end of the next rental period.

State Law Restrictions on Late Fees (continued)	
North Carolina	Late fee cannot be higher than $15 or 5% of the rental payment, whichever is greater, and may not be imposed until the tenant is five days late paying rent.
Oklahoma	Pre-set late fees are invalid.
Oregon	Landlord must wait four days after the rent due date to assess late fee, and must disclose the late fee policy in the rental agreement. A flat late fee must be "reasonable." A daily late fee may not be more than 6% of a reasonable late fee, and cannot add up to more than 5% of the monthly rent.
Tennessee	Landlord can't charge late fee until five days have passed. Fee can't exceed 10% of the amount past due.

Citations to these state laws on late rent fees are in "State Rent Rules" in Appendix I. States not listed here do not have statutes governing late rent charges, but case law may address the issue.

for a waiver or reduction of any late penalty—many landlords, appreciating your advance notice, will be willing to forgo that extra nickel. (The sample letter in Section H shows how.)

G. Returned Check Charges

Like any other business, your landlord has the legal right to charge an extra fee if your rent check bounces, but only if you knew in advance (in the lease or rental agreement, orally or by means of an obvious sign in the rental office where you bring your monthly check) that the fee would be imposed. And of course, if you regularly give your landlord rubber checks, don't be surprised if you receive a tenancy termination notice or, at least, a demand that you pay the rent by money order or another cash equivalent.

Like late charges, bounced check charges must be reasonable. Your landlord should charge no more than the amount the bank charges for a returned check, probably $10 to $20 per returned item, plus a few dollars for her trouble.

If your check has bounced, you might get a little breathing room if your landlord follows a policy of letting the bank present the check again to your bank. But don't count on it—experienced landlords instruct their banks to return bad checks after the first rejection, so they can confront the tenant and demand that the check be made good immediately.

Laws in some states allow landlords to charge interest on a bounced check, whether or not your lease or rental agreement says anything about late check charges. For example, California landlords may charge 10% per year interest on a bounced check—so, for example, on a $1,000 rent check that isn't made good for a month, the landlord can demand an additional $8.34. (Cal. Civ. Code §3289(b).) Your state's consumer protection office should be able to tell you whether your state has a similar law. (For the phone number, see "State Consumer Protection Offices" in Appendix I.)

H. Negotiating Partial or Delayed Rent Payments

Even a model tenant can suffer a temporary financial setback that makes it impossible to pay the rent on time or in full. If this happens to you, don't immediately assume that you will be evicted or even subjected to a late charge. A landlord who considers you a good tenant won't want to lose you, since it's often difficult and expensive to find and move in good tenants. This means you can probably get the landlord to accept a portion of the rent now—maybe even a small portion—and the rest later. Here are five sensible approaches to take:

1. **Give your landlord written notice (as much as possible) that you will not be able to pay on time.** By taking this responsible and courteous step, you seize the psychological high road. And even more important, you raise the issue *before* your landlord, faced with a bounced check or an empty rent envelope, has a chance to work up a righteous head of steam. This early warning approach could backfire—with your landlord simply giving you a legal demand to pay the rent or move out. But you don't have much to lose, because most landlords who receive no rent or your rubber check will promptly do exactly the same thing.

2. **Explain your difficulties and emphasize that they are only temporary.** If your landlord is a fairly decent sort and likely to empathize with your predicament, it's best to share at least some of the reasons behind your request. Emphasize your good, long-term relationship and—if you can—that your predicament will be short-lived and not likely to recur. The point, of course, is to put a human face on your situation. It's up to you to decide where your desire for privacy ends and your need to defer your rent begins.

3. **Offer to pay at least some of the rent on time.** Even if you have to borrow money, try to pay at least a portion of the rent on time. By putting even a small amount of money where your mouth is, you offer tangible evidence of your intention to follow through with the rest of your obligation. Your landlord knows that a tenant who has paid a portion of the rent is less likely to skip out than one who has had a totally free ride.

4. **Give your landlord written assurance of your plan to pay.** Most landlords, even the most accommodating, will want a written agreement of your promise to pay the full rent by a certain date, such as the 15th of the month. Your landlord will probably ask for a date that is tied to a verifiable outside event, such as your payday or after your taxes are due. And a written agreement will protect you if, despite an oral agreement, your landlord suddenly decides to evict you for nonpayment of rent. (If, however, you've already received an overdue rent notice and make a partial rent payment, your landlord may still give you a termination notice for the balance.) A sample letter asking the landlord to accept late rent is shown below. If the landlord agrees to your request to pay rent late, you should follow up with a written note confirming your exact agreement. Send your letter "return receipt requested," so that you can prove, if need be, that the landlord received it. In some situations, the landlord may want to draw up a more formal document.

5. **Keep your promise.** If you run into further difficulties and need to ask for an additional small extension, be sure that you have at least paid an additional portion of the overdue amount first. Obviously, your ability to re-negotiate is limited by the landlord's favorable opinion of you and his desire to keep you as a tenant, both of which will probably decline the more your payments are delayed.

I. Rent Increases

Rent increases are an inevitable part of any tenant's life. But landlords cannot raise the rent at whim. The timing of a rent increase, and the way your landlord communicates it, are governed by statute in most states.

Sample Letter Asking Landlord to Accept Late Rent

123 Shady Lane
Madison, Wisconsin 12345
(608) 555-1234

January 25, 200X

Mr. Max Mason
100 North Main Street
Madison, Wisconsin 12345

Dear Mr. Mason,

As you know, I have been your tenant at 123 Shady Lane for the past ten months, and I have always met the terms and conditions of my lease. Not only have I paid my rent fully and on time, but I have treated your property with care and respect. I enjoy living at Shady Lane and hope to stay here.

The reason for this letter is to ask you whether I may pay part of next month's rent, due on February 1st, late. I would like to pay half the rent on the 1st, and the balance on the 15th. Unfortunately and with practically no notice, I have been laid off from my job as a computer programmer as a result of downsizing at ABC Software. This layoff happened just after I had spent most of my savings on computer equipment I need for the freelance programming work I do on the side. I have been diligently looking for a new job and already have three interviews scheduled next week. I have also applied for unemployment benefits and I expect to start receiving checks in a few weeks. After February, I should have no problem paying the rent on time.

I would greatly appreciate it if you could accommodate my request. And since my finances are already stretched, I would also appreciate it if you would waive the late fee. I will be happy to sign an agreement laying out these terms.

Please call me (555-1234) so we can discuss this further. If I don't hear from you within a few days, I'll phone you at your office. Thank you very much for your consideration.

Yours truly,

Tom Tenant

Tom Tenant

1. When Your Landlord Can Raise the Rent

Except in cities with rent control, your landlord's legal right to raise the rent depends primarily on whether you have a lease or a month-to-month rental agreement.

a. Leases

Your landlord can't raise the rent until the end of the lease period, unless the lease itself provides for an increase or you agree. When the lease expires, the landlord can present you with a new lease that has a higher rent or other changed terms.

b. Rental Agreements

If you rent under a month-to-month rental agreement, the landlord can raise the rent by giving you proper written notice, which is 30 days in most states. (If you pay rent every 15 days, you may only be entitled to 15 days' notice.) In a few states, however, landlords must provide 45 or 60 days' notice to raise the rent for a month-to-month tenancy. (See "Notice Required to Increase Rent for a Month-to-Month Tenancy," below.)

c. Improper Notice

There are two ways in which landlords typically violate their notice obligations. Either they don't give enough notice before the increase is set to take effect or they fail to provide written notice at all. Your response should depend on which error is involved.

The notice period is too short. If your landlord writes you on June 20 that your rent, due on July 1, has gone up, you haven't been given enough notice. You absolutely do not have to pay the increased rent on July 1, but of course, you must still make your existing rent payment. However, if your land-lord has complied with other notice requirements (discussed below), you *will* be expected to pay the extra rent as of 30 days from the date you got the notice. In other words, your landlord's notice is effective as soon as the legal notice period has elapsed. This might mean you have to pay the next month's rent at the old rate; but, at some point during that month (when the notice period expires), you'll need to pay a pro-rated share of the rent at the new rate.

> **EXAMPLE:** Simon, a month-to-month tenant, paid his rent for the coming month on the first of the month. State law requires 30 days' notice before a rent increase can take effect. Simon's landlord gave him written notice of an increase on the 20th of June. On July 1, Simon paid full rent at the old rate. On July 20, Simon owed his landlord an additional sum: the rent per day at the new rate minus the rent per day at the old rate, times ten. On August 1, he paid the full increased rent.

The notice is oral or not properly delivered. State laws all require rent increase notices to be delivered to a tenant in writing; in some states, certified mail is required. Oral notices are ineffective and, unless you specifically agree to the rent in-crease, you are not obligated to pay any more money. But if you ignore a polite oral notice from a landlord you know well, be prepared for an angry confrontation followed by a speedily drafted written notice and a chill in your long-term relationship.

If you receive an oral notice and don't consider it worthwhile, in the long run, to fight your landlord on this issue, be sure to put details on the rent increase (and any other changes in your rental agreement) in writing. One way to do this is to ask the landlord to prepare a new rental agreement. (Chapter 15 shows how.) Another approach is to write a letter to the landlord confirming the new terms. Ask the landlord to sign and date it and return it to you. (Letters of understanding are explained in Chapter 2, Section C.) This will protect you against any misunderstanding as to the amount of the increase. The sample letter below shows you how to lock in an oral rent raise. You would be wise to send it return receipt requested, and to keep the receipt in a safe place with your other rental papers.

Sample Letter
Formalizing a Rent Increase

789 Walnut Street
Concord, CA 12345
(510) 555-4567

June 1, 200X

Mr. Mike Moskowitz
788 Walnut Street
Pleasanton, CA 12345

Dear Mr. Moskowitz,

In a conversation today you informed me that my rent, currently $650 per month, will go up $50, to $700, as of the first of July. Please sign and date this letter confirming this understanding and return it to me at the above address.

Yours truly,

William Ames

William Ames

_____ _____

s/Mike Moskowitz   Date

Local rent control laws also affect rent increase notices. If you live in an area covered by rent control and get a rent increase notice, be sure the notice (as well as the amount of the increase) complies with the laws of your city. Check your ordinance or contact the rent board.

2. How High Can the Rent Go?

In areas without rent control, there is no limit on the amount your landlord can increase the rent. The only exception to this rule is if a rent increase is in retaliation for a tenant for exercising a legal right.

Recognizing that most tenants want to know when and by how much the rent is likely to rise, some savvy landlords announce their rent increase policy in advance. For example, your landlord may say the rent will go up every January, based on a formula tied to the Consumer Price Index. Can you rely on this and successfully resist any other type of rent increase? It depends. If the policy is part of your written lease or rental agreement, the landlord is bound by it. But if it is an oral policy, or one that is part of another tenant's rental agreement but not yours, you'll have a very hard time convincing a judge to hold the landlord to it. If your landlord's policy is not in your lease or rental agreement, ask him to amend the lease or rental agreement to include it. (See Chapter 15 for advice on how to amend these documents.)

Rent increases often trigger security deposit increases. Many states limit the amount a landlord can charge for a security deposit. Typically, deposits are capped as a multiple of the monthly rent—for example, the maximum deposit may be twice the monthly rent. But this means that if the rent has gone up legally, the security deposit may also be legally increased. For example, if the deposit is twice the monthly rent, and your $500 rent has gone up $50, the deposit limit rises from $1,000 to $1,100. See Chapter 4 for more on security deposit increases.

3. Rent Increases as Retaliation or Discrimination

No landlord may raise the rent in a discriminatory manner—for example, only for members of a certain race or religion or for families with children. (Discrimination is explained in detail in Chapter 5.) And in most states your landlord can't use a rent increase (or evict you or decrease services, either) in retaliation against you for exercising a legal right—for example, in response to your legitimate complaint

Notice Required to Increase Rent for a Month-to-Month Tenancy

Alabama	No statute	Nevada	45 days
Alaska*	One month	New Hampshire*	30 days
Arizona*	30 days	New Jersey*	30 days
Arkansas*	30 days	New Mexico*	30 days
California*	30 days	New York*	30 days
Colorado	No statute	North Carolina	No statute
Connecticut	No statute	North Dakota*	30 days
Delaware	60 days	Ohio*	30 days
District of Columbia*	30 days	Oklahoma*	30 days
Florida	No statute	Oregon*	30 days
Georgia	60 days	Pennsylvania*	30 days
Hawaii	45 days	Rhode Island*	30 days
Idaho	15 days	South Carolina*	30 days
Illinois*	30 days	South Dakota*	One month
Indiana*	30 days	Tennessee	60 days
Iowa*	30 days	Texas*	30 days
Kansas*	30 days	Utah	No statute
Kentucky*	30 days	Vermont	60 days
Louisiana	No statute	Virginia*	30 days
Maine*	30 days	Washington*	20 days
Maryland*	30 days	West Virginia*	30 days
Massachusetts*	30 days	Wisconsin*	One month
Michigan*	30 days	Wyoming	No statute
Minnesota*	30 days		
Mississippi*	30 days		
Missouri*	30 days		
Montana*	30 days		
Nebraska*	30 days		

*The statutes in these states do not cover the notice required to raise the rent in a month-to-month tenancy. They do, however, specify one month to terminate a tenancy. Presumably, if you can terminate a tenancy on one month's notice, you can raise the rent with one month's notice.

Citations for these state laws are listed in "State Rent Rules" in Appendix I.

to a public agency about defective conditions or your decision to withhold rent because the landlord won't fix the broken water pipes in your rental unit. (Chapters 8 and 17 discuss your rights to demand fit and habitable housing, free from the threat of eviction.)

How will you know whether a rent increase is in response to your exercise of a legal right? In some states, if you get a rent increase soon—typically, within three to six months—after you've complained about defective conditions, the landlord is presumed to have been acting in retaliation. (See "State Laws Prohibiting Landlord Retaliation" in Appendix I.) If you refuse to pay the increase, and the landlord sues to evict you for nonpayment of rent, you should survive the eviction. Landlords in these states must prove to the judge that retaliation was not, in fact, the motive behind the increase. But if the increase follows a general policy that your landlord has announced before your use of a legal remedy, and if the landlord has applied the increase to all tenants, it will be hard to show that your recent exercise of a legal right such as rent withholding had anything to do with it.

For example, many landlords raise rent once a year in an amount that more or less reflects the increase in the Consumer Price Index. Other landlords use a more complicated formula that takes into account other rents in the area, as well as such factors as increased costs of maintenance or rehabilitation. They make sure to inform their tenants about the rent increase in advance and apply the increase uniformly to all their tenants. This kind of consistent approach usually protects the landlord against any claim of a retaliatory rent increase by a tenant who has coincidentally made a legitimate complaint about the condition of the premises or withheld rent.

If you think a rent hike is motivated by your assertion of a legal right, you can refuse to pay the increase, and if the landlord tries to evict you for nonpayment of rent, assert in court that the increase was done to retaliate against you. But before you do, ask yourself the following questions:

1. **Does state law presume landlord retaliation in some circumstances?** In some states, if rent is increased within a certain time following a tenant's legitimate complaint to a public agency, use of a remedy such as rent withholding or exercise of a legal right such as organizing a tenants' group, the law presumes that the landlord acted improperly. This brand of anti-retaliation statute gives you an important tactical advantage in the courtroom: It is up to the landlord to convince the judge that the increase was not based on retaliation. If the landlord can't convince the judge, you should win without even opening your mouth.

2. **How soon after your action did the rent increase come?** Obviously, the shorter the interval between your exercise of a legal right and the date of the increase, the more suspicious it becomes.

3. **How large was the increase?** Judges are more likely to view a large rent increase (rather than a small one) as the landlord's way to punish or drive away a troublesome tenant.

4. **Does the rent increase affect you alone, or does it apply to many others?** Your chances of proving a retaliatory motive will be greatly increased if you can show that you alone, or you and other activist tenants, but not tenants in similar units, received a rent increase.

5. **Is your landlord known for repeatedly and seriously trampling on tenants' rights?** Your landlord's reputation is certainly a relevant factor if you contemplate challenging a rent increase. You can learn whether the landlord is a frequent visitor to landlord-tenant or small claims court by asking the local tenants' organization or even your fellow tenants. Technically, you aren't supposed to argue in court that the landlord's past illegal rent raises prove guilt now, too; most judges will try to confine you to the facts of your case alone. But it's fairly easy to make sure the judge knows your landlord is a scofflaw—share your information succinctly and quickly, then

listen politely while the judge gives you a little lecture on the rules of evidence.

 If you are protected by rent control, your landlord's reputation before the rent control board is just as important as his track record in court. To find out whether your landlord has been repeatedly challenged before the board, check with the local tenants' union.

6. **How disruptive or expensive, from the landlord's point of view, was your exercise of a legal right?** It's easier to win these cases where you can convince a judge that the landlord has a strong motive to get even. Did you cause the landlord considerable time, expense, aggravation or embarrassment? For example, if you complained to the local health department that your housing is uninhabitable because the roof leaked, and the department ordered your landlord to put on a new roof, that's an expensive job that your landlord might resent highly. This anger could well, you'll claim, prompt a retaliatory rent hike. Similarly, a charge of discrimination (which

the landlord might even ultimately defeat) could easily generate strong feelings of bitterness. On the other hand, your isolated request for a necessary and inexpensive repair is far less likely in the eyes of a judge to engender serious landlord revenge. Of course, this theory is based on the assumption that retaliation is always linked to important matters— and we know that some landlords are inclined towards pettiness.

EXAMPLE: Ira rents a two-bedroom unit in a large apartment complex. Within the past year, he has asked his landlord for new carpets and drapes, which were grudgingly provided; and he has organized the rest of the tenants into a union so that they can collectively press for improvements in the property. Ira received a steep rent hike, which he refused to pay. When the landlord tried to evict him for nonpayment of the increased portion, Ira argued that the raise was in retaliation for his requests and political activities. Noting that none of the other two-bedroom tenants received similar hikes, the judge ruled in Ira's favor.

THIS IS A VERY STRONG APPEAL MR. HODGEKISS

J. Talking the Landlord Out of a Rent Increase

Legally, there is nothing you can do about a legal rent hike that doesn't violate a rent control ordinance and is not discriminatory or retaliatory. The landlord can charge as much as the market will bear. But practically, you can appeal to your landlord—to his business sense and to his heart. The first approach is built upon the *landlord's* reputation as a fair and human businessperson; the second approach emphasizes *your* good qualities as an attractive tenant. For the best results, use both.

No increase is good business. Landlording is a business, entered into to make money, but smart landlords realize that high rents are not the only route to high profits. Solvent, long-term tenants are the best tenants because they are low-maintenance—they don't have to be evicted, sued, coddled, cleaned up after, scolded for breaking the rules or interviewed and investigated as part of the time- and money-consuming new-tenant application process. If you are a good, long-term tenant and you can convince your landlord that the rent hike will make you move, your landlord might think twice, or at least moderate the increase. (On the other hand, if you have been less than straight in your dealings with the landlord, don't expect any accommodations.)

Obviously, your leverage with the landlord will increase if you can show that many other stable, long-term tenants are also upset and considering moving. If the rent hike affects others in your building, work together to present your collective plea. (See Chapter 19 for suggestions on working with other tenants.) Remember, even in a tight rental market, lots of long-term tenants are hard to find.

The increase is morally unfair. If you think your landlord will respond to an appeal based on kindness and fairness, give it a try. Design your appeal on the assumption that the landlord is a decent

person who wants to be a fair and honest landlord (hopefully, this won't be too much of a stretch). Let the landlord know you're sure that only some unusual circumstance would have led to the request for such an increase. Ideally, after reading your letter your landlord will be convinced that insisting on a big rent increase would be an uncharacteristic, somewhat embarrassing thing to do.

Below is a sample letter in response to a rent increase. Obviously, your letter will have to be closely tailored to your own situation. Note how the writers have documented the various ways in which they have been model tenants (the appeal to the landlord's business motives), and have acknowledged how decent the landlord has been in the past (the appeal to the heart). In addition, they have told the landlord, who lives in the same building, that there is a very real chance of losing quiet neighbors. Is all of this worth $300 a month? Hopefully, yes.

Sample Letter in Response to a Rent Increase

787, 788 & 789 Cherry Street
St. Louis, MO 12345
(314) 555-4567

June 15, 200X

Mr. Joe Jacks, Owner
790 Cherry Street
St. Louis, MO 12345

Dear Mr. Jacks,

We were dismayed to receive your notice of an intended rent increase of $100 per month. While we realize that you are within your legal rights to raise the rent, we would like to ask you to reconsider this decision.

As you know, the three families who have signed this letter have been your tenants and neighbors in your fourplex for the last four, five and seven years. None of us have ever been late with the rent; we all have always responded promptly to your requests to inspect and repair various aspects of the building, and have never intentionally damaged your property. During the time that we have lived here, no one has protested the two rent increases (the last being nine months ago). We have been careful to promptly notify you of any problems, and have not insisted on unnecessary, cosmetic improvements.

Having lived in many rentals over the years, we have appreciated your prompt attention to all the large and small details involved in running your business, and we have especially appreciated your kindness and understanding when things went a little bit awry. (Remember when Jimmy Spenser's basketball went through the front window?) The increased rent, however, will make it extremely difficult for us to continue living here.

We hope that you will take a few moments to consider our request that the increase be rescinded or, at the least, lessened significantly. We have enjoyed living here and hope to continue doing so.

Yours truly,

Alex Corinthos
Benny Spenser
Cathy Webber

Security Deposits

Almost all landlords require their tenants to pay a deposit before moving in, typically at the time you sign a lease or rental agreement. This payment, usually called a "security deposit" or "last month's rent," can amount to several hundreds, or even thousands, of dollars. Landlords charge security deposits to assure that you'll pay rent when due and keep the rental unit in good condition. If you damage the property or leave early owing rent, your landlord can use your deposit to cover what you owe.

Security deposits constitute a big investment on your part, and they are a major source of friction between landlords and tenants. Fortunately, most states impose fairly strict rules on how landlords can collect and use deposits and how they must return them when the tenant moves out. Many states even require landlords to put deposits in a separate account and pay interest on them. Landlords who violate security deposit laws are often subject to substantial financial penalties.

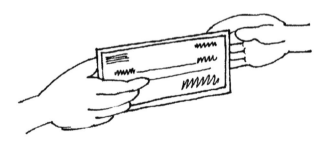

Related topics covered in this book include:
- Credit-check fees, holding deposits and other fees landlords may charge: Chapter 1.
- Lease and rental agreement provisions on security deposits: Chapter 2.
- State rules on how and when deposits must be returned, and deductions allowed for cleaning, damage and unpaid rent: Chapter 16.
- How to handle legal disputes involving deposits when you move out: Chapter 16.

Where to Get More Information on Security Deposits

For more information about security deposit rules in your state, get a current copy of your state's security deposit law (statute). Start by referring to "Citations for State Laws on Security Deposits" in Appendix I. Note that this table highlights exemptions to state security deposit laws. Then read the statute at a public library, law library or online. (See Chapter 20 for information on using the law library and accessing state statutes online.)

In addition, be sure to check local ordinances. Cities (particularly those with rent control) may add their own rules on security deposits, such as a limit on the amount landlords can charge or a requirement that landlords pay interest on deposits.

A. Dollar Limits on Deposits

Many states limit the amount a landlord can collect as a deposit to an amount equal to one or two months of rent. (Sometimes larger deposits are allowed for furnished rentals.) In some states, the rent a landlord collects in advance for the last month is not considered part of the security deposit limit, while in others it is. (Section C, below, covers last month's rent.)

Rent that a landlord collects in advance for the first month is never considered part of the security deposit limit. However, a landlord who demanded several months' rent in advance would almost always run afoul of state security deposit limits. Advance rent, beyond paying for the first month of your tenancy, is considered part of the deposit in most states. In highly competitive rental areas, such as New York City, tenants applying for desirable rental units occasionally offer to pre-pay several months' rent in order to convince landlords to choose them over other applicants. But is a landlord who collects this money (clearly in excess of the state's security deposit limit) in violation of the law?

Probably not, as long as it's the tenant's idea and the landlord has not made the extra rent payment a condition of getting the unit. In short, a tenant who wants to waive this protection of the state's deposit limit may; but the landlord cannot do it unilaterally.

The deposit limit in your state may depend on factors such as:

- your age (senior citizens may have a lower deposit ceiling)
- whether or not the rental unit is furnished
- whether you have a month-to-month rental agreement or a long-term lease
- whether or not you have a pet or waterbed, and
- the number of rental properties the landlord owns (smaller landlords may be exempt from security deposit limits).

For details, see "State Laws on Security Deposit Limits," below.

EXAMPLE: Jane, Reuben and Sandy, who live in different states, each pay $900 rent per month for an unfurnished apartment. The maximum security deposit they may pay ranges from $900 to $2,700:

- Reuben (Hawaii) pays $900 (one month's rent)
- Jane (California) pays $1,800 (two months' rent)
- Sandy (Nevada) pays $2,700 (three months' rent).

Don't pay an excessive deposit. If your landlord is requesting a deposit that exceeds your state's limit, show him a copy of your state's security deposit statute (if any) and ask him to lower the deposit. If your landlord refuses, contact your city or district attorney's office, tenants' rights group or state consumer protection agency (see the list in Appendix I) for advice.

If you have a hard time coming up with the deposit, see if the landlord will reduce the deposit or allow you to pay it in installments. Here are a few tips for approaching your landlord. Obviously,

these strategies are more likely to work if you have a good credit history and references and live in an area with lots of rentals. And don't ask for a lower deposit or an installment plan until you definitely have the place. A prospective landlord may be put off if you ask for special favors such as a lower deposit right off the bat. Wait until the landlord has offered you the rental unit before you start asking for special considerations.

- **Ask to pay in installments.** Offer to pay half the deposit up front with the rest on an affordable installment plan. Some landlords will say yes only if you can come up with the whole deposit in 30 to 60 days, but others will let you increase the amount a little each month until it's paid off in six months or more.
- **Suggest a cosigner.** A landlord may be reassured if a financially responsible friend or relative agrees to pay the deposit if you can't. (Chapter 2, Section F, discusses cosigners.)
- **Offer to buy renter's insurance.** A landlord who's worried about damage may be willing to reduce the deposit if you provide this extra measure of protection to cover any damage done to the rental property. (Chapter 2, Section D, explains renter's insurance.)
- **Offer to pay slightly more rent (assuming there are no rent control limits).** Some landlords may agree to a substantially lower deposit in exchange for a higher rent.

EXAMPLE: You offer to pay $25 more per month for rent in exchange for the landlord cutting the security deposit from $1,000 to $500. True, unlike the security deposit, the extra rent is not refundable. But if it allows you to rent a place you otherwise wouldn't qualify for, paying the extra money over time may be worth it.

Your landlord's security deposit policy cannot discriminate illegally. A landlord who charges some tenants the maximum deposit, and others less, should have a good explanation. This means if your landlord is charging the tenant next

State Laws on Security Deposit Limits

Here's the limit each state sets on the amount of security deposit landlords can charge. "No statutory limit" means that the state does not specify the amount landlords can charge. Appendix I contains "Citations for State Laws on Security Deposits."

State	Limit	State	Limit
Alabama	No statutory limit	Mississippi	No statutory limit
Alaska	Two months' rent, except where rent exceeds $2,000 per month	Missouri	Two months' rent
		Montana	No statutory limit
Arizona	One and one-half months' rent (unless tenant voluntarily agrees to pay more)	Nebraska	One month's rent (no pets); one and one-quarter months' rent (pets)
Arkansas	Two months' rent	Nevada	Three months' rent
California	Two months' rent (unfurnished, no waterbed); two and one-half months' rent (unfurnished, tenant has waterbed); three months' rent (furnished, no waterbed); three and one-half months' rent (furnished, tenant has waterbed)	New Hampshire	One month's rent or $100, whichever is greater
		New Jersey	One and one-half month's rent
		New Mexico	One month's rent (for rental agreement less than one year); no limit for leases of one year or more
Colorado	No statutory limit	New York	No statutory limit
Connecticut	Two months' rent (tenant under 62 years of age); one month's rent (tenant 62 years of age or older)	North Carolina	One and one-half months' rent for month-to-month rental agreements; two months' rent if term is longer than two months
Delaware	One month's rent on leases for one year or more; no limit for month-to-month rental agreements	North Dakota	One month's rent (or $1,500 if tenant has a pet)
		Ohio	No statutory limit
District of Columbia	One month's rent	Oklahoma	No statutory limit
		Oregon	No statutory limit
Florida	No statutory limit	Pennsylvania	Two months' rent for first year of renting; one month's rent during the second and subsequent years of renting
Georgia	No statutory limit		
Hawaii	One month's rent		
Idaho	No statutory limit	Rhode Island	One month's rent
Illinois	No statutory limit	South Carolina	No statutory limit
Indiana	No statutory limit	South Dakota	One month's rent (higher deposit may be charged if special conditions pose a danger to maintenance of the premises)
Iowa	Two months' rent		
Kansas	One month's rent (unfurnished, no pets); one and one-half months' rent (unfurnished with pets or furnished with no pets)		
		Tennessee	No statutory limit
		Texas	No statutory limit
Kentucky	No statutory limit	Utah	No statutory limit
Louisiana	30 days	Vermont	No statutory limit
Maine	Two months' rent	Virginia	Two months' rent
Maryland	Two months' rent or $50, whichever is greater	Washington	No statutory limit
Massachusetts	Two months' rent	West Virginia	No statutory limit
Michigan	One and one-half months' rent	Wisconsin	No statutory limit
Minnesota	No statutory limit	Wyoming	No statutory limit

door a lower deposit because she's purchased renter's insurance, you should be in good legal shape to ask for the same deal. If the landlord refuses, without good reason, to give you an equivalent deal, you may have a discrimination case if your race, religion, disability, age or family status place you in a protected category. See Chapter 5 for information on illegal discrimination.

B. How Landlords May Increase Deposits

Tenants often ask whether or not it's legal for a landlord to raise their security deposit after they move in. The answer is that it depends on the situation.

Leases: If you have a fixed-term lease, your landlord may not raise the security deposit during the term of your lease, unless the lease allows it (most don't). Security deposits may be increased, however, when the lease is renewed or becomes a month-to-month tenancy.

Written Rental Agreements: If you have a month-to-month tenancy, a security deposit can be increased just the same way the rent can be, typically by giving you a written notice 30 days in advance of the change (see Chapter 3). Of course, the deposit can't exceed the maximum amount allowed by your state's security deposit law. (See Section A, above.)

> EXAMPLE: Jules rents an apartment for $750 a month in a state that limits security deposits to one month's rent. If his landlord raises the rent to $1,000, the maximum deposit his landlord may collect goes up to $1,000. But the deposit doesn't go up automatically. To raise the deposit amount, his landlord must give Jules the required 30 days' notice.

Local rent control ordinances typically limit deposits as well as rents. (See Chapter 3 for more on rent control.)

C. Last Month's Rent

A landlord may want you to pay a sum of money called "last month's rent" before you move in, as a form of insurance against your leaving early and owing rent. Problems can arise when:

- the landlord tries to use last month's rent to cover repairs or cleaning, or
- the rent goes up—and the landlord wants you to top off the last month's rent.

We'll look at these situations below.

1. Applying Last Month's Rent to Damage or Cleaning

If you have paid your landlord a sum labeled last month's rent and your tenancy is ending (voluntarily or involuntarily), chances are that you will not write a rent check for your last month. After all, you've already paid for that last month, right? Surprisingly, many tenants do pay for the last month anyway, often forgetting that they have prepaid. What happens to that last month's rent?

Ideally, you'll leave the place clean and in good repair, enabling the landlord to refund the entire last month's rent and all or most of your security deposit. But if you leave the place a mess, most states allow your landlord to treat "last month's rent" as part of the security deposit and use all or part of it for cleaning or to repair or replace damaged items.

> EXAMPLE: Katie's landlord required a security deposit of one month's rent, plus last month's rent. Her state law allowed a landlord to use all advance deposits to cover a tenant's unpaid rent or damage, regardless of what the landlord called the deposit. When Katie moved out, she didn't owe any back rent, but she left her apartment a shambles. The landlord was entitled to use the entire deposit, including that labeled last month's rent, to cover the damage.

A few states, such as Massachusetts, restrict the use of money labeled as "last month's rent" to its stated purpose: the rent for the last month of your occupancy. In these states, if your landlord uses any of last month's rent to repair the cabinet you broke, he's violating the law.

> **EXAMPLE:** Mike's landlord collected a security deposit of one month's rent, plus last month's rent. Mike's state required that landlords use money collected for the last month as last month's rent only, not for cleaning or repairs. When Mike moved out, he didn't owe any rent but he, too, left his apartment a mess. Mike's landlord had to refund his last month's rent and, when the remaining security deposit proved too little to cover the damage Mike had caused, the landlord had to sue Mike in small claims court for the excess.

Last month's rent restrictions are often developed in court cases, not statutes. For this reason, we can't give you a neat list of states that restrict your landlord's use of your last month's rent. If you want to find out how courts in your state have ruled on the use of last month's rent, see our advice on doing legal research in Chapter 20.

Your landlord may want to use money labeled last month's rent before the end of your tenancy. As explained below in Section F, the landlord may use your security deposit during your tenancy to pay for repairs that your actions have necessitated. If he also holds last month's rent, in most states he can use that during your tenancy, too, if your security deposit is insufficient.

2. If Your Rent Goes Up

If you've paid the last month's rent in advance, and the rent at the end of your tenancy is the same as when you began, you're paid up. However, if the rent has increased, but you have not been asked to top off the last month's rent held by the landlord, questions arise. Do you owe the landlord for the difference? If so, can he take money from your security deposit to make it up?

Unfortunately, there are no clear answers. But because landlords in every state are allowed to ask you to top off the last month's rent at the time they increase the rent, judges would probably allow them to go after it at the end of the tenancy, too. Whether they get the difference from your security deposit or sue you in small claims court is somewhat academic.

> **EXAMPLE:** When Rose moved in, the rent was $800 a month, and she paid this much in advance as last month's rent, plus an additional $800 security deposit. Over the years the landlord, Artie, has raised the rent to $1,000. Rose does not pay any rent during the last month of her tenancy, figuring that the $800 she paid up front will cover it. Artie, however, thinks that Rose should pay the $200 difference. Artie and Rose may end up in small claims court fighting over who owes what. They could have avoided the problem by discussing the issue of last month's rent when Rose's tenancy began.

To avoid these disputes, we suggest that you get issues involving last month's rent straight with your landlord at the outset.

D. Nonrefundable Deposits and Fees

A few states, such as California, specifically prohibit landlords from charging any fee or deposit that is not refundable. Some states specifically allow landlords to collect a fee that is not refundable—such as for pets or cleaning. (See "States That Allow Nonrefundable Fees," below.) A few of these states require terms to be spelled out in the lease or rental agreement, but most don't, so find out your landlord's policy when you move in. A further complication is that nonrefundable fees are sometimes called "deposits"—a contradiction in terms.

If your landlord is charging a nonrefundable fee or deposit, make sure it is legal. This is not always easy, because most state security deposit statutes are silent on the subject of nonrefundable fees. Contact your city or district attorney's office, state or local consumer protection agency or tenants' rights organization for advice.

States That Allow Nonrefundable Fees

The following states have statutes that permit at least certain types of nonrefundable fees, such as for cleaning or pets:

Arizona	Nevada	Oregon
Florida	New Jersey	Utah
Georgia	North Carolina	Washington

Citations to these security deposit statutes appear in Appendix I.

In states that have no statute on the subject, the legality of nonrefundable fees and deposits is determined in court. For example, courts in Texas and Michigan have ruled that a landlord and tenant may agree that certain fees will be nonrefundable. (*Holmes v. Canlen Management Corp.*, 542 S.W.2d 199 (1976); *Stutelberg v. Practical Management Co.*, 245 N.W.2d 737 (1976).)

If this issue is of concern to you, you'll have to do some legal research. (Chapter 20 offers some research tips.)

E. Interest on Deposits and Separate Accounts

Unfair as it may seem, less than half of the states require landlords to pay interest on deposits or put the money in a separate bank account. In other words, your landlord can simply put your deposit in a personal bank account and use it, as long as the money is available when you move out. A number of years ago, when deposits were small, this may not have been such a big deal. But now, when deposits are often $1,000 or more, it's extremely unfair.

1. Separate Accounts

Several states (listed below) do require landlords to put security deposits in a separate account, sometimes called a "trust" account, rather than mixing the funds with their personal or business accounts.

Some states require landlords to give tenants information on the location of this separate trust account at the start of the tenancy, usually as part of the lease or rental agreement. The idea is that by isolating these funds from the landlord's other accounts and telling the tenant where they are kept, the deposit can be easily traced, and it will become immediately evident if the money is improperly used—for example, spent by the landlord for personal purposes, or grabbed by an over-eager creditor. Landlords are not usually required to set up separate accounts for every tenant, although they should maintain careful records of each tenant's contribution.

2. Interest

Ideally, your landlord should put your deposit into some kind of interest-bearing account and pay you the interest when you move out, After all, it's your money, not the landlord's.

Unfortunately, only a third of the states (listed below) require landlords to pay interest on security deposits.

States That Require Landlords to Maintain a Separate Account for Security Deposits	
Alaska	"Wherever practicable," deposit must be held in trust account or by escrow agent.
Connecticut	
Delaware	
District of Columbia	
Florida*	Instead of keeping separate account, landlord can post surety bond.
Georgia*	Instead of keeping separate account, landlord can post surety bond.
Iowa	
Kentucky*	
Maine	Deposit must be unavailable to landlord's creditors.
Maryland	Deposit must be held in Maryland banking or savings institution.
Massachusetts	Deposit must be held in Massachusetts and be unavailable to landlord's creditors.
Michigan*	
New Hampshire	
New Jersey	
New York*	
North Carolina*	
North Dakota	
Oklahoma	
Pennsylvania	
Tennessee*	
Washington	

* Landlords must give tenants written information on where the security deposit is being held.

Of course, excellent landlords are willing to pay interest on your deposit as an honest business practice, even if there is no law requiring it. If your landlord doesn't volunteer to do this, there's no harm in asking.

Even among the states that require interest, there are many variations. A few states, such as Illinois, don't require small landlords (less than 25 rental units) to pay interest on deposits. Others, such as Iowa, allow the landlord to keep the interest earned during the first five years of your tenancy.

State laws typically establish detailed requirements, including:

- The interest rate to be paid. Usually, it's a little lower than the bank actually pays because the landlord is allowed to keep a small portion for administrative expenses
- When interest payments must be made. The most common laws require payments to be made annually and/or when you leave, and
- Notification. Landlords must tell tenants where and how the security deposit is being held and the rate of interest. This should go in the lease or rental agreement.

Chicago, Los Angeles and several other cities (typically those with rent control), require landlords to pay or credit tenants with interest on security deposits even if the state law does not impose this duty. A few cities require that the funds be kept in separate interest-bearing accounts.

F. How the Deposit May Be Used

By law, your landlord must refund your deposit fairly promptly after you move out, unless there is a valid reason not to return part or all of it. Most states give landlords a set amount of time (usually from 14 to 30 days) to either return your entire deposit or provide an itemized written statement of deductions and refund the rest, if there's anything left.

Although state laws vary, your landlord can almost always withhold all or part of the deposit to pay for:

States That Require Landlords to Pay Interest on Deposits

Connecticut	Interest payments must be made annually and at termination of tenancy. The interest rate must be equal to the average rate paid on savings deposits by insured commercial banks, as published by the Federal Reserve Board Bulletin in November of the prior year, but not less than 1.5%.
Dist. of Columbia	Interest payments at the prevailing passbook rate must be made at termination of tenancy.
Florida	Interest payments (if any—account need not be interest-bearing) must be made annually and at termination of tenancy. However, no interest is due a tenant who wrongfully terminates the tenancy before the end of the rental term. If landlord is paying interest, details on interest rate and time of payment must be provided in lease or rental agreement.
Illinois	Landlords who rent 25 or more units in either a single building or a complex of buildings located on contiguous properties must pay interest on deposits held for more than six months. Interest must be paid annually and at termination of tenancy.
Iowa	Interest payment (if any—account need not be interest-bearing) must be made at termination of tenancy. Interest earned during first five years of tenancy belongs to landlord.
Maryland	Interest must be paid (at an annual rate of 4%) only on security deposits of $50 or more, at six-month intervals, not compounded.
Massachusetts	Landlord must pay tenant 5% interest per year or the amount received from the bank where the deposit has been held. Interest should be paid to the tenant yearly, and within 30 days of termination date. Interest will not accrue for the last month for which rent was paid in advance.
Minnesota	Landlord must pay 3% (simple, noncompounded) annual interest until 5/1/00. After that, 4% per year. Any interest amount less than $1 is excluded.
New Hampshire	A landlord who holds a security deposit for a year or longer must pay interest at a rate equal to the interest rate paid on regular savings accounts in the New Hampshire bank, savings and loan association or credit union where it is deposited. If a landlord mingles security deposits in a single account, the landlord must pay the actual interest earned proportionately to each tenant. Upon request, a landlord must give the tenant the name of any institution where the security deposit is held, the account number, the amount on deposit and the interest rate on the deposit, and must allow the tenant to examine his security deposit records. A tenant may request the interest accrued every three years, 30 days before that year's tenancy expires. The landlord must comply with the request within 15 days of the expiration of that year's tenancy.
New Jersey	Landlord must place the deposit in an insured money market account or other account where the fund matures in one year or less. Landlord must pay tenant interest on account, minus an amount not to exceed 1% per annum of the amount invested, or 12.5% of the aggregate interest, whichever is higher, less the amount of any service fee charged by the financial institution holding the deposit.
New Mexico	Landlord who receives more than one month's rent deposit on a year lease must pay the tenant, annually, interest equal to the passbook interest.
New York	Landlord must hold money in interest-bearing bank account and pay the tenant interest (less 1% for expenses) on it.
North Dakota	Landlord must pay interest if the period of occupancy is at least nine months. Money must be held in a federally insured interest-bearing savings or passbook account.
Ohio	Any security deposit in excess of $50 or one month's rent, whichever is greater, must bear interest on the excess at the rate of 5% per annum if the tenant stays for six months or more. Interest must be paid annually and upon termination of tenancy.
Pennsylvania	Tenant who occupies rental unit for two or more years is entitled to interest beginning with the 25th month of occupancy. Landlord must pay tenant interest (minus fee of 1%) at the end of the third and subsequent years of the tenancy.
Virginia	Landlord must accrue interest at an annual rate equal to the Federal Reserve Board discount rate as of January 1 of each year, on all money held as security. No interest is payable unless the landlord holds the deposit for over 13 months after the date of the rental agreement for continuous occupancy of the same unit. Interest begins accruing from the effective date of the rental agreement and must be paid only upon termination of tenancy.

- Unpaid rent
- Repairing damage to the premises (except for "ordinary wear and tear") that you or a guest caused
- Cleaning necessary to restore the rental unit to its condition at the beginning of the tenancy (over and above "ordinary wear and tear")
- Replacing rental unit property you've taken.

 Read your lease or rental agreement to be sure deposit refund procedures are spelled out. To protect yourself and avoid the all-too-common misunderstandings with your landlord, make sure your lease or rental agreement is clear on the use of security deposits and both your and your landlord's obligations. If it's not, follow our advice in Chapter 16, Section D. and write a letter of understanding to your landlord.

Landlords don't necessarily need to wait until you move out to tap into your security deposit. Your landlord may use some of your security deposit during your tenancy—for example, because you broke something and didn't fix it or pay for it. In this case, the landlord will probably require you to replenish the security deposit.

EXAMPLE: Millie pays her landlord Maury a $1,000 security deposit when she moves in. Six months later, Millie goes on vacation, leaving the water running. By the time Maury is notified, the overflow has damaged the paint on the ceiling below. Maury repaints the ceiling at a cost of $250, taking the money out of Millie's security deposit. Maury is entitled to ask Millie to replace that money, so that her deposit remains $1,000.

Chapter 16 provides details on rules landlords must follow when returning deposits, what kinds of deductions they can legally make and how to resolve disputes, including how to sue your landlord in small claims court.

G. If Your Landlord Sells the Property

In most states, the law requires a landlord who sells rental property to do one of two things: return the deposit to the tenant or transfer it to the new owner.

It's been known to happen, however, that a landlord does neither and simply walks off with the money. The tenant may not even be notified that the building has been sold until after the fact. Fortunately, the new owner—even one who never gets the deposit money—cannot require the tenant to replace any security deposit kept by the old landlord. And even better, in most states, whoever happens to be the landlord at the time a tenancy ends is legally responsible for complying with state laws requiring return of security deposits.

If Your Landlord Goes Bankrupt

If your landlord files for bankruptcy, your security deposit is beyond the reach of creditors. That's because, technically speaking, it's not your landlord's money—it's yours, which must be returned to you, unless you fail to pay the rent or damage the property. Chapter 15 explains what happens to your lease or rental agreement if the landlord goes bankrupt.

Discrimination

Not so long ago, a landlord could refuse to rent to you, or could evict you, for almost any reason—because of your skin color, or religion, or because you had children or were elderly or disabled. Some landlords even discriminated against single women, believing that they would be incapable of paying the rent or would have too many overnight guests.

Recognizing that all Americans who could afford to pay the rent should have the right to live where they chose, Congress and state legislatures passed laws prohibiting housing discrimination. Most notable of these are the federal Fair Housing Act of 1968 and the federal Fair Housing Amendments Act of 1988, which outlaw discrimination based on race or color, national origin, religion, sex, familial status or disability. (Throughout this chapter, we refer to this federal legislation as the federal Fair Housing Acts or the federal Acts.) In addition, many states and cities have laws making it illegal to discriminate based on additional factors, such as marital status or sexual orientation. Today, it is safe to say that unless a landlord has a legitimate business reason to reject a prospective tenant (for example, a poor credit history, terrible references from previous landlords or an application from a more solvent candidate), she risks a potentially costly legal challenge.

Because antidiscrimination laws are widely known, it is unusual to encounter a landlord who blatantly discriminates—for example, by stating a preference for all-white tenants or those without children. But it is still far too common to encounter more subtle—yet equally illegal—discrimination. For example, some landlords use overly restrictive occupancy standards to hide discrimination against families with children, or design advertisements that send powerful messages that applicants of a certain race are preferred. Or they may simply come up with superficially plausible—but nevertheless bogus—reasons not to rent to people of a certain race or religion.

In most situations with tenants, landlords have the upper hand. When it comes to discrimination, however, the balance of power shifts to the tenant. Because of strong antidiscrimination laws, a determined tenant or applicant for rental housing who has been wronged can often tie a landlord in legal knots. As discussed in Section C, tenants may complain to the U.S. Department of Housing and Urban Development (HUD), the federal agency that enforces the Fair Housing Acts, or to a state or local fair housing agency. Tenants may also file a lawsuit in federal or state court.

One of the reasons tenants have more clout in the housing discrimination area is that you don't always need to show that the landlord or manager intended to discriminate. As long as the landlord's conduct has a discriminatory effect or impact on members of a legally protected group (such as African-Americans), you may successfully win a discrimination case. And knowing that outrageous cases may result in large jury verdicts, insurance companies are often quick to offer settlements outside of court.

If you think that you have been a victim of housing discrimination and you want to do something about it, you face an important choice. You can take your story to the federal or state agency in charge of enforcing the federal and state laws, and hope that an agency investigator will pursue your case (you usually won't need your own lawyer). Or, you can talk to an attorney about suing in state or federal court. Successful tenants may win an order (or lever a settlement from the landlord's insurance company) forcing the landlord to rent to them or cease the discriminatory practice. You may also get a monetary award for your actual losses (having to rent another unit at a higher price, for example) or compensation for the humiliation you have endured.

 Related topics covered in this book include:
- Legitimate reasons landlords may use to turn down prospective tenants: Chapter 1.
- Discriminatory rent increases: Chapter 3.
- Discriminatory evictions: Chapter 16.

A. Kinds of Discrimination Prohibited by Federal Laws

Federal, state and local laws all forbid various kinds of discrimination against tenants. The most common kinds of discrimination—race or disability, for example—are prohibited by federal law, which must be followed by landlords in every state. (The key federal laws are the Fair Housing Acts, 42 U.S.C. §§ 3601-3619, 3631.)

Most state laws also make these forms of discrimination illegal, although some are not as inclusive as the federal laws. On the other hand, some states go even further; for example, some outlaw housing discrimination based on sexual orientation, something that is not addressed by federal law.

If you think you have been illegally discriminated against, it becomes important to know which law covers your situation, for two main reasons. First, if federal law has been violated, you can complain to

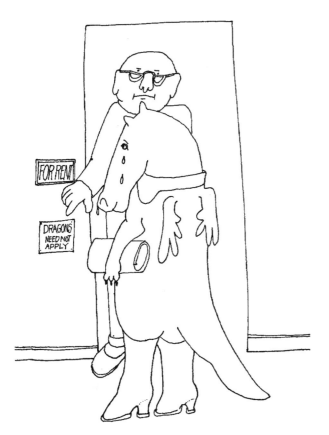

a federal agency or sue in federal court; if only state law covers your situation, you are limited to state agencies and courts. If your situation is addressed by both federal and state law, you have a choice between going to a federal agency or court or a state agency or court. Second, federal law (and many state laws) don't apply to every rental. As discussed below, some properties are exempt. Even if your situation is covered by both laws, you'll need to know whether an exemption would force you to use one law or the other.

Since federal law governs everyone, we'll start with it. The federal Acts prohibit discrimination on the following grounds (called "protected categories"):

- Race or color
- Religion
- National origin
- Familial status or age—includes families with children under the age of 18 *and* pregnant women
- Disability or handicap
- Sex, including sexual harassment.

The federal Acts apply to all aspects of the land-lord-tenant relationship. A landlord may not:

- advertise or make any statement that indicates a limitation or preference based on race, religion or any other protected category (advertising a building as a "quiet environment for mature adults" may be considered illegal familial status discrimination)
- falsely deny that a rental unit is available
- set more restrictive standards for selecting tenants
- refuse to rent to members of certain groups
- before or during the tenancy, set different terms, conditions, or privileges for rental of a dwelling unit, such as requiring larger deposits of some tenants, or adopting an inconsistent policy of responding to late rent payments
- during the tenancy, providing different housing services or facilities, such as making a community center or other common area available only to selected tenants, or
- terminate a tenancy for a discriminatory reason.

Unfortunately, not every rental is covered by the federal Acts. The following types of property are exempt:

- owner-occupied buildings with four or fewer rental units
- single-family housing rented without the use of discriminatory advertising or without a real estate broker
- certain types of housing operated by religious organizations and private clubs that limit occupancy to their own members, and
- with respect to age discrimination only, housing reserved exclusively for senior citizens. There are two kinds of senior citizen housing exempted: communities where every tenant is 62 years of age or older, or communities with individual units that have at least one person 55 years of age or older. To qualify as "55 and older housing," at least 80% of the occupied units in the housing facility must be occupied by at least one person 55 years or older.

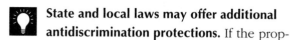 **State and local laws may offer additional antidiscrimination protections.** If the property you rent is exempt under federal law, similar state or local anti-housing discrimination laws may nevertheless protect you. For example, owner-occupied buildings with four or fewer rental units are exempt under federal law but not under California law.

1. Race or Religion

Discrimination based on race or religion isn't always as obvious as you might think. Especially when a person's beliefs are out of the mainstream or unpopular with other groups, it might even seem reasonable not to rent to that person. For example, a Jewish landlord might be offended by someone's anti-Semitic convictions, but nevertheless could not legally refuse to rent to that person for that reason.

EXAMPLE: Several tenants in Creekside Apartments reserved the common room for a meeting. Creekside management learned that the tenants were members of a white supremacist religion that believes in the inferiority of all non-whites and non-Christians. Creekside management was appalled at the thought of these ideas being discussed on its premises, and denied the group the use of the common room. The tenants who were members of this group filed a discrimination complaint with HUD on the basis of freedom of religion. HUD supported the religious group and forced Creekside to make the common room available.

Unintended discriminatory messages are just as illegal as overt ones. For example, an apartment ad that says "safe Christian community" or "Sunday quiet times enforced" violates federal law, since applicants might reasonably conclude that Christians are preferred as tenants. Landlords may not legally send these subtle messages to tenants after they have moved in, either. For example, tenant rules, signs, newsletters and other communication cannot legally convey any attempt to benefit, support or discriminate against a racial or religious group. The following examples are based on actual fair housing complaints of illegal discrimination:

- Management extends the use of the common room to tenants for "birthday parties, anniversaries and Christmas and Easter parties." Non-Christian tenants could understandably feel excluded.
- In an effort to accommodate Spanish-speaking tenants, management translates the move-in letter and house rules into Spanish. Regarding the use of alcohol in the common areas, the Spanish version—but not the English one—begins, "Unlike Mexico, where drinking is practiced in public places, alcoholic beverages may not be consumed in common areas...." To many people, this phrase implies an ethnic generalization.
- The metropolitan area where you live contains large numbers of both Spanish-

speaking and Cantonese-speaking people. Several apartment complexes advertise in Spanish only and offer nothing but Spanish-language leases. As an Asian-American who speaks Cantonese (or an Anglo who speaks only English), you naturally conclude that these complexes welcome Hispanics but not you. Advertisements and leases in English only do not violate fair housing laws unless your state, like California, requires lease translations if the negotiations were conducted in Spanish. (Cal. Civ. Code § 1632.)

2. National Origin

Discrimination based on national origin is illegal, whether it's practiced deliberately or unintentionally. For example, a landlord who required all residents to be U.S. citizens, or who advertised "Special discounts for members of the Irish-American Club," would likely face a charge of discrimination based on national origin.

Even if your landlord is motivated by what seems like a valid business concern, but rejects tenants in a way that singles out people of a particular nationality, it's still illegal. For example, since illegal aliens can be picked up and held in custody pending deportation at any time, their landlords might not receive the agreed-upon rent. In states such as California, Texas and Florida, many illegal aliens are from Central and South America. Does this mean that California or Texas landlords are entitled to ask every Hispanic applicant (but not others) for immigration papers or proof of citizenship? The answer is no and the reason, of course, is because of the impact this practice is almost sure to have on Hispanics who are citizens or in the U.S. legally. If you're an Hispanic, you're likely to reach the conclusion that you are not welcome because management assumes that everyone like you is living in the U.S. illegally. A fair housing agency or court would surely agree that this sort of selective "let me see your papers" policy is illegal discrimination.

On the other hand, a landlord who requires *all* prospective tenants to supply satisfactory proof of identity and eligibility to work is on solid ground. Why? Because every applicant, and not just members of one group, is subjected to an inquiry that is reasonably related to the landlord's right to choose credit-worthy tenants. It is not illegal for landlords to ask every applicant for the same type of citizenship or immigration documents that employers must use.

For information on how your landlord may legally verify your citizenship or immigration status, contact the Immigration and Naturalization Service (INS) at 800-755-0777. For a local INS office, check any metropolitan phone book under U.S. Department of Justice.

3. Familial Status or Age

A landlord may not legally turn away or evict families because they have children or because an applicant or tenant is pregnant. In addition, a landlord cannot exclude families by unreasonably limiting the maximum number of people permitted to occupy a rental unit, thereby indirectly preventing families with children from occupying smaller units. Finally, a landlord may not make tenancy decisions based on an applicant's age.

a. Discrimination Against Families

Discrimination based on family make-up can take unexpected forms. Even well-intentioned landlord motives will not justify a policy or rule that discriminates against families with children or younger people. Consider these examples:

- You and your 15-year-old daughter have applied to rent an apartment in an area of town that has experienced several muggings and rapes. Afraid that your daughter, when she returns from school alone each day, will be an easy mark, the manager refuses to accept your application.

- You, your spouse and teenage son and daughter have applied for a two-bedroom apartment. The occupancy policy is two-per-bedroom, but the landlord decides that it is inappropriate for children of different sexes to share a room.

The ban against familial status discrimination protects adults without children and singles, too. A landlord may not establish policies that adversely affect childless tenants. This means it is illegal to rent *only* to families, or even to segregate (or restrict) some tenants to certain floors or parts of a building. For example, a policy that requires tenants with children to rent ground floor units indirectly funnels childless tenants to the upper stories. A childless tenant who wanted a ground floor unit would have a valid claim of familial discrimination. Similarly, hosting "families only" social events in the common area excludes childless renters, who could raise a claim of discrimination.

b. Occupancy Limits: How Many People Can Live in the Rental Unit?

Landlords may try to avoid renting to families with children by setting occupancy policies that appear neutral but have the effect of discriminating. For example, a policy of no more than two people for a two-bedroom apartment would exclude a family with one or two children or a single parent with three children. To counter this subtle discrimination, the government has come up with rules that limit landlords' occupancy policies.

Illegal discrimination against families also occurs when an occupancy policy differentiates between adults and children. For example, consider the results of a landlord's policy allowing only one person per bedroom, with a couple counting as one person. Under these criteria, the landlord would rent a two-bedroom unit to a husband and wife and their one child, but would not rent the same unit to a mother with two children. The mother and her two children would have a valid discrimination claim.

Familial status discrimination also appears when a landlord applies an occupancy policy in an inconsistent manner. If in practice your landlord distinguishes between adults and children, you may be able to challenge those actions as a hidden form of familial discrimination, even if the landlord is following what he believes is a sensible and non-discriminatory policy.

EXAMPLE: Jackson owned and managed two identical one-bedroom units, one of which he rented out to three flight attendants who were rarely there at the same time. When the other unit became vacant, Jackson advertised it as a one-bedroom, two-person apartment. Harry and Sue Jones and their teen-age daughter were turned away because they exceeded Jackson's occupancy limit of two people. The Jones family learned that the companion unit was rented to three people, and decided to file a complaint with HUD, whose investigator helped negotiate a settlement. Jackson saw that he was legally in the wrong. He agreed to rent to the Jones family and to compensate them for the humiliation they had suffered as a result of being refused.

How do you know what is a reasonable occupancy limit? State and local health and safety codes typically limit the number of tenants allowed, based on the size of the unit and the number of bedrooms and bathrooms.

But the law also addresses the other end of the how-many-occupants issue, by setting policies that require a landlord to rent to *at least* a certain number of tenants per unit. The Department of Housing and Urban Development issues the federal guidelines, thus going a long way towards preventing discrimination against families with children. HUD generally considers a limit of two persons per bedroom a reasonable occupancy standard. Because the number of bedrooms is not the only factor—the size of the bedrooms, age of the children and configuration of the rental unit are also considered—the federal test has become known as the "two per bed-room plus" standard.

States and localities can set their own occupancy standards as long as they are more generous than the federal government's—that is, they allow more people per rental unit. If you live in a state or city whose occupancy standard is more generous than the federal rule, you are entitled to the benefit of the higher (or highest) number. For example, the California standard is two-per-bedroom plus one more person, which would result in three persons in a one-bedroom unit; under the federal rule, the result (without taking into consideration the size and configuration of the unit) would be only two. California landlords are bound by the state rule, since it's more generous than the federal one.

A landlord may, however, set an occupancy standard that is lower than the applicable federal, state or local figure if legitimate business reasons will justify it. This is hard to do—while the inability of the infrastructure to support more tenants (per-

haps the septic system or plumbing has a limited capacity) may validate a lower occupancy policy, a landlord's desire to ensure a quiet, uncrowded environment for upscale older tenants will not. If your landlord's occupancy policy limits the number of tenants for any reason other than health, safety and legitimate business needs, it may be illegal discrimination against families.

More Information on Occupancy Standards

To find out whether your state has its own occupancy standard, check the table below. It lists the states that have adopted the federal "two-per-bedroom plus" rule (some have modified it as well). If your state isn't listed, it has not legislated a policy of its own (which means that you are covered by the federal standard or any local one). For more information on federal occupancy standards, call HUD's Fair Housing Information Clearinghouse at 800-343-3442. Check your local and state housing departments for other occupancy standards that may affect your rental property.

IS THAT STUDIO APARTMENT STILL FOR RENT.?...

Exceeding the maximum allowable number of tenants is not always a bargain. Some tenants are delighted to find a landlord who will allow them to live with more than the maximum number of residents allowable under the applicable occupancy standard or even the local health and safety laws. Your rent share will be lower and, in tight rental markets, it may mean the difference between living in a good area and a really bad one, or not even having a home at all. But unless you are desperate, beware! The fact that a landlord is willing to live outside the law tells you a lot about how seriously he takes other legal responsibilities (like repairs and maintenance). And by agreeing to live in an overcrowded rental, you hamper your ability to assert your rights—you will naturally hesitate to do anything (like complain to a housing authority about substandard conditions or utilize a repair and deduct remedy) that will bring the illegal rental to the attention of courts or building inspectors.

States that Have Adopted All or Part of the Federal "Two-per-Bedroom Plus" Standard

Arizona[1]	Kansas[1]	Pennsylvania
California[2]	Kentucky[1]	Rhode Island
Colorado[1]	Louisiana	South Carolina[1]
Connecticut[1]	Maryland	Tennessee
Delaware	Massachusetts	Texas[5]
Florida[1]	Missouri[1]	Utah
Georgia[1]	New Mexico[3]	Virginia
Hawaii	New York[3]	West Virginia
Illinois	Ohio	Wisconsin[3]
Indiana	Oklahoma[4]	Wyoming[3]
Iowa[1]	Oregon[3]	

[1] Some cities or counties in these states have ordinances also.

[2] California has a state guideline of "two per bedroom and one more occupant" (who need not be a child). Localities can have ordinances also.

[3] The standard is roughly "two per bedroom," but these states did not copy the rest of the federal standard (involving age of unit, age of children and so on. New York City may fashion its own laws.

[4] The Oklahoma statute does not count children born to the tenants during the term of the lease.

[5] The Texas statute specifies a maximum occupancy of three persons per bedroom to prevent overcrowding, but the state uses a minimum standard of two per bedroom plus a child under the age of six months to evaluate fair housing discrimination complaints.

c. Age Discrimination

The federal Fair Housing Acts do not expressly ban discrimination based on age. Nevertheless, it is definitely forbidden under the broader concept of prohibiting discrimination on the basis of familial status.

A landlord cannot refuse to rent to an older person or impose special terms and conditions on the tenancy unless these same standards are applied to everyone else. If you have excellent references and credit history, a landlord has no legal basis for refusing you, even if you are 85 and rely to some degree on the regular assistance of a nearby adult child or friend. (Of course, he could legally give the rental to someone else with equal or better references or financial stability.) However, if your current landlord reveals that you suffer from advanced senility to the point that you often wander into the wrong apartment, frequently forget to pay the rent or are unable to undertake basic housekeeping chores, the prospective landlord can refuse to rent to you based on this age-neutral evidence that you are not likely to be a stable, reliable tenant.

EXAMPLE: Ethel, who is 80 years old, wants to find a smaller place closer to her daughter, Nora. She sells her home and applies for a one-bedroom apartment at Coral Shores. Ethel presents impeccable references from neighbors and employers and an outstanding credit history. Nonetheless, Lucy, the manager of Coral Shores, is fearful that Ethel, at her age, might forget to turn off the stove, fall on the front steps or do any number of other dangerous things, and decides not to rent to her. Ethel files a fair housing complaint with HUD, which she quickly wins on the basis of Coral Shores' policy of age discrimination.

The issue of age discrimination may also arise during a well-established tenancy. Suppose you have lived alone for years and now, with advanced age, must face the question of whether you are still able to live safely by yourself. Your landlord is honestly concerned that your physical incapacity or mental inattention might result in damage to the premises and injury to you or other tenants. Can your landlord, on the basis of these fears alone, decide not to renew your lease? Absolutely not—there must be real, serious and probably repeated violations of the criteria that apply to all tenants before non-renewal of a lease, or eviction, would be legal.

💡 **Elderly tenants may also qualify as disabled tenants, who are entitled to accommodation under the law.** An elderly tenant who cannot meet one of the landlord's policies may be entitled to special treatment as a disabled person. (See the discussion of discrimination on the basis of disability, below.) For example, an elderly tenant who is chronically late with the rent because of sporadic disorientation might justifiably ask for a grace period, or a friendly reminder when the rent is due; a non-disabled tenant who is chronically late with the rent would not be entitled to such special treatment. And if an elderly tenant can't negotiate the stairs, the legal solution is a ramp, not an eviction notice.

Additional Eviction Protections for Elderly Tenants

Some states and localities, including Connecticut and New York City, protect elderly tenants in the event that their building is sold or converted to condominiums, or if the owner of their rent-controlled unit attempts to evict them in order to move in themselves (or a member of their family). For information on eviction protections for elderly tenants, check your state's fair housing agency (listed in Appendix I).

The prohibition against age discrimination also applies to "emancipated" minors who have the same status as an adult and must be treated like any other adult applicant or tenant. (An emancipated minor is a 17-year-old—or possibly even a 16-year-old in some states—who is legally married, has a court order of emancipation or is in the military.) On the other hand, a landlord can reject an under-age applicant who is not emancipated because these minors lack the legal capacity to enter into a binding rental agreement.

4. Disability

Federal law prohibits discrimination against people who:

- have a physical or mental disability that substantially limits one or more major life activities—including, but not limited to hearing, mobility and visual impairments; chronic alcoholism (but only if it is being addressed through a recovery program); mental illness; HIV-positive, AIDS and AIDS-Related Complex; and mental retardation
- have a history or record of such a disability, or
- are regarded by others as though they have such a disability.

a. Mental or Emotional Impairments

If you had, have or appear to have mental or emotional impairments, you must be evaluated and treated by the landlord on the basis of your financial stability and history as a tenant, not on the basis of your mental health. A landlord may reject you only if he can point to specific instances of past behavior that would make you dangerous to others (such as information from a previous landlord that you repeatedly threatened or assaulted other residents). If you cannot meet the good-tenant criteria that the landlord applies to all applicants (such as a minimum rent-to-income ratio), you may be rejected on *that* basis.

b. Discriminatory Questions and Actions

Landlords are not allowed to ask you whether or not you have a disability or illness, or ask to see medical records. Even if it is obvious that you are disabled—for example, you use a wheelchair or wear a hearing aid—it is nevertheless illegal to inquire how severely you are disabled. In short, your landlord's actions and questions cannot be designed to treat you differently than other tenants.

The policy behind this rule is simple: No matter how well-intentioned, the landlord cannot make decisions about where and how you will live on the property that he would not make were you not disabled. For example, if there are two units for rent—one on the ground floor and one three stories up—the landlord must show both units to a wheelchair-bound applicant, however reasonable *he* thinks it would be for the person to consider only the ground floor unit.

c. The Rights of Disabled Tenants to Live in an Accessible Place

Federal law protects disabled tenants *after* they have moved into a rental unit as well as during the application process. Landlords must:

- accommodate the needs of disabled tenants, at the landlord's own expense (42 U.S.C. § 3604(f)(B)
- allow disabled tenants to make reasonable modifications of their living unit at their expense, if needed for the person to comfortably and safely live in the unit. (42 U.S.C. § 3604(f)(3)(A).)

Let's look briefly at each of these requirements.

Accommodations

As a disabled tenant, you may expect your landlord to reasonably adjust rules, procedures or services in order to give you an equal opportunity to use and enjoy your dwelling unit or a common space. Accommodations can include such things as:

- Parking—if the landlord provides parking in the first place, providing a close-in, spacious parking space for a wheelchair-bound tenant
- Service animals—allowing a guide dog, hearing dog or service dog in a residence that otherwise disallows pets
- Rent payment—allowing a special rent payment plan for a tenant whose finances are managed by someone else or by a government agency
- Reading problems—arranging to read all communications from management to a blind tenant, and
- Phobias—for example, providing a washtub and clothesline for a mentally ill tenant whose anxiety about machines makes her unable to use the facility's washer and dryer.

Does your landlord's duty to accommodate disabled tenants mean that you can expect every rule and procedure to be changed at your request? No. Although landlords are expected to accommodate "reasonable" requests, they need not undertake changes that would seriously impair their ability to run their business. For example, if a wheelchair-bound applicant prefers the third-story apartment in a walk-up building constructed in 1926 to the one on the ground floor, the landlord does not have to rip the building apart to install an elevator. HUD would consider the expense to be unreasonable.

Modifications

Fortunately, where your landlord's legal duty to reasonably accommodate the needs of disabled tenants ends, his obligation to allow you to modify your living space may begin. You have the right to modify your living space to the extent necessary to make the space safe and comfortable, as long as the modifications will not make the unit unacceptable to the next tenant, or you agree to undo the modification when you leave. Examples of modifications undertaken by a disabled tenant include:

- lowering countertops for a wheelchair-bound tenant
- installing special faucets or door handles for persons with limited hand use
- modifying kitchen appliances to accommodate a blind tenant, and
- installing a ramp to allow a wheelchair-bound tenant to negotiate two steps up to a raised living room.

These modifications must be reasonable and made with prior approval. A landlord is entitled to ask for a description of the proposed modifications, proof that they will be done in a workmanlike manner and evidence that you are obtaining any necessary building permits. In addition, if you propose to modify the unit in a way that will require restoration when you leave (such as the re-positioning of lowered kitchen counters), the landlord may require you to pay into an interest-bearing escrow account the amount estimated for the restoration. (The interest belongs to you.)

Landlords are also entitled to ask for proof that the accommodation or modification you have requested will address your needs. For some disabilities—for example, installing a ramp to accommodate a wheelchair—the solutions are obvious. But other disabilities, especially mental ones, are not obvious, and their accommodation isn't either—for example, removing doors to accommodate a person who is fearful of closed spaces. Without some proof, your landlord has no way of knowing whether your request is legitimate or a ruse to obtain special treatment.

If you want a specific accommodation or modification and your disability is not obvious (or if you anticipate an argument with your landlord regarding the necessity of what you have proposed), have your proof ready before you make your request.

Ask your physician or therapist for a letter attesting that what you are asking for will meet your needs. To protect your privacy, carefully explain to the physician or other writer that he need not explain the disability; he need only certify that the changes you would like are appropriate to your situation. A sample letter, in which the physician describes the tenant's requests but not the disability, is presented below.

New Buildings and the Disabled

The Fair Housing Amendments Act (42 U.S. Code § 3604(f)(3)(C) and 3604(f)(7)) imposes requirements on new buildings of four or more units that were first occupied after March 1991. All ground floor units and every unit in an elevator building must be designed or constructed so that:

- the main building is accessible and on an accessible route
- the public and common areas are "readily accessible to and usable by" the disabled, including parking areas (a good rule of thumb is to reserve 2% of the spaces)
- entryway doorways have 36" of free space *plus* shoulder and elbow room; and interior doorways are at least 32" wide
- interior living spaces have wheelchair-accessible routes throughout, with changes in floor height of no more than 1/4"
- light switches, outlets, thermostats and other environmental controls are within the legal "reach range" (15" to 48" from the ground)
- bathroom walls are sufficiently reinforced to allow the safe installation of "grab bars," and
- kitchens and bathrooms are large enough to allow a wheelchair to maneuver within the room (40" turning radius minimum) and have sinks and appliances positioned to allow side or front use.

Sample Letter
Attesting to the Appropriateness of an Accommodation or Modification

Marcus Welby, M.D.
400 Professional Way, Suite 100
Anytown, Colorado 12345
(719) 555-9999

September 19, 200X

Hilda Hanson, Manager
Royal Crest Apartments
Anytown, Colorado 12346

Dear Ms. Hanson:

John Anderson, who resides at Royal Crest Apartments, is a patient under my care. He has informed me that he will soon be asking you to modify certain aspects of his apartment. He will also ask you to make some accommodations regarding management policies at Royal Crest:

Modifications

1. Disconnect the electric doorbell and install a hand-knocker on the front door.

2. Allow Mr. Anderson to install curtain rods in the bedroom that will support heavy, light-blocking drapes.

3. Allow Mr. Anderson to put wall-to-wall carpet in the bedroom, which is currently bare hardwood.

Accommodations

1. Communicate any management requests in writing, left in Mr. Anderson's mailbox, rather than by phone.

2. Open the laundry room at 7 a.m., one hour earlier than the current schedule.

3. When management at Royal Crest calls a tenants' meeting to discuss and vote on issues of concern to tenants and management, allow Mr. Anderson to send a proxy who may speak and vote in his place.

In my professional opinion, these requests are necessary and appropriate to enable Mr. Anderson to live at Royal Crest in a safe and enjoyable manner.

Yours truly,

Marcus Welby, M.D.

Marcus Welby, MD
cc: Mr. John Anderson

d. Limited Protection for Alcoholics and Drug Users

Federal fair housing law extends limited protection to two carefully defined groups:

- **Recovering alcoholics.** An alcoholic who is "in recovery" may not be denied housing on the basis of his status as an alcoholic. Unfortunately, there is no clear definition of what "recovery" means, nor when it begins; but someone who actively and regularly participates in a medically based treatment or AA program probably qualifies.
- **Former drug addicts.** People who were previously addicted to illegal drugs cannot be denied housing on that basis alone. It is also illegal for a landlord to discriminate based on a conviction for illegal drug use. This protection does not extend to current addiction, nor does it protect someone who has a conviction for drug dealing or manufacture.

It is important to remember that other aspects of a recovering alcoholic's (or a former drug addict's) past might legally serve as the basis for a denial of housing. For example, if the recovering alcoholic also has bad credit, a spotty employment history or negative references from previous landlords, a landlord may reject him for these reasons just as readily as any other applicant with these flaws. What a landlord *cannot* do is reject the former addict or the recovering alcoholic on the basis of their *status* as former addicts or recovering alcoholics.

> **EXAMPLE:** Patsy applied for an apartment one morning and spoke with Carol, the manager. Patsy said she would have to return that afternoon to complete the application form because she was due at an Alcoholics Anonymous meeting. Carol decided on the spot that she did not want Patsy for a tenant, and she told Patsy that the unit "had just been rented," which was a lie. (Patsy continued to see the newspaper ad for the unit.)
>
> Patsy filed a complaint with HUD, alleging that she was a recovering alcoholic who had been discriminated against. Because Carol could not point to any reason for turning Patsy away other than her assumption that Patsy, as an alcoholic, would be a bad tenant, the judge awarded Patsy several thousand dollars in damages.

5. Sex and Sexual Harassment

You cannot be denied a place to live (or have special rules imposed on you) solely because you're female or male. Even well-intentioned policies are off-limits—for example, fearful that single women are more likely to be burglarized and assaulted than male tenants, a landlord cannot require single females to live in upper-story apartments, even if, in fact, those units are less prone to break-ins. Whether you consider it good intentions or unacceptable paternalism, it's illegal.

A landlord's policy that favors one sex over another may justify a claim of discrimination by either sex. In the example above, the landlord is discriminating against female applicants who want ground-floor apartments, *and* against male applicants who want an upper-story apartment that is reserved for single women.

Sexual harassment is another form of sexual discrimination. For example, it's illegal to refuse to rent to a person who resists the landlord's sexual advances or to make life difficult for a tenant who has resisted such advances. In the rental housing context, courts have defined sexual harassment as:

- a pattern of persistent, unwanted attention of a sexual nature, including the making of sexual remarks and physical advances, or a single instance of highly egregious behavior. A manager's persistent requests for social contact, or constant remarks concerning a tenant's appearance or behavior could constitute sexual harassment, as could a single extraordinarily offensive remark, or
- a situation in which a tenant's rights are conditioned upon the acceptance of the owner's or manager's attentions. For example, a man-

ager who refuses to fix the plumbing until the tenant agrees to a date is guilty of sexual harassment. This type of harassment may be established on the basis of only one incident.

EXAMPLE: Oscar, the resident manager of Northside Apartments, repeatedly asked Martha, a Northside tenant, for dates. Martha always turned Oscar down and, after his fourth proposition, asked that he leave her alone. Oscar didn't back off, and began hanging around the pool whenever Martha used it, watching her intently and making suggestive remarks about her to the other tenants.

Martha stopped using the pool and filed a sexual harassment complaint with HUD, claiming that Oscar's unwanted attentions made it impossible for her to use and enjoy the pool and even to comfortably live at Northside. Oscar refused to consider a settlement when the HUD investigator spoke to him and Martha about his actions. As a result, HUD pursued the case in court, where a federal judge ordered Oscar to leave Martha alone and awarded her several thousand dollars.

Deciding how to respond to an act of sexual harassment involves considerations that go beyond the usual housing discrimination case, because sexual harassment involves proving certain facts that aren't involved in other sex discrimination lawsuits. In Section C we suggest ways to evaluate the strength of your case and include suggestions as to how best to respond to sexual harassment.

B. Kinds of Discrimination Prohibited by State and Local Law

Most state and local laws prohibiting housing discrimination echo federal antidiscrimination law in that they outlaw discrimination based on race or color, national origin, religion, familial status, disability and sex. But state and local laws often go into more detail and may also forbid some kinds of

discrimination—such as discrimination based on marital status—that aren't covered by federal law. For example, in states that prohibit discrimination based on marital status, it would be illegal to refuse to rent to divorced people, something that is not covered by federal law.

Here we explain some of the common antidiscrimination laws that states and localities have adopted. For more information on state and local housing discrimination laws, contact your state fair housing agency, listed in Appendix I.

1. Marital Status

In most states, landlords may legally refuse to rent to you if you are an unmarried couple. About 20 states ban discrimination on the basis of marital status, and most of these extend protection to married couples only. Only a few states—California, Massachusetts, Michigan and New Jersey—have clearly ruled that the term "marital status" refers to *unmarried* couples. Oddly, courts in Maryland, Minnesota, New York and Washington have ruled that the term "marital status" only protects *single* people from being treated differently from married people, and vice versa, but does not protect unmarried couples.

Some landlords resist renting to unmarried couples on the grounds that cohabitation violates their religious beliefs. Courts in California and Massachusetts have refused to allow landlords to reject unmarried couples as tenants for this reason.

Until recently, Alaska also forbade landlords from rejecting unmarried tenants on that ground alone. A federal appellate court struck down Alaska's law in January, 1999 (*Thomas v. Anchorage Equal Rights Commission*, No. 97-35221 (9th Cir. 1999)). This holding could prove fatal to California's law if and when a California landlord rejects an unmarried couple on religious grounds, is sued and cites the case in his defense.

💡 **Unmarried couples may be protected by a city or county ordinance prohibiting discrimination on the basis of sexual orientation.** Although usually passed to protect the housing rights of gay and lesbian tenants, most local laws forbidding discrimination based on sexual orientation also protect unmarried heterosexual couples as well. In addition, unmarried people may be able to challenge a landlord's refusal to rent to them on the basis of sex discrimination, which is covered by the federal Acts.

Where Living Together Is a Crime

In a few states, it's illegal for an unmarried couple to live together. Although these anti-cohabitation laws are rarely enforced, they give legal backing to landlords who want to deny housing to unmarried couples.

Also, Georgia, Rhode Island and Utah still consider fornication to be a crime, so cohabitation is probably illegal in these states, too, unless the couple insists they are roommates, not lovers—something it is very hard for a landlord to prove or disprove.

📖 Unmarried tenants will find detailed information on all aspects of living together in *The Living Together Kit,* by Toni Ihara and Jake Warner (Nolo).

2. Sexual Orientation

Housing discrimination based on sexual orientation is prohibited in California, Connecticut, the District of Columbia, Massachusetts, Minnesota, New Jersey, Rhode Island, Vermont and Wisconsin. In addition, many cities prohibit discrimination against gays and lesbians, including Atlanta, Chicago, Detroit, Miami, New York, Pittsburgh, St. Louis and Seattle. For more information on state or local law, contact the National Gay & Lesbian Task Force, 2320 17th Street NW, Washington, DC 20009, 202-332-6483.

3. Source of Income

In a few states, including California (*Marina Point, Ltd. v. Wolfson,* 30 Cal. 3d 721 (1982)), Minnesota (Minn. Stat. § 363.03) and North Dakota (N.D. Cent. Code § 14.02.4-12), applicants who receive public assistance may not be turned away or otherwise discriminated against because of this fact. This doesn't mean, however, that being on public assistance entitles you to be considered for every rental. A landlord may refuse to rent to you if your available income (regardless of its source) falls below an established level, as long as that standard is applied to every applicant. (See Chapter 1, Section E, for information on how landlords may legally use income as a selection criterion.)

Arbitrary Discrimination Is Illegal in California

Federal and state laws clearly prohibit discrimination based on race, religion, sex and so on. But what about tenant-selection criteria that don't fit into these categories? Is it legal for a landlord to exclude bearded men and lawyers with Harleys?

In California, at least, the answer is no. Courts in that state have ruled that although California's Unruh Civil Rights Act (Cal. Civ. Code §§ 51-53, 54.1-54.8) contains only the words "sex, race, color, religion, ancestry or national origin" to describe types of discrimination that are illegal, these categories are just examples of illegal discrimination. The courts have construed the Unruh Act to forbid discrimination on the basis of a "personal characteristic or trait"—also known as "arbitrary discrimination." Other common examples of arbitrary discrimination include obesity, occupation or style of dress.

C. How to Fight Back

If you believe that a landlord has unlawfully discriminated against you, you don't just have to take it or move on. You can try to work things out with the landlord, or you can take advantage of the powerful antidiscrimination laws discussed earlier.

Your options (discussed in detail below) include:

- trying to negotiate an acceptable settlement with the landlord, possibly with the help of a neutral mediator
- filing a complaint with a federal, state or local government fair housing agency, or
- filing a lawsuit in federal or state court.

Any of these strategies may force the landlord to:

- rent you a particular unit
- pay you "actual" or "compensatory" damages. This amount covers your trouble in finding another rental, plus any additional rent you had to pay to rent elsewhere. In addition, you are entitled to money for any humiliation or emotional distress—if the landlord's conduct was truly awful, this amount can be substantial.
- pay you punitive damages—extra money as punishment for especially outrageous, intentional discrimination. It is not uncommon for juries to make large awards—$25,000 and up—if a landlord has persistently and obnoxiously violated fair housing laws.
- pay your attorney fees (if you hired an attorney to file a lawsuit)
- pay a penalty to the federal government. The maximum penalty under the federal Fair Housing Acts is $10,000 for a first violation and $50,000 for a third violation within seven years. Many states have comparable penalties.

1. Picking the Strategy That Suits Your Goals

Before you can make an intelligent decision about what strategy to pursue, you need to sit down and ask yourself what you're trying to achieve.

If you simply want the offensive or unfair behavior to stop, and aren't interested in seeking compensation for humiliation, inconvenience or added expense, you won't want to file a complaint or lawsuit right away. For example, if you're an established tenant, you may want a quick resolution of your own beef with the landlord, and be less interested in money damages. A frank discussion with the landlord, perhaps in the company of a mediator or other neutral third party, may work better than a frontal legal assault. Many a landlord will listen up quite quickly if you explain, for example, how an occupancy policy discriminates against families. With luck (and the specter of a lawsuit), the landlord may make amends. And if informal techniques don't work, you can still sue or complain to a government agency.

You may also be able to pressure the landlord by contacting his insurance company or mortgage lender. These parties have much to lose if your landlord gets hit with a large jury award. Consequently, they have a real interest in making sure that the landlord settles a potentially expensive lawsuit quickly and reasonably.

If, on the other hand, you see the incident as part of a bigger issue that ought to be settled for the sake of others to come, you may not want to broker your own separate peace. If you reach an informal resolution of your discrimination claim, you may be left with the disquieting thought that the same illegal behavior will simply be practiced on the next, unwitting applicant or tenant. Sexual harassment, in particular, is not likely to end as the result of one person's courageous confrontation.

Lawsuits and agency complaints, however, are adversarial and drawn-out procedures. As anyone who has been involved in a court case will tell you, it is no picnic—even if you win. If you have a strong case and can get a quick court order from a judge, your experience will be mercifully short. Or, if your facts are compelling and your lawyer good, you may be able to settle for a sizable amount of money without going to trial.

Not every case, however, proceeds so easily. If the landlord or his insurance company dig in their heels, it may take months, even years; in the meantime, the lawsuit may come to feel like an albatross around your neck. For example, you will need to be available for depositions (long, drawn-out sessions with the other side's lawyers in which you are questioned under oath) and court dates that are set without much, if any, consideration for your personal or business schedule. As the court or hearing day approaches, your stomach will be in knots and your mind consumed by the battle to come. Many litigants, including the successful ones, come out of the experience vowing never again to go near a lawyer or a courthouse if they can possibly avoid it.

Another important downside of filing a fair housing complaint or lawsuit is that it may hurt your chances of renting later. Future credit and background checks done by employers and landlords will probably reveal the fact that you filed a discrimination complaint. In spite of the existence of some legal protections against direct landlord retaliation (see Chapter 15) the reality is that you have no idea how this information will be used. It would be an unusual landlord indeed who would consider a lawsuit against a former landlord as a mark in your favor, even if your suit was totally justified.

Before making a final decision as to which path to take, ask for the opinion of a trusted and reasonable friend. Discrimination can be a highly emotional subject, and it's always a good idea to seek the counsel of someone who is not involved.

2. Special Issues in Sexual Harassment Cases

Sexual harassment cases are handled the same way as are other fair housing claims. But because of their special psychological and legal aspects, these cases involve several additional considerations.

As with other kinds of housing discrimination cases, you can directly confront the harasser or seek help from HUD (or a state fair housing agency) or a lawyer. Generally, annoying but not outrageous behavior merits an informal response, but serious, unbearable harassment needs the resources of professionals and courts. Is the behavior threatening? Or does it amount to the social ineptitude of one person? It is usually helpful to share your experience with a wise friend and ask for a candid evaluation of your perceptions.

If you conclude that the landlord's or manager's behavior warrants a confrontation, demand that it stop. Do so in writing or, at least, follow up your conversation with a written demand. Surprisingly often—some experts say up to 90% of the time— this works, especially in cases where the behavior is fairly low-level, such as comments about your appearance, tacky photos on the apartment manager's bulletin board or off-color jokes. Repeat your demands if necessary.

If the offensive behavior continues, in spite of your oral and written requests that it stop, you'll need to consider your next step. In general, you have three options:

Stay put and hope for the best. It's not a good idea to choose this option unless you simply cannot move or file a complaint. Many hard-core harassers escalate their behavior over time.

Break the lease and move out. The landlord has a legal responsibility to make sure you have the undisturbed, quiet enjoyment of your leased home. If a court decides that a landlord has not met this responsibility, the tenant is excused from the lease.

What this amounts to in the context of sexual harassment is that, if the landlord, manager or employee is harassing you and interfering with your ability to enjoy your tenancy, you may be able to point to this as a justification for breaking the lease. But the harassment must be serious and persistent in order for this strategy to work, and if your landlord challenges your decision to move without giving proper notice, you must be prepared to produce convincing evidence—for example, copies of your written demands that the behavior stop and, if possible, testimony from other tenants who have experienced similar mistreatment.

File a fair housing claim or lawsuit. In general, consider this option only if you can show clearly that the advances were unwanted, rebuffed, repeated and fairly serious; that you lost no time in confronting the harasser and, when repeated requests were unheeded, you promptly filed a complaint. Filing a sexual harassment complaint is almost sure to be a painful experience, especially if you alone have endured the mistreatment. The other side will probably base much of its defense trying to discredit you.

To prove a claim of sexual harassment, you must usually show that the behavior was *unwanted.* This can be hard to do, since it's usually a matter of your word ("I told him to stop and he persisted") against the harasser's ("She was just playing hard to get"). To help your lawyer or HUD investigator establish your case, you should:

- **Collect evidence.** Keep any offensive cards, notices or photographs; photograph evidence (such as off-color jokes or cartoons posted on bulletin boards) that you cannot seize.
- **Keep a detailed journal.** Keep a detailed journal of every offensive incident. Include the names of everyone involved, dates, times and locations. If your case goes to court, the contents of your journal may be admitted to substantiate your testimony; in any event, it will be an invaluable aid to the lawyer or investigator preparing your case.
- **Talk with other tenants.** If your story is echoed by other women, it's harder for the harasser to claim that you are lying or unreasonably

interpreting his ardent but innocent interest. Talk to other tenants and find out whether others are in the same boat. (Chapter 19 discusses ways for tenants to act together effectively.)

- **Talk with friends.** Promptly sharing your experience with trusted friends serves two purposes: First, it helps you sort out your emotions and relieves the burden of keeping an upsetting secret. Second, it creates potentially valuable witnesses who can testify that you were angry or upset. It will also preclude a harasser's inevitable argument that, had you been truly offended, you would have turned to a friend for solace and advice.

For more information on sexual harassment and how to stop it, see *Sexual Harassment on the Job,* by William Petrocelli and Barbara Kate Repa (Nolo). Although written primarily for employees, this book will also help tenants dealing with landlords or managers.

3. Negotiating With the Landlord

If the landlord's insurance company or lawyer realizes you have complained (or are about to do so) to a fair housing agency or are poised to file a lawsuit, they may offer to settle. Be wary of dealing with these professional types without the presence of a neutral third party—a mediator, for example. Chapter 19 explains the mediation process in detail, and gives you information on locating and working with a mediator.

During negotiations, you might be offered $5,000 to settle a sexual harassment or race-based discrimination claim. If you think that figure is too low, you may be tempted to go shopping for a lawyer in hopes of getting more money. Fine, but remember, once the lawyer's fee and pretrial expenses are figured in, you'll have to get quite a bit more in order to come out ahead.

EXAMPLE: Your landlord offers you $5,000 to settle your discrimination claim. Thinking that you can get more, you hire a lawyer, agreeing to an attorney's fee of one-third of your settlement or jury verdict plus court costs. Assuming costs amount to $1,500, this means you'll have to recover almost $10,000 in order to actually receive $5,000—what you were offered in the first place. If you end up getting only a couple of thousand dollars more with a lawyer than without, you'll recover less than you were originally offered.

Mediate Your Dispute, by Peter Lovenheim (Nolo), contains important information on choosing and working with a mediator.

4. How Strong Is Your Case?

If you've thought it through and decided you do want to file a complaint with a fair housing agency or sue the landlord, you need to evaluate the strength of your case and the chances of your success. How serious was the discrimination, and how convincing is your proof?

a. Severity of the Illegal Act

The more serious the harm you suffered, the more likely you are to win. For example, if you are a family of four and encounter a landlord who clearly uses occupancy standards to discriminate against families with children, an investigator at the local HUD office may be quite interested in your case. The key issue—being able to rent as a family—is extremely important. Less serious acts of discrimination might be better addressed in a meeting with the landlord.

Be realistic in your assessment of the harm. Remember, your fate will depend on how a judge, jury or insurance adjuster reacts to the landlord's behavior. For example, when a manager screams racial epithets at minority tenants, it's a big case in

anyone's book; if he puts all families with kids in the back of the building, it's less so.

Also try to determine whether the act was part of a pattern. Landlords who repeatedly discriminate against applicants and tenants are of far greater interest to enforcement agencies than those who commit an isolated wrong. Judges and juries, too, are more prone to punish inveterate bigots than first-timers.

b. Intentional vs. Unintentional Discrimination

Housing discrimination comes in two forms:
- Intentional, such as a statement that the owner doesn't rent to African-Americans, and
- Unintentional, such as a policy that lets only two people occupy a two-bedroom flat. It indirectly discriminates against families, even if the landlord's genuine reason is to limit noise and congestion.

Even though the law bans both kinds of discrimination, landlords who practice intentional discrimination are, in general, far more vulnerable to a fair housing charge. Indirect discrimination cases often must be proved by argument and statistics—you must show that the landlord's behavior or policy tends to hurt a protected group more than tenants in general. Also, intentional discrimination carries with it the possibility of punitive damages, which makes the case more attractive to a private attorney and often pressures landlords into settling.

c. Coming Up With Proof

However right you may be, to win in an administrative hearing or in court you'll have to prove it. If you're lucky, you can use the landlord's own words—like a printed ad that asks for "mature adults only"—as proof. But it's just as likely that there will be no hard proof of discrimination, and that your case will come down to your word against the landlord's.

For example, consider the landlord who tells you during the application process, when no one else is present, that he doesn't rent to single women because he is afraid of his liability if a woman is assaulted on his property. He can be expected to deny having made that statement. In this situation, your case would be greatly strengthened if you could find other women with decent credit and employment records who had also been turned down by this landlord.

Landlords are also sometimes caught by amateur testers. For example, if you are an African-American and think that you have been treated differently only because of your race, there is nothing to stop you from asking friends who are not African-American to apply for the same vacancy. Be sure that your "testers" have background and credit histories that are similar to yours. If they are offered the apartment, it's strong evidence that you were rejected because of your race.

How Landlords Get Caught

Landlords who turn away prospective tenants on the basis of race, ethnic background or other group characteristics don't come out and admit what they're doing. But especially if they own many rental units, their illegal practices often become known to private fair housing advocacy groups (sometimes known as "fair housing councils") or HUD investigators, who hear repeated complaints.

Commonly, a person who's a member of a racial minority or other protected group is told that no rentals are available, or that his income and credit history aren't good enough. If this person suspects that he isn't being told the truth, he contacts a private fair housing group or HUD. Both groups are adept at uncovering this discriminatory practice by having people called "testers" apply to the same landlord. Typically, a white tester applies for the same housing, listing credit and income information that is similar—or sometimes not even as good—as that given by the minority applicant. A landlord who offers to rent to a white tester, after having rejected the minority applicant with the same or better qualifications, is very likely to become the subject of a fair housing complaint or lawsuit.

5. Complaining to a Fair Housing Agency

You may file a discrimination complaint with HUD (if you believe a federal law has been violated) or a state antidiscrimination agency (if your state's antidiscrimination law has been violated), and in some places also with a local fair housing agency.

State fair housing agencies are listed in Appendix I, and regional HUD offices can be reached by calling HUD's Fair Housing Information Clearinghouse at 800-343-3442. A phone call to the state or regional federal agency should provide you with the complaint-filing procedure.

a. How It Works

A federal HUD complaint must be filed within one year of the alleged violation; state statutes and local ordinances may set shorter deadlines. The complaint form for HUD is short, simple and easily completed without the help of a lawyer. If the complaint is filed with HUD, the agency should (but doesn't always) conduct an investigation within 180 days. The response time of state housing agencies varies.

After HUD investigates (and this is true of most state agencies as well), it will decide whether to dismiss your complaint or take it further. If the agency proceeds with your complaint, they'll attempt to produce a conciliation agreement (compromise) between you and the landlord. For example, you might agree to drop your complaint in exchange for a sum of money and the landlord's written promise to rent you an apartment or, if you're a current tenant, to stop discriminatory policies.

If conciliation is unsuccessful, the fair housing agency will hold an administrative hearing, which is like a trial without a jury, to determine whether discrimination has occurred. If the administrative law judge decides there was a fair housing violation, he or she will order the landlord to pay you money damages, rent you the unit you were denied or take other appropriate action.

b. State or Federal Fair Housing Agency: Which Is Better?

If the fair housing violation you've encountered involves both federal and state law, you'll have a choice as to which enforcement agency to approach. Some points to consider are:

- **Your time frame.** HUD cases are typically long, drawn-out affairs—some have dragged on for years. If you want a court order that a landlord offer you a particular rental, you probably won't get quick action from HUD, but you could receive money damages later. Some states handle their cases more quickly.

Call your state's fair housing agency and ask how long it takes to resolve a typical case.

- **What you must prove.** It may be tougher to prove your case under one law than another. For example, the federal Fair Housing Acts do not require you to prove that the landlord acted intentionally, but some state laws (California's Unruh Act, for one) do. It may be wise to talk to a fair housing group or lawyer to compare the available laws.
- **What you may win.** Some state statutes put a cap on money damages, both compensatory and punitive; federal law does not. If your case is serious, you may give up a substantial amount of money by choosing a state agency.
- **Your state's reputation for protection of tenant rights.** A state fair housing agency will mirror the general attitude of the state towards tenants' rights. If you live in California, Massachusetts or New York, for example, you can expect more protection than if you live in a hands-off state such as Alabama. If you aren't familiar with your state's approach to housing discrimination law, you'll have to do a bit of homework, such as going to the public library and asking the reference librarian to guide you to helpful articles or books. The same questions may be asked of a librarian in your local law library. (See Chapter 20 for information on doing legal research.)

6. Filing a Lawsuit in Federal or State Court

If you have experienced clear and outrageous discrimination, going directly to court may be quicker and more rewarding than going to a government agency. You'll need the help of an experienced lawyer if you choose this route. With her help, you may be able to force the landlord to rent you the premises and to pay you money damages.

You may sue in federal court or state court even if you have filed a complaint with a fair housing agency (deciding whether to do both is one of the reasons you'll need to hire a good lawyer). The exception to this rule is if you have signed a conciliation agreement or a formal HUD administrative hearing has already begun. If you file in federal court, you must do so within two years of the alleged violation.

a.   How It Works

Your attorney may decide to file papers asking the court for an expedited hearing (often within a few days), with the hope that a judge will find that the landlord's actions or policies are discriminatory and order the landlord to cease them immediately. These orders are called "temporary restraining orders" (TROs) or sometimes "preliminary injunctions." They are granted only if you convince the judge that:

- You have a good chance of winning the case (that is, the landlord really did illegally discriminate), and
- You will suffer irreparable harm if immediate relief isn't granted.

In theory, the TRO remains in place until a more formal hearing is held. In practice, when discrimination is clear enough for a judge to issue a TRO, normally the parties settle out of court. A typical settlement might involve the tenant getting the rental unit plus attorney fees, plus money damages—which, depending on the severity of the discrimination, might be $2,000 to $20,000 or more.

b.   Hiring a Lawyer

Finding a lawyer to represent you in a federal or state lawsuit of this kind may be tough. In the past, legal aid attorneys, hired by government-financed law clinics, often handled discrimination cases for people with low incomes, but federal cutbacks have greatly reduced the availability of legal aid services. As a result, you will probably need to work with a private attorney. (Chapter 20 offers tips on how to find and work with a lawyer.)

If you have a strong case, an attorney may take it "on contingency." This means you pay nothing up front but agree to give the attorney a percentage, usually 20% to 40%, of whatever you win or agree to in a settlement. But the lawyer is reimbursed for the costs of filing the lawsuit and other expenses, such as those for depositions, investigators and expert witnesses, before the award is divided and distributed.

An attorney who is not confident your case is a winner will require an up-front retainer of at least several thousand dollars, to cover the costs of preparing the legal papers and filing the suit. When the case is over, the lawyer will return to you any amount that was not needed for costs and fees. If you have won, the whole award is divided according to your contingency fee agreement (since you've already paid for expenses). If the case settles or ends in your favor, you may also be awarded court costs, attorney fees and damages, but you can't count on it.

As explained above, if you've gotten a reasonable settlement offer from a landlord, your lawyer needs to win considerably more for you in order for you to come out ahead. To ensure that a lawyer doesn't end up actually costing you money, one strategy is to insist on paying a percentage of only the portion of any award or settlement that exceeds the amount you were already offered. If the lawyer balks at this, it's probably because she believes that the case isn't worth much more than your original offer. On the other hand, a lawyer who thinks that the case is really worth a lot more (for example, $25,000 to $50,000), will be pleased to base her fee on only a percentage of any recovery over $5,000.

If your lease or rental agreement has an "attorney fees" clause, it may not apply to a discrimination lawsuit. Typically, these clauses, which require the loser to pay the winner's attorney fees in a lawsuit between the landlord and tenant, apply only when the lawsuit is over a lease clause. For example, if you don't pay the rent and your landlord evicts you, the clause will apply because paying rent is part of the lease. But if your landlord's discriminatory behavior does not involve a lease term —you sue for sexual harassment, for example—the fees clause won't apply.

 For a detailed explanation of contingency fee contracts, see *Mad at Your Lawyer*, by Tanya Starnes (Nolo).

c. Who Gets Sued or Targeted in a Complaint

Landlords aren't the only targets of fair housing enforcement. Newspapers that publish discriminatory ads are also covered by the federal fair housing rules, and many have been sued or named by fair housing enforcement agencies for ads like "quiet and mature neighborhood" and "Tenant wanted: Christian handyman." Publishers are especially attractive targets, since they usually have hefty insurance policies that can pay a settlement or court judgment.

Management companies hired by landlords to oversee their rental properties may also be sued. Frequently, it's the manager who commits the discriminatory act—for example, by improperly screening tenants or setting discriminatory policies. Usually the company is every bit as liable as if the owner himself had done the deed; sometimes, an administrative judge or jury decides that both owner and management company are responsible. Large management companies that handle hundreds of rentals are often more solvent (have "deeper pockets") than the small-fry landlords they represent. ■

Inspecting the Rental Unit and Moving In

Legal disputes between tenants and landlords have gained a reputation for being almost as emotional as divorce court battles. One of the most common disputes doesn't even occur until your relationship with the landlord is over. Of course, we refer to the problem that occurs when your landlord keeps all or part of your security deposit, claiming you left the place filthy or damaged it—for example, stained the rug, cracked the bathroom mirror, or left behind a major cockroach problem, a grease-covered stove or a broken garbage disposal. Not surprisingly, you probably disagree for one of several reasons:

- the problems existed when you moved in
- the property damaged was so old that it wasn't worth anything in the first place, or was impossible to clean, or
- the landlord is substantially exaggerating the cost of cleaning up or fixing damage that did occur.

You consider suing your landlord in small claims court for your full deposit, but decide against it because you have no way to prove your case.

This chapter shows how you can avoid such disputes by inspecting and photographing the rental unit *before* you move in. (Chapter 16 covers the subject of moving out and getting your security deposit returned in detail.)

A. How to Inspect the Rental Unit

When you first visited your new place, you got a general impression of the rental unit's condition. To avert all sorts of future arguments with your landlord, you need to go much further. It is absolutely essential that you check the place over for damage, dirt, mildew and obvious wear and tear before moving in—ideally, before you've signed a lease or rental agreement or paid your first month's rent and deposit.

1. Filling Out a Landlord-Tenant Checklist

Filling in a Landlord-Tenant Checklist, inventorying the condition of the rental property at the beginning (and end) of the tenancy, is an excellent way to protect yourself when it comes time to getting your security deposit returned. It's also the law in some states, listed below.

A sample Landlord-Tenant Checklist is shown below and Appendix II includes a blank, tear-out copy.

You and your landlord or manager should fill out the checklist together. If that's impossible, complete the form on your own. It's a good idea to take along a friend as a potential witness, who could testify in court if there's a dispute over security deposit deductions when you move out.

Landlord-Tenant Checklist

GENERAL CONDITION OF RENTAL UNIT AND PREMISES

572 Fourth ST.

Street Address

Apt. 11   Washington, D.C.

Unit Number   City

	Condition on Arrival	Condition on Departure	Estimated Cost of Repair/Replacement
LIVING ROOM			
Floors & Floor Coverings	OK		
Drapes & Window Coverings	mini-blinds discolored		
Walls & Ceilings	OK		
Light Fixtures	OK		
Windows, Screens & Doors	window rattles		
Front Door & Locks	OK		
Fireplace	N/A		
Other			
Other			
KITCHEN			
Floors & Floor Coverings	Cigarette burn hole		
Walls & Ceilings			
Light Fixtures	OK		
Cabinets	OK		
Counters	Stained		
Stove/Oven	Burners filthy (grease)		
Refrigerator	OK		
Dishwasher	OK		
Garbage Disposal	N/A		
Sink & Plumbing	OK		
Windows, Screens & Doors			
Other			
Other			
DINING ROOM			
Floors & Floor Covering	OK		
Walls & Ceilings	Crack in ceiling		
Light Fixtures	OK		
Windows, Screens & Doors	OK		
Other			

	Condition on Arrival			Condition on Departure			Estimated Cost of Repair/Replacement
BATHROOM(S)	Bath 1	Bath 2		Bath 1	Bath 2		
Floors & Floor Coverings	OK						
Walls & Ceilings	OK						
Windows, Screens & Doors	OK						
Light Fixtures	OK						
Bathtub/Shower	Tub chipped						
Sink & Counters	OK						
Toilet		Base of toilet very dirty					
Other							
Other							
BEDROOM(S)	Bdrm 1	Bdrm 2	Bdrm 3	Bdrm 1	Bdrm 2	Bdrm 3	
Floors & Floor Coverings							
Windows, Screens & Doors	OK	OK					
Walls & Ceilings	OK	OK					
Light Fixtures	Dented	OK					
Other	OK	OK					
Other		Mildew in closet					
Other							
Other							
OTHER AREAS							
Heating System	OK						
Air Conditioning	OK						
Lawn/Garden	OK						
Stairs and Hallway	OK						
Patio, Terrace, Deck, etc.	N/A						
Basement	OK						
Parking Area	OK						
Other							
Other							
Other							
Other							
Other							

☒ Tenants acknowledge that all smoke detectors and fire extinguishers were tested in their presence and found to be in working order, and that the testing procedure was explained to them. Tenants agree to test all detectors at least once a month and to report any problems to Landlord/Manager in writing. Tenants agree to replace all smoke detector batteries as necessary.

FURNISHED PROPERTY

	Condition on Arrival	Condition on Departure	Estimated Cost of Repair/Replacement
LIVING ROOM			
Coffee Table	Two scratches on top		
End Tables	OK		
Lamps	OK		
Chairs	OK		
Sofa	OK		
Other			
Other			
KITCHEN			
Broiler Pan			
Ice Trays			
Other			
Other			
DINING AREA			
Chairs	OK		
Stools	N/A		
Table	Leg bent slightly		
Other			
Other			
BATHROOM(S)	Bath 1 Bath 2	Bath 1 Bath 2	
Mirrors	OK		
Shower Curtain	Torn		
Hamper	N/A		
Other			
BEDROOM(S)	Bdrm 1 Bdrm 2 Bdrm 3	Bdrm 1 Bdrm 2 Bdrm 3	
Beds (single)	OK N/A		
Beds (double)	N/A OK		
Chairs	OK OK		
Chests	N/A N/A		
Dressing Tables	OK N/A		
Lamps	OK OK		
Mirrors	OK OK		
Night Tables	OK N/A		
Other			

	Condition on Arrival	Condition on Departure	Estimated Cost of Repair/Replacement
Other			
OTHER AREAS			
Bookcases	N/A		
Desks	N/A		
Pictures	Hallway picture frame chipped		
Other			
Other			

Use this space to provide any additional explanation:

_____
_____
_____
_____
_____
_____
_____
_____
_____
_____
_____
_____

Landlord-Tenant Checklist completed on moving in on _____May 1_____, 200 _X_, and approved by:

*Bernard Cohen*_____ and _*Maria Crouse*_____
Landlord/Manager   Tenant

                                           _*Sandra Martino*_____
                                              Tenant

                                           _____
                                              Tenant

Landlord-Tenant Checklist completed on moving out on _____, 200 ___, and approved by:

_____ and _____
Landlord/Manager   Tenant

                                           _____
                                              Tenant

                                           _____
                                              Tenant

The checklist is in two parts. The first side covers the general condition of each room; the second covers furnishings.

You will be filling out the first column—*Condition on Arrival*—before you move in. The last two columns—*Condition on Departure* and *Estimated Cost of Repair/Replacement*—are for use when you move out and ideally the two of you inspect the unit again. At that time the checklist will document any damage to the rental unit during your tenancy, which the landlord may attempt to recoup by withholding all or part of your security deposit. (Chapter 16 discusses how to complete the Landlord-Tenant Checklist when you move out.)

items (especially in the kitchen or bathroom) that are dirty, including mildew, pest or rodent problems.

Mark "OK" next to items that are in satisfactory condition—basically, clean, safe, sanitary and in good working order.

Make a note—as specific as possible—on items that are broken, stained, worn, grime-covered, scratched, leaking, smelly, dented, chipped or simply not in the best condition. For example, instead of writing "stove dirty," state that the burners are covered with grease. Don't simply note that the refrigerator "needs fixing" if an ice maker doesn't work. It's just as easy to write "ice maker broken, should not be used." This way, the landlord can't claim you broke the ice maker and should pay for its repair or replacement.

States That Require a Landlord-Tenant Checklist

The following states require landlords to give new tenants a written statement on the condition of the rental premises at move-in time, including a comprehensive list of existing damages. Tenants in these states often have the right to inspect the premises to verify the accuracy of the landlord's list and to note any problems.

Check the statutes for the exact requirements in your state, including the type of inspection required at the end of the tenancy. (See "Citations for State Laws on Security Deposits" in Appendix I.)

Arizona	Maryland	North Dakota
Georgia	Massachusetts	Virginia
Hawaii	Michigan	Washington
Kentucky	Montana	

Home Inspection Resources

Here are two good books on how to inspect a home, including how to discover major problems such as a leaky roof or malfunctioning fireplace:

The Home Inspection Troubleshooter, by Robert Irwin (Dearborn)

Your Home Inspection Guide, by William L. Ventolo, Jr. (Dearborn)

---

a. General Condition of Rental Unit and Premises

In the *Condition on Arrival* column, you should note both serious problems, such as a broken heater or leaking roof, and minor flaws such as stained kitchen counters. Be sure to note areas or

b. Furnishings

The second part of the checklist covers furnishings, such as lamps or shower curtains. Obviously, you can simply mark "Not Applicable" or "N/A" in most of these boxes if your unit is not furnished.

If your rental property has rooms or furnishings not listed on the checklist, note them in "Other Areas" or cross out something that you don't have and write in the changes. If you are renting a large house or apartment or providing many furnishings, you may want to attach a separate sheet. Just make a separate list for additional items and staple it to the checklist.

What to Look For

Structure

- holes or cracks in floors, walls or ceiling
- dark round spots on the ceiling or dark streaks on the walls, indicating water leaks

Plumbing

- toilet takes too long to flush or leaks on the floor
- tap water is discolored
- low water pressure (scalding hot water in the shower when you flush the toilet)
- water drains slowly in sinks, tubs and showers

Heating

- no heat or inadequate or dangerous heating facilities

Light and Ventilation

- poor ventilation in bathrooms (no outside window or fan)
- inadequate natural light through windows
- poor lighting in hallways, stairs, entranceways or parking areas

Wiring and Electricity

- loose or exposed wiring
- insufficient outlets or light fixtures

Insects, Vermin and Rodents

- rodent trails or excrement
- evidence of cockroaches in cupboards, closets or behind appliances

Security

- flimsy or inadequate locks on doors and windows
- windows don't open and close easily (painted or nailed shut)

Fire Safety

- smoke detectors absent or not working
- fire extinguishers absent or not working
- exits leading to street or hallway unsafe or full of litter
- combustible materials in storage rooms, garages or basements

Trash and Garbage Receptacles

- inadequate garbage and trash storage and removal

Other Issues

Depending on where you live, you may note other problems—for example, earthquake and flooding hazards are important issues in some parts of the country.

Test Smoke Detectors and Fire Extinguishers

State and local laws often require landlords to provide fire extinguishers and smoke detectors in rental units. As part of your move-in procedures, make sure the landlord tests all smoke detectors and fire extinguishers in your presence and shows them to be in good working order. Be sure you understand how to:

- test the fire extinguisher and smoke detector
- recognize the signs of a failing detector—for example, a beeping noise, and
- replace the smoke detector battery.

Do not disable a smoke detector. Not only is it foolish–it could expose you to liability if a fire causes damage that could have been prevented had there been a working detector. Consider, for example, Texas Prop. Code § 92.211, which will also impose a civil fine for disabling a detector even if there is no fire.

The box on the bottom of the second page of the checklist acknowledges that you tested the smoke detector and fire extinguisher in the landlord's presence and found them to be in working order.

2. Signing the Checklist

After you and your landlord agree on all of the particulars on the rental unit, you each should sign and date every page of the checklist, including any attachments. The landlord will probably keep the original and give you a copy. If you filled out the checklist on your own, make sure the landlord reviews your comments, notes any disagreement and returns a copy to you promptly. You should ask the landlord to make the checklist part of your lease or rental agreement, as explained in Chapter 2.

A savvy landlord will update the checklist after making repairs or replacing, adding or removing items after you move in. You should both initial and date any changes.

B. Photographing the Rental Unit

Taking photos or videotapes of the unit before you move in is another excellent way to avoid disputes over your responsibility for damage and dirt. In addition to the checklist, you'll be able to compare "before" and "after" pictures when you leave. This should help refresh your landlord's memory, and if you end up in small claims court fighting over the security deposit, documenting your point of view with photos will be invaluable.

It's best to take "before" photographs with a Polaroid camera that develops pictures on the spot. This will allow both you and the landlord to date and sign the pictures, each keeping a set. Otherwise, use a camera that automatically imprints the date on each photo. If you don't have access to either type of camera, photograph the landlord or manager during the inspection. Then develop the pictures promptly and sign and date them on the back. If you go to a two-for-one developing place, you can send the landlord a set dated with a letter just a few days after the inspection. If you're doing the inspection on your own, bring a copy of that day's newspaper and photograph the front page as part of one of the photos. If you make a video, clearly state the date and time so that you can prove when the video was made.

You should repeat this process when you leave. Chapter 16 discusses moving out.

C. How to Handle Problems

If you discover any problems, try to get your new landlord to fix them before you move in.

1. Serious Problems

The landlord must fix certain defects—such as a broken heater or leaking roof—under state and local housing codes. (Chapter 8 discusses landlords' repair and maintenance responsibilities.) A landlord who does not immediately agree to fix serious problems, probably isn't taking the obligation to repair very seriously. You're probably best off refusing to rent the place and reporting the landlord to your local housing or building inspector.

If the landlord promises to make repairs or alterations after you move in, be careful. First, ask other tenants how good the landlord is at keeping promises. Second, get the promises in writing and signed, ideally as part of the lease or rental agreement. (See Chapter 2.) Your written agreement should specify the:

- exact repair or alteration to be made—for example, installation of a deadbolt lock
- deadline by which repairs will be made
- penalty for landlord's failure to complete repairs by the promised date—for example, a certain reduction in your rent.

Some samples are shown below.

Sample Agreements Regarding Repairs

Serious Problem:
Landlord will clear the drains and fix the leaking toilet by March 1, the day the Tenant's rental agreement begins. If Landlord fails to fix these plumbing problems by March 1, Tenant may withhold rent for each day Landlord is late fixing the problem.

Nonessential Repair or Improvement:
Landlord will supply up to $250 worth of paint and painting supplies. Tenant will paint the living room, hall and two bedrooms, using off-white latex paint on the walls and ceiling and water-based enamel paint on all wood surfaces (doors and trim). Paint and supplies shall be picked up by Tenant from ABC Hardware and billed to Landlord.

---

2. Nonessential Repairs or Improvements

If repairs are not essential—such as a new coat of paint or more electrical outlets in the study—try to work something out.

Many landlords are open to making reasonable improvements and alterations, especially in higher-rent areas where there are lots of places for rent and not too many people looking, or if you've impressed the landlord as a good, responsible tenant.

You might offer to pay part of the expense of nonessential repairs or improvements, such as up-grading the electrical system to accommodate your computer equipment or fixing the back yard fence so that your dog can't get out. If you want the apartment painted, offer to do the work if the landlord buys the paint. Chapter 10 provides advice on how to convince the landlord to improve or alter the premises, and how to keep your monetary outlay to a minimum.

If the landlord seems completely unreasonable, or really put out simply by your request, beware. This doesn't sound like a good way to start the tenancy.

If you are a disabled person seeking modification of your living space to meet your needs, your landlord will not be able to legally stand in your way. Under the federal Fair Housing Amendments Act of 1988, you are entitled to modify your rental to make it safe and enjoyable. Chapter 5 explains how to go about obtaining permission to perform necessary modifications.

D. Clarifying Important Terms of the Tenancy

A good lease or rental agreement should cover the basic issues of your tenancy, including rent, deposits, rent increases and sublets. (Chapter 2 discusses leases and rental agreements.)

If your landlord does little more than sign a tersely-worded lease or rental agreement and hand you a key, make sure you have all necessary information before you move in. For example, be sure you know:

- the landlord or manager's phone numbers (day and night)
- how to report maintenance and repair problems
- any rules for the use of grounds, garage and storage space
- location of garbage cans, recycling programs and trash pickup days, and
- other issues that affect the particular rental, such as pool hours or use of a laundry room.

E. Organizing Your Rental Records

Establishing a simple system to record all correspondence with your landlord, such as repair requests, will provide a valuable paper trail should disputes later develop—for example, regarding your landlord's failure to make necessary repairs. Without good records, the outcome of a dispute may come down to your word against your landlord's, always a precarious situation.

To get started right, set up a file folder for the following documents:

- a copy of your rental application, references and credit report (keeping these will also save you some work next time you move)
- your copy of the signed lease or rental agreement
- any building rules and regulations or move-in letter from the landlord
- deposit information, including the amount and (if known) the location and interest rate terms of your deposit (Chapter 4 discusses basic security deposit rules), and
- Landlord-Tenant Checklist and photos or video taken at move-in.

After you move in, add these documents to your file:

- your landlord's written requests for entry (Chapter 11 discusses tenant privacy rights)
- rent increase notices
- records of your repair requests, including how and when they were handled (Chapters 8, 9 and 10 discuss repairs, maintenance, improvements and alterations), and
- any other correspondence with your landlord.

■

Roommates

Many tenants decide to share a home rather than live alone. For some, living with roommates not only saves money but is also a social boon. Whatever the reasons you have roommates, one thing is likely: The make-up of your living group will change over time as jobs, schooling, friendships, love and even illness or death play their part in rearranging the names on your mailbox. Unfortunately, most landlords are not as flexible as you might wish when it comes to adding new roommates or letting one out of a lease.

This chapter discusses key issues about sharing rental housing, such as:

- Your legal obligations and responsibilities with respect to your roommate
- Moving in a roommate and what to do if your landlord objects
- What to do if your roommate becomes nasty or won't pay the rent, and
- Whether or not you can rent space to a roomer.

Common Terms

Original tenant. The initial tenant (or tenants) who signed the lease or rental agreement. This is a short-cut term with no precise legal meaning.

Tenant. Someone who has signed a lease or a rental agreement, or whose residency—or rent payments— has been accepted by the landlord.

Co-tenants. Two or more tenants who rent the same property under the same lease or rental agreement. Each is 100% responsible for carrying out the agreement (lawyers call this "joint and several liability"), including paying all the rent.

Roommates. Two or more people, usually unrelated, living under the same roof and sharing rent and expenses. Roommates are usually co-tenants, but a roommate may be a subtenant of the original tenant. In other situations, a roommate may have the legal status of a long-term guest, with no formal legal relationship with the landlord.

Joint and Several Liability. This refers to the sharing of legal obligations by two or more people. When co-tenants are "jointly and severally liable" for rent, it means each of them can be held responsible for paying the entire rent. You and your co-tenants are jointly and severally liable for rent and other obligations—*even if your lease or rental agreement does not include this clause.* It applies to oral leases, too.

Roomer. A person who rents space in your home. If you are a tenant, the roomer is your subtenant, and you are her landlord.

 Related topics covered in this book include:

- How to find a compatible roommate: Chapter 1.
- Lease or rental agreement restrictions on overnight guests, sublets and assignments: Chapter 2.
- Your right to sublet your apartment for a while, and what happens if your landlord objects: Chapter 15.

- Whether or not you can get someone else to take over the rest of your lease and, if you do, whether you are off the financial hook: Chapter 15.
- What happens if you break your lease and move out early: Chapter 15.
- Getting your security deposit back if you leave but your roommates stay: Chapter 16.

A. Renting a Place With Others

When two or more people all simultaneously sign the same rental agreement or lease—or enter into the same oral rental agreement—they are co-tenants and share the same legal rights and responsibilities. But there's a special twist. One co-tenant's negative behavior—not paying the rent, for example—can affect everyone's tenancy.

1. If One Roommate Doesn't Pay Rent

Co-tenants may decide to split the rent equally or unequally, depending on their own personal wishes. However, such agreements don't have any impact on the landlord. Each co-tenant is independently liable to the landlord for all of the rent. Landlords often remind co-tenants of this obligation by inserting into the lease a chunk of legalese which says that the tenants are "jointly and severally" liable for paying rent and adhering to terms of the agreement. (See "Common Terms," above.) If one tenant can't pay a share of the rent in a particular month, or simply moves out, the other tenant(s) must still pay the full rent.

EXAMPLE: James and Helen sign a month-to-month rental agreement for an apartment rented by Blue Oak Properties, for $800 per month. James and Helen agree between themselves to each pay half of the rent. After three months, James moves out without notifying Helen or Blue Oak. Helen is legally obligated to pay Blue Oak all the rent until she legally ends the tenancy. (This usually requires 30 days' written notice.) If Helen can't pay the rent, Blue Oak may evict her.

In the meantime, if she can prove the existence of her agreement with James, Helen could try to recover James' share of the rent by suing him in small claims court.

If, instead of leaving, she gets a new roommate who pays half the rent, Helen can recover from James only the extra rent she had to pay before the new person moved in.

Landlords often insist on receiving one rent check for the entire rent—they don't want to be bothered with multiple checks from co-tenants, even if each co-tenant pays on time and the checks add up to the full rent. As long as you have been advised of this policy in the rental agreement or lease, it's legal for your landlord to impose it.

2. If One Roommate Violates the Lease or Rental Agreement

Although it is painful for an innocent tenant to hear, the landlord can, legally, hold all co-tenants responsible for the negative actions of just one, and terminate everyone's tenancy with the appropriate notice. For example, two co-tenants can be evicted if one of them seriously damages the property, moves in an extra roommate on the sly, keeps a dog in violation of a no-pets rule or otherwise violates the lease or rental agreement.

EXAMPLE: Dan and Mike were co-tenants whose lease prohibited pets. Dan's friend Kate implored him to take Ralph, her cat, when she joined the Peace Corps. Mike didn't like the idea, but Dan won him over by promising that both he and Ralph would move if the landlord found out. To Mike's dismay, when the landlord discovered Ralph, he sent both Mike and Dan termination notices.

In practice, however, landlords sometimes ignore the legal rule that all tenants are equally liable for lease violations, and don't penalize a blameless one. If the non-offending roommates pay the rent on time, do not damage the landlord's property and can differentiate themselves from the bad apple in the landlord's eyes, the landlord will probably want to keep them.

If you want to remain after a co-tenant gets the boot, you would do well to understand the landlord's principal concerns—to have good, stable tenants who pay the rent on time. If you can convince the landlord that throwing everyone out and starting over doesn't best serve those goals, she may forgo her right to evict all of you. Of course, you will have to absorb the departed tenant's share of the rent for the time it takes to find an acceptable new co-tenant. And, your landlord will need to approve any new co-tenant. (Section B, below, shows the best way to find a roommate who passes your landlord's muster.)

Unfortunately, if you can't handle the increased rent until you find a new tenant, or the landlord feels you can't be trusted to find a trustworthy one, the landlord is likely to evict all of you at the same time. It's far simpler and quicker than first evicting the troublemaker for the lease violation and then later ousting the rest of you when you fail to come up with the entire rent.

3. Agreements—and Disagreements— Among Roommates

Roommates make lots of informal agreements about splitting rent, occupying bedrooms and sharing chores. Your landlord isn't bound by these agreements, and has no power to enforce them. For all sorts of reasons, roommate arrangements regularly go awry. If you have shared an apartment or house, you know about roommates who play the stereo too loud, never wash a dish, always pay their share of the rent late, have too many overnight guests, leave their gym clothes on the kitchen table or otherwise drive you nuts. If the situation gets bad

enough, you'll likely end up arguing with your roommates about who should leave.

Only Landlords Can Evict Tenants

As a general rule, you can't terminate your roommate's tenancy by filing an eviction action. (The situation is different if you rent to a subtenant; see Section C, below.)

The exception involves rentals governed by the few rent control statutes, such as the one in San Francisco, that allow a landlord to designate a "master tenant"—usually a long-term tenant who was there first—to perform many of the functions of a landlord. Master tenants have the right to choose—as well as to evict—tenants. If your municipality is subject to rent control, find out whether the scheme includes a provision for a master tenant.

The more you can anticipate possible problems from the start, the better prepared you'll be to handle disputes that do arise. First, try to choose compatible housemates. (Follow our advice in Chapter 1.) Before you move in, sit down with your roommates and create your own agreement covering major issues, such as:

1. **Rent.** What is everyone's share? Who will write the rent check if the landlord requires only one check?
2. **Space.** Who will occupy which bedrooms? How will you divvy up the extra closet?
3. **Household chores.** Who's responsible for cleaning, and on what schedule?
4. **Food sharing.** Will you be sharing food, shopping and cooking responsibilities? How will you split the costs and work?
5. **Noise.** When should stereos be turned off or down low?
6. **Overnight guests.** Is it okay for boyfriends/ girlfriends to stay over every night?

7. Moving out. If one of you decides to move, how much notice must be given? Must the departing tenant find an acceptable substitute?

It's best to put your understandings in writing. (See the sample roommate agreement, below.) Oral agreements are too easily forgotten or misinterpreted after the fact.

Be as specific as possible, especially on issues that are important to you. If dirty dishes in the sink drive you up the wall, write it down. If occasional guests are no problem, but you can't stand the thought of your roommate's (non-rent-paying) boyfriend hogging the bathroom every morning, make sure your agreement is clear on guests.

Most of this kind of agreement isn't legally binding—that is, a judge won't order a tenant to clean the bathroom. Judges will, however, enforce financial agreements, such as how rent is to be shared.

EXAMPLE: Roommates Janet and Jacob orally agree that Jacob will get the larger bedroom and pay 60% of the rent and Janet will pay 40%. Right after they move in, Jacob loses his job and is unable to pay his share. Janet pays the whole amount for two months until finally she talks Jacob into moving. Six months later, after landing a good job, Jacob still hasn't paid Janet, who sues him in small claims court. Jacob admits in court that he owes Janet his share of two months' rent, but says there was never a deal to split it 60-40. The judge, faced with two different stories and nothing in writing, decides to split the rental obligation 50-50.

If Janet and Jacob had shared the rental for some time and given separate rent checks to the landlord every month (Jacob paying 60% and Janet 40%), Janet would probably have been able to convince the judge of the 60/40 agreement by producing her string of canceled checks. Of course, a written and signed Roommate Agreement that reflected the 60/40 split would have won the case for Janet.

By far the greatest value of committing your understanding of co-tenant rights and responsibilities to writing is that it forces you and your housemates to take your co-tenancy responsibilities seriously. To underline this commitment, it's always wise to include a clause requiring co-tenants to participate in mediation before one of you breaks the agreement by moving out or running off to court. Our sample roommate agreement, below, includes such a clause. Chapter 19 discusses how mediation works.

It is usually best not to involve your landlord in disputes among roommates. The reasons—both practical and legal—include the following:

- The landlord can't enforce any decisions among tenants. For example, short of continual—and, of course, illegal—monitoring of your living situation, how could a landlord make tenants share housecleaning?
- Any complaint you make about a co-tenant is likely to be reciprocated, with the result that your landlord is likely to receive a negative picture of all of you. Especially if you have a month-to-month tenancy, your landlord may get tired of your constant complaining and decide to get rid of the whole bunch of you.

Don't change the locks. If a roommate dispute gets serious—especially if your co-tenant hasn't paid the rent—you may be tempted to change the locks or ask the landlord to do so. Don't. A landlord cannot legally bar entry to a tenant with-

Sample Roommate Agreement

Alex Andrews, Brian Bates and Charles Chew are co-tenants at Apartment 2, 360 Capitol Avenue, Oakdale, Kentucky, under a year-long lease that expires on February 1, 200__. They have all signed a lease with the landlord, Reuben Shaw, and have each paid $300 towards the security deposit of $900. Alex, Brian and Charles all agree as follows:

1. **Rent**. The rent of $900 per month will be shared equally, at $300 per person. Alex will write a check for the total month's rent and take it to the manager's office on the first of each month (or the next day if the 1st falls on a holiday). Brian and Charles will pay their share to Alex on or before the due date.

2. **Bedrooms**. Alex and Brian will share the large bedroom with the adjacent deck; Charles will have the small bedroom.

3. **Food**. Each co-tenant is responsible for his own food purchases.

4. **Cleaning**. Charles will clean his own room; Alex and Brian will clean theirs weekly. The household chores for the rest of the apartment—living room, dining room, kitchen and bathroom—will rotate, with each co-tenant responsible for vacuuming, dusting, mopping and bathroom maintenance on a weekly basis.

   Each co-tenant will promptly clean up after himself in the kitchen. No one will leave dishes in the sink for more than 24 hours, and everyone will promptly clean up when asked.

5. **Utilities**. Everyone will pay an equal share of the electricity and gas bills. Alex will arrange for service and will pay the bill. Within three days of receiving the bill, Charles and Brian will each pay Alex one-third of the total.

6. **Phone**. Alex will arrange for phone service and will pay the monthly bill. Within three days of receiving the bill, Alex, Brian and Charles will identify their own long-distance charges and Brian and Charles will each pay Alex their long-distance totals, plus one-third of the fixed charges.

7. **Guests**. Because of the apartment's small size, each tenant agrees to have no more than one overnight guest at a time and to inform the others in advance, if possible. Each co-tenant agrees to no more than four guests overnight in a month.

8. **Exam Periods**. During mid-term and final exam periods, no co-tenant will have overnight guests or parties.

9. **Violations of the Agreement**. The co-tenants agree that repeated and serious violations of one or more of these understandings will be grounds for any two co-tenants to ask the other to leave. If a co-tenant is asked to leave, he will do so within two weeks, and will forfeit any outstanding pre-paid rent.

Sample Roommate Agreement (continued)

10. **Leaving Before the Lease Ends**. If a co-tenant wants to leave before the lease expires on February 1, 199_, he will give as much notice as possible (and not less than one month) and diligently try to find a replacement tenant who is acceptable to the remaining co-tenants and the landlord.

11. **Security Deposits**. The co-tenant who leaves early (voluntarily or involuntarily) will get his share of the security deposit returned, minus costs of repairs, replacement and cleaning attributable to the departing tenant, when and if an acceptable co-tenant signs the lease and contributes his share to the security deposit. If an acceptable co-tenant cannot be found, the departing tenant will not receive any portion of his share of the security deposit until the tenancy of the remaining co-tenants is over and the security deposit is refunded (or not) by the landlord.

12. **Dispute Resolution**. If a dispute arises concerning this agreement or any aspect of the shared living situation, the co-tenants will ask the University Housing Office Mediation Service for assistance before they terminate the co-tenancy or initiate a lawsuit. This will involve all three tenants sitting down with a mediator in good faith to try to resolve the problems.

Alex Andrews	*February 5, 200X*
Alex Andrews	Date
Brian Bates	*February 5, 200X*
Brian Bates	Date
Charles Chew	*February 5, 200X*
Charles Chew	Date

out a court order. Similarly, if you unilaterally bar your roommate from the rental, you, too, risk legal liability if the locked-out roommate is forced to find shelter elsewhere and sues you for the cost of alternate housing. Finally, changing the locks without your landlord's permission is almost always prohibited in the lease, and gives your landlord a legal justification to evict all of you.

4. If You Fear Violence

If you ever fear for your immediate physical safety (or that of one of your co-tenants), or when serious law-breaking such as drug-dealing is involved, call the police. Short of that, if you have a sound factual basis to believe that one of your roommates intends to harm you (he's purchased a gun or has repeatedly told others he's going to get you), communicate these fears to your landlord, who may begin proceedings to evict the aggressor. Your landlord will probably be motivated by self-interest as much as a desire to protect you. A landlord who fails to sensi-

bly intervene where violence is clearly threatened may be successfully sued by the victim if the aggressor in fact carries through with the threat. (See a related discussion of assaults by one tenant against another tenant in Chapter 14.)

In the meantime, if you fear violence from a co-tenant, consider taking the following precautions:

- **Get out of harm's way.** This may mean spending a few days with a friend or at a motel, but if you feel seriously threatened, the inconvenience and possible cost of removing yourself from danger will be well worth it. If continuing your co-tenancy turns out to be impossible, taking a breather may give you a chance to plan your exit.

- **Contact the local police department or court clerk's office for information on obtaining a temporary restraining order.** In most areas, it's fairly quick and easy to bring this type of problem before a judge, without needing to pay a lawyer. And if the judge decides that the situation merits it, he or she will issue an order forbidding the aggressor from coming

near you. Temporary restraining orders (TROs)—and how to use them—are explained in Chapter 14.

If you and other blameless co-tenants want to stay, follow our suggestions for bringing in a substitute tenant as explained below in Section B.

EXAMPLE: Andy and his roommate Bill turned out to be completely incompatible. Before long, arguments about housekeeping, regular guests and late rent payments by Andy escalated to the point where Bill felt physically threatened. Bill asked their landlord, Anita, to evict Andy. Andy responded by telling Anita that he had never threatened Bill, and that Bill's complaints were a clear illustration of how paranoid and hard to live with he was.

After listening to Andy's and Bill's complaints, Anita referred them to a local mediation service. Both agreed to participate. The mediator's influence worked for a while, but Andy and Bill were soon back at loud, unpleasant shouting matches. After satisfying herself that Andy really had made a series of physical threats, Anita initiated eviction proceedings against him, on the grounds that he posed a real danger to the safety of another tenant. The lawsuit made Andy even madder, and Bill sensibly moved in with his girlfriend for a week, until Andy moved out. Bill posted a "roommate wanted" notice on a bulletin board at work and eventually found Charlie, who had a solid employment and rental history. After confirming Charlie's qualifications, Anita added him to the lease in place of Andy. Although Bill ended up paying some of Andy's share of the rent, he wisely decided that his peace of mind and safety were worth more than the money, and did not sue Andy for the debt.

If Your Roomie Is a Druggie

For all sorts of reasons, especially your physical safety, you should promptly inform your landlord if you reasonably suspect that your co-tenant is involved in illegal activity on the premises, especially drug dealing or serious drug use. It's also your only hope of salvaging your tenancy. If your landlord finds out from other sources, you will all probably be evicted. While the landlord has the right to evict all of you based on one tenant's illegal acts, your forthrightness might convince your landlord to let you stay and get a new (law-abiding) roommate.

5. When a Roommate Leaves

A co-tenant who wants to leave in the middle of a tenancy is legally responsible, if she is a month-to-month tenant, for giving the landlord proper written notice and paying rent through the end of the notice period. If there's a lease, the tenant must either get permission from the landlord to leave early or, if this is impossible, find a new tenant (acceptable to the landlord) to take over. If a co-tenant simply leaves, the fallout can be serious. Chapter 15 explains in detail the likely consequences to the departing tenant. Here we discuss the predicament of the remaining co-tenants.

a. What to Do If You Want to Stay

The unauthorized departure of a co-tenant gives the landlord the option of evicting the rest of you, even if you can pay the full rent. The landlord has this option because breaking the lease or rental agreement is a violation of a key lease term (the length of stay), for which all tenants are liable. (See Section A, above.)

In practice, however, your landlord will probably let you stay if it will keep a steady stream of rent money coming in and keep the place occupied by stable, non-destructive tenants. So if you pay the rent after a co-tenant has broken the lease and left, the landlord will probably not evict you and other tenants unless:

- you are a troublesome tenant, and this is a golden opportunity to be rid of you, or
- your income doesn't appear sufficient to cover the rent in the future. In this case, if you can assure the landlord that you can promptly bring in a good, law-and-lease-abiding new co-tenant, you might be able to salvage your tenancy. In the meantime, you may need to ask permission to pay the rent late or in installments. Or, ask the landlord to use the departed tenant's share of the security deposit to help pay the rent until you find an acceptable replacement. See Chapter 3 for ideas on how to approach your landlord.

⚠️ **Always get your landlord's approval before moving in a new roommate.** If a co-tenant takes off and leaves you facing the entire rent, you may be tempted to simply move in another roommate, bypassing the landlord's application process. Don't! Your lease or rental agreement probably prohibits unauthorized sublets. If it does, bringing in a new tenant—even a great one—without your landlord's okay violates your agreement and gives your landlord a watertight reason to evict you. Instead, keep your relationship on an honest footing and get your landlord's approval for a replacement tenant. Section B shows how.

b. How to Deal With a Departing Roommate

Remaining roommates need to cover their legal flanks with respect to the departed tenant as well as the landlord. If your housemate has left during the middle of a lease or without proper notice in a month-to-month tenancy, leaving you responsible for all the rent, your personal relations will be rocky at best. Probably the last thing you want is to have

your errant roommate reappear expecting to move back in.

To avoid such surprises, try to get your former roommate to sign an agreement, making it clear that the departing tenant:

- Will pay a stated amount of rent and utilities. If you rent under a written rental agreement, this will normally be rent and utilities for 30 days from the date the departing tenant gave written notice (or left without notice) unless a new roommate comes in earlier and covers these costs. If you rent under a lease, the amount owed will depend on when a new co-tenant, acceptable to the landlord, is ready to take over. If, despite your best efforts, you cannot find an acceptable replacement, the departing tenant will be liable for the rent for the balance of the lease.
- Will pay for any damage she caused to the rental unit. (See the Chapter 16 discussion of how landlords charge for damage. You can apply the same strategy.)
- Will pay for rent and damage no later than a stated date
- Has moved out for good and gives up any claim to be a tenant.

Chapter 16 discusses what happens to the departing co-tenant's security deposit.

But what if you and the departing roommate can't work things out, and the departed co-tenant shows no signs of paying? If your roommate is long gone or out-of-state, you may want to grit your teeth, pay his share and forget it, since trying to find him, sue him and then collect the judgment is likely to be more trouble than it's worth.

On the other hand, if your ex-roommate is still in town and has a source of income, consider taking the time to sue him in small claims court for unpaid rent, damage to the rental unit, unpaid utilities and your costs to find a replacement co-tenant, such as advertising. Then, if your ex-roommate still doesn't pay up, you can collect what you won in court from his bank account or wages. (Landlords often use these methods; see Chapter 16.)

c. What to Do If You Want to Move Out, Too

If your co-tenant skips out, leaving you in the lurch, you may decide that it's not worth the hassle of trying to stay and rustle up another roommate.

To ease your departure and forestall the landlord from keeping your security deposit to make up for unpaid rent, or listing you as a deadbeat at the credit bureau, follow these steps:

- If you are a month-to-month tenant, give the required amount of written notice (usually 30 days) immediately. Don't wait until you can't pay the next month's rent and receive a termination notice. (Chapter 15 shows how to give proper notice.)
- If you have a lease, let the landlord know in writing that you plan to move because you cannot afford the rent without your co-tenant. Before you move, be extra accommodating when it comes to showing the unit to prospective renters. Facilitating a quick re-rental is not just a courtesy to your landlord, but to your advantage as well, since the sooner a new tenant takes over, the sooner your liability for the balance of the rent due under the lease ends. In addition, do your best to find an acceptable replacement tenant yourself. (See Chapter 15 for an explanation of the landlord's responsibility to look for a new tenant, and Section B, below, for advice on finding and presenting a replacement.)

B. Adding a New Roommate

Suppose now that love, poverty or the desire for some friendly conversation convinces you to add a roommate—or you just need to replace a departing one. Most landlords will insist that the new roommate become a co-tenant, having the same rights and responsibilities as you do. This is normally best for you, too, but in a few situations, you may want the newcomer to be a subtenant, who rents from you and has no direct relationship with the landlord. For example, if you want to have the power to

evict your new roommate, you'll need to set up a subtenancy. Either way, though, you'll need the consent of the landlord. Here, we explain how to bring the roommate in as a co-tenant. Section C discusses how to sublet to a roomer.

1. Getting the Landlord's Approval

Obviously, you want to be sure that your choice of a new roommate is financially stable and compatible with you.

But even if you satisfy yourself as to your intended co-tenant's stellar qualifications, it doesn't mean the landlord will take your word for it. Landlords have their own good-tenant criteria. To increase your chances of getting an official okay, consider these questions before approaching the landlord:

- **Will adding a roommate exceed the occupancy limit?** Landlords are entitled to set reasonable limits on the number of occupants per rental unit. (See Chapter 5.)
- **Will the new roommate meet your landlord's good-tenant criteria?** Many landlords subject prospective tenants to a thorough screening process, checking credit, employment, rental history and references. Put yourself in your landlord's loafers and find out as much as you can about the person's financial status and rental history. It not only will help assure the landlord's approval, but protect you from

getting saddled with a deadbeat roommate. Ask your prospective roommate to request a credit report on himself. (See Chapter 1.) If the credit report is good, you'll want to hand it to the landlord with your proposed new tenant's application. Since the landlord will almost surely do this as well, doing it first gives you the opportunity to develop a plausible explanation for any negative information—for example, a prior eviction or bankruptcy.

Unless you are on fairly close personal terms with your landlord, it's usually a good idea to write your landlord a note about your desire to add a roommate. This gives the landlord an unpressured opportunity to think about it. It is also your chance to sell your proposal by pointing out that your rental is big enough for another tenant and, assuming you already have someone lined up, that your new roommate will be a great tenant. A sample letter is shown below.

2. Adding a Roommate to the Lease or Rental Agreement

If your intended roommate passes the landlord's credit and background checks, the landlord will probably ask both of you to sign a new lease or written month-to-month agreement. From your landlord's point of view, this is far more than a formality, since it makes the new arrival a co-tenant who is 100% liable to pay rent and make good on any damage. It's also desirable from your perspective, because it makes it completely clear that your new roommate shares the same legal rights and responsibilities as you do.

Sample Letter Requesting Permission to Add a Roommate

January 5, 200__

Barrie Newsome
247 Oakleaf Road
St. Paul, Minnesota 00000

Dear Ms. Newsome,

As you know, I rent a spacious one-bedroom apartment, #3A, at 250 Main Street, St. Paul, Minnesota. I would like to add my friend Marilyn Mason to my lease, as a co-tenant. Marilyn has just learned that her lease will not be renewed at the end of February because the owners of her flat, where she has lived for five years, have decided to move in themselves.

Marilyn and I have been friends for years. She works with me in the fulfillment department of Better Graphics, Ltd., and has been there for ten years. Her supervisor, Jim Barton, will be happy to answer any questions you might have, and Marilyn will be glad to provide a recent copy of her credit report. You can also contact her current and former landlords for references.

I would like to drop by the rental office this week and pick up a rental application for Marilyn.

Thank you very much for your consideration of my request.

Yours truly,

Tanya Tenant

3. More Roommates, More Rent

A landlord who agrees to an additional co-tenant will probably ask for a rent increase, on the theory that more residents means more wear and tear. By signing a new lease or rental agreement, you are in effect starting a new tenancy, so the landlord can increase rent immediately, rather than give you the usual 30 days' notice (for a month-to-month rental agreement) or wait until the lease ends.

Unless your rental unit is covered by rent control —or if the landlord is using a big rent increase as a not-so-subtle way to discriminate against you for an illegal reason (see Chapter 5)—your landlord can ask for as much extra money as the market will bear.

Negotiate the rent increase. Just because your landlord asks for a big rent increase doesn't mean you have to say yes. One good approach is to counter-offer a lower amount. Let the landlord know that you may rethink adding a roommate, or even move out yourself, if you can't reach an acceptable compromise.

4. Security Deposit Increases

The landlord also has the legal right to change other conditions of your tenancy when you add a roommate and sign a new agreement. One change that is particularly likely is an increase in the security deposit. However, this is one area where the sky is not the limit, because many states limit the amount of security deposits. Usually the limit is a multiple of the monthly rent. (See "State Laws on Security Deposit Limits," in Chapter 4.) Keep in mind that if the deposit is already at the maximum, but the landlord raises the rent for the new occupant, the maximum security deposit goes up, too.

C. Taking In a Roomer

What if you're reluctant to completely share your home with a roommate, but want someone to share costs of your rental? The answer may be to take in a roomer as a "subtenant," making it clear that this person is not a full-fledged co-tenant.

When you take in a subtenant, you're that person's landlord. We suggest that you sign a month-to-month rental agreement, specifying rent and any restrictions on the roomer's use of your home. And although your roomer doesn't sign the rental document you have with *your* landlord, he must comply with its rules as well as yours. Think of the arrangement as a set of nesting dolls: you live within your landlord's rules and regulations and your subtenant lives within yours. So if your landlord prohibits using the pool after 10 p.m., you can't promise your roomer the joy of midnight swims.

The main advantage of making your roomer a subtenant instead of a cotenant is that it gives you the legal right to terminate the roomer's tenancy if things don't work out as planned. By contrast, you can't end the tenancy of a roommate who is a full-fledged co-tenant—only the landlord can do this.

Don't get too enthusiastic about bringing someone in as a roomer without talking with your landlord. You'll need your landlord's approval to create a subtenancy—and many landlords would rather not. Even if your landlord gives approval, you may have problems getting a roomer out. You'll probably have to follow the same procedures all landlords use to terminate a tenancy.

For more on the pros and cons of subtenancies, see the discussion of subletting in Chapter 15.

The New York Roommates Law is special. Tenants in New York enjoy the benefits of its Roommate Law (N.Y. Real Property Law § 235(f)), which gives tenants the right to bring in specified roommates, subject only to local laws on overcrowding. ∎

Major Repairs and Maintenance

I n almost every state, you are legally entitled to rental property that meets basic structural, health and safety standards and is in good repair. But suppose a landlord comes up short? Depending on the state, you may have the legal right to:

- withhold rent
- pay for repairs yourself and deduct the cost from the rent
- sue the landlord, or
- move out without notice.

This chapter describes your right to basic, important things, such as hot water, a floor that will not collapse under your feet, decent heat and a roof that doesn't leak—in other words, your right to a safe and livable home. It also provides practical advice on how to get a reluctant landlord to perform needed repairs. Less important maintenance and repair issues—such as unclogging kitchen drains or mowing the front lawn—are covered in the next chapter.

Related topics covered in this book include:
- How to be sure your lease or rental agreement has clear provisions on repair and maintenance: Chapter 2.
- How to use a Landlord-Tenant Checklist to keep track of the condition of the premises before and after you move in: Chapter 6.
- Landlord's responsibility for minor repairs such as small plumbing jobs: Chapter 9.
- How to make improvements or alterations to your rental unit without violating your lease or rental agreement or donating your property to the landlord: Chapter 10.
- Landlord's liability for injuries caused by defective housing conditions: Chapter 12.
- Landlord's liability for cleaning up environmental hazards, such as asbestos and lead: Chapter 13.
- Landlord's responsibility to provide safe, reasonably crime-free rental housing: Chapter 14.

A. Your Basic Right to Livable Premises

Most landlords are legally required to offer livable premises when they originally rent a unit and to maintain it in that condition throughout the rental term. In legal terminology, this is given the lofty-sounding name "the implied warranty of habitability." If a landlord persists in failing to fulfill the obligation to provide habitable housing, tenants in most states may legally withhold rent or take other strong measures. (See Section G, below.)

The vast majority of American tenants have the right to a decent place to live even if they've moved into a place that's clearly below habitability standards, or even if the lease states that the landlord doesn't have to provide a habitable unit. In a rare showing of unanimity, almost all courts have rejected these sleazy arguments of tenant "waivers" and landlord "disclaimers." Except for a handful of states in very limited circumstances (including Florida, Maine and Texas), neither a tenant waiver (at the beginning of the tenancy or during its life) nor disclaimer in the lease will relieve the landlord of the responsibility to provide housing that begins—and remains—fit and habitable.

The landlord's responsibility to provide habitable housing generally includes:

- keeping basic structural elements of the building, including floors, stairs, walls and roofs, safe and intact
- maintaining all common areas, such as hallways and stairways, in a safe and clean condition
- keeping electrical, plumbing, sanitary, heating, ventilating and air-conditioning systems and elevators operating safely
- supplying cold and hot water and heat in reasonable amounts at reasonable times
- providing trash receptacles and arranging for their removal, and
- exterminating infestations of rodents and other vermin.

In some states, the building codes alone define what it means for housing to be habitable, while in others, court decisions define the concept. And in still other states, both apply. It can be important for you to know which source (building codes, court decisions or both) is the basis for the implied warranty of habitability in your state. The source of the warranty can define the landlord's responsibilities and determine your options for dealing with the landlord.

Are You Covered?

Every state except Alabama, Arkansas and Colorado has adopted the implied warranty of habitability. However, many local governments within these three states have enacted housing codes that protect their urban residents in ways similar to the implied warranty. And tenants in these three states who do *not* have the benefit of local laws may enjoy some of the same protections against dilapidated premises under a legal doctrine called the "covenant of quiet enjoyment." This rather quaint phrase amounts to an implied promise by your landlord to safeguard your ability to use the rented premises.

Examples of landlords' violations of the covenant of quiet enjoyment include:

- tolerating a nuisance, such as piled-up garbage or a major rodent infestation
- failing to provide sufficient electrical outlets, so that tenants cannot use appliances, and
- failing to fix a leaky roof, which deprives a tenant the use of that room.

Unfortunately, the covenant of quiet enjoyment is not as legally powerful or far-reaching as the implied warranty of habitability—that is, landlords can get away with more in Alabama, Arkansas and Colorado. For example, unless your landlord has promised a fit dwelling, you may not be able to break the lease and move out if he doesn't make needed repairs. Hopefully, your landlord will be subject to local government ordinances that impose specific requirements that make up for your state's lackadaisical approach.

B. State Laws and Local Housing Codes

If your state or local government has enacted building and housing laws, your landlord must comply with them. This section explains what these laws typically require of a landlord; if yours runs afoul of them, see Sections F and G, below, for what to do.

1. Local Ordinances

City or county building or housing codes regulate structural aspects of buildings and usually set specific space and occupancy standards, such as the minimum size of sleeping rooms. They also establish minimum requirements for light and ventilation, sanitation and sewage disposal, heating, water supply (such as how hot the water must be), fire protection and wiring (such as the number of electrical outlets per room). In addition, housing codes typically make property owners responsible for keeping hallways, lobbies, elevators and the other parts of the premises the owner controls clean, sanitary and safe.

Most local housing codes also have a catch-all provision that prohibits something called "nuisances." A nuisance is something that is dangerous to human life, detrimental to health or morally offensive and obnoxious—for example, overcrowding a room with occupants, providing insufficient ventilation or illumination, inadequate sewage or plumbing facilities, permitting illegal activities or allowing excessive noise or commotion, making it impossible to use or enjoy one's property. Drug use and dealing on the premises is also a legal nuisance.

Your local building or housing authority, and health or fire department, may have an informational booklet that describes the exact requirements your landlord must meet. In most urban areas, these local codes are more thorough than the state's general housing law—for example, many cities require landlords to install smoke detectors and some security items, such as dead bolt locks and peepholes, in exterior doors. However, local laws usually don't explain what you can do—withhold rent, for example—if your landlord fails to comply. To find out, you'll need to consult your state's general housing law.

Exemptions for Older Buildings

When a new housing code is adopted, or an old one changed, it doesn't necessarily mean that all existing buildings are illegal because they are not "up to code." Especially when it comes to items that would involve major structural changes, lawmakers will often exempt older buildings by writing a "grandfather clause" into the code, exempting all buildings constructed before a certain date. Typically, however, a landlord who later undertakes major renovations or remodeling must comply with the new rules. If you suspect that major work is being planned or done without bringing the building up to code, contact your local housing department. If you fear landlord retaliation, do so anonymously, if possible. (Tenants' protections against retaliatory conduct are discussed in Chapter 15.)

Other new code requirements that are easy and inexpensive to make—for example, installing locks, peepholes or smoke detectors—must be made regardless of the age of the building.

---

2. State Housing Laws

Legislatures in most states have enacted general laws requiring landlords to keep rental units in habitable condition. If you live in an urban area covered by a detailed building or housing code, the vaguer state regulations are likely to be of little importance to you. However, if you live in a small town or rural area not covered by a detailed building code, you'll want to refer to your state housing law. Some states have detailed laws—for example, requiring certain kinds of locks.

To find out whether your state has statutes that pertain to the maintenance of your rental, follow these steps:

- Refer to "Landlord-Tenant Statutes" in Appendix I. You'll need to look through these statutes in a law library or online, if your state has posted its statutes. (See Chapter 20 for a lesson on how to access your state and local statutes online, and for advice on using the law library.)
- Check out the laws that apply to you in more detail by looking in the index to your state's statutes for subentries under "Landlord-Tenant" such as "Landlord Obligations to Maintain Premises," "Repairs" and "Duty to Maintain."
- Contact your state consumer protection agency to see if it publishes pamphlets or brochures that describe landlords' repair and maintenance responsibilities in less legalistic terms. (The list in Appendix I tells you where to get informational booklets for tenants.)

What's "Common Law?"

This book often refers to "the common law." This term refers to the law that has been created and modified by courts over almost 1,000 years of English and U.S. history. Since it's made by judges, common law is different from statutory law, which is written by legislators and set out in code books.

In the landlord-tenant field, judges, not legislators, make at least a good portion of the rules. This means that researching the law often involves finding and understanding key court cases as well as statutes. (See Chapter 20 for a discussion of legal research sources.) Some legal concepts (for example, the implied warranty of habitability) are a mixture of both judge-made common law and statutory law.

C. Court-Imposed Rules

In many states, including California, New York, Iowa and Vermont, your right to habitable housing doesn't depend only on a state or local housing code. In these states, housing must be up to code *and* "fit for human occupation," or "fit and habitable." While a serious housing code violation will almost always qualify as a breach of the warranty of habitability, other shortfalls will constitute a violation of the warranty, too. This means that if your locality has nonexistent or poorly-written housing codes, a judge could still find that your landlord breached the warranty because, in the judge's opinion, the premises are not fit for human habitation. And even if there are local housing or building codes, a court may require more of a landlord than do the codes.

EXAMPLE: The city building code where Russell owned a few small apartment buildings required residential rental properties to have a kitchen sink, but said nothing about a separate kitchen. Russell rented dilapidated units to low-income families and assumed that he would not have to provide a separate room or additional kitchen facilities, except for the sink. One of his tenants refused to pay the rent, and Russell tried to evict her. He was dismayed to learn that the law in his state, developed in court cases over the years, also required that, to be habitable, a unit must contain a separate and sanitary cooking area.

In evaluating whether or not a landlord is providing habitable housing, courts may also consider the weather, the terrain and where the rental property is located. Features or services that might be considered nonessential extras in some parts of the country are legally viewed as absolutely necessary components of habitable housing in others. For example, in climates with severe winters, storm windows may be considered basic equipment. In wet, rainy areas, special waterproofing measures may be needed.

Finally, keep in mind that the meaning of the term "habitable housing" is not static, and court decisions are made in light of changes in living conditions and technology. For example, these days courts consider the prevalence of crime in urban areas when determining what constitutes habitable housing. Good locks, security personnel, exterior lighting and secure common areas are now seen, in some cities, to be as important to tenants as are water and heat. (Chapter 14 discusses your rights to adequate security measures.)

D. Your Repair and Maintenance Responsibilities

You now know that you can expect your landlord to provide safe and habitable housing and adhere to basic norms of cleanliness and behavior under a variety of overlapping legal rules. But your landlord isn't the only one with legal responsibilities. State and local housing laws generally require you to:

Keep your rental unit as clean and safe as the condition of the premises permits. For example, if your kitchen has a rough, unfinished wooden floor that is hard to keep clean, you should not be expected to keep it shiny and spotless—but a tenant with a new tile floor would be expected to do a decent job. If you don't, and your landlord has to do a major clean-up when you move out, expect a hefty deduction from your security deposit.

Dispose of garbage, rubbish and other waste in a clean and safe manner. For instance, if mice or ants invaded your kitchen because you forgot to take out the garbage before you left on a two-week vacation, you would be responsible for paying any necessary extermination costs.

Keep plumbing fixtures as clean as their condition permits. For example, bathtub caulking that has sprouted mold and mildew may render the tub unusable (or at least disgusting), but since it could have been prevented by proper cleaning, you are responsible. On the other hand, if the bathroom has no fan and the window has been painted shut, the bathroom will be hard to air out; resulting mildew might be your landlord's responsibility.

Use electrical, plumbing, sanitary, heating, ventilating, air-conditioning and other facilities and other systems, including elevators, properly. Examples of abuse by tenants include overloading electrical outlets and flushing large objects down the toilet.

Fix things you break or damage. If you cause a serious habitability problem in your unit—for example, you carelessly break the heater—you are responsible. A landlord who finds out about the problem can insist that you pay for the repair. Legally, you can't just decide to live without heat for a while to save money. If you drag your feet, the landlord can use your security deposit to pay for it, and if that isn't enough, sue you besides. Your landlord can't, however, charge you for problems caused by normal wear and tear—for example, a carpet that has worn out from use. (Chapter 16 discusses the difference between normal wear and tear and damage.)

Damage Caused by Criminals

If a burglar breaks into your home, smashing the cupboards and generally making a mess, who pays? Usually, the landlord, as long as your carelessness (failing to lock a window, for example) didn't facilitate the intruder's entry. If you *were* careless, are you 100% liable for the damage? If your landlord sues you and a jury is asked to apportion the blame between you and the burglar, it's anyone's guess what figure they'll come up with.

Carelessness is not the only way you might be liable for a criminal's acts. For example, if you and your landlord agree that you will maintain the doors and windows in your single-family rental and you fail to do so, you may be held partially liable for the burglar's damage. (If you live in Louisiana, you are required by law to maintain the locks. La. Civ. Code art. 2716.) And if the criminal happens to be someone whom you have let into the building, knowing that a criminal incident was likely, a jury will almost surely hold you responsible.

E. Making Tenants Responsible for Repairs

Your landlord may legally delegate some repair and maintenance responsibilities to you, typically in exchange for less rent. He cannot, however, force you to give up your rights to habitable housing.

Landlords rarely try to get tenants to take responsibility for major repair and maintenance duties (such as roof repairs and other structural work) in apartment rentals, since tenants do not have the time, skill or interest to devote to extensive construction. (Taking on responsibility for minor repairs and maintenance is discussed in Chapter 9.) In addition, many states have specific rules regarding the types of repairs that can be delegated and only allow licensed contractors to do the work.

The picture is often different, however, when you rent a single-family residence. In several states, the landlord and tenant may agree in writing that the tenant is to perform some of the landlord's legal duties—for example, to arrange for garbage disposal, running water, hot water and heat or other specified repairs. (In other states, agreements like this are void.) States allowing this arrangement typically require that each side completely understands their rights and responsibilities and that neither pressures the other (otherwise, a court won't enforce the agreement).

Agreeing to Do Repairs and Maintenance in Single-Family Rentals

In these states, landlords and tenants can agree in writing that the tenant will be responsible for some of the landlord's legal duties:

Alaska	Florida	Nebraska
Arizona	Kansas	New Mexico
Hawaii	Kentucky	South Carolina
Iowa	Montana	

F. How to Get Action From Your Landlord

Knowing that you have a legal right to habitable housing and getting it are, obviously, horses of very different colors. A lot depends on the attitude of your landlord. Here are some tips to maximize your chances of getting quick results.

1. Put Repair Requests in Writing

By far the best approach is to put every repair and maintenance request in writing, keeping a copy for your files. You may want to call first, but be sure to follow up with a written request.

Written communications to your landlord are important because they:

- are far more likely to be taken seriously than face-to-face conversations or phone calls, because it's clear to the landlord you're keeping a record of your requests
- are less likely to be forgotten or misunderstood
- satisfy the legal requirement that you give your landlord a reasonable opportunity to fix a problem before you withhold rent or exercise other legal rights (see Section G), and
- serve as potential evidence in case you ever need to prove that the serious problems with your unit were the subject of repeated repair requests.

In your request, be as specific as possible regarding the problem, its effect on you, what you want done and when. For example, if the thermostat on your heater is always finicky and often doesn't function at all, explain that you have been without heat during the last two days during which the nighttime low was below freezing—don't simply say "the heater needs to be fixed." If the problem poses a health or safety threat, such as a broken front door lock or loose step, say so and ask for it to be fixed immediately. Competent landlords will respond extra quickly to genuinely dangerous, as opposed to merely inconvenient, situations. Finally, be sure to note the date of the request and how many requests, if any, have preceded this one. For more tips on writing a persuasive repair request, see Chapter 9.

If your landlord provides a repair request form, use it. If not, do your own, (See the sample shown below.). Always make a copy of your request, and keep it in a safe place in your files.

In dangerous situations, you must take precautions, too. Once you're aware of a dangerous situation, you must take reasonable steps to avoid injury. Don't continue to use the outlet when you see sparks fly from the wall; don't park in the garage at night if the lights are burned out and there is a safer alternative. If you don't take reasonable care and are injured and sue the landlord, you can expect a judge or jury to hold the landlord only partially responsible. (See Chapter 12.)

Sample Request for Repair or Maintenance

TO: Kay Sera, Landlord, Stately View Apartments

FROM: Will Tripp, 376 Seventh Avenue, Apartment No. 45, Brighton, New Jersey

RE: Roof leak

DATE: March 10, 200X

As I mentioned to you on the phone yesterday, on March 9, 200X, I noticed dark stains on the ceilings of the upstairs bedroom and bath. These stains are moist and appear to be the result of the recent heavy rains. I would very much appreciate it if you would promptly look into the apparent roof leak. If the leak continues, my property may be damaged and two rooms may become unusable. Please call me so that I'll know when to expect you or a repair person. You can reach me at work during the day (555-1234) or at home at night (555-4546).

Thank you very much for your attention to this problem. I expect to hear from you within the next few days, and expect that the situation will be corrected within a couple of weeks.

Yours truly,

Will Tripp

Will Tripp

2. Deliver Your Repair Request to the Landlord

If your landlord has an on-site office or a resident manager, deliver your repair request personally. If you mail it, consider sending it certified (return receipt requested) or use a delivery service (such as Federal Express) that will give you a receipt establishing delivery. If you fax your request, ask for a call (or a return fax) acknowledging receipt. Although taking steps to verify delivery will cost a little more, it has two major advantages over regular mail:

- It will get the landlord's attention and highlight the fact that you are serious about your request.
- The signed receipt is evidence that the landlord did, in fact, receive the letter. You may need this in the event that the landlord fails to make the repair and you decide to do it yourself or withhold rent. If a dispute arises as to your right to use a self-help measure, you'll be able to prove in court that you satisfied the legal requirement of notifying the landlord first.

If your first request doesn't produce results—or at least a call or note from the landlord telling you when repairs will be made—send another. Mention that this is the second (or third) time you have brought the matter to the landlord's attention. If the problem is getting worse, emphasize this fact. And of course, be sure to keep a record of all repair requests.

3. Keep Notes on All Conversations

Besides keeping a copy of every written repair request, don't neglect to keep a record of oral communications, too. If the landlord calls you in response to your repair request, make notes during the conversation or immediately afterward; write down the date and time that the conversation occurred and when you made your notes. These notes may come in handy to refresh your memory and help you reconstruct the history of your case. In most states, if a dispute ends up in court, and you are unable to remember the details of the conversation, your notes can be introduced in court to fill the gap.

You can keep track of other kinds of communications, too. For example, if your dealings with your landlord are accomplished online, simply print out each message.

⚠ **Think twice before taping telephone conversations.** Many tenants are tempted to tape phone conversations with their landlords or managers, figuring that this is one sure-fire way to preserve evidence of a promise to repair. Under federal law (18 U. S. Code § 2511), phone conversations can be taped with the consent of one party (you), but some state laws are more strict. Laws in 12 states— California, Connecticut, Delaware, Florida, Illinois, Maryland, Massachusetts, Michigan, Montana, New Hampshire, Pennsylvania and Washington—require the consent of all parties before a conversation can be recorded. Penalties include fines and, in some instances, jail time. While it is unlikely that a one-time offender will be prosecuted, it is likely that this illegal conduct will weaken your case should you wind up in court defending your use of a tenant repair option. And it is possible that a landlord will turn around and sue *you* for your conduct.

4. Put the Landlord's Promises in Writing

If you and your landlord agree on a plan of action, it's especially wise to write down your understanding of this agreement. Send a copy to the landlord, inviting him to reply if he thinks that you have missed or misstated anything. (This is called a letter of understanding, which we explain in Chapter 2.) If he doesn't write back, the law presumes that he agreed with your version of the conversation. See the sample Letter of Understanding Regarding Repairs, below.

Sample Letter of Understanding Regarding Repairs

1234 Appian Way, #3
Bloom City, Indiana 00000

September 3, 200X

Ms. Iona Lott, Landlord
100 Civic Center Drive
Bloom City, Indiana 00000

Dear Ms. Lott,

Thank you for calling me yesterday, September 2, 200X, regarding my request for repairs, dated August 27, 200X. In that request, I told you that the hot water in my unit is very hot (123 degrees F. on my thermometer), even though the temperature gauge on the water heater is turned down as far as it can go. I am concerned that my young daughter may be injured by this scalding water, and am anxious that the temperature be lowered as soon as possible.

As I understand it, you agreed to have Ralph, your handyman, come check the problem on Saturday morning, September 6, between 9 and 10 a.m. Ralph will bring along a new thermostat should he need to replace the old one.

Please let me know if your recollection of our conversation and plans differs from mine.

Yours truly,

Howard Hillman

Howard Hillman

G. What to Do If the Landlord Won't Make Repairs

If your persistent and businesslike requests for repairs are ignored, you can take stronger measures. Your options will probably include one or more of what we call the "big sticks" in a tenant's self-help arsenal. These include:

- calling state or local building or health inspectors
- withholding the rent
- repairing the problem (or having it repaired by a professional) and deducting the cost from your rent
- moving out, or
- paying the rent and then suing the landlord for the difference between the rent you paid and the value of the defective premises.

If the landlord hasn't fixed a serious problem that truly makes your rental unit uninhabitable—rats in the kitchen, for example—you will want to take fast action. But not every case is so clear-cut. Before you withhold rent, move out or adopt another extreme remedy, make sure every one of these conditions is met:

- **The problem is serious, not just annoying, and imperils your health or safety.** Not every building code violation or annoying defect in your rental home (like your water heater's ability to reach only 107 degrees F, short of the code-specified 110 degrees) justifies use of a "big stick" against the landlord.
- **You (or a guest) did not cause the problem, either deliberately or through carelessness or neglect.** If so, you can't pursue the self-help options.
- **You told the landlord about the problem and gave him a reasonable opportunity to get it fixed, or the minimum amount of notice required by state law.** You can't use big stick options without first notifying the landlord and giving him a chance to fix the problem. You'll need to check your state's law for the exact requirements for the specific option you are pursuing.

- **You are willing to risk termination of your tenancy by an annoyed landlord.** Exercising any of the rights discussed here will not endear you to your landlord. Many states forbid your landlord from retaliating against you by raising the rent or terminating your tenancy but, unfortunately, some states don't. If your lease is about to run out (or you're a month-to-month tenant) and your state does not protect you from retaliatory rent increases or evictions, a complaint to health inspectors or use of a self-help big stick could end up causing you to lose your rental. (Chapter 15 discusses retaliation and gives information on state laws.)
- **You are willing to risk eviction if a judge decides that you shouldn't have used the big stick, and your credit rating can bear this negative mark.** Even if you're sure that you were justified in using a big stick, a judge may decide otherwise. For example, if you withhold rent, the landlord may sue to evict you based on nonpayment of rent. In most states and in most situations, you'll have a second chance to pay the balance before being sued for eviction, but not always. (See Chapter 17.) For some tenants, additional negative marks on their credit records will cause extremely serious problems for future rentals, loans and employment.
- **If you move out, either voluntarily or because the building is closed due to code violations you have reported, you can find a comparable or better unit.** In some states, landlords whose buildings are closed due to code violations must help their tenants with relocation expenses.

Before doing repairs yourself, withholding rent or using another "big stick," make sure you have proof of how bad the problem was. One good approach is to take pictures of the problem; another is to have witnesses. Also consider asking an experienced and impartial contractor or repair person to examine the situation and give you a written description of the problem and estimate for repair. Be sure the description is signed and dated.

1. Reporting Code Violations to Housing Inspectors

There are several ways a local building, health or fire department inspector may discover code violations, such as hazardous electrical wiring or a leaking roof. A tenant complaint may trigger an inspection, as may a change in property ownership or financing—for example, if the owner takes out a new loan. Code violations may also be discovered through routine inspections (discussed in Chapter 11).

After discovering a code violation, the housing inspector will give the owner an order to correct the problem. Fines and penalties usually follow if the owner fails to comply within a certain amount of time (often five to 30 business days). If there's still no response, the city or county may sue the landlord. In many cities, a landlord's failure to promptly fix cited violations of local housing laws is a misdemeanor (minor crime) punishable by hefty fines or even imprisonment. In rare cases, especially if tenants' health is imperiled, local officials may even require that the building be vacated.

In many areas, reporting a landlord to a building inspector is a very big deal—an inspector who finds lots of problems can force the landlord to clear them up immediately. But there is wild variation as to the effectiveness of building inspectors. In New Orleans, for example, there are woefully few inspectors compared to the number of tenant complaints, and courts are largely unable to follow up on the properties that are cited. It's just one of many cities where landlords have learned how to postpone, avoid and frustrate the process.

If You Must Move Because of Building Code Violations

If a judge decides that a building's condition substantially endangers the health and safety of its tenants, and repairs are so extensive they can't be made while tenants inhabit the building, the result may be an order to move. You usually won't have a chance to come to the court hearing to object to this dire consequence—you'll simply be told to get out, sometimes within hours.

In some states, the landlord must pay your rent in comparable temporary housing nearby. Some statutes also make the landlord cover moving expenses and utility connection charges and give you the first chance to move back in when the repairs are completed. In other states, however, you may be out of luck, which explains why tenants are often reluctant to call the inspectors.

If you're tempted to call the inspectors for major habitability problems, it might be wise to find out whether you can get relocation assistance if the building is closed. There's nothing to prevent you from calling the housing department for your city or state and simply asking, without registering a complaint. Or, you can check your state statutes (listed in "Landlord-Tenant Statutes" in Appendix I). If you go to the law library, try a more direct approach. Look in the index to your state's codes, under "Landlord-Tenant," for subheadings such as "Relocation Assistance" or "Padlock Orders." (See Chapter 20 for general advice on using the law library.)

2. Withholding the Rent

If you conclude that your landlord has not met the responsibility of keeping your unit livable, you may be able to stop paying any rent to the landlord until the repairs are made. This is called rent withholding. Many states have established rent withholding, either by statute or court decision. (See "Options in Your State," below.) Rent withholding can be done

Options in Your State

In every state, you can call the housing or building inspector and sue your landlord in small claims court if your rental unit is defective. In every state but Alabama, Arkansas and Colorado, you may have the option of moving out. This table lists states which give tenants additional options.

State	Withhold the rent	Repair and deduct	State	Withhold the rent	Repair and deduct
Alabama			New Jersey	✔	
Alaska	✔	✔	New Mexico	✔	✔
Arizona	✔	✔	New York	✔	✔
Arkansas			North Carolina		
California	✔	✔	North Dakota		
Colorado			Ohio	✔	
Connecticut	✔	✔	Oklahoma		✔
Delaware		✔	Oregon	✔	✔
District of Columbia			Pennsylvania	✔	
Florida	✔		Rhode Island	✔	✔
Georgia	✔		South Carolina	✔	✔
Hawaii	✔	✔	South Dakota	✔	✔
Idaho			Tennessee		✔
Illinois	✔		Texas		✔
Indiana			Utah		
Iowa	✔	✔	Vermont	✔	✔
Kansas	✔		Virginia	✔	
Kentucky	✔	✔	Washington	✔	✔
Louisiana		✔	West Virginia		
Maine	✔	✔	Wisconsin	✔*	
Maryland	✔		Wyoming		
Massachusetts	✔	✔			
Michigan	✔	✔			
Minnesota	✔	✔			
Mississippi		✔			
Missouri	✔				
Montana	✔	✔			
Nebraska	✔	✔			
Nevada	✔	✔			
New Hampshire	✔				

* Wisconsin tenants may withhold rent only for lead and asbestos problems.

Citations to the state statutes are listed in "State Laws on Rent Withholding and Repair and Deduct Remedies" in Appendix I.

Important: This table reflects statutes passed by the state legislatures and some court decisions. But your local government courts may authorized methods similar to these.

only in these states; if yours isn't one of them, you'll have to use another approach.

The term "withholding" is actually a bit misleading, since in some states and cities you can't simply keep the rent money until your landlord fixes the problem. Instead, you often have to deposit the withheld rent with court or a neutral third party or escrow account set up by a local court or housing agency until the repairs are accomplished. (And even if your statute doesn't require it, it's a good idea to escrow the rent yourself, as explained below.)

Before you can properly withhold the rent, three requirements must be met:

- The lack of maintenance or repair has made your dwelling unlivable (Section A, above, discusses habitability requirements).
- The problems were not caused by you or your guest, either deliberately or through neglect.

and

- You told the landlord about the problem and gave him a reasonable time to fix it or the minimum amount required by state law.

In addition, under most rent withholding laws, you cannot withhold rent if you are behind in the rent or in violation of an important lease clause. In short, you need to be squeaky clean.

Illegal Lease Clauses: Your Landlord Can't Limit Your Right to Withhold the Rent Under State Law

Some landlords insert clauses in their leases and rental agreements purporting to prohibit a tenant from withholding the rent, even if a property is uninhabitable. In many states, the rent withholding law itself makes this practice flatly illegal. But even where a state statute or court decision does not specifically disallow this side-step, these clauses may be tossed out if a tenant nevertheless withholds rent and is served with an eviction notice for nonpayment of rent. Why? Because a judge will approve your supposed waiver of your right to withhold rent only if your "waiver" has been the subject of real negotiations between you and the landlord, and not something the landlord insisted upon unilaterally. And since most leases are pre-printed forms that tenants are given in a take-it-or-leave-it situation, a judge is likely to decide that the so-called "waiver" was in fact imposed by the landlord and, consequently, invalid.

a. The Consequences of Withholding Rent

Your landlord will not be pleased when your rent check fails to arrive. His response will typically be to terminate your tenancy for nonpayment of rent and file for eviction if you don't move voluntarily. This may seem particularly unfair if you are meeting all your state requirements for withholding rent.

If you have met the requirements explained above and have carefully followed the procedures set out in your rent withholding statute, you'll have a good defense to the landlord's eviction lawsuit. You may feel confident enough to head into court without a lawyer or you may want to consult with an attorney first. If you have improperly used the remedy (for a minor repair, for example), you'll be evicted. Because of the possibility of this dire consequence, it's crucial to understand your rent withholding law and use it appropriately.

b. How to Withhold Rent

Here are the steps to follow when considering whether to withhold rent:

Step 1: Research the law.

If rent withholding is allowed in your state, the statute (law) will be listed in Appendix I. Also, check if any local laws apply. In a few localities subject to rent control, the procedure may be part of your local ordinance. In either case, read the law to find out:

- what circumstances justify rent withholding
- whether you must give the landlord a certain amount of notice (10 to 30 days are typical) and time to fix the defect, or whether the notice and response time simply be "reasonable" under the circumstances, and
- whether you must place the unpaid rent in a separate bank account or deposit it with a court or local housing agency and how this is done.

We explain how to find and look up your state's law in the library and online in Chapter 20.

Step 2: Notify your landlord.

Give your landlord written notice of the problem and your intent to withhold rent. A sample letter is shown below. Refer to your state's law or statute that allows withholding and include a copy of it. We recommend that you include in your letter a proposal that if for any reason your landlord disagrees that repairs are needed, you quickly mediate the dispute. (Chapter 19 discusses mediation services.) Send the letter "return receipt."

Sample Letter Telling the Landlord You Intend to Withhold Rent

58 Coral Shores, #37
Sandy Bay, FL 12345
407-555-5632

August 5, 200X

Mr. Roy Hernandez
3200 Harbor Drive
Sandy Bay, FL 12345

Dear Mr. Hernandez:

My family and I are your tenants at the above address. As you know, I called you on August 3 to report that the front porch has collapsed from dry rot at the top of the stairs, making it impossible to enter the flat except by the back door. You assured me that you would send a contractor the next day. No one came on August 4.

Under Florida Statutes § 83.51(b), you are responsible for keeping the porch in good repair. Florida law gives tenants the right to withhold rent if you fail to do so and the condition is serious (Florida Statutes § 83.201). Tenants may begin withholding if the landlord, after receiving 20 days' notice, fails to fix the problem.

By hand-delivering this notice to you today, August 5, I am giving you the notice as required by law. If the porch is not repaired by August 25, I will withhold rent until it is.

Yours truly,

Alicia Sanchez

Alicia Sanchez

Enclosure: Florida Statutes §§ 83.51 & 83.201

Step 3: Collect evidence.

In case your landlord tries to evict you for nonpayment of rent, you will want to prepare your defense from day one. You'll need to prove that the problem truly is serious and that you complied with the notice requirements of the rent withholding law. Of course, you'll want to keep copies of all correspondence with the landlord, plus photographs of the problem. Be sure to consider other ways (besides your own testimony) you can convince the judge that the problem was real and serious. For example, if your heater delivers a frigid blast, you'll want an estimate from a heating repairperson that corroborates the fact that the heater doesn't work. And because evictions are usually handled in a municipal court, which has stricter rules of evidence than small claims court, you cannot simply present a repair person's written description of the problem. The repair person would have to appear in court and testify about the condition of the repair job. Introducing evidence is covered in detail in "Rules of Evidence in Formal Court," Chapter 18.

Step 4: Repeat your request for repairs.

If the landlord hasn't responded satisfactorily to your first letter, give the landlord one last deadline—say, 48 hours or whatever period you feel is reasonable under the circumstances.

Step 5: File any court papers.

Under some state laws, you must ask a local court for permission to withhold rent, providing compelling reasons why your rental is not livable, and follow specific procedures. This filing process usually isn't difficult and doesn't require the use of a lawyer. You can get the necessary information and forms from the court or housing department that is named in your rent withholding statute.

Step 6: Deposit your rent in escrow.

In some states, you may have to deposit your rent with the specified local court or housing agency or in a separate bank account. Some states do not require a separate escrow account.

Even if your statute does not require this, we recommend that you deposit the withheld rent into an escrow account held by a neutral third party. This will dispel any suggestion that you are withholding rent simply in order to avoid paying it.

If a court or housing department is not set up to handle withheld rent, try asking a mediation service if it will establish an account for this purpose. Or, if you have an attorney, ask her to deposit the withheld rent in her "trust account." You can also set up a separate bank account of your own and use it only for withheld rent. If you must pay for any of these services, you can ask the court to order the landlord to reimburse you if the landlord brings an eviction action.

c. What Happens to the Withheld Rent

If the rent money is being held by a court or housing authority, landlords can sometimes ask for release of some of the withheld rent to pay for repairs. While repairs are being made, you may continue to pay the entire rent to the court or housing authority, or you may be directed to pay some rent to the landlord and the balance to the court or housing authority. When the dwelling is certified as fit by the local housing authorities or the court, any money in the account is returned to the landlord, minus court costs and inspection fees.

If your withholding law does not require you to escrow the rent and a court has not been involved, you and the landlord are free to make your own arrangements as to the distribution of the money. Once your landlord has made the repairs, he will probably expect full payment of the withheld rent. If you don't pay up, you can expect your landlord to file an eviction lawsuit for nonpayment of rent.

Depending on your state's law, whether or not a court is involved, the severity of the repair problem and your landlord's willingness to negotiate, you may seek compensation for the time you have spent living in a substandard home. You may want a retroactive reduction in rent, starting from the time that the premises became uninhabitable. (Some states will limit you to a reduction starting from the time you notified the landlord of the problem.). Reducing the rent is known in legalese as rent "abatement."

You may get a retroactive rent abatement through a court process or through negotiation with your landlord. The following section describes how a judge will determine how much the landlord should compensate you for the inconvenience of having lived in a substandard rental unit. If a court is not involved, you can use this same system in negotiating with your landlord.

d. Determining the Value of a Defective Rental Unit

How does a judge determine the difference between the withheld rent and what a defective, unlivable unit was really worth? There are two widely-used ways:

Figuring the market value. In some states, statutes or court cases say that if the landlord leaves your unit in a defective condition, all you owe the landlord is the fair market value of the premises in that condition. For example, if an apartment with a broken heater normally rented for $1,200 per month, but was worth only $600 without operable heating, the landlord would be entitled to only $600/month from the escrowed funds. Of course, the difficulty with this approach—as with many things in law—is that it is staggeringly unrealistic. An apartment with no heat in winter has *no* market value, because no one would rent it. As you can see, how much a unit is worth in a defective condition is extremely hard to determine.

By percentage reduction. Another slightly more sensible approach is to start by asking what part of the unit is affected by the defect, and then to calculate the percentage of the rent attributable to that part. For example, if the roof leaked into the living room of your $900/month apartment, rendering the room unusable, you could reduce the rent by the percentage of the rent attributable to the living room. If the living room were the main living space and the other rooms were too small to live in comfortably, the percentage of loss would be much greater than it would be in more spacious apartments. Obviously, this approach is far from an exact science, too.

We recommend you use both methods to calculate the unit's reduced, real value. Sometimes, the calculations will be simple—for example, using the fair market value approach, if a broken air conditioner reduces your flat to an oven, its rental value can be determined by consulting ads for non-air conditioned flats in your area. The percentage reduction method might, in some situations, yield a lower rental value. After you've used both methods, ask the judge to adopt the lower figure and to rule that the landlord is entitled only to that amount of rent per month, times the number of months that you endured the substandard conditions. The difference between the full rent and the realistic rent should go to you.

EXAMPLE: When Henry and Sue moved into their apartment, it was a neat and well-maintained. Soon after, the building was sold to an out-of-state owner, who hired an off-site manager to handle repairs and maintenance. Gradually, the premises began to deteriorate. At the beginning of May, 15 months into their two-year lease, Henry and Sue could count several violations of the building code, including the landlord's failure to maintain the common areas, remove the garbage promptly and fix a broken water heater.

Henry and Sue sent numerous requests for repairs to their landlord over a two-month period, during which they gritted their teeth and put up with the situation. Finally they had enough and checked out their state's rent withholding law. They learned a tenant could pay rent into an escrow account set up by their local court. Henry and Sue went ahead and deposited their rent into this account.

In response, Henry and Sue's landlord filed an eviction lawsuit. In their defense, Henry and Sue pointed to the numerous code and habitability violations. The court agreed with the couple, did not allow the eviction and ordered the following:

- During the time that they lived in these uninhabitable conditions, Henry and Sue were not required to pay full rent. Using the "market value" approach, the court decided that their defective rental was worth half its stated rent. Accordingly, since the landlord owed them a refund for portions of their rent for May and June, Henry and Sue would be paid this amount from the escrow account.

- The balance of the rent in the account would be released to the landlord (less the costs of the escrow and the tenants' attorney fees), but only when the building inspector certified to the court that the building was up to code and fit for human habitation.

- Henry and Sue could continue to pay 50% of the rent until needed repairs were made and certified by the building inspector.

Reducing the Rent on Your Own

If your state doesn't have a rent withholding statute, you may be tempted to reduce the rent on your own. For example, if the water heater is broken and the landlord won't fix it despite your repeated requests, you may feel like paying a few hundred dollars less per month, figuring that your cold-water flat is only worth that much.

It's very risky to give your landlord a short rent check. You can expect a speedily delivered termination notice, followed by an eviction lawsuit, for nonpayment of rent. Your theory—that the landlord was entitled to less rent because the premises weren't livable—is not likely to be well-received in a state that hasn't taken the issue seriously enough to establish orderly procedures (rent withholding) to insure that landlords live up to their duty to provide habitable housing. If you lose, you'll lose your rented home.

If your state does not give you the option of rent withholding, use one of the other remedies mentioned here, including repair and deduct (if available), moving out or filing a law suit in small claims court asking for a retroactive rent reduction for substandard conditions.

---

3. Making Repairs and Deducting the Cost—"Repair and Deduct"

You may, depending on where you live, also be eligible to use another powerful legal remedy, usually called "repair and deduct." Twenty-eight states and some large cities allow it. (See "Options in Your State," above.) If your state doesn't allow repair and deduct, check your local housing ordinances to determine whether your city has independently adopted it. If your state or city does not have a repair and deduct statute, this procedure is not available to you.

It works like this: If you have tried and failed to get the landlord to fix a serious defect, you can hire a repair person to fix it and subtract the cost from the following month's rent. In most states, the amount you can spend and deduct is limited to a specific figure or a percentage of the month's rent. Most states also limit the frequency with which you can use the procedure and require that you notify the landlord in writing and give him a specified or reasonable amount of time to repair the problem. Be sure to read your state statute for details on the repair and deduct option,

State laws vary greatly as to the amount of rent you can withhold and the frequency you can use for repairs. For example, in Massachusetts, you can spend up to four months' rent (for health code violations certified by an inspector only). (Mass. Gen. Laws ch. 111, § 127L.) In California, you can spend only one month's rent, and only use this option twice a year. (Cal. Civil Code §§ 1941 to 1942.5.) And in Louisiana, there is practically no guidance at all: You are simply allowed to repair and deduct for "indispensable" repairs that are the landlord's responsibility. (La. Civil Code art. 2694.)

These restrictions make the repair and deduct remedy a poor choice for tenants when it comes to big-ticket projects such as a major roof repair. Obviously, if you're limited to a twice-a-year expenditure of half your monthly rent, you are not going to be able to pay for a $20,000 roof retrofit. Sometimes, however, a number of tenants might pool their dollar limits to accomplish a costly repair. (Tenants working together is covered in Chapter 19.)

Most repair and deduct statutes require you to spend only a reasonable amount of money on repairs. In Washington, for example, you have to go with the lowest bid. If your landlord challenges the amount you spent on the repair, you'll need to be able to prove that the cost was the going rate for the job. Get bids from several reputable contractors or licensed repair persons, and choose wisely—in most states, not necessarily the lowest bid, but the best value for a decent job.

Sample Letter Telling the Landlord You Intend to Repair and Deduct

8976 Maple Avenue
Carson, WA 12345
360-555-6543

January 14, 200X

Hattie Connifer
200 Capitol Expressway, Suite 300
Carson, WA 12345

Dear Ms. Connifer:

On January 10, I called your office and spoke to you about a major problem: I have no hot water. As I explained on the phone, on the evening of January 9 the water heater for my flat sprang a leak. Luckily, I was home and was able to divert the water to the outside with a hose, turn off the intake valve and shut off the pilot.

At the end of our conversation on January 10, you assured me that you would send a repair person to the flat the next day, January 11. As of today, no one has showed up, and I am enduring my fourth day of no hot water.

Under Washington law, I am entitled to remedy the problem and deduct the cost from my rent if you do not attend to the problem within 24 hours (Washington Revised Code § 59.18.100). I intend to do this if the heater is not replaced within 24 hours after you receive this letter, which I am personally delivering to your office. As required by law, I have enclosed an estimate of the replacement cost: A-1 Appliance Repair has estimated the cost of a new, comparable heater at $400.

Yours truly,
Wanda Wright
Wanda Wright

Enclosure: Estimate of A1 Appliance Repair

4. Moving Out

If your dwelling isn't habitable and hasn't been made so despite your complaints and repair requests, you also have the right to move out—either temporarily or permanently. These drastic measures are justified only when there are truly serious problems, such as the lack of essential services, the total or partial destruction of the premises or the presence of environmental health hazards such as lead paint dust. (Chapter 13 explains your right to move out because of environmental toxins. This section covers the other two situations which justify moving out.)

a. The Landlord's Failure to Keep the Unit Habitable

The 47 states that recognize your right to habitable housing allow you to move out if you don't get it. Depending on the circumstances, you may move out permanently, by terminating the lease or rental agreement, or temporarily. This approach is borrowed directly from consumer protection laws. Just as the purchaser of a seriously defective car may sue to undo the contract or return the car for a refund, you can consider the housing contract terminated and simply return the rental unit to the landlord if the housing is unlivable.

The law, of course, has a convoluted phrase to describe this simple concept. It's called "constructive eviction," which means that the landlord, by supplying unlivable housing, has for all practical purposes "evicted" you. Once you have been constructively evicted (that is, you have a valid reason to move out), you have no further responsibility for rent.

Your state statute may have specific details, such as the type of notice you must provide before moving out because of a major repair problem. You may need to give your landlord anywhere from five to 21 days to fix it, depending on the state, and sometimes the seriousness of your situation. Check your state law for details.

Temporary Moves. In many states, if the landlord fails to provide heat or other essential services, you may procure reasonable substitute housing during the period of the landlord's noncompliance. You may recover the costs (as long as they're reasonable) of substitute housing up to an amount equal to your rent.

Permanent Moves. If you move out permanently because of habitability problems, you may also be entitled to money from the landlord to compensate you for out-of-pocket losses. For example, you may be able to recover for moving expenses and the cost of a hotel for a few days until you find a new place. Also, if the conditions were substandard during prior months when you did pay the full rent, you may sue to be reimbursed for the difference between the value of the defective dwelling and the rent paid. In addition, if you are unable to find comparable housing for the same rent, and end up paying more rent than you would have under the old lease, you may be able to recover the difference.

b. Damage to the Premises

If your home is severely damaged by natural disaster or any other reason beyond your control, it only makes sense that you have the legal right to consider the lease at an end and to move out.

If you must find another place to live because of damage to or destruction of the premises—no matter the cause—you must decide whether to terminate the lease or rental agreement or just suspend it while repairs are made. Depending on your situation, there are advantages to either course.

Terminating the lease or rental agreement. You'll want to terminate the lease if you can find new housing of comparable quality and cost. You won't have to live with the uncertainty of when you'll move back to the original dwelling, and it will save you the time and aggravation of an extra household move. And if your new housing comes with a lease, you may *have* to terminate the old one, since a lease won't allow you to move when you want.

If you decide to terminate the original lease or rental agreement, try to reach an agreement with the landlord as to what he owes you for your new housing—any difference between rent under the lease and what it will cost to rent a new place. Have the landlord write "Terminated" on each page of your lease or rental agreement. Both of you should sign and date each page. Your landlord should refund your security deposit according to your state's procedures. (See Chapter 16.)

Leaving temporarily without terminating the lease. If your rental is a particularly great deal, the local market is very tight or the repairs can be accomplished within a reasonable time, you'll want to hang on to your unit. If you are protected by rent control and you have lived in your rental for a significant period of time, you'll probably be loathe to move. Find a month-to-month rental while the original unit is repaired.

You and the landlord should add a page to the lease entitled "Suspension," which states that the landlord's and tenant's responsibilities have been suspended from a certain date until the day you move back in. Be sure to include the landlord's promise to notify you promptly as soon as the rental is ready. If relocation costs are being covered by the landlord, note them. Both of you should sign and date this document.

In some circumstances, and regardless of whether you decide to terminate or just suspend the original lease, you may have the legal right to financial assistance from the landlord to pay for tempo-rary substitute housing. It depends on how your rental unit was destroyed. If a natural disaster struck, the landlord is less likely to be obligated than if your home was destroyed by fire caused by the landlord botching an electrical repair job. And if your home burns down because of your own care-lessness, don't expect financial help—in fact, the landlord may be able to sue *you*.

Natural or third-party disasters. If your unit is destroyed by earthquake, tornado, flood or arson, your duty to pay rent is at an end. State laws vary on the extent of the landlord's responsibility to aid you with relocation or temporary housing costs. If you have renters' insurance, your best bet is to file a claim for help in resettlement and coverage for your lost or destroyed possessions. Let your insurance company try to recover all or a portion of what it pays you from the landlord. (Renters' insurance is covered in Chapter 2.)

If you have a month-to-month tenancy, the land-lord may be required by law to pay for your substi-tute housing for 30 days. If you have a lease, the landlord is probably obligated to pay for substitute housing for a longer period—often until you find a comparable replacement or, if you drag your feet, until a court thinks you should have been able to.

Destruction that is traceable to the landlord. If the landlord or his employees were even partially responsible for the damage, your legal right to assis-tance almost surely increases. Even if your tenancy is just month to month, the landlord is likely to be obligated by state law to pay for a reasonable period of temporary housing. If the permanent substitute housing you find is more expensive, the landlord may be obliged to pay the difference between your old rent and the new rent for one or two months. If you have a lease, the landlord's responsibility to pay the difference may extend to the end of your lease term.

If the landlord or his insurance company doesn't offer you a fair settlement, you may want to bring a lawsuit to recover the cost of temporary and substi-tute housing and the value of your lost possessions. Often, cases like these settle before trial, since your claims are likely to be covered by the landlord's in-surance policy. (Business policies generally include coverage for the landlord's negligent acts, but they exclude coverage for natural disasters.)

5. Suing the Landlord

A consumer who purchases a product—be it a car, a hair dryer or a steak dinner—is justified in expect-ing a minimum level of quality, and is entitled to compensation if the product is seriously flawed.

The same goes for tenants. Except in Alabama, Arkansas and Colorado, if your rental is not habitable, you can sue the landlord—whether or not you move out. You can probably use small claims court, which allows claims of up to several thousand dollars. (For your state's ceiling, see the table in Chapter 19.) You won't need to hire a lawyer.

Suing the landlord makes sense only if you can safely continue to live in your rental. For example, if the roof leaks only into the second bedroom, and you can move the kids into the living room for a while, you might want to stay and sue in order to avoid the hassle of moving, arranging for the repair yourself (repair and deduct) or figuring out the complications of rent withholding. But you wouldn't want to stay and sue if you are without heat in the winter or in danger of electrocution every time you use the kitchen stove.

What are the pros and cons of suing your landlord instead of using repair and deduct or rent withholding? On the positive side, if you lose your lawsuit you'll have lost some time and money, but you won't be evicted, as can happen with the unsuccessful use of repair and deduct or rent withholding. But suing isn't entirely risk-free, especially if you're a month-to-month tenant or nearing the end of a lease you would like to renew. Your annoyed landlord may simply decide to terminate or not renew. Tenants who are protected by state antiretaliation laws will have some protection, but to assert your rights you'll have to bring a lawsuit, a dreary prospect. (Landlord retaliation is covered in Chapter 15.)

In your lawsuit, you ask the judge to rule that your unrepaired rental was not worth what you've paid for it. You want to be paid the difference between the monthly rent and the real value of the unit, times the number of months that you've lived with the substandard conditions. In short, you'll ask for a retroactive rent decrease. In addition, you can sue your landlord for:

- lost or damaged property—for example, furniture ruined by water leaking through the roof
- compensation for personal injuries—including pain and suffering—caused by the defect (see Chapter 12), and
- your attorney fees and court costs if you had to hire a lawyer to sue the landlord (Chapter 2 discusses attorney fees).

In some states, you may ask the court for an order directing the landlord to repair the defects, with rent reduced until they are fixed. In others, small claims courts can only order the landlord to pay you for your losses, but usually the money judgment gets the landlord's attention and he makes the repairs. ■

Minor Repairs and Maintenance

Ask a group of tenants which rental problem is most annoying, and chances are you'd hear "Repairs!" And most wouldn't be referring to major problems that make a unit unlivable. What really bugs tenants are the day-to-day but nonetheless important problems: leaky faucets, malfunctioning appliances, security devices that don't work, worn carpets, noisy heaters, hot water heaters that produce a pathetic quantity of tepid water and dozens of other frustrating breakdowns.

Unfortunately, if your landlord refuses to attend to minor repairs, you don't have much legal clout. You can't withhold rent, move out or use most of the other "big stick" legal weapons discussed in Chapter 8. Even so, there are several proven strategies for getting results.

Related topics covered in this book include:
- How to clarify repair and maintenance duties at the start of your tenancy: Chapter 2.
- How to use a Landlord-Tenant Checklist to note problems with the rental unit when you move in: Chapter 6.
- Dealing with serious problems that make housing uninhabitable: Chapter 8.
- Your responsibilities to keep your rental unit clean, safe and in good condition: Chapter 8.
- Making improvements or alterations to your rental on your own: Chapter 10.
- Your landlord's liability for injuries caused by defective premises: Chapter 12.

A. Minor Repairs: What Are They?

If a landlord balks at making repairs, it's key to decide whether the problem is major (affecting the habitability of your rental unit) or minor. This distinction is necessary because you have different legal options depending on your conclusion.

Minor repair and maintenance includes:
- Small plumbing jobs, like replacing washers and cleaning drains
- System upkeep, like changing heating filters

- Structural upkeep, like replacing excessively worn flooring
- Small repair jobs like fixing broken light fixtures or replacing the grout around bathtub tile, and
- Routine repairs to and maintenance of common areas, such as pools, spas and laundry rooms.

Don't assume that inexpensive repairs are always minor repairs. Sometimes an extremely important repair costs very little. For example, if the only thing between you and a heated apartment is the replacement of a $45 furnace part, the repair is "major" because an unheated dwelling is uninhabitable, even though the repair cost is insignificant. And because this is true, if the landlord didn't replace the furnace part promptly, you would probably be entitled to withhold rent or use one of the other "big stick" strategies discussed in Chapter 8. By contrast, replacing the living room carpet, which is worn but not a hazard, will be very expensive, but will be considered a minor repair because the consequence of not replacing it is not an unfit dwelling.

Most often, minor repairs are the landlord's job. But landlords are not required to keep the premises looking just like new—ordinary wear and tear does not have to be repaired during your tenancy. (When you move out, however, the cost of dealing with ordinary wear and tear will fall on the landlord and cannot come out of your security deposit. See Chapter 16.)

B. The Landlord's Responsibilities

Not every minor problem is, legally, your landlord's responsibility. If you or one of your guests caused it, carelessly or intentionally, you are responsible for repairing it—or, if your lease or rental agreement prohibits you from doing so, paying the landlord to do it. Typically, landlords deduct the cost from your security deposit, as discussed in Chapter 16.

If you had nothing to do with the repair problem, and it's not a cosmetic issue, chances go way up that your landlord is responsible, for one of the following reasons:

Common Misconceptions About Routine Maintenance

Many tenants (and landlords) are under the mistaken impression that every time a rental unit turns over, or a certain number of years have passed, the landlord must supply a new paint job or clean drapes and carpets or some other kind of refurbishing. Unfortunately for tenants, the law almost never mandates cosmetic changes—even badly needed ones. (Of course, if the landlord doesn't spruce up the place now and then, it may be hard to find and keep tenants. But that's a market, not a legal, issue.)

Here are some of the common misconceptions regarding rental sprucing-up:

Paint. No state's law requires landlords to repaint the interior every so often. (Very rarely, local ordinances may impose minimal re-painting obligations.) Unless the paint creates a habitability problem—for example, it's so thick around a window that the window can't be opened, or flaking lead-based paint poses obvious health risks—it should comply with the law. (Lead-based paint creates so many potential problems that we discuss it separately in Chapter 13.)

Drapes and Carpets. So long as drapes and carpets are not so damp or mildewy as to amount to a health hazard, and so long as carpets don't have dangerous holes that could cause someone to trip and fall, your landlord isn't legally required to replace them.

Windows. You're responsible for fixing (or paying to fix) a broken window that you or your guest intentionally or carelessly break. If a burglar, vandal or neighborhood child breaks a window, however, the landlord is usually legally responsible for the repair. Broken windows can sometimes be a habitability problem; see Chapter 8.

Keys and Locks. Unfortunately, in many areas of the country, landlords are not legally required to change the locks for new tenants. (The exceptions are Texas and many cities.) However, if you tell a landlord in writing that you are worried about renting a unit secured by locks for which previous tenants (and perhaps their friends) have keys, most landlords re-key the locks. (If the landlord knows of your concern but does not respond, and you are attacked or your place is burglarized by someone using an old key, the chances of the landlord being held liable in a lawsuit go way up. See Chapter 14.)

- A state or local building code requires that the landlord keep the damaged item (for example, a kitchen sink) in good repair.
- A state or local law specifically makes it the landlord's responsibility.
- A lease or rental agreement provision or advertisement describes or lists particular items, such as hot tubs, trash compactors and air conditioners; by implication, this makes the landlord responsible for maintaining or repairing them.
- The landlord made explicit promises when showing you the unit—for example, regarding the security or air conditioning system.
- The landlord made an implied promise to provide a particular feature, such as a whirlpool bathtub, or because the landlord has fixed or maintained it in the past.

Each of these reasons is discussed below. If you're not sure whether or not a minor repair or maintenance problem is the landlord's responsibility, scan the discussion to find out.

1. Building Codes

States (and sometimes cities) write building codes that cover structural requirements, such as roofs, flooring and windows, and essential services, such as hot water and heat. If your repair problem is also a violation of the building code, you may be facing a habitability problem, as discussed in Chapter 8. But building codes often cover other, less essential, details as well. For example, codes may specify a minimum number of electrical outlets per room; if a broken circuit breaker means that you have fewer working outlets, the consequence is probably not an unfit dwelling, but the landlord is still legally required to fix the problem.

2. Landlord-Tenant Laws

Some state laws place responsibility for specific minor repairs and maintenance on the landlord. A common example is providing garbage receptacles and arranging for garbage pick-up. Many states have their own special rules. In Alaska, for example, the law makes landlords responsible for maintaining vacuum cleaners, dishwashers and other appliances supplied by them. (Alaska Stat. § 34.03.100 and following.)

In many states, renters of single-family residences may agree to take on responsibilities that would otherwise belong to the landlord, such as disposing of garbage. For details, check your state's landlord-tenant codes under "Landlord-Tenant Statutes," which are listed in Appendix I.

 While checking the statutes to find your landlord's duties, be sure to look at your duties as well. For example, Louisiana tenants are responsible for repairs to fireplaces, plastering, windows, shutters and locks. (La. Civ. Code art. 2717.) Chapter 8 provides details on tenant repair and maintenance responsibilities.

3. Promises in the Lease or Rental Agreement

When it comes to legal responsibility for repairs, your own lease or rental agreement is often just as important (or more so) than building codes or state laws. If your written agreement describes or lists items such as drapes, washing machines, swimming pools, saunas, parking places, intercoms or dishwashers, your landlord must provide them in decent repair. And the promise to provide them carries with it the implied promise to maintain them.

4. Promises in Ads

If an advertisement for your unit described or listed a feature, such as a cable TV hookup, that significantly affected your decision to move into the particular rental unit, you have the right to hold the landlord to these promises. Even if your written rental agreement says nothing about appliances, if the landlord's ad listed dishwasher, clothes washer and dryer, garbage disposal, microwave oven, security gates and Jacuzzi, you have a right to expect that all of them will be repaired by the landlord if they break through no fault of yours.

EXAMPLE: Tina sees Joel's ad for an apartment, which says "heated swimming pool." After Tina moves in, Joel stops heating the pool regularly, because his utility costs have risen. Joel has violated his promise to keep the pool heated.

The promise doesn't have to be in words.

EXAMPLE: Tom's real estate agent showed him a glossy color photo of an available apartment, which featured a smiling resident using an intercom to welcome a guest. The apartment Tom rented did not have a working intercom, and he complained to the management, arguing that the advertisement implied that all units were so equipped. The landlord realized that he would have to fix the intercom.

5. Promises Made Before You Rented the Unit

It's a rare landlord or manager who refrains from even the slightest bit of puffing when showing a rental to a prospective tenant. You're quite likely to hear rosy plans for amenities or services that haven't yet materialized ("We plan to re-do this kitchen—you'll love the snappy way that trash compactor will work!"). Whenever you hear promises like these, you would be wise to get them in writing, as part of (or attached to) your lease or rental agreement or, at the very least, in a prompt letter of understanding that cannot be repudiated later.

If this advice is coming to you now a bit late, and you don't in fact have anything in writing, don't give up hope. The oral promise is valid and enforceable—it's just a little harder to prove that it was made. If the promised trash compactor never appears, it's your word against the landlord's unless

you have witnesses to the conversation. You'll be in a stronger position, proof-wise, if the promised feature is present in your unit but just doesn't work or breaks down after you move in, as explained in subsection 6, just below.

EXAMPLE: When Joel's rental agent shows Tom around the building, she goes out of her way to show off the laundry room, saying, "Here's the laundry room—we have two machines now, but will be adding two more soon." Tom rents the apartment. Two months go by and Joel still hasn't added the new machines. Joel has violated his promise to equip the laundry room with four machines.

6. Implied Promises

Suppose your rental agreement doesn't mention a garbage disposal and neither does any ad you saw before moving in. And in fairness, you can't remember your landlord ever pointing it out when showing you the unit. But there is a garbage disposal and it was working when you moved in. Now the garbage disposal is broken and, despite repeated requests, your landlord hasn't fixed it. Do you have a legal leg to stand on in demanding that your landlord make this minor repair? Yes. Many courts will hold a landlord legally responsible for maintaining all significant aspects of your rental unit. If you rent a unit that *already has* certain features—light fixtures that work, doors that open and close smoothly, faucets that don't leak, tile that doesn't fall off the wall—many judges reason that the landlord has made an implied contract to keep them in workable order throughout your tenancy.

The flip side of this principle is that if you pay for a hamburger, the waiter doesn't have to deliver a steak. In other words, if your rental was shabby when you moved in, and the landlord never gave you reason to believe that it would be spruced up, you have no legal right to demand improvements—unless, of course, you can show health hazards or code violations. As when you buy secondhand goods "as is" for a low price, legally you are stuck with your deal. (But Section D, below, suggests some strategies—based on subtly showing your landlord the consequences of ignoring minor repairs—that may convince a reluctant landlord to take better care of business.)

Another factor that is evidence of an implied contract is the landlord's past conduct. If your landlord has consistently fixed or maintained a particular feature of your rental, he has made an implied obligation to continue doing so.

EXAMPLE: Tina's apartment has a built-in dishwasher. When she rented the apartment, neither the lease nor the landlord said anything about the dishwasher or who was responsible for repairing it. The dishwasher has broken down a few times and whenever Tina asked Joel to fix it, he did. By doing so, Joel has established a practice that he—not the tenant—is responsible for repairing the dishwasher.

Check your lease. Landlords who want to avoid responsibility for appliance repairs often insert clauses in their leases or rental agreements warning that the appliances are not maintained by the landlord. (See Chapter 2, Section D.)

Using the Landlord-Tenant Checklist at the start of your tenancy will give you a record of appliances and features—and their condition. If something needs repairs, you'll be able to use the Checklist as proof of its original condition.

C. Your Responsibilities

Leases and rental agreements usually include a general statement that you are responsible for keeping your rental unit clean, safe and in good condition, and for reimbursing your landlord for the cost of repairing damage you cause. Your lease or rental agreement will probably also say that you can't make alterations or repairs, such as painting the walls, installing bookcases or fixing electrical problems, without your landlord's permission. (See Chapter 2.)

Landlords who are tired of maintenance and repair jobs may use the lease, rental agreement or separate contract to give these responsibilities to a tenant. Especially if you rent a single-family home or duplex, you may be asked to agree to mow the lawn, trim the bushes and do minor plumbing jobs and painting.

Many state laws regulate the kind of repairs and maintenance that landlords can hand off to tenants. In general, if the landlord is not required to provide an item in the first place (a sauna, for example), the lease or rental agreement can delegate to the tenant responsibility for repairing it (which would normally be the landlord's, as discussed above). Landlords cannot, however, make tenants responsible for repairing or maintaining essential features of any rental, which are required by law. (See Chapter 8.) Also, laws in some states limit duties that landlords can delegate to tenants in multi-unit buildings, while allowing tenants in single-family dwellings and duplexes to assume more responsibilities.

Commonly, a landlord proposes a rent reduction in exchange for some work. Or the landlord may offer other perks (a parking space, for example), or will offer an amenity if the tenant will perform the maintenance—for example, a hot tub in exchange for your promise to clean it.

Although usually legal, these arrangements often lead to dissatisfaction—typically, the landlord feels that the tenant has neglected certain tasks, or the tenant feels that there is too much work. If the dispute boils over, the landlord tries to evict the tenant.

Here's how to protect yourself and avoid disputes:

- **Sign an employment agreement separate from your rental agreement or lease.** This is especially important if you plan to do considerable work for your landlord on a continuing basis, such as keeping hallways, elevators, or a laundry room clean or maintaining the landscaping. Tenants who are also building managers are in this position. Ask your landlord to pay you for your work, rather than give you a rent reduction. That way, if the landlord claims that the job is not done right, the worst that can happen is that you will be fired; your tenancy should not be affected. But if your maintenance duties are tied to a rent reduction and things go wrong, you and the landlord will have to amend the lease or

rental agreement in order to re-establish the original rent. And if the maintenance jobs are spelled out in a lease clause, the landlord also has the option of terminating the lease, on the grounds that your poor performance constitutes a breach of the lease.

- **Clearly write out your responsibilities and the landlord's expectations.** List your tasks and the frequency with which your landlord expects them to be done. Weekly tasks might include, for example, cleaning the laundry room, sweeping and wet-mopping of the lobby and mowing the grass between April 1 and November 1.

- **Make sure the agreement is fair.** Ideally, your landlord will pay you a fair hourly rate. If your only choice is a rent reduction, make sure the trade-off is equitable. If you're getting only a $50 rent reduction for work that would cost the landlord $200 if he hired a cleaning service, you're being ripped off.

- **Discuss problems with the landlord and try to work out a mutually satisfactory agreement**. If the landlord has complained about your work, maybe it's because he's underestimated what's involved in cleaning the hallways and grounds. Your landlord may be willing to pay you more for better results or shorten your list of jobs. If not, cancel the arrangement. In extreme cases, you may need to move out.

Watch Out for Illegal Retaliation

A landlord's delegation of some tasks does not relieve him of all repair and maintenance responsibilities. For example, if you and your landlord agree that you will do gardening work in exchange for a rent reduction, and he feels that you are not doing a proper job, he is not permitted to respond by shutting off your water.

Don't perform repairs involving hazardous materials. Any repair involving old paint or insulation (opening up a ceiling or wall cavity, for example) may expose you or others to dangerous levels of toxic materials. For example, sanding a surface for a seemingly innocuous paint job may actually create lead-based paint dust; the quick installation of a smoke alarm could involve disturbing an asbestos-filled ceiling. See Chapter 13 for more information on environmental hazards.

D. Getting the Landlord to Make Minor Repairs

By now you should have a pretty good idea as to whether or not your landlord is legally responsible for fixing the particular minor problem that is bedeviling you. Your next job is to get the landlord to do it. First, try to get the landlord to cooperate. If you can't, it may be time to take a confrontational approach.

Special Concerns for Month-to-Month Tenants

If you have a month-to-month tenancy, your landlord can, in most states, terminate your tenancy with just 30 days' notice. That means you should think twice before trying one of the adversarial strategies discussed below—reporting your landlord for building code violations or suing in small claims court—over minor problems with your rental.

An anti-retaliation law, if one is in force where you live, may protect you from a termination notice. But if you have to go to court to argue about it all, you may end up wishing you'd never complained about that cracked window. Remember, you can end your tenancy with 30 days' notice, too—so, if you're really unhappy with your place, maybe you should look for another.

---

1. Appealing to Your Landlord

Chances are you have already asked your landlord or manager to make repairs, only to be put off, ignored or even told to forget it. Your next step is to write a formal demand letter—or, if you have already done it, a second one.

Before you pick up your pen or turn on your computer, take a minute to think about what words will most likely get action. Begin by remembering your landlord's overriding business concerns: To make money, avoid hassles with tenants and stay out of legal hot water. A request that zeroes in on these issues will likely get the job done.

a. How to Write a Persuasive Repair Request

Whether this is your first or second formal demand letter, frame your repair request along one or more of the following lines, if possible:

- **It's a small problem now, but has the potential to be a very big deal.** A bathtub faucet that drips badly may be simply annoying now, but devastating later if the washer gives out while you're not home, flooding the tub and ruining the floor and downstairs neighbor's ceiling. When you ask that the faucet be repaired, point out the risk of letting things go.
- **There is a potential for injury.** Landlords hate to be sued. If a potential injury-causing problem is brought to their attention, it's likely that their fear of lawsuits will overcome their lethargy, and you'll finally get results. Say, for instance, you have asked your landlord to repair the electrical outlet in your kitchen so that you can use your toaster. If you've received no response, try again with a different pitch: Point out that, on occasion, you have observed sparks flying from the wall, and a short in the wiring could cause an injury or fire.
- **There is a security problem that imperils your safety.** Landlords are increasingly aware that

they can also be sued for criminal assaults against tenants if the premises aren't reasonably secure. (Chapter 14 discusses this topic in detail.) If you can figure out a way to emphasize the security risks of not fixing a problem—for example, a burned-out light bulb in the garage or a door that doesn't always latch properly— you may motivate the landlord to act promptly.

- **The problem affects other tenants.** If you can point to a disaster-waiting-to-happen that affects more than one tenant, you will greatly increase your chances of some action. For example, accumulated oil puddles in the garage threaten the safety of all tenants and guests, not just you. Faced with the possibility of a small army of potential plaintiffs, each accompanied by an eager attorney, even the most slothful landlord may spring into action. See Chapter 19 for tips on working with other tenants to accomplish common goals.

- **You're willing to try to fix it, but may make the problem worse.** Finally, you might try offering to fix the problem yourself in a way that is likely to elicit a quick "No, thanks, I'll call my contractor right away!" This is a bit risky, since your bluff might be called, but even the most dense landlord will think twice when you offer to make an electrical repair with a chisel and masking tape.

See the sample letter, below, for more ideas on writing a persuasive repair request.

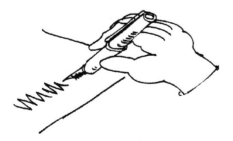

Sample Letter Asking for Minor Repairs

90 Willow Run, Apartment 3A
Morgantown, Arizona 00000

February 28, 200X

Mr. Lee Sloan
37 Main Street, Suite 100
Morgantown, Arizona 00000

Dear Mr. Sloan:

I would appreciate it if you could schedule an appointment with me to look at three problems in my apartment that have come up recently.

First, the kitchen sink is dripping, and it's getting worse. I'm concerned that a plate or dish towel might stop up the drain, leading to an overflow. At any rate, the water bill is yours, and I'm sure that you don't want to pay for wasted water.

I've also been having trouble opening the sliding doors on the bedroom closet. The track appears to be coming away from the wall, and the doors wobble and look like they might fall into the room when I open and close the closet.

Finally, it would really be great if you would give some thought to repainting the interior hallways. They looked clean when I moved in a year ago, but now are pretty grimy. I've spoken with the tenants in four of the other six units and they, too, would appreciate a return to your standards of old.

Thanks very much for thinking about my requests. I hope to hear from you soon.

Yours truly,

Chris Jensen

Chris Jensen

A written demand for repair or maintenance lets your landlord know that you are serious about the issue and are not content to just let it go. In addition, if your dispute ends up in small claims court, it can usually be introduced as evidence. Like this sample letter, your demand letter should:

- Be neatly typed and use businesslike language
- Concisely and accurately state the important facts (this is important in case your letter ends up before a judge, who will need to be made familiar with the situation)
- Be polite and non-personal. Obviously, a personal attack on your landlord may trigger an equally emotional response. Since you are appealing to the landlord's business interests, you want to encourage her to evaluate the issue soberly, not out of anger, and
- State exactly what you want—a new paint job, for example.

Always keep a copy of the letter for your files, and hand-deliver the letter or send it return-receipt requested.

b. Proposing Mediation

If your demand letter does not produce results, consider involving the help of a local mediation center. Most community services handle lots of landlord and tenant problems, for free or at a very low cost. If they can coax the landlord to talk with you, (and they're very good at doing that), you have a decent chance of ending up with an agreement. See Chapter 19 for more information on mediation.

2. Reporting Code Violations

If appealing to your landlord's business sensibilities doesn't work, other strategies are available to pry minor repairs out of your landlord.

If the problem you want fixed constitutes a code violation, such as inadequate electrical outlets or low water pressure, you should find an ally in the building or housing agency in charge of enforcing the code. (Chapter 8 covers how to find and what to expect from these local agencies.) Whether you'll get any action out of the agency will depend on the seriousness of the violation, the workload of the agency and its ability to enforce its compliance orders. Since by definition your problem is minor, don't expect lots of help if code enforcement officials are already overworked.

3. Suing in Small Claims Court

If you can reasonably argue that you aren't getting what you paid for, you might decide to sue in small claims court. But before you do, write a second demand letter. Like the first letter (see the sample above), your second letter should describe the problems and alert the landlord to the negative consequences (to him, not just to you) that may follow if repairs aren't made. In addition, state that you intend to sue if you don't get results. This may get the landlord's attention and save you a trip to the courthouse.

EXAMPLE: Chris Jensen wrote to her landlord on February 28, requesting repairs as shown in the sample letter in subsection 1a above. She got no reply. Ten days later, she sent a second letter that summarized the first and concluded with this paragraph:

"If you are unable to attend to these repairs, I'll need to call in a handyman to repair the faucet and doors, and I will seek reimbursement from you in small claims court if necessary. As for the deterioration of the paint, I believe I am entitled to a reduction in rent, which I will also seek in small claims court. Of course, I sincerely hope that this will not be necessary."

If the second letter doesn't produce results, it's time to head for small claims court. You won't need a lawyer; just go to the court and ask for the forms you need to sue someone. In small claims court, you can't get an order from the judge directing your landlord to paint, fix the dishwasher or repair the intercom. You may, however, be compensated in dollars for living in a rental unit with repair problems. Here's how it works.

When you file your small claims court suit, you'll ask for an amount that reflects the difference between your rent and the value of the unit with repair problems. (To calculate this amount, use one of the methods described in Chapter 8.) In court, your argument will be that you are not getting the benefit of what you're paying rent for—for example, a functioning dishwasher, presentable paint or a working air conditioner.

You're more likely to succeed with this line of argument if you have a lease rather than a month-to-month agreement. If you have a long-term lease, you can argue that you are locked into a set rent for an extended period of time and should be compensated accordingly—that is, month after month, you receive less than what you are obligated to pay for. In contrast, a month-to-month tenant has no long-standing obligation; if you don't like the fact that the shower door now won't close, you can leave after giving relatively short notice, with no legal liability for future rent. A judge is likely to point this out, and to tell you that, in effect, you agreed to the increasing shabbiness every month when you failed to send in a termination notice.

Don't stop paying rent. Although fairness dictates that if your rental unit is full of repair problems you ought to pay less rent, it's a mistake to pay your landlord less than the full monthly rent. Rent withholding, as discussed in Chapter 8, is legally appropriate only for major repairs. If you withhold even a portion of the rent because of a minor repair problem, you risk eviction for nonpayment of rent.

Your goal in small claims court is to convince the judge that these problems really make your rental unit worth less money. Use common sense—don't go running to court for small things. A small claims court judge is not going to adjust your rent because a little grout is missing from your bathroom tile. But if your dishwasher is broken, three faucets leak noisily and the bathroom door won't close properly, your chances of winning go way up. You'll need to show the judge that:

- There are lots of minor defects, not just an isolated one, and
- You've given the landlord plenty of time and notice to fix the problems.

Bring evidence. Winning in small claims court depends more on what you bring into court to prove your story than on what you say. Examples of key evidence include:

- copies of letters you've written asking for repairs
- your written notes on your landlord's response to your repair requests, including the number of times they were ignored or promised repairs didn't materialize
- witnesses—a family member, for example, who can describe the inoperable air conditioner
- photographs—your pictures of the cracked, flaking plaster, for example
- a copy of the local building or housing code, if the problem is covered there
- your lease or rental agreement, if it lists any of the items that need repair
- your lease or rental agreement, if it prohibits you from making repairs yourself
- a copy of the Landlord-Tenant Checklist, which you should have completed when you moved in and which is signed by you and the landlord, showing that the problem did not exist at the start of your tenancy, and
- ads, brochures or For Rent signs describing features of your rental are missing or malfunctioning.

For more advice on preparing for and filing a small claims court case, see Chapter 16.

EXAMPLE: Judy signed a one-year lease for a studio apartment at $750 a month. When she moved in, the place was in good shape. But six months into her tenancy, the condition of the apartment began to deteriorate. A water leak from the roof stained and buckled several areas of the hardwood floors; the kitchen cabinets, which were apparently badly made, warped and would not shut; the dishwasher became so noisy the neighbor banged on the wall when it was in use; the soap dish fell off the bathroom wall, and the white entryway rug started to fall apart. Judy asked her landlord to attend to these problems and followed up with several written demand letters. Two months after her original request, Judy wrote a final demand letter.

When the landlord still did nothing, Judy filed suit in small claims court, asking the judge to award her damages (money) representing the difference between her rent and the value of the deteriorated apartment. After considering Judy's evidence, including copies of her demand letter, photographs of the defects and the testimony of her neighbor, the judge agreed with Judy. She figured that the deteriorated apartment would have rented for $150 less a month, and ordered the landlord to pay Judy $450 to make up for the three months she had lived with the defects. Judy's landlord was quick to make repairs after learning this expensive lesson in court.

Everybody's Guide to Small Claims Court, by Ralph Warner (Nolo), has all the details you need to file a small claims court lawsuit.

E. Making Minor Repairs Yourself

If you've concluded that a repair job isn't your landlord's responsibility, that means it's in your lap.

Before you head out to the hardware store, pause for a moment. You need to know, first, whether it makes sense from a practical point of view for you to do the repair or maintenance, and second, whether it's legal .

1. Evaluating Your Skills and Time

Before you embark on a job, realistically assess its magnitude and your skills, tools and time. Seemingly easy repairs often have hidden complexities. A simple job, like replacing the flexible hoses under the sink that connect the pipes to the faucet, may require special wrenches because of the cramped workspace. Do you have this equipment, or are you willing to purchase it? Time is also an issue: Are you willing to commit precious weekend or evening time to a plumbing project? Only an experienced, equipped handyperson (or one willing to consult a good do-it-yourself manual) should consider doing most home repairs.

You must also consider whether or not you are willing to take the risk of being held liable if one of your repair projects goes awry and results in property damage or, worse, someone's injury. Your landlord's insurance policy will not cover your misdeeds, and unless you have renters' insurance, you stand to lose a lot of money.

EXAMPLE: Colin decided to replace a window that was broken by his daughter's basketball. He removed the shards of glass, fitted a new pane in place and caulked the circumference. He did not, however, paint the caulk; and a year later it had cracked, allowing rainwater to seep onto the windowsill and down the wall. The landlord was furious when he realized that he would have to replace the sill and the drywall, simply because Colin had not done a workmanlike job. The cost of these repairs was taken out of Colin's security deposit.

2. Getting the Landlord's Permission

First, look at your lease or rental agreement. You may see a clause that forbids you from undertaking any "repairs, alterations or improvements" without the landlord's consent. (Alterations and improvements are discussed in Chapter 10.) It may seem unfair, but such a clause is legal. And a "no repairs without consent" clause keeps the landlord in control of the property, while making you pay for it.

If your lease has a "no repairs" clause, you'll have to convince the landlord to give you permission. (See the sample letter, below.) And even if you *don't* have such a clause, check with the landlord first, anyway. You won't need to do this if the repair or replacement is truly insignificant and nontechnical (or if it's unlikely to be noticed by the landlord), like replacing the entryway rug or installing mini-blinds where old ones used to be.

But for jobs that have the potential to get complicated, expensive or have dire consequences if things go wrong, you'll want to have the official okay before proceeding. It may prevent your landlord from legally charging you if things go awry. Of course, a potential negative outcome may be the very reason your landlord will say "No way" and call for the bonded repair person. But many landlords—if they trust you—will be happy to save themselves the time and trouble of lining up a worker, scheduling a time to be in your apartment, getting you to pay the bill or deducting the expense from your security deposit and then getting you to bring the deposit up to its original level.

To protect yourself, put your repair proposal in writing, phrase it in a way that tells the landlord you'll proceed unless you hear to the contrary within a reasonable amount of time, and keep a copy for your records. That way, you have a record that your work was undertaken with the landlord's consent. A sample letter is shown below; notice how the tenant has communicated the problem, his experience with similar repairs and plan for repairing the item, all of which are designed to inspire the landlord's confidence.

Sample Letter Requesting Permission to Do a Minor Repair

890 Market Street, #3
Central City, Texas 00000
(214) 555-7890

January 4, 200X

Jackson Montgomery
234 Fourth Street
Central City, Texas 00000

Dear Mr. Montgomery,

Last night, a fork accidentally fell into my garbage disposal, jamming the blades and causing the unit to stop. The disposal will have to be taken out and the blade assembly examined. The shear key, which prevents the engine from seizing, will need to be replaced.

I am familiar with the installation and maintenance of these appliances, having worked on one at my former residence. I have the tools to do the job. I'll proceed with this repair unless I hear from you to the contrary. Please leave me a note or call me before January 10 if you do not wish me to do the job. If I don't hear from you by then, I'll go ahead.

Yours truly,

Janet Green

Janet Green

Making Improvements and Alterations

Your lease or rental agreement probably includes a clause prohibiting you from making any alterations or improvements to your unit without the express, written consent of the landlord. (Often, your landlord will forbid you to undertake repairs, too. This issue is discussed in Chapter 9.) Landlords use these clauses—some of which contain a long list of prohibitions—so that tenants don't change the light fixtures, knock out a wall, install a built-in dishwasher or even pound in a nail to hang a picture unless the landlord agrees first.

But what if you make one of these alterations or improvements without getting your landlord's permission—for example, you bolt a closet storage system to the wall? In most states, unless you get the landlord's permission to remove the item, such improvements and additions become the landlord's property when you leave.

Discovering too late that you must leave behind what you thought of as a portable improvement can be a real blow. To help you avoid problems, this chapter explains:

- what types of improvements and alterations become the landlord's property
- what you can do, ahead of time, to forestall losing your property
- how to minimize your losses if your landlord insists that the improvement remain on the property, and
- special rules for cable TV access and satellite dishes.

 Related topics covered in this book include:
- Disabled tenants' rights to modify their living space: Chapter 5.
- Performing minor repairs with the landlord's consent: Chapter 9.

A. Improvements That Become Part of the Property

Anything you attach to a building, fence, deck or the ground itself belongs to the landlord, absent an agreement saying it's yours. (Lawyers call such items "fixtures.") This is a basic legal principle, and it's also spelled out in most leases and rental agreements. This means when you move out, the landlord is legally entitled to refuse your offer to remove the fixture and return the premises to its original state. In addition, many leases and rental agreements make it even clearer what types of improvements belong to the landlord. A typical clause looks something like this: "Any alterations, installations or improvements, including shelving and attached floor coverings, will become the property of the owner and will remain with and as part of the rental premises at the end of the term."

In some cases, a landlord and departing tenant can't agree on who owns a particular piece of property, and the dispute ends up in court. Judges use a variety of legal rules to determine whether an object—an appliance, flooring, shelving or plumbing—is something that you can take with you or is a permanent fixture belonging to your landlord. Here are some of the questions judges ask:

- **Did you get the landlord's permission?** If you never asked the landlord to install a closet organizer, or you did and got no for an answer, a judge is likely to rule for your landlord—particularly if your lease or rental agreement prohibits alterations or improvements.
- **Did you make any structural changes that affect the use or appearance of property?** If so, chances are that the item will be deemed

the landlord's, because removing it will often leave an unsightly area or alter the use of part of the property. For example, if you modify the kitchen counter to accommodate a built-in dishwasher and then take the dishwasher with you, the landlord will have to install another dishwasher of the same dimensions or re-build the space. The law doesn't impose this extra work on landlords, nor does it force them to let you do the return-to-original work yourself.

- **Is the object firmly attached to the property?** In general, additions and improvements that are nailed, screwed or cemented to the building are likely to be deemed "fixtures." For example, hollow-wall screws that anchor a bookcase might convert an otherwise free-standing unit belonging to the tenant to a fixture belonging to the landlord. Similarly, closet rods bolted to the wall become part of the structure and would usually be counted as fixtures. On the other hand, shelving systems that are secured by isometric pressure (spring-loaded rods that press against the ceiling and floor) involve no actual attachment to the wall and for that reason are not likely to be classified as fixtures. Even if you have a very good reason for firmly attaching your addition—bolting a bookcase to the wall for earthquake protection, for example—you may still end up having to leave it behind.

- **What did you and the landlord intend?** Courts will look at statements made by you and the landlord to determine whether there was any understanding as to your right to remove an improvement. In some circumstances, courts will even infer an agreement from your actions—for instance, if your landlord stopped by and gave permission for you to install what you've described as a portable air conditioner, or helped you lift it into place. (Your chances of convincing the judge would be greatly enhanced if you had gotten permission in writing, as explained below in Section B.) By contrast, if you remove the landlord's light

fixtures and, without his knowledge, install a custom-made fixture that could not be used in any other space, it is unlikely that you could convince a judge that you reasonably expected to take it with you at the end of your tenancy.

Improvements That Plug or Screw In

The act of plugging in an appliance doesn't make the appliance a part of the premises. The same is true for simple wiring or pipe attachments to join an appliance to an electrical or water source. For example, a refrigerator or free-standing stove remains the property of the tenant. Similarly, portable dishwashers that connect to the kitchen faucet by means of a coupling may be removed.

B. Improving Your Rental Unit Without Enriching Your Landlord

Your best protection against losing an item you love is to not attach it to a wall in your unit. Fortunately, hundreds of items are on the market—bookcases, lighting systems, closet organizers and even dishwashers—that you can take with you when you leave. To get some good ideas, visit a large hardware store, home improvement center or a business devoted to closet organization systems.

If you are determined to attach something to the wall or floor, talk to the landlord before you get out your tools. If you can, get the landlord to agree to pay for the improvement, or let you remove it when you leave.

Decide beforehand which option you prefer. For example, since a custom-made track lighting system won't do you any good if you take it with you, find out whether the landlord will pay for it in the first place. On the other hand, if you want to take the fixture with you, impress upon the landlord your intent to carefully restore the property to its original condition. Keep in mind that if your restoration attempts are less than acceptable, the landlord will be justified in deducting from your security deposit the amount of money necessary to do the job right. And if the deposit is insufficient, the landlord can sue you in small claims court for the excess.

Approach your landlord as one businessperson dealing with another. If the improvement will remain and you seek reimbursement, point out that it will make the property more attractive. It might even justify a higher rent for the next tenant and thus pay for itself over the long run. Your landlord might agree to reduce your rent a little each month or simply reimburse you all at once. (You could also mention that the IRS will end up paying for a portion of the improvement, since it will be deductible as a business cost.)

If you and the landlord reach an understanding, put it in writing. As shown in the sample agreement below, you will want to carefully describe the project and materials and state whether you are to be reimbursed or allowed to take the improvement with you.

A blank, tear-out form of the Agreement Regarding Tenant Improvements to Rental Unit is in Appendix II.

Save all receipts for materials and labor.
Whether you will be reimbursed or will take the fixture with you when you leave, it is important to keep a good record of the amount of money you spend on the project. That way, there can be no dispute as to what you're owed if you are to be reimbursed. If the landlord changes his mind and doesn't let you remove the improvement at the end of your tenancy, you'll have receipts to back up your small claims lawsuit for the value of the addition.

C. Cable TV and Satellite Dishes

Major changes in technology have expanded entertainment services available from cable TV and satellite dishes. Unfortunately, your landlord may limit your ability to take advantage of all these options.

1. Cable TV Access

The wonders of cable TV come to your home through coaxial cables that are strung along telephone poles or underground and into your building. By now, many apartment buildings are wired for cable access, with a single "plug" on the exterior of the building and branches to individual units. Tenants who want to sign up need only call the cable provider to activate the existing cable line to their unit.

If your unit isn't wired for cable TV, you cannot force the landlord to allow you to install a junction box and wiring through the building. Similarly, if your building is already hooked up to one cable company, and you would prefer to buy the services of another, you may be out of luck. (Some states, however, are considering legislation that would force landlords to open the building to multiple providers.) Landlords quail at the thought of multiple service providers running a hodge-podge of wires through their buildings. Although an incumbent cable company can, in theory, share its cable wires, with other providers, they typically don't want to make their hardware available to competitors.

Agreement Regarding Tenant Improvements to Rental Unit

Mark Henderson _____ (Tenant) and

Robin Reese _____ (Landlord)

agree as follows:

Tenant may make the following improvement to the rental unit at ____370 Alpine Way, San Jose,____

California 00000: _____:

Install window unit air conditioner in the master bedroom. _____

_____

Tenant will accomplish the improvement by using the following materials and procedures:

Purchasing a Cold Spot window air conditioner unit, Model 34A, and anchoring it to the

window frame using manufacturer's enclosed brackets. _____

_____

Landlord and Tenant further agree that (check either 1 or 2):

[X] 1. The improvement will become Landlord's property and is not to be removed by Tenant.

Landlord will reimburse Tenant for (check a or b or both):

[X] a. the cost of material, and/or

[ ] b. labor costs at a rate of $_____ per hour, after Tenant provides receipts and the

Landlord determines that the work has been done in a workmanlike and acceptable manner.

Landlord will reimburse Tenant (check c or d):

[X] c. By lump sum payment, within a reasonable time, or

[ ] d. By reducing Tenant's rent, according to the following schedule: _____

_____.

[ ] 2. The improvement will be considered Tenant's personal property, and as such may be removed

by Tenant at any time up to the end of the tenancy. Tenant promises to return the premises to

their original condition upon removing the improvement. If Tenant fails to do this, Landlord

may deduct the cost of restoring the premises to their original condition from Tenant's security

deposit.

May 10, 200X _____ *Mark Henderson* _____

Date   Tenant

May 10, 200X _____ *Robin Reese* _____

Date   Landlord

Some opportunistic landlords, smelling the chance to make a little money, have negotiated exclusive contracts with cable providers. The landlords pay the cable company a flat monthly fee in exchange for consistent, uniform service to the tenants. The landlord makes money by charging you more than he pays the cable company. Allowing a different company would risk violating their agreement, jeopardizing the landlord's cut of the monthly revenue.

We doubt, however, that we have heard the last word on the issue of cable access. The Federal Communications Commission (FCC) will ultimately grapple with the problem and, to complicate matters further, the public utilities commissions of several states (including Arizona, Colorado, Connecticut, Indiana and New Jersey) have begun their own regulation-making process. To find out the current state of your rights to choose cable access, contact your state's public utilities commission.

Meanwhile, do some homework and find out whether there are multiple service providers in your area who will vie for your building's business. In a competitive situation, your landlord might be offered incentives that make the deal hard to turn down.

Talk to other tenants in the building and determine whether they are interested in cable TV (or alternative video service providers available in some areas) and are willing to pay for it. Signing up long-term tenants will help your case more than a group of month-to-month residents; there's no way of knowing whether the next batch will be interested in paying for the service. Present the results of your efforts to the landlord. If you can suggest a cable company or service provider that will give the landlord a monthly fee in exchange for exclusive access, the landlord can't lose.

And if nothing works: Read a book, take a walk, call a friend or go to the movies. Besides the *Larry Sanders Show*, do you really need cable TV?

2. Satellite Dishes and Wireless Antennas

Wireless communications have the potential to reach more people with less hardware than any cable system. But there is one, essential piece of equipment: A satellite dish or an antenna with wires connecting it to your television set or computer.

Many of us are familiar with the car-sized dishes often seen in backyards or on roofs of houses—the pink flamingo of the new age. Recently, however, smaller and cheaper dishes, two feet or less in diameter, have shown up in appliance stores. Wires from the dishes can easily be run under a door or through an open window to an individual TV or computer. Predictably, tenants have bought dishes or comparable wireless devices and attached them to roofs, windowsills, balconies and railings. And, sure enough, some landlords have howled, citing their unsightly looks and the potential for liability should a satellite dish or antenna fall and injure someone below.

The Federal Communications Commission has stepped in, however, on the side of tenants. Beginning in January 1999, landlords may not "unreasonably" interfere with a tenant's right to access the airways. (FCC Order 98-273.) This means that, while the landlord may flatly prohibit a tenant from installing a dish or antenna in common areas, on exterior walls or on the roof, she cannot forbid installation in areas where you have exclusive control, such as patios, yards and balconies.

The fact that the landlord cannot *forbid* installation of a dish in the areas mentioned above doesn't mean, however, that she can't set reasonable policies regarding their set-up. She can insist, for example, that the installation be done by a member of her maintenance staff (and she can charge reasonably for this service); or she might want to require installation by the dealer who sold the dish. Cautious landlords will write clear rules regarding placement and methods of attachment (for instance, they might insist that the dish not extend beyond the tenant's balcony), and may insist that you provide proof of renters' insurance that would cover you should someone be injured or property damaged as a result of an accident involving your dish or antenna. ∎

Your Right to Privacy

There's no place like home—unless, of course, you have a landlord who doesn't respect your right to privacy. The problem typically arises with a landlord or manager who cannot stop fussing over the property or who frequently tries to wangle an invitation into your home to look around. Even worse are landlords and managers who use a passkey to enter without notice when you're not at home and there is no emergency. The idea that a landlord might at any time violate your private space and even go through your personal belongings is, obviously, scary.

This chapter covers your basic rights to privacy and what to do about a landlord or manager who violates these rights. You can sue your landlord for entering unlawfully—but it's rarely worth the time or trouble. Unfortunately, the law won't solve all problems inherent in dealing with difficult people. In some instances, you may find that you'll either have to grin and bear the actions of an intrusive landlord or move on.

To avoid problems with obnoxious landlords at your next place, be sure to talk with other tenants before you move in. Chapter 1 provides advice on checking out prospective landlords.

State Laws on Landlord's Entry

About half the states have statutes specifying when and how landlords may legally enter rented property. See "State Laws on Landlord's Access to Rental Property" in Appendix I for details. In other states, your right to privacy is determined by your state's and the federal Constitution, as interpreted by the courts. If you want to know its precise extent, you'll have to research the law yourself or get help from a lawyer or tenants' right group.

A. Entry by the Landlord

When you rent residential property, the rental unit is your home and should be respected as such. Your landlord must have a good reason to enter your apartment and meet legal notice requirements.

1. Allowable Reasons

Landlords always can come in when you give permission or any time there is a genuine emergency that threatens life or property, like a fire or a serious water leak. Nearly every state has, by judicial decision or statute, decided that landlords can also enter, after notifying you beforehand, to:

- make needed repairs or improvements or assess the need for them, or

- show property to prospective tenants or purchasers.

In addition, a landlord who believes you have abandoned the property—that is, skipped out without giving any notice or returning the key—may legally enter.

The following sections provide details on each of these reasons.

Entry With Your Permission

Obviously, your landlord can always enter rental property if you agree. But don't let your landlord coerce your permission. A landlord who pressures you, perhaps implying or even threatening eviction if you don't allow immediate or virtually unrestricted access, is clearly violating your privacy rights. See Section D, below, for advice on how to deal with this situation.

a. Emergencies

In all states, landlords can enter your rental unit without giving notice to respond to a true emergency that threatens injury or property damage. Here are some examples:

- Smoke is pouring out of your apartment window. Your landlord calls the fire department and uses a master key—or even breaks in if necessary—to try to deal with the fire.
- Your landlord sees water coming out of the bottom of your back door. It's okay to enter and find the water leak.
- You hear screams coming from the rental unit next door and call the manager. She knocks on the apartment door, but gets no answer. After calling the police, the manager uses her passkey to enter and see what's wrong.
- Your family and friends, worried that you haven't been at work or reachable by phone over the long weekend, ask your landlord to enter your apartment to make sure every-

thing's okay. He does so and finds nothing amiss; you show up a day later, having taken a spur-of-the moment vacation.

On the other hand, a property owner's urge to repair a problem that's important but doesn't threaten life or property—say, a stopped-up drain that is not causing any damage—isn't a true emergency.

A landlord who does need to enter your apartment in an emergency should leave a note or call you explaining the circumstances and the date and time. If you don't get this kind of notification, make it clear in writing that you expect it.

 Your landlord is legally entitled to a key to your rental unit. Check your lease or rental agreement; many forbid tenants from re-keying, adding additional locks or installing a security system without the landlord's permission. If a landlord does grant you permission to change or add locks, you may need to provide duplicate keys. If you install a security system, you may need to give your landlord the name and phone number of the alarm company or instructions on how to disarm the system in an emergency.

b. Repairs

Many states, either by statute or court decision, allow a landlord or repairperson to enter rental property to make necessary or agreed-upon repairs, alterations or improvements—for example, to fix a broken oven or replace the carpet. This includes the landlord's entry to assess the need for or cost of repairs.

In these situations, the landlord generally must enter only at reasonable times and must give you at least the required amount of notice, usually 24 hours. (Notice requirements are discussed below.) However, if this is impracticable—for example, a repairperson is available on a few hours' notice—a landlord will probably be on solid ground by explaining the situation to you and giving shorter notice. Of course, if you agree to a shorter notice period, your landlord has no problem.

EXAMPLE: Amy told her landlord Brett that her bathroom sink was stopped up and draining very slowly. Brett called the plumber, who said that he had several large jobs in progress, but would be able to squeeze in Amy's repair at some point within the next few days. The plumber promised to call Brett before he came over. Brett relayed this information to Amy, telling her he would give her at least four hours' notice before the plumber came.

 Avoid hassles with repair people. Here's how:

- Be sure your landlord knows and trusts the service and repair people allowed to enter your rental unit. If new service providers are used, their references should be checked, and your landlord or manager should be present at all times.
- Try to be home (or ask your landlord to be present) when repairs will be made to avoid possible loss of or damage to your belongings or the rental unit.
- Always get the repair person's phone number in advance, so you can reschedule if need be.
- Make sure your landlord notifies you if plans change. You may be justifiably annoyed if the repair person shows up late or not at all.

c. Maintenance While You're Away

Several states with privacy statutes give landlords the legal right to enter rental premises if you are away for an extended period, often defined as seven days or more. The landlord is allowed to maintain the property as necessary and to inspect for damage and needed repairs. For example, if you live in a cold-weather place, such as Connecticut, your landlord may want to check the pipes in your house to make sure they haven't burst when you are away for winter vacation.

While many states do not address this issue, either by way of statute or court decision, your landlord is probably on safe legal ground to enter your rental

unit during your extended absence if there is a genuine need to protect the property from damage. But your landlord should enter only if something really needs to be done—that is, something you would do if you were home as part of your obligation to keep the property clean, safe and in good repair. (See Chapter 8 for a discussion of tenant repair and maintenance responsibilities.) For example, if you leave your windows wide open just before a driving rainstorm, your landlord would probably be justified in entering to close them.

 Check if your lease or rental agreement requires you to report extended absences. It may require you to inform your landlord when you will be gone for an extended time, such as two weeks, and give the landlord the right to enter the premises during these times. For example, in Alaska, where tenants are required by law to notify their landlords if they plan to be absent more than seven days, a landlord may enter without notice if the tenant has been gone for more than seven days without notification. (Alaska Stat. §§ 34.03.140, 34.03.230(b).) In general, if you plan to be gone for an extended time, it makes good sense to inform your landlord. Your landlord may be able to do the things (like draining the pipes) that will obviate the need to enter while you're gone.

d. Inspections

Some conscientious landlords schedule regular safety and maintenance inspections of their rental properties once or twice a year, in an effort to find small problems before they become big ones.

If this is your landlord's practice, your lease or rental agreement probably gives your landlord the right to enter your unit—after giving reasonable notice—to make this inspection. Even if it doesn't, your state law probably allows this type of entry. All states with privacy statutes, except California and Utah, grant landlords the right to inspect rental property. (See "State Laws on Landlord's Access to Rental Property" in Appendix I.)

⚠ **Don't put up with unnecessary, repeated inspections.** No unit should need inspecting more than once or twice a year absent a very specific reason—for example, to track down the source of a water leak, or to check the point of entry of a persistent ant or rodent infestation. If your landlord asks to inspect your unit too frequently, it may constitute illegal harassment. Section D, below, shows how to deal with this situation.

e. Showing the Property to Prospective Tenants or Purchasers

Most states with access laws allow landlords to enter rented property to show it to prospective tenants. If your landlord doesn't plan to renew your about-to-expire lease, or you have given or received a notice terminating your month-to-month tenancy, your landlord may show prospective new tenants around during the last few weeks (or even months) of your stay.

Also, a landlord may show your rental unit—whether an apartment in a multiple-unit building, single-family house or condominium unit—to potential buyers or mortgage companies.

Your landlord must follow the notice procedures discussed below. Typically, you are entitled to at least 24 hours' notice, and the landlord must enter at reasonable times.

It's no fun to have your last weeks or months in your current place constantly interrupted by prospective new tenants or buyers—after all, you are still paying the rent. Especially if you're not moving out voluntarily, it can seem like an intolerable intrusion to have your landlord or rental agent constantly parading people through.

If the landlord regularly wants to show the unit to prospective tenants or buyers on short notice, you have two options:

Notify your landlord in writing to follow the law or you will sue for invasion of privacy. (See Section D, below.) If you are planning to move out anyway, you might have nothing to lose by fully asserting your legal rights. But if you don't have a place lined up and are banking on a good recommendation, it just doesn't make sense to give your landlord a hard time.

Allow the unit to be shown on shorter notice in exchange for a reduction in the rent. This is a fair proposition since, after all, you are giving up some of the value of your rental home by letting lots of strangers waltz though. A smart landlord may well agree to pay a little something for your cooperation. For example, you might work out a deal with your landlord that two-hour notice is reasonable for up to three rental showings a week when you are home and three when you aren't, in exchange for having your rent reduced by a certain amount. Depending on how much you will be inconvenienced, a 10%-30% rent reduction might be reasonable.

For Sale or For Rent Signs

Occasionally, friction is caused by landlords who put "For Sale" or "For Rent" signs in front of an apartment building or a rented single-family house. Although your landlord may otherwise be very conscientious about respecting your privacy, putting a sign on the property is a flagrant invitation to prospective buyers or renters to disturb you.

In this age of computerized multiple-listing services, many real estate offices can, and commonly do, sell rental houses and buildings without ever placing a For Sale sign on the property, except perhaps when an open house is in progress. If a real estate office puts a sign in front of your building, you should insist that it clearly state a telephone number to call and warn against disturbing you, using words like "Inquire at 555-1357—Do Not Disturb Occupant." If this doesn't do the trick, and informal conversations with the landlord do not result in removal of the sign, write a firm letter explaining why your privacy is being invaded and ask your landlord to remove the sign. If this doesn't work, remove the sign yourself and return it to the landlord. If your landlord simply replaces the sign, you may sue for invasion of privacy, just as if the landlord personally had made repeated illegal entries.

![Warning icon] **Under no circumstances should your landlord place a key-holding "lock box" on the door.** This is a metal box that attaches to the front door and contains the key to that door. The box can be opened by a master key held by area real estate salespeople. Since a lock box allows any local salesperson to enter in disregard of any notice requirement, and when you're not home, it should not be used—period.

2. Notice Requirements

Most state access laws require landlords to give you 24 hours' to two days' notice before entering your rental unit in non-emergency situations. A few states simply require landlords to provide "reasonable" notice. See "How Much Notice Your Landlord Must Give You," below.

In many situations, you may not care a bit about getting the legally required amount of notice. You may be so delighted that your landlord is making needed repairs that you'll be standing by the door with coffee and a piece of cake. However, sometimes a landlord's request to enter to fix or inspect something is totally unreasonable. You won't welcome a surprise knock at your door by a landlord who wants to make a non-emergency repair or inspection when you are in the middle of cooking dinner for your book group, taking a nap or finish-

ing your income taxes. In such a situation, you have a legal right to deny entry and ask that a later appointment be scheduled. If you do so politely, and in a cooperative spirit, it shouldn't cause a problem.

Similarly, if your building is for sale and an over-eager real estate salesperson shows up on your doorstep with clients in tow, or your landlord calls on 20 minutes' notice and asks to be let in to show the place to a potential tenant, you are entirely within your rights to say politely but firmly, "I'm busy right now—try again in a day or so after we've set a time convenient for all of us."

![Tip icon] **Be sure your landlord knows how to reach you during the day, to give you notice of entry.** Without your work phone number, your landlord may be unable to give you adequate notice.

a. What's Reasonable Notice?

If your state only requires your landlord to give you "reasonable" notice before entering your rented home, you'll naturally want to know how this translates into hours and days. Twenty-four hours is generally presumed to be reasonable notice. In some circumstances, less notice (say, ten or fifteen hours) might be fine—for example, if your landlord finds out Thursday evening that an electrician is available Friday morning to put extra outlets in your apartment. Except for an emergency, less than four hours' notice is not ordinarily considered reasonable.

To find out precisely how your state's courts have interpreted the concept of reasonable notice, you'll need to look up their recent court decisions. (Chapter 20 explains how to find statutes and the cases that have dealt with them.)

![Tip icon] **Disabled tenants may be entitled to special notice.** A landlord who knows of a disabled tenant's unusual needs for privacy will be expected to accommodate the tenant's needs in all but true emergencies. (Chapter 5 discusses the rights of disabled tenants.)

How Much Notice Your Landlord Must Give You

This is a synopsis of state laws on the amount of notice landlords must give tenants before they enter. For details on reasons landlords may enter, and citations for state privacy laws, see "State Laws on Landlord's Access to Rental Property" in Appendix I.

State	Amount of notice required for landlord to enter	State	Amount of notice required for landlord to enter
Alabama	No statute	Montana	24 Hours
Alaska	24 Hours	Nebraska	One Day
Arizona	Two Days	Nevada	24 Hours
Arkansas	No statute	New Hampshire	Notice which is adequate under the circumstances
California	24 Hours		
Colorado	No statute	New Jersey	No statute
Connecticut	Reasonable notice	New Mexico	24 Hours
Delaware	Two Days	New York	No statute
District of Columbia	No statute	North Carolina	No statute
Florida	12 Hours	North Dakota	Reasonable notice
Georgia	No statute	Ohio	24 Hours
Hawaii	Two Days	Oklahoma	One Day
Idaho	No statute	Oregon	24 Hours
Illinois	No statute	Pennsylvania	No statute
Indiana	No statute	Rhode Island	Two Days
Iowa	24 Hours	South Carolina	24 Hours
Kansas	Reasonable notice	South Dakota	No statute
Kentucky	Two Days	Tennessee	No notice requirements in statute
Louisiana	No statute	Texas	No statute
Maine	24 Hours	Utah	No notice requirements in statute
Maryland	No statute	Vermont	48 Hours
Massachusetts	No notice requirements in statute	Virginia	Reasonable notice
Michigan	No statute	Washington	Two Days
Minnesota	Reasonable notice	West Virginia	No statute
Mississippi	No statute	Wisconsin	Reasonable notice
Missouri	No statute	Wyoming	No statute

b. Must Notice Be in Writing?

Not all states require that notice be in writing. But it's a good idea to ask your landlord for written notice whenever possible, especially if the landlord has entered without permission previously. Keep copies of these written notices in your rental file and also make a note of any oral requests for entry. Most importantly, if your landlord has entered without your permission or giving proper notice, make a note of the time, date and circumstances, listing the names of anyone else who witnessed or knows about the incident. This information will come in handy should you end up in a legal dispute with your landlord over this issue. (See Section D.)

c. Time of Day Landlord May Enter

Most state access laws either do not specify what hours a landlord may enter your rental unit or simply allow entry at reasonable times. Weekdays between 9 a.m. and 6 p.m. would seem to be reasonable times, and perhaps Saturdays between 10 a.m. and 1 p.m.

Some statutes are more specific. Delaware allows entry between 8 a.m. and 9 p.m. California specifies "normal business hours," leaving it open to whether Saturday or Saturday mornings are included.

3. Clarifying Access Rules

To make sure you and your landlord are operating on the same wavelength, be sure your lease or rental agreement includes a clause regarding landlord access to the property. If it doesn't, you may want to add a clause, or write a letter of understanding after you and the landlord have discussed the issue and come to an agreement. (Chapter 2 covers how to write a letter of understanding. Chapter 15 explains how to amend a lease or rental agreement.)

Spelling out clear guidelines is especially important if your state does not set specific rules regarding your landlord's entry. Ask your landlord to give you at least 24 hours' notice before entering your unit, except when there is a genuine emergency or you invite the landlord to enter. You might point out that this is the standard in many states. See the suggested lease clause in Chapter 2 for a good model.

4. Cooperating With Requests to Enter

Common sense suggests that if your landlord does not have a history of invading your privacy, you're better off accommodating requests for entry, especially if the purpose is to make repairs that will benefit you. By taking a reasonably cooperative approach, you'll go a long way toward avoiding disputes and legal problems. Here's why:

You might be evicted. In every state, your landlord has certain legal rights of access, regardless of any desire you have to be left alone. As long as your landlord complies with your state law as to reasons for entry and notice periods, your refusal to allow access can result in an eviction lawsuit.

Your tenancy might be terminated. Unless you have a long-term lease or live in a rent control city that requires the landlord to state a good reason (just cause) for eviction, you face the threat of losing your rental unit if your landlord concludes you are too difficult to deal with. Even though you may feel you are within your legal or moral rights to deny your landlord access to your rental unit, your landlord may simply give you a 30-day notice and terminate your tenancy rather than put up with you.

Your landlord might be less cooperative when you want a favor. If your landlord considers your desire for absolute privacy hard to cope with, don't expect much help when you make other requests. And you may get a negative reference when you eventually move on.

Adopting a reasonable attitude to landlord requests doesn't mean you should surrender your right to privacy and let your landlord enter at all hours of the day or night. No question—you should respond quickly to a landlord (or manager) who is entering without notice or good reason and make it clear that you won't tolerate clear violations of your privacy. (Section D, below, provides advice.) But don't be hard-nosed just for the principle involved.

B. Entry by Others

Your landlord is not the only one who may enter your rental unit. This section describes situations when other people, such as municipal inspectors, may want entry to your home.

1. Health, Safety or Building Inspections

While your state may give you significant protections against entry by your landlord, the rules are different when it comes to entry by state or local health, safety or building inspectors.

a. Neighbor's Complaints

If inspectors have credible reasons to suspect that your unit violates housing codes or local standards—for example, your neighbor has complained about noxious smells coming from your home or about your 20 cats—they will usually knock on your door and ask permission to enter. Except in the case of genuine emergency, you have the right to say no.

Inspectors have ways to get around tenant refusals. A logical first step (maybe even before they stop by your rental unit) is to ask your landlord in advance to let them in. Since your landlord can usually enter on 24 hours' notice, this is probably the simplest approach. If inspectors can't reach your landlord, or get cooperation, their next step will probably be to get a search warrant based on the information from your neighbor. The inspectors must first convince a judge that the source of their information—the neighbor—is reliable, and that there is a strong likelihood that public health or safety is at risk. Inspectors who believe that you

will refuse entry often bring along police officers who, armed with a search warrant, have the right to do whatever it takes to overcome your objections.

b. Random Inspections

Fire, health and other municipal inspectors sometimes randomly inspect apartment buildings even if they don't suspect noncompliance. These inspections may be allowed under state law or local ordinance. (Most ordinances exempt single-family homes and condominiums.) The inspectors may contact your landlord first and ask permission to enter. If the landlord says yes and gives you 24 hours' notice (or whatever your state requires), the inspection can proceed. If the landlord refuses entry, the inspector will almost surely have a judge issue a search warrant, allowing him to enter to check for fire or safety violations. Again, if there is any expectation that you may resist, a police officer will usually accompany the inspector.

An inspector who arrives when you're not home may ask the landlord to open your door on the spot, in violation of your state's privacy laws. If the inspector's come with a warrant, the landlord can probably give consent, since even you couldn't prevent entry. But if the inspector is there without a warrant, your landlord probably cannot speak for you and say "Come on in." However, the answer will depend on each state's interpretation of its laws regarding warrantless entries. Since municipal inspection programs are relatively new, few courts have decided the issue. Cautious landlords will ask an inspector without a warrant to enter after the landlord has given you the proper amount of notice, under your state's law or the terms of your lease or rental agreement.

States With Municipal Inspections

Some cities in these states have municipal inspection programs. Since the idea is a popular one (at the very least, it's a revenue generator for the city), you can expect that the list will steadily grow.

California	New Jersey (statewide and
Colorado	additional city ordinances)
Florida	North Carolina
Indiana	Ohio
Kansas	Pennsylvania
Louisiana	South Dakota
Minnesota	Texas
Missouri	Virginia (statewide)

To find out whether your city has an inspection ordinance, ask your landlord. You can also call your city manager's or mayor's office.

c. Inspection Fees

Many cities impose fees for inspections, on a per unit or building basis or a sliding scale based on the number of a landlord's holdings. Some fees are imposed only if violations are found. If your ordinance imposes fees regardless of violations, you may find the inspection cost passed on to you in the form of a rent hike. It's not illegal for your landlord to do this, and even in rent-controlled cities, the cost of an inspection might justify a rent increase. (See Chapter 3 for information on how landlords may legally increase rents.)

If your ordinance imposes a fee only when violations are found, your landlord should not pass the cost on to you if the non-compliance is not your fault. For example, if inspectors find that the landlord has failed to install state-mandated smoke alarms, the landlord should pay for the inspection; but if you have allowed garbage to pile up in violation of city health laws, you can expect the inspector's bill.

2. Police

Even the police may not enter your rental unit unless they can show you or your landlord a recently-issued search or arrest warrant, signed by a judge. The police do not need a search warrant, however, if they need to enter to prevent a catastrophe, such as an assault or fire, if they are in hot pursuit of a fleeing criminal or if they need to enter to preserve evidence of a serious crime.

3. Your Landlord's Right to Let Others In

Your landlord has no right to give others permission to enter your home. (Municipal inspections and the police, however, may pose an exception. See subsection 1, above.)

Occasionally a landlord or resident manager will be faced with a very convincing stranger who will tell a heart-rending story:

- "I'm Nancy's boyfriend and I need to get my clothes out of her closet now that I'm moving to New York"
- "If I don't get my heart medicine that I left in this apartment, I'll die on the spot," or
- "I'm John's father and I just got in from the North Pole, where a polar bear ate my wallet, and I have no other place to stay."

Of course, if the landlord asks you and you authorize entry, there's no problem. But what if the landlord can't contact you at work or elsewhere to ask whether it's okay to let the desperate individual in? This is one reason why your landlord should always know how to reach you during the day.

The story the desperate person tells your landlord may be the truth, and chances are that if you could be contacted, you would say "Yes, let Uncle Harry in immediately." But the landlord can't know this, and letting anyone enter your home without your permission invades your privacy. The landlord risks being legally responsible should your property be stolen or damaged. If your landlord does let a stranger in without your permission, you can sue her for any loss you suffer as a result.

C. Other Invasions of Privacy

Entering your home without your knowledge or consent isn't the only way a landlord can interfere with your privacy. Here are a few other common situations, with advice on how to handle them.

1. Giving Information About You to Strangers

Your landlord may be asked by strangers, including creditors, banks and prospective landlords, to provide credit or other information about you. Did you pay the rent on time? Did you maintain the rental property? Cause any problems? As with letting a stranger into your home, what your landlord says may cause you considerable anxiety.

Basically, your landlord has a legal right to give out truthful business information about you to people and businesses who ask and have a legitimate reason to know—for example, your bank when you apply for a loan or a prospective landlord who wants a reference. An extra-cautious landlord will ask for your written permission to release credit and similar information, but as long as the landlord's answer is in response to a legitimate request, a formal release is not legally required. (See the release form at the bottom of the rental application in Chapter 1.)

If a landlord gives out negative information on you, it should be absolutely factual. If your landlord spreads false stories about you—for example, says you filed for bankruptcy if this isn't true—and you suffer a loss as a result (for example, you don't get a job)—you can sue the landlord for defamation (libel or slander).

A landlord (or, more typically, an on-site manager) who makes a big effort to spread negative information (whether or not true) risks an invasion of privacy lawsuit. Examples include calling other landlords in your area to bad-mouth you, broadcasting that you haven't paid the rent or telling others that you drink too much. This sort of gossip has no legitimate purpose and is malicious and damaging.

It amounts to an invasion of privacy for which you may have a valid reason to sue.

2. Bothering You at Work

Your landlord should have your work phone number in case there's an emergency. However, situations justifying a landlord calling you at work are fairly rare. If a landlord calls you to complain about late rent payments or other problems, politely say you'll talk when you're at home. If this doesn't work, follow up with a brief note.

If the landlord persists or tries to talk to your boss or other employees about the problem ("Tell your deadbeat employee I'll evict her if she doesn't pay the rent"), your privacy is definitely being invaded. Write a letter asking the landlord to stop immediately. If the conduct continues, consider going to small claims court to sue for damages. If as a result of the landlord's conduct you lose your job or a promotion, see a lawyer. You may have the basis for a successful lawsuit.

3. Unduly Restricting Guests

Some landlords limit guests' visits—for example, no more than ten days in any six-month period—to avoid having a guest turn into an illegal subtenant. (See Chapter 7.) A few landlords, overly concerned about possible new occupants, go overboard in keeping tabs on legitimate guests who stay overnight or for a few days. Some leases, rental agreements or rules and regulations will require you to register any overnight guest. While your landlord has a legitimate concern about persons who begin as guests becoming permanent unauthorized residents of the property, it is overkill to require you to inform your landlord of a guest whose stay is only for a day or two.

In short, while your landlord does have a right to control who lives in the rental unit, your social life is your own business. Extreme behavior in this area—whether by an owner or a management employee—can be considered an invasion of privacy for which you may sue.

4. Spying on You

A few landlords have attempted to interrogate visitors, knock on tenants' doors at odd hours to see who answers or even peek through windows. Needless to say, this sort of conduct can give you cause to sue a landlord for invasion of privacy.

Drug dealing is an exception. A landlord's intrusive behavior may be excused if a tenant, guest or family member is dealing drugs or engaging in other illegal behavior on the rental property. Landlords have a responsibility to keep their properties safe, which includes kicking drug dealers out pronto when they are discovered. Other tenants and neighbors, as well as government agencies, may bring costly lawsuits against landlords who allow drug dealing on their properties. Chapter 14 discusses how this affects a tenant's privacy rights.

5. Self-Help Evictions

It is generally illegal for the landlord to come on the property and do such things as take off windows and doors, turn off the utilities or change the locks. (Chapter 18 discusses illegal "self-help" evictions.)

6. Sexual Harassment or Assault

If your landlord or manager comes onto your property or into your home and harms you in any way, sexually harasses you (see Chapter 5), threatens you or damages any of your property, see an attorney pronto. You should also report the matter to the police. Some local police departments have taken the excellent step of setting up special landlord-tenant units. The officers and legal experts in these units have been given special training in landlord-tenant law and are often helpful in settling disputes and setting straight a landlord who has taken illegal measures against a tenant.

You might have a discrimination claim. As we explain in Chapter 5, if you are single, female, disabled or of a certain race, religion or ethnicity, and only you have been harassed by the landlord, he may be violating fair housing laws.

D. What to Do About Invasions of Privacy

Suppose now your landlord does violate your rights of privacy—what can you do about it?

As you have undoubtedly long since figured out, it is one thing to have a right, and quite another thing to enforce it. This is especially true for tenants who do not have a long-term lease and do not live in a city where a rent control ordinance requires just cause for eviction. In these situations, if you set about aggressively demanding your rights, you may end up with a termination notice. So perhaps a softer approach is the most sensible. None of this means you shouldn't be firm and determined in asserting your rights, but rather, that being strident may be counterproductive.

Landlords often don't know what their managers are doing. If your manager is invading your privacy, don't assume the landlord is at fault. Instead, it's best to assume the landlord doesn't know and won't approve when he does. So tell the landlord promptly and politely that you expect better. Follow up with a written note if the problem continues.

Here is a step-by-step approach that usually works in dealing with a landlord who is violating your right to privacy.

1. Talk to the Landlord or Manager

As a first step, voice your concerns in a friendly but firm way. If you come to an understanding, follow up with a note to confirm it.

Sample Letter When Landlord Violates Privacy (Friendly Approach)

February 5, 200X

Joan Smith
123 Main St.
Portland, Oregon 00000

Dear Ms. Smith:

Thanks for sending your plumber over yesterday to fix my bathtub leak. I really appreciate your prompt response. As I mentioned, I would have preferred to be home when the plumber came because I often work at home and need to be able to count on uninterrupted periods of time. As we discussed, next time you'll give me at least 24 hours' notice so I can plan accordingly.

Thanks again.

Sincerely,

Jon Klein

Jon Klein
Green Gables Apartment #4B
526 Grover Road
Portland, Oregon

Work with other tenants. Chances are that if your landlord has entered your home repeatedly and without good reason or notice, other tenants in the building or complex have had the same problem. Talk to your neighbors and find out. If so, you have a golden opportunity to organize your neighbors and exert concerted pressure by using, together, the steps outlined in this section. For all the obvious reasons, your group complaints will be taken more seriously and given more attention than if you are acting alone. (See Chapter 19 for tips on how to organize fellow tenants.)

2. Write a Tough Letter

If the friendly, informal approach doesn't work, or if your landlord doesn't follow the agreement that you have worked out, it's time for a stronger, more formal letter that sets forth your legal rights and explains what you'll do if they aren't respected. Assuming you are willing to risk alienating your landlord—perhaps because you have a lease and don't feel vulnerable or because your relationship is already bad—your letter should threaten a small claims lawsuit if the landlord's illegal conduct doesn't stop pronto. This can be an especially effective technique if a group of tenants is working together.

A sample letter is shown below.

 **Writing a demand letter like this will greatly improve your chances of winning a small claims court lawsuit, if you decide to go ahead and sue.** For advice on using small claims court, see Chapter 19.

Sample Letter When Landlord Violates Privacy (Get Tough Approach)

September 19, 200X

Jan Roper Real Estate Co.
11 Peach Street
Cleveland, Ohio 00000

Dear Mr. Roper:

Several times in the last two months your resident manager, Pete Tuttle, has entered my apartment when I was not at home and without notifying me in advance. Following the second such visit, I wrote to you on August 20, demanding that these unannounced entries stop at once.

In spite of my letter, Pete continued to enter when I was not home and without notice. One time when I was home sick from work, he simply walked in without knocking.

In no situation was any emergency involved, and there was no real purpose for these visits. These intrusions have caused me considerable anxiety and stress, to the point that my peaceful enjoyment of my tenancy has been seriously disrupted.

This letter is to formally notify you that I value my privacy highly and insist that my legal rights to that privacy, as guaranteed to me under Ohio Rev. Code Ann. §§ 5321.04(B), 5321.05(B), be respected. Specifically, in non-emergency situations, I am entitled to 24 hours' notice of your (or your employee's) intent to enter my home, and a clearly stated purpose of the entry.

I assume this notice will be sufficient to correct this matter. If you want to talk about this, please call me at home (555-7890) at night before 10 p.m.

Yours truly,

Sally South

Sally South
789 Porter St., #3
Cleveland, Ohio

Try mediation before filing a lawsuit. It's always preferable in terms of cost, energy and outcome. Mediation by a neutral third party is an especially good way to resolve disputes with your landlord when you want to continue living in your current rental unit. See Chapter 19 for details on finding and using a mediation service.

3. Sue Your Landlord

If, despite your second letter, the invasions of your privacy continue, document them and either see a lawyer or take your landlord to small claims court.

Depending on the circumstances, you may be able to sue your landlord for:

- Trespass: entering your rental space without consent or proper authority
- Invasion of privacy: interfering with your right to be left alone
- Breach of implied covenant of quiet enjoyment: interfering with your right to undisturbed use of your home. (Chapter 8, Section A, discusses the implied covenant of quiet enjoyment.)
- Infliction of emotional distress: a pattern of illegal acts by someone (in this case, the landlord or manager) who intended to cause serious emotional consequences to you.

One difficulty with a lawsuit against a landlord guilty of unlawful entry is that it may be hard to prove much in the way of money damages. Most likely, a judge will figure that you have not been harmed much by the fact that your landlord walked on your rug and opened and closed your door—and you won't be awarded much money to compensate you.

However, if you can show a repeated pattern of illegal entry (and the fact that you asked the landlord to stop it) or even one clear example of outrageous conduct, you may be able to get a substantial recovery. You'll probably want an attorney for this kind of case, especially if you bring your case in a court other than small claims court.

Here are examples of two recent court cases based on a landlord's unlawful entry.

EXAMPLE: Debra rented a townhouse from Grace. Grace approached Debra with a suggestion that they go into business together, but Debra declined. Feeling spurned, Grace demanded that Debra's co-tenant leave. She called both tenants at home and at work, changed their locks, yelled obscenities and ripped out their phone jack. Debra moved out, losing her pre-paid rent, security deposit and incurring temporary housing costs. Debra sued Grace for trespass and, because the trespass was deliberate and outrageous, for emotional distress as well. The state appellate court directed the trial court, which had initially thrown the case out, to let it go to the jury. (*Johnson v. Marcel*, 465 S.E. 2d 815. Va. 1996).)

EXAMPLE: In New York, a landlord entered his tenant's apartment several times without permission. Although the entries did not make the premises unusable, they violated the tenant's reasonable expectation of privacy and New York's law that required the landlord to provide habitable premises. A judge ruled that the tenant was entitled to a retroactive rent abatement of 15%. (*Steltzer v. Spesaison*, 614 N.Y.S.2d 488 (1994).)

 Chapter 20 shows how to find and work with a lawyer. Chapter 19 discusses small claims court suits and dollar limits in each state.

4. Move Out

Repeated abuses by a landlord of your right of privacy may give you a legal excuse to break a lease or end a tenancy early, without liability for further rent. If the landlord sues you for the rent after you leave, your defense can be that repeated intrusions made it impossible for you to "quietly enjoy" your rented home—a right guaranteed to every tenant. Or you can argue that the landlord's repeated entries amounted to an eviction (lawyers call it "constructive eviction"), justifying your departure.

Don't take the law into your own hands.
You do not have the right to attack a landlord who invades your privacy. If you have good reason to fear that you or your property may be harmed, call the police. ■

12

Injuries on the Premises

I f you have been injured on your landlord's property, you may have a good legal claim against your landlord. That doesn't mean you'll have to file a lawsuit—over 90% of valid claims against landlords are settled without trial. It may well be to your advantage to negotiate with the landlord's insurance adjuster or lawyer yourself, rather than to immediately hire a lawyer, who will typically take one-third of your recovery. If the landlord or insurer proves unreasonable, you can always hire a lawyer.

This chapter explains how to evaluate whether your landlord is liable for your injury, and what to do to maximize your chances of a just settlement or lawsuit verdict.

Related topics covered in this book include:
- Landlords' repair and maintenance responsibilities: Chapters 8 and 9.
- Landlords' legal responsibility to provide premises that are safe from criminal acts: Chapter 14.
- How to recognize and deal with common environmental hazards: Chapter 13.
- How to sue for a landlord's tolerance of a legal "nuisance": Chapter 14.
- How to research your state's laws on personal injuries: Chapter 20.
- How to choose and work with a lawyer: Chapter 20.

A. What to Do If You're Injured

What is the best course of action to take if you're injured? If your injury is significant and costly—it has resulted in lost work, doctor's bills and physical or emotional discomfort—and you think the landlord is at fault, you'll want to consider legal action. But don't go rushing off to the nearest personal injury lawyer just yet. Especially if your injury isn't very severe, you may be better off—at least initially—handling the claim yourself.

But if your injury is severe, see a lawyer right away. Injuries in this category include:

- a long-term or permanently disabling injury, such as the loss of a limb
- an injury that results in medical costs and lost income over $10,000, or
- heavy-duty toxic exposure, such as pesticide poisoning.

This book can't cover all the ins and outs of pursuing a personal injury claim. Here, however, is an outline of the basic steps you should follow.

An injured guest may have a hard time pinning liability on your landlord. In all states, landlords are expected to take reasonable steps to avoid tenant injuries. (See Section B1.) But in some states, landlords get by with a lower standard of care when it comes to non-tenants. If you're reading this chapter on behalf of an injured guest, you'll need to know your state's approach to injuries suffered by non-tenants. Chapter 20 gives tips on how to approach a legal research task in the library.

1. Get Immediate Medical Attention

The success of an accident claim often depends on what you do in the first hours and days after your injury. Although you may be in pain, angry or even depressed, attention to these details immediately following the incident will pay off later.

It is essential to get prompt medical attention for your injury, even if you consider it to be of marginal help to your physical recovery. No insurance company, judge or jury will take your word alone for the extent of your injury, pain and suffering. It may seem obvious to you that a sprained ankle caused immobility, swelling and pain and made you miss a week's work. Nonetheless, you'll need the confirmation of a physician, and the professional opinion that you didn't suffer a mere soft tissue bruise, when it comes to convincing a skeptical insurance adjuster or jury of your injury's impact.

Moreover, if you intend to hold the landlord financially responsible for your injuries, the law expects you to take whatever steps are possible to lessen the extent of your injuries and speed your recovery. Oddly, the reason has little to do with concern for your physical well-being; rather, the law expects you to take reasonable steps to lessen the accident's financial impact on the landlord. In short, you'll need the verification of a doctor that you were a conscientious patient who did not prolong or ignore your injuries.

> EXAMPLE: May-Ling, a new tenant, slipped on a puddle of oil-slicked rainwater that habitually accumulated at the base of the garage stairs. She fell on and badly twisted her back. Thinking that time would heal her wounds, she did not seek medical attention, though she did stay home from work for a week.
>
> She then filed a claim with the landlord's insurance company, seeking compensation for her pain and suffering and lost wages. The insurance adjuster questioned the severity of her injury, and suggested that, had she consulted a doctor, she might have recovered sooner with the aid of muscle-relaxing medication. Unable to verify the extent of her injury and having no way to effectively answer the claim that medical attention might have helped her, May-Ling settled her claim for a disappointing amount.

2. Write Everything Down

As soon as possible after the accident, jot down everything you can remember about how it happened. Include a complete list of everyone who was present and what they said. For example, if, after you tripped on a loose stair, the manager rushed over and blurted out, "I told Jim [the landlord] we should have replaced that last month!", be sure to write it down and note the names of anyone who heard the manager say it.

Describe the precise nature of your injuries, including pain, anxiety and loss of sleep. Make notes of every economic loss, such as lost wages, missed classes and events and transportation and medical costs. If you have a conversation regarding the incident with anyone (the landlord, other tenants, an insurance adjuster or medical personnel), make a written summary of the conversation.

3. Preserve Evidence

Claims are often won by the production of a persuasive piece of physical evidence: the worn or broken stair that caused the fall, the unattached throw rug that slipped when stepped on, the electrical outlet faceplate that showed burn marks from a short. Remember that physical evidence that is not preserved within a short time can be lost, modified by time or weather, repaired or destroyed. For example, the landlord, not wanting more accidents, may quickly replace a loose stair that caused you to fall, and throw the old one away.

If preservation of the evidence would involve dismantling the landlord's property, you may have to settle for the next best alternative, photographs or videos. Don't wait—make your record before repairs are made. Be sure to develop the film immediately and have the date stamped on the reel or the back of the prints, or at least get a dated receipt. And to forestall challenges to the accuracy of your pictures (or a claim they were doctored), have someone else take them and be prepared to testify in court that they are a fair and accurate depiction of the scene.

4. Contact Witnesses

Having an eyewitness can be an immeasurable help. Witnesses can corroborate your version of events and may even have seen important aspects of the situation that you missed. But you must act very quickly to find and preserve the observations and memories of those who could bolster your case—people's memories fade quickly, and strangers can be very hard to track down later.

Don't tell witnesses not to talk to the "other side." Witnesses have no legal obligation to talk to you, although most will if they feel you have been wronged. Similarly, you have no legal right to tell them not to talk to others. Moreover, trying to do so may come back to haunt you via a suggestion that you had something to hide. If a favorable witness tells an insurance adjuster a different story, you can expose the inconsistencies later in court.

If you find people who witnessed the incident, get their names, addresses and as much information about what they saw as possible. Talk with them about what they saw and write it up. Ask them if they would be willing to review your summary for accuracy; if so, mail them a copy and ask them to correct it, sign it and return it to you in the stamped envelope you have provided.

Don't overlook the witness who heard or saw another witness. It can often be important to have a witness to what another witness said or did. For example, the manager who blurted out "I told him we should have fixed that last month"

will have every incentive to deny making that statement, since it pins knowledge of the defect on the property owner. If someone besides you also heard the manager say it, he'll have a tougher time disowning it.

5. Evaluate Your Case

Before you go making demands for money from your landlord or an insurance company, you need to know whether or not you have a legal leg to stand on. That's what most of the rest of this chapter explains.

6. Notify the Landlord and the Insurance Carrier

Write to the owner of the rental property, stating that you have been injured and need to deal with the owner's liability insurance carrier. You should have the owner's name and address on your lease or rental agreement. If you deal with a manager or management company, you should also notify them.

If a third party is involved, it won't hurt to notify them, too, if there is some basis for thinking that they may have been at least partially responsible. For example, a contractor or subcontractor may have created or contributed to the dangerous situation, or a repair person may have done a faulty job, causing your injury.

A sample letter is shown below. If your case is substantial, you can expect that the owner will contact the insurer right away. On the other hand, a landlord who suspects that the claim is phony or trivial may hold off notifying the insurance company, fearing a rate increase. You cannot force the landlord to refer the case or disclose the name of the insurer; all you can do is persevere until your persistence and the threat of a lawsuit become real enough for the landlord to call in the insurance company's help.

Sample Letter to Landlord Regarding Tenant Injury

Alice Watson
37 Ninth Avenue North
South Fork, RI 00000
401-555-4567

February 28, 200X

Fernando Diaz
3757 East Seventh Street
South Fork, RI 00000

Dear Mr. Diaz:

On February 25, 200X, I was injured in a fall on the front steps of the duplex that I rent from you. The middle step splintered and collapsed as I walked down the stairs. Please refer this matter to the carrier of your business liability insurance and have them contact me at the above address.

Thank you for your cooperation.

Yours truly,

Alex Watson

Alex Watson

7. Negotiate, Mediate or Sue

If you are successful at reaching the landlord's insurance carrier, chances are that you'll negotiate a settlement. You may choose mediation (in which a neutral third party helps both sides reach a settlement) if you feel that the landlord is interested in settling the matter and will deal with you fairly. (If the result isn't adequate, you can always file a lawsuit.) But if the landlord stonewalls you, refusing to refer your claim to the insurance carrier or a lawyer, you may need to consider a lawsuit. Chapter 19 gives detailed information on negotiating with, mediating with and suing your landlord if necessary. It

also helps you decide whether to take your case to small claims court yourself, saving time and the expense of hiring a lawyer, or whether you are better off in a formal court with a lawyer.

Don't wait too long before filing suit. You must file your lawsuit within the time specified by your state's "statute of limitations." Most states give you one to four years after your injury. Check your state statutes for the deadline that applies to personal injury cases. Chapter 20 gives information on how to look up a statute.

How to Win Your Personal Injury Claim, by Joseph L. Matthews (Nolo), explains personal injury cases and how to work out a fair settlement without going to court

Everybody's Guide to Small Claims Court, by Ralph Warner (Nolo), provides great advice on small claims courts, which, in most states, allow you to sue for amounts up to $3,000 to $7,500.

Represent Yourself in Court, by Paul Bergman and Sara Berman-Barrett (Nolo), will help you prepare and present your case should you end up in court.

Mediate Your Dispute, by Peter Lovenheim (Nolo), gives detailed information on the mediation process.

How to Sue for Up to $25,000…and Win! by Roderic Duncan (Nolo), is a step-by-step guide to suing (and defending) in municipal court in California.

B. Is the Landlord Liable?

It isn't always easy to determine whether or not the landlord is legally responsible for an injury. Basically, your landlord may be liable for your injuries if those injuries resulted from:

- the landlord's unreasonably careless conduct
- the landlord's violation of a health or safety law
- the landlord's failure to make certain repairs

- the landlord's failure to keep the premises habitable, or
- the landlord's reckless or intentional acts.

And in rare instances, the landlord may be liable because courts or the legislature in your state have decided that landlords are automatically liable for certain kinds of injuries, even though they haven't been careless.

Keep in mind that several of these legal theories may apply in your situation, and you (and your lawyer) can use all of them when pressing your claim. The more plausible reasons you can give for your landlord's liability, the better you will do when you negotiate with the landlord's insurance company.

1. The Landlord Was Unreasonably Careless

Most personal injury claims against landlords charge that the landlord acted negligently—that is, acted carelessly, in a way that wasn't reasonable under the circumstances—and that the injury was caused by that carelessness.

Negligence is always determined in light of the unique facts of each situation. For example, it may be reasonable to put adequate lights in a dark, remote stairwell. If your landlord doesn't, and you're hurt because you couldn't see the steps and fell, your landlord's failure to install the lights might be negligence. On the other hand, extra lights in a lobby that's already well-lit might not be a reasonable expectation.

To determine whether or not your landlord was negligent and should be held responsible for your injury, you must answer six questions. The insurance adjuster will use these same questions to evaluate your claim. If your case looks strong, you'll probably be able to wrest a good settlement offer from the company. And if you don't, you'll be able to head to court confidently, where a judge or jury will use the same questions when deciding your case.

Evaluating Negligence Cases

If you think your landlord's carelessness caused your injury, you'll need answers to these questions before you can expect to recover damages:

1. Did your landlord control the area where you were hurt or the thing that hurt you?
2. How likely was it that an accident would occur?
3. How difficult or expensive would it have been for the landlord to reduce the risk of injury?
4. Was a serious injury likely to result from the problem?
5. Did your landlord fail to take reasonable steps to prevent an accident?
6. Did your landlord's failure to take reasonable steps to keep you safe cause your injury?

Question 1: Did your landlord control the area where you were hurt or the thing that hurt you? For example, the property owner normally has control over a stairway in a common area, and if its chronic disrepair causes a tenant to fall, the owner will likely be held liable. The owner also has control over the building's utility systems. If a malfunction causes injury (like boiling water in your sink because of a broken thermostat), he may likewise be held responsible.

Question 2: How likely was it that an accident would occur? The landlord isn't responsible if the accident wasn't foreseeable. For example, common sense would tell anyone that loose handrails or stairs are likely to lead to accidents, but it would be unusual for injuries to result from peeling wallpaper or a thumbtack that's fallen from a bulletin board. If a freak accident does happen, chances are your landlord will not be held liable.

Question 3: How difficult or expensive would it have been for the landlord to reduce the risk of injury? The chances that your landlord will be held liable are greater if a reasonably priced response could have averted the accident. In other words, could something as simple as warning signs, a bright light or caution tape have prevented people from tripping over an unexpected step leading to the patio, or would major structural remodeling have been necessary to reduce the likelihood of injury? But if there is a great risk of very serious injury, a landlord will be expected to spend money to avert it. For example, a high-rise deck with rotten support beams must be repaired, regardless of the cost, since there is a great risk of collapse and dreadful injuries to anyone on the deck. A landlord who knew about the condition of the deck and failed to repair it would surely be held liable if an accident did occur.

Question 4: Was a serious injury likely to result from the problem? The amount of time and money your landlord is expected to spend on making his premises safe will also depend on the seriousness of the probable injury if he fails to do so. For example, if the umbrella on a poolside table wouldn't open, no one would expect it to cause serious injury. If you're sunburned at the pool as a result, it's not likely that a judge would rule that your landlord had the duty of keeping you from getting burned. But if a major injury is the likely result of a dangerous situation—the pool ladder was broken, making it likely you'd fall as you climbed out—the owner is expected to take the situation more seriously and fix it faster.

The answers to these four questions should tell you (or an insurance adjuster or judge) whether or not there was a dangerous condition on the landlord's property that the landlord had a legal duty to deal with. Lawyers call this having a "duty of due care."

Let's look at how these first four questions would get answered in a few possible scenarios.

EXAMPLE 1: Mark broke his leg when he tripped on a loose step on the stairway from the lobby to the first floor. Since the step had been loose for several months, chances are the landlord's insurance company would settle a claim like this.

Mark's position is strong because of the answers to the four questions:

1. The landlord was legally responsible for (in control of) the condition of the common stairways.
2. It was highly foreseeable to any reasonable person that someone would slip on a loose step.
3. Securing the step would have been simple and inexpensive.
4. The probable result of leaving the stair loose—falling and injuring oneself on the stairs—is a serious matter.

EXAMPLE 2: Lee slipped on a marble that had been dropped on the public sidewalk outside his apartment by another tenant's child just a few minutes earlier. Lee twisted his ankle and lost two weeks' work. Lee will have a tough time establishing that his landlord had a duty to protect him from this injury. Here's what the questions turn up:

1. The landlord has little control over the public sidewalk.
2. The likelihood of injury from something a tenant drops is fairly low.
3. The burden on the landlord to eliminate all possible problems at all times by constant inspecting or sweeping the sidewalk is unreasonable.
4. Finally, the seriousness of the likely injury as a result of not checking constantly is open to great debate.

EXAMPLE 3: James suffered a concussion when he hit his head on a dull-colored overhead beam in the apartment garage. When the injury occurred, he was standing in the back of his pickup, loading items onto the roof rack. Did the landlord have a duty to take precautions in this situation? Probably not, but the answers to the four questions are not so easy.

1. The landlord exercises control over the garage, and certainly has a responsibility to reasonably protect tenants from harm there.
2. The likelihood of injury from a beam is fairly slim, since most people don't stand

on trucks, and those who do have the opportunity to see the beam and avoid it.

3. As to eliminating the condition that led to the injury, it's highly unlikely anyone would expect the landlord to rebuild the garage. But it's possible that a judge might think it reasonable to paint the beams a bright color and post warning signs, especially if lots of people put trucks and other large vehicles in the garage.

4. As to the seriousness of probable harm, injury from low beams is likely to be to the head, which is a serious matter.

In short, this situation is too close to call, but if an insurance adjuster or jury considered the case, they might decide that James was partially at fault (for not watching out for the beams) and reduce any award accordingly. (See Section C, below.)

If, based on these first four questions, you think the landlord had a legal duty to deal with a condition on the premises that posed a danger to you, keep going. You have two more questions to answer.

Question 5: Did your landlord fail to take reasonable steps to prevent an accident? For example, if you've demonstrated that a stair was in a dangerous condition, you also need to show that the landlord's failure to fix it was unreasonable in the circumstances. Let's take the broken step that Mark (Example 1, above) tripped over. Obviously, leaving it broken for months is unreasonably careless—that is, negligent—under the circumstances.

But what if the step had torn loose only an hour earlier, when another tenant dragged a heavy footlocker up the staircase? Mark's landlord would probably concede that he had a duty to maintain the stairways, but would argue that the manager's daily sweeping and inspection of the stairs that same morning met that burden. In the absence of being notified of the problem, he would probably claim that his inspection routine met his duty of keeping the stairs safe. If a jury agreed, Mark would not be able to establish that the landlord acted unreasonably under the circumstances.

Question 6: Did your landlord's failure to take reasonable steps to keep you safe cause your injury? This last question establishes the crucial link between the landlord's negligence and your injury. Not every dangerous situation results in an accident. You'll have to prove that your injury was the result of the landlord's carelessness, and not some other reason. Sometimes this is self-evident: One minute you're fine, and the next minute you've slipped on a freshly waxed floor and have a broken arm. But it's not always so simple. For example, in the case of the loose stair, the landlord might be able to show that the tenant barely lost his balance because of the loose stair and that he had really injured his ankle during a touch football game he'd just played.

Here's a final example, applying all six questions to a tenant's injury.

EXAMPLE: Scotty's apartment complex had a pool bordered by a concrete deck. On his way to the pool, Scotty slipped and fell, breaking his arm. The concrete where he fell was slick because the landlord had cleaned the pool and spilled some of the cleaning solution earlier that morning. To assess his chances of collecting against his landlord for his injury, Scotty asked himself these questions:

1. Did the landlord control the pool area and the cleaning solution? Absolutely. The pool was part of a common area, and the landlord had done the cleaning.

2. Was an accident like Scotty's foreseeable? Certainly. It's likely that a barefoot person heading for the pool would slip on slick cement.

3. Could the landlord have eliminated the dangerous condition without much effort or money? Of course. All that was necessary was to hose the deck down.

4. How serious was the probable injury? Falling on cement presents a high likelihood of broken bones, a serious injury.

Having established that the landlord owed him a duty of care, Scotty considered the rest of his case.

5. Had his landlord also breached this duty? Yes; Scotty was sure a jury would conclude that leaving spilled cleaning solution on the deck was an unreasonable thing to do.

6. Did the spilled cleaning solution cause his fall? This one is easy, because several people saw the accident and others could describe Scotty's robust fitness before the fall. Scotty hadn't himself been careless (see Section C, below), so he decided he had a pretty good case.

Examples of Injuries From Landlord Negligence

Here are some examples of injuries for which tenants have recovered money damages due to the landlord's negligence:

- Tenant falls down a staircase due to a defective handrail.
- Tenant trips over a hole in the carpet on a common stairway not properly maintained by the landlord.
- Tenant injured and property damaged by fire resulting from an obviously defective heater or wiring.
- Tenant gets sick from pesticide sprayed in common areas and on exterior walls without advance notice.
- Tenant's child is scalded by water from a water heater with a broken thermostat.
- Tenant slips and falls on a puddle of oil-slicked rainwater in the garage.
- Tenant's guest injured when she slips on ultra-slick floor wax applied by the landlord's cleaning service.
- Tenant receives electrical burns when attempting to insert the stove's damaged plug into the wall outlet.
- Tenant slips and falls on wet grass cuttings left on a common walkway.

---

2. The Landlord Violated a Health or Safety Law

Many state and local governments have enacted health and safety laws requiring smoke detectors, sprinklers, inside-release security bars on windows, childproof fences around a swimming pools and so on. To put real teeth behind these important laws, legislators (and sometimes the courts) have decided that if a landlord doesn't take reasonable steps to comply with certain health or safety statutes, he will be legally considered negligent. And if that negligence results in an injury, the landlord is liable for it. You don't need to prove that an accident was foreseeable or likely to be serious; nor do you have to show that complying with the law would have been relatively inexpensive. The legal term for this rule is "negligence per se."

> EXAMPLE: A local housing code specifies that all kitchens must have grounded power plugs. There are no grounded plugs in your kitchen. As a result, you're injured when using an appliance in an otherwise safe manner. In many states, the law would presume negligence on the part of your landlord. If you can show that the ungrounded plug caused your injury, the landlord will be held liable.

Bear in mind that landlords are only expected to take reasonable steps to comply with safety and health laws that fall within the negligence *per se* realm. For example, most states require landlords to supply smoke detectors. If your landlord has supplied one, but you have disabled it, your landlord won't be held responsible if you are hurt by a fire that could have been stopped had you left the detector alone.

The landlord's violation of a health or safety law may also indirectly cause an injury. For example, if the landlord lets the furnace deteriorate in violation of local law, and you are injured trying to repair it, the landlord will probably be liable unless your repair efforts are extremely careless themselves.

EXAMPLE: The state housing code requires landlords to provide hot water. In the middle of the winter, your hot water heater has been broken for a week, despite your repeated complaints to the landlord. Finally, to give your sick child a hot bath, you carry pots of steaming water from the stove to the bathtub. Doing this, you spill the hot water and burn yourself seriously.

You sue the landlord for failure to provide hot water as required by state law. If the case goes to court, it will be up to the jury to decide whether or not the landlord's failure to provide hot water caused your injury. Many juries would think that your response to the lack of hot water was a foreseeable one and, knowing this, your landlord's insurance company would probably be willing to offer a fair settlement.

3. The Landlord Didn't Make Certain Repairs

For perfectly sensible reasons, many landlords do not want tenants to undertake even relatively simple tasks like painting, plastering or unclogging a drain. Your lease or rental agreement may prohibit you from making any repairs or alterations without the owner's consent, or limit what you can do. (Chapter 10 discusses this.)

But in exchange for a landlord's reserving the right to make all these repairs, the law imposes a responsibility. If, after being told about a problem, the landlord doesn't maintain or repair something you aren't allowed to touch, and you are injured as a result, the landlord is probably liable. The legal reason is that the landlord breached the contract (the lease) by not making the repairs. (The landlord may be negligent as well; remember, there is nothing to stop you from presenting multiple reasons why the landlord should be held liable.)

EXAMPLE: The Rules and Regulations attached to Lori's lease state that management will inspect and clean the fan above her stove every six months. Jake, an affable but somewhat scatterbrained graduate student in charge of maintenance at the apartment complex, was supposed to do the fan checks. But deep into his studies and social life, Jake scheduled no inspections and, ten months later, Lori was injured when the accumulated grease in the fan filter caught fire.

Lori sued the landlord, alleging that his failure to live up to his contractual promise to clean the fan was the cause of her injuries. The jury agreed and awarded her a large sum.

Some other common examples might include:
- Environmental hazards. If your lease forbids repainting without the landlord's consent, the landlord is obligated to maintain the painted surfaces. If an old layer of lead paint begins to crack, deteriorate and enter the air, the landlord will be liable for the health problems that follow. (Chapter 13 covers environmental health hazards such as lead-based paint.)
- Security breaches. Landlords typically forbid tenants from installing locks of their own. That means your landlord may be liable if his failure to provide secure locks contributes to a crime. (See Chapter 14.)

4. The Landlord Didn't Keep the Premises Habitable

One of a landlord's basic responsibilities is to keep the rental property in a "habitable" condition.

Failure to maintain a habitable dwelling may make the landlord liable for injuries caused by the substandard conditions. For example, a tenant who is bitten by a rat in a vermin-infested building may argue that the owner's failure to maintain a rat-free building constituted a breach of duty to keep the place habitable, which in turn led to the injury. You must show that the landlord knew of the defect and had a reasonable amount of time to fix it.

This theory applies only when the defect is so serious that the rental unit is unfit for human habitation. For example, a large, jagged broken picture window would probably make the premises unfit for habitation in North Dakota in winter, but a torn screen door in southern California obviously would not. The North Dakota tenant who cut herself trying to cover the window with cardboard might sue under negligence and a violation of the implied warranty of habitability, while the California tenant would be limited to a theory of negligence.

EXAMPLE: Jose notified his landlord about the mice that he had seen several times in his kitchen. Despite Jose's repeated complaints, the landlord did nothing to eliminate the problem. When Jose reached into his cupboard for a box of cereal, he was bitten by a mouse. Jose sued his landlord for the medical treatment he required, including extremely painful rabies shots, and alleged that the landlord's failure to eradicate the rodent problem constituted a breach of the implied warranty of habitability, and that this breach was responsible for his injury. The jury agreed and gave Jose a large monetary award.

The injury sustained by Jose in the example above could also justify a claim that the injury resulted from the landlord's negligence. And, if Jose's landlord had failed to take reasonable steps to comply with a state or local statute concerning rodent control, the landlord might automatically be considered negligent. Finally, the owner may also be liable if the lease forbade Jose from make repairs, such as repairing improper sewage connections or changing the way garbage was stored. As you can see, sometimes there are several legal theories that will fit the facts and support your claim for damages.

5. The Landlord Acted Recklessly

In the legal sense of the word, "recklessness" usually means extreme carelessness regarding an obvious defect or problem. A landlord who is aware of a long-existing and obviously dangerous defect but neglects to correct it may be guilty of recklessness, not just ordinary carelessness.

If your landlord or an employee acted recklessly, your monetary recovery could be significant. This is because a jury has the power to award not only actual damages (which include medical bills, loss of earnings and pain and suffering) but also extra, "punitive" damages. (See Section D, below.) Punitive damages are almost never given in simple negligence cases, but are appropriate to punish recklessness and to send a sobering message to others who might behave similarly. But don't count your millions before you have them: In any situation the line between ordinary negligence and recklessness is wherever the unpredictable American jury thinks it should be. The size of the punitive award is likewise up to the jury.

The very unpredictability of punitive damage awards, however, can be to your advantage when negotiating with the landlord. The landlord may settle your claim rather than risk letting an indignant jury award you punitive damages.

> **EXAMPLE:** The handrail along the stairs to the first floor of the apartment house Jack owned had been hanging loose for several months. Jack attempted to fix it two or three times by taping the supports to the wall. The tape did no good, however, and the railing was literally flapping in the breeze. One dark night when Hilda, one of Jack's tenants, reached for the railing, the entire thing came off in her hand, causing her to fall and break her hip.
>
> Hilda sued Jack for her injuries. In her lawsuit, she pointed to the obviously ineffective measures that Jack had taken to deal with an obviously dangerous situation, and charged that he had acted with reckless disregard for the safety of his tenants. (Hilda also argued that Jack was negligent because of his unreasonable behavior and because he had violated a local ordinance regarding maintenance of handrails.) The jury agreed with Hilda and awarded her punitive damages.

6. The Landlord Intentionally Harmed You

Intentional injuries are rare, but, unfortunately, they occur more often than you might guess. For example, if a landlord or manager struck and injured you during an argument, obviously that would be an intentional act for which the landlord would be liable.

Less obvious, but no less serious, are emotional or psychological injuries which can, in extreme circumstances, also be inflicted intentionally. Intentional infliction of emotional distress often arises in these situations:

- **Sexual harassment.** Repeated, disturbing attentions of a sexual nature that the harasser refuses to stop, which leave the victim fearful, humiliated and upset. (See Chapter 5, Section C2, for a detailed discussion of possible responses.)

> **EXAMPLE:** Rita's landlord Brad took advantage of every opportunity to make suggestive comments about her looks and social life. When she asked him to stop, he replied that he was "just looking out for her," and he stepped up his unwanted attentions. Rita finally had enough, broke the lease and moved out. When Brad sued her for unpaid rent, she turned around and sued him for the emotional distress caused by his harassment. To his surprise, Brad was slapped with a multi-thousand dollar judgment, including punitive damages.

- **Assault.** Threatening or menacing someone without actually touching them is an assault, which can be enormously frightening and lead to psychological damage.
- **Repeated invasions of privacy.** Deliberately invading a tenant's privacy—by unauthorized entries, for example—may cause extreme worry and distress. (Chapter 11 covers tenants' privacy rights.)

7. The Law Makes the Landlord Liable

In a few rare circumstances, a landlord may be responsible for a tenant's injury even though the landlord did his best to create and maintain a safe environment. In other words, even if the landlord did his best to provide a safe premises—the landlord was not negligent—he's responsible. This legal principle is called "strict liability," or liability without fault. It's a very similar concept to "no fault" auto insurance—you collect without having to prove that the accident was the other person's fault.

In most states, strict liability is imposed by courts or lawmakers only when a hidden defect poses an unusually dangerous risk of harm to a group of persons unable to detect or avoid the danger. For example, Massachusetts landlords are subject to strict liability if tenants are poisoned by lead-based paint. In New York, strict liability has been applied to injuries from radon.

Louisiana is the only state that makes strict liability available for a wide range of tenant injuries, but the quirkiness of the law (you must have been injured by an "original aspect" of the structure that has succumbed to "ruin") make it little used in practice. Most injured Louisiana tenants sue their landlords for negligence.

C. If You're at Fault, Too

If you sue your landlord for negligence, the landlord may turn right around and accuse you of negligence, too. And if you are partially to blame for your injury, the landlord's liability for your losses will be reduced accordingly.

1. Your Own Carelessness

If you are also guilty of unreasonable carelessness—for example, you were drunk and, as a result, didn't (or couldn't) watch your step when you tripped on a loose tread on a poorly-maintained stairway—in most states the landlord's liability will be proportionately reduced.

The legal principle is called "comparative negligence." Basically, this means that if you are partially at fault, you can collect only part of the value of your losses. For example, if a judge or jury ruled that you had suffered $10,000 in damages (such as medical costs or lost earnings) but that you were 20% at fault, you would recover only $8,000.

Comparative negligence is applied in different ways in different states. In some states (listed below), injured tenants can collect something no matter how careless they were—even if they were 99% at fault.

In many others, however, you can recover only if your own carelessness was not too great. In Arkansas and Colorado, for example, you'll get something only if your carelessness was less than the landlord's. If it's equal to or greater than his, you'll get nothing. In a majority of states, including New Jersey, Texas and Wisconsin, you can recover if your negligence was *equal to* or lower than the landlord's; so if the jury concludes that you were equally at fault, you'll collect half your damages.

In a few states—Alabama, Maryland, North Carolina and Virginia—the doctrine of comparative negligence doesn't exist. If you were even the least bit negligent, you can collect nothing.

Generous Comparative Negligence States

In these states, injured tenants can collect something even if they were 99% at fault:

Alaska	Louisiana	New Mexico
Arizona	Maine	New York
California	Missouri	Rhode Island
Florida	Mississippi	Washington
Kentucky		

2. Your Risk-Taking

Carelessness on your part is not the only way that your monetary recovery can be reduced. If you deliberately chose to act in a way that caused or worsened your injury, another doctrine may apply. Called "assumption of risk," it refers to a tenant who knows the danger of a certain action and decides to take the chance anyway.

> EXAMPLE: In a hurry to get to work, you take a short cut to the garage by using a walkway that you know has uneven, broken pavement. You disregard the sign posted by your landlord—"Use Front Walkway Only." If you trip and hurt your knee, you'll have a hard time pinning blame on your landlord because you deliberately chose a known, dangerous route to the garage.

In some states, if you are injured as a result of putting yourself in harm's way, you may not be entitled to recover anything, even if the landlord's negligence contributed to the injury. In other states, your recovery will be diminished according to the extent that you appreciated the danger involved.

D. How Much Money You're Entitled To

If you were injured on your landlord's property and have convinced an insurance adjuster or jury that the landlord is responsible, at least in part, you can ask for monetary compensation, called "compensatory damages." Injured tenants can recover the money they have lost (wages) and spent (doctors' bills), plus compensation for physical pain and suffering, mental anguish and lost opportunities.

Medical care and related expenses. You can recover for doctors' and physical therapists' bills, including future care. If your bills were covered by your own insurance company or medical plan, you can seek reimbursement for any co-payments and deductibles.

Missed work time. You can sue for lost wages and income while you were unable to work and undergoing treatment for your injuries. You can also recover for expected losses due to continuing care. The fact that you used sick or vacation pay to cover your time off from work is irrelevant. You are entitled to save this pay to use at your discretion at other times. In short, using up vacation or sick pay is considered the same as losing the pay itself.

Pain and other physical suffering. The type of injury you have suffered and its expected duration will affect the amount you can expect for pain and suffering. But insurance adjusters won't take your word for the level of discomfort you're experiencing. If you can show that your doctor has prescribed strong anti-pain medication, you'll have some objective corroboration of your distress. And the longer your recovery period, the greater your pain and suffering.

Permanent physical disability or disfigurement. If your injury has clear long-lasting or permanent effects—such as scars, back or joint stiffness or a significant reduction in your mobility—the amount of your damages goes way up.

Loss of family, social, career and educational experiences or opportunities. If you can demonstrate that the injury prevented you from advancing in your job or landing a better one, you can ask for compensation representing the lost income. Of course, it's hard to prove that missing a job interview resulted in income loss (after all, you didn't yet have the job). But the possibility that you might have moved ahead may be enough to convince the insurance company to sweeten their offer.

Emotional damages resulting from any of the above. Emotional pain, including stress, embarrassment, depression and strains on family relationships can be compensated. Like pain and suffering, however, it's hard to prove. If you have consulted a therapist, physician or counselor, their evaluations of your reported symptoms can serve as proof of your problems. Be aware, however, that when you choose to sue for mental or emotional injuries, your doctor's notes and files regarding your symptoms and treatment will usually be made available to the other side.

In some cases, injured tenants can collect more than compensatory damages. Punitive damages are awarded if a judge or jury decides that the landlord acted outrageously, either intentionally or with extreme carelessness. Punitive damages are punishments for this conduct.

Injuries Without Impact: Legal Nuisances

You may be able to successfully sue and recover damages in some situations where you are not physically hurt. If the landlord maintains a legal nuisance—a serious and persistent health or safety condition that adversely affects a tenant's (or neighbor's) enjoyment of the property—a tenant can sue for damages, even if no physical injury occurs. For example, a tenant who is repeatedly plagued by the stench of garbage scattered about because the landlord hasn't provided enough garbage cans for the apartment building can sue for the annoyance and inconvenience of putting up with the smell. Similarly, a tenant or neighbor—or a group of them—may sue if the landlord does nothing to evict a notorious drug-dealing tenant, whose dangerous associates genuinely frighten them. (See Chapter 14 for a discussion of legal nuisances.)

And as discussed in Chapter 5, a landlord may also be sued for the non-physical distress caused by illegal discrimination or harassment.

Environmental Hazards

Because of some relatively recent changes in the law, landlords must now do more than provide housing that meets minimum health and safety standards. They are also expected to deal with some serious environmental health hazards. Simply put, laws now require the landlord to take steps to ensure that you and your family aren't sickened by several common hazards, including lead, asbestos and radon.

This chapter explains landlords' obligations and offers some suggestions on how to spot problem areas, work with the landlord (or housing authorities) and take steps to protect yourself.

 Related topics covered in this book include:
- Your right to safe and habitable housing: Chapters 8 and 9.
- Your legal options if you are injured by defective housing conditions: Chapter 12.

A. Asbestos

Exposure to asbestos has long been linked to an increased risk of cancer, particularly for workers in the asbestos manufacturing industry or in construction jobs involving the use of asbestos materials. More recently, the danger of asbestos in homes has also been recognized.

Homes built before the mid-1970s often contain asbestos insulation around heating systems, in ceilings and in other areas. Until 1981, asbestos was also widely used in other building materials, such as vinyl flooring and tiles. Asbestos that is intact (or covered up) is generally not a problem, and the current wisdom is to leave it in place but monitor it for signs of deterioration. However, asbestos that has begun to break down and enter the air—for example, when it is disturbed during maintenance or renovation work—can become a significant health problem to people who breathe it.

1. OSHA Regulations

Until quite recently, landlords had no legal obligation to test for the presence of asbestos absent clear evidence that it was likely to be a health hazard.

Fortunately for tenants in every state, owners of buildings constructed before 1981 must now install warning labels, train staff and notify people who work in areas that might contain asbestos. Unless the owner rules out the presence of asbestos by having a licensed inspector test the property, the law presumes that asbestos is present.

These requirements are imposed by the U.S. Occupational Safety and Health Administration (OSHA) to protect workers. But they are also a boon to tenants. In the process of complying with OSHA's requirements to inform and protect employees or outside contractors, your landlord learns whether or not there is asbestos on the property and (based on its type and quantity) what must be done to protect the workers. Unless the landlord never hires an employee or outside contractor or learns about asbestos on the property, these precautions also benefit tenants. And once a landlord knows about the presence of any dangerous defect on the rental property, including asbestos, the law imposes a duty to take reasonable steps to make sure that tenants aren't harmed. In short, once the asbestos genie is out of the bottle, the landlord must take reasonable steps to protect your health or face the legal consequences.

Deteriorating Asbestos: An Obvious, Dangerous Defect

Problems with asbestos often arise when neither the landlord, nor the tenant, realize that the material is embedded in ceilings and floors. Sometimes, however, the situation is not so subtle. Deteriorating asbestos that is open and obvious is a dangerous defect that your landlord must address pronto. It's no different than a broken front step or an inoperable front door lock. As the owner, the landlord is responsible for fixing conditions that could cause significant injury.

OSHA regulations cover two classes of materials: Those that definitely contain asbestos (such as certain kinds of flooring and ceilings) and those that the law presumes contain asbestos. The second class is extremely inclusive, describing, among other things, any surfacing material that is "sprayed, troweled on or otherwise applied." Under this definition, virtually every dwelling built before 1980 must be suspected of containing asbestos. Asbestos or asbestos-containing materials are typically found in or on:

- sprayed-on "cottage cheese" ceilings
- acoustic tile ceilings
- vinyl flooring, and
- insulation around heating and hot water pipes.

2. When the Landlord Must Test for Asbestos

Your landlord is required to comply with OSHA's asbestos testing and protective rules when he undertakes a major re-modeling or renovation job of a pre-1981 building, as well as when he undertakes lesser projects (such as the preparation of an asbestos-containing ceiling or wall for repainting). Even relatively non-invasive custodial work—such as stripping floor tiles containing asbestos—comes within the long reach of OSHA.

OSHA has concluded that post-1981 buildings are unlikely to contain asbestos, but if your post-1981 building *does* have asbestos (perhaps the builder or remodeler used recycled building materials), OSHA regulations cover it, too.

3. Protection From Asbestos

OSHA is very specific regarding the level of training, work techniques and protective clothing for employees whose work involves disturbing asbestos. But they do not specifically address the measures that a landlord must take to protect *tenants* from exposure. However, the worker protection requirements give very useful clues as to what you can reasonably expect from your landlord in the way of tenant protections. In short, the more your landlord must do to protect workers, the more he must do to warn and protect tenants, too. If he doesn't and you are injured as a result, he risks being found liable. (See Chapter 12.)

- **Custodial work.** At the low end of the asbestos-disturbing spectrum, workers doing custodial work—for example, stripping the floor tiles in the lobby—must be trained (and supervised by a trained superior) in safe asbestos-handling techniques. Your landlord should warn all tenants that the work is planned, giving you an opportunity to avoid the area if you choose. The landlord should also make sure that tenants, their guests and children don't come into contact with the debris. Conscientious landlords will use written notices to alert tenants, and place cones and caution tape around the area.
- **Major repairs or renovations.** If renovation or repair work is planned for a pre-1981 building, the landlord must test for asbestos and provide more protection, including air monitoring, protective clothing and medical surveillance of workers. You are entitled to appropriate warnings and your landlord should minimize your exposure, through fastidious work site procedures and isolation of dangerous materials.

EXAMPLE: Sally returned home to her apartment to find that workers were removing the ugly, stained ceiling tile in the lobby and hallways. She learned from the contractor that the project would last four days. Sally was concerned that her young sons, returning home from school in the afternoon and curious about the renovations, would hang around the halls and lobby or at least pass through them as they went in and out to play. Either way, Sally's sons would be exposed to the airborne fibers. Sally wrote a note to the landlord, explaining her concerns.

Sally's landlord recognized the reasonableness of her fears and the potential for injury. He spoke with the contractor, one who had been specially trained in asbestos removal, and arranged for the work to be done between the hours of 8 a.m. and 3 p.m. He insisted, and the contractor readily agreed, that the old tiles be removed, and any asbestos-containing material covered, at the end of each work day. Finally, the landlord hired two adults to monitor foot traffic in and around the renovation site, to ensure that no one lingered near the workers or came into contact with the removed materials.

4. Alerting and Motivating Your Landlord

Many landlords, unfortunately, have no idea about their duty to deal with the risks posed by asbestos. If you live in an older building and suspect that there is asbestos on the premises that is not being managed properly, alert your landlord and see to it that your health is protected. Here are some strategies.

When the asbestos is obvious but intact. Asbestos that is intact—for example, asbestos insulation that is covered with foil or wrapped with tape—probably does not pose a significant health risk to you, since the fibers can't enter the air. It is important, however, that asbestos be monitored for signs of deterioration. For example, if the tape wrapping is tearing or falling away, it is no longer doing its job of containment. If you are worried about whether asbestos-containing materials in your home are dangerous, ask your landlord, in writing, to have the material inspected by a trained professional.

Never disturb asbestos-containing materials. You shouldn't drill holes in walls or ceilings that contain asbestos, or sand asbestos tiles in preparation for a new coat of paint. First, you want to protect your health. Second, intentionally disturbing asbestos will almost certainly reduce, if not defeat, any legal claim you might have if your health is harmed by an asbestos-related problem. The law won't hold your landlord responsible for an injury that you deliberately courted, ignoring a risk you knew about. (See Chapter 12.)

When the asbestos is obvious and airborne. Take immediate action if asbestos in your living space has begun to break down or slough off. Asbestos that has begun to break down is extremely dangerous. If it is present in your living space in any significant amount, it makes your premises legally uninhabitable. (See Chapter 8, for your legal options, which may include withholding rent. Also, subsection 6, below, discusses the option of moving out.) A sample letter from a tenant concerned about deteriorating asbestos is shown below.

Sample Letter Regarding Deteriorating Asbestos

37 Ninth Avenue North
Chicago, Illinois 00000
312-555-4567

February 28, 200X

Margaret Mears
3757 East Seventh Street
Chicago, Illinois 00000

Dear Ms. Mears:

As you know, the ceilings in my apartment are sprayed-on acoustical plaster. I have begun to notice an excessive amount of fine, white dust in the apartment, and I believe it is the result of the breakdown of the asbestos fibers in the plaster. I am quite concerned about this, since inhaling asbestos can cause serious illness. Please contact me immediately so that you can take a look and arrange for a licensed inspector to examine the ceilings.

Yours truly,

Terry Lu

Terry Lu

Keep copies of all correspondence regarding asbestos or other environmental health hazards. If your landlord fails to take the right steps and you want to move out or seek other legal remedies, you'll need to be able to prove that you notified the landlord of the problem and waited a reasonable amount of time for a response.

When custodial or repair work is done improperly. When it comes to asbestos removal, the people who suffer most from a landlord's disregard of workplace safety are the workers themselves. But improper asbestos removal or disturbance is likely to affect you, too. Fortunately, there is something you can do about it. OSHA wants to hear about violations of workplace safety rules. You can reach OSHA by calling the phone number listed below in "Asbestos Resources." Many states have state equivalents of OSHA, and you can also call your state's consumer protection agency for information. (See the list in Appendix I.)

Beware of landlord retaliation. A landlord who learns about your complaint to OSHA won't be pleased. Many (but not all) states have laws that prohibit landlords from taking actions against tenants (such as rent hikes, diminution of services or ending a tenancy) after tenants have exercised their legal rights by contacting a federal or state agency regarding a violation of law. (See "State Laws Prohibiting Landlord Retaliation" in Appendix I.) If you aren't protected by an anti-retaliation statute, proceed carefully and, if possible, anonymously.

5. Moving Out If Necessary

Sometimes it isn't possible to shield yourself from the effects of deteriorating asbestos, or even your landlord's major repairs or renovations involving asbestos. For example, if the acoustic ceilings in your apartment are being removed, it is unlikely (even if you and your landlord are prepared to take every precaution) that you can avoid inhaling some dangerous airborne fibers. In situations like this,

especially if you or your family have health problems that make you especially vulnerable to the effects of asbestos, the best alternative might be to move out temporarily until the work is completed. (See Chapter 8 for a discussion of moving out because your rental is uninhabitable.) Since the responsibility to repair and maintain the structure is the landlord's, the cost of temporary shelter should be covered by the landlord as long as you can convincingly establish that remaining on the premises would constitute a significant health risk. See the sample letter, below.

If you are able to give valid reasons why you should be temporarily absent while the asbestos removal work is done, and if you have a reasonable landlord who appreciates the potentially serious legal consequences of denying your reasonable request, chances are you'll be able to come to an agreement. (Don't ask to stay at the Ritz, however!)

But what if the landlord stubbornly refuses? Obviously, to protect your health, you'll want to move out anyway. And assuming the asbestos problems really are serious, you should stand a good chance of prevailing in a small claims court lawsuit for the cost of your temporary housing. Be sure to keep a copy of the letter you have sent (preferably by certified mail) to the landlord, a record of his refusal to pay for temporary accommodations and all receipts for your expenses.

Sample Letter Requesting Reimbursement for Temporary Housing

1289 Central Avenue, Apartment 8
Toofar, TX 00000
713-555-7890

June 13, 200X

Mr. Frank Brown, Owner
Sunshine Properties
75 Main Street
Toofar, TX 00000

Dear Mr. Brown:

I have just received the notice you sent to all tenants on the first floor, alerting us to the fact that you intend to tear out the heating ducts and insulation during the week of July 6. The work will involve removal of heating vents inside our apartment and removal of the asbestos insulation through the openings. You estimate that the work will take two days for each apartment.

I do not think that it would be a good idea for me and my elderly mother to live in the apartment during this process. I am concerned that we will inhale airborne fibers that may cause difficulties in breathing. My mother suffers from chronic bronchitis and cannot risk exposure to anything that might worsen the condition. Dr. Jones, who treats my mother, would be happy to corroborate this fact.

I think that the best solution would be for us to move out while this work is being done. The nearby Best Midwestern Motel has reasonable rates and would be convenient to our jobs and transportation. Please contact me so that we might discuss this before the renovation work begins. You can call me at home at the above number most nights and weekends.

Yours truly,

Sharon Rock

Sharon Rock

cc: Dr. Jones

Come to court prepared with asbestos-related information. If you go to small claims court, be prepared to explain the serious dangers of breathing asbestos fibers to the judge and why the landlord's work was so invasive that temporarily moving out was your only sensible alternative. See "Asbestos Resources" below. Also, see Chapter 19 for a discussion of small claims lawsuits.

Instead of suing in small claims court, you may be tempted to utilize what the law calls a "repair and deduct" remedy (discussed in Chapter 8) by simply deducting the cost of replacement housing from your rent. It seems logical, but a judge might not allow it. Seizing upon this uncertainty, your landlord's response will probably be to terminate your tenancy and file for eviction for nonpayment of rent. If you lose, you will not only have to pay for the cost of the temporary housing, but face eviction from your rental as well. (In addition, you may be stuck with the landlord's attorney fees if there is an "attorney fees" clause in your lease. See Chapter 2, Section D.) Far better to file a straightforward lawsuit asking for reimbursement, where the risk is simply losing the suit, not your home.

If your landlord refuses to cover temporary housing expenses, you might also want to consider moving out permanently. This option is most appropriate when the risk is great and the length of exposure relatively long. But to justify breaking the lease (and to avoid liability for future rent), you will have to be able to show that airborne asbestos really did make the premises uninhabitable. (See Chapter 8 for a full discussion of breaking the lease due to uninhabitability.) If the landlord is ripping out whole ceilings over a month's time, this argument will be strong. However, it will not amount to much if the landlord is drilling two small holes in the ceiling to install a smoke detector.

Check to see if your state law allows the landlord to terminate a tenancy for major renovation work if he provides relocation assistance for tenants. "State Rent Rules" in Appendix I gives citations to your state's landlord-tenant codes and

"State Laws on Unconditional Quit Terminations" gives citations to laws that explain when landlords may terminate your tenancy. In one or another of those sets of laws, you may find that your state requires your landlord to pay for moving expenses if your tenancy is terminated because a major project (such as wide-scale asbestos removal) makes it impossible for you to stay on the premises.

Asbestos Resources

For further information on asbestos rules, inspections and control, contact the nearest office of the U.S. Occupational Safety and Health Administration (OSHA) or call 202-219-8148.

OSHA has also developed interactive computer software for property owners, called "Asbestos Advisor," designed to help identify asbestos and suggest ways to handle it. It may help you, or interested members of any tenants' association in your building, to determine whether asbestos is present and whether your landlord is managing it properly. The Asbestos Advisor is available free through the U.S. Department of Labor's electronic bulletin board, LaborNews, by telephoning 202-219-4784. You will also find it online at OSHA's Web site, www.OSHA.GOV.

B. Lead

As we all know, exposure to lead-based paint and lead water pipes may lead to serious health problems, particularly in children. Brain damage, attention disorders and hyperactivity have all been associated with lead poisoning. Studies show that the effects of lead poisoning are lifelong, affecting both personality and intelligence. In adults, the effects of lead poisoning can include nerve disorders, high blood pressure, reproductive disorders and muscle and joint pain.

Buildings constructed before 1978 are likely to contain some source of lead: lead-based paint, lead pipes or lead-based solder used on copper pipes. In 1978, the federal government required the reduction of lead in house paint; lead pipes are generally only found in homes built before 1930, and lead-based solder in home plumbing systems was banned in 1988. Pre-1950 housing in poor and urban neighborhoods that has been allowed to deteriorate is by far the greatest source of lead-based paint poisonings.

Discovering (or being told by the landlord) that there is lead on the premises is not necessarily the end of a healthy and safe tenancy. Subsection 4, below, gives you advice on how to cope with a lead problem.

How Lead Poisoning Occurs

Lead-laden dust caused by the deterioration of exposed lead-based paint is the greatest source of lead poisoning. Falling on window sills, walls and floors, this dust makes its way into the human body when it is stirred up, becomes airborne and is inhaled, or when it is transmitted directly from hand to mouth. Exterior lead-based house paint is also a potential problem because it can slough off walls directly into the soil and be tracked into the house.

Lead dust results from renovations or remodeling—including, unfortunately, those very projects undertaken to rid premises of the lead-based paint. Lead poisoning can also occur from drinking water that contains leached-out lead from lead pipes or from deteriorating lead solder used in copper pipes.

Children between the ages of 18 months and five years are the most likely to be poisoned by lead-based paint. Their poisoning is detected when they become ill or, increasingly, in routine examinations that check for elevated blood levels of lead.

1. Federal Protections

Unfortunately, federal law does *not* require land-lords to test for lead, nor does it require them to get rid of it if they know it's present. Still, federal law aimed at reducing lead poisoning does give some important benefits to tenants:

a. Disclosure to New Tenants

Since December 6, 1996, all property owners must inform tenants, before they sign or renew a lease or rental agreement, of any information they possess on lead paint hazard conditions on the property. They must disclose information on its presence in individual rental units, common areas and garages, tool sheds, other outbuildings, signs, fences and play areas. If the property has been tested (testing must be done only by state-certified lead inspectors), a copy of the report, or a summary written by the inspector, must be shown to tenants.

With certain exceptions (listed below), every lease and rental agreement must include a disclo-sure page, even if the landlord has not tested. A copy of the federally approved disclosure form, "Disclosure of Information on Lead-Based Paint or Lead-Based Paint Hazards" is reproduced below.

If you were a tenant in your current home on December 6, 1996, your landlord must comply with these disclosure requirements according to whether you are a tenant with a lease or are renting month to month.

- **Tenants with leases**. Your landlord need not comply until your lease is up and you renew or stay on as a month-to-month tenant.
- **Month-to-month tenants.** Your landlord should have given you a disclosure statement when you wrote your first rent check dated after December 6, 1996 (September 6, 1996, if the landlord owns five or more units).

Lead Inspections

While inspections are not required by federal law, landlords may voluntarily arrange an inspection in preparing their disclosure forms in order to certify that the property is lead-free and exempt from federal regulations. (See list of exemptions, below.) Also, when a property owner takes out a loan or buys insurance, the bank or insurance company may require a lead inspection.

Professional lead inspectors don't always inspect every unit in large, multifamily properties. Instead, they inspect a sampling of the units and apply their conclusions to the property as a whole. Giving you the results and conclusions of a building-wide evaluation satisfies the law, even if your particular unit was not tested. If, however, your landlord has specific information regarding your unit that is inconsistent with the building-wide evaluation, he must disclose it to you.

For information on arranging a professional lead inspection or using a home testing kit, see subsection 3, below.

b. Information

The landlord must give all tenants the lead hazard information booklet "Protect Your Family From Lead In Your Home," written by the Environmental Protection Agency (EPA). If they choose, landlords may reproduce the booklet in a legal-size, 8½ x 14-inch format, and attach it to the lease. The graphics in the original pamphlet must be repro-duced. State agencies may develop their own pamphlets, but they may not be used in place of the EPA version unless the EPA has approved them. California's pamphlet, *Environmental Hazards: A Guide for Homeowners, Buyers, Landlords and Tenants,* has been approved.

If your landlord has not given you a disclosure form or an EPA booklet, ask for them. If you get no results, notify the EPA. This will probably result in no more than a letter or call from the inspectors, since the EPA will not cite landlords unless their noncompliance with the laws is willful and continuing. But a landlord who continues to ignore the law may find himself subject to the penalties described below.

c. Disclosure Prior to Renovation or Remodeling

If your landlord renovates or remodels your pre-1978 rented home, you must be given another copy of the federal booklet, "Protect Your Family from Lead in Your Home." This disclosure duty falls on the contractor or management company; however, if the landlord himself is doing the actual work, he must distribute the information. It may seem silly to be given this information twice; but at the very least, seeing (and hopefully reading) the booklet again will serve to remind you that you must take precautions when lead dust is likely to be in the air.

d. Penalties

Property owners who willfully fail to comply with EPA regulations face penalties of up to $10,000, and may have to pay an injured tenant three times what the tenant suffered in damages.

Rental Properties Exempt From Federal Regulations

- Housing for which a construction permit was obtained, or on which construction was started, after January 1, 1978. Older buildings that have been completely renovated since 1978 are *not* exempt, even if every painted surface was removed or replaced.
- Housing certified as lead-free by a state-accredited lead inspector. Lead-free means the absence of any lead paint, even paint that has been completely painted over and encapsulated.

- Lofts, efficiencies, studios and other "zero-bedroom" units, including dormitory housing and rentals in sorority and fraternity houses. University-owned apartments and married student housing are not exempted.
- Short-term vacation rentals
- A single room rented in a residential home
- Housing designed for persons with disabilities (as explained in HUD's Fair Housing Accessibility Guidelines, 56 Code of Federal Regulations 9472, 3/6/91), *unless* any child less than six years old resides there or is expected to reside there
- Retirement communities (housing designed for seniors, where one or more tenant is at least 62 years old) *unless* children under the age of six are present or expected to live there.

The Residential Lead-Based Paint Hazard Reduction Act was enacted in 1992 to reduce lead levels. It is commonly referred to as Title X [Ten] (42 U.S. Code § 4852d). The Environmental Protection Agency (EPA) has written regulations that explain how landlords should implement lead hazard reduction (24 Code of Federal Regulations Part 35 and 40 Code of Federal Regulations Part 745). For more information, see "Lead Hazard Resources," below.

2. State Laws on Lead Affecting Tenants

Many states acted long before the federal government did, outlawing the use of lead-based paint in residences and requiring the careful maintenance of existing lead paint and lead-based building materials. None of the state laws explicitly direct landlords to test for lead. However, landlords are indirectly forced to test in Washington, D.C., where landlords with resident children under eight years old must keep the premises lead-free, and in Massachusetts, where owners must remove or cover lead hazards.

Disclosure of Information on Lead-Based Paint or Lead-Based Paint Hazards

LEAD WARNING STATEMENT

Housing built before 1978 may contain lead-based paint. Lead from paint, paint chips and dust can pose health hazards if not managed properly. Lead exposure is especially harmful to young children and pregnant women. Before renting pre-1978 housing, lessors must disclose the presence of known lead-based paint and/or lead-based hazards in the dwelling. Lessees must also receive a federally approved pamphlet on lead poisoning prevention.

Lessor's Disclosure

(a) Presence of lead-based paint and/or lead-based paint hazards. Check (i) or (ii) below:

☐ (i) Known lead-based paint and/or lead-based paint hazards are present in the housing (explain): _____.

☐ (ii) Lessor has no knowledge of lead-based paint and/or lead-based paint hazards in the housing.

(b) Records and reports available to the lessor. Check (i) or (ii) below:

☐ (i) Lessor has provided the lessee with all available records and reports pertaining to lead-based paint and/or lead-based paint hazards in the housing (list documents below):

_____.

☐ (ii) Lessor has no reports or records pertaining to lead-based paint or lead-based paint hazards in the housing.

Lessee's Acknowledgment (initial)

___ (c) Lessee has received copies of all information listed above.

___ (d) Lessee has received the pamphlet Protect Your Family From Lead In Your Home.

Agent's Acknowledgment (initial)

___ (e) Agent has informed the lessor of the lessor's obligations under 42 U.S.C 4852d and is aware of his/her responsibility to ensure compliance.

Certification of Accuracy

The following parties have reviewed the information above and certify, to the best of their knowledge, that the information they have provided is true and accurate.

_____	_____	_____	_____
Lessor	Date	Lessor	Date
_____	_____	_____	_____
Lessee	Date	Lessee	Date
_____	_____	_____	_____
Agent	Date	Agent	Date

States With Lead Hazard Reduction Laws

The following states have laws on lead-based paint and hazards. For details on each state's law, see "State Lead Hazard Reduction Laws" in Appendix I.

Arizona	Iowa	New York
Arkansas	Kentucky	North Carolina
California	Louisiana	Ohio
Colorado	Maine	Oregon
Connecticut	Maryland	Pennsylvania
Delaware	Massachusetts	Rhode Island
District of	Minnesota	South Carolina
Columbia	Mississippi	Tennessee
Georgia	Missouri	Texas
Hawaii	Nebraska	Vermont
Illinois	New Hampshire	Virginia
Indiana	New Jersey	Wisconsin

3. Recognizing Lead in Your Home

If your landlord has tested for lead and complied with federal disclosure requirements, you can skip this section. However, most landlords have not tested for lead. (This situation will surely change as banks and insurance companies begin to require testing as a prerequisite to loans and insurance coverage.) There are several clues as to whether or not there is lead in or around your home, and ways that you (or, ideally, your landlord) can find out for sure.

You will need to hire a licensed lead tester to get a precise assessment of the risk of lead in your home. Unfortunately, the cost is high—a few hundred dollars at least. If you (and possibly other tenants) choose to do an assessment, you'll be in a good position to lobby the landlord to do something about containing the risk. But even if you do not get a professional's opinion, but are fairly sure that lead is present in your home, you can still act prudently on your own to reduce the risk. (Subsections 4 and 5, below, explain what you can do yourself and how to get the landlord to act.)

a. Paint

Your first step should be to determine the age of the building. If the landlord doesn't know or won't say, go to the local building permit office and ask to see the building's construction permit. If there is no permit on file, you'll have to estimate the structure's age.

As noted above, housing that was built before January 1, 1978, is almost certain to have lead-based paint. But buildings constructed later may have it, too, since the 1978 ban did not include a recall and lead-based paint remained on the shelves.

You can do your own test for lead. Home testing kits work like this: After swabbing a chemical solution over a painted surface, the swab will turn a certain color if lead is present. Kits are widely available at hardware and paint stores and are inexpensive, but unfortunately are unreliable about 30% of the time. For more reliable results, hire a professional tester who will use an x-ray gun to give an instant reading through all the layers of paint. A professional inspection will cost a few hundred dollars; if you can, share the cost with other tenants. (See "Lead Hazard Resources," below, for information on finding a HUD-approved contractor to test for lead.)

b. Lead Pipes

Pre-1930 construction generally used lead pipes. It's difficult to know for sure whether you have lead pipes until you examine the plumbing. When you look under the sink, you may be able to see the pipe coming out from the wall; if so, look for the tell-tale dark gray color. A plumber should be able to identify the pipes without difficulty.

WHILE YOU'RE HERE, I WAS WONDERING IF YOU COULD DO SOMETHING ABOUT THE ANTS.

c. Lead Solder

Lead solder was used to join sections of pipe as recently as 1988. You won't know whether it was used unless you can look at several soldered junctions; even then, you will probably need a plumber to tell you whether the solder was leaded or not.

d. Imported, Non-Glossy Vinyl Mini-Blinds

Mini-blinds from China, Taiwan, Indonesia and Mexico are likely to contain lead, but are not banned by the Consumer Product Safety Commission. As the surface vinyl deteriorates in the sun, lead dust enters the air. Even if your landlord knows your pre-1978 apartment has leaded mini-blinds, he doesn't have to tell you *unless* the landlord knows that the blinds have begun to deteriorate and produce lead dust. Be smart: Ask the landlord to replace the blinds now, before a problem occurs.

e. Soil

For decades, American cars ran on leaded gasoline—and the effects are still with us. Exhaust from lead-burning cars contains lead, which falls to the ground where it remains, relatively inert, for years. Neighborhoods adjacent to heavily traveled roadways have significant amounts of lead in the soil; the readings drop off dramatically as the distance from the roads diminishes. If you live near a busy freeway or throughway, assume the worst and take care of yourself. See subsection 4, below, for suggestions on self-help.

4. Dealing With Lead on Your Own

You don't need to automatically reject, or move out of, a rental that contains lead. Remember, only deteriorating lead is the culprit.

If you do discover hazardous lead, an aggressive approach is often the best idea. If you live in older housing where lead is almost surely present and deteriorating, assume a worst-case scenario and adjust your housekeeping and hygiene habits accordingly. (Ideally, you'll want the landlord to eventually take more drastic measures, such as careful re-painting as discussed below. Here's what the experts recommend that you do.

- Vacuum thoroughly and regularly, using a "HEPA" ("high energy particle arresting") vacuum that will filter out the fine lead dust. Ask your landlord to provide one.
- Even where a unit has been repainted, the old lead paint layer will eventually be re-exposed on some painted surfaces that get a lot of wear, such as door and windowsill areas. Wash them with a phosphate-based cleaner or a solution (like "Leadisolve") designed for lead pick-up.

⚠ **Don't disturb lead paint in buildings built before 1978.** Do not sand walls, window sills, doors or other surfaces—it risks releasing lead into the air (possibly even from paint several layers down), creating the very hazards you are attempting to avoid. Renovations of this order should be handled by painters who have been trained and equipped to capture and remove lead dust and chips. If you intentionally disturb lead and suffer an injury, it will be difficult to place legal responsibility on your landlord.

- If your unit has lead pipes or copper pipe with lead solder, draw water out of the pipes by letting the taps run for 30 seconds before using—even if you plan to boil it for tea. Don't use hot water for cooking. Better yet, use bottled water for drinking and cooking.
- If lead is in the soil outside, provide throw rugs at each entrance or ask folks to remove their shoes before entering.
- Consider covering lead-laced soil with sod or an impermeable material.
- If your household has young children (especially those who are still crawling), use extra care to clean floors, especially around windows. Wash children's toys and hands frequently, and clean pacifiers and bottles after they fall on the floor.
- Test your children for lead poisoning. Elevated blood levels in young children can be picked up in a simple blood test. Increasingly, the test is being done as part of routine checkups. If you live in a building that you suspect places your child at risk for lead poisoning, you need this information to protect your child. The Centers for Disease Control recommend giving children a blood level test at age six months to one year. Do follow-up tests as needed.

⚠ **If a child's blood lead level is very high, move promptly and see a lawyer.** Evidence of lead poisoning will almost certainly entitle you to move out on the grounds of uninhabitability. (See subsection 6, below.) In Connecticut, a dwelling with lead is considered unfit by law. You will definitely need expert legal assistance if you sue for damages.

5. Getting the Landlord to Act

Getting your landlord to hire a professional to test and assess the risk of lead poisoning may be a tall order—after all, no federal or state law requires it. And it may be next to impossible to get your landlord to paint over deteriorating lead paint. But even the most penurious, callous or short-sighted landlord may respond to an appeal to the bottom line.

Many landlords have learned (sometimes the hard way) that testing for lead and taking measures before tenants get sick is well worth the cost and time. Although landlords aren't liable for lead poisoning unless it can be shown that they knew that lead was present, these days it is increasingly difficult for landlords to plausibly argue that they were ignorant of this well-publicized issue. Lawsuits for lead poisoning can result in astronomical jury awards or settlements if the landlord is held responsible for the lifetime effects of an infant's brain damage. The cost of testing, risk assessment and lead management pales in comparison.

If the landlord isn't aware of the potentially enormous liability for lead poisoning, suggest she read *Every Landlord's Legal Guide* (Nolo Press), which makes clear that tenants can bring, and win, lawsuits for lead poisoning. Many state health agencies publish their own pamphlets that also explain the risks to landowners who ignore the writing (and the paint) on the wall.

a. Notify the Landlord of Problems

If you discover a lead hazard on the property, tell the landlord at once, in writing. A sample letter is shown below.

Although the goal of your efforts is a safe place to live, not a successful lawsuit, don't lose sight of the fact that your landlord may avoid liability for lead injuries unless you can show that he knew (or should have known) of lead hazards and failed to take reasonable steps to reduce them. In short, if you believe there is a lead risk on your property, you want to make it impossible for the landlord to plausibly deny knowing about it. If you use a kit to test your rental unit or its water supply and find the presence of lead, send the results (certified mail) to the landlord. If your child has elevated blood levels, do the same. Keep these receipts and any other evidence of the landlord's knowledge, such as notes of a conversation in which the landlord acknowledged the presence of pre-1978, chipping paint but refused to buy a HEPA vacuum.

Sample Letter Regarding Lead Test Results

45 East Avenue North
Central City, MO 00000
816-555-7890

February 28, 200X

Lester Levine
3757 East Seventh Street
Central City, MO 00000

Dear Mr. Levine:

We recently hired the environmental engineering firm of Checkit & Howe to test our duplex for the presence of lead-based paint. A report of their findings is enclosed. As you can see, there is indeed old, unstable lead paint on most of the windowsills and in the upstairs hall.

We are concerned about the effect that this deteriorating paint will have on the health of our children, aged three months and three years. At a minimum, we would like to discuss a safe and effective response to this problem. Please contact us as soon as possible so that we can arrange a meeting. We're home in the evenings and on weekends.

Yours truly,

Maynard G. and Zelda Krebs

Maynard G. and Zelda Krebs

Encl: Report of Checkit & Howe

b. Involve State, Local or Federal Inspectors

Some states with aggressive lead-containment laws (such as Maryland, Connecticut and California), and even some cities (such as San Francisco) have the power to inspect and order clean-ups when a tenant complains to their enforcement agencies or reports a child's elevated blood level. Check the list of states with lead hazard reduction laws, above, to see whether or not your state has a lead abatement law; if so, read the summary in Appendix I and contact the enforcing agency for help.

If your state does not have a lead hazard reduction law or effective enforcing agency, contact the EPA for advice.

c. Consider a Lawsuit

Some lead-management measures, such as scrupulous housekeeping, are more time-consuming than expensive. However, money enters the picture when there's so much lead dust that containment is the only reasonable response—for example, sealing lead-based paint by covering it with a durable finish. If actual removal of the painted surfaces is necessary (perhaps the underlying structure is so deteriorated that it must be replaced), considerable expense is in the offing.

Forcing the landlord to deal with lead on the property will involve asking a judge to issue an order that directs that the work be accomplished in a certain way within a certain time. Lawsuits like this cannot be filed in small claims court. These lawsuits are typically complicated affairs that require lawyers. They can be very effective when a group of tenants sue together. See Chapter 20 for suggestions on finding and working with a lawyer.

If you spend time and money dealing with lead containment—using special detergents or vacuums, devoting extra time to fastidious housekeeping, putting up with the intrusion of contractors trying to deal with the lead problem—ask your landlord to reduce the rent accordingly. (See Chapter 8 for advice on how to determine the value of a defective rental unit.) After all, these expenses are necessitated by the dilapidation of the property. If he refuses and you have a lease requiring that you live in the unit for months or years, consider going to small claims court for an order reducing your rent; and ask that you be compensated for past labor and expenses, too. See Chapter 8 and *Everybody's Guide*

to Small Claims Court, by Ralph Warner (Nolo), for help.

6. Moving Out If Necessary

If the risk of lead poisoning is high and cannot be controlled, the smartest move may be moving out. Here are two scenarios that usually justify a move:

The rental is permeated with lead that you cannot effectively control. If lead constitutes a serious danger to your health—perhaps deteriorating paint has caused a serious lead dust problem, or old lead pipes have contaminated the water supply—you would be justified in breaking the lease and moving out on the grounds that your unit is legally uninhabitable. (See Chapter 8 for more on this topic.) To help counter any possible lawsuit by the landlord against you for future unpaid rent, be sure that you have your evidence in hand, such as a report from an EPA inspector or a state agency in charge of enforcing your state's lead law.

Renovations will create a lead problem. If the landlord plans repairs or renovations in an effort to contain a serious lead problem, you may be wise to leave the premises. Even meticulous clean-up procedures cannot eliminate the risk of inhaling lead dust created by renovation. Some state statutes require the landlord to cover temporary housing expenses incurred during lead abatement work; check your state's lead laws, listed in Appendix I. Even in the absence of such a statute, however, nothing prevents you from suing in small claims court. (Section A, above, discusses reimbursement for housing during asbestos-removal work).

Lead Hazard Resources

Information on the evaluation and control of lead dust may be obtained from the regional offices of the federal EPA or by calling the National Lead Information Center at 800-424-LEAD, http://www.epa.gov/lead/nlic.htm. You can also get information by going to the National Lead Information website at www.nsc.org/ehc/lead.htm.

The Department of Housing and Urban Development has issued a useful booklet entitled "Guidelines For the Evaluation and Control of Lead-Based Paint Hazards In Housing," which may be obtained by calling the National Lead Information Center.

For the most recent interpretations of federal law, go to the HUD Lead Office site on the World Wide Web, at www.hud.gov/lea/leahome.html. Information is also available from the EPA on its website: www.epa.gov/opptintr/lead/index.html.

HUD maintains a "Lead Listing" of names, addresses and phone numbers of trained lead paint contractors (for testing and abatement) in every state. Call 1-888-LEAD-LIST or access the list on the Web at www.leadlisting.org.

State housing departments have information on state laws and regulations. Start by calling your state consumer protection agency. (See the list in Appendix I.)

are over-insulated or poorly ventilated. Radon is a smaller risk when it escapes from building materials that have incorporated uranium-filled rocks and soils (like certain types of composite tiles or bricks) or is released into the air from aerated household water that has passed through underground concentrations of uranium. Problems occur most frequently in areas where rocky soil is relatively rich in uranium and in climates where occupants keep their windows tightly shut to maintain heat in the winter and air conditioning in the summer. No state is immune, however—according to the EPA, high levels of radon have been detected in every state. If you smoke and your house has high radon levels, your risk of developing lung cancer is especially high.

State Laws on Radon

New Jersey and Florida have been at the forefront in addressing the radon problem. New Jersey has an extensive program that includes an information and outreach program. (N.J. Rev. Stat. §§ 26:2d-61, 26:2d-70 and 26:2d-71f.) The New Jersey Department of Environmental Protection maintains a toll-free radon hotline staffed by scientists (609-292-2121). Florida taxes new construction to raise funds for the development of a radon-resistant construction code, and it requires landlords to warn renters about the known presence of radon. (Fla. Stat. § 404.056.)

C. Radon

Radon is a naturally occurring radioactive gas that is associated with lung cancer. The U.S. Environmental Protection Agency (EPA) estimates that over one-quarter of American homes have unacceptably high levels of radon. Radon can enter and contaminate a house built on soil and rock containing uranium deposits. It can also enter through water from private wells drilled in uranium-rich soil.

Radon becomes a lethal health threat when it enters from the soil and is trapped in homes that

Fortunately, there are usually simple, inexpensive ways to measure and reduce radon levels in buildings. For example, good ventilation will disperse the gas in most situations. Solutions range from the obvious (open the windows) to the somewhat complex (use fans), but none of them involves tremendous expense.

There are currently no laws that require a private landlord to try to detect or get rid of radon. The radon problem has not become the subject of national laws requiring testing or even disclosure.

But if you find radon in your rented property, there are still things you can do.

1. Finding Radon

Radon is invisible and odorless. To test the air in your house, you can buy a do-it-yourself kit (make sure it says "Meets EPA Requirements") or hire a professional (get one who is certified by the EPA's Proficiency Program). Testing takes at least three days, and sometimes months.

Testing for radon makes sense if you live in an area that is naturally rich in uranium soil and rock. (In Alaska, for instance, radon is rarely a problem.) To find out, you'll need to do a bit of sleuthing: Start with the public library and find out about your local geology. City planning departments, insurance brokers (who may have experience in dealing with radon-related claims), architects (who ought to understand the local geology), environmental engineers and neighbors may be fruitful sources.

2. Solving Radon Problems

If radon is present in significant amounts, it needs to be kept out or blown out of the building.

Getting it out. Once radon has entered the house, it needs to be dispelled with fans and open windows. Because of the increased costs of heating and air conditioning, and the loss of security when windows are left open, these methods should be only temporary. The only good long-term solution is keeping radon out.

Keeping it out. Sealing cracks and other openings in the foundation is a basic radon reduction technique. Another method is soil suction—sucking the radon out of the soil before it enters the foundation or basement, and venting it into the air above the roof through a pipe. Increasing the air pressure within a house can also work, because radon enters houses when the air pressure inside is less than that of the surrounding soil. Equalizing the pressure in the basement or foundation reduces this pull.

3. The Landlord's Responsibility

Keeping radon out of your dwelling involves major expenditures and modifications of the building's structure. Obviously, this kind of work is your landlord's responsibility.

If your landlord is unaware of the radon issue, give him a copy of the EPA booklet explaining it. (See "Radon Resources," below.) If you have grounds for concern—you notice radon detection devices in local stores, your neighborhood has several buildings that are vented for radon control, or the geology of the area suggests the presence of uranium-rich soils—suggest that your landlord hire a testing firm. As always, if a group of tenants voices their concern, the landlord is more likely to pay attention than if you act alone. Obviously, if you perform a test, send the landlord a certified letter with a copy of the report.

Keep copies of letters and reports, and write a letter of understanding to the landlord summarizing any oral discussions of the issue. (A sample letter of understanding can be found in Chapter 2.) Meticulous business practices like these impress your landlord with your seriousness and willingness to take legal action if necessary.

4. Moving Out If Necessary

Unacceptably high levels of radon render a home unfit for habitation. If a certified tester has reached that conclusion, you have all that you need to demand that the landlord take prompt steps to remedy the problem. If the landlord fails to address it within a very short time, you can break your lease or month-to-month rental agreement and move out, citing a breach of the implied warranty of habitability (see Chapter 8). Your suspicion alone that radon is present (perhaps because your neighbor has a radon problem) will probably not protect you if the landlord sues you for unpaid rent.

It may be appropriate to move out temporarily if the landlord plans to install pumps or vents, which may take some time. See the discussion above in Section A, which suggests strategies for recouping expenses of temporary housing.

Radon Resources

For information on the detection and removal of radon, call the U.S. Environmental Protection Agency Radon Hotline at 800-767-7236. You can ask for a copy of the booklet, "Consumer's Guide To Radon Reduction," which includes a list of every state's agency or department in charge of radon reduction.

D. Carbon Monoxide

Carbon monoxide (CO) is a colorless, odorless, lethal gas. Unlike radon, whose deadly effects work over time, CO can build up and kill within a matter of hours. And, unlike any of the environmental hazards discussed so far, CO cannot be covered up or managed.

When CO is inhaled, it enters the bloodstream and replaces oxygen. Dizziness, nausea, confusion and tiredness can result; high concentrations bring on unconsciousness, brain damage and death. It is possible to be poisoned from CO while you sleep, without waking up.

1. Sources of Carbon Monoxide

Carbon monoxide is a byproduct of fuel combustion; electric appliances cannot produce it. Common home appliances, such as gas dryers, refrigerators, ranges, water heaters or space heaters; oil furnaces, fireplaces, charcoal grills and wood stoves all produce CO. Automobiles and gas gardening equipment also produce CO. If appliances or fireplaces are not vented properly, CO can build up within a home and poison the occupants. In tight, "energy-efficient" apartments, indoor accumulations are especially dangerous.

 If you smell gas, it's not CO. Carbon monoxide has no smell. Only a CO detector will alert you to its presence. To help identify leaking natural gas, utility companies add a smelly ingredient; when you "smell gas," you are smelling that additive. Because natural gas is so combustible, call the utility company or 911 immediately if you smell it.

2. Preventing Carbon Monoxide Problems

If your landlord has a regular maintenance program, it should prevent the common malfunctions that cause CO build-up. But even the most careful service program cannot rule out unexpected problems like the blocking of a chimney by a bird's nest or the sudden failure of a machine part.

Fortunately, relatively inexpensive devices, similar to smoke detectors, can monitor CO levels and sound an alarm if they get too high. If you purchase one, make sure it is UL certified.

If your CO detector sounds an alarm, leave immediately and do a household head count. Since one of the effects of CO poisoning is confusion and disorientation, get everyone out immediately—then check for signs of poisoning and call the fire department or 911.

Avoiding Carbon Monoxide Problems

- Check chimneys and appliance vents for blockages.
- Never use portable gas grills or charcoal grills inside your home.
- Never use a gas range, clothes dryer or oven for heating.
- If you use a non-electric space heater, have it inspected annually. You can get recommendations from fuel suppliers.
- Never run a car engine or any gas-powered equipment in an attached garage; the fumes may seep into the house.
- Check the pilot lights of gas appliances every few months. They should show a clear blue flame; a yellow or orange flame may indicate a problem.

Unlike smoke detectors, which are required by many local ordinances, CO detectors are not legally required. But that doesn't mean that you cannot persuade your landlord to install one. Detectors that are connected to the interior wiring of the house and backed up with emergency batteries are best. In a letter, emphasize your concerns and the relative ease with which the landlord could put your mind at rest. A sample letter is set out below.

Sample Letter Asking for CO Detector

34 Maple Avenue North, #3
Badlands, CO 00000
303-555-1234

February 14, 200X

Cindy Cerene
1818 East Seventh Street
Badlands, CO 00000

Dear Ms. Cerene:

The kitchen in the apartment we rent from you has a gas stove and cook-top, which are about 15 years old, and there is a gas furnace in the hallway. These appliances appear to be working normally, but especially in the winter, when storm windows make the house airtight, I am concerned about the possible buildup of carbon monoxide. I would like to ask you to install a CO detector in the hallway near the bedrooms.

As you know, CO is a deadly gas that can kill within hours. We can't see it or smell it, and it could accumulate and poison us during the night. The only way to protect ourselves (besides your regular maintenance of these appliances) is with a detector. These devices are not very expensive, and can be easily installed. I would do it myself, except that our lease prevents me from undertaking alterations or improvements without your consent.

I hope that you'll give some thought to my request. Thanks very much for your consideration of this matter.

Yours truly,

Brian O'Rourke

Brian O'Rourke

3. Responsibility for Carbon Monoxide

Most CO hazards are caused by a malfunctioning appliance or a clogged vent, flue or chimney. It follows that the responsibility for preventing a CO buildup depends on who is responsible for the upkeep of the appliance.

Appliances. Appliances that are part of the rental, especially built-in units, are typically the responsibility of the landlord, although you are responsible for intentional or unreasonably careless damage. For example, if the pilot light on the gas stove that came with the rental is improperly calibrated and emits high amounts of CO, the landlord is responsible for fixing it. On the other hand, if you bring in a portable oil space heater that malfunctions, that is your responsibility.

Vents. Vents, chimneys and flues are part of the structure, and their maintenance is typically handled by the landlord. In single-family houses, however, it is not unusual for landlord and tenant to agree to shift maintenance responsibility to the tenant.

If you have or suspect a CO problem that can be traced to the landlord's faulty maintenance, promptly request that the landlord fix it. If you are poisoned because your landlord failed to routinely maintain the appliances or to respond promptly to your repair request, the landlord will have a difficult time avoiding legal responsibility. (See Chapter 12.) To motivate your landlord to fix the CO-spewing gas dryer, it might be sufficient to subtly point out that failure to do so could cause a tragedy—and a lawsuit.

A sample letter bringing a CO problem to the landlord's attention is shown above. If you write such a letter, you would be smart to hand-deliver it to your landlord or manager, since the problem needs immediate attention. And in the meantime, don't use the appliance you suspect of causing the problem.

Carbon Monoxide Resources

Local natural gas utility companies often have consumer information brochures available to their customers. You can also contact the American Gas Association for consumer pamphlets on carbon monoxide. It can be reached at 1615 Wilson Boulevard, Arlington, VA 22209, 703-841-8667.

E. Electromagnetic Fields

Electromagnetic fields (EMFs) are the newest, and until recently, the most controversial, of the household "environmental hazards" that concern tenants.

Power lines, electrical wiring and appliances emit low-level electric and magnetic fields. The intensity of both fields are thousands of times lower than the natural fields generated by the electrical activity of the human heart, brain and muscles. The further away you are from the source of these fields, the weaker their force.

The controversy surrounding EMFs concerns whether or not exposure to them increases a person's chances of getting certain cancers–specifically, childhood leukemia. Government scientists have looked repeatedly at data and have come up with inconsistent answers. (In July 1999, one government researcher was discovered to have faked his data, which supposedly established a link between EMFs and cancer.) On balance, there is very little solid scientific support for the fear that EMFs cause cancer. But that won't stop many people from worrying about exposure.

Landlords cannot control EMFs any more than they can control the weather. If your apartment or rented house sits under or near a set of power lines and you're worried about possible effects on your health, your only recourse is to move at the end of the term.

Electromagnetic Fields Resources

The National Institute of Environmental Health Sciences and the U.S. Department of Energy publish an excellent booklet entitled "Questions and Answers About EMF (1995)." For a free copy, contact the U.S. Government Printing Office, Washington DC, 20402, 202-512-1800.

■

Crime on the Premises

Landlords in most states have at least some degree of legal responsibility to provide secure housing. This means they must take reasonable steps to:

- protect tenants from would-be assailants, thieves and other criminals
- protect tenants from the criminal acts of fellow tenants
- warn tenants about dangerous situations they are aware of but cannot eliminate, and
- protect the neighborhood from their tenants' illegal and noxious activities, such as drug dealing.

If landlords don't live up to this responsibility, they may be liable for any injuries or losses that occur as a result.

This chapter explores the security measures that you can legally expect from your landlord—and how to insist on them if your landlord doesn't do enough to safeguard tenants.

 Related topics covered in this book include:
- Lease and rental agreement ban on tenants' illegal activities and disturbances: Chapter 2.
- Landlords' responsibilities for repair and maintenance: Chapters 8 and 9.
- Your right to privacy: Chapter 11.
- Landlords' liability for injuries from defective housing conditions: Chapter 12.

A. The Landlord's Basic Duty to Keep You Safe

In every state, a landlord is expected to take reasonable precautions to protect tenants from foreseeable harm. You can't expect your landlord to build a moat around the rental property and provide round-the-clock armed security. On the other hand, your landlord can't just turn over the keys, trusting to the local constable and fate to assure your safety.

1. State and Local Laws

In many areas of the country, local building and housing codes are rich with specific rules designed to protect tenants. For example, some city ordinances require peepholes, deadbolt locks and specific types of lighting.

Only a few states have specific laws as to landlords' responsibilities to provide secure premises. For example:

- Under Florida law, landlords must provide locks and keep common areas in a "safe condition." A Florida tenant who was assaulted by someone who entered because of a broken back door lock was allowed to argue to a jury that the landlord was partially responsible. (*Paterson v. Deeb,* 472 So. 2d 1210 (Fla. Dist. Ct. 1985).)
- In Alabama, a statute that requires locks to "function safely and effectively" has been used to require landlords to try to protect

FUNNY. I DON'T REMEMBER LEAVING THE SILVER AND STEREO ON THE PORCH

tenants from foreseeable criminal acts. *Brock v. Watts Realty Co.*, 582 So. 2d 438 (Ala. 1991).

- Texas has the most stringent law in the country. All Texas rental units must be equipped with keyless bolts and peepholes on all exterior doors and pin locks on sliding glass doors, as well as a handle latch or security bar. If a landlord doesn't supply this equipment, the tenant may do so and deduct the cost from the rent, or legally break the lease and move out. (Tex. Prop. Code §§ 92.151-170.)

Unfortunately, many state and local laws offer little specific guidance. For example, they may require "clean and safe" or "secure" housing, without defining these terms. Courts in several states have ruled that these requirements apply only to the condition of the physical structure. In other words, "safe" stairways are those that will not collapse or otherwise cause injury, not those that are well-lit, protected and unlikely to be the site of a criminal incident.

But as the following example shows, some courts have taken a broader view of the term "safe."

EXAMPLE: The housing code in the city where Andrew owned rental property set minimum standards for apartment houses, including a requirement that all areas of rental property be kept clean and safe. The garage in Andrew's apartment building was poorly lit and accessible from the street because the automatic door worked excruciatingly slowly. The tenants met to discuss the situation and decided to send a group letter to Andrew, setting out their concerns. They had done a little legal research first, and were able to explain to Andrew that if a tenant (or guest) were hurt by an assailant who had entered through the unsecured entrance, Andrew might be liable.

Andrew showed the letter to his lawyer, who explained that the apartment building's dark and easy-to-enter parking garage violated the "clean and safe" requirement of the housing code, and that the tenants were right regarding

his potential liability. Andrew fixed the door and added lights in the garage.

If your state and local laws are vague, you may want to see how local agencies or the courts have interpreted the meaning of fuzzier terms.

If your landlord does not comply with specific equipment requirements, you can complain to the agency in charge of enforcing the codes, often a local building or housing authority. (See Section D, below.)

If you are injured as a result of your landlord's violation of a safety law—for example, an intruder enters your apartment building because of a lock that's been broken for weeks—the landlord may be liable for your injuries. The landlord's liability in this situation is explained in Chapter 12.

To get a copy of your local housing code or ordinance, call your city manager's or mayor's office or look it up at your local public library. In addition, you may be able to get information from a state or local housing agency (see Chapter 8) or local tenants' association.

2. The Landlord's General Responsibility

In addition to complying with local and state laws that require basic security measures, landlords have a general common law duty to act reasonably under the circumstances—or, expressed in legal jargon, to "act with due care." For example, common areas must be kept clean and safe, so that they do not create a risk of accidents. When it comes to security, too, courts in most states have ruled that landlords must take reasonable precautions to protect tenants from foreseeable criminal assaults and property crimes.

What precautions are reasonable depends on the situation. If you have been the victim of a crime on the premises—or are afraid you will be, sooner or later—ask yourself six questions to help you determine your landlord's responsibility.

1. Did your landlord control the area where the crime occurred?

Your landlord isn't expected to police the entire world. For example, a lobby, hallway or other common area is an area of high landlord control. However, the landlord exerts much less control over the sidewalk outside the front door.

2. How likely was it that a crime would occur?

Landlords are duty-bound to respond to the foreseeable, not the improbable. Have there been prior criminal incidents at the particular spot you are worried about? Elsewhere in the neighborhood? A landlord who knows that an offense is likely (because of a rash of break-ins or prior crime on the property) has a heightened legal responsibility in most states to guard against future crime.

3. How difficult or expensive would it have been for the landlord to reduce the risk of crime?

If relatively cheap or simple measures could significantly lower the risk of crime, it is likely that a court would find that your landlord had a duty to undertake them, especially in an area where criminal activity is high. For instance, would reasonably inexpensive new locks and better lighting discourage thieves? However, if the only solution to the problem is costly, such as structural remodeling or hiring a full-time doorman, it is doubtful that a court would expect it of your landlord unless the danger is very great.

4. How serious an injury was likely to result from the crime?

The consequences of a criminal incident (break-in, robbery, rape or murder) may be horrific.

Let's look at how these first four questions might be answered in three crime situations.

EXAMPLE 1: Sam was accosted outside the entryway to his duplex by a stranger who was lurking in the tall, overgrown bushes in the front yard next to the sidewalk. There had been many previous assaults in the area. Both the bushes and the lack of exterior floodlights near the entryway prevented Sam from seeing his assailant until it was too late. If Sam filed a claim with the landlord's liability insurance company, or sued the landlord, an adjuster or judge would probably conclude that the landlord was bound to take measures to protect Sam's safety, because:

1. The landlord controlled the common areas outside the duplex.
2. It was foreseeable that an assailant would lurk in the bushes and that another assault would occur.
3. The burden of trimming the shrubbery and installing lights was small in comparison to the risk of injury.
4. There are usually serious consequences from a criminal assault.

EXAMPLE 2: Caroline was assaulted in the house she rented by someone whom she let in, thinking that he was a gas company repairperson. There was a peephole in the front door, as required by law, which she could have used had she asked to see proof of his identification. When Caroline sued her landlord, the judge tossed the case out. Her case collapsed on question 1: The landlord had no control over Caroline foolishly opening the door to someone whom she could have safely questioned (and excluded) from inside.

EXAMPLE 3: Max was assaulted and robbed in the open parking lot next to his apartment house when he came home from work late one night. The landlord knew that several muggings had recently been reported in the neighborhood. The parking lot was thoroughly lit by bright floodlights, but it was not fenced and gated. Here's how the four questions got answered:

1. The lot was under the landlord's control.
2. An assault seemed reasonably foreseeable in view of the recent nearby muggings.
3. However, the burden of totally eliminating the danger (fencing the lot) would have been very expensive.

4. The seriousness of the probable injury was great.

When Max sued, the judge ruled in favor of the landlord, concluding that it wasn't reasonable to expect the landlord to fence and lock the parking lot. In a high-crime area in another state or where tenants had previously been assaulted in the parking lot, a judge's decision might be different.

If, based on these first four questions, you think the landlord had a legal duty to deal with a condition on the premises that exposed you to the risk of crime, keep going. You have two more questions to answer.

5. Did your landlord fail to take reasonable steps to prevent a crime?

As ever, "reasonableness" is evaluated within the context of each situation. For example, returning to Sam (Example 1, above), the fact that the landlord let the bushes grow high and didn't replace the lights clearly was unreasonable. But suppose the landlord had cut the bushes back halfway and installed one light. Would that have been enough? It would be up to a jury to decide.

The greater the danger, the more a landlord must do. Past criminal activity on the premises increases your landlord's duty to keep tenants safe. "Reasonable precautions" in a crime-free neighborhood are not the same as those called for when three apartments in the landlord's building have been burglarized within the past month.

EXAMPLE: Allison rented an apartment in Manor Arms after being shown the building by the resident manager. Nothing was said about recent criminal activity in the building. A month after moving in, Allison was assaulted by a man who stopped her in the hallway, claiming to be a building inspector. Unbeknownst to Allison, similar assaults had occurred in the building in the past six months, and the manager even had a composite drawing of the suspect done by the local police. Allison's assailant was captured and proved to be the person responsible for the earlier crimes.

Allison sued the building owners after their insurance carrier refused to offer her a reasonable settlement. In her lawsuit, Allison claimed that the owners were negligent (unreasonably careless) in failing to warn her of the specific danger posed by the repeat assailant and in failing to beef up their security (such as hiring a guard service) after the first assault. The jury agreed and awarded Allison a large sum of money.

Many courts have ruled that prior criminal activity in the neighborhood increases a landlord's duty to tenants only if the prior crimes were similar to the current one. For example, a string of car break-ins in the neighborhood will probably not obligate a landlord to provide extra security measures to prevent apartment break-ins.

EXAMPLE: In New Jersey, a fight between two tenants in a downstairs apartment knocked loose their light fixture; later, another altercation between the same tenants resulted in a shotgun blast through the ceiling, injuring the upstairs tenant. The trial court found that the landlord was not negligent for failing to evict the rowdy tenants, and was not liable for the neighbor's injuries, because the second incident was not reasonably foreseeable as a result of the first. *Williams v. Gorman,* 214 N.J. Super. 517 (1986). Similar limitations on a landlord's liability have been drawn in California, Illinois, Massachusetts, Michigan and Missouri.

Landlords cannot eliminate all danger to tenants. In some situations, it may be enough to warn them. Just as caution tape and warning cones alert tenants to a freshly washed floor, landlords can warn tenants about possible criminal problems by using:

- newsletters that remind tenants to be on the alert and use good sense

- letters that communicate specific information, such as a physical description of an assailant who has struck nearby, and

- signs that remind tenants to use the building's safety features, such as a notice posted in the lobby asking tenants to securely lock the front door behind them.

6. Did your landlord's failure to take reasonable steps to keep you safe contribute to the crime?

You must be able to connect the landlord's failure to provide reasonable security with the criminal incident. It is often very difficult for tenants to convince a jury that the landlord's breach caused (or contributed to) the assault or burglary.

Think of it this way: If you fall because the rotten front step collapsed, you can trace the collapse directly to the landlord's failure to maintain the property. But when an intruder enters through an unsecured front door, you have another ingredient: the burglar's independent decision to commit the crime. The landlord is not responsible for the criminal's determination to break the law, and many juries simply won't place any responsibility on the landlord, even if, for example, failure to install a lock made the entry possible. To convince a jury otherwise, you must emphasize that a crime of this nature was highly foreseeable and would probably have been prevented had the landlord taken appropriate measures.

If a jury decides that the landlord didn't meet the duty to keep you safe, and that this failure facilitated the crime, it will typically split the responsibility for the crime between the landlord and the criminal. For example, jurors might decide that the landlord was 60% at fault and the criminal 40%. The landlord must compensate you accordingly. Not surprisingly, the criminal's share is usually never collected.

In Sam's case (Example 1, above), he convinced the jury that, had the bushes been properly trimmed and the area well-lit, he could have seen the assailant or, more likely, the assailant wouldn't have chosen this exposed place to commit a crime. The jury found that the landlord was 70% at fault for Sam's injuries.

How Much Money You're Entitled To

To get financial compensation, you must show that you were harmed by the criminal incident. Tragically, this is often quite obvious, and the only issue that lawyers argue about is the worth, in dollars, of dreadful injuries. Compensation may also be awarded for mental anguish and continuing psychological effects of the encounter.

Now let's look at two final, realistic cases, applying all six questions.

EXAMPLE 1: Elaine was assaulted and robbed by an intruder who entered her apartment through a sliding window that was closed but could not be locked. To determine whether or not the landlord would be liable, Elaine asked herself the six questions and came up with these answers:

1. The landlord controlled the window and was responsible for its operation.
2. This burglary was foreseeable, since there had been break-ins at the building in the past.
3. Installing a window lock was a minor burden.
4. The seriousness of foreseeable injury was high.
5. The landlord had done nothing to secure the window or otherwise prevent an intrusion.
6. The intruder could not have entered so easily and silently had the window been locked.

Putting these answers together, she concluded that the landlord owed her the duty to take reasonable steps to fix the problem. She filed a claim with the landlord's insurance company, but it failed to offer a fair settlement and Elaine's case went to trial. The jury decided that the landlord should have installed a window lock and that since the burglar might not have entered at all through a properly secured window, the landlord was partially responsible for Elaine's injuries. The jury fixed the value of her injuries at $500,000 and decided that the landlord was 80% responsible.

EXAMPLE 2: Nick was assaulted in the underground garage of his apartment building by someone who hid in the shadows. Nick's neighborhood had recently experienced several muggings and assaults. Nick couldn't identify the assailant, who was never caught. The automatic garage gate was broken and wouldn't close completely, allowing anyone to slip inside.

Nick decided that (1) the landlord controlled the garage, (2) in view of the recent crimes in the neighborhood, an assault was foreseeable, (3) fixing the broken gate wouldn't have been a great financial burden, and (4) the likelihood of injury from an assault was high. Nick concluded that the landlord owed him a duty of care in this situation.

Nick then considered the last two questions. The garage door was broken, which constituted a breach of the landlord's duty. But the garage was also accessible from the interior of the building, making it possible that the assailant had been another tenant or a guest. Nick's case fell apart because the landlord's failure to provide a secure outside door hadn't necessarily contributed to the crime. If the assailant were another tenant or guest, the landlord's failure to fix the gate would have been completely unconnected to the crime. Nick probably would have had a winning case if he could have proved that the assailant got in through the broken gate.

3. The Landlord's Promises

A landlord who promises specific security features—such as a doorman, security patrols, interior cameras or an alarm system—must either provide them or be liable (at least partially) for any criminal act that they would have prevented. Remember, your lease is a contract, and if it includes a "24-hour security" promise or a commitment to have a doorman on duty at night, you have a right to expect it. Even oral descriptions of security bind the landlord, if they were a factor that led you to rent the unit. You can often also rely on statements about security in advertisements.

Your landlord won't be liable for failing to provide what was promised, however, unless this failure caused or contributed to the crime. Burned-out light bulbs in the parking lot won't mean anything if the burglar got in through an unlocked trap door on the roof.

EXAMPLE 1: The manager of Jeff's apartment building gave him a thorough tour of the "highly secure" building before he decided to move in. Jeff was particularly impressed with the security locks on the gates of the high fences at the front and rear of the property. Confident that the interior of the property was accessible only to tenants and their guests, Jeff didn't hesitate to take his kitchen garbage to the dumpsters at the rear of the building late one evening. There he was accosted by an intruder who got in through a rear gate which had a broken lock. Jeff's landlord was held liable because he had failed to maintain the sophisticated, effective locks that had been promised.

EXAMPLE 2: The information packet given to Maria when she moved into her apartment stressed the need to keep careful track of door keys: "If you lose your keys, call the management and the lock will be changed immediately." When Maria lost her purse containing her keys, she immediately called the management company but was couldn't reach them because it was after 5 p.m. and there was no after-hours emergency procedure. That evening, Maria was assaulted by someone who got into her apartment by using her lost key.

Maria sued the owner and management company on the grounds that they had completely disregarded their own standard (to change the locks promptly) and so were partially responsible (along with the criminal) for the assailant's entry. The jury agreed and awarded Maria a large sum.

B. Problems With Other Tenants

Sometimes danger lurks within as well as beyond the gate. And your landlord has a duty to take reasonable steps to protect you if another resident on the property (including a roommate) threatens to harm you or your property.

Your landlord should respond to a troublesome tenant in essentially the same way he would respond to a loose stair or broken front-door lock. A landlord who knows about a problem (or should know about it) is expected to take reasonable steps to prevent foreseeable harm to other tenants. If the landlord fails to do that, and you are injured or robbed by another tenant, you may sue and recover damages.

If your roommate's the problem, be sure to read the related discussion of violent roommates in Chapter 7.

1. When the Landlord Must Act

The landlord won't be held partially responsible for a tenant's illegal acts unless the problem tenant had done or threatened similar criminal conduct in the recent past, and the landlord knew about it. In short, you'll need to convince an insurance adjuster, judge or jury that:

- it was reasonable to expect the landlord to know or discover the details of a tenant's past, and
- once known, the landlord could have taken steps to control or evict the troublemaker.

Unless there's a clear history of serious problems with the offending tenant, landlords usually win these cases.

EXAMPLE 1: Evelyn decided to rent an apartment to David, although she knew that he had been convicted of spousal abuse some years earlier. For several months David appeared to be a model tenant, until he hit another tenant, Chuck, in the laundry room over a disagreement as to who was next in line for the dryer. Chuck was unable to convince the jury that Evelyn should bear some responsibility for his injuries, because he could not show that the incident was foreseeable.

EXAMPLE 2: Mary rented an apartment to Carl, who appeared to be a nice young man with adequate references. Carl stated that he had no criminal convictions when he answered this standard question on the rental application. Several months later, Carl was arrested for the burglary and assault of another tenant in the building. At trial, it came out that Carl had recently been released from state prison for burglary and rape. Because Mary had no knowledge of his criminal past, she was not held liable for his actions.

On the other hand, tenants sometimes win if they can show that the landlord knew about a resident's tendency towards violence and failed to take reasonable precautions to safeguard the other tenants.

EXAMPLE: Bill received several complaints from his tenants about Carol, a tenant who had pushed another resident out of the elevator, slapped a child for making too much noise and verbally abused a tenant's guest for parking in Carol's space. Despite these warning signs, Bill didn't terminate Carol's tenancy or even speak with her about her behavior. When she picked a fight with a resident whom she accused of reading her newspaper and badly beat her up, Bill was held partly liable on the grounds that he knew of a potentially dangerous situation and failed to take appropriate steps to safeguard his tenants.

If you fear violence from another tenant, let your landlord know in writing. Not only does this underscore the seriousness of the situation, but it will be irrefutable proof that the landlord was on notice that problems were brewing. When more than one resident complains, the landlord will face more pressure to take action. And if there is an altercation later, the landlord cannot plausibly claim ignorance.

Get your facts straight before making accusations. If you believe that certain individuals are breaking the law—or just causing trouble—be certain that you have the facts straight before telling others about them. Otherwise, you might find yourself on the wrong end of a libel or slander lawsuit.

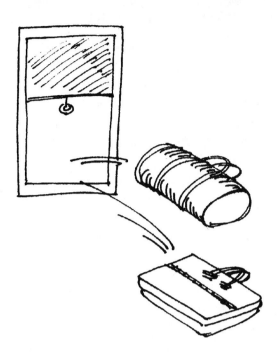

2. What the Landlord Must Do

A landlord who knows about the potential for danger from another tenant must do something about the problem tenant, such as warn other tenants or evict the troublemaker.

For example, suppose your neighbor bangs on the walls every time you practice the violin during the afternoon—and the pounding is getting louder. If you've tried to talk things out and been greeted with a raised fist, it's time to alert the landlord. You can reasonably expect the landlord to intervene and attempt to broker a solution—perhaps an adjustment of your practice schedule or some heavy-duty earplugs for the neighbor. If the circumstances are more threatening—for example, your neighbor brandishes a gun—your landlord might be legally expected to call the police, post a security guard and warn other tenants pending the speedy eviction of the dangerous tenant.

To make this legal responsibility easier for landlords to meet, many states now make it relatively simple for landlords to evict troublemakers. These laws specify that harm or the threat of harm to other persons justifies a quick eviction. (See Chapter 17 for details on expedited evictions.)

Intervention and eviction of the troublemaker are the usual ways that landlords meet their duty to take care that residents don't harm other residents. But the law doesn't require your landlord to have a crystal ball.

EXAMPLE: Abbot and his mother rented a duplex from Xavier, who knew that Abbot was emotionally disabled and took regular medication to control his behavior. Unknown to his mother or Xavier, Abbot began skipping his medication and eventually attacked Larry, the other tenant in the duplex, with a baseball bat. Xavier was not held liable, since it would have been illegal to refuse to rent to Abbot, a disabled person under the Federal Fair Housing Amendments Act. Xavier did not know that Abbot had discontinued his medication, nor would it have been reasonable to expect Xavier to monitor Abbot's dosages. If Xavier had known that Abbot was off his medication, however, he would have been duty-bound to speak to Abbot and his mother and possibly warn the other residents.

Getting a Restraining Order

If you are seriously threatened by another tenant who will not leave you alone, and your landlord either won't evict the aggressor or the eviction is taking some time, consider obtaining a court restraining order.

These orders are signed by a judge after you demonstrate that you really are in danger—for example, the aggressor has made repeated verbal threats to harm you or your family. The order directs the person to stay away from you. Its principal value is that the police will react faster and more firmly than they might otherwise. To obtain a restraining order, call your local courthouse for information.

If you obtain a restraining order, make a copy and give it to your landlord and to the manager, if any. Ask him to alert other on-site personnel, such as security guards and maintenance personnel of the existence and meaning of the order. A wise landlord will usually consider a restraining order as ample grounds for a swift termination and eviction. If the aggressor returns after he is evicted, request that the landlord order him off the property and call the police.

If you get no cooperation from your landlord and are still fearful, move. Your safety is worth far more than your right to live in a particular rental space. Your landlord may feel that you have broken the lease and may try to keep your security deposit to cover unpaid rent for the balance of the lease or rental agreement, but if you go to court to contest this, your chances of winning are good. (Chapter 16 discusses small claims suits over security deposits.) You can argue that by failing to evict the troublemaker, the landlord has breached the covenant of quiet enjoyment and made your rental unfit and uninhabitable, which justifies your moving out. (See Chapter 8.)

C. Illegal Activity on the Property and Nearby

Illegal activities on the premises create problems for law-abiding tenants, and enormous financial risks and penalties for landlords. Law-abiding tenants move out, and landlords may be hit with:

- Lawsuits by tenants who are hurt or annoyed by drug dealers or other criminals
- Fines by local, state or federal authorities for tolerating a legal nuisance
- Criminal charges for tolerating illegal behavior, and
- In extreme cases, loss of their rental properties when they are seized by the courts.

Understanding your landlord's legal responsibilities and risks will help you and other tenants convince the landlord to take steps to avoid trouble before it strikes. (See Sections D and E for suggestions on what you can do to convince the landlord to take action against drug dealing and other activities and, at the same time, take steps to protect yourself.)

Nice Properties Are Not Immune

If you live in a safe neighborhood, you may think that drug crime is largely a problem in seedy neighborhoods. Think again. Illegal drug use is spread widely throughout American society—the notion that it is a ghetto phenomenon is just plain wrong. A study by the Crime Control Institute, a nonprofit group in Washington, D.C., found that smaller apartment complexes with some measure of security are preferred by drug dealers over large, unprotected housing units. The reason may surprise you: A drug dealer, like a law-abiding tenant, is interested in a safe, controlled environment. But a drug dealer who's smart enough to choose a nice property isn't always smart enough not to hassle the other tenants.

1. Government Lawsuits Against the Landlord

The legal meaning of "nuisance" bears only a little resemblance to its meaning in everyday life. A legal nuisance is a pervasive, continuing and serious condition—like a pile of stinking garbage or a group of drug dealers—that threatens public health, safety or morals. In some states, it also includes activity that is simply offensive, like excessive noise or open sexual conduct.

Every state has some type of nuisance abatement law, which allows the government, and sometimes the neighbors, to sue to stop these sorts of problems. Using public nuisance abatement laws against crime-tolerant landlords is increasingly common in large cities with pervasive drug problems. In extreme cases, where the conduct giving rise to the nuisance complaint is illegal (drug dealing or prostitution, for example), landlords themselves face civil fines or criminal punishment for tolerating the behavior.

Public nuisance laws come in two forms: civil and criminal. The table below explains the differences between the two types.

Civil and Criminal Nuisance Laws

	Civil Nuisance Laws	Criminal Nuisance Laws
Activities the laws target	Unhealthy, immoral or obnoxious behavior which may be, but is not necessarily, a violation of the criminal law as well	Criminal behavior
Examples of targeted activities	Excessive noise, piles of garbage and trash and inordinate amounts of foot or car traffic	Drug dealing, prostitution, gambling and gang activities
Who can sue	Public agencies such as city health departments, law enforcement agencies and, in many states, affected neighbors, who may band together and sue for large sums in small claims court. (See Section D, below.)	Law enforcement agencies only
Possible consequences to the landlord	A court ordering the offending tenant, and sometimes the landlord, to compensate other tenants. If a health, fire or other enforcement agency brings the nuisance action based on many violations, it can result in a court order closing down the entire building.	Liability for money damages plus fines and imprisonment

Designer Nuisance Laws

The public nuisance statutes in some states are fine-tuned to efficiently deal with offending tenants with a minimum of court entanglement.

- Laws in Rhode Island and Missouri specify that if the landlord is aware of certain illegal activity, including drug dealing, occurring on the premises, the lease is rendered void and the tenant must vacate. The landlord does not need to take any legal action—that is, file an eviction lawsuit—even if there isn't a criminal conviction for the tenant's offense. Of course, the physical removal of the tenant is still up to the landlord and the local sheriff.
- Florida's way to deal with drug dealing involves local administrative boards that receive complaints and hold hearings regarding alleged nuisances. These boards have the power to shut down the premises for up to one year.
- In Texas, 10% of the voters in any voting district may require the district attorney to call a public meeting regarding any alleged nuisance. The property owner is notified of the meeting, and the results of the meeting are forwarded to the district attorney, who may take steps to close the property.

2. Seizure of the Landlord's Property

It's rare, but the government sometimes seizes property because of the illegal activities of one or more tenants. A successful forfeiture proceeding is absolutely devastating from the landlord's point of view. The landlord loses not only the property, but also all the rent money that the landlord received from the drug-dealing tenants.

If you're a tenant, forfeiture won't improve your lot. Few tenants want to live in government-run housing that starts off as a drug den. But a landlord who hears the word "forfeiture" will probably be highly motivated to get rid of the offending tenants.

EXAMPLE: Sterling Properties hired a management firm to run several apartment buildings in a high-crime area. At one of the buildings, there were repeated drug arrests and complaints from neighbors regarding incessant comings and goings of people at all hours. The federal government initiated forfeiture proceedings. Sterling Properties argued that because it had not been informed by its management company of the situation, it had no knowledge of the illegal activities of the tenants. The court ruled that the neighborhood was a virtual "anthill" of illegality that any reasonable person would know about and that the knowledge of the management company could be imputed to the owners. The building was forfeited and became the property of the United States government.

Other landlords in the area, shocked at this result, began meeting to work out strategies to rid their neighborhood of residents suspected of drug dealing.

3. Small Claims Lawsuits Filed by Neighbors

Overworked and understaffed police and health departments are often unable to make a real dent in problem-plagued neighborhoods.

Determined tenants and neighbors have stepped into the breach, bringing their own lawsuits, seeking the elimination of the offensive behavior. Basically, tenants and neighbors may sue a landlord for failing to take steps to clean up the property, and seek:

- monetary compensation for each of them for having put up with the situation. Each neighbor generally sues for the maximum allowed in state small claims court ($3,000 to $7,500 in most states), and the landlord often pays the maximum to *each* one. (See the discussion of small claims courts in Chapter 19.)
- an order from the judge directing the landlord to evict the troublemakers, install security and

repair the premises. Such orders are not available in all states.

Many lawsuits of this nature have been successfully filed across the nation.

Many laws proscribing nuisances are "neighbor friendly"—that is, an offended neighbor doesn't need to have the resources of Scotland Yard to successfully use them. For example, in New York City a local ordinance allows neighbors within 200 feet of property used as a "bawdy house" or for other illegal activity to begin summary eviction proceedings (in a court other than small claims) against the tenants if the owner does not take steps to correct the problem after being given five days' notice. (New York City Admin. Code §§ C16 and following.) A notable aspect of the ordinance is that the neighbors need not prove specific acts of illegality; all they need show is the ill repute of the premises or of those renting or using it. (*Kellner v. Cappellini*, 516 N.Y.S.2d 827 (N.Y. City Civ. Ct. 1986).)

Small (But Sometimes Mighty) Claims Court

The private enforcement of public nuisance laws has been creatively and successfully pursued in small claims courts in California and several other states, where groups of affected neighbors have brought multiple lawsuits targeted at drug houses. This approach makes sense whenever a landlord is confronted by a large group of tenants all suing for the small claims maximum dollar amount, thus motivating the landlord to clean up the property.

In one case in Berkeley, California, after failing to get the police and city council to close down a crack house, neighbors sought damages stemming from the noxious activities associated with a crack house. Each of the 18 plaintiffs collected the maximum amount allowed in small claims court ($3,500 at the time), avoided the expense of hiring counsel and sent the landlord a very clear and expensive message. The problem was solved within a few weeks.

Resources: Organize Against Drug Dealers

Contact "Safe Streets Now" for help in organizing beyond your building. This nonprofit organization is headquartered in Oakland, California, and has helped tenants throughout the United States combat drug dealing, gangs, blighted property and the problems associated with all-night convenience stores, bars and cheap motels. It can be reached at 408 13th Street, Suite 452, Oakland, CA 94612, 510-836-4622.

D. Getting Results From the Landlord

Here are some suggestions on how to encourage your landlord to fulfill the responsibility to provide a safe place to live.

1. Evaluate the Situation

Before approaching your landlord with requests for improved security, collect hard evidence concerning the building's vulnerability to crime. The best way to evaluate the safety of your rented home is to conduct a security inspection of the rental property. Your goal is to answer two questions:

- If I (or a family member, roommate or guest) were here alone at night, would I feel safe? and
- If I were an assailant or a thief, how difficult would it be to get into the building or individual rental unit?

Involve Other Tenants

If you are a renter in a multi-unit building, chances are that you aren't the only one concerned with safety. Working with other tenants on this issue (or others) has definite advantages:

- **Landlords respond to armies more readily than to individuals.** Once you get other tenants involved, your chances of getting the landlord to implement anti-crime measures greatly increase. The consequences of rent withholding, complaints to the police or small claims actions are much greater if done by a group than by a sole tenant. (These tactics are discussed below.)

- **Involving others reduces the chances of retaliation.** Tenants in most states are protected against landlord retaliation (such as terminations, rent hikes and withdrawal of services) for exercising their rights to voice their opinions to the landlord, complain to enforcement agencies and organize collectively. (See Chapter 15 for a thorough explanation of anti-retaliation laws.) But if your state does not protect you against retaliation, acting as a group may make it harder for your landlord to retaliate—few landlords want instantly empty buildings, or worse, buildings full of angry residents.

- **You'll learn more about security problems.** For example, maybe the upstairs neighbor, who is home during the day, can tell you that the 24-hour security guard really lounges in the manager's office all afternoon, watching the soaps.

- **Involving others increases your safety.** Once you and your neighbors realize that you are all in the same boat, it is more likely that you will look out for each other.

See Chapter 19 for tips on working with other tenants.

a. Analyze the Building

Start by circulating a letter to other residents explaining your concerns and suggestions for improved security on the property, and solicit their comments. Call a meeting to discuss the results and plan your next moves.

You'll learn the most about your building's vulnerability if several tenants walk or drive around the rental property at different times of the day and night—you might see something at 11 p.m. that you wouldn't notice at 11 a.m. A reasonably safe and secure single-family home, duplex or multi-unit rental will have strong locks on windows and doors, good interior and exterior lighting and other features that will hinder unwanted intrusions. To see how your rental unit, building and grounds measure up, use the checklist of Important Security Features, below.

You may also want to get a security evaluation and advice from your renter's insurance agent. Because insurance companies are potentially liable for large settlements or awards, they are concerned with reducing crime on rental property. So talk to your insurance company and, even more important, encourage your landlord to talk to hers about equipment and safety systems that can prevent break-ins and assaults.

Important Security Features

- Exterior lighting directed at entrance ways and walkways that is activated by motion or a timer, and not dependent on the memory of managers or tenants to turn them on. The absence or failure of exterior lights is regarded by many security experts as the single most common failing that facilitates break-ins and crime.
- Good, strong interior lights in hallways, stairwells, doorways and parking garages.
- Sturdy deadbolt door locks on individual rental units and solid window and patio door locks, as well as peepholes (with a wide-angle lens for viewing) at the front door of each unit. Lobby doors should have deadbolt locks. Solid metal window bars or grills over ground floor windows are often a good idea in higher-crime neighborhoods, but landlords may not be able to install them due to restrictions of local fire codes. All grills or bars should have a release mechanism, allowing the tenant to open them from inside. Too many tenants have tragically died in fires because they could not escape an apartment with window bars or grills that had no release mechanism.
- Intercom and buzzer systems that allow you to control the opening of the front door from the safety of your apartment.
- Neat and compact landscaping that does not obscure entryways or afford easy hiding places adjacent to doorways or windows.
- In some areas, a 24-hour doorman is essential and may do more to reduce crime outside the building than anything else.
- Driveways, garages and underground parking that are well-lit and secure from unauthorized entries. Fences and automatic gates may be a virtual necessity in some areas.
- Elevators that require a passkey for entry. If this won't solve the problem, you may even want to request the landlord to install closed-circuit monitoring. Obviously this is expensive, since it requires someone to watch the monitor, but it may be worth suggesting if your building has fairly high rents or is in a particularly crime-prone area.

b. Consider the Neighborhood

The extent of your vulnerability depends not only on the security systems in your building, but the surrounding neighborhood. If there has been little or no crime in your area, you have less to worry about and less legal reason to expect your landlord to equip the property with extensive security devices. On the other hand, if crime is a problem where you live, gather information on local crime from people in the neighborhood and the police department. Then, armed with what you have learned, you are in a good position to suggest ways both your landlord and other tenants can keep the rental property safe.

2. Request Improvements

Once you and other tenants have gathered information about your vulnerability to crime and what can be done to reduce your risk, you'll be ready to take specific steps to make your lives safer.

It's quite likely that you know more about the security needs of the rental units and building (and landlords' legal responsibilities) than the owner, especially if the owner is an absentee landlord. To improve security in your rental, you may first have to educate your landlord about:

- **Statutory security requirements.** If local or state ordinances or laws require specific security devices, such as deadbolts, peepholes or window locks, start by asking your landlord to comply with the law. Put your request in writing. (Of course, keep copies of all correspondence.) Attach a copy of the ordinance or statute to your request. If you get no response, submit a second request. Then, if there is still no compliance, consider your options (see Section E, below).
- **Promised security measures that are missing or malfunctioning.** If the landlord has promised security beyond the basics dictated by law—such as an advertisement promising garage parking or security personnel—you have a legal right to ask that the landlord

deliver. (See Section A, above.) Send a written reminder to the landlord and attach a copy of the advertisement or lease provision that backs up your request.

- **Security required by the surroundings and circumstances.** Your own assessment of the property and the neighborhood may lead you to conclude that the landlord is shirking his duty to protect tenants. But because you do not have a clear-cut ordinance or statute to point to, you will have to do some extra work motivating the landlord. Use the information you've gathered to convince the landlord that, given the area's crime problems, more effective security measures are required—and that if security isn't improved the landlord could be legally liable for injuries that result.

Oral requests sometimes get results, but more often they are ignored. Putting security requests in writing and having them signed by as many tenants as possible is a far better way to get results. Even the most dim-witted landlord understands that if tenants have a written record of their complaints about personal safety issues—especially when the landlord has not kept promises to provide security systems—and nothing is done, the chances of a successful lawsuit go way up.

So write a letter even if you think it's hopeless, even if your landlord is notoriously stingy or impossibly stubborn. By creating a paper trail, you have provided the landlord with a considerably increased incentive to take action. Your letter should:

- remind the landlord that he has control of the problem
- set out the foreseeable consequence (an assault) of not dealing with the property's obvious lack of security
- propose that the solution is relatively easy, and
- suggest that the consequences—a burglary or assault—are serious.

A sample letter alerting the landlord to dangerous conditions, is shown below.

Sample Letter Alerting the Landlord to Dangerous Conditions

789 Westmoreland Avenue, #5
Central City, WA 00000
555-123-4567

January 3, 200X

Mr. Wesley Smith, Landlord
123 East Street
Central City, WA 00000

Dear Mr. Smith:

As tenants of the Westmoreland Avenue building, we are concerned that there is a dangerous condition on the property that deserves your prompt attention.

As you know, the large sliding windows on the bottom floor (in the lobby) are secured by turn locks that can be easily forced open. On occasion we have seen a dowel placed in the track to prevent the windows from being opened, but lately the dowels have often been missing. Several times, the windows have even been left open all night.

We are worried that an intruder will have an easy time of getting into the building. There have been several burglaries in the neighborhood within the past two months. The situation would be greatly helped if you could send a glass repair person to replace the locks with much stronger ones. Needless to say, a burglary or assault is a worrisome prospect.

Thank you for your prompt consideration of this matter.

_____

[as many tenants as possible]

Contact the landlord's insurance company. If you can find out who insures the landlord (a tenant who has filed any type of previous claim may know) and the landlord persists in not taking reasonable safety precautions, send copies of all your correspondence to the company. Since it may have to pay a substantial claim or jury award if a tenant is assaulted, it has an obvious interest in getting the landlord to act, now. Pressure from the insurance company (and the worry that it may cancel the policy or increase rates) may have an immediate effect on a lazy or stubborn landlord.

3. Meet With the Landlord

If your written requests don't produce results, invite your landlord to meet with you (and other tenants, if possible) to discuss your concerns. You may want to involve a local mediation service, which has the advantage of giving you a skillful and neutral moderator. You'll be especially glad for the presence of the mediator if your landlord arrives with an attorney. If you or other tenants end up in court over your landlord's failure to keep the premises safe, the refusal to discuss the situation with you will hardly help the landlord's case. (Chapter 19 gives suggestions on finding and working with a mediator.)

Ask other tenants if they're willing to pay for better security. For example, you may find that fellow tenants will agree to a small rent increase in order to get a doorman, a locking garage gate or an intercom system. A landlord may be very interested in such a proposal.

4. Get Help From the Government

If gentle (or even concerted) persuasion fails to get desired security improvements, call in the reinforcements. Depending on what the exact problem is and where you live, contact either building or health inspectors or local law enforcement agencies, who have the power to order the landlord to comply with the law. For example, if there is a local ordinance requiring deadbolts on all exterior doors, it probably names the agency (such as the health department or the building inspectors) responsible for enforcing the code. Often, all you need to do is

to contact that agency and begin the complaint procedure. Send copies of your complaint (signed by as many tenants as possible) to the landlord. This alone may result in the landlord taking the desired actions.

The effectiveness of turning to building or health inspectors varies hugely. In some areas, such as New York City, inspectors are so overwhelmed with complaints that they are rarely able to respond promptly. On the other hand, enforcement agencies are quite effective in many areas, and you may get a quick and satisfying response. Since they respond fastest to situations that pose serious and immediate threats to health or safety, emphasize the seriousness of the problem.

EXAMPLE: When Lucy moved into her apartment two years ago, the neighborhood was reasonably safe and untroubled. In the last two months, however, Lucy's street had become the site of rival gang activity. After two muggings nearby and a burglary next door, Lucy was worried about her safety and decided to do something about it.

Lucy went to the local library and looked at the city ordinances, which included a requirement that multi-unit rental property be equipped with deadbolts and locks on lower-level windows. Along with several other tenants, she also evaluated the property and concluded that the shrubbery needed trimming, the exterior lights were inadequate and the parking garage was unsafe. They talked with the other tenants, and decided to present their concerns to the landlord as a group.

When a meeting failed to produce significant change, they contacted the building inspector, who cited the landlord for code-related violations of the deadbolt lock law. At that point, another tenant had an idea that proved to be a small stroke of genius: She complained to the fire department about the condition of the bushes, which resulted in a scheduled inspection. Even though the size of the bushes might not have resulted in a citation, notification of the inspection was enough to motivate the landlord to immediately cut them back.

Finally, realizing that the tenants were determined to make changes—and to avoid being hassled in the future—the landlord hired a regular landscaper, installed floodlights and added a locking gate to the garage.

5. Withhold Rent or Break the Lease

If your rented home becomes truly dangerous, it may be legally considered uninhabitable—which means that you might be justified in withholding rent. (Chapter 8 explains this option.)

Because this is a relatively new and fast developing area of the law, we cannot give you a neat list of the states in which these options are available for serious security problems. We can, however, suggest some guidelines that must be met by any claim that a unit is uninhabitable because of high crime danger.

- **The problem is truly serious now, not merely annoying or a potential problem.** For example, having to walk past dope dealers on your way through the front hall is unavoidable, frightening and loaded with potential for violence. On the other hand, unverified stories regarding prostitution in your neighborhood or even in your building are less compelling.
- **You've given the landlord notice of the problem and time to respond.** In general, as discussed in Chapter 8, you must tell the landlord about it and give him time to respond, either by fixing the problem or approaching the legal authorities (police or city attorney) who are better equipped to deal with it. For example, if drug dealers have moved in next door, you must alert the landlord and give him time to begin eviction procedures; if gangs have invaded your neighborhood, you must complain to the landlord and give the police time to act.

⚠️ **Withholding rent, even if it's totally justified, may prompt the landlord to terminate your tenancy if you're a month-to-month renter.** Although many states have laws that are supposed to protect you from such retaliation, you may still have to fight it out in court if your landlord sues to evict you. (See Chapter 8.)

6. Break the Lease

If your rented home is legally considered uninhabitable, you might be justified in moving out, for the same reasons you may be able to withhold rent. (See subsection 5, above.)

You may also be justified in breaking the lease and moving out if the promised security was an important factor in your decision to rent your place, and the landlord failed to follow through on that promise (see Section A, above). This remedy is explained in Chapter 8 in connection with repairs or maintenance that have been promised but not delivered.

EXAMPLE: Wendy, a flight attendant, rented her apartment in Safe Harbor after reading its advertisement in the local newspaper that promised "Security personnel on duty at all times." When she was shown around the property, Wendy told the manager that she often came home late at night. She was assured that there was a 24-hour guard service. However, after coming home several nights in the early morning hours and discovering that there were no security guards on duty, Wendy confronted the management and was told that financial constraints had made it necessary to cut back on the guards' hours. Wendy wrote the landlord a letter asking that the guard service be restored. When it wasn't, she promptly moved out.

Safe Harbor kept Wendy's entire security deposit (one month's rent), claiming that her departure violated the lease and that management had been unable to find a replacement tenant for four weeks. Wendy sued Safe Harbor for the return of her entire deposit, arguing that in fact it was Safe Harbor who had broken the lease by failing to provide security as promised. The judge decided that the promise of 24-hour security was an important part of Safe Harbor's obligations and that *its* failure to deliver constituted a breach of the lease, which excused Wendy from her obligation to stay and pay rent. And the judge ordered Safe Harbor to refund Wendy a portion of the rent she had already paid, on the grounds that she had paid for an apartment with a guard but had not received it.

You may be able to break a lease and move with little or no financial consequence. In most states your landlord will have a duty to make reasonable efforts to re-rent your unit and apply the new rent to what you owe on the balance of your lease. (This duty is discussed in detail in Chapter 15.) If the rental market is tight and your rental is reasonably attractive and competitively priced, your landlord may have little excuse for not re-renting quickly. Of course, if the dangerous conditions that prompted your early departure are noticed by prospective tenants (who reject the rental for that reason), the landlord may have a hard time re-renting. Fortunately for you, the harder it is for the landlord to re-rent, the stronger your case that the rental was unacceptably unsafe, justifying your breaking the lease. In short, you win either way.

7. Sue in Small Claims Court

Your most effective response to inadequate security or dangerous surroundings might be aggressive action in small claims court. Interestingly, small claims court can be an appropriate tool to deal both with simple problems like the installation of a deadbolt and complex ones like ridding the building of drug-dealing tenants. (See Section C, above.)

If you're lucky, the difference between a secure apartment and an unsecured one might be the simple addition of a code-mandated door or window lock, trimming some bushes or replacing burned-out light bulbs in the garage or hall. If your repeated requests for action have fallen on closed ears, and local inspectors can't or won't come to your aid, what should you do?

Small claims court might be the answer. Simply perform the work yourself (preferably with other tenants) and then sue the landlord for the cost. This route does, however, put you at risk, especially if your lease or rental agreement says "no improvements or alterations without the landlord's consent." Your risk of eviction for violating a lease clause will probably be less if the job you do is required by local law, such as a code-required deadbolt, rather than a modification like trimming the bushes that *you* have concluded is required for your safety. In short, if it's something clearly required of the landlord, he'll have a hard time laying blame on you for doing his job, and your lease clause violation will appear almost necessary.

E. Protecting Yourself

Faced with an unsafe living situation, your only option may be to pursue self-help remedies, such as installing your own security protections or moving out.

1. Use Good Judgment

If you live in a dangerous building or high-crime neighborhood, your first thought must be to watch out for yourself. Just as defensive driving techniques may do more to keep you safe than confronting dangerous drivers or equipping your car with every imaginable safety device, you'll want to rely primarily on your own good judgment and willingness to change your habits.

If you have identified vulnerable aspects of your building or rental unit, chances are that others have too. If you were a burglar or mugger, how would you strike? Avoid dangerous situations—for example:

• Don't use an isolated parking lot late at night.

- Consider curtailing your evening's activities. No late-night movie is worth the risk of an assault.
- Use a fan for air circulation instead of opening easily-accessible windows at night.

2. Install Your Own Security Protections

In some situations, you may be able to take matters into your own hands, at least as regards your own rented space. Although your lease may prohibit you from making alterations or repairs without the landlord's permission (see Chapter 10), lots of effective security devices do not require permanent installation. For example, sliding windows can often be secured with removable interior blocks, and sliding doors can be tightly locked with specially designed rods. In addition, local or state law may expressly permit you to install certain devices when the landlord has failed to do so. In Texas, the tenant may install code-required locks and peepholes. (Tex. Prop. Code §§ 92.151 to 170.) (For suggestions on supplying code-required equipment and not footing the bill, see Section D, above.)

⚠ **Involve your landlord if you install an alarm or permanent locks.** Many tenants install locks or alarms, no matter what the law or their lease says. If you live in a high-crime area, your landlord may not squawk as long as you provide keys to the locks and a way to disarm the alarm.

Remember, your landlord has the right to enter in an emergency, and you cannot make this impossible. (Chapter 11 discusses your landlord's right of entry.) We suggest that you ask your landlord before you install locks or alarms, since installation of these devices constitutes an "improvement or alteration" that your lease or rental agreement may prohibit. If you don't get the landlord's OK, the lease violation could serve as grounds to terminate your tenancy.

3. Consider Moving

Sad to say, often your most effective response to a dangerous rental situation is to move. Many tenants on a tight budget believe they can't afford any better alternatives. While understandable, this view is often wrong. Look around your area for places where low rents don't mean high crime. Although sometimes well-kept secrets, these neighborhoods often exist. Or consider the possibility of getting a roommate or sharing a house, so you can afford to live in a better part of town.

If you have a month-to-month rental agreement you can usually move out with 30 days' notice. Breaking a lease may be a little more difficult, unless you're moving out because your rental is uninhabitable or your landlord failed to follow through with promised security measures, as discussed in Section D, above. (Chapter 15 discusses notice requirements for ending a tenancy.) ■

How Tenancies End or Change

Sooner or later, all tenancies end. Whether you move often, or tend to stay put for years, you should understand the important legal issues that arise at the end of a tenancy, including:

- the type of notice a landlord or tenant must provide to end a month-to-month tenancy
- legal restrictions on your landlord's ability to end a month-to-month tenancy, including the ban on "retaliatory evictions"
- what happens if you leave without giving required notice
- the landlord's legal options if you don't leave after receiving (or giving) a termination notice or after the lease has expired
- your options if you want to get out of a lease early or sublet your home temporarily, and
- what happens if your landlord goes out of business or declares bankruptcy.

This chapter starts with a brief discussion of a related topic—how your landlord may change your lease or rental agreement during your tenancy. For example, your landlord would be a pretty rare bird if he never increased the rent for a month-to-month tenancy. And you, too, may want to make a change—for example, by adding a roommate or keeping a pet.

Related topics covered in this book include:
- Lease and rental agreement provisions on notice required to end a tenancy: Chapter 2.
- Notice required for rent increases: Chapter 3.
- Getting your security deposit back after you leave: Chapter 16.
- When the landlord can terminate your tenancy because you violated the lease or rental agreement: Chapter 17.
- Overview of eviction lawsuits: Chapter 18.

A. Changing Terms During Your Tenancy

Once you sign a lease or rental agreement, it's a legal contract between you and your landlord. All changes should be in writing and signed by both of you.

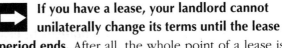 **If you have a lease, your landlord cannot unilaterally change its terms until the lease period ends.** After all, the whole point of a lease is to fix the terms of the tenancy—including rent—for the length of the lease. If you have a lease, skip ahead to Section C.

1. Amending a Month-to-Month Rental Agreement

A landlord who wants to change something in a month-to-month rental agreement doesn't need your consent. Legally, your landlord need simply send you a notice of the change. The most common reason landlords amend a rental agreement is to increase the rent. Chapter 3 provides a detailed discussion of this issue.

To change a month-to-month tenancy, most states require 30 days' notice, subject to any local rent control ordinances. (See "Notice Required to Change or Terminate a Month-to-Month Tenancy" in Appendix I for a list of each state's notice requirements.) In most states, the landlord can deliver the notice by first-class mail.

A landlord doesn't legally have to re-do the entire rental agreement in order to make a change or two. It's just as legal and effective to attach a copy of the notice making the change to the rental agreement. However, many landlords will want the change to appear on the written rental agreement itself.

If the change is small and simply alters part of an existing clause—such as increasing the rent or making the rent payable every 14 days instead of every 30 days—your landlord can cross out the old language in the rental agreement, write in the new and sign in the margin next to the new words. He'll probably also want you to sign and date the change.

If the changes are lengthy, your landlord may either add an amendment page to the original document or prepare a new rental agreement, as discussed below. If an amendment is used, it should clearly refer to the agreement it's changing and be signed by the same people who signed the original agreement. See the sample amendment, below.

Amendment to Lease or Rental Agreement

This is an Amendment to the lease or rental agreement dated _____March 1_____, 200_X_,

(the Agreement) between _____Olivia Matthew_____

(Landlord) and _____Steve Phillips_____

(Tenant) regarding property located at _____1578 Maple St., Seattle_____

_____ (the premises).

Landlord and Tenant agree to the following changes and/or additions to the Agreement:

1. Beginning on June 1, 200X, Tenant shall rent a one-car garage, adjacent to the main premises,

   from Landlord for the sum of $75 per month.

2. Tenant may keep one German shepherd dog on the premises. The dog shall be kept on a leash in

   the yard unless tenant is present. Tenant shall clean up all animal waste from the yard on a

   daily basis. Tenant agrees to repair any damages to the yard or premises caused by his dog, at

   Tenant's expense.

_____

_____

_____

_____

_____

_____

_____

_____

_____

_____

May 20, 200X	_Olivia Matthew, Landlord_
Date	Landlord
May 20, 200X	**Steve Phillips, Tenant**
Date	Tenant
Date	Tenant
Date	Tenant

A blank, tear-out form Amendment to Lease or Rental Agreement is in Appendix II. Copy the tear-out and save the original for later use.

2. Preparing a New Rental Agreement

In the age of computers and word processing, a landlord who is adding a new clause or making several changes to your rental agreement will probably find it easiest to substitute a whole new agreement for the old one. For example, your landlord will probably want a new agreement if you're adding or replacing a roommate or if a "no pets" clause is being added. If your landlord prepares an entire new agreement, it's best that you both write "Canceled by mutual consent, effective (date)" on the old one, and sign it. All tenants should sign the new agreement. (Chapter 7 discusses having a roommate sign a new agreement.) The new agreement should take effect on the date the old one is canceled.

B. How Month-to-Month Tenancies End

This section discusses how you or the landlord can end a month-to-month tenancy.

Ending a rental agreement involuntarily. If your landlord terminates your tenancy because you have violated a rental clause—for example, by not paying rent or by disturbing your neighbors—turn to Chapter 17.

1. How Landlords May End a Tenancy

It's easy for a landlord to end a month-to-month tenancy. No reasons are required in most states. (New Hampshire and New Jersey are exceptions because landlords in these states must have a just cause or valid reason to end a tenancy.) A landlord can simply give you a written notice to move,

allowing you the minimum number of days required by state law (typically 30) and specifying the date on which your tenancy will end. (See "Notice Required to Change or Terminate a Month-to-Month Tenancy" in Appendix I.) After that date, you no longer have the legal right to occupy the premises.

Most rent control laws do not allow a landlord to terminate a month-to-month tenancy except for just cause, or a legally recognized reason. Chapter 3 discusses rent control rules.

If you want more security, your only real alternative is to sign a fixed-term lease. But if you want to stay, after getting a 30-day notice telling you to leave, either for a short time (until you find another place) or indefinitely, there is nothing to stop you from negotiating with the landlord. (Section E, below, gives some practical advice on how to approach this.)

Each state, and even some cities, has its own very detailed rules and procedures for how landlords must prepare and serve termination notices. For example, some states specify that the notice be printed in a certain size or style of typeface. If your landlord doesn't follow these procedures, the notice terminating your tenancy may be invalid. But once you point out the mistake, either informally or as a defense to an eviction lawsuit, your landlord will probably do it right the next time. If you want information on your state's exact requirements, consult your state statutes. (See "Landlord-Tenant Statutes" in Appendix I.) Your state consumer protection agency or local tenants' rights organization may also have useful advice.

If you stay on despite receiving a properly written and served termination notice, you'll be a candidate for an eviction lawsuit. (See Section C, below.)

The 30-day period may start on the day the notice is mailed, not received. Say your landlord mailed a 30-day notice on June 1, asking you to be out by July 1. If you don't get the notice until June 4, you might believe you are legally entitled to stay until July 4, even though the notice gives a July

1 termination date. Not necessarily. In some states, putting the notice in the mail is enough to start the 30-day notice period running. If you need every day possible to move out and can't arrange a compromise date with your landlord, check this point in your state's statutes. (Chapter 20 discusses how to look up a statute.)

2. How You Can End a Month-to-Month Tenancy

The landlord isn't the only one who can end a month-to-month tenancy easily and quickly; you can do it, too. In fact, the overwhelming number of rental relationships are ended when the tenant voluntarily decides to move on.

a. How and When to Give Notice

In most states, and for most rentals, you must provide the same amount of notice as (sometimes less than) a landlord—typically, 30 days.

For details on your state's rules, see "Notice Required to Change or Terminate a Month-to-Month Tenancy," in Appendix I. You'll see that in some states, if you pay rent more frequently than once a month, you can give notice to terminate that matches your rent payment interval. For example, if you pay rent every two weeks, you need give only 14 days' notice.

If your state allows you to mail your termination notice, use first-class mail, and mail it a few days early. Depending on the state, it may be legal to mail your 30-day notice exactly 30 days before you wish to end your tenancy, even though the landlord gets it a few days later. But in other states, a landlord is entitled to receive the notice at least 30 days before you plan to leave. If you intend to leave on July 1 and mail your notice on June 1, your landlord might not get it until June 4. If the notice period is 30 days, your tenancy won't end

until July 4. Your landlord might try to withhold four days' worth of "unpaid rent" from your security deposit if you move out as planned on July 1.

To protect yourself, mail a notice in plenty of time to give the landlord 30 days' notice. To be on the safe side, don't count the last day if it falls on a Sunday or holiday. Or, if time is tight, deliver it in person, requesting a receipt.

Even if you try to give your notice orally, many landlords will insist that you provide it in writing. Especially if you know the landlord well, you may feel that your word is enough, but the law usually requires written notice. Use our form Tenant's Notice of Intent to Move Out. A filled-out sample is shown below.

A Tenant's Notice of Intent to Move Out tear-out form is included in Appendix II. Copy this form, fill it out and give it to your landlord when you plan to move.

In most states, you can give notice at any time. In other words, you don't have to give notice so that your tenancy will end on the last day of the month. If your tenancy ends mid-month, you'll be paying rent until that date. For example, if you pay rent on the first of the month but give notice on the tenth, you will be obliged to pay for ten days' rent for the next month, even if you move out earlier. To calculate the amount, pro-rate the monthly rent.

The only exception to this general rule comes if your rental agreement states that notice may be given only on a certain date, typically the date the rent is due. This means that if you decide on the tenth that you need to move, you'll have to wait until the first to give notice, and will be obliged to pay for the entire next month, even if you leave earlier.

You are legally free to give your landlord more notice than is required by law. But giving extra notice does not give you an initial period of time in which to change your mind. For example, if you give 45 days' notice in a state that legally requires 30, you cannot change your mind during the first 15 days.

Tenant's Notice of Intent to Move Out

April 3, 200X
_____
Date

Anne Sakamoto
_____
Landlord

888 Mill Avenue
_____
Street Address

Nashville, Tennessee 37126
_____
City and State

Dear___Ms. Sakamoto_____,
            Landlord

This is to notify you that I/we will be moving from ___999 Brook Lane, Apartment Number 11___

_____,

on __May 3, 200X_____, __30 days_____ from today.

This provides at least ___30 days_____ written notice as required in our

rental agreement.

Sincerely,

Patti Ellis
_____
Tenant

Joe Ellis
_____
Tenant

_____
Tenant

b. If You Change Your Mind

For all sorts of reasons, you may change your mind after giving your landlord formal notice of your intent to move. But if you can't convince the landlord to reinstate your tenancy, or the unit has already been rented again, it's too late. You'll have to move.

If you now want to stay on, promptly call the landlord, explain your change of heart and ask for a meeting. Explain why your plans have changed—for example, you were moving because you thought you had just bought a house, but the deal collapsed in escrow. You are more likely to influence the landlord to reinstate your tenancy if you can show that you now plan to stay for an extended period of time, not just a few weeks.

If the landlord agrees to reinstate your tenancy informally—perhaps over the phone—fine, but be sure to follow up with a confirming letter. If your landlord doesn't immediately write back disagreeing with your understanding, this is probably enough to legally reinstate the old rental agreement. But, to be safe, offer to sign a new rental agreement. A sample letter to a landlord is shown below. Note how the tenant has built in a favorable outcome: The letter states that if she doesn't hear from her landlord within a reasonable time, the old rental agreement will be back in force. (Locking the landlord into your position is the essence of this kind of letter, which is explained in detail in Chapter 2, Section C2.)

If you are having trouble communicating with your landlord, see if a local mediation program can help. (See Chapter 19 for more on mediating land-lord-tenant disputes.)

Sample Letter Asking for Reinstatement of Tenancy

945 Willow Road, #8
Marysville, RI 00000

June 10, 200X

Mr. Paul Johnston
123 Capitol Mall
Capital City, RI 00000

Dear Mr. Johnston,

On June 1, I gave you written notice of my intent to move on the first of July, in order to accept a transfer to my company's headquarters in New York.

After I gave notice, however, my job transfer was canceled, and I would like to continue living here. I hope that you have not rented my apart-ment already, and will cancel my 30-day notice and continue to rent to me as you have done for the past two years. My hope is to continue to live here for at least six months.

Thank you very much for considering my request. Assuming I can stay on, I would be happy to sign another rental agreement or, if you prefer, we can resume using the old agreement. If I don't hear from you within a few days, I'll assume that we'll be operating under the old rental agreement. I have enclosed a copy of my supervisor's recent memo canceling my job transfer.

Yours truly,

Sally Blum

Sally Blum

c. Extending Your Tenancy a Few Days

Suppose that, after giving notice, you need a little more time to move. Assuming no new tenant is set to move in right away, your landlord may be willing to let you pay pro-rated rent for a specified number of extra days. If so, you should sign an agreement setting out what you have agreed to.

If your landlord refuses your request to stay a few days, and you simply don't move at the end of the notice period, you'll probably receive a termination notice from the landlord right away. The landlord will probably also promptly file papers to evict you, or, if it's allowed in your state, go directly to court. (See Section C.)

d. Leaving on Short Notice

There are times when even the most conscientious tenant may not be able to give the landlord the required amount of notice (usually 30 days). Perhaps a family medical emergency or a new job requires you to move out immediately. If you leave without giving enough notice, you lose your right to occupy the premises, but are still obligated to pay rent through the end of the required notice period.

EXAMPLE: Edna moves out after giving her landlord 15 days' written notice of her intent to move. Since Edna lives in a state that requires 30 days' notice, she owes rent for an additional 15 days. Of course, Edna's landlord may let her leave early without paying the additional rent, especially if another tenant is ready to move in very soon. But if the landlord can't rent the apartment within 15 days Edna's landlord can deduct any unpaid rent from Edna's security or last month's rent deposit.

Many landlords must try to minimize their losses when tenants leave early. In many states, your landlord has a legal duty to try to limit ("mitigate," in legalese) the amount lost because you leave early. To do that, the landlord must try to re-rent the property promptly. (This responsibility is discussed in detail in Section F.) But few courts expect a landlord to accomplish this in less than a month. So if you leave without giving enough notice, expect to pay rent for the next month.

C. How Fixed-Term Leases End

A lease lasts for a fixed term, typically one year. As a general rule, neither you nor your landlord may unilaterally end the tenancy, unless you have violated the terms of the lease or the landlord has failed to meet a responsibility, such as to provide a habitable place to live.

If you and your landlord both live up to your promises, however, the lease simply ends of its own accord at the end of the lease term. At this point, you must either:

- move
- sign a new lease (with the same or different terms), or
- stay on as a month-to-month tenant with your landlord's approval.

If you do none of these things and your landlord wants you to move on, you are considered a "holdover" tenant and will probably be evicted.

Your lease renewal may be protected in a rent control area. If your tenancy is covered by rent control, your landlord may be required to renew your lease unless there is a legally approved reason (just cause) not to. (See Chapter 3 for more on rent control.) Reasons such as your failure to pay rent or your landlord's desire to move in a close relative commonly justify non-renewal. If your landlord does not renew your lease, but the reason given does not meet the city's test, you will probably become a month-to-month tenant. Your landlord will still need a good reason to get you out. Check your city's rent control ordinance carefully. (Major cities' ordinances are summarized in Appendix I.)

1. What to Do Before the Lease Expires

A lease clearly states when it will expire, and you are responsible for knowing this date. Some states or cities (especially those with rent control), however, require landlords to remind you in writing a reasonable period (often 30 days) before the lease expiration date if they want you to leave.

If you want to renew your lease or stay on as a month-to-month tenant, talk to your landlord well before your lease expires. If you have been a good tenant, your landlord will probably want you to stay, assuming you agree to any new terms, such as, possibly, a rent increase. This is also the time to suggest changes you want—for example, if you want to add a roommate or bring in a pet.

If you plan to leave at the end of the lease, it's courteous to give your landlord notice of your intent. If you plan to move but need an extra few days, weeks or even months, chances are your landlord will be accommodating.

2. Staying On and Paying Rent Without a New Lease

It's fairly common for landlords and tenants not to care, or not even to notice, that a lease has expired. The tenant keeps paying the rent, and the landlord keeps cashing the checks. Is everything just the same as it was before the lease expired? The answer depends on where you live.

Creating a month-to-month tenancy. In most states, you will have created a new, oral month-to-month tenancy on the terms that appeared in the old lease. Now your landlord can treat you as a month-to-month tenant—for example, the rent can be raised with 30 days' notice.

> **EXAMPLE:** Shawn's lease ended on July 1, but neither he nor his landlord Helen realized that the lease was up. Shawn paid the regular month's rent on July 1. On July 20, Helen realized that the lease had expired, and decided that she wanted Shawn to stay—but at a higher rent. She decided not to offer Shawn another lease, since rents were going up in her area and she wanted to be able to raise his rent as she saw fit. She sent him a note, telling him that he would have to pay $100 more on August 1.
>
> When Shawn got Helen's note, he realized that he was no longer renting under his old lease. But he understood that, by accepting rent on July 1, Helen had created a month-to-month tenancy. This meant that Helen could not change any terms unless she gave Shawn the proper amount of notice—30 days in their state. Since Helen gave notice on July 20, Shawn's rent could not go up until August 20.

Of course, your landlord can belatedly present you with a new lease. If you decide not to sign it, you can stay on as a month-to-month tenant, under the terms of the old lease, until the landlord gives you proper written notice to move on. As discussed above, this is usually 30 days.

Automatically renewing the lease. However, in a few states, including Pennsylvania, the rule is quite different. If your lease expires and your landlord continues to accept rent, the two of you have created a new lease for the same length (such as one year) and terms (such as the amount of rent) as in the old lease. In other words, you have automatically renewed the lease. The effects are dramatic: You and the landlord are now legally obligated for a new lease with the same term as the old one.

To avoid inadvertently signing up for an entire new term, never pay rent past the date the lease expires without discussing it first with your landlord.

3. When a Lease Ends and Your Landlord Wants You Out

Once the lease expires, your landlord doesn't have to keep you on as a tenant. If you stay on after the lease ends and offer rent that your landlord *does not* accept, you're a "holdover" tenant. In some states, the landlord must still give you notice, telling you to leave within a few days; if you don't leave at the end of this period, you can be evicted. A few states allow the landlord to file for eviction immediately, as soon as the lease expires.

Unless you have a reasonably good chance of proving that your landlord's refusal to renew the lease is illegal (see Section D, below), or you believe you can work out a compromise with your landlord (see Section E, below), it's probably time to pack up and move. There's no reason to head into an eviction lawsuit that's a pretty sure loser.

First, if your intent is to buy time, you'll get relatively little of it by staying on and going to court. That's because holdover eviction lawsuits, where the tenant has no good defense, are given speedy treatment in most states. And while the exact time will vary depending on state law and how fast the landlord jumps through required procedural hurdles, it can often be accomplished in two to three weeks. (See the overview of evictions in Chapter 18.)

Second, take a good look at your lease or rental agreement. Chances are it has an "attorney fees and costs" clause in it. (See Chapter 2, Section D.) This means that if you lose (or even if you capitulate on the courthouse steps before the actual hearing), you'll probably be on the hook for your landlord's attorney fees and costs. Those can add up to a few thousand dollars for even the most perfunctory eviction lawsuit. These costs will come out of your security deposit. If that doesn't cover them, the landlord can come after your wages or bank account.

Finally, remember that the fact that an eviction lawsuit was filed against you will show up on any credit report perused by future employers, banks, landlords and stores where you wish to establish credit. In short, holding on to your apartment for no legally defensible reason in an effort to avoid moving for a few weeks is very rarely worth the negative consequences.

⚠️ **Watch out for lease and rental agreement clauses that make holdover tenants pay a higher rent.** Your landlord may attempt to discourage you from staying past the end of your tenancy by making you agree, in advance, to pay as much as three times the rent if you do. Clauses like this may not be legal—they are a form of "liquidated damages" (damages that are set in advance, without regard to the actual harm suffered by the landlord), which are illegal in residential rentals in many states, including California. (However, they have been upheld in Texas.) The clause would probably not hold up in a rent control city; nor would it survive a challenge if the clause describes the rent hike as a "penalty."

D. Retaliation and Other Illegal Tenancy Terminations

Landlords can terminate a tenancy for a variety of reasons, such as nonpayment of rent, serious violations of the lease and illegal activity such as drug-dealing on the rental property. And unless state or local laws require a reason, a landlord can, with proper notice, terminate a month-to-month rental agreement or decline to renew a lease without giving any reason at all. But they can't terminate a tenancy for the *wrong* reason—in retaliation against you for exercising your legal rights or in a way that discriminates illegally.

1. Illegal Discrimination

Just as landlords can't engage in illegal discrimination when they rent a unit in the first place, they can't unlawfully discriminate when it comes to terminating a month-to-month tenancy or deciding not to renew a lease—for example, by deciding not to continue to rent to persons of a certain ethnicity or because of the landlord's political beliefs. Discrimination is covered in detail in Chapter 5, which also explains what you can do if you think you have been illegally discriminated against. All of the options discussed there—such as complaining to the federal Department of Housing and Urban Development and filing a lawsuit—are available to you if your lease or rental agreement is not renewed for discriminatory reasons.

2. Retaliation

The second major landlord "no-no" when it comes to tenancy non-renewals is retaliation. In most states, landlords may not end a tenancy in retaliation for your legally protected activities, such as complaining to a building inspector that a rental unit is uninhabitable. If they do, and you stay on despite the landlord's wishes, you can defend yourself against a lawsuit to evict you by proving retaliation.

Prohibitions against retaliatory evictions were the natural outgrowth of tenant protection laws that began to appear in the 1970s. Lawmakers reasoned, quite rightly, that it made no sense to arm tenants with the legal right to insist on fit and habitable housing (see discussion in Chapter 8) if the landlord could simply evict a tenant who exercised this right. Only eight states—Alabama, Colorado, Georgia, Indiana, Oklahoma, Pennsylvania, South Dakota and Wyoming—do not have statutes or court decisions protecting tenants against retaliation. The rest protect you if you have:

- complained to government agencies, such as housing authorities, health departments or fire departments
- exercised your First Amendment rights to assemble and present your views collectively, as in joining or organizing a tenant union, and
- availed yourself of strategies allowed by your state's law, such as deducting money from the rent and using it to fix defects in the rental unit, or even withholding the rent entirely for an uninhabitable unit (see Chapter 8).

See "State Laws Prohibiting Landlord Retaliation" in Appendix I for the specifics of these state laws.

How do you prove your landlord is trying to retaliate against you? In the real world, landlords are rarely so foolish as to say directly, "If you complain to the housing department, I'll evict you!" Instead, they're likely to terminate a tenancy for a trumped-up reason, hoping to mask the fact that the real motive is to get rid of a tenant whom they regard as a troublemaker. Common examples of cover-ups that are really retaliations are:

- A termination that follows hard on the heels of a long-term tenant's legitimate decision to withhold the rent
- An unexplained refusal to renew a lease following a tenant's complaint to the health department, and
- Sending a termination notice alleging misuse of common facilities after a tenant has used the common room to bring tenants together to fight a proposed rent increase.

Fortunately, however, many states give tenants an edge when it comes to unmasking illegal reasons to end a tenancy. In 15 states, the landlord is presumed to be retaliating against you if a tenancy is ended (or services decreased) within a certain amount of time, typically six months but sometimes 90 days or one year, following your exercise of a legal right. These rights include such things as withholding rent, complaining to a public agency about safety problems, or legitimately using any of the other remedies discussed in Chapter 8. (For a related discussion of rent hikes as retaliation, see Chapter 3.)

E. How to Stay When Your Landlord Wants You Out

Even if you do not have a legally valid response to your landlord's tenancy termination notice—for example, you can't convincingly claim that your landlord is retaliating for your exercise of a legal right, or you can't characterize it as an instance of illegal discrimination—all is not necessarily lost. In fact, your best chance of staying comes not from legal arguments but from honest negotiations. Not only does this strategy save the money and aggravation that you would otherwise spend defending yourself in an eviction lawsuit, but it also allows you to clear the air with your landlord. Even if your landlord has been behaving in a highly unreasonable way, it is still in your interest to try to arrive at an acceptable compromise. The following steps may help get your lease or rental agreement renewed.

1. Promptly Ask for a Meeting

Set up an appointment with the landlord or manager. Don't wait—the more time that passes, the less chance you have to get the landlord to come around. If possible, save the specifics of what you want to talk about until you meet face-to-face. It's harder to say no across a table than it is on the phone.

2. Prepare Your Case in Advance

If the termination or non-renewal is apparently not based on something the landlord thinks you did wrong (these situations are covered in Chapter 17), try to figure out the reason behind the landlord's decision before you meet. The manager (if any) or other tenants may have some insight.

Common reasons for a landlord to end a tenancy include:

- **A misunderstanding.** For example, maybe your landlord's been told—incorrectly—that you'll be moving in a couple of months, and wants to rent the unit now, when a renter is lined up
- **A matter of personal taste.** Your landlord is annoyed with the family parties you hold around the outdoor grill every Saturday night, or has been influenced by the manager, who doesn't like you, your teenage son, or any one of a dozen other things.
- **Irrational whim.** Your landlord likes to periodically rotate tenants, even stable ones, on the theory that—contrary to accepted landlord lore—regular turnover makes it easier to push through rent increases.

3. Negotiate With Your Landlord

When you meet with your landlord, explain why you want to stay, and be prepared with convincing arguments to counter the landlord's concerns. Chapter 19 discusses how to negotiate with your landlord.

4. Try Mediation

If you're unsuccessful negotiating your own case, enlist the help of a neutral third-party mediator, often available at little or no cost. Chapter 19 discusses how to find and use an outside mediator.

 Look for hidden, illegal reasons behind your landlord's termination. It's just possible that, in the process of negotiation, you'll discover that the true motivation is, indeed, illegal—such as your proper exercise of a repair-and-deduct statute or the addition of a baby to an apartment that is roomy enough to accommodate another occupant. In that event, you may want to stay and fight, even up to and including an eviction lawsuit. Chapter 18 gives you some tips on how to defend an eviction lawsuit.

5. If You're Successful, Sign a New Lease or Rental Agreement

Sage negotiators never leave the table without a written version of the conclusions reached. Neither should you. Ask to sign a new lease or rental agreement or, at the very least, write a summary of your understandings, date it and ask the landlord to sign it. If that can't be accomplished, immediately write a

letter of understanding detailing the promises made by each of you, including the reinstatement of your tenancy. Letters of understanding are explained in Chapter 2.

F. Getting Out of a Lease

Ideally, you'll sign a lease for just the amount of time you need the rental—a year to attend school, for instance. But despite your best efforts to match your lease term with your plans, you may need to move, temporarily or permanently, before the lease is up.

If you have no intention of returning, one option is to simply move out without sweating the legalities. Leaving before a fixed-term lease expires, without paying the remainder of the rent due under the lease, is called breaking the lease.

Breaking the lease may not cost you much. If the landlord re-rents the property quickly, all you'll be responsible for paying is the rent for the brief time the unit was vacant.

But if you want to leave early, there are better options than just moving out and hoping your landlord gets a new tenant quickly. There's a lot you can do to minimize your financial responsibility—and ensure a good reference from the landlord when you're looking for your next place to live.

This section discusses all your options:

1. **Get the landlord to cancel the lease.** By far the most painless method.

2. **Find a new tenant to sign a new lease.** A little more trouble, but usually worth it if the landlord won't just let you off the hook.

3. **Assign your lease**. Turn over your lease to someone else—not a bad choice, but it keeps you on the legal hook to some extent.

4. **Sublet, leave temporarily and return later.** Subletting makes sense only if you truly want go back to your rental later.

5. **Break the lease.** The landlord probably has a legal duty to try to find a new tenant, so you may not lose much by following this simple route.

When Breaking a Lease Is Justified

There are some important exceptions to the blanket rule that a tenant who breaks a lease owes the rent for the entire lease term. You may be able to legally move out without providing the proper notice in the following situations.

- **The rental unit is unsafe or otherwise uninhabitable.** If your landlord does not provide habitable housing—for example, if the unit violates health or safety codes—a court would probably conclude that you have been "constructively evicted." That releases you from further obligations under the lease. (See Chapter 8.)

- **State law allows you to leave early in the circumstances.** A few states' laws list reasons that allow a tenant to break a lease. For example, in Delaware you need only give 30 days' notice to end a long-term lease if you must move because your present employer has relocated or because of health problems (yours or a family member's). In New Jersey, a tenant who has suffered a disabling illness or accident can break a lease and leave after 40 days' notice upon presenting proper proof of disability. Some states, such as Georgia, allow members of the military to break a lease because of a change in orders. If you have a good reason for a sudden move, check your state's law.

- **The rental unit is damaged or destroyed.** If your home is significantly damaged—either by natural disaster or any other reason beyond your control—you have the right to consider the lease terminated and to move out. (See Chapter 8.)

- **Your landlord harasses you or violates your privacy rights.** (See Chapter 11.)

1. Getting the Landlord to Cancel the Lease

Lots of tenants assume that their landlord will never agree to end their lease early. This is a mistake. And anyway, it can't hurt to ask. Depending on the circumstances, you landlord may actually be delighted to see you go.

Reasons why your landlord may cheerfully tear up your lease include:

- **It's a chance to raise the rent.** Especially if you are a long-term tenant and your rent is below the current going rate, your departure gives your landlord the chance to offer the unit at a higher rate.

 **Most rent control cities, including those in California and Washington, D.C., let landlords raise rent to the market rate when a tenant moves out.** This gives landlords a huge financial incentive to get rid of old tenants. In the few rent control cities that limit rent increases even when a tenant voluntarily moves out, the landlord's profit motive to end your tenancy will be weaker. (Chapter 3 discusses rent control.)

- **The landlord will be able to make major repairs or renovations.** Laws in many states require the landlord to pay for relocation and temporary housing costs if a tenant must move because of renovations or repairs. Or the landlord might have to reduce the rent if a part of an apartment becomes unusable. (See Chapter 8.) So landlords usually put these jobs off until the unit is vacant; your departure might be just what your landlord was waiting for.

- **The landlord doesn't like you.** Here is one situation where a less-than-perfect tenant might have an edge. If, in your landlord's eyes, you are a pain in the neck (but your actions have not justified eviction), your request to leave early might be met with a sigh of relief.

- **Your landlord is a decent sort.** If you have been honest and considerate with the landlord, and you have a good reason for leaving—for example, to nurse a sick parent or find a new job after getting laid off—your landlord might be willing to extend you the favor of letting you go. In fact, your landlord may be legally required to allow you to leave early because of a job change or health problem. (See "When Breaking a Lease Is Justified," above.)

When you ask to get out of your lease, be prepared to sweeten the deal by offering to pay a little bit extra. In the world of big business, this is known as a "buy-out." There's no reason why you can't do it, too. For example, if you want to leave three months early, you might offer to pay half a month's extra rent and promise to be extra accommodating when the landlord wants to show the unit to prospective tenants. A sample Buy-Out Agreement is shown below.

Sample Buy-Out Agreement Between Landlord and Tenant

This Agreement is entered into on January 3, 200X, between Colin Crest, Tenant, who leases the premises at 123 Shady Lane, Capitol City, California; and Marie Peterson, Landlord.

1. Under the attached lease, Tenant agreed to pay Landlord monthly rent of $600. Tenant has paid rent for the month of January, 200X.

2. Tenant's lease expires on June 30, 200X, but Tenant needs to break the lease and move out on January 15, 200X.

3. Landlord agrees to release Tenant on January 15, 200X, from any further obligation to pay rent in exchange for Tenant's promise to pay one-and-one-half month's rent ($900) by January 15, 200X.

4. Tenant agrees to allow Landlord to show his apartment to prospective new tenants on two hours' notice, seven days a week. If Tenant cannot be reached after Landlord has made a good-faith effort to do so, Landlord may enter and show the apartment.

5. If Tenant does not fulfill his promises as described in paragraphs 3 and 4 above, the attached lease, entered into on January 3, 200X, will remain in effect.

Colin Crest   1/3/0X
Colin Crest, Tenant   Date

Marie Peterson   1/3/0X
Marie Peterson, Landlord   Date

Help With Moving Costs From Your Employer

If you need to move because of a new job or transfer, check to see if your company will cover the cost of getting out of a lease. Many will, recognizing that relocation expenses aren't limited to hiring movers and storing furniture. Especially if your transfer is involuntary or you have been aggressively courted by a new company, use your leverage as a valued employee to ask the company to buy out at least a month or two of your lease. In most areas, that should give the landlord plenty of time to find a new tenant.

If your landlord agrees to let you out of your lease early—even if your parting is friendly—it's vital to get the agreement in writing. (See the sample Termination of Lease, below.) It protects you in the event that the landlord changes his mind (or sells to a new owner) and tries to hold you responsible for future rent or damages done by the next tenant.

 A blank, tear-out copy of the Termination of Lease form is in Appendix II.

2. Terminating the Lease and Providing a New Tenant

If your landlord is not willing to end your lease early, another approach will probably let you break your lease at little or no cost. Simply present your landlord with an acceptable substitute tenant, who will take over right away and continue the flow of rent uninterrupted. Another benefit of this strategy is that it prevents the landlord from passing along to you the costs of finding a new tenant.

To come up with an acceptable new tenant, you'll need to advertise the unit and screen applicants. Doing this is similar to finding someone to be a co-tenant. (See Chapter 7.) If you find a good person whom the landlord accepts, be sure the

---

Termination of Lease

Robert Chin _____ (Landlord)

and ____ Carl Mosk _____

(Tenant) agree that the lease they entered into on ____ November 1, 200X _____ , for premises at

_____ 56 Alpine Terrace, Hamilton, Tennessee _____ , will terminate

on _____ January 5, 200X _____ .

____December 28, 200X_____   *Robert Chin*_____
Date   Landlord

____December 28, 200X_____   *Carl Mosk*_____
Date   Tenant

---

landlord signs a "Termination of Lease" form, shown above.

In many states, your landlord is legally bound to accept a suitable tenant you propose or to try to find one without your help. (See the discussion below.) But what if your landlord simply refuses to talk to the perfectly acceptable people you find, and demands that you pay rent for the rest of the lease? You'll need to preserve the evidence that you presented one or more good, new tenants, and that the landlord unreasonably refused to consider them or unreasonably rejected them. Without good evidence, you may lose your deposit, be liable for unpaid future rent and suffer other negative consequences of breaking a lease.

Keep good records of suitable new tenants. This should include their employment and rental history and letters of reference. Better yet, have candidates fill out the rental application in Chapter 1 and give you a copy of their credit report. If your prospective sub's background and credit history is as good as or better than your own, the landlord is going to have a tough time explaining a rejection to a judge, if the dispute ever goes to court.

3. Assigning Your Lease

If you intend to leave permanently, but your landlord will not cancel the lease, and you don't want the hassles of finding a replacement tenant, consider the third option: assignment. Because you face some potential legal liability with assignments, this option is always less attractive than the previous two.

a. How Assignments Work

Assigning a lease means you turn over the entire rest of your lease to another person, called an "assignee." (You're the "assignor.") You move out, and the new person takes over the lease and moves in. If a dispute erupts over the lease—for example, the assignee fails to pay the rent, or the landlord fails to maintain the property—the new tenant can sue or be sued by the landlord.

But making an assignment doesn't completely sever your legal relationship with the landlord. *Unless you agree otherwise, you remain responsible for the rent if the assignee fails to pay.* You are not, however, liable for damage to the premises caused by the assignee. The bottom line: It's much better to get your lease officially terminated and have the new tenant sign a new lease. Then you're totally off the hook.

Generally, the landlord and new tenant are bound by all the terms of the lease you, the original tenant, signed. For example, a lease provision in which the landlord agreed to return the security deposit in a certain manner is still in effect; but it now benefits the new tenant. Only in very unusual situations, where a lease provision is personal, does the obligation not transfer. For example, under the law of most states, a promise by a tenant to do a landlord's shopping in exchange for a rent reduction would not automatically pass to an assignee.

Some landlords will agree to an assignment when they might not agree to terminate your tenancy and simply rent to a new tenant. The reason is obvious: under an assignment, you are still legally responsible to pay the rent if the assignee doesn't. Of course, if you are moving out of state and will be beyond the power of a local court, the landlord is unlikely to be able to collect from you.

b. Finding an Assignee

Finding someone to take over your lease is little different than finding an acceptable new tenant. The advice in Chapter 7 will help you locate and present someone whom your landlord is likely to accept.

There is one important added consideration, however. Because you remain on the hook financially if the new tenant falls behind on the rent, you will want to be absolutely sure that the assignee is solvent and responsible. In short, you may want to be even fussier than your landlord is. Once you move, you never want to hear about your old rental unit again.

If You Take Over Someone's Lease

If you move in as an assignee of an old tenant's lease, your legal position is very good. You can stay until the lease runs out and enjoy all the rights of a regular tenant—for example, you can sue your landlord for failure to fix a hole in the roof, insist on the use of a parking space as promised in the lease, or use your state's repair-and-deduct statute for appropriate repairs. In addition, if you don't pay the rent, you'd still get evicted, but if it turns out that the original tenant is easier to locate or collect from, the landlord may even pursue her, not you.

But keep in mind that if you take over a lease that has only a few more months to run, you may face a rent increase if you want to stay longer. It might be better to sign a new, year-long lease and lock in the current rent, if the landlord agrees.

c. How to Assign a Lease

Accomplishing an assignment isn't difficult. One simple, legal approach is to print "Assigned to John Doe" on your current lease at each place your name appears. This will usually be the first clause that identifies the "parties" of the lease (see Chapter 2) and the signature line at the end of the lease. The new tenant, you and the landlord should then sign your names next to the words "Assigned to John Doe," each place these words are inserted on the lease.

However, there is a less messy approach. Simply present your landlord with a formal "Consent to Assignment of Lease," like the sample shown below. Using this form protects you in two important respects:

- It tells the newcomer (the assignee) that he is responsible for every term and condition of the lease, and
- It gives you an opportunity to have the landlord agree that you are off the hook if the

new tenant fails to pay the rent. (If the land-lord doesn't agree, you'll have to pay the rent if the assignee doesn't.)

In this assignment document, the landlord specifically gives up the right to collect any further rent from you. The landlord may balk and demand that this provision be removed. But then again, lots of landlords, not that worried about this issue, may just go ahead and sign.

 A blank, tear-out copy of the Consent to Assignment of Lease is in Appendix II.

4. Subletting Your Home Temporarily

If you have a fairly long lease and a particularly wonderful rental, you may want to move out for a while but then move back in. If you really want to keep your place, you can sublet it—that is, rent it to a short-term tenant who will leave when you wish to return.

Subletting may sound good, but think long and hard before you dive in. There are some serious drawbacks, explained below. As a general rule, sublease only if all four of these conditions are met:

1. You are completely confident of the integrity, financial stability and housekeeping habits of your intended subtenant.
2. Your landlord has approved the person you have presented.
3. You are sure you will return, and
4. You really want your old rental unit back.

EXAMPLE: Denis has lived in his apartment in a university town for 20 years. His landlord, Sally, happily renews the lease every year, appreciating the fact that Denis pays the rent on time and takes good care of the property. When Denis began planning a four-month trip to Europe, he asked Sally if he could sublet to his cousin Ralph, who would be a visiting professor during that time.

Sally was hesitant, having heard from other landlords that sublets were loaded with legal problems. But Denis gave Sally a copy of Ralph's excellent resume and explained that he just couldn't afford to leave the unit empty for four months; he might have to move out permanently if Sally didn't let Ralph take over. After checking Ralph's references and credit report, Sally agreed to the sublet. The subtenancy proceeded without a hitch and Denis returned to a well-kept home.

a. Downsides of Subletting

Here are some important issues to consider before you go hunting for a subtenant.

You're still on the hook, financially. If the new tenant (the subtenant) fails to pay the rent or damages the premises, you will be 100% legally responsible.

It's hard to find good subtenants. The pool of reliable short-term tenants is fairly small: visiting students or professors, people waiting for escrow to close on a home they've purchased and so on. And it's important to find a very, very reliable subtenant; if you don't, you may end up getting sued by the landlord for losses caused by the subtenant. (See Chapter 7 for advice on choosing a replacement tenant.)

Your landlord may refuse. Most leases require the landlord's permission before you can sublet. (See Chapter 2.) But your landlord will probably prefer to end your tenancy and rent to a new tenant, let you assign the rest of your lease to a new tenant or, if you want a roomer (discussed in Chapter 7), insist that the new occupant become a full-fledged co-tenant.

The big reason is that if the subtenant screws up, the landlord may not be able to sue the subtenant directly. For example, in some states, if a subtenant ruins the premises and the security deposit doesn't cover the loss, the landlord can only sue you, the tenant, not the subtenant who caused the damage. If you are far away and suddenly decide not to return, the landlord has a big problem. Or if the subtenant's behavior is grounds for eviction—for

Consent to Assignment of Lease

Maurice Mountjoy _____ (Landlord) and

Samuel Taylor _____ (Tenant) and

Umberto Echo _____ (Assignee)

agree as follows:

1. Tenant has leased the premises at ___ 3457 Walker Avenue, Number 5A, Pico, Arizona ___

_____ from Landlord.

2. The lease was signed on _____ March 1 _____, 200_X_, and will expire on

February 28 _____, 200_X_.

3. Tenant is assigning the balance of Tenant's lease to Assignee, beginning on _____ August 1 _____

_____, 200_X_, and ending on February 28 _____, 200_X_.

4. Tenant's financial responsibilities under the terms of the lease are ended by this assignment. Specifically, Tenant's responsibilities for future rent and future damage are ended.

5. As of the effective date of the assignment, Tenant permanently gives up the right to occupy the premises.

6. Assignee is bound by every term and condition in the lease that is the subject of this assignment.

July 25, 200X _____ *Maurice Mountjoy* _____

Date / Landlord

July 25, 200X _____ *Samuel Taylor* _____

Date / Tenant

July 25, 200X _____ *Umberto Echo* _____

Date / Assignee

Comparing Subleases and Assignments		
	Sublease	**Assignment**
Rent	New tenant (subtenant) is liable to the original tenant, not to the landlord. Original tenant is liable to landlord.	New tenant (assignee) is liable to the landlord. Absent an agreement to the contrary, old tenant is liable if new tenant doesn't pay.
Damage to premises	Original tenant is liable for damage caused by new tenant.	Absent an agreement to the contrary, original tenant is not liable for damage caused by new tenant.
Violations of lease	Landlord can't sue new tenant for money losses caused by violating lease, because new tenant never signed lease. New tenant can't sue landlord for lease violations, either.	New tenant and landlord are bound by all terms in lease except those that were purely personal to the landlord and old tenant.
Eviction	Landlord can sue to evict new tenant for any reason old tenant could have been evicted. But to evict subtenant, landlord must also evict old tenant.	Landlord can evict new tenant for any reason old tenant could have been evicted.

example, the subtenant is dealing drugs on the rental property or disturbing the neighbors—the landlord may need to evict you in order to get rid of the subtenant.

From a landlord's perspective, there are other problems as well:

- If the subtenant won't move out when you return, the landlord could become embroiled in a lawsuit between you and the subtenant.
- Few landlords are willing to grant eviction powers to tenants, fearing that sooner or later the power will be abused.

The subtenant might refuse to leave when you return. This puts you in an awkward legal situation. The only way the landlord may be able to evict the subtenant is to evict you, too.

A subtenant can turn into a tenant. If you and the landlord treat a subtenant like a tenant, that subtenant can gain the legal status of the landlord's

tenant. For example, a subtenant who repeatedly pays rent directly to the landlord and not to you may be able to claim the status of a tenant. And once that happens, the new tenant has all the rights and responsibilities of a co-tenant which can have important legal consequences for you. (See the Chapter 7 discussion of co-tenants and the joint and several liability rule.) To avoid this, make sure that the subtenant pays *you* the rent, no matter what it says in a written subtenancy agreement. Either send it to the landlord or, better yet, deposit it in your account and write a personal check for the rent.

b. Creating a Sublease

If you have decided to sublease—and have gotten your landlord's okay—you have just donned a new legal hat: You are your subtenant's landlord. As a landlord, it makes sense to take steps to protect your interests and, above all, ensure that your tenant will not do anything that will jeopardize your own tenancy.

You'll need a clear written agreement, signed by you and the subtenant, which will specify rent, duration of the tenancy, a security deposit and so on. For example, you'll need to state whether the subtenant has a month-to-month tenancy or a lease for a certain period. One way is to simply use the same form you signed with your landlord, changing the title from "Lease" to "Sublease" and making yourself the sublessor and the other person the subtenant. Attach a copy to your original lease, the terms and conditions of which the sublessee agrees to follow as well.

Now That You're a Landlord

Once you take on a subtenant, you must meet your responsibilities as a landlord. Follow these steps to make sure you cover the basics:

- Screen and choose your subtenant carefully.
- Get a security deposit equal to the maximum allowed by law.
- Do your best to provide the subtenant a safe place to live. As you would do for your own safety, alert the property owner about any hazards and clean up any dangerous situation you've created within your rental unit.
- Use a Landlord-Tenant Checklist to note the condition of the premises when the subtenant moves in.
- Use the Landlord-Tenant Checklist again when the subtenant moves out and promptly refund the security deposit, less any legitimate deductions for unpaid rent, cleaning or damage. If you make deductions, immediately give the subtenant a written explanation.

For much more information on your duties as a landlord, check out *Every Landlord's Legal Guide* by Stewart, Warner and Portman (Nolo).

Don't discriminate illegally. As a sublessor, you must abide by fair housing laws. (See Chapter 5.) Be especially careful in your advertisements. An index card tacked to a grocery store bulletin board advertising "Room to rent, single Christian lady preferred," may be a violation of your state's law.

c. Ending a Subtenancy

If your subtenant rents month-to-month and you'd like to end the arrangement, you'll need to give the amount of notice required by your state to terminate a month-to-month tenant. Typically, this is 30 days. (Appendix I lists every state's rule.) If your subtenant has a lease that you would prefer not to renew, send a reminder towards the end of the term that the end is approaching and that you do not intend to renew the lease or start a month-to-month relationship.

If the tenant doesn't leave, do not accept any more rent. You'll probably need to follow regular eviction procedures, like any other landlord.

You also may find it necessary to evict if the subtenant hasn't paid you the rent, or has broken the house rules or a lease clause. You'll probably need to follow your state's procedures for eviction "for cause." (Chapter 17 discusses termination notices for tenant wrongdoing. Read Chapter 18 for an overview of evictions.)

Rent control may limit your options. Check your ordinance to see if it applies to subtenants. If it's unclear, ask the local rent control board or a tenants' group.

5. Breaking the Lease

When you sign a lease, you are legally bound to pay rent for the full lease term, whether or not you continue to occupy the dwelling. Simply moving out, whether or not you notify the landlord in advance, does not get you off the hook as far as paying rent is concerned.

There's good news, though: You may not have to pay much, if any, additional rent. You must pay only the amount your landlord loses because you move out early. If the rental market is tight, the landlord will probably get a new tenant quickly, at the same rent you paid (or even more). Once there's a new rent-paying tenant, that ends your obligation to pay rent.

a.   Your Landlord's Duty to Find a New Tenant

Most states require a landlord to take reasonable steps to keep losses to a minimum—in legalese, to "mitigate damages." (Each state's rule is listed below.) So if you break your lease and move out without legal justification, your landlord usually can't just sit back and wait until the end of the term of the lease, and then sue you for the total amount of lost rent. In most states, your landlord must try to re-rent the property reasonably quickly and subtract the rent received from new tenants from the amount you owe. The landlord can also, however, add legitimate expenses to your bill—for example, the cost of advertising the property or using credit reporting agencies to investigate potential renters.

Negotiate over the landlord's normal tenant-finding expenses. Why should you pay for the landlord's costs of advertising, showing the apartment and screening applicants? After all, these are expenses that your landlord would have incurred anyway if you had stayed and left at the end of your term.

Especially if you left only a month or so early, tell the landlord that you are willing to pay lost rent, but shouldn't have to underwrite regular business expenses. If the landlord doesn't buy it, and withholds a sizable portion of your security deposit for this purpose, consider suing in small claims court. Many judges will conclude that your landlord should bear at least a portion of the cost of finding a new tenant. (Chapter 16 explains the use of small claims court to dispute security deposit deductions.)

Your landlord is required to make reasonable efforts to re-rent the property to a good tenant at a reasonable rent. The landlord does not need to relax standards for acceptable tenants—for example, to accept applicants with poor credit or rental histories. Also, the landlord is not required to rent the premises for below their fair market value or to immediately turn all her attention to renting your unit, disregarding other business.

EXAMPLE: Susan rented an apartment from Stephen in January for a term of one year, at the monthly rent of $1,000. At the end of August, Susan gave notice of her intent to move at the end of September to be closer to her invalid mother. Susan is legally liable to Stephen for $3,000—the rent for October, November and December.

However, Stephen takes out an ad, checks out prospective tenants and rents the apartment again on October 15. The new tenant pays $500 for the last half of October and $1,000 in November and December. Stephen must subtract this $2,500 from Susan's $3,000 debt. This leaves her liable for only $500, plus Stephen's advertising costs of $20 and credit bureau fees of $50, for a total of $590.

The Landlord's Duty to Re-Rent the Premises

State	Landlord must take reasonably prompt steps to re-rent	Landlord has no duty to look for and rent to another tenant	Law is unclear or courts have not addressed the issue	State	Landlord must take reasonably prompt steps to re-rent	Landlord has no duty to look for and rent to another tenant	Law is unclear or courts have not addressed the issue
Alabama		X		Nevada	X		
Alaska	X			New Hampshire	X		
Arizona	X			New Jersey	X		
Arkansas			X	New Mexico	X		
California	X			New York			X
Colorado			X	North Carolina	X		
Connecticut	X			North Dakota	X		
Delaware	X			Ohio	X		
Dist. of Columbia	X			Oklahoma	X		
Florida	X			Oregon	X		
Georgia			X	Pennsylvania			X
Hawaii	X			Rhode Island	X		
Idaho			X	South Carolina	X		
Illinois	X			South Dakota			X
Indiana	X			Tennessee	X		
Iowa	X			Texas	X		
Kansas	X			Utah	X		
Kentucky	X			Vermont			X
Louisiana	X			Virginia	X		
Maine	X			Washington	X		
Maryland	X			West Virginia			X
Massachusetts			X	Wisconsin	X		
Michigan			X	Wyoming			X
Minnesota		X					
Mississippi		X					
Missouri			X				
Montana			X				
Nebraska			X				

If you need citations to a statute or court opinion, look in Footnotes 1, 2 and 3 of *Austin Hill Country Realty, Inc. v. Palisades Plaza, Inc.*, # 95-1273, 1997 WL7268 (July 9, 1997) (Texas Supreme Court).

b. If the Landlord Sues You

If you move out and break your lease, your land-lord can, and probably will, charge you for the time and cost of advertising for a new tenant, particularly if the rental market is slow.

Your landlord will probably first use your security deposit to cover these amounts. (See Chapter 16.) But if your deposit does not cover what you owe, your landlord may sue you. The landlord can go to court as soon as the property is rented again. At this point, his losses—his expenses and the rent differ-ential, if any—are known. In many states, the land-lord has up to four, or even five, years to sue.

Demands for "Liquidated Damages"

If your lease contains a liquidated damages clause—a provision requiring you to pay the landlord a certain amount of money if you break the lease—the landlord may sue you for that amount. In some states, liquidated damages clauses in residential leases are flatly illegal, so a court would rule for you.

In some states that allow these provisions, the amount of money called for must not be excessive. If the amount you are supposed to pay greatly exceeds what the landlord actually lost—or would have lost if she had actively looked for another tenant—a court may consider it an invalid "pen-alty," and order you to compensate the landlord only for actual losses. But even if you ultimately don't have to pay the whole amount, you'll expend considerable time and energy fighting your land-lord in court.

If you are sued, you will receive legal documents setting out the landlord's claim. Read them care-fully, to see if the amount the landlord asks for is fair. As explained above, if you took the proper steps to protect yourself by finding an acceptable replacement tenant, your landlord's suit may be bogus, and you will definitely want to defend your-self.

You may be sued in small claims court, assum-ing the amount the landlord claims isn't above the court's upper limit—about $2,000 to $5,000 in most states. But if it is, and if your lease contains a clause allowing your landlord to recover attorney fees, he may file in regular court, where you stand to lose much more.

> EXAMPLE: Cree has a year's lease at $800 per month. She moves out with six months ($4,800 of rent) left on the lease. Cree's landlord, Robin, cannot find a new tenant for six weeks, and when she finally does, the new tenant will pay only $600 per month.
>
> Unless Cree can show Robin acted unrea-sonably, Cree would be liable for the $200 per month difference between what she paid and what the new tenant pays, multiplied by the number of months left in the lease at the time she moved out. Cree would also be responsible for $1,200 for the time the unit was vacant, plus Robin's costs to find a new tenant. Cree would thus owe Robin $2,400 plus advertising and applicant screening costs. If Robin sues Cree for this money, and there is an "attorney fees and costs" in her lease, Cree will also owe Robin these costs, which can be upwards of a few thousand dollars.

If you are sued in small claims court for an amount that seems excessive, simply tell the judge your side of the case. Bring with you any witnesses and documentation that would help tell your story—for example, any evidence that the landlord did not advertise the rental unit, failed to consider prospec-tive tenants you suggested or overpriced the unit, making it harder to find new tenants.

In some states, such as Ohio, in order to win, you may be required to prove that the landlord took no steps to find a new tenant. In other states, it's up to the landlord to prove that he *did* take reasonable steps. To be on the safe side, assume that the burden of proof is on you, and be prepared to make your case in court if your landlord sits back and makes no attempts to re-rent.

Chapter 16 discusses how to defend yourself in small claims court. If you are sued in regular court and want legal advice, see Chapter 20 which covers how to find and work with a lawyer.

Everybody's Guide to Small Claims Court, by Ralph Warner (Nolo), explains how to defend yourself against a landlord who sues you in small claims court.

How to Represent Yourself in Court, by Paul Bergman and Sara Berman-Barrett (Nolo). Few people can afford a lawyer to handle a $400 case. But you can represent yourself and level the playing field somewhat by understanding the mechanics of a civil lawsuit and how to conduct yourself in court. This book gives you the basics.

G. Condominium Conversions

Landlords can sometimes make a lot of money by converting their rental properties into condominiums, which probably means the end of your tenancy. Condo conversions can be especially attractive to landlords in areas with rent control, because rent control restricts the profit a landlord can make by renting, but doesn't regulate the selling price of condominiums.

Many states, such as California, Connecticut and New York, regulate the conversion of rental property into condominiums—that is, they limit the number of conversions and give existing tenants considerable rights, as explained below. Here are some of the basic issues that your state's condo conversion law may address:

Government approval. An owner who intends to convert rental property to condos must usually get a plan approval (often called a "subdivision map approval") from a local planning agency. If the property is subject to rent control, there are probably additional requirements.

Public input. In most situations, the public—including current tenants—can speak out at planning agency hearings regarding the proposed condominium conversion and its impact on the rental housing market. Owners are usually required to give tenants notice of the time and place of these hearings.

Tenants' right of first refusal. Most condominium conversion laws demand that the owner offer the units for sale first to the existing tenants, at prices that are the same as or lower than the intended public offering. Often, to keep tenant opposition to a minimum, landlords voluntarily offer existing tenants a chance to buy at a significantly lower price.

Tenancy terminations. Month-to-month tenants who don't buy their units will receive notice to move at some point during the sales process. Tenants with leases usually have a right to remain through the end of the lease. The entire condo conversion approval process typically takes many months—time enough for current leases to expire before the final okay has been given.

Renting after the conversion has been approved. If you sign a lease or rental agreement *after* the condo conversion has been approved, many statutes require the owner to give you plenty of clear written warnings (in large, bold-faced type) that your unit may be sold and your tenancy terminated on short notice. But landlords who continue to rent units after they've gotten their subdivision approval usually do so on a month-to-month basis, so the short notice really won't be any different from what any month-to-month tenant would receive.

Relocation assistance and special protections. Some statutes require owners to pay current tenants a flat fee to help with relocation. Some also require owners to provide more notice or additional relocation assistance for elderly tenants or those with small children. There is nothing to stop you from bargaining with the owner for additional compensation—in exchange for your agreement to vacate earlier, for example.

What can you do if your landlord fails to comply with your state or city's conversion laws? Generally, you may be able to delay the conversion and possibly obtain money damages (if you sue your landlord), but you can rarely, if ever, stop the process.

For advice on researching your state's statutes and court cases on condominium conversions, see the discussion of legal research in Chapter 20.

H. If the Landlord Goes Out of Business

What happens to your lease if your landlord goes out of the business of renting residential property before the end of the lease term? If a new owner buys the property, in most cases the new owner must honor the existing leases. There are three other common and more complicated scenarios, discussed below.

1. The Landlord Declares Bankruptcy

If your landlord files for bankruptcy, the bankruptcy court will appoint someone called a "bankruptcy trustee" to oversee the case. The trustee decides whether to carry on with or terminate the leases held by the landlord's tenants. Typically, the trustee will keep leases held by stable, rent-paying tenants, but terminate those of tenants who owe back rent or have damaged the premises. Keep in mind, however, that the trustee can always initiate eviction procedures later in appropriate situations, such as nonpayment of rent.

2. The Rental Property Is Foreclosed

If the landlord falls behind on mortgage payments on the rental property, the bank can have the property sold, and pay the landlord's debt out of the proceeds of the sale. In short, when there is a foreclosure sale, there's a new owner who becomes your new landlord.

Foreclosure sales generally wipe out existing leases, and the harsh reality is that the new owner may terminate your tenancy on short notice with an Unconditional Quit notice. (Unconditional Quit notices are explained in Chapter 17.) However, in some states you are protected from eviction as long as your lease was signed before the deed of trust or mortgage was put on file (recorded) in the local land records office. (The recording date will be on file at your local land records office.) Rules vary greatly from state to state. Consult a tenants' rights group or an attorney for specific information.

3. The Landlord Puts the Property to Another Use

If a landlord no longer wants to be a landlord, you can't just be tossed out. The regular rules discussed in Sections B and C, above, apply. If you don't have a lease, the landlord can give you a 30-day notice. If you do have a lease, it must be honored. But when your lease is up, the landlord has no obligation to continue renting to you or anyone else. A landlord who really wants lease-holding tenants out early will offer to buy them out.

Phony going-out-of-business ploys. Some landlords claim to go out of business and then pop up a few months later, in order to charge a market-rate rent—which may be higher than the current, controlled rent—to a new batch of tenants. To prevent this, a rent control ordinance may require withdrawn property to remain off the market for a lengthy amount of time (penalties result if the landlord re-rents too soon). It may also specify that former tenants be given the right of first refusal when the property is returned to the residential rental market. ■

16

Moving Out and Getting Your Security Deposit Back

ights over security deposits make up a large percentage of the landlord-tenant disputes that wind up in small claims court. Many suits are brought by tenants against landlords who unfairly withheld deposit money for cleaning or refused to return the deposit at all.

Fortunately, you can take some simple steps to minimize the possibility that you'll spend hours haggling in court with your landlord. This chapter shows you how, and if you do end up in court, how to prepare a winning case. It includes:

- when and how landlords must return deposits and what deductions are allowed under the law
- how to make sure you meet your landlord's expectations for the condition in which the unit should be left
- how to protect yourself by documenting the condition of the rental unit when you move out
- how to write demand letters for the return of your deposit
- how to negotiate with your landlord, and use a mediation service, if appropriate, and
- how to sue your landlord in small claims court, if necessary, over your deposit.

 Related topics covered in this book include:

- State laws on the amount and collection of deposits and what happens to your deposit if the landlord sells the property: Chapter 4.
- How to use a Landlord-Tenant Checklist to document the condition of the rental unit when you move in: Chapter 6.
- Landlord and tenant repair and maintenance responsibilities: Chapters 8, 9 and 10.
- What happens to your deposit if the landlord files for bankruptcy or the property is foreclosed: Chapter 15.

A. Basic Rules for Returning Deposits

Most states hold landlords to a strict set of rules regarding security deposits. Landlords are expected to account for your money promptly or face stiff penalties. For example, in many states a landlord who deliberately violates the security deposit statute may have to return all of your deposit plus two or three times the amount wrongfully withheld, plus attorney fees and costs.

1. Deadlines

Depending on the state, landlords generally have between 14 and 30 days after you leave—whether voluntarily or by eviction—to return your entire deposit.

The landlord must mail the following to your last known address (or forwarding address, if known):

1. Your entire deposit, with interest if required (Chapter 4 lists state laws requiring interest), or

2. A written, itemized statement as to how the deposit has been applied toward back rent and costs of cleaning and damage repair, together with whatever is left of the deposit, including any interest that is required. (See subsection 2, below.) In most states, landlords send the itemization along with any deposit balance. A few states add an additional step that gives tenants time to respond to proposed deductions before they are actually made. (See "Advance Notice of Deposit Deductions," below.)

For specifics on your state's law, see "Deadlines for Landlords to Itemize and Return Security Deposits," below.

Unfortunately, landlords in some states, including Alabama, Idaho, Louisiana, Wisconsin and Wyoming, are not subject to any deadline or rules governing the return of deposits. If you live in one of these states, ask your landlord when you move out when you can expect to get your deposit back. A reasonable landlord should return your deposit within one month. If more than a month has passed or you suspect you may never see your deposit again, follow the steps in Section F, below.

⚠️ **Make sure your landlord knows how to reach you.** If you don't give your landlord a forwarding address, you may never see your deposit. In some states, including Arkansas, Delaware, Iowa, Georgia and Kentucky, a landlord is allowed to keep the deposit if you cannot be found after a reasonable effort, or after searching for a very short period, sometimes as little as 60 or 90 days. To protect yourself, send your landlord a written

---

Advance Notice of Deposit Deductions

Laws in the following five states give tenants the opportunity to inspect the rental unit to determine the accuracy of the landlord's list of damages before the final itemization is done. If you disagree with the landlord's proposed deductions, you must explain your disagreement in writing and send it to the landlord within a specified time. Only then can you sue the landlord for deductions you consider improper.

State	Rule
Florida	Landlord must send tenant a list of proposed deductions within 15 days after tenant vacates; tenant must send objections within 15 days of receiving landlord's list.
Georgia	Landlord must send tenant a list of proposed deductions within three days of the lease or rental agreement termination; tenant has a right to examine the premises within five days of lease termination.
Kentucky	Landlord must inspect and give tenant a list of deductions; tenant may inspect to ascertain the accuracy of the list. No time periods are specified for this process, but the landlord must still meet the state deadline for returning deposits.
Michigan	Landlord must send tenant an itemized list of proposed deductions within 30 days after the lease terminates; tenant must mail response within seven days of receiving landlord's list.
Tennessee	Landlord must mail a list of deductions to tenant; tenant may inspect to ascertain the accuracy of the list. No time periods are specified for this process, but the landlord must still meet the state deadline for returning deposits.

Citations to these statutes are in "Citations for State Laws on Security Deposits" in Appendix I.

Deadlines for Landlords to Itemize and Return Security Deposits

State	Deadline for Returning Security Deposit	State	Deadline for Returning Security Deposit
Alabama	No statutory deadline	Michigan	30 days
Alaska	14 days if the tenant gives proper notice to terminate tenancy; 30 days if the tenant does not give proper notice	Minnesota	Three weeks after tenant leaves and landlord receives mailing address; five days if tenant must leave due to building condemnation
Arizona	14 days	Mississippi	45 days
Arkansas	30 days	Missouri	30 days
California	Three weeks	Montana	30 days
Colorado	One month, unless lease agreement specifies longer period of time (which may be no more than 60 days); 72 hours if a hazardous condition involving gas equipment requires tenant to vacate	Nebraska	14 days
		Nevada	30 days
		New Hampshire	30 days
		New Jersey	30 days; five days in case of fire, flood, condemnation or evacuation
Connecticut	30 days, or within 15 days of receiving tenant's forwarding address, whichever is later	New Mexico	30 days
		New York	Reasonable time
Delaware	15 days	North Carolina	30 days
District of Columbia	45 days	North Dakota	30 days
		Ohio	30 days
Florida	15 to 45 days depending on whether tenant disputes deductions	Oklahoma	30 days
		Oregon	30 days
Georgia	One month	Pennsylvania	30 days
Hawaii	14 days	Rhode Island	20 days
Idaho	No statutory deadline	South Carolina	30 days
Illinois	30-45 days depending on whether deductions were made	South Dakota	Two weeks
Indiana	45 days	Tennessee	No statutory deadline
Iowa	30 days	Texas	30 days
Kansas	30 days	Utah	30 days, or within 15 days of receiving tenant's forwarding address, whichever is later
Kentucky	30-60 days depending on whether tenant disputes deductions	Vermont	14 days
Louisiana	No statutory deadline	Virginia	30 days
Maine	21 days (tenancy at will) or 30 days (written rental agreement)	Washington	14 days
Maryland	30-45 days depending on whether tenant has been evicted or has abandoned the premises	West Virginia	No statutory deadline
		Wisconsin	No statutory deadline
		Wyoming	No statutory deadline
Massachusetts	30 days		

For details check, your statute. See "Citations for State Laws on Security Deposits" in Appendix I.

request for the return of your security deposit, and include your forwarding address. (A sample letter is in Section D, below.)

2. Itemized Statements

You are entitled to a statement that explains the purpose of each deduction and states the dollar amount withheld. Your landlord should never send a statement that simply says, "$200 deduction for cleaning and repairs." If you get this kind of vague statement, you have the legal right to ask for more details.

If cleaning and repair work have already been done, your landlord should provide details on labor and supplies, including receipts, in the final itemization. For example:

- "Carpet cleaning by ABC Carpet Cleaners, $160, required by several large grease stains and candle wax imbedded in living room rug," or
- "Plaster repair, $400, of several fist-sized holes in bedroom wall."
- "$250 to replace drapes in living room, damaged by cigarette smoke and holes."

See the sample "Security Deposit Itemization," below.

If your landlord can't get necessary repairs made or cleaning done within the time required to return the security deposit, the statement should contain a reasonable estimate of the cost. But if you end up subsequently suing your landlord, he will need to produce receipts for the amount deducted.

If you damaged or substantially shortened the useful life of an item, it can be a little tougher to put a dollar amount on damages. Generally, you must take into account how old it was, how long it might have lasted otherwise and the cost of replacement.

EXAMPLE: Your dog ruined an eight-year-old rug that had a life expectancy of ten years. If a replacement rug would cost $1,000, your landlord would charge you $200 for the two years of life that would have remained in the rug had your dog not ruined it.

B. Deductions for Cleaning and Damage

Legally, a landlord may charge for any cleaning or repairs necessary to restore the rental unit to its condition at the beginning of the tenancy. The landlord may not use your security deposit for the cost of remedying ordinary wear and tear.

Unfortunately, it's not always easy to decide what constitutes ordinary wear and tear, or what must be done to leave a rental unit clean. Must you leave the premises perfectly clean? "Reasonably" clean?

1. Reasonable Deductions

In general, landlords may charge only for cleaning and repairs that are really necessary, such as replacing stained or ripped carpets or drapes (particularly smoke-contaminated ones), fixing damaged furniture and cleaning dirty stoves, refrigerators and kitchen and bathroom fixtures. Your landlord may also need to take care of such things as flea infestations left behind by your dog or mildew in the bathroom caused by your failure to clean properly.

Your landlord can't set unreasonable standards for cleaning. For example, if the place was less than immaculate when you moved in, your landlord has no legal right to require a perfect cleaning job now. And no judge would uphold a requirement that you clean the floor with a toothbrush.

That said, every move-out is different in its details, and there are simply no hard and fast rules on what is wear and tear (your landlord's problem) and what is your responsibility. But here are some basic guidelines:

- You should not be charged for filth or damage that was present when you moved in.
- You should not be charged for replacing an item when a repair would be sufficient. For example, if you damaged the kitchen counter by placing a hot pan on it, you shouldn't be required to replace the entire counter if an expertly done patch will do the job. Of course,

Security Deposit Itemization

Date: November 8, 200X

To: Rachel Tolan   From: Lena Coleman

      123 Larchmont Lane   456 Penny Lane, #101

      St. Louis, Missouri   St. Louis, Missouri

Property Address: 789 Cora Court, St. Louis, Missouri

Rental Period: January 1, 200X, to October 31, 200X

1. Security Deposit Received .... $ 600

2. Interest on Deposit (if required by lease or law): .... $ N/A

3. Total Credit (sum of lines 1 and 2) .... $ 600

4. Itemized Repairs and Related Losses:

    repainting of living room walls, required by

    crayon and chalk marks

                                       Total Repair Cost: $ 260

5. Necessary Cleaning:

    sum paid to resident manager for 4 hours cleaning

    at $20/hour: debris-filled garage, dirty stove and refrigerator

                                       Total Cleaning Cost: $ 80

6. Unpaid Rent:

                                       Total Rent Due: $ 0

7. Amount Owed (line 3 minus the sum of lines 4,5 and 6)

    ☐ A. Total Amount Tenant Owes Landlord: .... $

    ☒ B. Total Amount Landlord Owes Tenant: .... $ 260

Comments:

    A check for $260 is enclosed.

you have to evaluate the overall condition of the unit—if it is a luxury property that looks like an ad in *Architectural Digest*, don't expect your landlord to make do with a patch.

- The longer you've lived in a place, the more wear and tear can be expected on things like carpets, floors and walls.

- You should not be charged for cleaning if you paid a nonrefundable cleaning fee. Landlords in some states are allowed to charge a cleaning fee, which is separate from the security deposit and is specifically labeled as nonrefundable. (See Chapter 4.) If you paid a cleaning fee, the landlord should not deduct anything from your security deposit for cleaning.

- You should be charged a fair price for repairs and replacements. You should not be asked to foot the bill for a high-priced handyman or unreasonably expensive replacement items. Legally, your landlord is obligated to spend only what is needed to accomplish the job in a workmanlike manner. You cannot expect the landlord to drive 500 miles for a bargain or to hire the very cheapest laborer, but neither should you be overcharged.

Check prices yourself. If you believe you are being price-gouged, it might be worth your while to get a few quotes from repair persons and compare them with the landlord's bill, or to shop around for the item that the landlord replaced. Say, for example, your landlord charges you $800 to replace a stove you damaged. If you find the same stove on sale at a nearby discount warehouse for $500, you have the makings of a winning small claims case if, after learning of the discrepancy, the landlord doesn't reduce your bill by $300.

See "What Can Your Landlord Charge For?" below for some examples of what a court will consider to be ordinary wear and tear, and what crosses the line and is commonly considered to be a condition for which you must pay for cleaning, replacement or repair.

Your rent control ordinance may give a clue as to what is "normal wear and tear" and what is "damage." Most rent control ordinances allow the landlord to raise the rent for specific capital expenses. Typically, maintenance expenses, spent in response to normal wear and tear, are not considered capital expenses. But if the landlord must replace an item, it may qualify as a capital expense, which justifies a rent increase. Pro-tenant rent boards have reacted against this rent-increase justification by classifying the replacement of appliances, carpets, repainting and so on as mere "maintenance" necessitated by normal wear and tear. Your argument: If it's maintenance to the rent board, it ought to be maintenance with respect to your security deposit, too, and your deposit shouldn't be used for it.

2. Common Disagreements

Common areas of disagreement between landlords and tenants concern repainting, carpets and fixtures.

a. Painting

Although state laws provide no firm guidelines as to who is responsible for repainting when a rental unit needs it, courts usually rule that if you have lived in your unit for several years, it should be done at your landlord's expense, not yours. On the other hand, if you have lived in a unit for less than a year, and the walls were freshly painted when you moved in but are now a mess, your landlord is probably entitled to charge you for all costs of cleaning the walls. If repainting badly smudged walls is cheaper and more effective than cleaning, however, the landlord can probably charge for repainting.

b. Rugs and Carpets

If the living room rug was already threadbare when you moved in a few months ago and looks even worse now, it's pretty obvious that your footsteps

What Can Your Landlord Charge For?

Ordinary Wear and Tear: Your Landlord's Responsibility	Damage or Excessive Filth: Your Responsibility
Curtains faded by the sun	Cigarette burns in curtains or carpets
Water-stained linoleum by shower	Broken tiles in bathroom
Minor marks on or nicks in wall	Large marks on or holes in wall
Dents in the wall where a door handle bumped it	Door off its hinges
Moderate dirt or spotting on carpet	Rips in carpet or urine stains from pets
A few small tack or nail holes in wall	Lots of picture holes or gouges in walls that require patching as well as repainting
A rug worn thin by normal use	Stains in rug caused by your leaking fish tank
Worn gaskets on refrigerator doors	Broken refrigerator shelf
Faded paint on bedroom wall	Water damage on wall from hanging plants
Dark patches of ingrained soil on hardwood floors that have lost their finish and have been worn down to bare wood	Water stains on wood floors and windowsills caused by windows being left open during rainstorms
Warped cabinet doors that won't close	Sticky cabinets and interiors
Stains on old porcelain fixtures that have lost their protective coating	Grime-coated bathtub and toilet
Moderately dirty mini-blinds	Missing mini-blinds
Bathroom mirror beginning to "de-silver" (black spots)	Mirrors caked with lipstick and makeup
Clothes dryer that delivers cold air because the thermostat has given out	Dryer that won't turn at all because it's been over-loaded
Toilet flushes inadequately because mineral deposits have clogged the jets	Toilet won't flush properly because it's stopped up with a diaper

have simply contributed to the inevitable, and that this wear and tear is not your responsibility. On the other hand, a brand-new good quality rug that becomes stained and full of bare spots within months has probably been subjected to the type of abuse you will have to pay for. In between, it's anyone's guess. But clearly the longer you have lived in a unit, and the cheaper or older the carpet was when you moved in, the less likely you are to be held responsible for its deterioration.

c. Fixtures

The law considers pieces of furniture or equipment that are physically attached to the rental property, such as bolted-in bookshelves, to be your landlord's property, even if you paid for them. This means that if you leave behind a row of bookshelves, your landlord can legally remove them, subtract the cost from your security deposit *and* keep the bookshelves.

(Chapter 10 discusses how to avoid disputes over fixtures when you move out.)

Report damage immediately to your landlord. If your landlord doesn't take action and the problem gets worse, you have a record of your attempts to nip it in the bud. You shouldn't have to pay, at move-out time, for the landlord's inaction.

C. Deductions for Unpaid Rent

If you move out owing rent, your landlord can deduct any unpaid rent from your security deposit, including any unpaid utility charges or other financial obligations required under your lease or rental agreement. Even if your debt far exceeds the amount of the security deposit, the law still requires your landlord to itemize and notify you of how the security deposit was applied to your debt.

Chapter 15 discusses how month-to-month tenancies and fixed-term leases end, including notice requirements and what happens if you leave early or stay late.

1. Month-to-Month Tenancies

If you rent on a month-to-month basis, ideally you'll give the right amount of notice and pay for your last month's rent. Usually, the notice period is the same as your rental period, 30 days. Then, when you leave as planned, the only issue with respect to your security deposit is whether you've caused any damage or left the place dirty. But there are three common variations on this ideal scenario, and they all result in deductions from your security deposit for unpaid rent:

- You leave as announced, but with unpaid rent behind you.
- You leave later than planned, and haven't paid for your extra days, or
- You leave as announced, but you haven't given the right amount of notice.

Let's look at each situation.

a. Leaving Unpaid Rent Behind

If you've been behind on the rent for months, convincing a good-hearted (or lazy) landlord to let matters slide, the landlord is entitled to deduct what you owe from the security deposit—either during the tenancy or when you leave.

b. Staying After Your Announced Departure Date

If you fail to leave when planned (or when requested, if the landlord has terminated the rental agreement), you obviously aren't entitled to stay on rent-free. When you eventually do leave, your landlord will figure the exact amount you owe by prorating the monthly rent for the number of days you have failed to pay.

EXAMPLE: Erin gives notice on March 1 of her intent to move out. She pays her landlord Ann the rent of $600 for March. But because she can't get into her new place on time, Erin stays until

April 5 without paying anything more. Ann is entitled to deduct $5/30$ (one-sixth) of the total month's rent, or $100, from Erin's security deposit.

c. Giving Inadequate Notice

When you terminate a month to-month-tenancy, you must give your landlord the legally required amount of notice before leaving; in most states, that's 30 days. You must pay rent for that entire period. If you gave less than the legally required amount of notice and moved out, your landlord is entitled to rent money for the balance of the notice period unless the place is re-rented within the 30 days. (Chapter 15 covers notice requirements for terminating a tenancy.)

> **EXAMPLE:** Tom pays his rent on the first of every month. State law requires 30 days' notice to terminate a tenancy. On June 20, Tom gives notice that he will leave on July 1. The rental market is soft and Jim, his landlord, is unable to re-rent for two months. Since Tom gave only ten days' notice, Jim is entitled to deduct two-thirds of a months' rent (representing the 20 days of unpaid rent) from Tom's deposit.

2. Fixed-Term Leases

If you leave before a fixed-term lease expires, your landlord is entitled to the balance of the rent due under the lease. That rule is softened considerably by the fact that in most states your landlord is required to try to re-rent the property, and once a new tenant starts paying rent, your obligation ends.

If you leave less than a month before your lease is scheduled to end, you can be almost positive that, if the case goes to court, a judge will conclude you owe rent for the entire lease term. It would be unreasonable to expect a landlord to immediately find a new tenant to take over the few days left of your lease. But if you leave more than 30 days be-

fore the end of a lease, your landlord's duty to look for a new tenant will be taken more seriously by the courts. (See Chapter 15 for more on your land-lord's duty to try to re-rent the property promptly.)

> **EXAMPLE:** On January 1, Anthony rents a house from Will for $1,200 a month and signs a one-year lease. He moves out on June 30, even though six months remain on the lease, making him responsible for a total rent of $7,200. Will re-rents the property on July 10, this time for $1,250 a month (the new tenants pay $833 for the last 20 days in July), which means that he'll receive a total rent of $7,083 through December 31. That's $117 less than the $7,200 he would have received from Anthony had he lived up to the lease, so Will may deduct $117 from Anthony's deposit. In addition, if Will spent a reasonable amount of money to find a new tenant (for newspaper ads, rental agency com-missions and credit checks), he may also deduct this sum from the deposit.

3. After an Eviction

If you lose an eviction lawsuit, the landlord can legally expect payment for rent until you actually leave.

> **EXAMPLE:** When Allen fails to pay May's rent of $450, Marilyn sues to evict him. On June 10, she gets an eviction judgment from the court, ordering Allen to pay rent through that date. He doesn't actually leave until June 17th. Marilyn can deduct the following items from the deposit:
> - costs of necessary cleaning and repair, as allowed by state law
> - the amount of the judgment (for rent through June 10)
> - rent for the week between June 10 and June 17 at $15/day, or $105.

If the security deposit is not large enough to cover everything you owe, the landlord can collect the balance in all sorts of ways—for example, by going after your wages or bank account.

D. Avoiding Fights Over Deposits

Most security deposit hassles between landlords and tenants concern cleaning, not repairs or replacement costs. That's because replacement and repair costs are objective and can be verified, but cleanliness is a matter of each person's individual tastes. You need to ferret out what your landlord expects, and adopt those standards—at least until you've moved out.

1. Your Cleaning Plans

Some landlords are wise enough to establish fair cleaning and damage guidelines right in the lease or rental agreement, a move-out letter or set of building rules and regulations. But what if your lease says nothing beyond obligating you to leave the unit in "clean and acceptable condition"? If you've lived in your place long enough, you may have a good idea of your landlord's standards.

But if you have any doubt, you should seize the initiative by giving your landlord written notice of your cleaning plans—for example, washing the kitchen floor, laundering the cotton bedroom drapes, thoroughly cleaning all appliances and bathroom fixtures and so on. Your letter should also ask your landlord to respond within a few days with any comments or disagreements with your cleaning plans. See the sample letter #1, below.

Is it really necessary to take the time and trouble to give your landlord a preview of your cleaning plans? Yes.

First, giving the landlord the chance to respond in advance to your cleaning plans puts you in the driver's seat. This type of letter of understanding legally obligates your landlord to tell you if your cleaning plans aren't sufficient. If the landlord fails to respond to your letter, you can assume that she agrees with your cleaning intentions. If, later, the

landlord deducts for an unwaxed kitchen floor when you stated that you intended to do a thorough washing only, you have solid evidence that she is being unreasonable.

But keep in mind that you must do a thorough job on the tasks you set yourself, and that it is always possible for you and the landlord to argue whether or not you washed the floor well enough.

Telling your landlord in advance how you intend to clean might save you some trouble, too. For example, if your landlord intends to replace the bedroom drapes that you plan to wash, repaint the walls you intend to clean or junk the old stove you plan to scrub, she might let you know, saving you a pile of work.

A letter of understanding may also save you money. For example, when you suggest washing the walls with a strong cleaner, your landlord may react in horror, saying that it could strip the paint of its glossy finish. If you don't know about these risks, and your cleaning makes things worse, you can be sure that your landlord will tap into your deposit.

Legally speaking, you are required only to return your rental in the same condition in which you found it, minus ordinary wear and tear. If your rental was on the grubby end of the cleanliness spectrum when you moved in, you'll hardly be in the mood to return it any cleaner. But leaving a dirty apartment, even for good reason, all but guarantees that your landlord will dip into your deposit for cleaning charges. Knowing this, you must be willing and equipped to assert your rights in a lawsuit in small claims court if you wish to get the entire deposit back. To win, you'll need to have a good deal of evidence of the rental unit's original filthy or damaged condition (such as a signed Landlord-Tenant Checklist, photos and witnesses).

The sample letter #2 below shows you how to set up a less-than-perfect cleaning job for an apartment that was presented in less-than-perfect shape. Note how the tenant, Stephan, lets his landlord know that he has plenty of hard evidence concerning the miserable condition of the unit when he moved in.

Letter #1:
Tenant's Cleaning Plans

1492 Fraser Avenue, #363
Chicago, Illinois, 00000

May 15, 200X

Brett Steiner
5 Hilton Ave.
Chicago, Illinois 00000

Dear Ms. Steiner:

As you know, I gave notice on April 30, 200X, that I intended to terminate my tenancy effective May 30, 200X.

I intend to leave the apartment clean and undamaged. Specifically, I plan to:

1. Vacuum all floors and carpets and strip and wax kitchen and bathroom floors.

2. Wash bathroom tile and all painted surfaces.

3. Clean all bathroom and kitchen appliances with cleaning products designed for these areas; clean oven and turn off and clean refrigerator.

4. Cold-water wash the drapes in the kitchen and bathroom. Vacuum drapes in the living room and bedroom.

5. Wash the interior surfaces of the windows.

6. Remove all rubbish and personal items.

I believe that thoroughly accomplishing these tasks will satisfy my obligations under Illinois law to leave my rental unit clean. And since my apartment has not been damaged (beyond ordinary wear and tear), I expect a full and prompt refund of my $750 security deposit. Please let me know within five days if my cleaning plan is not acceptable to you. If I don't hear from you, I'll assume that you are in agreement with it.

Yours truly,

Stephan Pierce

Stephan Pierce

Of course, there is the possibility that your landlord will use your letter as a point of departure, adding extra tasks from replacing degraded tile grout to painting the ceiling. If so, politely refuse, explaining that such requests are excessive.

2. Cleaning Thoroughly

You can't expect to get your deposit back if you've left the place a mess. So clean the place thoroughly, including all the items you promised in the letter (if any) you sent to your landlord. This doesn't normally mean you have to dry clean the drapes or wash the ceiling. A good thorough cleaning, including all appliances, fixtures, floors and window coverings should be adequate. Be sure to apply some extra elbow grease when cleaning the kitchen and bathrooms.

Remove all your belongings before you leave. That includes bags of garbage, clothes, food, newspapers, furniture, appliances, dishes, plants, cleaning supplies or other items. Leaving them causes extra work for your landlord, which you'll end up paying for from your deposit.

Letter #2: Tenant's Cleaning Plans

1492 Fraser Avenue, #363
Chicago, Illinois, 00000

May 15, 200X

Brett Steiner
5 Hilton Ave.
Chicago, Illinois 00000

Dear Ms. Steiner:

As you know on April 30, 200X, I gave notice to terminate my tenancy effective May 30, 200X.

When I moved in on October 1, 200X, the previous tenant had just left a day earlier. There were full garbage bags in the kitchen and entry hall; the kitchen, hallway and bathroom floors had been swept but not washed or waxed; the kitchen cabinets had peeling, sticky shelf paper; the windows had not been washed; the refrigerator still had containers of food; the oven had not been cleaned and the burners on the stove were encrusted with charred spills. After we toured the apartment and noted all of these problems on the Landlord-Tenant Checklist (copy attached), you promised to have a cleaning service come the next day.

Despite my written reminder to you the next day (copy attached), the cleaning crew never materialized. I was forced to spend six hours dealing with the mess. In case you don't remember just how bad it was, I have a set of date-stamped photos showing all the disgusting details, which I'd be happy to show you. I also have receipts for my cleaning materials.

Under state law, I am required to return the rental unit to you in substantially the same condition as I found it, minus ordinary wear and tear. I intend to live up to my legal duty. In fact, the condition of the apartment is far better than it was when I moved in. I will be here to go over the apartment with you on my last day as we arranged, and will have with me our original Checklist, my Polaroid and my co-worker Ray, who helped me clean when I moved in.

Yours truly,

Stephan Pierce
Stephan Pierce

If you leave anything you want back, you may be out of luck. Some states require the landlord to try to locate you, to store your belongings and sell them only after a certain period of time has elapsed. Other states allow landlords to immediately sell or use the items as they see fit. It's far easier to take your stuff with you than to research your state's laws on abandoned property, but if you need to look up the law, see Chapter 20.

3. Documenting the Condition of the Unit

In Chapter 6, we recommend that you fill out a Landlord-Tenant Checklist when you move in, documenting the condition of the rental unit. We also suggest you photograph and videotape the unit. You should do the same when you move out. Pictures will provide great visual proof of your claim if you later have to sue the landlord to get your deposit returned. (See Chapter 6 for suggestions on taking photos that you can rely on later.)

Also be sure to keep all your receipts for cleaning and repair materials, such as rental of a carpet cleaning machine or hiring a professional cleaning service as evidence that you did clean, in case you later have to sue in small claims court in order to get your deposit back.

Finally, be sure to have a friend or neighbor witness the final result. A person who helped clean often makes a very convincing witness. Make sure it's someone who will be willing to testify in court on your behalf, if necessary, should you end up in small claims court.

4. Arranging a Final Inspection

After you've moved your belongings out and cleaned up, and just before you return the key, ask your landlord to inspect the unit in your presence to determine whether any deductions from your security deposit are necessary.

Try to avoid having your landlord do the final inspection alone. A landlord is less likely to claim dirty or damaged conditions when a tenant is present. A few states, including Arizona, Maryland and Virginia, actually give the tenants the legal right to be present when landlords conduct the final inspection. But wherever you live, you'll want to insist on being there. Write the landlord a brief note such as the one below.

Request to Be Present at Inspection

1492 Fraser Avenue, Apt. #363
Chicago, Illinois 00000

May 24, 200X

Brett Steiner
5 Hilton Ave.
Chicago, Illinois 00000

Dear Ms. Steiner:

As you know on April 30, 200X, I gave notice terminate my tenancy effective May 30, 200X. On May 15, I wrote to you explaining my plans for cleaning the apartment. Since I didn't hear back from you, I went ahead and cleaned as planned.

I would like to arrange to meet you and conduct a final inspection of my apartment this week. Saturday morning is best for me, but I can be somewhat flexible. I have a copy of the Checklist we completed when I moved in two years ago. I'm sure that you will be pleased with the condition of the apartment.

Please call me at 123-4567 so that we can arrange for a convenient time to meet.

Yours truly,

Stephan Pierce

Stephan Pierce

When you meet to tour the apartment together, give your landlord a copy of the Landlord-Tenant Checklist you completed when you moved in and any other before-and-after proof you have that the unit is in essentially the same condition, excluding normal wear and tear. Any item that your landlord claims needs cleaning, repair or replacement should be noted in the middle column, Condition on Departure. Where possible, also note the estimated cost of repair or replacement in the third column. An excerpt of the Checklist is shown here. See Chapter 6 for a complete Checklist.

Be ready to calmly and pleasantly assert your point of view, backed up, if possible, with photos showing the condition of the unit when you moved in. Try to work out any disagreements on the spot. If your landlord points to a damaged or dirty item that would be inexpensive to clean or replace, be willing to compromise. It is usually better to give up a few dollars than go to all the trouble of suing later. (You would sue for the portion improperly withheld.) If you come to an agreement, ask the landlord to return your security deposit before you leave.

If your landlord claims that your unit needs more cleaning or repairs, ask for a second chance to do it. By law, at least one state (Montana) requires landlords to offer tenants a second chance at cleaning (if it's done within 24 hours) before deducting cleaning charges from the security deposit.

As long as you are still technically a tenant (your 30-day notice period hasn't run out), you should have no problem. But if your time to move out is up, and your landlord needs to get the apartment ready quickly for another tenant, the answer may be no, especially if repairs are required, not just cleaning.

If that happens, put your request in writing. (A sample letter is shown below.) A written request that is also turned down might serve you well if you decide later to sue in small claims court over deposit money withheld for cleaning. Especially if the case is close, a judge is likely to look askance at a landlord who refused your repeated offers to do a better job.

Landlord-Tenant Checklist

GENERAL CONDITION OF RENTAL UNIT AND PREMISES

572 Fourth St
Street Address

Apt. 11   Washington, D.C.
Unit Number   City

	Condition on Arrival	Condition on Departure	Estimated Cost of Repair/Replacement
LIVING ROOM			
Floors & Floor Coverings	OK	OK	Ø
Drapes & Window Coverings	Mini-blinds discolored	Dirty	$10
Walls & Ceilings	OK	Several holes in wall	$100
Light Fixtures	OK	OK	Ø
Windows, Screens & Doors	Window rattles	OK	Ø

Request to Clean Further

75 Bolton Road
Evanston, Illinois, 00000

May 28, 200X

Brett Steiner
5 Hilton Ave.
Chicago, Illinois 00000

Dear Ms. Steiner:

Thank you for meeting me today to go over the condition of my old apartment on Fraser Avenue (#363). My tenancy expires on May 30, although I have already moved my belongings and have moved out. I had hoped that you would approve completely of my cleaning job.

It is my understanding that you approved of the condition of the apartment except for the bathroom walls and tiles. I used a conventional household cleaner, not wanting to risk marring the surface of the tiles with anything stronger. As a result, I could not remove every bit of discoloration and mildew in the grout. You expressed disappointment at this and stated that you would have to hire a cleaning crew to do the job over, and would deduct two hours of their time (at $40 an hour) from my security deposit.

I asked you at the time, and I repeat the request now, to have the opportunity to do the work myself. I am sure that I can remove the offending stains with a stronger cleanser just as well as a cleaning company could. I know that this will mean that you will need to inspect again, but since you visit the property daily, it seems to me that this would not be an undue imposition. And because I am no longer occupying the unit, you would need to look at this one room only, since the rest of the apartment is acceptable. I can arrange to meet you at any time.

Please extend me the favor of another 10-minute inspection of the bathroom walls. Getting my entire security deposit ($750) back is very important to me, since I am facing a hefty security deposit obligation in my new duplex.

Yours truly,

Stephan Pierce
Stephan Pierce

5. Requesting Your Deposit in Writing

It's always a good idea to ask for the return of your deposit in a letter to your landlord. (See the sample below.) In some states you *must* make a written "demand" for its return—if you don't, you risk losing it altogether. Even if your state does not require it, promptly writing to your landlord when your tenancy is up is important for several reasons:

- **Your letter gives the landlord your forwarding address**. This simple, essential information is often overlooked by tenants in a hurry to pack up and move. In some states, your landlord may keep the deposit if he can't locate you within a specified amount of time.

- **Writing a demand letter is another opportunity to build your case if you decide later to sue for the return of your security deposit**. Writing down what you think your landlord owes invites one of two responses: paying up or disputing your version. If your landlord doesn't pay and doesn't take the time or trouble to discuss the matter with you, you're in a good position to argue in court that he lost his opportunity to work things out and should now pay up.

- **Your letter makes it more likely that you'll get penalty damages if the landlord fails to follow the law.** Laws in many states penalize landlords who intentionally break security deposit laws. If you have written a clear letter that tells the landlord exactly what to do and you still don't get your deposit, the landlord certainly can't claim ignorance of the law or of your whereabouts.

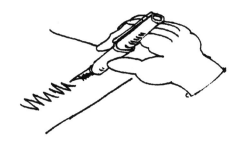

Demand for Return of Security Deposit

75 Bolton Road
Evanston, Illinois, 00000

June 2, 200X

Brett Steiner
5 Hilton Ave.
Chicago, Illinois 00000

Dear Ms. Steiner:

As you doubtless remember, I was your tenant in Apartment #363 at 1492 Fraser Avenue in Chicago. My tenancy ended on May 30.

Thanks for giving me the opportunity to re-do the bathroom tiles and clean them to your satisfaction. We agreed yesterday that the entire apartment was cleaned and returned to you in a satisfactory condition, without damage or more than usual wear and tear. Since I have no unpaid rent to account for, I expect that my security deposit will be refunded in full. Please send me a check in the amount of $750 to the address above.

Yours truly,

Stephan Pierce

Stephan Pierce

If Stephan doesn't hear from Brett within a month, he'll want to send a stronger letter. An example is shown in Section F, below.

6. Using the Deposit as Last Month's Rent

If you have not paid the rent for your last month of residence, the landlord can always apply your security deposit to this unpaid sum. It's just another way of saying that the deposit can be used to cover unpaid rent. In fact, this is exactly what you may want the landlord to do. It saves you from writing a check for the last month's rent and having to wait until after you move out to get your deposit refund.

(If your landlord collected a separate sum, labeled "last month's rent," see Chapter 4.)

If you want your landlord to apply your deposit for the last month's rent, get approval in writing. Why should your landlord object? Because the landlord can't know in advance what the property will look like when you leave. If you leave the property a mess, but the whole security deposit has gone to pay the last month's rent, there will be nothing left to use to repair or clean the property. The landlord will have to absorb the loss or sue you.

If you're a fastidious tenant who is almost sure to leave the unit in tip-top shape, your landlord may decide to take a chance that the deposit won't be needed for repairs or cleaning. Offer to let the landlord make a quick inspection first, to see that the property is clean and undamaged.

Even if your landlord objects to your decision not to write a final rent check, the chances that you will be evicted for nonpayment of rent are slim, since you'll be out of there in a month anyway. (But don't expect a stellar recommendation from this landlord when your next one calls for a reference.)

⚠ **If the landlord doesn't agree to your request, be sure you know your state's law before deciding not to write your last month's rent check.** In a few states, acting without your landlord's approval can be disastrous. In Kansas, if you attempt to use the security deposit for the last month's rent, you lose the entire deposit and can be sued for the last month's rent besides. Minnesota and Texas also impose statutory penalties when tenants try this maneuver. Court cases in other states may reach similar conclusions. Check your state's statutes and the cases that have interpreted them before you act. (Citations to the statutes mentioned above are in "Citations for State Laws on Security Deposits" in Appendix I.)

E. Security Deposits From Co-Tenants

A common dispute among roommates is what happens to the security deposit when one leaves and the others stay. If you're the one leaving, you would most certainly like your share of the deposit back when you move out. Unfortunately, you may have to wait a while.

When co-tenants all sign a lease or rental agreement together, your landlord has no legal duty to return or account for any portion of the deposit until they all leave. Practically speaking, this means co-tenants must work out among themselves what to do when one roommate leaves.

It's common for a new tenant to pay a departing one his share of the deposit. From the new tenant's point of view, however, this is wise only if the unit is being maintained properly, since the new tenant won't want to end up paying for damage that was caused by the former tenant. If no one is replacing you, see if the other co-tenants will chip in and pay you your share.

Some landlords, however, will refund your share of the deposit when you leave even though it's not legally required. However, as part of doing so, the landlord will probably want to inspect the property. That's good for the new tenant, too, who gets to start with a clean slate, knowing that all damage has been noted and paid for from the former tenant's portion of the security deposit.

> EXAMPLE: Bill and Mark were co-tenants who had each contributed $500 toward the $1,000 security deposit. Bill needed to move before the lease was up, and asked Len, their landlord, if he would accept Tom as a new co-tenant. Len agreed.
>
> Bill wanted his $500 back, and although Tom was willing to contribute his share of the deposit, he did not want to end up paying for damage that had been caused before he moved in. To take care of this, Len agreed to inspect if Tom would first give him a check for $500. When he got the check, Len inspected and found $200 worth of damage. Bill disagreed, and they compromised on $150. Len deducted this amount from Bill's share of the deposit and wrote Bill a check for $350. Len left it up to Bill and Mark to fairly apportion the responsibility for the damage.

If the landlord refuses your request to inspect and return a portion of the security deposit to the departing tenant, get together with your roommates and realistically appraise the situation. The new co-tenant should be asked to pay the departing tenant a full share of the deposit if there is no damage, or a portion if there is damage attributable to the departing tenant.

F. How to Handle Deposit Disputes

Let's assume that several weeks have passed since you moved out and wrote to your landlord asking for your deposit to be returned. However, you haven't gotten either a check or an explanation of why the landlord is keeping your money. Or maybe you have received an itemization from the landlord—and you're convinced that the deductions are unjustified. Or maybe your landlord has violated another law, such as a requirement that you receive interest on your deposit.

Clearly, it's time to take action. Start with a simple phone call to your landlord, follow up, and if all else fails, go to court.

1. Call the Landlord

Start by phoning the landlord to discuss the problem. Especially if your deposit is only a few days late, there may be a reasonable explanation for your landlord's tardiness—maybe the landlord is waiting for some repair work and doesn't yet know its exact cost. Make a note of the date and time of your phone call, and write down as many specifics of the conversation that you can remember. If you go to court, you may need to show these notes to the judge.

2. Make a Second Written Demand

If you didn't get a good answer and a firm promise that you'll get the deposit or itemization right away, it's time for stronger action. Write another demand letter like the one shown below. (If this if your first letter, you might want to soften the tone a bit.)

If you're tempted to skip this step because you're sure it's a waste of time, don't. Your demand letter may serve as a catalyst to get your landlord to agree to a fair settlement. Even if the landlord never reads it, setting out your case in a formal letter gives you an excellent opportunity to prepare your case for small claims court. And remember: Some state security deposit statutes require you to make a written request; and in some states, small claims court rules require you to write a demand letter before you can sue. (See Section G, below.)

Your letter should lay out the reasons your landlord owes you deposit money and make it clear that if you don't get it, you plan to go to small claims court. Now, instead of being just another cranky voice on the telephone, you and your dispute assume a sobering reality to your landlord. Your landlord will realize that you won't simply go away and stop bothering him, but plan to have your day in court.

Here are some tips on writing a demand letter:

1. Concisely review the main facts. If you end up in small claims court, your letter will be read by a judge. This will explain what happened.

2. Be polite. Don't personally attack your landlord—even if you think it's deserved. The more annoying you are, the more you invite your landlord to respond similarly. Your goal is to get your landlord to make a businesslike analysis of the dispute and ask:

- What are my risks of losing?
- How much time will a defense take?
- Do I want the dispute to be decided in public?
- Even if I think the tenant is partly at fault, isn't it more cost-effective to return the deposit?

3. Ask for exactly what you want. For example, if you want your full deposit returned, ask for it.

4. Explain your legal rights. Cite state security deposit law, using the summaries in this book and the "Citations for State Laws on Security Deposits" in Appendix I.

If your state allows extra, punitive damages when a landlord intentionally withholds a deposit, point out that you are entitled to them now. (Check your state security deposit statutes for details on punitive damages.)

5. Conclude by stating you will promptly sue in small claims court if necessary. If you will be suing for extra (punitive) damages allowed under your state law, make this point, too. It will be hard for your landlord to claim blissful ignorance of the law or simple inadvertence—which might protect her from being hit by punitives—when you show the judge the letters you've written.

Keep a copy of all correspondence. You'll need it if you go to court.

Second Demand for Return of Security Deposit

75 Bolton Road
Evanston, Illinois, 00000

July 15, 200X

Brett Steiner
5 Hilton Ave.
Chicago, Illinois 00000

Dear Ms. Steiner:

As you know, until May 30, 200X, I rented Apartment #363 at 1492 Fraser Avenue in Chicago. When I moved out, the apartment was thoroughly cleaned. I re-cleaned the bathroom and you inspected it May 28, pronouncing the bathroom (and the rest of the unit) acceptable. Actually, I left the place in far better shape than it was when I moved in. In addition, the apartment was not damaged in any way. I left owing no rent.

On June 2, 200X, I sent you a letter asking that my deposit be refunded in full and gave you my new address. I called you on June 20 to remind you about returning my deposit and again gave you my new address. You assured me that you'd "Get right on it in a day or two."

As of today, I have received neither my $750 security deposit nor any accounting from you for that money. Under Illinois law (Ill. Rev. Stat. ch. 765 para. 710, 715), I was entitled to receive my deposit, including an itemization of any deductions, 30 days after my tenancy ended—that is, by June 30, 200X. You are now over two weeks late.

If I do not receive my money by July 25, I will regard your retention of my deposit as showing bad faith and will sue you in small claims court for $1,500, which is double the amount of my deposit as allowed under Illinois law.

Please mail my deposit immediately to the above address.

Very truly yours,

Stephan Pierce

Stephan Pierce

3. Consider Compromise

If you've written your landlord a demand letter and you don't get a satisfactory response, in most states you are eligible to file suit immediately. (Some states require that you try mediation first; check your state's statute.) But before you do, try to meet the landlord halfway. You don't need to go overboard trying to reach a compromise, especially if you believe your landlord's original assessment of the cost of repairs and cleaning was grossly unfair and you believe you can prove your position in court. Just the same, it usually doesn't make sense for you to prepare a small claims case and spend time in court to argue over $50 or even $100. This is especially true because, fair or not, some judges are prone to split the difference between the landlord's and the tenant's claims.

If you and the landlord reach a compromise, it's wise to sign an agreement right away. Writing things down gives you a chance to make sure you and your landlord really agree. And if the landlord fails to honor the agreement, you can take it to small claims court. You won't have to argue over any of the underlying facts (concerning your clean or not-so-clean apartment, for example); the agreement will clearly show that the landlord promised you a certain amount of money. A sample agreement is shown below.

Sample Agreement Regarding Return of Security Deposit

Brett Steiner, Landlord and Stephan Pierce, Tenant agree as follows:

1. Tenant's tenancy at 1492 Fraser Avenue, Apartment #363, Chicago, terminated on May 30, 200X.

2. Tenant left owing no unpaid rent.

3. Tenant requested the return of his entire $750 security deposit but has not yet received any of it.

4. Landlord will deduct $25 from the deposit for re-cleaning of the bathroom tiles and will return $725 to Tenant by mailing a check no later than three days after the date of this Agreement.

5. In exchange for receiving the $725 as required by this Agreement, Tenant will not sue Landlord for failing to return the deposit within the time required by state law.

6. This Agreement is a final and complete resolution of the dispute over use and retention of Tenant's security deposit.

Brett Steiner   1/20/0X

Brett Steiner, Landlord   Date

Stephan Pierce   1/20/0X

Stephan Pierce, Tenant   Date

If you and your landlord can't arrive at a reasonable compromise, you may wish to try mediation. That's a procedure in which you meet with a neutral third person, who helps you arrive at your own solution. Many cities, counties and nonprofit organizations offer mediation services designed to help tenants and landlords. In addition, mediation may be an essential prerequisite to filing a lawsuit in small claims court. Check your state's small claims court procedures, and read the discussion on how to negotiate with landlords on various issues in Chapter 19. It also covers mediation.

G. Suing Your Landlord in Small Claims Court

If the formal demand doesn't work and there is no reasonable prospect of compromise, consider suing your landlord in small claims court. It's inexpensive, usually $10 to $50, to file a case. You don't need a lawyer, and disputes typically go before a judge (there are no juries) within 30 to 60 days. The trial itself, which consists of both sides explaining what happened from their point of view and presenting any evidence or witnesses, seldom takes more than 15 or 20 minutes. The judge either announces a decision right there in the courtroom or mails it out within a few days.

By Any Other Name

We use the term small claims court here, but the exact name depends upon the state. These courts are called "Justice of the Peace," "Conciliation," "District," "Justice," "City" or "County" in different places.

You can sue your landlord for your security deposit and for interest if it's required in your state or city. In many states, you can also sue for extra punitive damages if the landlord intentionally failed to return your deposit on time. (See Section A, above.) Whether or not the landlord's conduct was bad enough to entitle you to punitive damages is up to the judge, but it never hurts to ask. In practice, your chances of collecting significant punitive damages will be good only if the landlord has delayed a considerable time—probably at least ten days, and possibly longer. As a general rule, you have to request damages when you file your suit. If you win, the judge will add court costs, such as filing fees, later.

The maximum amount for which you can sue in small claims court varies among the states, but in most states it's about $2,500 to $7,500. (Chapter 19 lists each state's limit.)

Don't wait to file your case. Each state limits the time within which lawsuits can be filed. In a dispute over a written rental agreement or lease, you probably have up to four or five years to sue. Just the same, it's foolish to wait very long, since the memories of witnesses fade (or the witnesses themselves may be impossible to find), and your landlord may even go out of business. Also, judges are not very sympathetic to old disputes.

Everybody's Guide to Small Claims Court, by Ralph Warner (Nolo), explains small claims court strategy and procedure, including how and where to serve court papers, how to collect your money and details on appeals.

1. Preparation: The Key to Winning

Winning your small claims court case can be easy or difficult, depending on the facts of the situation and how much homework you do before appearing in court.

First, get a copy of your state's security deposit law and any local ordinances that apply. Read these thoroughly before you go to court. You can get copies from the library or, in many states, online. (See Chapter 20 for advice on legal research.)

Second, gather tangible evidence. If you simply testify that your apartment was clean and in good shape, and your landlord says just the opposite, the judge is stuck making a decision that is little more than a guess. Most judges will split the difference. If your landlord comes to court with a witness who reads off a long list of damaged and dirty conditions he claims you left behind, you may even lose.

To win, you must have enough evidence to convince the judge you are right. Ideally, preparation should start when you move into the rental unit and make a record of its condition. When you moved out, you should have made another similar written record and taken photos. (See Section D, above.)

But even if you weren't so thorough, there are still good ways to convince the judge that you left the place in good shape. Here are kinds of evidence you can take to court:

- A clear statement of how much money your landlord owes you, the interest (if any) owed, penalties you seek and expenses such as cleaning supplies
- A copy of your signed lease or rental agreement and any written guidelines your landlord provided on cleaning, damage repair and security deposits.
- Photos or a video of the premises before you moved in which show how dirty or damaged the place was.
- Photos or a video after you left which don't show additional mess or damage.
- One, or preferably two, witnesses who were familiar with the property, saw it just after you left and who will testify that the place was clean or that certain items were not damaged.
- If it's difficult for a witness to come to court, a signed letter or a statement (declaration) signed "under penalty of perjury" can be used in most states. Make sure the statement includes the date of the event, exactly what the witness saw, any credentials that make the person qualified to testify on the subject and any other facts that bear on the dispute.
- Details on the amount of time you spent cleaning the unit.
- Copies of receipts for cleaning supplies you used in the final clean-up or for professional cleaning (such as carpets and drapes) or repair.
- A copy of the Landlord-Tenant Checklist that you filled out with the landlord when you moved in and when you moved out, signed by both you and your landlord. This is particularly important if the landlord admitted, on the Checklist, to damaged or dirty conditions when you moved in.

- Copies of all correspondence: a letter outlining your cleaning plans (if any), the demand letters and written notes of your conversations about the deposit.
- If the landlord is overcharging for cleaning or repairs, a written estimate from another cleaning or repair service showing it would have done the job for less. For example, if your landlord claims to have paid $400 for cleaning, you could submit a statement from ABC cleaning that they charge $20 per hour and can clean a one-bedroom apartment in six hours, for a total bill of $120.
- If you dispute your landlord's claim that you broke or damaged an item such as an appliance, the opinion of a repair person or other expert as to why the appliance failed.

If you take the trouble to understand your state's law and to gather good evidence, you should have no trouble convincing a judge to rule in your favor.

EXAMPLE: Shawna's landlord claims that Shawna is responsible for the broken refrigerator ice maker, claiming that she must have caused the problem by blocking the air circulation when she stuffed too much food in the freezer. Shawna, who rarely has more than a half-gallon of ice cream in her freezer, is not about to stand by and give up the $400 the landlord claims it will cost to fix the ice maker, which she is convinced was on its last legs when she moved in.

To fight back, Shawna talks to a local refrigerator repair person. He scoffs at the idea that the problem could be caused by over-filling the freezer and tells Shawna that this particular model is notorious for ice maker failures. Shawna asks him to write a letter to the court saying this, and then follows up by going to the library and looking in Consumer Reports magazine, which lists this brand of ice maker as a problem. Shawna brings the letter and article to court, shows them to the judge, testifies that she never misused the freezer and wins the case.

2. How to Present Your Case in Court

Small claims courts are informal places, intended to be used by regular folks presenting their own cases. If you do not have any experience with a court, consider watching a few cases a day or two before your case. You will see that it is a very simple procedure. Many small claims courts also provide helpful pamphlets, videos and even computer tutorials on how small claims courts work. A few offer free legal advisor programs to help you prepare your case properly.

A few days before your case will be heard, practice your presentation in front of a tough-minded friend acting as the judge. Present your case from start to finish, introducing any witnesses and explaining evidence. Chances are that your presentation will be awkward and you may even forget key points. Fine, keep practicing until you can make your presentation in an efficient and convincing way. Keep in mind that the judge will give you only a few minutes to make your case. Stick to the important facts.

On the day your case is to be heard, get to the court a little early and check for your courtroom (in some places, referred to as a "department"). Tell the clerk or bailiff that you are present and sit down and wait until your case is called. When your turn comes, stand at the large table at the front of the room to speak. Remember, judges hear many cases every day and will not be particularly excited by yours. If you are long-winded, your judge may stop listening and start thinking about lunch.

If Your Landlord Doesn't Show Up

In the unlikely event your landlord doesn't show up, you'll probably win. In most states, the judge will ask you to briefly state the basic facts of your case and to provide some evidence, such as a set of photos showing the condition of the rental unit when you moved in and out. The judge may also check to see that your landlord was properly served with the court papers and may ask you a question or two to make sure there is no obvious flaw in your case. Of course, you'll still have to collect the judgment, and the landlord may appeal in some cases.

Start your presentation with the problem—for example, "Brett Steiner hasn't returned my $750 security deposit to me, and it's been almost two months since I moved out of her apartment at 1492 Fraser Avenue. State law says she is supposed to return it within 30 days." Then present the directly relevant facts that explain why you should win—for example, "The apartment was clean, nothing was damaged and my rent was paid in full." Again, be brief and to the point; don't ramble. You may show pictures and documents to the judge. When you are done with your oral presentation, tell the judge you have witnesses who want to testify.

The landlord, of course, will also have a chance to speak. In most states, the landlord has the responsibility of proving that he's entitled to keep all or part of a deposit. If the landlord exaggerates the extent of any damage or dirt, stay cool. You should get another chance to speak—and your evidence should back up your version. If you don't have a lot of tangible evidence or witnesses, simply state the facts as you see them. For example, you might say, "Your Honor, when I moved in three years ago, the walls had not been freshly painted. And since the previous tenant lived in the unit for two years, I'm pretty sure it's been at least five years since the unit was painted. The fact that they need freshening up now is due to ordinary wear and tear, and it should be the landlord's responsibility."

When to see a lawyer. Although generally it's not cost-effective to hire a lawyer when you head to small claims court, there is one possible exception to this rule. If your lease or rental agreement requires you to pay the landlord's attorney fees if the landlord wins a lawsuit, then in most states, you, too, are entitled to attorney fees if you win a lawsuit. In short, if there's a fair sum of money involved and you're confident of winning, you might look for a lawyer experienced in representing tenants to handle the matter for you if your state allows lawyers to appear in small claims court. (If it doesn't the lawyer can at least advise you, and you should be able to collect for that, too.) Be sure you thoroughly discuss fee arrangements ahead of time. (See Chapter 20 for advice on finding and working with an attorney.)

H. If Your Deposit Doesn't Cover What You Owe

Tenants aren't the only ones who can use small claims court. If the security deposit doesn't cover what you owe for back rent, cleaning or repairs, your landlord may file a small claims suit against you.

If you are sued, you should show up in court even if you think the landlord is in the right or you know you can't pay what you owe. Even if your landlord has a good case, it gives you a chance to present any facts that might reduce the amount of the judgment a little. Also, in some states, you can ask the judge to allow you to make payments in installments.

If you don't show up, the landlord will probably win by default and can collect the judgment by garnishing your wages or going after other assets, like a bank account. The judgment can be collected against you for many years and will be a negative mark on your credit file.

If you have good evidence of a valid defense, you definitely want to argue your side of things. For example, if you feel that the landlord charged too much for the cleaning job, get estimates from at least two reputable cleaning firms as to how much they would have charged. Calmly and clearly present your side of the dispute. If you have no proof about the dispute itself, you'll need to demonstrate that the landlord's case is flawed in some procedural respect—for example, the landlord failed to send an itemized list of proposed deductions, as required by your state's law. ■

17

Termination Notices Based on Nonpayment of Rent and Other Illegal Acts

If a tenant screws up in any of a hundred possible ways—by paying the rent late, keeping a dog in violation of a no-pets clause in the lease, throwing loud parties that disturb neighbors—the landlord can terminate the tenancy. Termination is the first step toward an eventual eviction. The landlord sends you a notice announcing that your tenancy is over, and that if you don't leave, he'll go to court and sue for eviction. Or the notice may give you a few days to clean up your act (pay the rent, find a new home for the dog). If you leave (or reform) as directed, no one goes to court.

Eviction itself—that is, physically throwing you and your possessions out of the property—generally can't be done until the landlord has gone to court and proved that you've done something wrong that justifies eviction. And even if the landlord wins the eviction lawsuit, he can't just move you and your things out onto the sidewalk. In most states, he has to hire the sheriff or marshal to perform that unpleasant task.

This chapter explains when and how a landlord can terminate your tenancy. It also explains some strategies you may want to consider if you are the unhappy recipient of a landlord's pink slip.

Related topics covered in this book include:
- Terminations when you haven't done anything wrong: Chapter 15.
- Overview of the eviction process, including illegal "self-help" evictions: Chapter 18.
- State laws that require your landlord to give you proper notice before beginning an eviction: Appendix I.

A. Termination Notices

In most states, landlords must follow specific rules and procedures to end a tenancy. Before filing an eviction lawsuit (sometimes called an unlawful detainer, or UD lawsuit), the landlord must give you a properly written notice describing a valid reason why the landlord wants you to leave.

An eviction lawsuit may be thrown out if the termination notice is not written and delivered correctly. Most states require termination notices to be written and delivered ("served") according to very picky rules that dictate the information contained and dates mentioned. Some states even specify the type size of the notice and method of delivery. Check your state's statutes to determine whether the notice you received complies with the law. If it does not, you may be able to defeat the landlord's eviction lawsuit on this basis. But a determined landlord will be simply delayed, not deterred. If you prove that the landlord's notice was faulty, you'll probably receive a correct one very soon after.

If a landlord wants you to leave because of some wrongdoing on your part, you'll receive one of three different types of termination notices. Although terminology varies somewhat from state to state, the substance of the three types of notices is remarkably the same.

- **Pay Rent or Quit** notices are used when the tenant has not paid the rent. You are given a few days (three to five in most states) to pay or move out ("quit"). If you don't, the landlord can file for eviction. But not every state requires a landlord to give you this second chance to pay the rent; in a few states, if you fail to pay rent on time, the landlord can simply demand that you leave (see Unconditional Quit, below).

- **Cure or Quit** notices are typically given after a violation of a term or condition of the lease or rental agreement, such as a no-pets clause or the promise to refrain from making excessive noise. Typically, you are given a set amount of time in which to correct, or "cure," the violation; if you fail to do so, you must move in order to avoid an eviction lawsuit.

- **Unconditional Quit** notices are the harshest of all. They order you to vacate the premises with no chance to pay the rent or correct your violation of the lease or rental agreement. In most states, unconditional quit notices are allowed only when the tenant has repeatedly:
  - violated a lease or rental agreement clause
  - been late with the rent
  - seriously damaged the premises, or
  - engaged in illegal activity.

Many states have all three types of notices on the books. But Unconditional Quit notices are the only notice statutes in Arkansas and Texas. Of course, Arkansas and Texas landlords may voluntarily give you a chance to correct your behavior, but no state law requires them to do it.

The tables in Appendix I ("State Laws on Termination for Nonpayment of Rent," "State Laws on Termination for Violation of Lease" and "State Laws on Unconditional Quit Terminations") give the details and citations to your state's statutes.

B. Late Rent

The number one reason for getting kicked out of a rental is—surprise!—not paying the rent on time. If you are late with the rent, landlords in most states can immediately send you a termination notice.

Fortunately, in most states the termination notice must give you a few days—usually three to five—in which to pay up. The exact number of days varies from state to state. (For details, see "State Laws on Termination for Nonpayment of Rent" in Appendix I.)

EXAMPLE: Willy's $400 rent was due on the first of the month. When he had not paid by the third, his landlord sent him a Five-Day Pay or Quit notice. Willy understood that he had to pay his rent by the end of the eighth day of the month in order to avoid being sued for eviction. On the seventh, Willy paid the entire rent of $400, avoiding a lawsuit that would have surely led to his eviction.

Unfortunately, if your state does not require the landlord to give you a few days to scrape the rent together, your landlord may immediately terminate your tenancy for not paying the rent. Usually you have a few days before the landlord can file for eviction. Of course, some landlords will allow you to stay on if you pay reasonably quickly and convincingly argue that you'll pay your rent on time in the future.

1. Required Grace Periods

A handful of states (Connecticut, Delaware, Maine, Oregon and Rhode Island) do not let the landlord send a termination notice (either a Pay or Quit notice or an Unconditional Quit notice) until the rent is a certain number of days late. In these states, tenants enjoy a statutory "grace period." (Details are in "State Laws on Termination for Nonpayment of Rent" in Appendix I.) If you live in one of these states, haven't paid the rent and receive a Pay or Quit notice, you have a pretty good cushion before your landlord can file for eviction: the grace period plus the time specified in the Pay or Quit notice.

EXAMPLE: Lara, a Maine tenant, couldn't pay her rent on time. State law required the landlord to wait until the rent was seven days late before he could send a termination notice. He did so on the eighth, giving Lara notice that she must pay or move within seven days. In all, Lara had fourteen days in which to pay the rent before her landlord could file for eviction.

Late rent fees are unaffected by Pay or Quit time periods or statutory grace periods. If you are subject to late rent fees, they'll kick in as soon as your lease or rental agreement (or in some states, state law) says they can. The number of days specified in your Pay or Quit notice will not affect them, nor will a legally required grace period. (Chapter 3 discusses late fees.)

2. Paying Rent After You Get a Termination Notice

If you are late with the rent and get a termination notice—whether or not it gives you a few days to pay the rent—call the landlord immediately and try to work something out. Section F, below, offers some pointers on dealing with the landlord. Here are the legal rules.

a. Paying the Whole Rent

If the landlord has sent you a termination notice but then accepts rent for the entire rental term, you are entitled to stay for that period. In most states, it's as if you paid on time in the first place.

> EXAMPLE: Zoe's rent was due on the first of the month. She didn't pay on time, and her landlord sent her a Three-Day Pay or Quit notice. Zoe borrowed money from her parents and paid on the third day, saving her tenancy and avoiding an eviction lawsuit.

In some states, however, your late payment may come back to haunt you if you are late again, as explained below.

b. If You're Chronically Late

In several states, landlords don't have to give you a second chance to pay the rent if you are habitually late. Typically, they are legally required to give you

a chance to pay and stay only once or twice within a certain period. For example, in Connecticut, if you are late with the rent more than once in six months, the next time you don't pay on time the landlord doesn't have to give you the option of paying the rent or leaving. Instead, he can send you an Unconditional Quit notice that simply tells you to leave within five days.

Some states insist that the landlord must have given you a written Pay or Quit notice for the first late payment, so that there is proof that you were late. Other statutes allow the Unconditional Quit notice merely for "repeated lateness." In that case, the landlord need not have given you a notice to pay or quit for the first tardiness.

Don't wear your landlords' patience thin. Even if your landlord accepts late rent without giving you a Pay or Quit notice ("writing you up," landlords call it), don't count on endless forbearance. Remember, unless you have a lease, in most states the landlord can terminate your tenancy with a 30-day notice. Even if you live in a rent control area that requires landlords to have good reason to evict you, repeatedly paying late is ample legal reason to evict. (Section F explains how to protect yourself when negotiating late rent payments.)

If you receive a Pay or Quit notice, don't assume that you have to pack up and move immediately. Section F, below, explores your options.

c. Making a Partial Rent Payment

Some tenants believe that having the landlord accept a partial payment of overdue rent after receiving a Pay or Quit (or Unconditional Quit) notice means that the landlord can't go ahead with an eviction. Sorry, but the most that you've bought is a little time. If the landlord accepts an amount of rent that covers only part of what you owe (for past months or even just the current month), that will, in most states, cancel the effect of the notice. But your

States That Limit Number of Times You Can Pay and Stay

State	Number of late rent payments required before landlord can send Unconditional Quit notice	Notice to Pay or Quit required for all prior late payments?
Connecticut	Two within six months	yes
Georgia	Two within 12 months	yes
Maryland	Three within 12 months, but Landlord must have won an eviction lawsuit for each prior nonpayment of rent episode*	yes
Massachusetts	Two within 12 months	yes
New Hampshire	Three within 12 months	yes
New Jersey	Habitual failure to pay rent on time	no
South Carolina	Repeated nonpayment of rent	no
Vermont	Three within 12 months	yes
Virginia	Two within 12 months	yes

* Tenants in Maryland can reinstate their tenancy by paying rent and court costs after the landlord has won the eviction lawsuit, but before physical eviction.	Citations to the code sections are found in "State Laws on Unconditional Quit Terminations" in Appendix I.

landlord can pocket your offering with one hand and simultaneously serve you with a new notice with the other, demanding that you pay the new balance or leave.

EXAMPLE: Danny's rent of $600 was due on the first of the month. Danny didn't pay January's rent and didn't have enough for February, either. On February 2, his landlord sent him a Three-Day notice to pay $1,200 or leave. Danny paid $600 on February 3 and thought that he'd saved his tenancy. He was amazed when, later that day, his landlord handed him a new three-day notice to pay $600 or leave. The landlord filed for eviction on February 7 when Danny failed to pay.

C. Other Violations of the Lease or Rental Agreement

In addition to nonpayment of rent, landlords may terminate a tenancy if you violate other terms of the lease or rental agreement. Common examples are:

- keeping a pet in violation of a no-pets rule
- bringing in an unauthorized tenant
- subleasing or assigning without the landlord's permission
- repeatedly violating "house rules" that are part of the lease or rental agreement, such as using common areas improperly, making too much noise, having unruly guests or abusing recreation facilities.

The laws in most states insist that the landlord give you an opportunity to correct, or "cure," the violation before the tenancy can end. You'll get a

"Cure or Quit" notice, giving you about five to 30 days to mend your ways. However, there are two important "but ifs" that can limit your chances to clean up your act and avoid the premature end of your tenancy:

Repeated violations. If you have violated the same lease clause two or more times within a certain period of time, you'll probably lose the right to a second chance. The landlord may give you an Unconditional Quit notice instead.

The violation cannot be corrected. Some lease violations cannot be corrected because the effect of the violation is permanent. For instance, suppose your lease contains the common prohibition against making alterations or improvements without the landlord's consent. Without asking, you remove and discard the living room wallpaper, which you think is surpassingly ugly but your landlord considers a national treasure. He can hardly demand that you cease violating the lease clause because it is simply too late to save the wallpaper. If a lease violation cannot be cured, the landlord may serve you with an Unconditional Quit notice.

If you get a notice telling you to cease a curable violation of your lease or rental agreement, your response will depend on the legitimacy of the landlord's claim. See Section F, below, for suggestions.

D. Violations of Your Legal Responsibilities as a Tenant

Virtually every state allows landlords to terminate a tenancy if a tenant has violated basic responsibilities imposed by law. These include the duty to maintain at least minimally acceptable housekeeping standards and to refrain from highly disruptive activities. For example, a tenant who commits any of the following acts is a likely candidate for a termination notice:

- grossly deficient housekeeping practices that cause an unhealthy situation, such as allowing garbage to pile up
- seriously misusing appliances, like damaging the freezer while attempting to defrost it with an ice pick
- repeatedly interfering with other tenants' ability to peacefully enjoy their homes, such as hosting late parties, playing incessant, loud music or running a noisy small business (repairing cars in the driveway of a rental duplex, for example)
- substantially damaging the property—for instance, knocking holes in the walls or doors, and
- allowing or participating in illegal activities on or near the premises, such as drug dealing or gambling.

Many careful landlords incorporate these obligations into their leases or rental agreements. But

even if they are not mentioned in these documents, you are still legally bound to observe them.

"Waste" and "Nuisance"

If you receive a termination notice based on your behavior, you may encounter two archaic legal terms that need a bit of explaining:

Waste. A tenant who either intentionally or through extreme carelessness damages the landlord's property is said to have committed waste. Waste does not include normal wear and tear or accidents that are the result of simple carelessness. For example, a carpet that needs to be replaced because your fish tank inexplicably sprung a leak would probably not constitute waste; but if you turn the dining room into a motorcycle repair shop, ruining the carpet in the process, you can expect a termination notice based on waste.

Nuisance. Public nuisances are activities that result in a substantial danger to the health or safety of occupants or neighbors, such as drug dealing. Private nuisances are activities, not necessarily illegal, that seriously limit the neighbors' ability to use and enjoy their homes, such as playing music so loudly that no one can sleep or using the backyard for midnight volleyball tournaments every Friday and Saturday night. Many state statutes allow a landlord to terminate a tenancy based on either form of nuisance. (Chapter 14 explains how to use public nuisance laws to pressure a landlord to evict troublemaking tenants.)

If you or your guests substantially damage the premises, expect an Unconditional Quit notice. The law does not require landlords to give tenants accused of serious misbehavior a second chance. You'll probably get only five to ten days to move out. The details are in "State Laws on Unconditional Quit Terminations" in Appendix I.

E. Illegal Activity on the Premises

In recent years, many states have responded aggressively to widespread drug dealing in residential neighborhoods by making it easier for landlords to evict based on these activities. Indeed, in some states a landlord must evict known drug dealers or users or risk having authorities close down or even confiscate the entire property. (This process, known as "forfeiture," is explained in Chapter 14). To say the least, the threat of losing their rental property has motivated many landlords to quickly evict tenants they suspect are engaging in illegal acts.

The landlord usually doesn't have to wait until the tenant is convicted of a crime or even arrested. In Texas and North Carolina, the landlord may evict as long as he has a "reasonable suspicion" that illegal activity is afoot and the tenant or the tenant's guests are involved. By contrast, in New Jersey an eviction for illegal activity may not begin unless there's been a criminal conviction for criminal acts on the rented premises.

Evictions based on criminal activity are often called "expedited evictions" because courts push them through and send law enforcement out to finish the job quicker than for a normal eviction. Expedited evictions are preceded by an Unconditional Quit notice that tells the tenant to move out (and do it quickly). If the tenant stays, the landlord can go to court and file for eviction. The court hearing on the eviction is typically held within a few days, and if the landlord wins, the tenant is given little time to move. In Missouri, a tenant who uses the premises for gambling or prostitution is not entitled to *any* termination notice; the landlord may file for eviction immediately. In Oregon, the tenant has 24 hours to vacate after a landlord wins in court. Details are set out in "State Laws on Unconditional Quit Terminations" in Appendix I.

F. Negotiating With the Landlord

If you receive a termination notice, you may experience at least a momentary surge of panic, despair or anger. Do you have to move immediately, or can you buy some time? What if you think the landlord is wildly exaggerating the problem? What will happen if you don't move out when you're supposed to?

Your best response to a termination notice will depend on whether and how long you would like to stay and whether you have a good defense to the landlord's justification for giving you the termination notice. You'll also want to consider the big picture: the time and trouble it will take you to fight an eviction, and the possible effect a lawsuit may have on your credit rating and chances for future rentals, even if you win.

If you don't want to move, negotiation should be your first response—regardless of the merits of your defense. For example, if there is some validity behind your landlord's termination notice—if you are, in fact, late with the rent, or your last two parties truly were a bit raucous—your best bet is to meet with your landlord and agree on making some changes in the future. Don't be shy about negotiating. After all, from your landlord's point of view, striking a deal can make far more sense than going to court to evict you. Remember, lawsuits are time-consuming, expensive and filled with technicalities; they are certainly a lot less attractive, business-wise, than negotiating a firm settlement that the landlord believes you will abide by.

It goes without saying that a landlord who perceives you as an inveterate troublemaker is unlikely to want to bargain. And of course, some landlords are so unapproachable or irrational that meeting on a one-to-one basis is sure to be fruitless. If so, you'll have to consider one of the options in Sections G and H, below.

Suggestions on how to negotiate with the landlord are covered in Chapter 15. All of the considerations explained there also apply in the situations discussed in this chapter. But there are additional strategies to consider.

1. When You're at Fault

If the landlord has a valid reason for terminating your tenancy, you'll find that negotiation is most likely to work under two conditions:

- you have generally been a stable, law-abiding tenant, and
- the alleged violation is relatively minor and can be completely remedied.

For example, if you've kept your son's dog for a couple of weeks in violation of the no-pets rule, and the animal has not caused substantial damage or annoyance, your landlord might give you a few extra days (beyond the time specified in the Cure or Quit notice) to find a home for the pooch. Similarly, if the landlord is mad because you've had an overnight guest a few too many times in violation of the lease clause, offer proof of your changed ways, in that your pal has:

- moved on (show him your friend's new lease)
- agreed not to stay over in a regular basis in the future, or
- wants to become a tenant (your roommate) for a reasonable increase in your rent.

If you're late with the rent, an offer to pay part now and the rest on your next payday might mollify the landlord. (It's even better to tell the landlord if you anticipate a payment problem and set up a partial payment agreement in advance: see Chapter 3.) Other strategies include offering to make payments in person for the next three months or, if checks have been bouncing, paying with a money order rather than a check. To ensure that there will be a sure source of rent money, offer to add a parent or friend as a cosigner on the lease or rental agreement.

As you negotiate, keep these points in mind:

- Emphasize your track record as a desirable tenant.
- Explain that the problem can be easily resolved, will leave no lasting ill effects, and won't happen again.
- If possible, offer to compensate the landlord in place of moving out—for example, if the landlord is furious at your "remodeling" work in the kitchen, which he believes was done

badly, offer to pay for further work that will remedy the situation.

- As subtly as possible, point out to the landlord that compromising with you is far less expensive and time-consuming than going to court to evict you.

- Remember that it may be to your advantage, too, to live with a less-than-perfect solution rather than take the time to respond to—and possibly lose—an eviction lawsuit.

 If the manager is unreasonable, try to meet and deal with the owner.

2. When You've Done Nothing Wrong

If a termination notice accuses you of something you did not do—or, at least, did not intend to do— you're in a difficult position. True, if the case goes to court, the landlord will have the job of proving your misdeeds. But short of that, during informal negotiations you must convince the landlord that you're not guilty. And of course, it's never easy— and sometimes impossible—to get some people to contemplate the possibility that they have exaggerated the situation or are just plain mistaken. Here are some approaches that may be useful in your situation:

- **The landlord has made a mistake.** The landlord thinks you were the one responsible for the mess left in the common room, or were the host of the destructive wild party. Unlike TV lawyers like Perry Mason, you may not be able to produce the culprit, but you may be able to bring evidence—for example, statements from neighbors—that will establish your blamelessness. Here you need not only evidence, but a good deal of tact. Don't rub your landlord's face in his error. Not only may this poison your future relations, it's likely to cause him to terminate your month-to-month tenancy or refuse to renew your lease when it runs out.

- **You made a good-faith error.** You violated a lease or rental agreement term, but really didn't intend to do so. For example, perhaps you made the common mistake of assuming that all tenants enjoy a legal grace period when it comes to paying rent late before a termination notice can be sent. Arriving with your entire month's rent and honestly explaining your confusion to the landlord may get results.

G. Getting Help From a Mediator

In many areas, community mediation programs—or sometimes even mediation programs limited to landlord-tenant disputes—are available to help feuding landlords and tenants. They can be a huge help when direct negotiation with your landlord fails or your landlord refuses to negotiate. To find out if such a program exists, call your city government (manager or mayor), county offices or court clerk.

Even if you are sure your landlord is an unmovable rock, mediation is worth a try. One big advantage to this approach is that you don't have to call a person whom you are mad at (and who may even refuse to talk to you). Instead, case workers at the mediation program will contact the landlord for you and set up the session. At the mediation session, a skilled person—the mediator—will attempt to help you both craft an acceptable compromise. Remarkably, most mediation programs report a better than 50% success rate working with people who believed no compromise was possible. Chapter 19 gives details on using mediation to resolve landlord-tenant disputes.

How to Mediate Your Dispute, by Peter Lovenheim (Nolo), is an excellent step-by-step guide that explains how to prepare for and succeed in a mediation session.

H. Refusing to Move Out

When the deadline in your termination notice passes, you will not be automatically evicted. In almost every state, the landlord must file and win an eviction lawsuit before the sheriff or marshal can physically evict you. It follows that if you and the landlord haven't arrived at a solution, you face two choices:

- abide by the demands of the termination notice, or
- force the landlord to start eviction proceedings.

Refusing to obey a termination notice makes sense in three situations: When the landlord's reasons for terminating your tenancy are wrong, when they are illegal or (possibly) if you need to buy time to find another place.

Depending on the state, your case will be heard in a formal trial court, a small claims court or an informal landlord-tenant court. If you're headed for formal court, you may want to hire a lawyer. Chapter 18 gives an overview of eviction lawsuits.

1. When You're In the Right

The most obvious reason to ignore a termination notice and fight an eviction lawsuit is if you're right and you're prepared to take the time and the risk of going to court to prove it. For example, suppose, despite your repeated requests over a reasonable period of time, your landlord failed to replace your broken heater, with the result that you eventually called a heater service and had it fixed yourself. After deducting the cost of the repair from the next month's rent, you received a Pay or Quit notice. If you carefully read Chapter 8 and followed your state's law allowing you to make the repair, and have documented your communications with the landlord, you will probably be in no mood to move or even compromise.

As any lawyer or citizen who has been through a lawsuit will tell you, however, being in the right is no guarantee that you will prevail in court. You must have the law and the facts on your side—and sometimes a fair amount of luck besides.

If you're headed for court, no matter what the reason, check these points:

Did the landlord comply with the notice requirements to end your tenancy? Carefully read your state's entries on the three tables in Appendix I ("State Laws on Termination for Nonpayment of Rent," "State Laws on Termination for Violation of Lease" and "State Laws on Unconditional Quit Terminations") and compare them with the notice that you have received. Here are some common landlord mistakes you'll want to check for:

- Did the landlord give you the correct notice? For example, if you received an Unconditional Quit notice when you were entitled to a Cure or Quit notice, this is a serious error. Failure to use the right notice is probably the most common landlord mistake, and often results in a judge refusing to grant an eviction. A landlord can start over with the proper notice.
- Did the landlord deliver the notice to you in the way required by your state law? For example, did the person who served the notice attempt to do so personally?

- Did the termination notice contain the legally required wording? For example, many states require the landlord to explain, in plain English, exactly what you've done (or not done) that justifies the notice. In these states, a notice is legally insufficient if it simply says that you have five days to cease violation of the lease or leave. The landlord must explain, for example, that you owe a specified amount of rent, or that the lease violation consists of your repeated use of the pool at night, which is prohibited in your lease.

Consider doing some legal research. You may want to go to your local law library or online to read the termination notice laws and the cases that have interpreted them before concluding whether the notice was properly chosen, drafted and given. See Chapter 20 for advice.

Do you have documentary evidence? Obviously, it's helpful in court to back up your claims with as much hard-copy evidence as possible. For example, if the basis of the termination is that you have violated a rental rule (by using the pool at midnight), yet no rule prohibiting night swimming appears in the lease or house rules, be sure that you have a copy of the lease and rules.

Do you have visual evidence? The chances for winning will increase if you can give a judge or jury a real picture of the situation. If you withheld rent because of a leaking roof, take a picture of the sodden wall and your bucket of water.

Do you have live testimony? A neutral witness who supports your side of the story is invaluable. For instance, if you withheld rent because the landlord refused to repair your stove, ask a repair person to examine the stove and call him to testify as to its condition. Or, if the landlord claims that you've made excessive noise, ask a neighbor to testify that, in fact, there was really no problem.

2. When the Landlord Is Retaliating

In most states, landlords are not allowed to terminate your tenancy as punishment for exercising a legal right, such as complaining to a health inspector, organizing a tenants' group or properly withholding rent or using repair and deduct. (Landlord retaliation is discussed in detail in Chapter 15.) But suppose you have spoken to a housing inspector but you are *also* late with the rent—will it do you any good to prove that the landlord's real motive is retaliation? Or, put another way, does your conduct have to be "squeaky clean" in order to get a judge to stop an eviction lawsuit based on your landlord's retaliatory conduct?

It stands to reason that you'll always be in a better position if you can present yourself as a completely blameless tenant. But even if you are less than perfect, all may not be lost. Some states address this issue in their written law; others leave it to the courts to decide. If you plan to mount a retaliatory eviction defense but you know that there is a skeleton or two hiding in your closet, be sure to read your state's retaliation statutes and look for court decisions interpreting them. (Chapter 20 gives advice on how to do basic legal research.)

3. Buying Time (at a Price)

If you do not have a good legal reason for ignoring a termination notice, you may still choose to force the landlord to proceed to an eviction lawsuit if you have no place to move. The process (other than expedited evictions) normally takes from two to six weeks, time which you may need in order to find another rental or finish a job or school year. And depending on the law and practice in your state, you may be able to obtain additional delays for hardship circumstances (see Chapter 18).

Understand that buying time often comes at a price: When an eviction lawsuit is filed against you, that fact will inevitably become part of your credit record, which can be consulted by future employers, landlords, banks and stores. This negative mark will appear even if you voluntarily move (and the case is dismissed) before the landlord gets a court order that allows him to evict you. And if your lease or rental agreement allows your landlord to recover for attorney fees, you'll be charged for these, too. Courts in some states can order you to pay these fees even in the absence of such a clause, if the judge decides that your conduct has been extreme and outrageous. These fees can total $500 to $1,000 or even more. (Chapter 2 explains attorney fees.)

I. Cutting Your Losses and Moving

Even if you believe you are in the legal right, finding another place to live may be your best option after getting a termination notice. There are many times in life when it is not worth your time and money to fight. Consider moving to a more congenial situation if:

- You can find comparable or better housing without major inconvenience.
- The landlord has always been difficult to deal with and you can expect future hassles.
- You cannot afford the time off from work, school or your personal life to get involved in a lawsuit, nor can you afford to hire a lawyer.

- You are not absolutely sure you will win and your lease or rental agreement contains an attorney "fees and costs" clause, meaning that if you lose you'll pay the landlord's costs as well as your own, or
- Your credit record is shaky, you are in the process of trying to clean it up and you are absolutely determined not to damage it further.

Moving in response to a termination notice, or even an eviction, does not mean that you forfeit your security deposit. Of course, if you have failed to pay the rent or have damaged the rental unit beyond normal wear and tear, the landlord can subtract what you owe from the deposit. (Chapter 16 discusses basic rules on returning security deposits.) The landlord can also usually take attorney fees and costs from the deposit.

What about any future rent you owe under a lease the landlord terminates early? Chances are that even if the landlord has a good reason to end your lease early, a court will not hold you liable for rent for any period after you leave. However, this may not always be true if your conduct has been highly outrageous or illegal (dealing drugs from your bedroom, for example). In this situation, a judge might charge you for future rent and subtract it from your deposit for an additional period, to give the landlord a reasonable chance to re-rent the unit. ■

Evictions: An Overview

This chapter is for those readers who, despite the fact their landlord has told them to move on, have decided to stay put. If you count yourself as one of this intrepid group, read this chapter to get an idea of what you'll face if the landlord goes ahead and files a lawsuit to evict you.

We can't tell you exactly how to fight back—laws vary too much from state to state, and every situation is unique. But we can give you a good overview of the eviction procedure that follows a termination notice (see Chapter 17) and tell you what your landlord can—and cannot—do under the law. To win an eviction lawsuit, you'll need to hire a lawyer or learn the particulars of your state's laws on your own. (Chapter 20 tells you how to get started by looking up your state's eviction statutes.)

 Consider hiring a lawyer if your lease or rental agreement has an attorney fees clause. If you will be entitled to attorney fees if you win, and you are confident that you have a strong case, you may want to hire an attorney. Some lawyers even take eviction defense cases on a contingency—that is, you owe nothing if you lose, and they collect their fees from the landlord if you win. (Chapter 20 discusses contingency fees.)

 California tenants should consult *Tenants' Rights,* by Myron Moskovitz and Ralph Warner (Nolo). It contains eviction defense information and tear-out court forms.

A. When to Fight—And When to Move

Unless you have the law and provable facts on your side, fighting a termination notice is usually short-sighted. If you lose an eviction lawsuit, you may end up hundreds (even thousands) of dollars in debt and face a negative credit rating.

So when does it make sense to fight an eviction? Here is a bare bones list of the main legal reasons (grounds) on which to contest an eviction:

- Your landlord gave you the wrong notice—for example, an unconditional notice to quit when you were entitled, under state law, to a "Pay or Quit" notice. (Fighting an eviction on this ground only buys you a bit of time.) See Chapter 17.
- Your landlord canceled the termination notice—for example, your landlord accepted rent after giving you a Pay or Quit notice—but filed for eviction anyway. See Chapter 17.
- You got a Pay or Quit notice and you offered rent within the specified time, but the landlord wouldn't accept it. See Chapter 17.
- The premises are legally uninhabitable, which excuses you from paying rent. See Chapter 8.
- You didn't pay all the rent because you properly used a repair and deduct procedure or rent withholding. See Chapter 8.
- An agreement with your landlord justified your paying less rent—for example, because you had taken on responsibility for maintenance. See Chapter 9.
- You're being evicted because you've exercised a legal right, such as complaining to a housing inspector about your unit. See Chapter 15.
- Your landlord has an illegal discriminatory motive for eviction—for example, your race, sex, age, family status or disability. See Chapter 5.

B. Illegal "Self-Help" Evictions

In years past, there was nothing to stop a landlord from changing the locks, removing the front door, cutting off the utilities or even moving the furniture onto the street if the tenant failed to pay rent, violated a lease clause or damaged the property. Fortunately, today practically every state has forbidden these "self-help" evictions. Instead, landlords must get a court order directing you to leave and, if you don't, authorizing a local sheriff or marshal to physically remove you.

Many states that have outlawed self-help evictions have put some teeth behind the ban. If you have been locked out, frozen out by having the heat cut off or denied electricity or water by the landlord, you can sue not only for your actual money losses (such as the need for temporary housing, the value of food that spoiled when the refrigerator stopped running or the cost of an electric heater when the gas was shut off), but also for penalties as well. For example, in Arizona a landlord can be ordered to pay the tenant up to two months' rent or the tenant's actual damages, whatever is higher. And in Connecticut, the landlord may even be prosecuted for a misdemeanor. In some states, you can collect and still remain in the premises; in others, you are entitled to monetary compensation only. (See "Suing the Landlord for Self-Help Evictions," below.)

If you decide to sue your landlord for an illegal eviction, research your state's statutes and consider consulting an experienced tenants' lawyer. (See Chapter 20 for advice on legal research and using an attorney as a coach.)

Watch out for the landlord who removes your property under the guise of handling "abandoned" property. A few states allow the landlord to freely dispose of a tenant's property when the tenant has permanently moved out. So when a landlord has locked up, taken or moved a tenant's property, it's not surprising to hear the landlord claim that the tenant had abandoned the property—even when it's not clear. If a tenant who in fact didn't intend to abandon sues over the property, the landlord must prove by clear and decisive evidence that the tenant intended to leave permanently and turn the place (and its contents) over to the landlord.

C. How Eviction Lawsuits Work

Here's a guide to the basic elements of an eviction lawsuit.

"Expedited evictions" are fast and do not follow the typical path. If you are being evicted for serious illegal activity, such as drug dealing or use, you may be subject to a speedy eviction procedure that will give you little, if any, time to prepare a defense. In Arizona, for example, a landlord who suspects you of engaging in serious illegal activity on the premises can immediately terminate a tenancy and get a court date within three days. (Ariz. Rev. Stat. §§ 33-1368 and 1377.)

1. What Court Hears Evictions?

Your landlord will file an eviction lawsuit in a formal trial court (called "municipal," "county" or "justice"), or in small claims court. Some states give landlords the choice; others confine eviction lawsuits to one or the other. If your landlord has a choice, the decision of which court to use will depend on:

- **Amount of unpaid rent.** If the landlord is also suing for unpaid rent which is higher than the small claims court's jurisdictional amount, the

Suing the Landlord for Self-Help Evictions

These states prohibit self-help evictions by statute. If your state is not listed, do not despair. Your state's court cases may address the issue. See Chapter 20 for tips on doing legal research.

State	Amount Tenant Can Sue For	Tenant's Court Costs & Fees Also Covered?	Can Tenant Choose to Stay?	Statute or Legal Authority
Alaska	Up to one and one-half times the actual damages.	No	Yes	Alaska Stat. § 34.03.210
Arizona	Up to two months' rent or twice the actual damages, whichever is greater.	No	Yes	Ariz. Rev. Stat. § 33-1367
Arkansas	Actual and punitive damages.			*Gorman v. Ratliffe*, 712 S.W.2d 888 (1986)
California	Actual damages plus up to $100 per day of violation ($250 minimum). Tenant may ask for an injunction prohibiting any further violation during the court action.	Yes	Yes	Cal. Civil Code § 789.3
Connecticut	Landlord may be prosecuted for a misdemeanor. Tenant may collect up to double actual damages.	Yes	Yes	Conn. Gen. Stat. Ann. §§ 47a-43, 47a-46, 53a-214
District of Columbia	Actual and punitive damages.	No	No	*Mendes v. Johnson*, 389 A.2d 781 (DC 1978)
Hawaii	Two months' rent or free occupancy for two months (tenant must have been excluded "overnight"). Court may order landlord to stop illegal conduct.	Yes	Yes	Hawaii Rev. Stat. § 521-63(c)
Iowa	Actual damages. If tenant elects to terminate, landlord must return entire security deposit.	Yes	Yes	Iowa Code § 562A.26
Kansas	Actual damages or up to one and one-half months' rent, whichever is greater.	No	Yes	Kan. Stat. Ann. § 58-2563

Suing the Landlord for Self-Help Evictions (continued)

State	Amount Tenant Can Sue For	Tenant's Court Costs & Fees Also Covered?	Can Tenant Choose to Stay?	Statute or Legal Authority
Kentucky	Up to three months' rent.	Yes	Yes	Ky. rev. Stat. Ann. § 383.655
Maine	Actual damages or $250, whichever is greater. If the tenant loses, the court may award costs and fees to the landlord if the court finds that the tenant brought a frivolous lawsuit or one intended to harass.	Yes	No	Me. Rev. Stat. Ann. tit. 14, § 6014
Massachusetts	Three months' rent or three times the actual damages.	Yes	Yes	Mass. Gen. Laws Ann. ch. 186 § 15F
Michigan	Actual damages or $200, whichever is greater.	No	Yes	Mich. Comp. Laws § 600.2918
Minnesota	$500 or three times the actual damages, whichever is greater.	Yes	Yes	Minn. Stat. § 504A.521
Montana	Up to three months' rent or three times the actual damages, whichever is greater.	Yes	Yes	Mont. Code Ann. § 70-24-411
Nebraska	Up to three months' rent	Yes	Yes	Neb. Rev. Stat. § 76-1430
Nevada	Up to $1,000 or actual damages, whichever is greater, or both.	No	Yes	Nev. Rev. Stat. Ann. § 118A.390
New Hampshire	Actual damages or $1,000, whichever is greater; if court finds that the landlord knowingly or willingly broke the law, two to three times this amount. Each day that a violation continues is a separate violation. If the court finds tenant brought a frivolous suit or one intended to harass, it may order tenant to pay landlord's costs and fees.	Yes	Yes	N.H. Rev. Stat. Ann. §§ 540-A:3, A:4, 358-A:10
New Mexico	A pro-rated share of the rent for each day of violation, actual damages and civil penalties.	Yes	Yes	N.M. Stat. Ann. § 47-8-36
North Carolina	Actual damages	No	Yes	N.C. Gen. Stat. § 42-25.9

	Suing the Landlord for Self-Help Evictions (continued)			
State	Amount Tenant Can Sue For	Tenant's Court Costs & Fees Also Covered?	Can Tenant Choose to Stay?	Statute or Legal Authority
Ohio	Actual damages	Yes	No	Oh. Rev. Code Ann. § 5321.15
Oklahoma	Up to twice the average monthly rental or twice the actual damages, whichever is greater.	No	Yes	Okla. St. tit. 41, § 123
Oregon	Up to two months' rent or twice the actual damages, whichever is greater.	No	Yes	Ore. Rev. Stat. § 90.375
Pennsylvania	Self-help evictions are not allowed.	Judge decides	Judge decides	*Wofford v. Vavreck,* 22 D. & C. 3d 444 (1981); and *Kuriger v. Cramer,* 1985.PA.1209
Rhode Island	Up to three months' rent or three times the actual damages, whichever is greater.	Yes	Yes	R.I. Gen. Laws § 34-18-34
South Carolina	Three months' rent or twice the actual damages, whichever is greater.	Yes	Yes	S.C. Code Ann. § 27-40-660
South Dakota	Two months' rent. If the tenant elects to terminate the lease, tenant is entitled to the return of the full security deposit.	No	Yes	S.D. Codified Laws Ann. § 43-32-6
Tennessee	Actual and punitive damages. If the tenant elects to terminate the lease, teneant is entitled to the return of the full security deposit.	Yes	Yes	Tenn. Code Ann. § 66-28-504
Texas	Actual damages, one month's rent or $500, whichever is greater. Tenant who files a lawsuit in bad faith is liable to the landlord for the landlord's actual damages, one month's rent or $500, whichever is greater. NOTE: If tenant has not paid the rent, landlord may follow specified steps to cut utilities or change locks.	Yes	Yes	Texas Prop. Code §§ 92.008, 92.0081, 92.009

		Tenant's Court	Can Tenant	
		Costs & Fees	Choose to	Statute or
State	**Amount Tenant Can Sue For**	**Also Covered?**	**Stay?**	**Legal Authority**
Vermont	Actual damages. Court may award costs and fees to the landlord if the court finds that the tenant brought a frivolous lawsuit or one intended to harass.	Yes	Yes	Vt. Stat. Ann. tit. 9, § 4464
Virginia	Actual damages	Yes	Yes	Va. Code Ann. §§ 55-248.26, 55-225.2
Washington	Actual damages. For utility shut-offs only, actual damages and up to $100 per day of no service. Court may award costs and fees to the prevailing party.	Yes (includes costs of arbitration)	Yes	Wash. Rev. Code Ann. §§ 59.18.290, 59.18.300

Suing the Landlord for Self-Help Evictions (continued)

landlord must use a higher court. (States' small claims court jurisdictional limits are listed in Chapter 19.)

- **Attorney fees clause.** If your lease or rental agreement contains an attorney fees clause, and your landlord has a strong case against you, she's likely to hire an attorney and go to formal court, figuring that the fee will come from your pocket when she wins. On the other hand, if she realizes that you have little or no funds, she'll understand that her chances of collection are dim and may choose small claims instead. Big landlords (who usually include attorney fees clauses in their rental contracts) are especially likely to choose the formal court, regardless of the strength of their case, since they do not have the time to go to court themselves.

Evictions in Small Claims Court

Landlords in these states may file evictions in small claims court:

Arizona (Justice Court)	New Mexico
Delaware	North Carolina
Florida	Pennsylvania
Georgia	South Carolina
Indiana	Tennessee
Iowa	Virginia
Kentucky	West Virginia
Louisiana	Wisconsin
Maine	Wyoming
Maryland	

A few states, including Illinois, New York and Massachusetts, have separate "landlord-tenant" courts in larger cities, similar to a small claims court, specifically set up to handle evictions.

There are important differences between regular trial courts and small claims (or landlord-tenant) court.

- In small claims court, the regular rules of evidence are greatly relaxed, and you can show or tell the court your side of the story without adhering to the "foundation" requirements that apply in higher courts. ("Laying a foundation" is explained in "Rules of Evidence in Formal Court," below.)

- In regular court, you and the landlord may engage in a pretrial process called "discovery," in which you ask each other about the evidence that supports your positions. Discovery includes depositions (where witnesses are questioned under oath) and interrogatories (discussed in subsection 5, below). This process is normally available in formal court, but not in small claims or landlord-tenant courts.

- In regular court, you and the landlord may each attempt to wash the case out of court quickly by filing pretrial requests to the court to dismiss or limit the case (discussed in subsections 3 and 4, below). In small claims and landlord-tenant court, the idea is to decide the entire case after one efficient court hearing, and these motions are not used.

Everybody's Guide to Small Claims Court, by Ralph Warner (Nolo), describes the workings of your state's small claims court in detail.

Represent Yourself in Court, by Paul Bergman and Sara Barrett-Berman (Nolo), explains how to present evidence and arguments in formal court.

2. First Steps: The Complaint and Summons

An eviction lawsuit begins when the landlord files a legal document called a "Complaint." The Complaint, which is usually loaded with legal jargon, lists the facts that the landlord thinks justify your eviction. It also asks the court to order you to leave, pay back rent, damages directly caused by your unlawfully remaining on the property, court costs and sometimes attorney fees.

Normally, your landlord cannot sue you for anything but back rent and damages. Because an eviction procedure is so quick, most states do not allow a landlord to add other legal beefs to an eviction Complaint. For example, if your landlord claims that you have damaged the sofa and your security deposit won't cover the cost of replacement, he must sue you in small claims court in a separate lawsuit. Similarly, if you would like to bring up an unrelated bit of landlord misbehavior, such as your landlord's repeated violations of your privacy, you will have to do so in a separate legal action.

When the landlord files a Complaint, the clerk will assign a date on which the case will be heard by the court. That date is entered on the Summons, a piece of paper that says that you've been sued and must answer the landlord's charges and appear in court within a specified number of days or lose the lawsuit. The landlord must then give you the Complaint and the Summons, which officially inform you of your right to appear before a judge. In legal jargon, this is called "service of process."

State laws are quite detailed as to the proper way to give you, or "serve," court papers. Typically, the preferred method is "personal" service, which means that a law enforcement officer or professional process server personally hands you the papers. (Don't think that you can slam the door in his face and avoid service—when the process server leaves them on the doorstep, you're served.) In some states, any adult not involved in the lawsuit can serve papers.

If, despite repeated attempts, the process server cannot locate you, most states allow something called "substituted service." This means the process server leaves a copy of the papers with a competent adult at your home, or mails the papers first-class and also leaves a copy in a place where you'll likely see it, such as posted on your front door.

Failure to properly serve the tenant is one of the most common errors landlords make. For example, the landlord may serve the papers himself, violating the typical rule that does not permit parties to a

Rules of Evidence in Formal Court

Depending on the state, evictions are heard in a formal trial court, small claims court or an informal landlord-tenant court. In small claims court, you can present any evidence you want to the judge. But if you are in a formal court, the judge will not examine documentary evidence until you have established that it is likely to be trustworthy. Presenting the legal background of evidence is called "laying a foundation." Here are a few hints on how to prepare evidence for formal court.

- **Photographs**. If your landlord's termination notice is based on your knocking a hole in the kitchen wall, you'll want to show the judge a photograph of the place where, in fact, there is a mere scuff mark. But before the picture can be admitted into evidence, someone will have to testify that the picture is a fair and accurate depiction of the way the wall looked. It's best to ask a neutral witness to come to your apartment, look at the wall and come to court prepared to testify that, yes, the photo is an accurate portrayal. Your witness need not take the photo.

- **Letters.** You may have received a termination notice because your landlord thinks that you improperly used the repair and deduct remedy by failing to notify him of the problem in the first place. In court, this means you'll need to introduce into evidence your copy of the letter you sent your landlord requesting repairs as proof that you complied with this requirement. To do this, you can simply testify that the letter is a true copy, that the signature is your own and that you mailed or handed it to your landlord.

- **Petitions.** Perhaps your defense to your termination and eviction is that the landlord is retaliating against you because you circulated a petition asking for cleaner common areas or because you protested a rent increase. To introduce the petition, you can testify that you circulated it, or even better, have someone who signed it testify that it is genuine.

- **Government documents.** If you've withheld rent because of what you claim are uninhabitable conditions (an inoperable toilet, for example), your landlord may attempt to evict you for nonpayment of rent. If you made a complaint to a local health department and they issued a report critical of your landlord, you'll want to have the report considered by the court (admitted into evidence). You'll have to have the inspector testify that he wrote the report as part of his normal duties when investigating possible health violations. To get him to court, you'll need to use an order, called a "subpoena," that you can serve on the inspector.

lawsuit to serve papers. Or, the landlord may not make enough attempts at personal service before resorting to substituted service. The most common violation of the service rules is that the process server simply lies about having personally contacted you. This happens especially in rough areas of town, where process servers are afraid to go.

If your landlord did not follow state statutes correctly, you can usually ask the judge to dismiss the lawsuit before trial. However, in some states the fact that you did, in fact, receive the papers will defeat your claim. And even if you win, your landlord may be prepared with a new Summons, which will be handed to you right in court.

⚠️ **Don't ignore a Summons.** If you have already ignored a notice telling you to move out, you may be tempted to also ignore a Summons and Complaint, too, figuring that you'll move out just before the case goes to court or the sheriff arrives to escort you out. This is usually a mistake. Far better to immediately call the landlord and negotiate a move-out date. If you owe back rent and attorney fees and costs, which amount to more than the security deposit, maybe the landlord will agree not to sue you for the excess in exchange for your speedy departure. But don't expect more than a few days at this point.

If you don't respond to the Summons and Complaint, the landlord will automatically win the eviction lawsuit. The court will grant what's called a "default judgment" against you, ordering you to pay unpaid rent and, if your lease or rental agreement has an attorney fees and costs clause, those expenses as well. The default will show up, to your obvious disadvantage, on future credit reports.

3. Knocking the Lawsuit Out of Court Before Trial

Failure to properly serve you isn't the only procedural objection you can raise to the landlord's lawsuit. Other landlord mistakes may also justify dismissal of the case before trial. To get the case dismissed, you may need to file brief documents called a "motion to dismiss" the landlord's case, or to "strike" (eliminate) a key part of it. In California, you use a response called a "demurrer." You must also serve a copy of your motion on the landlord, in the manner required by law in your state. Here are the main grounds for these challenges.

The landlord used the wrong notice. In many states, a landlord must give you a certain amount of time—often three to five days—to pay the rent or cure the lease violation before filing an eviction lawsuit. (See Chapter 17.) However, very serious misbehavior (such as damage to the property), illegal activities or repeated late rent or lease violations may allow the landlord to serve you with an unconditional quit notice, which gives you no second chance to cure the problem. If you are being evicted for behavior that triggers a "Pay or Quit" or "Cure or Quit" notice, but the landlord gave you an "Unconditional Quit" notice instead, you can challenge it in court. If you win, the landlord will be told to start over and use the right termination notice. So you'll buy yourself some time, but you'll still have to argue the merits of the case later.

The landlord filed the lawsuit too soon. If you've been given a termination notice that does give you time to pay or cure, the landlord cannot file for eviction until that time has run out. For example, if you have five days to pay the rent or move, and you don't pay, the lawsuit cannot be filed until the sixth day.

4. Your Answer to the Complaint

The next step in a typical eviction lawsuit involves your response to the landlord's claims that something you've done (or not done) justifies your eviction. At this point, you've gone beyond the technicalities of the way your landlord filed the lawsuit, and are meeting the reasons for the eviction head-on.

You must file a document called an Answer on or before the date printed on the Summons. Fortunately, your answer need not take the shape of a lengthy legal brief. In some states, you can even use a preprinted Answer form, prepared by the court, that allows you to simply check an appropriate box, depending on what you intend to argue. And even in states which still follow the old-fashioned approach of requiring documents typed-up on numbered legal paper, law libraries contain form books which you can use to copy out the required language. (Lawyers use them, too.)

In general, your Answer may contain two kinds of responses:

- **Denials.** You may dispute that what the land-lord says is true. For example, if you paid your rent to the manager, but the landlord claims it was never received, you will simply deny that the rent is unpaid. Or, if the land-lord is evicting you because you have a dog, but the animal actually belongs to the tenants in the next unit, you'll also simply check the "denials" box. Or, if there is no form, you would type something like this: "Defendant denies the allegations in Paragraph X of Plaintiff's Complaint." (The landlord is the plaintiff in the lawsuit; you're the defendant.)
- **Affirmative Defenses.** The Answer is also the place to state what the law calls "affirmative defenses"—good legal reasons that excuse what would otherwise be grounds for evic-tion. For example, if you're being evicted for not paying the rent, you could explain that you used some of the rent money to pay for repairing a serious problem your landlord had ignored, as is allowed under your state's law. Some preprinted Answer forms actually list the common defenses, which we set out for you in Section A, above. Normally, you'll need to provide a one-paragraph statement of the facts that justify your use of the affirmative defense you have selected.

EXAMPLE: Wilson, an African-American man, was sure that his termination and eviction were racially motivated. On the Answer form, he checked "Discrimination" and, below, simply wrote "Plaintiff served me with a 30-day notice because he doesn't want Black people living in his building."

Not every state, however, gives you the conve-nience of a list of preprinted affirmative defenses. But don't worry: You won't have to write your Answer entirely from scratch. You can find a fill-in-the-blanks form at your local law library. Form books are designed to cover every typical situation, so you're sure to find a "canned" form that will fit your situation. When you sign your Answer, be sure to note under your typed name that you are appear-ing "Pro per" or "Pro se," which means that you are representing yourself and have not hired a lawyer. A sample is shown below.

5. Pre-Trial Discovery

You or the landlord may wish to find out more about each other's case before you go to trial. Called "discovery," this process is not available in small claims court. It can involve:

- depositions, in which witnesses, experts or parties to the lawsuit are questioned under oath and a transcript of the session is prepared
- requests for documents, such as the landlord's repair request form or a landlord's letter to all tenants
- sets of preprinted questions, called "interroga-tories," that cover information normally in-volved in a landlord-tenant dispute. For example, the landlord might be asked to "State the names and addresses of all owners of record of the property," and
- specific statements of fact that the other side is asked, under oath, to admit or deny (called "requests for admissions"), such as a state-ment "Landlord does not maintain an on-site office at [your apartment complex]."

Information gathered during discovery can be used at trial.

Answer Raising Affirmative Defense

First Affirmative Defense

1. Defendant admits that she did not pay the amount of rent due as stated in the Complaint. She argues, however, that the entire rent was not due because she was legally entitled to pay less than the stated rent because of her valid use of the repair and deduct statute of the state of California, Civil Code § 1942.

2. Plaintiff is required by law to provide hot water of at least 110 degrees Fahrenheit, as specified by California Civil Code § 1941.1. However, the water temperature in defendant's apartment did not rise above 50 degrees as of January 4, 200X.

3. Plaintiff had actual knowledge of the inability of defendant's water heater to deliver legally sufficient hot water, since defendant wrote him two letters (dated January 5 and 10, 200X), asking that the situation be corrected, but he failed to do so.

4. The defective condition was not caused by any willful or negligent act of the defendant or any person acting under her authority.

5. As a direct and proximate result of plaintiff's failure to correct the violation of law within a reasonable time, defendant hired a plumber on January 25, 200X, to inspect and repair the water heater. The heater was fixed by installing a new valve, at a reasonable cost of $125.

6. Defendant deducted $125 from her rent check on February 1, 200X.

7. Defendant has not used this state's repair and deduct statute more than the number of times allowed by law, nor is the amount deducted more than one month's rent.

THEREFORE, DEFENDANT ASKS THAT:

1. Plaintiff take nothing by his action;

2. Costs of this action be awarded to defendant; and

3. Defendant be awarded such further relief as the Court considers proper.

Dated: __February 9, 200X__   *Sally Strong*
                          Sally Strong, in Pro Per

6. The Trial

The way your trial will look and sound will depend primarily on whether it's in a formal court or a small claims or landlord-tenant court. In formal court, you'll have to abide by your state's rules of evidence. But in an informal court, you may be able to introduce letters and secondhand testimony ("I heard her say that..."). Also, you can introduce evidence without elaborate "foundations." (See "Rules of Evidence in Formal Court," above.) See Chapter 19 for an explanation of the kinds of evidence you'll need to win.

7. The Judgment

If you win, the landlord cannot evict you, and you'll likely get a judgment for your court costs and fees. You may also be awarded money damages if the landlord acted illegally, as in the case of discrimination. If the landlord wins, you must move out. The landlord may also be awarded unpaid rent, damages, court costs and attorney fees.

If you win by asserting a habitability defense, the court may hold onto your case even after the trial is over. That's because the court doesn't want to simply return you to an unfit dwelling. In some states, a judge may order the landlord to make repairs while the rent is paid into a court account; when an inspector certifies that the dwelling is habitable, the judge will release the funds.

8. If You Lose: Stopping or Postponing an Eviction

If you lose the eviction lawsuit, you can expect your landlord to move quickly to physically remove you from the property. In rare instances, you may be able to get the trial judge to stop the eviction, but only if you can convince the court of two things:

- Eviction would cause a severe hardship for you or your family. For example, you may be able to persuade the judge that alternate housing is unavailable and your job will be in jeopardy if you are forced to move, and
- You are willing and able to pay any back rent owed (and the landlord's costs to bring the lawsuit) and future rent, as well.

It's very unusual for a judge to stop an eviction, for the simple reason that if your sympathetic predicament (and sufficient monetary reserves) weren't persuasive enough to win the case for you in the first place, it's unlikely that these arguments can prevail after the trial.

It may, however, be more realistic to ask for a postponement of the eviction. Typically, evictions are postponed in three situations:

- **Pending your appeal.** If you file an appeal, you may ask the trial judge to postpone ("stay") the eviction until the appellate court decides the case. If you've been evicted in small claims court, in a few states you may enjoy an automatic postponement during the appeal. Of course, this is one reason why smart landlords never use small claims court in these states.

- **Until your circumstances improve.** You may be able to persuade a judge to give you a little more time to find a new home.
- **Until the weather improves.** Contrary to popular belief, judges in many cold-climate states (including Alaska, Minnesota and North Dakota) are not required to postpone an eviction on frigid days. But there's nothing to stop you from asking the judge anyway. In the District of Columbia, however, a landlord may not evict on a day when the National Weather Service predicts at 8:00 a.m. that the temperature at the National Airport will fall below freezing within the next 24 hours. (D.C. Code § 45-2551(k).)

To convince a judge to order your eviction postponed, you'll need to show that it would pose an extreme hardship to you or your family, and that your continued presence will not harm the landlord. This will at least involve proving that you are capable of continuing to pay the rent.

9. Eviction

In most states, a landlord cannot move your belongings out on the street, even after winning an eviction lawsuit. (See Section B, above.) Typically, the landlord must give the judgment to a local law enforcement officer, along with a fee which you've been charged for as part of the landlord's costs. The sheriff or constable gives you a notice telling you that he'll be back, sometimes within just a few days, to physically remove you if you aren't gone. At this point, it's time to move. No one, even the most outrageously wronged tenant, wants the experience of being tossed out.

D. Stopping Eviction by Filing for Bankruptcy

If you have significant financial burdens, you may decide to declare bankruptcy. There are several kinds of bankruptcy; the most common are "Chapter 7," in which most debts are wiped out after as many creditors as possible have been paid; or "Chapter 13," in which the debts remain but are paid off over time according to a court-approved plan.

As soon as you file a bankruptcy petition—and whether or not the landlord knows about it—an automatic "stay" (court order) takes effect. It bars the landlord from terminating your tenancy or starting or continuing an eviction proceeding. This is true even if your lease or rental agreement says the landlord can immediately terminate your tenancy if you file for bankruptcy. (11 U.S. Code § 365(e).)

This means that if you have filed for either Chapter 7 or 13 bankruptcy and are behind in the rent, become unable to pay the rent or violate another term of your tenancy (such as keeping a pet in violation of a no-pets clause), your landlord can't give you a termination notice and proceed with an eviction. Even if your landlord has already gone to court and obtained an eviction order, the eviction process must stop if you file for bankruptcy. Be aware, however, that Congress has been continuously lobbied by landlords' groups to remove the automatic stay for evictions. By the time you read this, they may have succeeded.

Don't jump to the conclusion, however, that filing for bankruptcy enables you to violate your lease or not pay the rent with impunity. At most, filing for bankruptcy buys you a little time. Your landlord will simply go to the federal bankruptcy court and ask the judge to remove the automatic stay. (11 U.S. Code §§ 362(a)(1), (2) &(3).) In most cases, the landlord gets the stay lifted within a matter of days and is allowed to continue with the termination and eviction.

Don't file for bankruptcy just to postpone an eviction. Even if you voluntarily withdraw your petition yourself before the case concludes, the fact that you have filed will remain on your credit record for ten years. Future landlords can legally turn you away when they learn of it, and it will cause problems with employers and would-be creditors, too. For less drastic solutions to financial difficulties, see *Money Troubles,* by Robin Leonard (Nolo).

What Happens to Your Lease

Filing for bankruptcy affects your tenancy even if you are not behind in the rent or otherwise in violation of your lease. After you file, the "bankruptcy trustee" (a person appointed by the bankruptcy court to oversee the case) must decide whether to carry on with or terminate your lease or rental agreement. In most situations, the trustee will let you keep the lease since it wouldn't be of any benefit to your creditors to force you to incur the expense of finding a new home and moving. First, however, you must pay any unpaid back rent.

If the trustee keeps the lease, your landlord has the right to ask the bankruptcy court to demand that you show proof of your ability to pay future rent. (11 U.S. Code §§ 365(b)(1)(A), (B) & (C).) Of course, if you become unable to pay the rent after the lease is assumed, you can expect your landlord to ask the bankruptcy court to lift the stay so that he can terminate and, if necessary, evict.

■

Resolving Problems Without a Lawyer

L egal disputes between tenants and landlords come in all shapes and sizes. Here are some of the more common ones:

- **Rent.** You disagree about the validity, timing or method of a rent increase.
- **Habitability.** You've complained several times about the leaky roof that has made the living room unusable. After getting no response from your landlord, you don't pay the next month's rent. Your landlord is threatening eviction.
- **Privacy.** You don't want the landlord to show your apartment to prospective new tenants on very short notice and at inconvenient times. Your landlord thinks you're being unreasonable.
- **Security deposits.** At the end of your tenancy, you claim that you left the rental unit reasonably clean and undamaged. The landlord says it didn't pass the white glove test.
- **Lease or rental agreement violation.** Your landlord complains that you are violating your lease by having noisy parties and frequent overnight guests. You feel your private life is your business, and that your landlord is mostly mad that you have more fun than she does.

How you handle problems with your landlord can have a profound effect on your ability to enjoy your rental home. In some cases, such as when a landlord persistently refuses to attend to major repairs, enters unannounced and generally makes your life miserable on a number of fronts, your best bet may be to simply end the tenancy and move to a more congenial place.

Often, however, you can take steps that will improve matters—or at least resolve the dispute in your favor. But rarely should lawyers, lawsuits and all their attendant expenses and tensions be your first approach. Instead, try:

- negotiation
- mediation, or
- small claims court.

In many cases, you will be dealing with your landlord either alone or with your roommates. But if other tenants will share your concerns, you'll find it effective to approach your landlord as a group. We show how later in this chapter.

A. How to Negotiate a Settlement

No matter how serious the problem, you're almost always better off trying to resolve disputes directly with your landlord. This is especially true if your concerns don't warrant the use of a heavy-duty legal strategy in the first place. So put aside the possibility of suing—except possibly in small claims court (see Section C, below)—and instead direct your efforts towards negotiating a settlement.

You'll be most successful if you focus on what exactly you want the landlord to do, rather than fighting for the principle involved. Berating your landlord for insensitivity or ignorance may give you a sense of righteous vindication, but not necessarily better results.

Here are some helpful pointers for negotiating with landlords:

- **Set up an appointment to discuss the problem.** Try to arrange sufficient time, without distractions such as children, so you can both express your concerns and work out an agreement.
- **Solicit the landlord's point of view.** Once the landlord starts talking, listen closely and don't interrupt, even if some points are not true or some opinions are inflammatory.
- **State that you understand and respect the landlord's key points.** Even if you strongly disagree with your landlord's position, it's often a good idea to accurately restate his concerns. This should discourage him from endlessly repeating the same point.
- **Avoid personal attacks.** Even if true, suggesting that your landlord is a slumlord or is profiteering at the expense of tenants will only raise the level of hostility and make settlement more difficult. Equally important, it's usually best to stay calm and not to react impulsively or emotionally to your landlord's misstatements.

- **Be courteous, not weak.** If the law is on your side or you have the firm backing of most other tenants, let the landlord know that you're coming from a position of strength. Make it clear that you prefer negotiating an agreement but, if necessary, you have the resources and evidence to fight and win.
- **Emphasize problem solving.** Try to structure the negotiation as a mutual attempt to solve a problem. For instance, if you're complaining about a landlord's policy of entering tenants' apartments to make unannounced repairs, seek solutions that recognize the interests of both parties—for example, an understanding that repairs are necessary and even desirable but most can be pre-arranged.
- **Put yourself in the landlord's shoes.** How would you want to work with unhappy tenants if roles were reversed? Your answer may be something like "I'd want to feel that I've won." As it turns out, this is a great insight—the best settlements are often those in which both sides feel they've won, or at least not given up anything fundamental.
- **If you reach an understanding with your landlord, promptly write it down and sign it.** You should volunteer to prepare the first draft. If you agree to pay the landlord some money as part of the settlement, make it clear that the payment fully satisfies the landlord's claim: "Tenant's $200 payment of August 1, 199X, fully satisfies any claim Landlord has against Tenant regarding damaged patio furniture."

Getting to Yes: Negotiating Agreement Without Giving In, by Roger Fisher and William Ury (Penguin Books). This classic book offers a strategy for coming to mutually acceptable agreements in all kinds of situations, including landlord-tenant disputes.

Getting Past No: Negotiating Your Way From Confrontation to Cooperation, by William Ury (Bantam Books). This sequel to *Getting to Yes* discusses techniques for negotiating with obnoxious, stubborn and otherwise difficult people.

B. Using a Mediator

If you're unsuccessful negotiating a settlement with your landlord, or relations are so strained that no meeting seems possible, you may be ready to give up on the idea of negotiation. This would be a mistake. Instead, your best approach is often to enlist the help of a neutral third party mediator. Even if your landlord won't speak to you, a skilled and experienced mediator may get him to the table.

Many people confuse mediation with arbitration, which is seldom, if ever, used in residential landlord-tenant disputes. While both are nonjudicial ways to resolve disputes, there's a huge difference: Arbitration, like lawsuits, results in a binding decision. Mediators, by contrast, have no power to impose a decision. Their job is simply to help the parties work out a mutually acceptable solution to their dispute. Put another way, if you and your landlord don't agree on a solution, there is no solution.

Mediation can make especially good sense if:
- Your landlord doesn't realize what a poor job the resident manager or management company has been doing, and you want the opportunity to bring this up
- You are dealing with a good or at least halfway decent landlord, and you think there's hope for resolution, or
- You think the landlord is savvy enough to want to avoid a protracted court battle.

Mediation can also help resolve roommate disputes. If you and your roommate disagree about noise, overnight guests or some other issue, consider trying mediation.

Does mediation really work? Surprisingly, yes. One big reason is the cooperative spirit that emerges. By agreeing to mediate a dispute in the first place, you and the landlord implicitly agree to solve your own problems. Also, the fact that no judge or arbitrator has the power to impose what may be an unacceptable solution reduces fear and defensiveness on both sides. This, in turn, often means both landlord and tenant take less extreme—and more conciliatory—positions.

Sometimes mediation is not the best approach. For example, if your landlord has discriminated against you based on your race, sex or some other illegal reason, you should probably file a fair housing complaint or a lawsuit, as explained in Chapter 5.

1. How to Find a Mediation Group

Many cities offer free or low-cost community mediation programs that handle landlord-tenant disputes. For information, call your mayor's or city manager's office and ask for the staff member who handles landlord-tenant mediation matters or housing disputes. That person should refer you to the public office or community group that attempts to informally—and at little or no cost—resolve landlord-tenant disputes before they reach the court stage. You can also get referrals from the American Arbitration Association (you can reach the main office in New York City at 212-484-4000) or a neighborhood dispute resolution center.

 If there's a charge for the mediation service, offer to split it with your landlord. That way, you'll both feel equally vested in the outcome.

2. How Mediation Works

Mediation in landlord-tenant disputes is fairly informal. More likely than not, the mediator will have you and your landlord sit down together. Each side is usually asked to discuss all issues they consider important—even emotional ones. This process of airing the entire dispute often cools people off considerably and can lay the foundation for a fairly quick compromise.

If the dispute is not resolved easily, the mediator may suggest ways to resolve the problem, or may even keep everyone talking long enough to realize that the real problem goes deeper than the one being mediated. Typically this is helped along through a caucus process, where each side is asked to occupy a separate room, with the mediator shuttling back and forth with offers and counteroffers. When settlement appears near, everyone gets back together, and the mediator helps guide the parties to an agreement everyone approves.

For example, assume you and you landlord are mediating because you have threatened to withhold rent due to a serious defect in the premises, such as a broken heater. In a court hearing, this issue would be the only one considered. In contrast, the mediator may use the looser mediation process to discover that a major part of your grievance is that the manager has been slow to make all types of repairs, and the heat problem is simply the final straw.

You're not the only one who will have a chance to discuss other issues. You may discover that your landlord is angry at you for letting your kids run wild and ruin the garden, or is sick and tired of getting calls from the police responding to noise complaints filed by your neighbors. Once all of this is on the table, a compromise solution may fall easily into place: You may agree to provide better supervision of your kids and cut out overly loud parties in exchange for the manager getting the heat fixed and doing other repairs quickly.

And to keep future conflicts from developing, both sides might agree to meet monthly so that misunderstandings can be resolved before they grow into major battles.

How to Mediate Your Dispute, by Peter Lovenheim (Nolo). This book explains the mediation process from start to finish, including how to get the other side to the mediation table (even if they oppose the idea), prepare for mediation and draft a legally enforceable agreement.

C. Suing in Small Claims Court

If your attempts at settling a dispute with your landlord fail, you may end up in a lawsuit. Fortunately, there are many situations when you can competently and efficiently represent yourself in court. This is almost always true when your case is worth less than a few thousand dollars and you choose to use small claims court.

You can use small claims court for many legal problems:

- To force a landlord to perform needed major repairs. (See Chapter 8.)
- To pressure a landlord to do minor repairs. (See Chapter 9.)
- To deal with a landlord who repeatedly and seriously intrudes upon your privacy. (See Chapter 11.)
- To win a money judgment against a landlord who has failed to get rid of drug dealing tenants. (See Chapter 14.)
- To get your security deposit back. (See Chapter 16.)

Most people who go to small claims court handle their own cases. In fact, in some states, including California, Michigan and New York, lawyers aren't allowed to represent clients in small claims court. In any event, representing yourself is almost always the best choice—after all, the main reason to use the small claims court is because the size of the case doesn't justify the cost of hiring a lawyer.

1. Learning the Rules

Small claims court procedures are relatively simple and easy to master. Basically, you pay a small fee, file your lawsuit with the court clerk, see to it that the papers are served on your landlord (this can often be done by mail), show up on the appointed day, tell the judge your story and present any witnesses and other evidence.

Evidence that backs up your story is usually the key to winning in small claims court. For example, if you are suing your landlord to get your security deposit returned, all you need to win is a photograph of a clean and undamaged apartment and the convincing testimony of someone who helped you clean up. (Chapter 16 explains how to gather and present evidence in small claims court disputes about security deposits.)

Court rules that cover such things as where you file your lawsuit, how legal papers must be delivered to your opponent ("service of process") and how promptly you must sue, are usually available from the small claims clerk. In addition, clerks in small claims court are expected to explain procedures to you. In some states, they may even help you fill out the necessary forms, which are quite simple anyhow. If necessary, be persistent. If you ask enough questions, you'll get the answers you need to handle your own case comfortably. Also, in some states such as California, you can consult a free small claims court advisor.

2. How Much Can You Sue For?

Exactly how much can you sue for in small claims court? The maximum varies from state to state. In most, it is $3,000 to $4,000. (See "Small Claims Court Limits," below.)

Many states regularly increase the size of the cases their small claims courts can consider. In California, landlords can now sue for $5,000. In Minnesota, the small claims limit is $7,500, and in Tennessee's Court of Simplified Procedure it is $10,000. Ask your court clerk for the most current limit.

Don't assume that your case can't be brought in small claims court if it's slightly over the limit. Rather than hiring a lawyer or trying to go it alone

Small Claims Court Limits

State	Amount	State	Amount
Alabama	$3,000	Nevada	$3,500
Alaska	$7,500	New Hampshire	$2,500
Arizona	$2,500 (Small Claims Court) $5,000 (Regular Justice Court)	New Jersey	$2,000 (Small Claims Court) $10,000 (Regular Special Civil Court)
Arkansas	$5,000	New Mexico	$5,000
California	$5,000	New York	$3,000
Colorado	$5,000	North Carolina	$3,000
Connecticut	$2,500	North Dakota	$5,000
Delaware	$15,000	Ohio	$3,000
District of Columbia	$5,000	Oklahoma	$4,500
Florida	$5,000 (Small Claims Court) $15,000 (County Court)	Oregon	$3,500
Georgia	$5,000	Pennsylvania	$5,000
Hawaii	$3,500[1]	Rhode Island	$1,500
Idaho	$3,000	South Carolina	$5,000
Illinois	$5,000	South Dakota	$4,000
Indiana	$6,000[2]	Tennessee	$15,000[3]
Iowa	$4,000	Texas	$5,000
Kansas	$1,800	Utah	$5,000
Kentucky	$1,500	Vermont	$3,500
Louisiana	$2,000	Virginia	$15,000[4]
Maine	$4,500	Washington	$2,500
Maryland	$2,500	West Virginia	$5,000
Massachusetts	$2,000	Wisconsin	$5,000[5]
Michigan	$1,750	Wyoming	$4,000; County Court, $7,000
Minnesota	$7,500		
Mississippi	$2,500		
Missouri	$3,000		
Montana	$3,000		
Nebraska	$2,100		

[1] No limit in deposit cases.

[2] $6,000 in Marion and Lake Counties; $3,000 in others.

[3] $25,000 if county population over 700,000.

[4] Depends on jurisdiction. $15,000 is maximum.

[5] No limit on eviction suits.

in formal court, your most cost-effective option may be to sue for the small claims maximum and forget the rest.

 Everybody's Guide to Small Claims Court, by Ralph Warner (Nolo Press), provides detailed advice on bringing or defending a small claims court case, preparing evidence and witnesses for court and collecting your money judgment when you win. Especially if you have never been to small claims court, you'll want to closely study the material on how to present your testimony and witnesses in court. *Everybody's Guide to Small Claims Court* will also be useful in defending yourself against a landlord who sues you in small claims court—for example, claiming that you owe money for damage to the premises.

D. Tenants Working Together

When it comes to tenants confronting a recalcitrant landlord, one strategy is potentially more productive than all others: Working together with other tenants. A landlord who has the resources and determination to outwait, outspend or outmaneuver one tenant will often be much more willing to compromise when a number of tenants all threaten to act together. For example, you and other tenants could file a complaint with a government agency, sue, threaten a rent strike or move out.

Keep in mind, however, that a group of tenants will be effective only if they speak with a clear, consistent voice. For a variety of reasons, it can be hard or even impossible to form a tenants' group— for example, if tenant turnover is high or many tenants fear or dislike one another. But even if it's only a handful of tenants, you may find that there's power in numbers.

1. What Tenants' Groups Can Do

A tenant organization can be an informal group that comes together on one major issue, such as getting

the landlord to make repairs or fighting a rent increase. Or a group can be more formally organized with regular meetings and address a wide variety of issues, such as getting the landlord to stop arbitrary mistreatment of tenants or making the building safer.

The tenant organization may use negotiation or mediation to convince the landlord to work more cooperatively with tenants. If push comes to shove, however, the tenants' group may even sue the landlord in small claims court. Faced with a multi-tenant lawsuit, many landlords suddenly become more willing to sign a formal agreement giving the tenants all or some of what they request. A cohesive tenant organization should be able to convince the landlord to deal with it on a continuing basis.

Tenants' organizations can also help work out problems among tenants. As any tenant in a multi-unit building knows, a neighbor with a loud stereo (or child, dog or spouse) can cause more day-to-day misery than the most obnoxious landlord. To deal with ongoing problems, an effective tenants' group can set up a voluntary mediation procedure to help members settle problems before they fester. And when it comes to drugs, prostitution and gang activity, a tenants' organization can be very effective in pressuring the landlord to evict the troublemaker.

Beware of retaliation against tenant groups. Laws in most states protect tenants from landlord retaliation when the tenant exercises a legal right such as withholding rent when conditions justify it. Unfortunately, some states don't extend this legal protection to activist tenants, which means that a hostile landlord may try to get rid of those who organize or participate in tenant groups. Of course, the stronger and more unified the group, the harder this will be to do. See "State Laws Prohibiting Landlord Retaliation" in Appendix I, and the discussion of retaliation in Chapter 15. Proceed at your own risk if tenants' organizing activities are not protected by your state's anti-retaliation laws.

2. Getting Tenants Together

Two or three concerned tenants can start an effective tenants' group. Start by holding a meeting so people can get to know each other and speak about problems they have had with the building or the landlord.

You'll need a small group to get things started. If there are members of different races or ethnic groups on the property, get someone from each group to participate in your core organizing group. If you live in a large apartment complex or more than one building is involved, make sure you have the active involvement of someone from each building.

To get other tenants interested, identify one or more problems most tenants face. A big rent increase, fear of crime, safety of children and parking problems are common. Focus on problems that should concern most tenants, not just your personal beef with your landlord.

Set a convenient meeting time and place to discuss these issues and contact tenants individually to ask them to come. If you and the other organizers can afford the time, do this in person, door-to-door. Post or distribute notices only as a last resort or as a supplement to personal contact. Don't be too confrontational. You don't want to present yourselves to moderate tenants as a bunch of hotheads and, of course, you don't want to alienate the landlord, whom you hope to persuade to work with your group.

The first meeting should begin informally. People should be given a chance to get to know each other and see that they really do have common problems that can be tackled by a group.

Try to anticipate and deal with tenants' fears about participating in the group. Some people may worry about being evicted if they ask for better treatment, while others may be concerned that the tenants' group is controlled by unreasonable or self-centered people. Even if not expressed, these fears are likely to be present. If they are not brought into the light and dealt with, they may cause tenants to drop out later, when the action starts.

At the close of your first meeting, assuming you have clearly identified one or more key problems that badly need to be addressed, you'll want to assign a little legal homework. For example, if your landlord has refused to repair the front door lock, someone needs to see if state or local laws require specified security equipment. Fortunately, the research you need to do shouldn't be difficult. If this book doesn't answer your questions, Chapter 20 goes into considerable detail about how you can learn more.

Bring a copy of laws that back up your position. Wavering tenants are often convinced to support a tenants' group when they see that the law is on their side. If you have a copy of your state's anti-retaliation statute or repair and deduct statute, for example, it will reassure other tenants.

3. How to Structure Your Group

At some point, your group will need to decide how to structure itself. Do you want a formal organization, with officers, committees, chairpersons and regular meetings? Or are you content with a looser, as-needed organization that requires less work and commitment? If you are lucky enough to have a relatively small, committed group of long-term tenants, you may be able to create a cohesive, structured organization. But in most places, the tenant population is ever-changing, and tenants are not particularly connected to each other. Most tenant organizations look less like a labor union and more like a group of neighbors responding to a particular problem.

Contact groups that are concerned with tenants' rights. Some communities have city-wide tenant associations. They can furnish technical and legal advice as well as publicity and moral support.

If you live in a city covered by rent control, be sure to study the ordinance and its regulations. You may be able to bring your group's grievance before the rent board, and you may be required to do so before going to court.

4. Petitioning the Landlord and Taking Action

Especially if you face a serious problem, your group's second meeting should be devoted to developing a strategy to deal with the landlord. First, report on what you've found out about the legal options available to you. For example, if you all are fed up with the building's lack of hot water and have determined that its temperature often falls below the minimum mandated by your state's building codes, you will probably have learned that it's legal to withhold rent until the situation is corrected. (See

Chapter 8.) But you should have also learned that you cannot legally do this until you have notified the landlord in writing and given her a reasonable amount of time in which to attend to the problem. (This is a good idea, regardless of whether it's legally required or not.)

Draw up a list of your complaints and concerns, present them to the landlord and ask for a meeting. Your letter or petition should:

- be worded politely but firmly
- clearly set out your requests, and
- ask for a response within a specific time (such as seven days).

Unless the situation is extremely serious (for example, drug dealers are shooting at each other in the parking lot, or the building's sewage systems are backing up daily), your first letter should not threaten specific repercussions if the landlord is not cooperative. Better to have your letter carry the clear implication that your group takes its requests seriously and that it will act in some as-yet unspecified way if a favorable response is not forthcoming. To reinforce this point, it is usually best if all the tenants in the group sign the petition. See the sample Petition to the Landlord, below.

5. Meet With the Landlord

Follow our suggestions for negotiating, in Section A, above. But be careful not to overwhelm the landlord with sheer numbers. Consider nominating one or two people to speak on behalf of the group.

If that doesn't work, follow through with mediation and then, as a final resort, sue in small claims court or take other appropriate court action.

Petition to the Landlord

Harbor View Apartments
3700 Marina Way
Shady Bay, OR

September 1, 200X

PETITION TO RENEE ECKER, LANDLORD

We are all tenants at Harbor View Apartments. We direct your attention to the following problems, and ask that prompt action be taken to correct them.

1. Closed laundry facility. Because advertisements for Harbor View state that there are two on-site laundry facilities, and the apartment tour includes a visit to one of the two laundry rooms, we are entitled to the use of both rooms. Since June 15, 200X, the laundry room in the West building has been closed, forcing all tenants to use the one remaining room. There are not enough washing machines in that room to reasonably accommodate the needs of the tenants.

2. Inadequate security. We request that the security of Harbor View be improved. At present, there are no deadbolt locks on residents' doors, no peepholes in front doors and no lighting (other than a softly-lit decorative sign) in the front of the building. This situation is intolerable given the fact that there have recently been three burglaries at a neighboring apartment building, Sea Breeze. In addition, Officer Friday, who covers this beat on a regular basis, has informed us that there has been an increase in the number of robberies, car thefts and incidents of vandalism in this neighborhood.

We ask that you immediately install deadbolt locks, peepholes and better lighting. We also ask that you consult a security specialist to develop an overall plan for improved building security.

3. Dirty common areas. We request that the cleanliness and maintenance of our building be improved. As the landlord, you have the responsibility under state law to keep these common areas neat and clean by maintaining them on a regular basis. The lobby, hallways and stairways are not being cleaned on a regular basis. Specifically, the lobby has large dustballs, piles of discarded junk mail and unwashed windows. The stairways and halls are not regularly swept and washed, and the exterior breezeways have not been thoroughly cleaned since last spring.

We would like to meet with you to discuss these issues. Please contact Andy Ableson, in Apartment 3C, within the next five days to arrange for a mutually convenient time and place. A weekday evening in the Clubhouse common room might work best. We look forward to talking with you and working out a solution to these concerns.

Signed,

[As many tenants as possible] _____

_____

_____

Lawyers and Legal Research

Throughout this book, we point out instances when an attorney's advice or services may be useful—usually, disputes that involve lots of money or are very complicated. For example, if you become involved in a lawsuit over housing discrimination, withhold rent because your rental unit is uninhabitable or claim that your landlord's wrongful acts resulted in your being seriously injured, you'll likely benefit from a lawyer's help. This chapter explains how to work with a lawyer efficiently, to get the most for your money.

But, if you attempt to buy much legal information at the rates lawyers charge—$150 to $250 an hour—you'll quickly go broke. Fortunately, you don't need a lawyer to acquire a good working knowledge of the basic legal principles that apply to problems with landlords. You've probably learned a lot already by reading this book. When more questions come up, turn to this chapter for advice on how to research the law for yourself.

A. How a Lawyer Can Help You

Here are some important ways lawyers can help tenants:

Make a quick phone call or write a letter to the landlord. For example, say your landlord persists in entering your apartment to perform non-emergency repairs upon 20 minutes' notice and ignores your complaints about these intrusions. In this case, a letter from your lawyer explaining your state's interpretation of "reasonable notice" requirements should do the trick, especially if it outlines repercussions of your landlord's continued violation of the law.

Help you with research. A lawyer can point you to the statutes, regulations and possibly court cases that apply in a given situation, if you can't find them yourself.

Help with a complicated case. If you're being sued for eviction, a lawyer can help prepare your defense. Or, you may want a lawyer to confirm that you have a good claim, especially in cases involving significant amounts of money.

Handle big lawsuits for a contingency fee. If you have a legal problem that may involve a big recovery, such as a personal injury lawsuit or discrimination charge, the lawyer may be willing to accept a contingency fee, which means the lawyer gets paid only if you win.

Represent you in disputes over terms of your lease or rental agreement. If the lease or agreement has an "attorney fees" clause and your position appears to be a solid winner, the landlord will end up paying for the lawyer if you win. Obviously, this provision makes your case more attractive to a lawyer.

Review a long-term lease before you sign it. Most people don't need to involve a lawyer when they sign a lease. But if you plan to lease a place for several years, and especially if you're adding custom provisions such as an option to purchase, the advice of a knowledgeable lawyer will probably be worth the expense.

B. Finding a Good Lawyer

Most lawyers in general practice have limited experience in landlord-tenant legal issues. (In fact, by now you may know more than many of them.) So if you just pick a name out of the telephone book, or go with the attorney who prepared your will, you're unlikely to get someone who's qualified to deal with your problem. And the lawyers who are thoroughly familiar with landlord-tenant law often represent property owners; they may be unwilling to take a tenant's case—or charge so much that you can't afford them anyway.

But the good news is that in every metropolitan area, there are competent tenants' lawyers who charge fairly for their services. Not only do these attorneys already know the law (you don't pay while they look it up), they understand how the landlord-tenant business works and can often suggest effective strategies that general practitioners don't even know about.

1. Compile a List of Prospects

The best way to find a suitable attorney is through one or more of these sources:

A trustworthy person or organization with experience in the landlord-tenant field. A local tenants' organization is often a good place to get a referral.

Organizations that focus on a particular area of the law or special interest groups. Fair housing groups can give referrals for discrimination cases. Women's organizations may recommend attorneys who handle sexual harassment cases.

An experienced local lawyer. Ask for a referral to someone who regularly represents tenants. For example, if you or a friend have been pleased with the services of a local family law practitioner, chances are that this attorney will steer you to an equally good tenants' lawyer.

Local legal aid (legal services) office. Legal aid usually has lawyers experienced in representing tenants. If you have a limited income, you may be eligible for their services. Even if you are not eligible, ask for a reference—the legal aid office may know local lawyers who are experienced, honest and skillful.

Where there's rent control, there are lawyers. Since many rent control ordinances are complicated or poorly written, attorneys are almost always on the scene. Ask the rent control board, or visit a meeting or hearing and see who shows up on behalf of the tenants.

Attorneys who write articles about landlord-tenant law in trade magazines and newspapers. Even if these lawyers live in other parts of the country, it can make sense to track them down. Experts in this increasingly complex field share information at national conferences or online, and may be able to provide top-notch referrals in your area.

Your state's continuing legal education program —usually run by a bar association, a law school or both. These programs offer seminars and publications for attorneys and can often identify lawyers with expertise in landlord-tenant law.

How Not to Find a Lawyer

The worst sources for lawyers are:

- **Heavily advertised legal clinics.** While they may offer low flat rates for routine services such as drafting a will, most make their money on personal injury cases. Few legal clinics offer good, affordable representation to tenants. This is because resolving tenant cases requires solutions that cannot be mass-produced.

- **Referral panels set up by local bar associations.** While bar association panels usually do minimal screening before qualifying lawyers as experts in landlord-tenant law, the emphasis is on the word "minimal." While you might get a good referral from these panels, usually these lists are full of inexperienced practitioners and those who have not been able to attract enough clients on their own. Experienced lawyers with plenty of business rarely put their names on these panels.

- **Private referral services.** When it comes to services that advertise on TV and billboards, forget it. These groups typically make little effort to evaluate a lawyer's skill and experience. They simply supply names of lawyers who have paid to list with the service or have agreed to give the referral service a kickback based on the fees the lawyer collects.

Don't forget your renters' insurance. If you followed our advice in Chapter 2 and purchased renters' insurance, you have bought legal representation if you are sued by your landlord, a guest or other tenant for specified acts. (Your policy does not entitle you to a lawyer in an eviction or if you are the one who intends to file a lawsuit.) Contact your insurance company immediately if you are served with legal papers (usually called a Complaint and Summons).

Help From Non-Lawyers

In large metropolitan areas, look to tenants' organizations and legal typing services (often called independent paralegals) for help if you're sued for eviction. Some tenants' groups provide free one-on-one eviction defense help, and others offer classes or seminars on particular issues, such as eviction defense or rent withholding.

Legal typing services, on the other hand, are private businesses that help consumers do their own legal paperwork, for fees that are usually much lower than lawyers. They normally specialize in typing your eviction papers (such as your Answer to the landlord's Complaint) so they'll be accepted by the court, arranging for filing and then serving court papers on the landlord. Fees for this work should not exceed a few hundred dollars.

Typing services can't give legal advice about your specific case and can't represent you in court at the eviction trial. You must decide what steps to take in your case, and provide the information to complete the needed forms.

To find a non-lawyer typing service, look in the telephone book under "Eviction Services" or "Paralegals." Ask how many years they have been in business, and also ask for and check references.

2. Shop Around

After several reliable organizations or individuals give you the names of prospective lawyers, your job has just begun. First, take a look at your list of names. If several people recommend the same attorney, start with that one.

The best way to evaluate a prospective lawyer is to arrange a brief meeting to evaluate your case. If your case has the potential for a significant monetary award (as do discrimination or personal injury cases), many lawyers will be glad to speak to you for a half hour or so at no charge, or at a reduced rate.

When you meet, briefly explain your legal problem and how much work you plan to do yourself. Try to get a feeling for the lawyer's experience and accessibility:

Does the lawyer frankly answer your questions about fees, experience in landlord-tenant matters and your specific legal issue? Stay away from lawyers who make you feel uncomfortable asking questions. And be sure you understand how the lawyer charges for services. (Section C discusses various fee arrangements.)

Will the lawyer provide the kind of legal help you want? If you plan to be actively involved in dealing with your legal problem, look for a lawyer who doesn't resent your participation. If it will make the lawyer uncomfortable, you have the wrong lawyer.

Does the lawyer clearly lay out all your options? A good lawyer should almost always discuss the possibility of trying to resolve your dispute through negotiation or mediation instead of immediately going to court.

Will the lawyer be accessible ? This is a huge issue—probably the most common complaint against lawyers is that they don't return phone calls or faxes and are not available to their clients in times of need. If every time you have a question there's a delay of several days before you can talk to your lawyer, you'll lose precious time, not to mention sleep. So be sure to discuss with any lawyer how fast you can expect to have phone calls returned and how you can contact the lawyer in an emergency.

Is the lawyer experienced in your particular legal problem? If your property is in a rent-controlled city, be sure the lawyer knows its particular rent control laws and practices.

Does the lawyer represent landlords, too? Chances are that a lawyer who represents both landlords and tenants has the knowledge to do a good job for you. On the other hand, you'll want to steer clear of lawyers who represent landlords almost exclusively, since their sympathies and world view are likely to be different from yours.

Lawyer Ratings

One source for background information about lawyers is a book called the *Martindale-Hubbell Law Directory,* available at most law libraries and some public libraries. It contains biographical sketches of most practicing lawyers and information about their experience, specialties, education and the professional organizations to which they belong. Be aware, however, that lawyers purchase the space for the biographical sketches, so don't be overly impressed by long ones.

Of more significance is the fact that almost every lawyer listed is rated AV, BV or CV. These ratings come from confidential opinions that Martindale-Hubbell solicits from lawyers and judges.

The first letter is for Legal Ability, which is rated as follows:

    A—Very High to Preeminent

    B—High to Very High

    C—Fair to High

The V part of the rating stands for Very High General Recommendation—meaning that the rated lawyer adheres to professional standards of conduct and ethics. In truth, it's practically meaningless, because lawyers who don't qualify for it aren't rated at all. Also realize that some excellent new lawyers may not yet be rated, since they are too new to the legal community to be known among the local lawyers and judges. So don't make the rating system your sole criterion for deciding on a potential lawyer. On the other hand, it is reasonable to expect that a lawyer who gets high marks from other clients and an "AV" rating from *Martindale-Hubbell* will have experience and expertise.

Talk with other tenant clients. It's a good idea to ask for references from some of the lawyer's other tenant clients, particularly those with similar legal problems. Find out how satisfied other tenants were with the lawyer's work.

C. Fee Arrangements With Lawyers

How you pay your lawyer depends on the type of legal service you need and the amount of legal work involved. Once you choose a lawyer, ask for a written fee agreement explaining how fees and costs will be billed and paid. In some states, a written agreement is required by law; even if it isn't, it's always a good idea. Be sure to include an overall cap on what you can be billed absent your specific agreement.

If your case involves a significant amount of attorney time, and your lawyer will be delegating some of the work to a less experienced associate, paralegal or secretary, the delegated work should be billed at a lower hourly rate. Be sure this information is recorded in your written fee agreement.

1. Lawyers' Billing Practices

There are four basic ways that lawyers charge for their services.

Hourly fees. In most parts of the United States, you can get competent representation for $125 to

$225 an hour. Most lawyers bill in ten- or 15-minute increments. If you're doing much of the legal legwork yourself, and just want specific questions answered, you'll probably be billed this way. Comparison shopping among lawyers can help you avoid overpaying, but only if you are comparing lawyers with similar expertise. A highly experienced tenants' attorney may be cheaper in the long run than a general practitioner, even at a higher hourly rate. The fact that the tenants' attorney is further along the learning curve means it should take less time to come up with good answers and advice.

Flat fees. Sometimes a lawyer will quote you a flat fee for a specific job—for example, to defend you in an eviction lawsuit. In a flat fee agreement, you pay the same amount regardless of how much time the lawyer spends on the particular job. If a lawyer is highly recommended by others as trust-worthy, and the flat fee is moderate, this can be a great arrangement for you.

Contingency fees. This is a percentage—commonly, one-third—of the amount the lawyer obtains for you in a negotiated settlement or through a trial. If the lawyer recovers nothing for you, you pay only for the costs of filing suit and other expenses (for example, expert fees and depositions). Contingency fees are common in personal injury and discrimination cases, but relatively unusual for eviction defense. (For more details on contingency fees, see Chapter 5.)

The landlord pays. If your lease or written rental agreement has a two-way ("loser pays") attorney fees provision (discussed in Chapter 2), you are entitled to recover your attorney fees if you win a lawsuit that concerns the meaning or implementation of that agreement. The clause does not cover fees if the dispute arose independently of the lease or rental contract, such as a discrimination claim, personal injury lawsuit or sexual harassment case. If you have a strong case that's backed up with a loser-pays clause, many lawyers will take your case for little or nothing, in the expectation that they will get paid by the losing landlord.

How Legal Costs Can Mount Up

In addition to the fees they charge for their time, lawyers bill for a variety of items as well—and if you're not wary, these costs can add up quickly. Costs can include charges for:

- photocopying
- faxes
- overnight mail
- messenger service
- expert witness fees
- court filing fees
- long distance phone calls
- process servers
- work by investigators
- work by legal assistants or paralegals
- deposition transcripts
- online legal research, and
- travel.

Many sensible lawyers absorb the cost of photocopying, faxes, local phone calls and the like as normal office overhead—part of the cost of doing business—but that's not always the case. So in working out the fee arrangements, ask for a list of costs you'll be expected to pay. If a lawyer seems intent on nickel-and-diming you to death, look elsewhere. For example, if you learn the law office charges $3 or more for each page it faxes, red flags should go up. On the other hand, it is reasonable for a lawyer to pass along expenses like court costs, process server fees and work by investigators.

---

2. Saving on Legal Fees

Here are some key ways to hold down the cost of legal services:

Do your own research. Read any consumer-oriented legal materials in your state or city, such as informational booklets prepared by your state's attorney general's office or consumer protection agency. (See the chart in Appendix I, which lists the information available from many states.) Also, see

the suggestions in Section E, below, as to how you can easily find relevant statutes, ordinances and court decisions that affect your problem.

Be organized. Especially when you are paying by the hour, it's important to gather important documents, write a short chronology of events and concisely explain a problem to your lawyer. Since papers can get lost in a lawyer's office, keep a copy of everything that's important, such as your lease or rental agreement, move-in letter from your landlord, correspondence with the landlord, repair requests and other records.

Be prepared before you meet your lawyer. Whenever possible, put your questions in writing and mail, fax or deliver them to your lawyer before all meetings or phone conversations. That way your lawyer can be prepared to answer your questions and won't have to schedule another conference or phone conversation. Early preparation also helps focus the meeting so there is less chance of digressing (at your expense) into unrelated topics.

Carefully review lawyer bills. Like everyone else, lawyers make mistakes. For example, a ".1" of an hour (six minutes) may be transposed into a "1." (one hour) when the data are entered into the billing system. That's $200 instead of $20 if your lawyer charges $200 per hour. Don't hesitate to politely question your bill. You have the right to a clear explanation of costs.

D. Resolving Problems With Your Lawyer

If you see a problem emerging with your lawyer, don't just sit back and fume; call or write your lawyer. Whatever it is that rankles—a shockingly high bill or a missed deadline—have an honest discussion about your feelings.

If you can't frankly discuss these sometimes sensitive matters with your lawyer, fire that lawyer and hire another one. If you don't, you'll surely waste money on unnecessary legal fees and risk having matters turn out badly.

If you decide to change lawyers, be sure to fire your old lawyer before you hire a new one. If you don't, you could find yourself being billed by two lawyers at the same time. Also, be sure to get all important legal documents back from the first lawyer. Tell your new lawyer what your old one has done to date and pass on the file.

Here are some tips on resolving specific problems:

- If you have a dispute over fees, the local bar association may be able to mediate it for you, although the extent to which they are willing to go after one of their own varies greatly.
- If a lawyer has violated legal ethics—for example, had a conflict of interest, overbilled you or didn't represent you zealously—the state agency that licenses lawyers may discipline or even disbar the lawyer. Although lawyer oversight groups are typically biased in favor of the legal profession, they will often take action if your lawyer has done something seriously wrong.
- Where a major mistake has been made—for example, a lawyer missed the deadline for filing your papers in response to an eviction lawsuit—you can sue for malpractice. Many lawyers carry malpractice insurance, and your dispute may be settled out of court.

Mad at Your Lawyer, by Tanya Starnes (Nolo), shows you in detail how to successfully handle almost every imaginable problem with your lawyer.

Your Rights as a Client

As a client, you have the right to expect the following:

- courteous treatment by your lawyer and staff members
- an itemized statement of services rendered and a full advance explanation of billing practices
- charges for agreed-upon fees and no more
- prompt responses to phone calls and letters
- confidential legal conferences, free from unwarranted interruptions
- up-to-date information on the status of your case
- diligent and competent legal representation, and
- clear answers to all questions.

E. Doing Your Own Legal Research

Using this book is a good way to educate yourself about the laws that affect your rights as a tenant. But given the fact that the laws and court decisions of 50 states, plus the ordinances of many thousands of municipalities, are involved, no one book can do the whole job. If you face a serious problem with your landlord, sooner or later you'll probably need more information. For example, if you were assaulted in the hall of your apartment building, you'll almost surely want to look up your state court decisions involving similar incidents.

Fortunately, lawyers aren't the only source of legal help. There's a lot you can do on your own. Law libraries and even some larger public libraries are full of valuable information, such as state statutes that regulate the landlord-tenant relationship. Look for a law library that's open to the public—often, there will be one in your main county courthouse or at your state capitol. Publicly funded law schools generally permit the public to use their libraries,

and even some private law schools grant access to the public, sometimes for a modest fee.

If there is no law library nearby, don't overlook the reference department of the public library. Especially in metropolitan areas, many large public libraries have fairly decent legal research collections. Also, if you work with a lawyer, ask about using the research materials in the lawyer's office

 Legal Research: How to Find and Understand the Law, by Stephen Elias and Susan Levinkind (Nolo). This book gives easy-to-use, step-by-step instructions on how to find legal information.

Legal Research Made Easy: A Roadmap Through the Law Library Maze, by Robert C. Berring, (Nolo), is a videotape presentation on the subject.

1. Statutes and Ordinances

Every tenant and every landlord is governed by a mix of state, local and federal law, with state law almost always being the most important. In some areas, such as discrimination, federal, state and local laws overlap. When this happens, the laws that give tenants the most protection usually prevail.

If you're starting out to find the answer to a legal question, it's usually best to start by looking for a state, federal or local law that covers your issue.

a. State Statutes

State law regulates, among other things, rent rules, deposits, your right to privacy, housing standards, maintenance responsibilities and eviction procedures. Your state consumer protection agency or attorney general may provide helpful publications, or phone advice, summarizing and explaining these laws. (Appendix I includes a list of state consumer protection agencies and helpful publications.) Unfortunately, not every agency does a good job of publishing practical legal information for tenants.

If you need more information, begin with the legal references (citations) to your state's key landlord-tenant laws contained in this book. Next, get a copy of your state's laws (statutes), which are collected in well-indexed volumes (often called "codes"), available in many public libraries and all law libraries. More and more states are also making their statutes available online (see subsection 3, below). In some states, statutes are organized by subject matter, with each title or chapter or code covering a particular legal area—for example, the vehicle code or the corporations code. In most states, statutes are simply numbered sequentially, without regard to subject matter, meaning you'll usually need to spend considerable time using the index to find what you need.

EXAMPLE: Susan, a Florida tenant, wanted to look up the state statute that controlled the amount of notice she had to give her landlord when terminating a month-to-month tenancy. From a table in Appendix I of this book, she learned that the statute's citation was "Florida Statutes Annotated § 83.57." The law librarian directed her to the bookshelves containing the Florida codes, and she chose the volume that included Section 83. Within that book, she found § 83.57.

Annotated codes contain not only all the text of the laws (as do the regular codes), but also an extremely valuable summary of all or some of the court decisions interpreting each law (discussed in

subsection 2, below). In addition, annotated codes list articles and books that further discuss and explain the particular law. Annotated codes have comprehensive indexes by topic, and are kept up-to-date with paperback supplements ("pocket parts") stuck inside the back cover of each volume.

⚠️ **Never rely on old law.** Many laws change every year. Make sure you are up to date by referring to the insert you'll almost always find inside the back cover of code books. (If there isn't an insert, it's because the hardbound book was published that year and is completely current.) These pocket parts, which are organized by code number, should contain all law changes through the end of your state's last legislative session.

b. Local Ordinances

Local ordinances, such as rent control rules, health and safety standards and requirements that your landlord pay interest on your security deposit, are also important. Contact your city manager's or mayor's office or a local tenants' organization for information on local ordinances that affect tenants. If you are protected by rent control, be sure to get a copy of the ordinance, as well as all rules issued by the rent board covering rent increases and hearings.

c. Federal Statutes and Regulations

Congress has enacted laws, and federal agencies such as the U.S. Department of Housing and Urban Development (HUD) have adopted regulations, that cover important aspects of landlord-tenant law. Examples include antidiscrimination laws, wage and hour rules that affect the employment of tenant-managers and statutes requiring the disclosure of environmental health hazards.

Federal laws affecting tenants are contained in a multi-volume series of books called the U.S. Code. It consists of 50 separate numbered titles. Each title covers a specific subject matter. For example, the

federal Fair Housing Acts are contained in title 42 and begin with section 3601.

Federal regulations which explain the law in detail are usually published in the Code of Federal Regulations (C.F.R.), organized by subject into 50 separate titles. For example, regulations issued by the Environmental Protection Agency interpreting the federal lead paint legislation ("Title Ten") can be found in Title 24, Part 35, and Title 40, Part 745.

2. Court Decisions

Sometimes the answer to a legal question cannot be found in a statute. This happens when:

- court cases and opinions have greatly expanded or explained the statute, taking it beyond its obvious or literal meaning, or
- the law that applies to your question has been made by judges, not legislators.

a. Court Decisions That Explain Statutes

Statutes and ordinances rarely explain themselves. For example, a state law may guarantee you the right to housing that is weatherproofed, but that statute alone may not tell you whether that means your landlord must provide storm windows. However, other tenants may have asked the same question and ended up in court. If a judge interpreted the statute and wrote an opinion on the matter, that written opinion, once published, will become the law as much as the statute itself. If a higher court (an appellate court) has also examined the question, then its opinion becomes the law statewide.

To find out if there are written court decisions that interpret a particular statute or ordinance, a good place to start is an annotated code (discussed in subsection 1, above). If a case that seems to answer your question or relate to your problem is listed in the code, your first step is to find and read it. (See subsection c, below.)

Next, if you find a court decision that's useful to your case, make sure the decision is still good law—that a more recent opinion from a higher court has not reached a different conclusion. To do this, use a set of books known as *Shepard's*. Explaining how to do this takes more space than is available here, but a friendly law librarian can guide you. *Legal Research: How to Find and Understand the Law*, by Stephen Elias and Susan Levinkind (Nolo Press), has a good, easy-to-follow explanation of how to use the Shepard's system to expand and update your research.

b. Court Decisions That Make Law

Some laws that govern your rights will not have a starting point in a statute or ordinance. These laws, which are entirely court-made, are known as common law. An example of common law in many states is the landlord's responsibility to provide tenants with habitable housing, discussed in Chapter 8.

Researching common law is more difficult than researching statutory law, because you do not have the launching pad of a statute or ordinance. But with a little perseverance, you can find your way to the court cases that have developed and explained the legal concept you wish to understand.

A good beginning is to ask the librarian for any lawyer's practice guides in the field of landlord-tenant law. These outlines of the law, which are written to provide basic information to lawyers, are usually up-to-date. Because lawyers' practice guides are so popular, they are usually kept behind the reference counter and cannot be taken out of the library.

c. How to Read a Case Citation

If you find a citation to a case that looks important, you may want to read the opinion. You'll need the title of the case and its citation, which is like an address for the set of books, volume and page where the case can be found. Ask the law librarian for help.

Although it may look about as decipherable as hieroglyphics, once understood, a case citation gives lots of useful information in a small space. It tells you the names of the people or companies involved, the volume of the reporter (series of books) in which the case is published, the page number on which it begins and the year in which the case was decided.

> EXAMPLE: *Smith v. Jones Int'l*, 123 N.Y.S.2d 456 (1994). Smith and Jones are the names of the parties having the legal dispute. The case is reported in volume 123 of the New York Supplement, Second Series, beginning on page 456; the court issued the decision in 1994.

Most states publish their own official state reports. All published state court decisions are also included in seven regional reporters. There are also special reports for U.S. Supreme Court and other federal court decisions. (See "Common Abbreviations in Case Citations," below.)

Law Review Articles

Law schools and other state and local bar associations publish periodicals that may contain timely articles on legal issues that affect tenants. But academic journals rarely contain useful, practical information. Local bar association journals and other publications aimed at practicing lawyers are likely to be much more helpful.

Common Abbreviations in Case Citations

Abbreviation	Title	Courts Covered
A. and A.2d	Atlantic Reporter (first and second series)	Connecticut, Delaware, the District of Columbia, Maine, Maryland, New Hampshire, New Jersey, Pennsylvania, Rhode Island and Vermont
N.E. and N.E.2d	Northeastern Reporter (first and second series)	New York (except for appellate court decisions), Illinois, Indiana, Massachusetts and Ohio
N.Y.S.	New York Supplement (first and second series)	New York appellate court
N.W. and N.W.2d	Northwestern Reporter (first and second series)	Iowa, Michigan, Minnesota, Nebraska, North Dakota, South Dakota and Wisconsin
P. and P.2d	Pacific Reporter (first and second series)	Alaska, Arizona, California (except for appellate court decisions), Colorado, Hawaii, Idaho, Kansas, Montana, Nevada, New Mexico, Oklahoma, Oregon, Utah, Washington and Wyoming
Cal. Rptr.	California Reporter (first and second series)	California appellate court
S.E. and S.E.2d	Southeastern Reporter (first and second series)	Georgia, North Carolina, South Carolina, Virginia and West Virginia
So. and So.2d	Southern Reporter (first and second series)	Alabama, Florida, Louisiana and Mississippi
S.W. and S.W.2d	Southwestern Reporter (first and second series)	Arkansas, Kentucky, Missouri, Tennessee and Texas
U.S.	United States Reports	U.S. Supreme Court
S. Ct.	Supreme Court Reporter	U.S. Supreme Court
F.2d or F.3d	Federal Reporter (second or third series)	Federal court other than the U.S. Supreme Court
F. Supp.	Federal Supplement	Federal court other than the U.S. Supreme Court

Figure 1

3. Online Legal Research

Many states have made their statutes available online. If your state has done so, you can use your computer and browser to read any of the statutes cited in this book.

To show you how to find landlord-tenant statutes online, we're going to assume that you have a basic familiarity with your computer, your browser and the Internet. For more detailed descriptions of how to do legal research online, see *Legal Research: Online and in the Library,* by Stephen Elias and Susan Levinkind (Nolo Press).

Let's suppose that you are a tenant in Missouri and would like to read your state's statute on security deposits. After consulting "State Security Deposit Laws" in Appendix 2, you know that the statute's number is Section 535.300. The following steps show you how to find that statute.

Step 1: Go to Findlaw. We suggest that you use the Internet search engine known as Findlaw (www.findlaw.com). When you enter Findlaw's URL in your browser, you'll see their Homepage, as shown in Figure 1.

Step 2: Choose the link that will take you to state statutes. In Figure 1, you see a number of links. Since you're looking for state statutes, you'll want to click on the State Laws link, under the Laws: Cases & Codes main link. The resulting page is shown in Figure 2.

Figure 2

Step 3: Choose your state. As you look at the page shown in Figure 2 (you may have to scroll down a bit), you'll see the 50 states listed under State Resources Indexes. When you click on the state you're interested in—for this example, Missouri—you'll see the page shown in Figure 3.

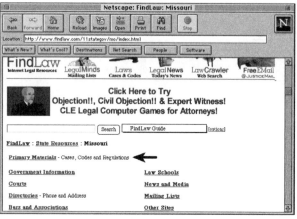

Figure 3

Step 4: Choose the link that will take you to the state statutes. In Figure 3, you'll see that Findlaw has put Missouri cases, codes and regulations under its Primary Materials link. (Remember, "codes" is another word for statutes.) When you choose that link, you'll get the screen shown in Figure 4.

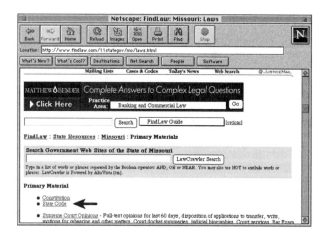

Figure 4

Step 5: Choose the State Code. Under the Primary Materials link, you could choose to go to the Constitution or the Code. When you click on the State Code link, you'll get the page shown in Figure 5.

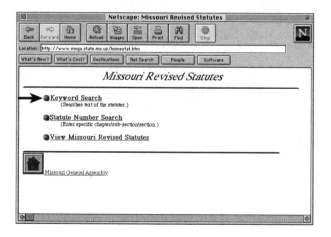

Figure 5

Step 6: Search for your statute. You'll see that the Missouri site gives you three ways to read the statutes:

1. If you don't know the statute's number, you can enter a "keyword" that is likely to be in it. For example, you could ask Findlaw to look for statutes containing the words "security" and "deposit."

2. If you know the statute number, you could ask Findlaw to take you directly there.

3. If you just want to browse through the statutes, you could ask Findlaw to give you the code's table of contents, which is linked to the codes.

For our example, we'll ask Findlaw to do the Number search described in 2, above. Clicking on the Statute Number Search link brings us to a page with a query box, shown in Figure 6.

When you do a search like this for your state, you may find that your state's statute page is designed differently than the one shown in Figure 5. But the basic choice of initial "clicks" in Findlaw is the same for every state. Usually, you can figure out how to get to the codes with a little trial and error.

Step 8: Ask for the statute. Finally, you're close to the statute itself. Clicking on the Section 535-300 link brings you to the page shown in Figure 8.

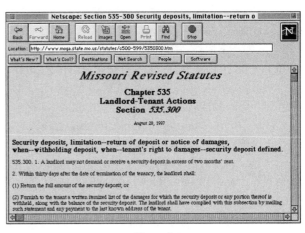

Figure 6

Figure 8

Step 7: Type in the statute number. When you enter the statute number, as directed in the page's instructions, you'll be taken to another page with a link to the statute, shown in Figure 7.

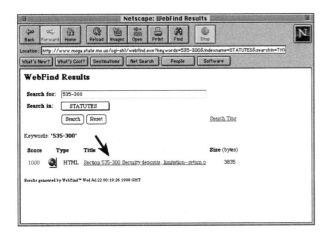

Figure 7

Computerized Research Services: Helpful but Costly

Several companies now offer full-scale legal research services, which make it relatively easy to search a huge database of statutes, court decisions, regulations and legal articles.

If you are not connected with a large law office or law school, you will likely find it difficult to get access to either of the two main legal research systems, Westlaw and Lexis. A small but growing number of law libraries or public libraries, however, offer these services.

Once found, there are two other major barriers to using these systems. One is cost. Be prepared for sticker shock—you can end up paying as much as $300 per hour. Second, it takes time and training to learn how to navigate these legal research systems efficiently. However, if you are already savvy on how to use computerized information retrieval services and are involved in a dispute worth a considerable sum, you may want to give it a try.

If you wish to use one of these systems, either ask a law librarian where the nearest terminal available to the public is located, or write to the companies directly.

For more information about Westlaw, contact West Publishing Co., 50 West Kellogg Boulevard, P.O. Box 3526, St. Paul, MN 55165, 800-WESTLAW or 800-937-8529.

For Lexis, contact Lexis Mead Data Central, 200 Park Ave., New York, NY 100017, 800-45LEXIS or 800-455-3947.

Helpful Websites

There are many websites that provide basic information and advice. Here are a few of our favorites:

- **Municipal codes**. The Seattle Public Library has links to many cities that have posted their ordinances online. http://www.spl.org/govpubs/municode.html
- **Federal codes, regulations, bankruptcy laws and consumer protection laws**. The U.S. House of Representatives Internet Law Library is complete and easy to use. http://law.house.gov
- **Rent control**. TenantNet provides information on tenants' rights. It focuses on New York City laws and issues, but also has links to other rent control cities. http://tenant.net

Appendix 1:

State Laws and Agencies

Landlord-Tenant Statutes

Here are some of the key statutes pertaining to Landlord-Tenant law in each state.

Alabama	Ala. Code §§ 35-9-1 to -100	**Missouri**	Mo. Ann. Stat. §§ 441.010-.650; and §§ 535.150-.300
Alaska	Alaska Stat. §§ 34.03.010 to .380	**Montana**	Mont. Code Ann. §§ 70-24-101 to -25-206
Arizona	Ariz. Rev. Stat. Ann. §§ 12-1171 to -1183; §§ 33-1301 to -1381	**Nebraska**	Neb. Rev. Stat. §§ 76-1401 to -1449
Arkansas	Ark. Code Ann. §§ 18-16-101 to -306	**Nevada**	Nev. Rev. Stat. Ann. §§ 118A.010-.520
California	Cal. [Civ.] Code §§ 1925-1954, 1961-1962.7, 1995.010-1997.270	**New Hampshire**	N.H. Rev. Stat. Ann. §§ 540:1-540-A:8
		New Jersey	N.J. Stat. Ann. §§ 46:8-1 to -49
Colorado	Colo. Rev. Stat. §§ 38-12-101 to -104, -301 to -302	**New Mexico**	N.M. Stat. Ann. §§ 47-8-1 to -51
Connecticut	Conn. Gen. Stat. Ann. §§ 47a-1 to 50a	**New York**	N.Y. [Gen. Oblig.] Law §§ 7-101 to -109; N.Y. [Real Prop.] Law §§ 220-238; N.Y. [Mult. Dwell.] Law §§ 1-11; N.Y. [Mult. Resid.] Law §§ 305
Delaware	Del. Code. Ann. tit. 25, §§ 5101-7013		
Dist. of Columbia	D.C. Code Ann. §§ 45-1401 to -1597, -2501 to -2593	**North Carolina**	N.C. Gen. Stat. §§ 42-1 to -56
Florida	Fla. Stat. Ann. §§ 83.40-.66	**North Dakota**	N.D. Cent. Code §§ 47-16-01 to -41
Georgia	Ga. Code Ann. §§ 44-7-1 to -81	**Ohio**	Ohio Rev. Code Ann. §§ 5321.01-.19
Hawaii	Haw. Rev. Stat. §§ 521-1 to -78	**Oklahoma**	Okla. Stat. tit. 41, §§ 1-136
Idaho	Idaho Code §§ 6-301 to -324 and §§ 55-201 to -313	**Oregon**	Or. Rev. Stat. §§ 90.100-.435
		Pennsylvania	Pa. Stat. Ann. tit. 68, §§ 250.101-.342
Illinois	Ill. Rev. Stat. ch. 765 para. 705/0.01-740/5	**Rhode Island**	R.I. Gen. Laws §§ 34-18-1 to -19
		South Carolina	S.C. Code Ann. §§ 27-40-10 to -910
Indiana	Ind. Code Ann. §§ 32-7-1-1 to 37-7-19	**South Dakota**	S.D. Codified Laws Ann. §§ 43-32-1 to -26
Iowa	Iowa Code Ann. §§ 562A.1-.36	**Tennessee**	Tenn. Code Ann. §§ 66-28-101 to -517
Kansas	Kan. Stat. Ann. §§ 58-2501 to -2573	**Texas**	Tex. [Prop.] Code Ann. §§ 91.001-92.301
Kentucky	Ky. Rev. Stat. Ann. §§ 383.010-.715		
Louisiana	La. Rev. Stat. Ann. §§ 9:3201-:3259; La. Civ. Code Ann. art. 2669-2742	**Utah**	Utah Code Ann. §§ 57-17-1 to -5, -22-1 to -6
Maine	Me. Rev. Stat. Ann. tit. 14, §§ 6001-6045	**Vermont**	Vt. Stat. Ann. tit. 9, §§ 4451-4468
Maryland	Md. Code Ann., [Real Prop.] §§ 8-101 to -501	**Virginia**	Va. Code Ann. §§ 55-218.1 to -248.40
		Washington	Wash. Rev. Code Ann. §§ 59.04.010-.900, .18.010-.910
Massachusetts	Mass. Gen. Laws Ann. ch. 186 §§ 1-21		
Michigan	Mich. Comp. Laws Ann. § 554.601-.640	**West Virginia**	W. Va. Code §§ 37-6-1 to -30
Minnesota	Minn. Stat. Ann. §§ 504.01-.35	**Wisconsin**	Wis. Stat. Ann. §§ 704.01-.40
Mississippi	Miss. Code Ann. §§ 89-8-1 to -27	**Wyoming**	Wyo. Stat. §§ 34-2-125 to -130

State Rent Rules

Here are citations for statutes that set out rent rules in each state. When a state has no statute, the space is left blank.
See the "Notice Required to Change or Terminate a Month-to-Month Tenancy" Chart in this Appendix for citations to statutes for raising rent.

State	When Rent is Due	Grace Period	Where Rent is Due
Alabama			
Alaska	Alaska Stat. § 34.03.020(c)		Alaska Stat. § 34.03.020(c)
Arizona	Ariz. Rev. Stat. Ann. § 33-1314(C)		Ariz. Rev. Stat. Ann. § 33-1314(C)
Arkansas			
California	Cal. [Civ.] Code § 1947		
Colorado			
Connecticut	Conn. Gen. Stat. Ann. § 47a-3a	Conn. Gen. Stat. Ann. § 47a-15a	Conn. Gen. Stat. Ann. § 47a-3a
Delaware	Del. Code Ann. tit. 25, § 5501(b)	Del. Code Ann. tit. 25, § 5501(d)	Del. Code Ann. title 25, § 5501(b)
D.C.			
Florida	Fla. Stat. Ann. § 83.46		
Georgia			
Hawaii	Haw. Rev. Stat. § 521-21(b)		Haw. Rev. Stat. § 521-21(b)
Idaho	Idaho Code §§ 55-201 to -313		
Illinois			
Indiana	*Watson v. Penn*, 108 Ind. 21 (1886), 8 N.E. 636 (1886)		
Iowa	Iowa Code Ann. § 562A.9(3)		Iowa Code Ann. § 562A.9(3)
Kansas	Kan. Stat. Ann. § 58-2545		Kan. Stat. Ann. § 58-2545
Kentucky	Ky. Rev. Stat. Ann. § 383.565(2)		Ky. Rev. Stat. Ann. § 383.565(2)
Louisiana			
Maine		Me. Rev. Stat. Ann. tit. 14, § 6028	
Maryland			
Massachusetts		Mass. Gen. Laws Ann. ch. 186 § 15B(1)(c)	Mass. Gen. Laws Ann. ch. 186 § 15B(1)(c)
Michigan	Hilsendegen v. Scheich, 55 Mich. 468 (1885), 21 N.W. 2d 894 (1885)		
Minnesota			

State Rent Rules (continued)

State	Returned Late Charges	Check Charges
Alabama		
Alaska		
Arizona	Ariz. Rev. Stat. Ann. § 33-1368(B)	
Arkansas		
California	*Jack v. Sinsheimer*, 125 C563 (1899); *Ricker v. Rombough*, 120 Cal App 2d Supp 912 (1953), but see *Canal-Randolph Anaheim, Inc. v. Wilcowski*, 78 Cal.App. 3d 477 (1978)	
Colorado		
Connecticut	Conn. Gen. Stat. Ann. §§ 47a-4(a)(8), 47a-15a	
Delaware	Del. Code Ann. tit. 25, § 5501(d)	
D.C.		
Florida		
Georgia		
Hawaii		
Idaho		
Illinois		
Indiana		
Iowa		
Kansas		
Kentucky		
Louisiana		
Maine	Me. Rev. Stat. Ann. tit. 14, § 6028	
Maryland	Md. Code Ann., [Real Prop.] § 8-208(3)	
Massachusetts	Mass. Gen. Laws Ann. ch. 186 §11; Mass. Gen. Laws Ann. ch. 186 §15B(1)(c)	
Michigan		
Minnesota		

State Rent Rules

State	When Rent is Due	Grace Period	Where Rent is Due
Mississippi			
Missouri			
Montana	Mont. Code Ann. § 70-24-201(2)(c)		Mont. Code Ann. § 70-24-201(2)(b)
Nebraska	Neb. Rev. Stat. § 76-1414(3)		Neb. Rev. Stat. § 76-1414(3)
Nevada	Nev. Rev. Stat. Ann. §§ 118A.210-.250		
New Hampshire			
New Jersey			
New Mexico	N.M. Stat. Ann. § 47-8-15(B)		N.M. Stat. Ann. § 47-8-15(B)
New York			
North Carolina		N.C. Gen Stat. § 42-46	
North Dakota	N.D. Cent. Code § 47-16-07		
Ohio			
Oklahoma	Okla. Stat. tit. 41, § 109		Okla. Stat. tit. 41, § 109
Oregon	Or. Rev. Stat. § 90.240(5)(a)	Or. Rev. Stat. § 90.260	Or. Rev. Stat. § 90.240(4)(a)
Pennsylvania			
Rhode Island	R.I. Gen. Laws § 34-18-15(c)	R.I. Gen. Laws § 34-18-35	R.I. Gen. Laws § 34-18-15(c)
South Carolina	S.C. Code Ann. § 27-40-310		S.C. Code Ann. § 27-40-310
South Dakota	S.D. Codified Laws Ann. § 43-32-12		
Tennessee	Tenn. Code Ann. § 66-28-201(c)		Tenn. Code Ann. § 66-28-201(c)
Texas			
Utah			
Vermont			
Virginia	Va. Code Ann. § 55-248.7(C)		
Washington			
West Virginia			
Wisconsin			
Wyoming			

State Rent Rules (continued)

State	Late Charges	Returned Check Charges
Mississippi		
Missouri		
Montana		
Nebraska		
Nevada		Nev. Rev. Stat. Ann. § 118A.200(3)(c)
New Hampshire		
New Jersey	N.J. Stat.Ann. § 2A-42-6.1	
New Mexico	N.M. Stat. Ann § 47-8-15(D)	
New York		
North Carolina	N.C. Gen. Stat. § 42-46	
North Dakota		
Ohio		
Oklahoma	*Sun Ridge Investors, Ltd. v. Parker* 956 P.2d 876 (1998)	
Oregon	Or. Rev. Stat. § 90.260	Or. Rev Sat. § 90.302(3)(b)
Pennsylvania		
Rhode Island		
South Carolina		
South Dakota		
Tennessee	Tenn. Code Ann. § 66-28-201(d)	
Texas		
Utah		
Vermont		
Virginia		
Washington		
West Virginia		
Wisconsin		
Wyoming		

Selected Rent Control Ordinances

CALIFORNIA

Los Angeles

Ordinance Adoption Date

4/21/79 (Los Angeles Municipal Code, Chapter XV); latest amendment 7/95.

Exceptions

Units constructed (or substantially renovated with at least $10,000 in improvements) after 10/1/78, "luxury" units (defined as 0, 1, 2, 3, or 4+ bedroom units renting for at least $302, $420, $588, $756, or $823, respectively, as of 5/31/78), single-family residences, except where two or more houses are located on the same lot. [Sec. 151.02.G,M.]

Administration

Appointed seven-member Rent Adjustment Commission, 111 N. Hope Street, Lobby, Los Angeles, CA 90012. For information regarding ordinance, call 213-367-9099; or 800-994-4444. Website: http://www.tenantnet/Other_Areas/Calif/losangel/index.html.

Registration

Required. (The ordinance's provision that tenants may withhold rents for non-registration is unconstitutional, unless ordinance allows the landlord a hearing first. Floystrup v. Berkeley Rent Stabilization Board, 219 Cal. App. 3d 1309 (1990).) [Sec. 151.11.B.]

Tenant may defend any unlawful detainer action on the basis of the landlord's failure to register the property. [Sec. 151.09.F.]

Rent Formula

Except with permission of Commission or Community Development Department, rents may not be increased by more than a 3% to 8% percentage based on the "Urban All Items Consumer Price Index" for the Los Angeles/Long Beach/Anaheim/Santa Monica/Santa Ana areas. The figure is published each year by the Community Development Department on or before May 30th, and applies to rent increases to be effective the following July 1st through June 30th of the next year. The actual percentage is calculated by averaging the CPI over the previous 12-month period beginning the September 30th before that, but in any event cannot fall below 3% or exceed 8%. In addition, if the landlord pays for gas or electricity for the unit, she may raise the rent an additional 1% for each such type of utility service. [Secs. 151.06.D, 151.07.A.6.]

Individual Adjustments

Landlord may apply to the Rent Adjustment Commission for higher increase to obtain "just and reasonable return." (This does not include "negative cash flow" based on recent purchase, but does include negative "operating expense," not counting landlord's mortgage payment.) [Sec. 151.07.B.] Also, landlord may apply to Community Development Department for permission to pass on to the tenant 50% of the cost of capital improvements not directly benefiting the landlord—for example, new roof costs would be considered, but not costs of renovations to manager's units or advertising signs—spread out over five or more years. [Sec. 151.07.A.]

Rent-Increase Notice Requirements

Landlord must post conspicuously or give tenant a copy of current registration statement showing that the property is registered with Board. [Sec.151.05.A.] Landlord who applies to Board for a rent higher than maximum is required to provide written justification for the difference. [Sec. 151.05.C.]

Vacancy Decontrol

Landlord may charge any rent after a tenant either vacates voluntarily or is evicted for nonpayment of rent, breach of a rental agreement provision or to substantially remodel. Controls remain if landlord evicts for any other reason, fails to remodel after evicting for that purpose or terminates or fails to renew a subsidized-housing lease with the city housing authority. Once a vacated unit is re-rented, it is subject to rent control based on the higher rent. [Sec. 151.06.C.]

Eviction

Landlord must show just cause to evict. For other restrictions, see Landlord's Law Book, Volume 2: Evictions.

Penalties

Violation of ordinance, including failing to include proper information in eviction notices, is a misdemeanor punishable by maximums of $500 fine and six months imprisonment. [Sec. 151.10.B.] Tenant may sue in court for three times any rent in excess of legal rent collected, plus attorney fees. [Sec. 151.10.A.]

Other Features

Landlord must pay 5% annual interest rate on deposits held over a year. Interest payments need only be made every five years, and when deposit refunded at end of tenancy. (This part of the ordinance, however, is not being enforced at this time, while a legal challenge proceeds through the appeals courts.)

Los Angeles also has a Rent Escrow Adjustment Program (REAP) ordinance that applies to all rent-controlled units. Under this ordinance, a tenant whose landlord has received a 30-day notice from local health or building inspectors to correct serious housing code violations may withhold rent and pay it to a city escrow fund, if the landlord has failed to correct the violation within the 30-day period. (See Chapter 11 for details on REAP.)

Oakland

Ordinance Adoption Date

10/7/80; latest amendment 11/97.

Exceptions

Units constructed after 1/1/83, buildings "substantially rehabilitated" at cost of 50% of that of new construction (as determined by Chief Building Inspector), properties with HUD-insured mortgages. [Sec. 8.22.030.] Controls may be permanently removed if landlord spends at least 50% of new construction costs to "substantially rehabilitate" the property. [Sec. 8.22.060.]

Administration

Appointed seven-member Residential Rent Arbitration Board, 1333 Broadway, 4th Floor, Oakland, CA 94612. 510-238-3721 (to leave message) or call Sentinel Fair Housing, 510-836-2687.

Registration

Not required.

Rent Formula

Rents may not be increased more than 3% in any 12-month period for occupied units, and 6% in any 12-month period for units vacated after the landlord terminated the tenancy. The 6% increase is one time only. [Secs. 8.22.060.]

Individual Adjustments

Tenant can contest an increase in excess of that allowed (but only if his rent is current) by filing a petition with the Board. The petition must be filed within 30 days. Hearing officer may consider costs of capital improvements, repairs, maintenance and debt service, and past history of rent increases. [Secs. 8.22.080, 8.22.060.]

Rent-Increase Notice Requirements

Landlords are required to notify tenants of the Residential Rent Arbitration Board at outset of the tenancy, in an addendum to the lease or rental agreement. [Sec. 050.d.]

Vacancy Decontrol

Landlord may charge any rent after a tenant vacates voluntarily. If tenant vacates involuntarily, landlord may not charge the new tenant more than twice the annual allowable increase.

Once property is re-rented, it is subject to rent control based on the higher rent. [Sec. 8.22.060.]

Eviction

Ordinance does not require just cause to evict, but there are other requirements. For other restrictions, see Landlord's Law Book, Volume 2: Evictions.

Penalties

Violation of ordinance is infraction (petty offense) punishable on first, second and third offenses within 12-month period by fines of up to $100, $200 and $500, respectively. A fourth offense within 12 months is a misdemeanor punishable by maximums of a $1,000 fine and/or six months imprisonment. [Sec. 9.1.]

San Francisco

Ordinance Adoption Date

6/79 (San Francisco Administrative Code, Chapter 37); latest amendment 11/98.

Exceptions

Units constructed after 6/79, buildings over 50 years old and "substantially rehabilitated" since 6/79. [Sec. 37.2(p).]

Administration

Appointed five-member Residential Rent Stabilization and Arbitration Board [Sec. 37.4], 25 Van Ness Avenue, Suite 320, San Francisco, CA 94102, 415-252-4600 (auto. info. system) and 415-252-4602 (counselor). Website: http://tenant.net/Other_Areas/Calif/sf/index.html.

Registration

Not required.

Rent Formula

Rents may not be increased by more than 7% in any 12-month period. (Increase allowed each year is 60% of the "Urban All Items Consumer Price Index" for the San Francisco-Oakland Metropolitan Area, but not more than 7%.) The figure is published each year by the Board. [Sec. 37.3.] A landlord who has not increased the rent during a previous 12-month period may accumulate his/her rights to increases and impose them in later years. Landlord may apply to Board for certification of capital improvements, the amortized cost of which may also be passed through to the tenant, but such increases are limited to 10% of the base rent each year. [Sec. 37.7.]

Individual Adjustments

Landlord may apply to Board for higher increase based on increased costs, including utility and capital-improvement costs. Hearing officer decides case based on various factors, including operating and maintenance expenses, but not "negative cash flow" based on recent purchase. Hearing officer may also consider rent-increase history and failure to make repairs. Tenant may contest any claimed pass through of utility costs, or request rent reduction based on decrease of services or poor maintenance. Either party may request an "expedited hearing." [Secs. 37.8.]

Rent-Increase Notice Requirements

Landlord must give tenant written itemized breakdown of rent increases—for example, what portion reflects costs of capital improvements—on or before the date of service of the rent-increase notice. [Sec. 37.6(b).]

Vacancy Decontrol

Landlord may charge any rent after a tenant vacates voluntarily or is evicted for cause. Once property is re-rented for a year, it is subject to rent control based on the higher rent. [Section 37.3(a).]

Eviction

Landlord must show just cause to evict. There is a moratorium on certain owner move-in evictions, protecting tenants who are 1) 60 years old or older and have lived in the rental for at least ten years; 2) disabled or blind and have lived in the rental for at least 10 years; or 3) disabled and have a "catastrophic illness" and have lived in the rental for at least five years. The moratorium does not apply in certain situations. Owner move-in evictions are further restricted; see ordinance for details.

Penalties

Violation of ordinance, including wrongful eviction or eviction attempts, is a misdemeanor punishable by maximums of a $2,000 fine and six months imprisonment. [Sec. 37.10.]

Other Features

Landlord must pay 5% annual interest on deposits held over a year, with payments made on tenant's move-in anniversary date each year, and when deposit refunded at end of tenancy. [Administrative Code, Chapter 49.]

San Jose

Ordinance Adoption Date

7/7/79 (San Jose Municipal Code, Title 17, Chapter 17.23); latest amendment 7/19/91.

Exceptions

Units constructed after 9/7/79, single-family residences, duplexes and condominium units. [Sec. 17.23.150.]

Administration

Appointed seven-member Advisory Commission on Rents, 4 N. Second St., Suite 600, San Jose, CA 95113-1305, 408-277-5431.

Registration

Required.

Rent Formula

Rents may not be increased more than 8% in any 12-month period, and may not be increased more than once within the 12 months. However, a landlord who has not raised the rent for over 24 months is entitled to a 21% increase. [Secs. 17.23.180, 17.23.210.]

Individual Adjustments

Tenant can contest an increase in excess of that allowed by filing a petition before rent increase takes effect (30 days), or lose the right to object. Disputes initiated by tenant petition are heard by a mediation hearing officer, who may consider costs of capital improvements, repairs, maintenance and debt service, and past history of rent increases. Either party may appeal mediator's decision and invoke binding arbitration. Tenant can also petition to contest rent based on housing-code violations or decrease in services. [Secs. 17.23.220-17.23.440.]

OTHER STATES

Rent-Increase Notice Requirement

Where rent increase exceeds 8%, rent-increase notice must advise tenant of her right to utilize the Rental Dispute Mediation and Arbitration Hearing Process, giving the address and telephone number of the city's rent office. The notice must also indicate the time limit within which the tenant may do this. [Sec. 17.23.270.]

Vacancy Decontrol

Landlord may charge any rent after a tenant vacates voluntarily or is evicted following three-day notice for nonpayment of rent or other breach of the rental agreement. Once the property is re-rented, it is subject to rent control based on the higher rent. [Sec. 17.23.190.]

Eviction

Ordinance does not require showing of just cause to evict.

Penalties

Violation of ordinance by charging rent in excess of that allowed following mediation/arbitration, by retaliation against the tenant for asserting his rights or by attempting to have tenant waive rights under ordinance is a misdemeanor punishable by maximums of a $500 fine and six months imprisonment. [Secs. 17.23.515-17.23.530.] Tenant may sue landlord in court for excess rents charged, plus treble damages or $500 (whichever is greater.) [Sec. 17.23.540.]

District of Columbia

Ordinance Adoption Date

7/17/85; (Rental Housing Act of 1985, District of Colombia Code §45-2501 et seq.); latest amendment in §18, Omnibus Budget Support Congressional Review Emergency Act of 1995 (D.C. Act 11-124, July 27, 1995; 42 DCR 4160).

Exceptions

Any rental unit in any federally or District-owned housing accommodation, buildings constructed after 12/75, rental additions after 1/80, buildings with four or less rental units, cooperative housing, housing which receives rehabilitation assistance. [D.C. Code §42-2515.]

Administration

Appointed three-member Rental Housing Commission, [D.C. Code §45-2511], North Potomac Building, 614 H Street, N.W., Room 1105, Washington, DC 20001, 202-727-7400.

Registration

Required and landlord cannot increase the rent if the building is not registered. [D.C. Code §45-2518, §45-2515.]

Rent Formula

Rents may not be increased by more than 10% in any 12-month period. (Increase allowed each year equal to the change during the previous year in the DC Standard Metropolitan Statistical Area Consumer Price Index for Urban Wage Earners and Clerical Workers for all items during the preceding calendar year.) [D.C. Code §45-2516(b).]

Rent-Increase Notice Requirements

Landlord must give tenant 30 days written Notice of any rent adjustment with a statement of the current rent, the increased rent, and the utilities covered by the rent which justify the adjustment. [D.C. Code §45-2518(a)(1)(E) and (f).] In addition, any notice must include a summary of tenants' rights and a list of sources of technical assistance.

Vacancy Decontrol

If tenant vacates voluntarily or is evicted for not paying rent or using the rental unit for illegal purposes, the landlord may increase the rent 12% above the rent ceiling. Landlord may do this only once per 12-month period. [D.C. Code § 45-2523.]

Eviction

Landlord must show just cause to evict. [D.C. Code § 45-2551.]

Penalties

A landlord who demands or receives any rent in excess of the maximum allowable rent or substantially reduces or eliminates related services previously provided for a rental unit, will be liable for the amount by which the rent exceeds the applicable rent ceiling or for three times that amount (in the event of bad faith) and/or for a rollback of the rent to the amount the Rental Housing Commission allows. A landlord who violates the chapter in any way will be subject to a civil fine of not more than $5,000 for each violation. [D.C. Code § 45-2591.]

Tenant may challenge a rent increase by filing a petition with the Rent Administrator within three years of the increase. [D.C. Code §45-2516(e).]

Newark, New Jersey

Ordinance Adoption Date

November 20, 1973 (Title 15, Housing Chapters 9A and 9B). Last amended in 12/96.

Exceptions

Owner-occupied one-, two-, three- and four-unit dwellings and public housing. Units that have been rehabilitated by federal or state programs and that receive Section 8 rent subsidies or federal housing vouchers may raise rents only up to fair market value, as determined by the federal Department of Housing and Urban Development. These units lose their exemption if they are withdrawn from Section 8 or the Rental Rehabilitation Program. [15:9B2.] New construction, previously vacant properties and substantially rehabilitated vacant units are all exempt from rent control for five years. [15:9B-17.]

Administration

Appointed five-member Rent Control Board. [15:9B-9.] Office of Boards, City of Newark, Room 112, 920 Broad Street, Newark, New Jersey 07102. For information regarding ordinance, call 973-733-3675.

Registration

Required. [15:9A-10.]

Rent Formula

Rents may not be increased by more than 5% for dwellings of 49 units or less, or 4% for dwellings of 50 units or more. [15:9B-3.]

Individual Adjustments

Landlord may increase the rent for hardship, for a capital improvement surcharge, a substantial rehabilitation exemption, a utilities surcharge and after a unit is vacated. [15:9B-7, 15:9B-8, 15:9B-17(c), 15:9B-16.]

Rent-Increase Notice Requirements

Landlord must notify the Board and tenant at least 60 days before the effective date of the increase.

The Board or the tenant may request a hearing within 30 days of receipt of notice from the landlord. [15:9B-7 and 8.] For a utilities surcharge, the landlord must send notice to the tenant within 14 days after the landlord applies to the Board. [15:9B-16.]

Vacancy Decontrol

Vacant units which remain vacant for a minimum of 18 months remain outside of the rent control ordinance for a period of five years. [15:9B-17(b).] Apartments which become vacant and in which the landlord spent more than $100 times the number of rooms in the unit for the purpose of rehabilitating the apartment may have their rent increased a maximum of 25% of the prior rent. Landlord must post his application to the Board for this rent increase in a conspicuous place in the apartment building on the date of the application. [15:9B-17(d).]

Eviction

Landlord must show just cause to evict.

Penalties

Violation of ordinance is punishable by a maximum of $500 fine and/or 90 days imprisonment. [15:9A- 14 and 15:9B-18.]

Other Features

Landlord may seek a tax surcharge from a tenant because of an increase in municipal property taxes after giving the tenant one month's notice. [15:9B-5.] If there is a tax decrease, the tenant is also entitled to a rent reduction. [15:9B-6.]

New York

New York's rent regulation programs, which affect mainly New York City tenants, are divided into those apartments that are under rent control and those that are under rent stabilization.

Rent Control The rent control program applies only to residential buildings constructed before February 1, 1947, and containing three or more units (there are only about 100,000 rent control units). In order for an apartment that meets these specifications to be under rent control, the tenant must have lived there continuously since July 1, 1971. In addition, rent control covers one-family dwellings and apartments in two-family dwellings built before February 1, 1947, if the same tenant has lived there continuously since May 1, 1953. When a rent controlled apartment is vacated, it either becomes rent stabilized or completely removed from regulation.

Since there are no new rent control tenants, the program is dying out.

Rent Stabilization: Apartments are under rent stabilization if they are in buildings of more than six units, built between February 1, 1947, and January 1, 1974. There are over 1,100,000 rent stabilized units. Tenants in buildings built before February 1, 1947, who moved in after June 30, 1971, are also covered by rent stabilization. In addition, buildings of three or more apartments constructed or extensively renovated since 1974 with special tax benefits are also covered by rent stabilization.

Ordinance Adoption Date

Emergency Housing Rent Control Law of 1946, Emergency Tenant Protection Act of 1974, and New York City Administrative Code Sections 26-501 to 26-520, adopted 1969, all amended by the Rent Regulation Reform Act of 1993. Further amendments were made in June 1997.

Exceptions, Rent Control and Rent Stabilization

Buildings with more than six units or built after 1974. Tenants who are 62 years or older may qualify for a full or partial exemption from rent increases. Seniors are eligible if their incomes are below a maximum limit set by local law, they are paying at least 1/3 of their income for rent and their leases are for one- or two-year terms. [Senior Citizen Rent Increase Exemption-SCRIE, NYC Admin. Code Sections 26-601 to 26-615.]

Vacated apartments that rent for more than $2,000, including any rent increases that are the result of passed-on renovation costs, are deregulated immediately.

Administration

New York State Division of Housing and Community Renewal (DHCR) administers rent regulations both in and outside NYC. DHCR has a Central Rent Information Hotline, 718-739-6400; 163 W. 125th Street, 5th Floor, New York, NY 10027, or 156 William Street, 9th Floor, New York, NY 10038. In addition, NYC has an appointed nine-member Rent Guidelines Board (RGB) which establishes the guidelines for annual rent adjust-ments. [NYC Admin. Code Sec. 26-510.] Rent Guide-lines Board, 51 Chambers Street, Room 202, New York, NY 10007 212-349-2262.

Registration

Owners had to register with the DHCR, no later than 6/30/84. For apartments which became subject to rent stabilization after 1984, an owner is required to file an initial registration within 90 days after the property becomes subject to rent stabilization. After the initial registration, owners must file an annual registration state-ment giving the April 1st rent for each unit and provide tenants with a copy of their statement. Owners who don't comply can't increase the rent and are subject to additional penalties. [NYC Admin. Code Sec. 26-517.]

Rent Formula

Rent Control: A Maximum Base Rent (MBR) system is established for each apartment and adjusted every two years to reflect changes in operating costs. The rent that rent-controlled tenants pay is called the Maximum Collectible Rent (MCR), which is usually less than the MBR. Owners who certify that they are providing "essential" services are entitled to raise rents up to 7.5% each year until they reach the MBR. Tenants can challenge the proposed increase on the grounds that the building has safety or health code violations or that the owner's expenses do not warrant an increase.

Rent Stabilization: Landlord can increase the rent when an apartment is vacated based on city guidelines plus an adjustment called the "vacancy allowance." The rent may be increased at least 20% if the lease is for two or more years and the previous tenant has either moved or died. When a landlord renovates a vacant unit, the rent may be increased by $1 for every $40 spent.

Rent-Increase Notice Requirements

Owner can increase the rent for increase in services, capital investments or hardship, but must first file an application with the DHCR, which then serves the tenants notice of the increase in rent. The increase in the monthly stabilization rent can only be 1/40th of the total cost of the improvements. [NYC Rent Stabilization Code Part 2522.4.] Landlords can also include the price of fuel in a rent increase in rent controlled apartments only. This is known as a "pass-along."

Vacancy Decontrol

When a rent-controlled apartment becomes vacated, it falls under rent stabilization if it is in a building with six or more units; otherwise it becomes deregulated. [NYC Rent Stabilization Law Sec. 26-504.]

Luxury Decontrol: Units rented by tenants whose combined yearly income exceeds $175,000 for two consecutive years and who pay $2,000 or more in rent will be deregulated.

Eviction

Landlord must show just cause to evict. [NYC Rent Stabilization Code Part 2524.1, .3.] In addition, a land-lord can't refuse to renew a lease of a tenant who is over 62 or disabled because the landlord wants the apartment for personal use. [Rent Stabilization Code 2524.4(a).] A landlord may demolish a building with few units if the tenants are relocated to comparable housing.

Penalties

If a tenant's rights are violated, DHCR can reduce rents and levy civil penalties against the owner ranging from $100 to a maximum of $2,500 for subsequent offense, depending on the violation. If the landlord overcharged the rent, the DHCR can assess treble damages. There is a retroactive four-year maximum on rent overcharge refunds for complaints filed after April 1, 1984, and a two-year maximum on treble damages. Landlords who harass tenants in an effort to get them to vacate their apartments may be charged with a class B felony, punishable by up to four years in state prison. [NYC Admin. Code Sec. 26-516.]

Other Features

An owner must include a copy of the Rent Stabilization Rider with a tenant's lease, which describes the rights and obligations of tenants and owners under the Rent Stabilization Law. The Rider informs a rent-stabilized tenant signing a vacancy lease of the legal regulated rent in effect immediately prior to the vacancy and explains how the present rent was computed.

In most cases, tenants must place rent into escrow accounts during disputes with landlords.

Tenants' succession rights extend to spouses and unmarried domestic partners only, and are limited to one generation.

Citations for State Laws on Security Deposits

Here are citations for statutes pertaining to security deposits in each state. Details on various aspects of security deposits are provided in Chapters 4 and 16.

This table is limited to security deposit statutes. Some states—Alabama, Idaho, West Virginia and Wyoming—do not have statutes on security deposits. That doesn't mean that there is no law on the subject. Court decisions (what lawyers call "case law") in your state may set out quite specific requirements for refundability of deposits, whether they should be held in interest-bearing accounts and the like. This book doesn't cover all this case law; you may need to check it out yourself. To find out whether courts in your state have made decisions you need to be aware of, you may need to do some legal research on your own (see Chapter 20).

Alabama	No statute
Alaska[1]	Alaska Stat. § 34.03.070
Arizona	Ariz. Rev. Stat. Ann. §§ 33-1321
Arkansas[2]	Ark. Code Ann. §§16-303 to -306
California	Cal. [Civ.] Code § 1950.5
Colorado	Colo. Rev. Stat. §§ 38-12-102 to -104
Connecticut	Conn. Gen. Stat. Ann. § 47a-21
Delaware	Del. Code Ann. tit. 25, § 5514
District of Columbia	D.C. Code Ann. § 45-2527 and D.C. Mun. Regs. tit. 14, §§ 308-311
Florida	Fla. Stat. Ann. § 83.49
Georgia[3]	Ga. Code Ann. §§ 44-7-30 to -36
Hawaii	Haw. Rev. Stat. § 521-44
Idaho	Id. Code § 6-321
Illinois[4]	Ill. Rev. Stat. ch. 765 para. 710, 715
Indiana	Ind. Code Ann. §§ 32-7-5-1 to -19
Iowa	Iowa Code Ann. § 562A.12
Kansas	Kan. Stat. Ann. § 58-2550
Kentucky	Ky. Rev. Stat. Ann. § 383.580
Louisiana	La. Rev. Stat. §9.3251
Maine[5]	Me. Rev. Stat. Ann. tit. 14, §§ 6031-6038
Maryland	Md. Code Ann. [Real Prop.] § 8-203
Massachusetts	Mass. Gen. Laws Ann. ch. 186 § 15B
Michigan	Mich. Comp. Laws Ann. §§ 554.602-.613
Minnesota	Minn. Stat. Ann. § 504A.221
Mississippi	Miss. Code Ann. § 89-8-21
Missouri	Mo. Ann. Stat. § 535.300

Montana	Mont. Code Ann. §§ 70-25-101 to -206
Nebraska	Neb. Rev. Stat. § 76-1416
Nevada	Nev. Rev. Stat. Ann. §§ 118A.240-.250
New Hampshire[6]	N.H. Rev. Stat. Ann. §§ 540-A:5 to :8
New Jersey[7]	N.J. Stat. Ann. §§ 46:8-19 to -26
New Mexico	N.M. Stat. Ann. § 47-8-18
New York[8]	N.Y. Gen. Oblig. Law §§ 7-101 to -109
North Carolina	N.C. Gen. Stat. §§ 42-50 to -56
North Dakota	N.D. Cent. Code § 47-16-07.1
Ohio	Ohio Rev. Code Ann. § 5321.16
Oklahoma	Okla. Stat. tit. 41 § 115
Oregon	Or. Rev. Stat. § 90.300
Pennsylvania	Pa. Stat. Ann. tit. 68, §§ 250.511a-.512
Rhode Island	R.I. Gen. Laws § 34-18-19
South Carolina	S.C. Code Ann. § 27-40-410
South Dakota	S.D. Codified Laws Ann. §§ 43-32-6.1, -24
Tennessee[9]	Tenn. Code Ann. § 66-28-301
Texas	Tex. Prop. Code Ann. §§ 92.101-.109
Utah	Utah Code Ann. §§ 57-17-1 to -5
Vermont	Vt. Stat. Ann. tit. 9, § 4461
Virginia	Va. Code Ann. § 55-248.11
Washington	Wash. Rev. Code Ann. §§ 59.18.260 -.285
West Virginia	No statute
Wisconsin	Wisc. Admin. Code ATCP § 134.06
Wyoming	No statute

Exemptions from State Security Deposit Laws

[1] Any rental unit where the rent exceeds $2,000 per month (Alaska)

[2] Landlord who owns five or fewer rental units, unless these units are managed by a third party for a fee (Arkansas)

[3] Landlord who owns ten or fewer rental units, unless these units are managed by an outside party (Georgia)

[4] Landlord who owns four or fewer dwelling units (Illinois)

[5] Rental unit which is part of a structure with five or fewer units, one of which is occupied by landlord (Maine)

[6] Landlord who leases a single-family residence and owns no other rental property or landlord who leases rental units in an owner-occupied building of five units or less. (Exemption does not apply to any individual unit in owner-occupied building that is occupied by a person 60 years of age or older.) (New Hampshire)

[7] Owner-occupied building with two or less units where tenant fails to provide 30 days' written notice to landlord invoking provisions of act (New Jersey)

[8] Landlord who rents out fewer than six rental units (New York)

[9] Rental properties outside of Davidson, Knox, Hamilton and Shelby Counties (Tennessee)

State Fair Housing Agencies

The name, address and phone number of the state organization responsible for administering and enforcing state fair housing laws or handling discrimination complaints is listed here. In states where there is no state agency, contact the U.S. Department of Housing and Urban Development (HUD) for information.

Alabama
No state agency. Contact HUD.

Alaska
Commission on Human Rights
800 A Street, Suite 204
Anchorage, AK 99501
907-274-4692

Arizona
Office of the Attorney General,
   Civil Rights Section
1275 W. Washington Street
Phoenix, AZ 85007
602-542-5263 Phoenix
520-628-6500 Tucson

Arkansas
Department of Housing & Urban
   Development
TCBY Tower
425 West Capitol Avenue, Suite 900
Little Rock, AR 72201
501-324-6296

California
Department of Fair Employment & Housing
1330 Broadway, Suite 1336
Oakland, CA 94612-2512
800-233-3212

Colorado
Civil Rights Division
1560 Broadway, Suite 1050
Denver, CO 80202
303-894-2997

Connecticut
Commission on Human Rights &
   Opportunities
90 Washington Street
Hartford, CT 06115
203-566-4895

Delaware
Division of Human Relations
Carvel State Office Building
820 North French Street
Wilmington, DE 19801
302-577-3485

District of Columbia
Commission on Human Rights
2000 14th Street NW
Washington, DC 20009
202-939-8740

Florida
Commission on Human Relations
325 John Knox Road
Building F, Suite 240
Tallahassee, FL 32399
904-488-7082

Georgia
Fair Housing and Equal Opportunity
   Commission
75 Spring Street SW
Atlanta, GA 30303-3388
404-331-3356

Hawaii
Civil Rights Commission
888 Mililani Street, 2nd Floor
Honolulu, HI 96813
808-586-8636

Idaho
Commission on Human Rights
450 West State Street
Boise, ID 83720
208-334-2873

Illinois
Department of Human Rights
100 West Randolph Street, Suite 10-100
Chicago, IL 60601
312-917-6200

Indiana
Civil Rights Commission
100 North Senate Avenue, Room N103
Indianapolis, IN 46204
317-232-2600

Iowa
Civil Rights Commission
211 East Maple
Des Moines, IA 50319
800-457-4416

Kansas
No state agency. Contact HUD.

Kentucky
Commission on Human Rights
Heyburn Building
332 W. Broadway, 7th Floor
Louisville, KY 40202
502-588-4024

Louisiana
Department of Justice, Equal Opportunity
   Section
P.O. Box 94095
Baton Rouge, LA 70804-9095
504-342-9764

Maine
Human Rights Commission
State House
Augusta, ME 04333
207-624-6050

Maryland
Commission on Human Relations
20 East Franklin Street
Baltimore, MD 21202
410-333-1700

Massachusetts
Commission Against Discrimination
One Ashburton Place
Boston, MA 02108
617-727-7310

Michigan
Department of Civil Rights
Executive Plaza Building
1200 6th Street
Detroit, MI 48226
313-256-2663

Minnesota
Department of Human Rights
Bremer Tower
Seventh and Minnesota Street
St. Paul, MN 55101
612-296-5663

State Fair Housing Agencies (continued)

Mississippi
No state agency. Contact HUD.

Missouri
Commission for Human Rights
3315 West Truman
Jefferson City, MO 65102
314-751-3325

Montana
Human Rights Commission
616 Helena Avenue
Helena, MT 59624
406-444-2884

Nebraska
Equal Opportunity Commission
P.O. Box 94934
Lincoln, NE 68509
402-471-2024

Nevada
No state agency. Contact HUD.

New Hampshire
Commission for Human Rights
163 Loudon Road
Concord, NH 03301
603-271-2767

New Jersey
Division on Civil Rights
383 West State Street
Trenton, NJ 08618
609-292-4605

New Mexico
Human Rights Commission
Aspen Plaza
1596 Pacheco Street
Santa Fe, NM 87501
505-827-6838

New York
Division of Human Rights
55 West 125th Street, 13th Floor
New York, NY 10027
212-961-8400

North Carolina
Human Relations Commission
121 West Jones Street
Raleigh, NC 27603
919-733-7996

North Dakota
No state agency. Contact HUD.

Ohio
Civil Rights Commission
220 Parsons Avenue
Columbus, OH 43215
614-466-2785

Oklahoma
Human Rights Commission
2101 North Lincoln Boulevard, Room 480
Oklahoma City, OK 73105
405-521-3441

Oregon
Bureau of Labor and Industry,
  Civil Rights Division
800 NE Oregon Street
Portland, OR 97232
503-731-4075

Pennsylvania
Human Relations Commission
101 South Second Street, Suite 300
Harrisburg, PA 17105
717-787-4410

Rhode Island
Commission for Human Rights
10 Abbott Park Place
Providence, RI 02903
401-277-2661

South Carolina
Human Affairs Commission,
  Fair Housing Division
2611 Forest Drive
Columbia, SC 29204
803-253-6336

South Dakota
Division of Human Rights
222 East Capitol Street
Pierre, SD 57501
605-773-4493

Tennessee
Human Rights Commission
530 Church Street
Nashville, TN 37243
615-741-5825

Texas
Commission on Human Rights
8100 Cameron Road, Suite 525
Austin, TX 78754
512-837-8534

Utah
Industrial Commission,
  Anti-Discrimination Division
160 East 300 South
Salt Lake City, UT 84114
801-530-6801

Vermont
Human Rights Commission
135 State Street
2nd Floor
Montpelier, VT 05633-6301
802-828-2480

Virginia
Office of Fair Housing
3600 West Broad Street
Richmond, VA 23230
804-367-8530

Washington
Human Rights Commission
402 Evergreen Plaza Building
711 South Capitol Way
Olympia, WA 98504
360-753-6770

West Virginia
Human Rights Commission
1321 Plaza East
Charleston, WV 25301
304-348-6880

Wisconsin
Department of Industry, Labor and Human
  Relations, Equal Rights Division
P.O. Box 8928
201 East Washington Avenue
Madison, WI 53708
608-266-7552

Wyoming
No state agency. Contact HUD.

State Laws on Rent Withholding and Repair and Deduct Remedies

Here are citations for state laws that allow tenants to withhold rent or use the repair and deduct remedy for landlord's failure to provide habitable premises.

State	Statute on rent withholding	Statute on repair and deduct
Alabama	No statute	No statute
Alaska	Alaska Stat. § 34.03.190	Alaska Stat. § 34.03.180
Arizona	Ariz. Rev. Stat. Ann. § 33-1365	Ariz. Rev. Stat. Ann. §§ 33-1363, -1364
Arkansas	No statute	No statute
California	*Green v. Superior Court,* 10 Cal. 3d 616 (1974)	Cal. [Civ.] Code § 1942
Colorado	No statute	No statute
Connecticut	Conn. Gen. Stat. Ann. §§ 47a-14a to -14h	Conn. Gen. Stat. Ann. § 47a-13
Delaware	Del. Code Ann. tit. 25 §§ 5306(b), 5308(b)(3)	Del. Code Ann. tit. 25, §§ 5307, 5308
District of Columbia	*Javins v. First Nat'l Realty Corp.,* 428 F.2d 1071 (D.C. Cir. 1970)	No statute
Florida	Fla. Stat. Ann. § 83.60	No statute
Georgia	No statute	No statute
Hawaii	Haw. Rev. Stat. § 521-78	Haw. Rev. Stat. § 521-64
Idaho	No statute	No statute
Illinois	Ill. Rev. Stat. ch. 765 para. 735/2-/2.1	No statute
Indiana	No statute	No statute
Iowa	Iowa Code Ann. § 562A.24	Iowa Code Ann. § 562A.23
Kansas	Kan. Stat. Ann. § 58-2561	No statute
Kentucky	Ky. Rev. Stat. Ann. § 383.645	Ky. Rev. Stat. Ann. §§ 383.635, 383.640
Louisiana	No statute	La. Civ. Code Ann. art. 2694
Maine	Me. Rev. Stat. Ann. tit. 14, § 6021	Me. Rev. Stat. Ann. tit. 14, § 6026
Maryland	Md. Code Ann., [Real Prop.] §§ 8-118, -211, -211.1	No statute
Massachusetts	Mass. Gen. Laws Ann. ch. 239, § 8A	Mass. Gen. Laws Ann. ch. 186 § 14
Michigan	Mich. Comp. Laws § 125.530	No statute
Minnesota	Minn. Stat. Ann. §§ 504.26, 504A.135S, 504A.171, 504A.585	No statute
Mississippi	No statute	Miss. Code Ann. § 89-8-15
Missouri	Mo. Ann. Stat. §§ 441.580, 441.570	No statute
Montana	Mont. Code Ann. § 70-24-421	Mont. Code Ann. §§ 70-24-406, -407, -408
Nebraska	Neb. Rev. Stat. §§ 76-1425, -1428	Neb. Rev. Stat. § 76-1427
Nevada	Nev. Rev. Stat. Ann. § 118A.490	Nev. Rev. Stat. Ann. §§ 118A.360, -.380
New Hampshire	N.H. Rev. Stat. Ann. § 540:13d	No statute
New Jersey	N.J. Stat. Ann. §§ 2A: 42-85 to -96	No statute
New Mexico	N.M. Stat. Ann. § 47-8-27.2	No statute
New York	N.Y. [Mult. Resid.] Law § 305-a	N.Y. [Mult. Resid.] Law § 305-c and N.Y. [Real Prop.] Law § 235-a
North Carolina	No statute	No statute
North Dakota	No statute	N.D. Cent. Code § 47-16-13
Ohio	Ohio Rev. Code Ann. § 5321.07	No statute
Oklahoma	Okla. Stat. tit. 41, § 121	Okla. Stat. tit. 41, § 121
Oregon	Or. Rev. Stat. § 90.370	Or. Rev. Stat. § 90.365
Pennsylvania	Pa. Stat. Ann. tit. 68, § 250.206	Pa. Stat. Ann. tit. 68, § 339.6
Rhode Island	R.I. Gen. Laws § 34-18-32	R.I. Gen. Laws §§ 34-18-30, -31
South Carolina	S.C. Code Ann. §§ 27-40-640, -790	S.C. Code Ann. § 27-40-630
South Dakota	S.D. Codified Laws Ann. § 43-32-9	S.D. Codified Laws Ann. § 43-32-9
Tennessee	Tenn. Code Ann. § 68-111-104	Tenn. Code Ann. § 66-28-502
Texas	No statute	Tex. [Prop.] Code Ann. §§ 92.0561, 92.056
Utah	No statute	No statute
Vermont	Vt. Stat. Ann. tit. 9, § 4458	Vt. Stat. Ann. tit. 9, § 4459
Virginia	Va. Code Ann. §§ 55-248.25 to .30	No statute
Washington	Wash. Rev. Code Ann. § 59.18.115	Wash. Rev. Code Ann. § 59.18.100
West Virginia	No statute	No statute
Wisconsin	Wisc. Stat. Ann. § 704.07(4)	No statute
Wyoming	No statute	No statute

State Laws on Landlord's Access to Rental Property

This is a synopsis of state laws that specify circumstances when a landlord may enter rental premises and the amount of notice required for such entry.

State	State law citation	Amount of notice required for landlord to enter	To deal with an emergency	To inspect the premises	To make repairs, alterations, or improvements	To show property to prospective tenants or purchasers	During tenant's extended absence
			Reasons landlord may enter				
Alabama	No statute						
Alaska	Alaska Stat. § 34.03.140	24 Hours	✔	✔	✔	✔	✔
Arizona	Ariz. Rev. Stat. Ann. § 33-1343	Two Days	✔	✔	✔	✔	
Arkansas	No statute						
California	Cal. Civ. Code § 1954	24 Hours	✔		✔	✔	
Colorado	No statute						
Connecticut	Conn. Gen. Stat. Ann. §§ 47a-16 to -16a	Reasonable notice	✔	✔	✔	✔	✔
Delaware	Del. Code Ann. Tit. 25 §§ 5509, 5510	Two Days	✔	✔	✔	✔	✔
District of Columbia	No statute						
Florida	Fla. Stat. Ann. § 83.53	12 Hours	✔	✔	✔	✔	✔
Georgia	No statute						
Hawaii	Haw. Rev. Stat. § 521-53, -70(b)	Two Days	✔	✔	✔	✔	✔
Idaho	No statute						
Illinois	No statute						
Indiana	No statute						
Iowa	Iowa Code Ann. §§ 562A.19, .28, .29	24 Hours	✔	✔	✔	✔	✔
Kansas	Kan. Stat. Ann. §§ 58-2557, -2565	Reasonable notice	✔	✔	✔	✔	✔
Kentucky	Ky. Rev. Stat. Ann. §§ 383.615	Two Days	✔	✔	✔	✔	✔
Louisiana	No statute						
Maine	Me. Rev. Stat. Ann. Tit. 14 § 6025	24 Hours	✔	✔	✔	✔	
Maryland	No statute						
Massachusetts	Mass. Gen. Laws Ann. ch. 186 § 15B1(a)			✔	✔	✔	
Michigan	No statute						
Minnesota	Minn. Stat. Ann. § 504.183	Reasonable notice	✔	✔	✔	✔	

State Laws on Landlord's Access to Rental Property (continued)

State	State law citation	Amount of notice required for landlord to enter	To deal with an emergency	To inspect the premises	To make repairs, alterations, or improvements	To show property to prospective tenants or purchasers	During tenant's extended absence
			Reasons landlord may enter				
Mississippi	No statute						
Missouri	No statute						
Montana	Mont. Code Ann. § 70-24-312	24 Hours	✔	✔	✔	✔	✔
Nebraska	Neb. Rev. Stat. § 76-1423	One Day	✔	✔	✔	✔	✔
Nevada	Nev. Rev. Stat. Ann. § 118A.330	24 Hours	✔	✔	✔	✔	
New Hampshire	N.H. Rev. Stat. Ann. § 540-A:3	Notice which is adequate under the circumstances	✔	Tenant's prior consent is necessary.			
New Jersey	No statute						
New Mexico	N.M. Stat. Ann. § 47-8-24	24 hours	✔	✔	✔	✔	✔
New York	No statute						
North Carolina	No statute						
North Dakota	N.D. Cent. Code § 47-16-07.3	Reasonable notice	✔	✔	✔	✔	
Ohio	Ohio Rev. Code Ann. § 5321.04(B), .05(B)	24 Hours	✔	✔	✔	✔	
Oklahoma	Okla. Stat. Tit. 41, § 128	One Day	✔	✔	✔	✔	
Oregon	Or. Rev. Stat. § 90.322	24 Hours	✔	✔	✔	✔	
Pennsylvania	No statute						
Rhode Island	R.I. Gen. Laws § 34-18-26	Two Days	✔	✔	✔	✔	✔
South Carolina	S.C. Code Ann. § 27-40-530	24 Hours	✔	✔	✔	✔	✔
South Dakota	No statute						
Tennessee	Tenn. Code Ann. § 66-28-403		✔	✔	✔	✔	✔
Texas	No statute						
Utah	Utah Code Ann. § 57-22-5(c)		✔		✔		
Vermont	Vt. Stat. Ann. Tit. 9 § 4460	48 Hours	✔	✔	✔	✔	
Virginia	1 Va. Code Ann. § 55-248.18	Reasonable notice	✔	✔	✔	✔	✔
Washington	Wash. Rev. Code Ann. § 59.18.150	Two Days	✔	✔	✔	✔	
West Virginia	No statute						
Wisconsin	Wis. Stat. Ann. § 704.052	Reasonable notice	✔	✔	✔	✔	
Wyoming	No statute						

State Lead Hazard Reduction Laws

State	Statute	Summary
Alabama	Ala. Code § 22-37-3	Requires plumbing components to be lead-free at time of installation or repair.
	Ala. Code §§ 22-37A-1 and following	Allows state health officer to investigate lead contamination generally or at request of owner or occupant.
		Requires certification of lead hazard reduction professionals.
Arizona	Ariz. Rev. Stat. Ann. §§ 36-1671 and following	Ariz. Rev. Stat. Ann. §§36-1671 and following
		Forbids the use of lead-based paint on any interior surface of a dwelling that may be within reach of a child under seven years.
		Authorizes Department of Health to develop local programs to detect and prevent lead-based paint poisoning in interior and exterior of buildings built before 1978 that are accessible to children under age seven.
		Provides for promulgation of regulations concerning certification of lead abatement professionals.
Arkansas	Ark. Stat. §§ 20-27-601 to 20-27-608	Permits the state to investigate the sources of lead hazards when a child is diagnosed with an elevated blood-lead level.
		Requires the state to notify the owner/occupier of a dwelling of detected lead hazards and requires abatement.
		Prohibits evicting the occupants of an affected residence.
		Mandates licensing for lead abatement workers as well as standards for removal of lead hazards.
California	Cal. Health and Safety Code §§ 105185 and following	Establishes training, certification and accreditation for lead abatement professionals.
	Cal. Civ. Code §§ 1102 to 1102.6	Requires an owner of a property to disclose lead-based paint hazards to prospective buyers.
	Cal. Labor Code §§ 6716-6717	Establishes standards for lead abatement workers.
	Cal. Health & Safety Code §§ 124160 and 124165	Directs Department of Health to take steps necessary to reduce children's excessive exposure to lead.
Colorado	Co. Rev. Stat. § 25-5-1104	Requires the Department of Public Health to establish a plan to reduce children's lead levels and control exposure to lead paint hazards in residences and child-occupied facilities.
Connecticut	Conn. Gen. Stat. § 8-219e	Provides government loans to persons seeking to remove lead-based paint.
	Conn. Gen. Stat. §§ 19a-111 to 19a-111d	Owners of dwellings with reported high blood-lead levels in occupants under six years old are required to abate the lead hazard. An owner may be responsible for relocating residents.
	Conn. Gen. Stat. § 21a-82	Forbids the use of lead-based paint in tenements or municipally owned buildings unless it adheres to state and federal regulations.
	Conn. Gen. Stat. § 47a to 54f	Prohibits paint in tenement houses that is cracked, chipped, blistered, flaking, loose or peeling so as to constitute a health hazard.
Delaware	Del. Code Title 31 § 4114(d)	Bans the use of lead-based paint on any dwelling unit surface, including fences and outbuildings.
District of Columbia	D.C. Code Ann. §§ 6-997.1 and following	Establishes lead-based paint abatement program under Mayor's office.
		Provides for certification and permits for lead abatement activities.
		Requires owners to keep records of lead-based paint abatement activities

State Lead Hazard Reduction Laws (continued)

State	Statute	Summary
District of Columbia (continued)		Provides for random inspections of lead-based paint abatement activities.
		Prohibits use of lead-based paint in any structure, fixture, appliance or furniture.
		Law does not apply to efficiencies or housing built after 1978.
Georgia	Ga. Code § 31-41-2	Requires the enactment of regulations to train, license and certify lead hazard abatement professionals.
Hawaii	Hi. Rev. Stat. § 321-11(27)	Places lead abatement practices and training programs within the Department of Health.
Illinois	410 Ill. Comp. Stat. 45/2 and following	An owner of a dwelling has between 30 and 90 days to mitigate the lead hazard. Abatement must be conducted by a licensed contractor. If abatement requirements are not met, the department may withhold rent from the owner or relocate the occupants until the procedures are complied with.
		Requires an owner to give written notice to prospective residents that a lead hazard has been identified in the dwelling unit. All owners of pre-1978 residential buildings must give prospective lessees a brochure on the potential hazards posed by lead in dwelling units.
Indiana	In. Code Ann. §§ 13-17-14-1 and following	Regulates abatement when children six years old and younger will be affected; requires lead-based paint workers to be licensed. Establishes trust fund to provide money for programs in target housing.
Iowa	Iowa Code § 135.100 to 135.105	Department of Public Health must design programs to eliminate or reduce dangerous levels of lead in children by implementing an abatement grant program to assess homes and assist in abatement.
Kentucky	Ky. Rev. Stat. §§ 211.900 to 201-905 and 211-.994	Permits the Human Resources Department to inspect a dwelling if an occupant is reported to have an elevated blood-lead level.
		Gives the owner of a residential unit 30 days to remove, replace or cover any lead hazard surfaces that are accessible to children under the age of six.
		If the Department determines that a child under six is in immediate danger from the presence of a lead hazard, the occupant may terminate the rental agreement without reprisal.
Louisiana	La. Rev. Stat. 40:1299.26-29	Mandates that an owner of residential property must remove or cover any lead-bearing materials within 30 days of a violation, if a child under six or a mentally retarded person resides at the premises.
	La. Rev. Stat. 30:2351-2351.59	Requires licenses for lead contractors, reduction planners and inspectors. The statute also includes a whistle blower provision to facilitate reporting the improper handling of lead-containing substances.
Maine	Me. Rev. Stat. Title 22 §§ 1314 to 1326	Restricts the use of any lead-based paint on any fixtures or exposed surface of a dwelling.
		Permits the Department of Human Services to inspect residences, provide notice to owners and occupants of any lead hazards and order abatement of exposed surfaces containing a lead hazard.
Maryland	Md. Ann. Code 83B §§ 2-307 and 1402 and following	Establishes lead hazard reduction grant and load programs for owners of residential property to fund lead hazard reduction activities with the emphasis on replacement of windows containing lead-based paint on friction surfaces and concentrating on residential properties constructed prior to 1950; with children who have been diagnosed with elevated blood-lead; families of limited income; or to test innovative methods of lead hazard reduction.
	Md. Env. Code § 6-301	Prohibits the use of lead-based paint on any interior or exterior surface commonly within the reach of children.
		Requires the training and licensure of lead abatement professionals.
	Md. Env. Code §§ 6-801 to 6-852	Requires owners to register their properties containing lead hazards and abate. Provides immunity from liability under certain circumstances. Requires owners to give tenants a lead poisoning information packet.
	Md. Real Prop. Code § 8-211.1	Allows lessee to ask the District Court to hold rent in escrow without reprisal where an owner has failed to comply with lead abatement laws.

State Lead Hazard Reduction Laws (continued)

State	Statute	Summary
Massachusetts	Mass. Gen. Laws Chapter 111, §§ 127b1/2, 189A-199	Requires training and licensing of lead abatement professionals.
		Permits inspection of the premises for lead hazards.
		Owners of residential dwellings must remove or cover lead hazards.
		Owners must disclose lead hazards to prospective buyers of the property.
	Mass. Gen. Laws Chapter 23B	Provides for a grant and load program for abatement of lead-based materials in dwellings.
Michigan	Mich. Comp. Laws Ann. § 565.957	Provides for Department of Public Health to make recommendations to governor for lead-based paint poisoning program.
	Mich. Comp. Laws. Ann. § 333.12101	Requires disclosure of lead-based paint to prospective buyers.
Minnesota	Minn. Stat. §§ 144.9501 to 144.9509	Requires lead abatement contractors to be registered with the state.
		Provides for the development of residential lead abatement procedures.
		Requires owners to abate lead hazards if residents are children under six or pregnant women.
Mississippi	Ms. Code §§ 49-17-501 and following	Authorizes the Department of Environmental Quality to establish certification programs for lead abatement workers. Requires licensing and certification of lead-based paint abatement professionals.
Missouri	Mo. Stat. §§ 701.300 and following	Requires residential lead hazard abatement.
		Provides for the licensure of abatement professionals.
Nebraska	Neb. Rev. Stat. § 71-6319 to § 71-6333	Lead abatement workers must be licensed; law establishes a training and certification program.
New Hampshire	N.H. Rev. Stat. § 130-A	Permits the Health Department to inspect residential dwellings.
		Requires an owner to abate lead hazards within 90 days of notice. Owners are prohibited from evicting occupants with children under six upon finding the presence of a lead hazard.
		Owners must disclose lead hazard violations to prospective buyers.
		Prohibits knowingly leasing a property with a lead hazard to occupants with children under six.
		Prohibits use of paint with more than .06% lead in any dwelling unit.
New Jersey	N.J. Rev. Stat. §§ 26:2-130 to 26:2-137	Provides screening for every child five years old and younger; results must be given to parents or guardians.
		Requires certification for lead abatement professionals.
		Establishes a grant program for local health boards to abate lead hazards.
	N.J. Rev. Stat. §§ 24:14A-1 to 24:14A-11	Forbids the use of lead-based paint on residential surfaces reachable by children.
		Mandates the removal and disposal of lead paint within ten days of a violation.
		Prohibits retaliatory eviction for the purpose of avoiding abatement.
New York	N.Y. Stat. Public Health Code §§ 1370 to 1375	Forbids the use of lead-based paint on any residential porches or interior surfaces.
		Notification of owner/occupant about the lead hazard and suggested abatement procedures.
		Mandatory screening of children in pre-school or day care.
North Carolina	N.C. Gen. Stat. § 130A-131.5	Establishes lead poisoning prevention program and authorizes commission to adopt rules for prevention of lead poisoning in children.
	N.C. Gen. Stat. § 130A-131.7(9)	Requires certain cleaning and maintenance procedures to prevent lead hazards.
	N.C. Gen. Stat. §§ 130A-453.02, .03	Requires certification of lead abatement professionals.

State Lead Hazard Reduction Laws (continued)

State	Statute	Summary
Ohio	Ohio Rev. Code §§ 3742 and following	Requires licensure for lead abatement professionals. Permits the Health Department to inspect dwellings for lead hazards.
Oklahoma	Ok. Rev. Stat. Title 27A §§ 2-12-101 to 2-12-501	Establishes certification requirements for workers in federally assisted housing (private property owners may use certified workers, but are not required to do so).
Oregon	Or. Stat. §§ 431.920, 701.500 to 701.515	Establishes training and licensing programs for lead-based paint workers; authorizes education and screening programs.
Pennsylvania	Pa. Stat. Ann. tit. 35, §§ 5901 to 5916	Establishes guidelines for the certification of lead hazard reduction contractors.
Rhode Island	R.I. Gen. Laws Title 23 § 24.6	Requires lead inspectors and abatement professionals to be licensed. Prohibits the use of lead-based paint in residential property accessible to children under six. Permits inspections of dwellings by the Health Department. Provides for emergency abatement if occupants have lead poisoning. Owners must disclose lead hazards to potential buyers or lessees.
South Carolina	S.C. Code § 44-53-1310 and following	Provides for state inspections and requires owner to remove or cover lead hazards within 30 days of a violation. Prohibits use of lead-based paint on interior or exterior of dwelling or on fixtures or furniture.
Tennessee	Tn. Code Ann. § 68-131-401	Department of Environment and Conservation to establish a certificaiton program for lead-based paint workers.
Texas	Tx. Civil Stat. Art. 9029	Department of Health to establish a training, certification and accreditation program for lead-based paint workers who work in child-occupied facilities.
Vermont	Vt. Stat. tit. 18 §§ 1751 to 1765	Establishes training and certification for lead abatement professionals. Requires owners to disclose lead hazards to prospective buyers or lessees. Allows the commissioner of the department of health to inspect other dwelling units in a building upon receiving a report that a child who lives in one unit has been severely lead poisoned. Establishes essential maintenance practices. Requires insurers to provide liability coverage of lead-based paint hazards.
Virginia	Va. Uniform Statewide Building Code, Vol. 11, §§ 1701, R224, PM 305.4	Prohibits application of lead-based paint on any interior or exterior surface of a dwelling. Requires lead hazards to be removed or covered.
	Va. Code Ann. § 54.1-503	Requires license for lead abatement activities.
	Va. Code Ann. § 55-519	Requires owner to disclose lead-based paint to prospective buyers.
West Virginia	W. Va. Code §§ 16-35-1 and following	Requires licensure of lead risk assessment, inspection and abatement professionals. Requires owner of building to notify health department before undertaking a lead abatement project. Directs the health department to establish a lead abatement and education program.
Wisconsin	Wisc. Stat. §§ 254.11 to 254.178	Prohibits the use of lead-bearing paint; requires doctors to report lead poisoning or exposure; establishes guidelines for screening children under six years of age. When notified that a child under six years of age has been lead poisoned, department of health shall inspect the dwelling and may order the owner to abate the hazard within 30 days. Requires insurance coverage in certain circumstances.

In order to completely understand your compliance duties, read the entire statute or regulation. Tips on using the law library are in Chapter 18. Some cities may have additional requirements.

Summaries courtesy of Barbara Ann Vassallo, Esq., coordinator of state and local government affairs for the National Apartment Association, Washington, D.C., and Doug Farquhar, National Conference of State Legislatures, Denver, Colorado.

Notice Required to Change or Terminate a Month-to-Month Tenancy

Except where noted, the amount of notice a landlord must give to increase rent or change another term of the rental agreement in month-to-month tenancy is the same as that required to end a month-to-month tenancy. Be sure to check state and local rent control laws, which may have different notice requirements.

State	Tenant	Landlord	Statute	Comments
Alabama	10 days	10 days	Ala. Code § 35-9-3	No state statute on the amount of notice required to change rent or other terms.
Alaska	One month	One month	Alaska Stat. § 34.03.290(b)	
Arizona	30 days	30 days	Ariz. Rev. Stat. Ann. § 33.1375	
Arkansas	30 days	30 days	Polk v. State, 772 S.W.2d368 (1989)	
California	30 days	30 days	Cal. Civ. Code § 1946	Landlord and tenant may agree to a shorter termination period, but not less than seven days.
Colorado			No statute	
Connecticut			Conn. Gen. Stat. § 47a-23	Three days do not include the day the notice is served or the day the termination or change is to take effect.
Delaware	60 days	60 days	Del. Code Ann. tit. 25, § 5106 and 5107	After receiving notice of landlord's proposed change terms, Tenant has 15 days to terminate tenancy. Otherwise, changes will take effect as announced.
District of Columbia	30 days	30 days	D.C. Code Ann. § 45-1402	No state statute on the amount of notice required to change rent or other terms.
Florida	15 days	15 days	Fla. Stat. Ann. § 83.57	No state statute on the amount of notice required to change rent or other terms. Tenant can terminate with seven days notice if landlord doesn't comply with a material provision of the lease.
Georgia	30 days	60 days	Ga. Code Ann. § 44-7-7	No state statute on the amount of notice required to change rent or other terms.
Hawaii	28 days	45 days	Haw. Rev. Stat. §§ 521-71 and 521-21(d)	
Idaho	30 days	30 days	Idaho Code § 55-208 and 55-307	Landlords must provide 15 days' notice to increase rent or change tenancy.
Illinois	30 days	30 days	Ill. Rev.stat.ch. 735 ¶ 5/9-207	
Indiana	30 days	30 days	Ind. Code Ann. § 32-7-1-3	
Iowa	30 days	30 days	Iowa Code Ann. §§ 562A.34, 562A.13.5	
Kansas	30 days	30 days	Kan. Stat. Ann. § 58-2570	No state statute on the amount of notice required to change rent or other terms.
Kentucky	30 days	30 days	Ky. Rev. Stat. Ann. § 383.695	
Louisiana	10 days	10 days	La. Civ. Code Ann. art. 2686	No state statute on the amount of notice required to change rent or other terms.
Maine	30 days	30 days	Me. Rev. Stat. Ann. tit. 14 § 6002	
Maryland	30 days	30 days	Md. Code Ann. [Real Prop.] § 8-402	
Massachusetts	30 days	30 days	Mass. Gen. Laws Ann. ch. 186 § 12	
Michigan	30 days	30 days	Mich. Comp. Laws Ann. § 554.134	No state statute on the amount of notice required to change rent or other terms.
Minnesota	30 days	30 days	Minn. Stat. Ann. § 504A.225	No state statute on the amount of notice required to change rent or other terms.
Mississippi	30 days	30 days	Miss. Code. Ann. § 89-8-19	No state statute on the amount of notice required to change rent or other terms.
Missouri	30 days	30 days	Mo. Ann. Stat. § 441.060	No state statute on the amount of notice required to change rent or other terms.

Notice Required to Change or Terminate a Month-to-Month Tenancy (continued)

State	Tenant	Landlord	Statute	Comments
Montana	30 days	30 days	Mont. Code Ann. § 70-24-441	No state statute on the amount of notice required to change rent or other terms.
Nebraska	30 days	30 days	Neb. Rev. Stat. § 76-1437	No state statute on the amount of notice required to change rent or other terms.
Nevada	30 days	30 days 118A.300	Nev. Rev. Stat. Ann. §§ 40.251, to increase rent.	Landlords must provide 45 days' notice
New Hampshire	30 days	30 or 7 days	N.H. Rev. Stat. Ann. §§ 540:2 and 540:3	Landlord may terminate only for just cause.
New Jersey	No statute	No statute	No statute	Landlord may terminate only for just cause.
New Mexico	30 days	30 days	N.M. Stat. Ann. § 47-8-37	Landlord most deliver rent increase notice at least 30 days before rent due date.
New York	one month	one month	N.Y. Cons. Laws Real Property § 232-b	No state statute on the amount of notice required to change rent or other terms.
North Carolina	7 days	7 days	N.C. Gen. Stat. § 42-14	No state statute on the amount of notice required to change rent or other terms.
North Dakota	30 days	30 days	N.D. Cent. Code § 47-16-15	Tenant may terminate with 25 day's notice if landlord has changed the terms of the lease.
Ohio	30 days	30 days	Ohio Rev. Code Ann. § 5321.17	No state statute on the amount of notice required to change rent or other terms.
Oklahoma	30 days	30 days	Okla. Stat. tit. 41 § 111	No state statute on the amount of notice required to change rent or other terms.
Oregon	30 days	30 days	Or. Rev. Stat. § 91.060	
Pennsylvania	No statute	No statute	No statute	
Rhode Island	30 days	30 days	R.I. Gen. Laws §§ 34-18-16.1 and 34-18-37	
South Carolina	30 days	30 days	S.C. Code Ann. § 27-40-770	No state statute on the amount of notice required to change rent or other terms.
South Dakota	30 days	30 days	S.D. Codified Laws Ann. §§ 43-32-13and 43-32-22	Tenant can terminate within 15 days of receiving landlord's modification notice
Tennessee	30 days	30 days	Tenn. Code Ann. § 66-28-512	No state statute on the amount of notice required to change rent or other terms.
Texas	30 days	30 days	Tex. [Prop.] Code Ann. § 91.001 (but only if property is sold)	No state statute on the amount of notice required to change rent or other terms.
Utah	No statute	No statute	No statute	
Vermont	30 days	30 days	Vt. Code Ann. tit. 9 § 4467, 4456	If there is no written rental agreement, the landlord must provide 60 days' notice to notice to terminate (but only 30 days if property is sold). Landlord must give 60 days' notice to incease rent.
Virginia	30 days	30 days	Va. Code Ann. § 55-248-37	No state statute on the amount of notice required to change rent or other terms.
Washington	30 days	20 days	Wash. Rev. Code Ann. §§ 555.248.37, 59.18.200, 59.18.140, 59.18.352	Tenant may terminate without notice if threatened with a weapon by another tenant and landlord fails to begin an eviction proceeding within seven days of the arrest of that tenant.
West Virginia	30 days	30 days	W. Va. Code § 37-6-5	No state statute on the amount of notice required to change rent or other terms.
Wisconsin	28 days	28 days	Wis. Stat. Ann. § 704.19	No state statute on the amount of notice required to change rent or other terms.
Wyoming	No statute	No statute	No statute	

State Laws Prohibiting Landlord Retaliation

This chart lists states that do not allow landlords to retaliate—by eviction, rent hikes or other negative treatment—when tenants complain about living conditions, exercise legal rights such as the use of repair and deduct statutes and rent withholding and organize other tenants.

State	Tenant's Complaint to Landlord or Government Agency	Tenant's Involvement in Tenants' Organization	Tenant's Exercise of a Legal Right	Retaliation Is Presumed If Negative Reaction by Landlord Within Specified Time of Tenant's Act	Statute
Alabama					No statute
Alaska	✔	✔	✔		Alaska Stat. § 34.03.310
Arizona	✔	✔		6 months	Ariz. Rev. Stat. § 33-1381
Arkansas	✔				Ark. Stat. Ann. § 20-27-608
California	✔	✔	✔	6 months	Cal. Civ. Code §§ 1942.5, 1942.5a
Colorado					No statute
Connecticut	✔	✔	✔	6 months	Conn. Gen. Stat. §§ 47a-20, 47a-33
Delaware	✔	✔	✔	90 days	Del. Code Ann. tit. 25 § 5516
D.C.	✔	✔	✔	6 months	D.C. Code § 45-2552
Florida	✔	✔			Fla. Stat. § 83.64
Georgia					No statute
Hawaii	✔				Hw. Rev. Stat. § 521-74
Idaho	✔				Idaho Code § 55-2015; *Wright v. Brady*, 126 Idaho 671, 889 P.2d 105. (Ct. App. 1995).
Illinois	✔				765 Ill. Comp. Stat. 720/1
Indiana					No statute
Iowa	✔	✔		1 year	Iowa Code § 562A.36
Kansas	✔	✔			Kan. Stat. Ann. § 58-2572
Kentucky	✔	✔		1 year	Ky. Rev. Stat. § 383.705
Louisiana					No statute
Maine	✔		✔	6 months	14 Me. Rev. Stat. § 6001
Maryland	✔	✔	✔		Md. Real Property Code Ann. § 8-208.1
Massachusetts	✔	✔	✔	6 months	Mass. Ann. Laws ch. 239 § 2A; ch. 186 § 18
Michigan	✔	✔	✔	90 days	Mich. Stat. Ann. § 27A.5720
Minnesota	✔		✔	90 days	Minn. Stat. §§ 566.03 & .28
Mississippi					No statute

State Laws Prohibiting Landlord Retaliation (continued)

State	Tenant's Complaint to Landlord or Government Agency	Tenant's Involvement in Tenants' Organization	Tenant's Exercise of a Legal Right	Retaliation Is Presumed If Negative Reaction by Landlord Within Specified Time of Tenant's Act	Statute
Missouri	✔		✔		Mo. Rev. Stat. §441.620
Montana	✔	✔		6 months	Mont. Code Ann. §70-24-431
Nebraska	✔	✔			Neb. Rev. Stat. § 76-1439
Nevada	✔	✔	✔		Nev. Rev. Stat. Ann. §118A.510
New Hampshire	✔	✔	✔	6 months	N.H. Rev. Stat. Ann. §§ 540:13-a & 540:13-b
New Jersey	✔	✔	✔	90 days	N.J. Stat. §2A:42-10.10 & 2A:42-10.12
New Mexico	✔	✔	✔		N.M. Stat. Ann. § 47-8-39
New York	✔	✔	✔	6 months	N.Y. Consolidated Laws Real Prop. §§223-b & 230
North Carolina	✔	✔	✔		N.C. Gen. Stat. § 42-37.1
North Dakota					No statute
Ohio	✔	✔			Ohio Rev. Code Ann. 5321.02
Oklahoma					No statute
Oregon	✔	✔	✔		Or. Rev. Stat. §90.385
Pennsylvania					No statute
Rhode Island	✔		✔		R.I. Gen. Laws Ann. §§34-20-10 & .11
South Carolina	✔				S.C. Code Ann. §27-40-910
South Dakota					No statute
Tennessee	✔		✔		Tenn. Code Ann. § 66-28-514 & §68-111-105
Texas	✔		✔		Tex. Prop. Code § 92.331
Utah	✔				*Building Monitoring Sys. v. Paxton*, 905 P.2d 1215 (Utah 1995).
Vermont	✔	✔			9 Vt. Stat. Ann. §4465
Virginia	✔	✔	✔		Va. Code Ann. § 55-248.39
Washington	✔		✔	90 days	Wash. Rev. Code §§59.18.240 & 59.18.250
West Virginia	✔				W. Va. Code §55-3A-1, -3;*Imperial Colliery Co. v. Fout*, 179 W. Va. 776, 373 S.E.2d 489 (1988)
Wisconsin	✔		✔		Wis. Stat. § 704.45
Wyoming					No statute

State Laws on Termination for Nonpayment of Rent

If you are late with the rent, in most states your landlord cannot immediately file for eviction. Instead, you must get written notice that you have a specified number of days in which to pay up or move. If you do neither, the landlord can file. In a few states, the landlord must wait a few days before giving you the notice. And some states, as noted, allow the landlord to file for eviction immediately.

State	Statute	Time You Have to Pay Rent or Move Before Landlord Can File for Eviction	Legal Late Period: How Long Landlord Must Wait Before Giving You Notice to Pay or Quit
Alabama		Landlord can file for eviction immediately.	
Alaska	Alaska Stat. §§ 09.45.090, 34.03.220	7 days	
Arizona	Az. Rev. Stat. § 33-1368	5 days	
Arkansas	Ak. Stat. §§ 18-16-304 and 18-16-101	3 days; and tenant may be prosecuted for a misdemeanor if the rent is not paid after 10 days' notice.	
California	Cal. Code of Civil Procedure § 1161	3 days	
Colorado	Colo. Rev. Stat. § 13-40-104	3 days	
Connecticut	Conn. Gen. Stat §§ 47a-15, 47a-23, 47a-15a	1. 15 days 2. If you are late more than once in a six-month period, landlord can use an Unconditional Quit notice. You have 3 days to leave before landlord can file.	
Delaware	25 Del. Code §§ 5501(d), 5502	5 days	If rental agreement provides for a late charge, but landlord does not maintain an office in the county in which the rental unit is located, due date for the rent is extended 3 days; thereafter, landlord may serve a 5-day notice.
District of Columbia	D.C. Code § 45-2551	30 days	
Florida	Fla. Stat. §§ 83.20, 83.56(3)	3 days	
Georgia	Ga. Code Ann. §§ 44-7-50 and 44-7-52	Landlord may demand the rent as soon as it is due and, if not paid, can file eviction lawsuit. Tenant then has 7 days to pay to avoid eviction.	
Hawaii	Hawaii Rev. Stat. § 521-68(a)	5 days	
Idaho	Idaho Code § 6-303	3 days	
Illinois	Ill. Comp. Stat. chap. 735 para. 5/9-209	5 days	
Indiana	Ind. Code Ann. § 32-7-1-5	10 days	
Iowa	Iowa Code § 562A.27	3 days	
Kansas	Kan. Rev. Stat. §§ 58-2507, 58-2508, 58-2564	3 days or, at landlord's option, 10 days for tenancies over 3 months	

State Laws on Termination for Nonpayment of Rent (continued)

State	Statute	Time You Have to Pay Rent or Move Before Landlord Can File for Eviction	Legal Late Period: How Long Landlord Must Wait Before Giving You Notice to Pay or Quit
Kentucky	Ky. Stat. Ann. § 383.660	7 days	
Louisiana	La. Civil Code Art. 2712	Landlord can file for eviction immediately; tenant has 5 days to vacate.	
Maine	Me. Rev. Stat. tit. 14, § 6002	7 days	Notice cannot be delivered until the rent is 7 days late.
Maryland	Md. Real Property Code § 8-401	5 days' notice to appear in court; if you don't pay and the landlord wins, you have 4 days to vacate. If tenant pays all back rent and court costs before execution of eviction, tenant can stay.	
Massachusetts	Mass. Ann. Laws ch. 186 § 11 & § 12	10 days; additional 4 days to quit if you don't pay.	
Michigan	Mich. Comp. Laws § 554.134	7 days	
Minnesota	Minn. Stat. § 504B.135	Landlord may terminate as soon as rent is overdue; tenant has 14 days to vacate.	
Mississippi	Miss. Code §§ 89-7-27, 89-7-45	3 days, but tenant may stay if rent and costs are paid prior to removal.	
Missouri		Landlord can file for eviction immediately.	
Montana	Mont. Code Ann. § 70-24-422(2)(a)	3 days	
Nebraska	Neb. Rev. Stat. § 76-1431	3 days	
Nevada	Nev. Rev. Stat. Ann. §§ 40.251, 40.253, 40.2512	5 days	
New Hampshire	N.H. Rev. Stat. Ann. §§ 540:2, 540:3, 540:9	7 days, but you must also pay landlord $15	
New Jersey	N.J. Stat. §§ 2A:18-61.2, 2A:42-9	30 days, and landlord must accept rent any time up to the day of trial.	
New Mexico	N.M. Stat. Ann. § 47-8-33	3 days	
New York	N.Y. Real Prop. Actions Law § 711	3 days	
North Carolina	N.C. Gen. Stat. § 42-3	10 days	
North Dakota	N.D. Cent. Code § 33-06-01	Landlord can file for eviction when rent is 3 days overdue. No notice or option to pay required.	
Ohio		Landlord can terminate with an Unconditional Quit notice.	
Oklahoma	41 Okla. Stat. §131	5 days	

State Laws on Termination for Nonpayment of Rent (continued)

State	Statute	Time You Have to Pay Rent or Move Before Landlord Can File for Eviction	Legal Late Period: How Long Landlord Must Wait Before Giving You Notice to Pay or Quit
Oregon	Ore. Rev. Stat. § 90.400(2)(b)	72 hours (3 days) or

144 hours (6 days), but only if lease or rental agreement so provides. | Notice cannot be delivered until the rent is 8 days late.

Notice cannot be delivered until the rent is 5 days late. |
Pennsylvania	Pa. Stat. Ann. § 250.501(G)	10 days	
Rhode Island	R.I. Gen. Laws § 34-18-35	5 days, but tenant can stay if he pays back rent prior to commencement of suit. If tenant has not received a pay or quit notice within the past 6 months, tenant can stay if he pays back rent and costs prior to hearing on eviction.	Notice cannot be delivered until rent is 15 days late.
South Carolina	S.C. Code Ann. § 27-40-710	5 days	
South Dakota	S.D. Codified Laws Ann. § 21-16-1	Landlord can file for eviction after giving you 3 days' notice to move.	
Tennessee	Tenn. Code Ann. § 66-28-505	14 days to pay; you have an additional 16 days to vacate if you fail to pay.	
Texas	Tx. Prop. Code Ann. § 24.005	No statute: Landlord can file for eviction after giving 3 days' notice to move (lease may specify a shorter time).	
Utah	Utah Code Ann. § 78-36-3	3 days	
Vermont	Vt. Stat. Ann. tit. 9, § 4467	Tenant gets 14 days' notice, but the 14 days cannot begin until the 16th day of the rental period.	
Virginia	Va. Code Ann. §§ 55-225, §55-243	5 days. Tenant who pays rent, costs and reasonable attorney fees before the first court date can stay.	
Washington	Wash. Rev. Code § 59.12.030	3 days	
West Virginia	W. Va. Code § 55-3A-1	Landlord can file for eviction immediately.	
Wisconsin	Wis. Stat. Ann. § 704.17	Month-to-month tenants: 5 days, but landlord may also use an Unconditional Quit notice.

Tenants with a lease less than one year, and year-to-year tenants: 5 days (landlord may not use an Unconditional Quit notice).

Tenants with a lease longer than one year: 30 days (landlord may not use an Unconditional Quit notice). | |
| **Wyoming** | Wy. Stat. §§ 1-21-1002 and 1-21-1003 | Landlord can file for eviction when rent is 3 days or more late and landlord has given at least 3 days' notice. No option to pay required. | |

State Laws on Termination for Violation of Lease

Many states give you a specified amount of time to cease the lease or rental agreement violation or move before the landlord can file for eviction. In some states, if you have not ceased or cured the violation at the end of that period, you get additional time to move before the landlord files; in others, you must move as soon as the cure period expires. And some states allow the landlord to terminate with an Unconditional Quit notice, without giving you a chance to cure or cease the violation.

State	Legal Authority	Time Tenant Has to Cure the Violation or Move Before Landlord Can File for Eviction
Alabama		Landlord can terminate with an Unconditional Quit notice.
Alaska	Alaska Stat. §§ 09.45.090, 34.03.220	10 days, except for failing to pay utility bills, resulting in shut-off—then, 3 days to cure (additional 2 to vacate)
Arizona	Ariz. Rev. Stat. § 33-1368	5 days for violations materially affecting health and safety; 10 days for other violations of the lease terms
Arkansas		Landlord can terminate with an Unconditional Quit notice.
California	Cal. Code of Civil Procedure § 1161	3 days
Colorado	Colo. Rev. Stat. § 13-40-104(1)(e)	3 days
Connecticut	Conn. Gen. Stat. § 47a-15	15 days to cure, additional 15 to vacate
Delaware	25 Del. Code § 5513	7 days
District of Columbia	D.C. Code § 45-2551	30 days
Florida	Fla. Stat. §83.56(2)	7 days
Georgia		Landlord can terminate with an Unconditional Quit notice.
Hawaii	Hawaii Rev. Stat. §§ 521-69, 666-3	10 days, except 24 hours to cease a nuisance
Idaho	Idaho Code § 6-303	3 days
Illinois		Landlord can terminate with an Unconditional Quit notice.
Indiana		Landlord can terminate with an Unconditional Quit notice.
Iowa	Iowa Code § 562A.27	7 days
Kansas	Kan. Stat. Ann. § 58-2564	14 days to cure and additional 16 to vacate
Kentucky	Ky. Rev. Stat. § 383.660	15 days
Louisiana		Landlord can terminate with an Unconditional Quit notice.
Maine		Landlord can terminate with an Unconditional Quit notice for rental violations and if tenant has failed to pay rent twice within 12 months.
Maryland	Md. Real Property Code § 8-402.1	30 days
Massachusetts	Mass. Ann. Laws ch.186 §§ 11 and 12	Landlord can terminate with an Unconditional Quit notice.
Michigan	Mich. Comp. Laws § 554.134	7 days
Minnesota	Minn. Stat § 504.B135(A)	Landlord can terminate with an Unconditional Quit notice, which must be as long as the interval between rent or 3 months, whichever is shorter.
Mississippi	Miss. Code § 89-8-13	30 days

State Laws on Termination for Violation of Lease (continued)

State	Legal Authority	Time Tenant Has to Cure the Violation or Move Before Landlord Can File for Eviction
Missouri		Landlord can terminate with an Unconditional Quit notice.
Montana	Mont. Code Ann. § 70-24-422	14 days, except 3 days if unauthorized pet or person on premises
Nebraska	Neb. Rev. Stat. § 76-1431	For all violations: 14 days to cure, 16 additional days to vacate
Nevada	Nev. Rev. Stat. Ann. § 40.2516	For all violations: 3 days to cure, 2 additional days to vacate
New Hampshire		Landlord can terminate with an Unconditional Quit notice.
New Jersey	*Jijon v. Custodio,* 598 A2d. 251 (N.J. Supr. L. 1991)	No statute, but case law requires that the tenant be given an opportunity to cure the violation or condition up to the entry of judgment in favor of the landlord
New Mexico	N.M. Stat. Ann. § 47-8-33	7 days
New York	N.Y. Real Prop. Actions Law § 711(6) & §711(3)	30 days (in cities with a population of 1 million or more) for twice removing the batteries from or disassembling a smoke or fire detector; and if specified in the lease, 3 days for failure to pay taxes or assessments
North Carolina		Landlord can terminate with an Unconditional Quit notice.
North Dakota		Landlord can terminate with an Unconditional Quit notice.
Ohio	Ohio Rev. code § 5321.11	30 days for violations of tenant's statutory obligations concerning health or safety.
Oklahoma	Okla. Stat. tit. 41, § 132	10 days to cure, additional 5 days to vacate
Oregon	Ore. Rev. Stat. §§ 90.400, 90.405	14 days to cure, additional 16 days to vacate; for an illegal pet: 10 days to remove pet
Pennsylvania		Landlord can terminate with an Unconditional Quit notice.
Rhode Island	R.I. Gen. Laws § 34-18-36	20 days
South Carolina	S.C. Code Ann. § 27-40-710	14 days
South Dakota		Landlord can terminate with an Unconditional Quit notice.
Tennessee	Tenn. Code Ann. § 66-28-505	14 days to cure; tenant has an additional 16 to vacate
Texas		Landlord can terminate with an Unconditional Quit notice.
Utah	Utah Code Ann. § 78-36-3	3 days
Vermont	Vt. Stat. Ann, tit.9 § 4467(b)	30 days
Virginia	Va. Code. Ann. § 55-248.31	21 days to cure, additional 9 to quit
Washington	Wash. Rev. Code Ann. § 59.12.030	10 days
West Virginia	W. Va. Code §55-3A-1	Landlord can terminate with an Unconditional Quit notice.
Wisconsin	Wis. Stat. § 704.17(3)	If you have a lease of more than one year: 30 days. Otherwise landlord can terminate with an Unconditional Quit notice
Wyoming		Landlord can terminate with an Unconditional Quit notice.

State Laws on Unconditional Quit Terminations

Every state allows landlords to terminate a tenancy for specified reasons, without giving you a second chance. Some states allow landlords to deliver Unconditional Quit notices for late rent or any lease violation; others reserve this harsh measure only for repeated violations or serious misbehavior, such as illegal activity.

State	Statute	Time to Move Out Before Landlord Can File for Eviction	When Unconditional Quit Notice Can Be Used
Alabama	Ala. Code § 35-9-6	10 days	Violation of any lease term
Alaska	Alaska Stat. §§ 34.03.220 (a)(1); 09.45.090)a)(2)(G), 34.03.220(e), 34.03.300(a)	24 hours	Tenant or guest intentionally causing more than $400 of damage to landlord's property
		5 days	Illegal activity on the premises
		3 days	Failure to pay utility bills twice within six months
		10 days	Refusal to allow the landlord to enter
Arizona	Ariz. Rev. Stat. §§ 33-1368, 33-1377	5 days	Material misrepresentation of criminal record or current criminal activity, or prior eviction record
		10 days	Second violation materially affecting health and safety
		Immediately	Discharging a weapon, prostitution, use or sale of illegal drugs, assaults, any material and irreperable breach of the rental agreement or a breach that threatens harm to others
Arkansas	Ark. Stat. Ann. §§ 18-60-304, 18-16-107, 18-16-101	3 days	Nonpayment of rent
		10 days	Failure to vacate after giving notice (tenant is liable for twice the rent, and can be prosecuted for a misdemeanor)
California	Cal. Code of Civil Procedure § 1161	3 days	Assigning or subletting without permission, committing waste or a nuisance, illegal activity on the premises
Colorado	Colo. Rev. Stat. §§ 13-40-104(1)(e.5), 13-40-107.5	Immediately	Any repeated violation of a lease clause, endangering the landlord or another tenant or their property, commiting a violent or drug-related felony, any criminal act in common areas
Connecticut	Conn. Gen. Stat. §§ 47a-23, 47a-31	3 days	Repeated nonpayment of rent, nuisance, violation of the rental agreement, illegal sublet/occupant, owner move-in, removal of unit from housing market
		Immediately	Conviction for prostitution or gambling
Delaware	25 Del. Code § 5513	7 days	Material violation of lease rule other than nonpayment of rent or same violation repeated within 12 months
		Immediately	Violation of law or breach of the rental agreement that causes or threatens to cause irreparable harm to the landlord's property or other tenants
District of Columbia	D.C. Code § 45-2551(c)	30 days	Committing an illegal act within the rental unit if tenant performed the act or should have known the act was taking place
Florida	Fla. Stat. § 83.56	7 days	Intentional destruction of the landlord's or other tenants' property or repeated unreasonable disturbances
Georgia	Ga. Code Ann. §§ 44-7-50 to 52	Immediately	Nonpayment of rent twice within 12 months, holding over
Hawaii	Hawaii Rev. Stat. §§ 521-71(e), 521-70(c), 521-72, 666-3	Immediately	Holding over, using the dwelling for any purpose other than as a residence, causing or threatening to cause injury, violating housing or building laws concerning health or safety, damaging the premises or allowing another person to do so
		5 days	Failure to abate a nuisance within 24 hours of receiving notice

State Laws on Unconditional Quit Terminations (continued)

State	Statute	Time to Move Out Before Landlord Can File for Eviction	When Unconditional Quit Notice Can Be Used
Idaho	Idaho Code § 6-303	3 days	Assigning or subletting without the consent of the landlord or causing serious damage to the property
Illinois	Ill. Rev. Stat. chap. 735 para. 5/9-210, chap. 740 para. 40/11	10 days	Failure to abide by any term of the lease
		5 days	Unlawful use or sale of any controlled substance
Indiana	Ind. Code Ann. § 32-7-1-7	Immediately	Nonpayment of rent, holdover tenants, committing waste
Iowa	Iowa Code Ann. §§ 562A.27, 562A.27A	3 days	Creating a clear and present danger to the health or safety of the landlord, tenants or neighbors within 1,000 feet of the property boundaries, possession of a controlled substance
		7 days	Second material noncompliance with a rented term within 6 months (written notice for first violation required)
Kansas	Kan. Stat. Ann. § 58-2564	30 days	Failure to correct a material violation of the lease (or repeating the same violation) within 14 days of being notified
Kentucky	Ky. Rev. Stat. § 383.660	14 days	Repeating the same material violation of the lease within 6 months of being given a first cure or quit notice
Louisiana	La. Civil Code Arts. 2712, 2729	Immediately	Failure to pay rent or fulfill your legal obligations
Maine	Me. Rev. Stat. Ann. tit. 14, § 6002	7 days	Violations of law, damage to the premises or maintaining a nuisance
Maryland	Md. Real Prop. Code Ann. § 8-401(e)	Immediately	Third court judgment within 12 months for nonpayment of rent
Massachusetts	Mass. Gen. Laws Ann. Ch. 186 § 11	14 days	Receiving a second notice to pay rent or quit within one year
Michigan	Mich. Comp. Laws Ann. § 554.134	7 days	Willfully or negligently causing a serious and continuing health hazard or damage to the premises or possession of illegal drugs (but landlord must first file a police report)
Minnesota	Minn. Stat. § 504B.135, 540B.171	Immediately	Nonpayment of rent (tenant has 14 days to vacate), violation of a condition of the lease, allowing drugs, prostitution, unlawful firearm possession or stolen property on the premises
Mississippi	Miss. Code Ann. §§ 89-8-13, 89-8-25	14 days	Repeating the same act, which is a violation of tenant's statutory duties, within 6 months (notice of first violation required); includes tenant's duties to maintain property and not engage in illegal acts upon the premises
Missouri	Mo. Ann. Stat. §§ 441.030, 441.040	10 days	Assigning or subletting without consent, seriously damaging the premises or violating the lease
		5 days	Drug activity by someone other than the tenant
	Mo. Ann. Stat. §§ 441.020, 441.710 et seq., 535.020	Immediately	Using the premises for gambling, prostitution or sale or use of a controlled substance; nonpayment of rent
Montana	Mont. Code Ann. § 70-24-422	5 days	Repeating the same act—which constituted a lease violation and for which notice was given—within 6 months; or destroying or removing any part of the premises
Nebraska	Neb. Rev. Stat. § 76-1431(1)	14 days	Repeating the same act—which constituted a lease violation and for which notice was given—within 6 months
Nevada	Nev. Rev. Stat. Ann. §§ 40.2514, 40.2516	3 days	Assigning or subletting in violation of the lease, substantial damage to the property, conducting an unlawful business, permitting or creating a nuisance or unlawful possession for sale, manufacture or distribution of illegal drugs
		Immediately	Violation of a lease term where the consequences cannot be undone

State Laws on Unconditional Quit Terminations (continued)

State	Statute	Time to Move Out Before Landlord Can File for Eviction	When Unconditional Quit Notice Can Be Used
New Hampshire	N.H. Rev. Stat. Ann. §§ 540:2, 540:3, 540:9	7 days	Causing substantial damage to premises, behavior that adversely affects the health and safety of other tenants, third notice for non-payment of rent within 12 months
		30 days	Failure to comply with a material term of lease
New Jersey	N.J .Stat. §§ 2A:18-53, 2A:18-61.2, 2A:18-61.1	3 days	Disorderly conduct; willful or grossly negligent destruction of landlord's property; assaults upon or threats against the landlord; termination of tenant's employment as a building manager, janitor or other employee of the landlord; conviction for use, possession or manufacture of an illegal drug either on the property or adjacent to it within the last two years *unless* the tenant has entered a rehabilitation program (includes harboring anyone so convicted)
		30 days	Habitual failure to pay rent; continued violations, despite repeated warnings, of the landlord's reasonable rules and regulations
New Mexico	N.M. Stat. Ann § 47-8-33	3 days	Substantial violation of the lease
		7 days	Repeated violation of a term of the rental agreement within 6 months
New York	N.Y. Laws Real Prop. Actions Law § 711(5)	Immediately	Using the premises for illegal purposes; being adjudicated a bankrupt by a court (questionable validity)
North Carolina	N.C. Gen. Stat. § 42-26	Immediately	Violation of a lease term that specifies that eviction will result from noncompliance, holding over
	N.C. Gen. Stat. §§ 42-59 to -76; 90-95	Immediately	Tenant or guest engaging in illegal drug or other criminal activity on or near the property, failure of tenant to immediately notify landlord or law enforcement about the re-entry into the tenant's dwelling of someone who has been previously banned from the property pursuant to this law (no criminal conviction or arrest necessary for banned trespasser)
North Dakota	N.D. Cent. Code §§ 33-06-01, 33-06-02	3 days	Violation of a material term of the lease, failure to pay rent or unreasonably disturbing other tenants, holding over
Ohio	Ohio Rev. Code Ann. §§ 1923.02 to 1923.04, 5321.11, 5321.17	3 days	Nonpayment of rent; violation of a written lease or rental agreement; when the landlord has "reasonable cause to believe" that the tenant has used, sold or manufactured an illegal drug on the premises (conviction or arrest not required)
Oklahoma	Okla. Stat. tit. 41, § 32	Immediately	When the tenant has threatened or caused immediate and irremediable harm to the premises or any person and has not remedied the problem "as promptly as conditions require" upon being made aware of it

State Laws on Unconditional Quit Terminations (continued)

State	Statute	Time to Move Out Before Landlord Can File for Eviction	When Unconditional Quit Notice Can Be Used
Oregon	Ore. Rev. Stat. §§ 900.400(3), 166.165, 90.405	24 hours	Tenant, guest or pet inflicting (or threatening to inflict) immediate, substantial personal injury to landlord, other tenants, neighbors or guests; intentionally causing substantial property damage; subletting without permission; committing any act "outrageous in the extreme," including prostitution or manufacture or sale of illegal drugs; intentionally or recklessly injuring someone (or placing that person in fear of imminent danger) because of the tenant's perception of that person's race, color, religion, national origin or sexual orientation
		10 days	Second failure to remove an illegal pet within 6 months
Pennsylvania	Pa. Stat. Ann. tit. 68, §§ 250.501, 250.505-A	15 days (for lease 1 yr. or less, but lease may specify a shorter time)	Violations of the terms of the lease
		30 days (for lease more than 1 yr., but lease may specify a shorter time)	Nonpayment of rent only
		10 days (any tenancy)	First conviction for illegal sale, manufacture or distribution of an illegal drug; or a repeated use of an illegal drug; or the seizure by law enforcement of an illegal drug within the leased premises
Rhode Island	R.I. Gen. Laws §§ 34-18-24, 34-18-36	20 days	Committing an act which violates the lease or rental agreement or affects health or safety twice within 6 months (notice must have been given for the first violation)
		Immediately	"Seasonal tenant" whose lease begins no earlier than May 1 and expires no later than October 15, with no right of extension or renewal, who has been charged with violating a local occupancy ordinance, making excessive noise or disturbing the peace; any tenant who uses the premises to use or sell illegal drugs or commits or attempts to commit any crime of violence on or in any public space adjacent to the premises
South Carolina	S.C. Code Ann. § 27-40-710	Immediately	Repeated nonpayment of rent, allowing illegal activities on the property or failure to maintain the dwelling as required by law
South Dakota	S.D. Cod. Laws §§ 21-16-1, 21-16-2	3 days	Nonpayment of rent, holding over
		Immediately	Committing waste, violations of the lease which are grounds for termination under the lease
Tennessee	Tenn. Code Ann. §§ 66-28-505, 66-28-517	14 days	Repeating an act which violates the lease or rental agreement or affects health or safety twice within 6 months (notice must have been given for the first violation)
		Immediately	Committing a violent act or behaving in a manner that threatens the person or property of other tenants or persons, or allowing others to do so

State Laws on Unconditional Quit Terminations (continued)

State	Statute	Time to Move Out Before Landlord Can File for Eviction	When Unconditional Quit Notice Can Be Used
Texas	Tex. Prop. Code § 24.005	3 days (lease may specify a shorter time)	Any violation of the lease, including nonpayment of rent
Utah	Utah Code Ann. § 78-36-3	3 days	Assigning or subletting without permission, holding over, carrying on an unlawful business on the premises or maintaining a nuisance
Vermont	Vt. Stat. Ann. tit. 9, §§ 4467(a), 4467(b), 4456	30 days	Third time tenant is late with the rent (and has received proper notice) within a 12-month period, any violation of the lease or landlord/tenant law, disturbing other tenants, destruction of premises or fixtures
Virginia	Va. Stat. Ann. tit. 9, §§ 55-225, 55-243, 55-248.31	5 days	Second time tenant is late with the rent (for which he received proper notice) within a 12-month period
		30 days	Material, unremediable breach of the lease or rental agreement or acts which materially and permanently affect others' health and safety
		Immediately	A breach of the lease or rental agreement that is willful or a criminal act, is not remediable and is a threat to the health or safety of others
Washington	Wash. Rev. Code § 59.12.030	3 days	Serious damage, carrying on an unlawful business, maintaining a nuisance
		Immediately	Committing or permitting gang activity on the premises
West Virginia	W. Va. Code §55-3A-1	Immediately	Nonpayment of rent, violation of lease clause, deliberate or negligent damage to the property
Wisconsin	Wis. Stat. Ann. §§ 704.17	14 days (month-to-month tenants)	Failure to pay rent, violation of the rental agreement or substantial damage to the property
		14 days (tenants with a lease of less than one year, or year-to-year tenants)	Failing to pay the rent on time twice within one year (must have received proper notice for the first violation)
		5 days (all tenants)	Causing a nuisance on the property (landlord must have written notice from a law enforcement agency regarding the nuisance)
Wyoming	Wyo. Stat. §§ 1-21-1002, -1003	3 days	Nonpayment of rent, hold-over tenants

State Consumer Protection Offices

Your state consumer protection agency can provide general information and referrals on your state law. Many also provide free written brochures on landlord-tenant law. If brochures are available from a different state agency or organization, we also note that here. Check the publication date of any booklet that you receive and do not rely on outdated information. When a state provides no written materials, the space is left blank.

State	State Consumer Protection Offices (Source for Information Publications, if different)	Phone Number	FAX
Alabama	Office of the Attorney General, Consumer Assistance, 11 South Union Street, Montgomery, AL 36130	334-242-7334 800-392-5658	334-242-2433
Alaska	The Consumer Protection section in the office of the Attorney General has been closed.		
Arizona	Office of the Attorney General, Consumer Information and Complaints, 1275 West Washington Street, Phoenix, AZ 85007	602-542-5673 800-352-8431 602-542-5002 (TTY)	602-542-1275
Arkansas	Office of the Attorney General, Advocacy Division, 200 Tower Building, 323 Center Street, Little Rock, AR 72201	501-682-2341 800-482-8982 501-652-6073 (TTY)	501-682-8084
	(Office of the Attorney General, Consumer Protection Division, 200 Catkett-Prien Building, 323 Center Street/Little Rock, AR 72201)	800-482-8982	501-682-8084
California	Department of Consumer Affairs, Consumer Assistance Office, 400 R Street, Room 1040, Sacramento, CA 95814	916-445-1254 800-344-9940	
Colorado	Office of the Attorney General, Consumer Protection Unit, 1525 Sherman Street, 5th Floor, Denver, CO 80203	303-866-5189 800-332-2071	303-866-5691
	(Housing Information & Referral Services, 1905 Sherman Street, Suite 920, Denver, CO 80203)	303-831-1935	
Connecticut	Department of Consumer Protection, 165 Capitol Avenue, Hartford, CT 06106	800-842-2649 203-566-2534	203-566-1531
	(Department of Banking, 260 Constitution Plaza, Hartford, CT 06103)	203-240-8200	203-240-8178
Delaware	Department of Justice, Consumer Protection Unit, 820 North French Street, 4th Fl., Wilmington, DE 19801	302-577-3250	302-577-6499
District of Columbia	Department of Consumer and Regulatory Affairs, 614 H Street NW, Room 1120, Washington, DC 20001	202-727-7120	202-727-8073
Florida	Division of Consumer Services, Department of Agriculture and Consumer Services, 407 S. Calhoun St., Room 235, Tallahassee, FL 32399	800-435-7352 904-488-2221	904-487-4177

State Consumer Protection Offices (continued)

State	State Consumer Protection Offices (Source for Information Publications, if different)	Phone Number	FAX
Georgia	Governor's Office of Consumer Affairs, 2 Martin Luther King Jr. Drive, S.E., Plaza Level-East Tower, Atlanta, GA 30344	404-651-8600 404-656-3790	404-651-9018
	(Georgia Housing & Finance Authority, Tenant/Landlord Authority, 60 Executive Park South, NE, Suite 250, Atlanta, GA 30329-2231)	404-679-4840	404-679-4837
Hawaii	Department of Commerce and Consumer Affairs, Office of Consumer Protection, 828 Fort St. Mall, Suite 600 B, P.O. Box 3767, Honolulu, HI 96813	808-586-2636	808-586-2640
Idaho	Office of the Attorney General, Consumer Protection Division, 210 State House, P.O. Box 83720, Boise, ID 83720-1000	208-334-2424 800-432-3545	208-334-2840
Illinois	Office of the Attorney General, Consumer Protection Division, 100 West Randolph, 12th Floor, Chicago, IL 60601	312-814-3000 800-252-8666	
Indiana	Office of the Attorney General, Consumer Protection Division, Indiana Gov't Center South, 5th Floor, 402 West Washington, Indianapolis, IN 46204-2270	317-232-6330 800-382-5516	317-232-7979
Iowa	Office of the Attorney General, Consumer Protection Division, Hoover State Office Building, Des Moines, IA 50319	515-281-5926	515-281-6771
Kansas	Office of the Attorney General, Consumer Protection Division, Kansas Judicial Center, 2nd Floor, Topeka, KS 66612	913-296-3751 800-432-2310	913-291-3699
Kentucky	Consumer Protection Division, Office of Attorney General, P.O. Box 2000, Frankfort, KY 40602-2000	502-564-2200 800-432-9257	
Louisiana	Office of the Attorney General, Consumer Protection Section, P.O. Box 94095, Baton Rouge, LA 70804-9095	504-342-9638	504-342-9637
Maine	Department of the Attorney General, Public Protection Unit, 6 State House Station, Augusta, ME 04333-0006	800-332-8529 207-624-8527	207-582-7699
Maryland	Office of the Attorney General, Consumer Protection Division, 200 St. Paul Place, Baltimore, MD 21202-2022	410-528-8662	410-576-6566
Massachusetts	Office of the Attorney General, Consumer Complaint & Information Section, 1 Ashburton Place, Boston, MA 02108	617-727-5765	617-227-5765
Michigan	Office of the Attorney General, Consumer Protection Division, P.O. Box 30213, Lansing, MI 48909	517-373-1140	517-241-1850
Minnesota	Office of the Attorney General, Consumer Services Division, 1400 NCL Tower, 445 Minnesota Street, St. Paul, MN 55101-2130	612-296-3353 800-657-3787	612-297-4193

	State Consumer Protection Offices (continued)		
State	**State Consumer Protection Offices (Source for Information Publications, if different)**	**Phone Number**	**FAX**
Mississippi	Office of the Attorney General, Consumer Protection Division, P.O. Box 22947, Jackson, MS 39225-2947	601-359-4230 800-281-4418	601-359-4198
Missouri	Office of the Attorney General, Consumer Protection Division, P.O. Box 899, Jefferson City, MO 65102	314-751-3321 800-392-8222	314-751-7948
Montana	Department of Commerce, Consumer Affairs Unit, 1424 Ninth Avenue, Helena, MT 59620	406-444-3553	406-444-2903
Nebraska	Office of the Attorney General, Consumer Protection Division, 2115 State Capitol Building, P.O. Box 98920, Lincoln, NB 68509-8920	402-471-2682	402-471-3297
Nevada	Commissioner of Consumer Affairs, Department of Business and Industry, State Mail Room Complex, Las Vegas, NV 89158	702-486-7355	702-486-7901
New Hampshire	Department of Justice, Consumer Protection Bureau, 33 Capitol Street, Concord, NH 03301	603-271-3641	603-271-2110
	(New Hampshire Legal Assistance, 15 Green Street, Concord, NH 03301)	603-224-3333	603-224-6067
New Jersey	Consumer Protection Office, 124 Halsey St., Newark, NJ 07101	201-504-6534	201-648-3538
	(Administrative Division of the Courts, Civil Practice Division, R.J.H. Justice Complex, Courts Building, 7th Floor CN 037, Trenton, NJ 08625)	609-984-0275	609-292-3320
New Mexico	Office of the Attorney General, Consumer Protection Division, P.O. Drawer 1508, Santa Fe, NM 87504	505-827-6060 800-678-1508	505-827-5826
New York	Assistant Attorney General, Bureau of Consumer Fraud and Protection, Office of Attorney General, State Capital, Albany, NY 12223-12224	518-474-5481	
North Carolina	Office of the Attorney General, Consumer Protection Section, Department of Justice, P.O. Box 629, Raleigh, NC 27602	919-733-7741	919-715-0577
North Dakota	Office of the Attorney General, Consumer Protection Division, 600 East Boulevard, Bismarck, ND 58505-0400	701-224-3404 800-472-2600	
Ohio	Office of the Attorney General, Consumer Protection Division, State Office Tower, 30 East Broad Street, 25th Floor, Columbus, OH 43215-3428	614-466-4986 800-282-0515	
	(Ohio Legal Services Association, 861 North High Street, Columbus, OH 43215)	614-299-2114 800-589-5888	
Oklahoma	Office of the Attorney General, Consumer Affairs Division, 2300 N. Lincoln Blvd., Oklahoma City, OK 73105-3498	405-521-4274	405-528-1867

State Consumer Protection Offices (continued)

State	State Consumer Protection Offices (Source for Information Publications, if different)	Phone Number	FAX
Oregon	Department of Justice, Financial Fraud Division, 1162 Court Street, NE, Salem, OR 97310	503-378-4732	503-373-7067
Pennsylvania	Office of the Attorney General, Bureau of Consumer Protection, Strawberry Square, 14th Floor, Harrisburg, PA 17120	717-787-9707 800-441-2555	717-787-8242
Rhode Island	Department of the Attorney General, Consumer Protection Division, 72 Pine St., Providence, RI 02903	401-277-4400	401-277-1331
South Carolina	Department of Consumer Affairs, 1101 Williams Street, Columbia, SC 29211	803-734-3970 800-922-1594	803-734-9365
South Dakota	Office of the Attorney General, Division of Consumer Affairs, State Capitol Building, 500 East Capitol, Pierre, SD 57501	605-773-4400 800-300-1986	605-773-4106
Tennessee	Department of Commerce and Insurance, Division of Consumer Affairs, 500 James Robertson Parkway, 5th Floor, Nashville, TN 37243-0600	615-741-3491 800-342-8385	615-741-4747
Texas	Office of the Attorney General, Consumer Protection Division, P.O. Box 12548, Austin, TX 78711	512-463-2070	512-463-2063
Utah	Division of Consumer Protection, Dept. of Commerce, 160 East 300 South, P.O. Box 45804, Salt Lake City, UT 84145-0804	801-530-6001	801-530-6601
Vermont	Office of the Attorney General, Consumer Assistance, 109 State Street, Montpelier, VT 05609-1001	802-828-3171 800-649-2424	802-828-2154
Virginia	Department of Agriculture and Consumer Services, Office of Consumer Affairs, 1100 Bank St., Richmond, VA 23219	804-786-2042 800-552-9963	804-371-7479
Washington	Office of the Attorney General, Consumer Resource Center, 1125 Washington Street SE, P.O. Box 40100, Olympia, WA 98504-0100	360-753-6210 800-551-4636	360-586-8474
West Virginia	Office of the Attorney General, Consumer Protection Division, 812 Quarrier St., Charleston, WV 25301	304-558-8986 800-368-8808	304-558-0140
	(West Virginia Legal Services Plan, Inc., 922 Quarrier Street, Charleston, WV 25301)	800-642-8279 304-342-6814	304-342-3011
Wisconsin	Department of Agriculture, Trade and Consumer Protection, Consumer Protection Bureau, P.O. Box 8911, Madison, WI 53707	608-224-4939	608-224-5045
Wyoming	Office of the Attorney General, Consumer Affairs Division, 123 State Capitol Building, Cheyenne, WY 82002	307-777-7874	307-777-7841

Appendix II: Tear-Out Forms

Rental Priorities Worksheet

Address: _____

Contact: _____ Phone #: _____

Rent: _____ Deposit: _____ Other fees: _____

Term: _____ Date seen: _____ Date available: _____

Brief description of rental unit and building: _____
_____
_____

Mandatory Priorities:

☐ _____
☐ _____
☐ _____
☐ _____
☐ _____
☐ _____
☐ _____

Secondary Priorities:

☐ _____
☐ _____
☐ _____
☐ _____
☐ _____
☐ _____

Absolute No Ways:

☐ _____
☐ _____
☐ _____
☐ _____
☐ _____
☐ _____

Other Comments: _____
_____
_____
_____
_____

Apartment-Finding Service Checklist

Name of Company: _____

Address: _____

Phone Number: _____

Hours: _____

Date: _____

1. Description of listings:

   - geographic areas covered _____

   - type of rentals _____

   - total number of listings _____

   - number of new listings/day _____

   - exclusivity _____

   - type of information available/listing _____

   _____

   _____

2. Type of access to listings, cost and duration of service:

   ☐ phone _____

   ☐ fax _____

   ☐ e-mail _____

   ☐ pager _____

   ☐ books available in-office _____

3. Free phone available in office for members' use?   ☐ Yes   ☐ No

4. Other services and costs:

   ☐ roommate referrals _____

   ☐ credit screening _____

   ☐ other _____

5. Percentage of members who find a rental unit through service: _____

6. Refund if rental not found through company: _____

7. Length of time in business: _____

8. Other comments: _____

Rental Application

Separate application required from each applicant age 18 or older.

THIS SECTION TO BE COMPLETED BY LANDLORD

Address of Property to Be Rented: _____

_____

Rental Term: ☐ month-to-month ☐ lease from _____ to _____

Amounts Due Prior to Occupancy

First month's rent .... $_____

Security deposit .... $_____

Credit check fee .... $_____

Other (specify): _____ $_____

TOTAL .... $_____

Applicant

Full Name—include all names you use(d): _____

Home Phone: (_____)_____ Work Phone: (_____)_____

Social Security Number: _____ Driver's License Number/State: _____

Vehicle Make: _____ Model: _____ Color: _____ Year: _____

License Plate Number/State: _____

Additional Occupants

List everyone, including children, who will live with you:

Full Name _____ Relationship to Applicant _____

_____

_____

_____

_____

Rental History

Current Address: _____

Dates Lived at Address: _____ Reason for Leaving: _____

Landlord/Manager: _____ Landlord/Manager's Phone: (_____)_____

Previous Address: _____

Dates Lived at Address: _____ Reason for Leaving: _____

Landlord/Manager: _____ Landlord/Manager's Phone: (_____)_____

Previous Address: _____

Dates Lived at Address: _____   Reason for Leaving: _____

Landlord/Manager: _____   Landlord/Manager's Phone: (_____)

Employment History

Name and Address of Current Employer: _____

_____   Phone: (_____)

Name of Supervisor: _____   Supervisor's Phone: (_____)

Dates Employed at This Job: _____   Position or Title: _____

Name and Address of Previous Employer: _____

_____   Phone: (_____)

Name of Supervisor: _____   Supervisor's Phone: (_____)

Dates Employed at This Job: _____   Position or Title: _____

Income

1. Your gross monthly employment income (before deductions): $ _____

2. Average monthly amounts of other income (specify sources): $ _____

_____

_____

TOTAL: _____ $ _____

Credit and Financial Information

Bank/Financial Accounts	Account Number	Bank/Institution	Branch
Savings Account:			
Checking Account:			
Money Market or Similar Account:			

Credit Accounts & Loans	Type of Account (Auto loan, Visa, etc.)	Account Number	Name of Creditor	Amount Owed	Monthly Payment
Major Credit Card:					
Major Credit Card:					
Loan (mortgage, car, student loan, etc.):					
Other Major Obligation:					

Miscellaneous

Describe the number and type of pets you want to have in the rental property: _____

_____

Describe water-filled furniture you want to have in the rental property: _____

_____

Do you smoke? ☐ yes ☐ no

Have you ever: Filed for bankruptcy? ☐ yes ☐ no   Been sued? ☐ yes ☐ no

                 Been evicted? ☐ yes ☐ no   Been convicted of a crime? ☐ yes ☐ no

Explain any "yes" listed above: _____

_____

References and Emergency Contact

Personal Reference: _____   Relationship: _____

Address: _____

                                          Phone: (___) _____

Personal Reference: _____   Relationship: _____

Address: _____

                                          Phone: (___) _____

Contact in Emergency: _____   Relationship: _____

Address: _____

                                          Phone: (___) _____

I certify that all the information given above is true and correct and understand that my lease or rental agreement may be terminated if I have made any false or incomplete statement in this application. I authorize verification of the information provided in this application from my credit sources, current and previous landlords and employers, and personal references.

_____
Date   Applicant

Notes (Landlord/Manager): _____

_____

_____

_____

_____

_____

Receipt and Holding Deposit Agreement

This will acknowledge receipt of the sum of $_____ by _____

_____ (Landlord) from _____

_____ (Applicant) as a holding deposit to

hold vacant the rental property at _____

_____ ,

until _____ at _____. The property will be rented to Applicant

on a _____ basis at a rent of $_____ per month, if Applicant

signs Landlord's written _____ and pays Landlord the

first month's rent and a $_____ security deposit on or before that date, in which

event the holding deposit will be applied to the first month's rent.

This Agreement depends upon Landlord receiving a satisfactory report of Applicant's references and credit history. Landlord and Applicant agree that if Applicant fails to sign the Agreement and pay the remaining rent and security deposit, Landlord may retain of this holding deposit a sum equal to the pro-rated daily rent of $_____ per day plus a $_____ charge to compensate Landlord for the inconvenience.

_____   _____
Date   Applicant

_____   _____
Date   Landlord

Landlord-Tenant Checklist

GENERAL CONDITION OF RENTAL UNIT AND PREMISES

Street Address   Unit Number   City

	Condition on Arrival	Condition on Departure	Estimated Cost of Repair/Replacement
LIVING ROOM			
Floors & Floor Coverings			
Drapes & Window Coverings			
Walls & Ceilings			
Light Fixtures			
Windows, Screens & Doors			
Front Door & Locks			
Fireplace			
Other			
Other			
KITCHEN			
Floors & Floor Coverings			
Walls & Ceilings			
Light Fixtures			
Cabinets			
Counters			
Stove/Oven			
Refrigerator			
Dishwasher			
Garbage Disposal			
Sink & Plumbing			
Windows, Screens & Doors			
Other			
Other			
DINING ROOM			
Floors & Floor Covering			
Walls & Ceilings			
Light Fixtures			
Windows, Screens & Doors			
Other			

	Condition on Arrival			Condition on Departure			Estimated Cost of Repair/Replacement
BATHROOM(S)	Bath 1	Bath 2		Bath 1	Bath 2		
Floors & Floor Coverings							
Walls & Ceilings							
Windows, Screens & Doors							
Light Fixtures							
Bathtub/Shower							
Sink & Counters							
Toilet							
Other							
Other							
BEDROOM(S)	Bdrm 1	Bdrm 2	Bdrm 3	Bdrm 1	Bdrm 2	Bdrm 3	
Floors & Floor Coverings							
Windows, Screens & Doors							
Walls & Ceilings							
Light Fixtures							
Other							
Other							
Other							
Other							
OTHER AREAS							
Heating System							
Air Conditioning							
Lawn/Garden							
Stairs and Hallway							
Patio, Terrace, Deck, etc.							
Basement							
Parking Area							
Other							
Other							
Other							
Other							
Other							

☐ Tenants acknowledge that all smoke detectors and fire extinguishers were tested in their presence and found to be in working order, and that the testing procedure was explained to them. Tenants agree to test all detectors at least once a month and to report any problems to Landlord/Manager in writing. Tenants agree to replace all smoke detector batteries as necessary.

FURNISHED PROPERTY

	Condition on Arrival	Condition on Departure	Estimated Cost of Repair/Replacement
LIVING ROOM			
Coffee Table			
End Tables			
Lamps			
Chairs			
Sofa			
Other			
Other			
KITCHEN			
Broiler Pan			
Ice Trays			
Other			
Other			
DINING AREA			
Chairs			
Stools			
Table			
Other			
Other			
BATHROOM(S)	Bath 1 Bath 2	Bath 1 Bath 2	
Mirrors			
Shower Curtain			
Hamper			
Other			
BEDROOM(S)	Bdrm 1 Bdrm 2 Bdrm 3	Bdrm 1 Bdrm 2 Bdrm 3	
Beds (single)			
Beds (double)			
Chairs			
Chests			
Dressing Tables			
Lamps			
Mirrors			
Night Tables			
Other			

	Condition on Arrival	Condition on Departure	Estimated Cost of Repair/Replacement
Other			
OTHER AREAS			
Bookcases			
Desks			
Pictures			
Other			
Other			

Use this space to provide any additional explanation:

_____

_____

_____

_____

_____

_____

_____

_____

_____

_____

_____

_____

_____

Landlord-Tenant Checklist completed on moving in on _____, _____, and approved by:

_____ and _____
Landlord/Manager   Tenant

                                                        _____
                                                        Tenant

                                                        _____
                                                        Tenant

Landlord-Tenant Checklist completed on moving out on _____, _____, and approved by:

_____ and _____
Landlord/Manager   Tenant

                                                        _____
                                                        Tenant

                                                        _____
                                                        Tenant

Agreement Regarding Tenant Improvements to Rental Unit

_____ (Tenant) and

_____ (Landlord)

agree as follows:

Tenant may make the following improvement to the rental unit at _____

_____:

_____

_____

Tenant will accomplish the improvement by using the following materials and procedures:

_____

_____

_____

Landlord and Tenant further agree that (check either 1 or 2):

☐ 1. The improvement will become Landlord's property and is not to be removed by Tenant.

   Landlord will reimburse Tenant for (check a or b or both):

   ☐ a. The cost of material, and/or

   ☐ b. Labor costs at a rate of $_____ per hour, after Tenant provides receipts and the

       Landlord determines that the work has been done in a workmanlike and acceptable manner.

   Landlord will reimburse Tenant (check c or d):

   ☐ c. By lump sum payment, within a reasonable time, or

   ☐ d. By reducing Tenant's rent, according to the following schedule: _____

       _____.

☐ 2. The improvement will be considered Tenant's personal property, and as such may be removed

   by Tenant at any time up to the end of the tenancy. Tenant promises to return the premises to

   their original condition upon removing the improvement. If Tenant fails to do this, Landlord

   may deduct the cost of restoring the premises to their original condition from Tenant's security

   deposit.

_____   _____
Date   Tenant

_____   _____
Date   Landlord

Amendment to Lease or Rental Agreement

This is an Amendment to the lease or rental agreement dated _____, _____,

(the Agreement) between _____

(Landlord) and _____

(Tenant) regarding property located at _____

_____ (the premises).

Landlord and Tenant agree to the following changes and/or additions to the Agreement:

_____

_____

_____

_____

_____

_____

_____

_____

_____

_____

_____

_____

_____

_____

_____

_____

_____

_____   _____
Date   Landlord

_____   _____
Date   Tenant

_____   _____
Date   Tenant

_____   _____
Date   Tenant

Tenant's Notice of Intent to Move Out

_____

Date

_____

Landlord

_____

Street Address

_____

City and State

Dear_____,

Landlord

This is to notify you that I/we will be moving from _____

_____,

on _____ , _____ from today.

This provides at least _____ written notice as required in our

rental agreement.

Sincerely,

_____

Tenant

_____

Tenant

_____

Tenant

Termination of Lease

_____ (Landlord)

and _____

(Tenant) agree that the lease they entered into on _____, for premises at

_____, will terminate

on _____.

_____   _____
Date   Landlord

_____   _____
Date   Tenant

Consent to Assignment of Lease

_____ (Landlord) and

_____ (Tenant) and

_____ (Assignee)

agree as follows:

1. Tenant has leased the premises at _____

_____ from Landlord.

2. The lease was signed on _____, _____, and will expire on

_____, _____.

3. Tenant is assigning the balance of Tenant's lease to Assignee, beginning on _____

_____, _____, and ending on _____, _____.

4. Tenant's financial responsibilities under the terms of the lease are ended by this assignment.
   Specifically, Tenant's responsibilities for future rent and future damage are ended.

5. As of the effective date of the assignment, Tenant permanently gives up the right to occupy the
   premises.

6. Assignee is bound by every term and condition in the lease that is the subject of this assignment.

_____   _____
Date   Landlord

_____   _____
Date   Tenant

_____   _____
Date   Assignee

Index

CATALOG
...more from Nolo Press

	PRICE	CODE

BUSINESS

		PRICE	CODE
⊙	The CA Nonprofit Corp Kit (Binder w/CD-ROM)	$39.95	CNP
▣	Consultant & Independent Contractor Agreements (Book w/Disk—PC)	$24.95	CICA
▣	The Corporate Minutes Book (Book w/Disk—PC)	$69.95	CORMI
	The Employer's Legal Handbook	$31.95	EMPL
▣	Form Your Own Limited Liability Company (Book w/Disk—PC)	$34.95	LIAB
▣	Hiring Independent Contractors: The Employer's Legal Guide (Book w/Disk—PC)	$29.95	HICI
▣	How to Create a Buy-Sell Agreement and Control the Destiny of your Small Business (Book w/Disk—PC)	$49.95	BSAG
▣	How to Form a California Professional Corporation (Book w/Disk—PC)	$49.95	PROF
▣	How to Form a Nonprofit Corporation (Book w/Disk —PC)—National Edition	$39.95	NNP
⊙	How to Form a Nonprofit Corporation in California	$34.95	NON
▣	How to Form Your Own California Corporation (Binder w/Disk—PC	$39.95	CACI
▣	How to Form Your Own California Corporation (Book w/Disk—PC)	$34.95	CCOR
▣	How to Form Your Own Florida Corporation (Book w/Disk—PC)	$39.95	FLCO
▣	How to Form Your Own New York Corporation (Book w/Disk—PC)	$39.95	NYCO
▣	How to Form Your Own Texas Corporation (Book w/Disk—PC)	$39.95	TCOR
	How to Write a Business Plan	$24.95	SBS
	The Independent Paralegal's Handbook	$29.95	PARA
	Legal Guide for Starting & Running a Small Business, Vol. 1	$24.95	RUNS
▣	Legal Guide for Starting & Running a Small Business, Vol. 2: Legal Forms (Book w/Disk—PC)	$29.95	RUNS2
	Marketing Without Advertising	$19.00	MWAD

▣ Book with disk
⊙ Book with CD-ROM

	PRICE	CODE
⊡ Music Law (Book w/Disk—PC)	$29.95	ML
Nolo's California Quick Corp (Quick & Legal Series)	$19.95	QINC
◉ Open Your California Business in 24 Hours (Book w/CD-ROM)	$24.95	OPEN
⊡ The Partnership Book: How to Write a Partnership Agreement (Book w/Disk—PC)	$34.95	PART
Sexual Harassment on the Job	$18.95	HARS
Starting & Running a Successful Newsletter or Magazine	$24.95	MAG
Take Charge of Your Workers' Compensation Claim (California Edition)	$29.95	WORK
Tax Savvy for Small Business	$29.95	SAVVY
Trademark: Legal Care for Your Business and Product Name	$34.95	TRD
Wage Slave No More: Law & Taxes for the Self-Employed	$24.95	WAGE
Your Rights in the Workplace	$21.95	YRW

CONSUMER

	PRICE	CODE
Fed Up with the Legal System: What's Wrong & How to Fix It	$9.95	LEG
How to Win Your Personal Injury Claim	$26.95	PICL
Nolo's Everyday Law Book	$24.95	EVL
Nolo's Pocket Guide to California Law	$12.95	CLAW
Trouble-Free Travel...And What to Do When Things Go Wrong	$14.95	TRAV

ESTATE PLANNING & PROBATE

	PRICE	CODE
8 Ways to Avoid Probate (Quick & Legal Series)	$15.95	PRO8
9 Ways to Avoid Estate Taxes (Quick & Legal Series)	$22.95	ESTX
How to Probate an Estate (California Edition)	$39.95	PAE
Make Your Own Living Trust	$24.95	LITR
Nolo's Law Form Kit: Wills	$14.95	KWL
⊡ Nolo's Will Book (Book w/Disk—PC)	$29.95	SWIL
Plan Your Estate	$24.95	NEST
Quick & Legal Will Book (Quick & Legal Series)	$15.95	QUIC

FAMILY MATTERS

	PRICE	CODE
Child Custody: Building Parenting Agreements That Work	$26.95	CUST
The Complete IEP Guide	$24.95	IEP
Divorce & Money: How to Make the Best Financial Decisions During Divorce	$26.95	DIMO
Do Your Own Divorce in Oregon	$19.95	ODIV
Get a Life: You Don't Need a Million to Retire Well	$18.95	LIFE
The Guardianship Book (California Edition)	$39.95	GB

⊡ Book with disk
◉ Book with CD-ROM

▣ Book with disk
◉ Book with CD-ROM

| | | **PRICE** | **CODE** |

HUMOR

29 Reasons Not to Go to Law School	$9.95	29R
Poetic Justice	$9.95	PJ

IMMIGRATION

How to Get a Green Card: Legal Ways to Stay in the U.S.A.	$24.95	GRN
U.S. Immigration Made Easy	$44.95	IMEZ

MONEY MATTERS

⌨ 101 Law Forms for Personal Use (Quick & Legal Series, Book w/disk—PC)	$24.95	SPOT
Bankruptcy: Is It the Right Solution to Your Debt Problems? (Quick & Legal Series)	$15.95	BRS
Chapter 13 Bankruptcy: Repay Your Debts	$29.95	CH13
Credit Repair (Quick & Legal Series)	$15.95	CREP
⌨ The Financial Power of Attorney Workbook (Book w/disk—PC)	$24.95	FINPOA
How to File for Chapter 7 Bankruptcy	$26.95	HFB
IRAs, 401(k)s & Other Retirement Plans: Taking Your Money Out	$21.95	RET
Money Troubles: Legal Strategies to Cope With Your Debts	$19.95	MT
Nolo's Law Form Kit: Personal Bankruptcy	$16.95	KBNK
Stand Up to the IRS	$24.95	SIRS
Take Control of Your Student Loans	$19.95	SLOAN

PATENTS AND COPYRIGHTS

⌨ The Copyright Handbook: How to Protect and Use Written Works (Book w/disk—PC)	$29.95	COHA
Copyright Your Software	$24.95	CYS
How to Make Patent Drawings Yourself	$29.95	DRAW
The Inventor's Notebook	$19.95	INOT
⌨ License Your Invention (Book w/Disk—PC)	$39.95	LICE
Patent, Copyright & Trademark	$24.95	PCTM
Patent It Yourself	$46.95	PAT
Patent Searching Made Easy	$24.95	PATSE
◉ Software Development: A Legal Guide (Book with CD-ROM)	$44.95	SFT

⌨ Book with disk
◉ Book with CD-ROM

ORDER FORM

Code	Quantity	Title	Unit price	Total
		Subtotal		
		California residents add Sales Tax		
		Basic Shipping ($3.95)		
		UPS RUSH delivery $8.00—any size order*		
		TOTAL		

Name

Address

(UPS to street address, Priority Mail to P.O. boxes)   * Delivered in 3 business days from receipt of order.
S.F. Bay Area use regular shipping.

FOR FASTER SERVICE, USE YOUR CREDIT CARD AND OUR TOLL-FREE NUMBERS

Order 24 hours a day	1-800-992-6656
Fax your order	1-800-645-0895
Online	www.nolo.com

METHOD OF PAYMENT

☐ Check enclosed
☐ VISA   ☐ MasterCard   ☐ Discover Card   ☐ American Express

Account #   Expiration Date

Authorizing Signature

Daytime Phone

PRICES SUBJECT TO CHANGE.

VISIT OUR OUTLET   VISIT US ONLINE!

You'll find our complete line of books and software, all at a discount.

BERKELEY
950 Parker Street
Berkeley, CA 94710
1-510-704-2248

on the Internet
www.nolo.com

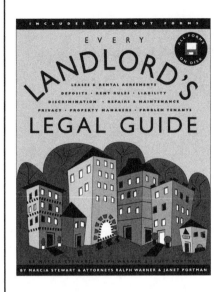

Take 2 Minutes & Give Us Your 2 cents

Your comments make a big difference in the development and revision of Nolo books and software. Please take a few minutes and register your Nolo product—and your comments—with us. Not only will your input make a difference, you'll receive special offers available only to registered owners of Nolo products on our newest books and software. Register now by:

PHONE
1-800-992-6656

FAX
1-800-645-0895

EMAIL
cs@nolo.com

or **MAIL** us
this registration card

REMEMBER:
Little publishers have big ears. We really listen to you.

- - - - - - - - - - - - - fold here - - - - - - - - - - - - -

  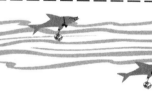

REGISTRATION CARD

NAME _____ DATE _____

ADDRESS _____

_____

CITY _____ STATE _____ ZIP _____

PHONE _____ E-MAIL _____

WHERE DID YOU HEAR ABOUT THIS PRODUCT? _____

WHERE DID YOU PURCHASE THIS PRODUCT? _____

DID YOU CONSULT A LAWYER? (PLEASE CIRCLE ONE)   YES   NO   NOT APPLICABLE

DID YOU FIND THIS BOOK HELPFUL?   (VERY)   5   4   3   2   1   (NOT AT ALL)

COMMENTS _____

_____

_____

WAS IT EASY TO USE?   (VERY EASY)   5   4   3   2   1   (VERY DIFFICULT)

DO YOU OWN A COMPUTER? IF SO, WHICH FORMAT? (PLEASE CIRCLE ONE)   WINDOWS   DOS   MAC

❑ If you do not wish to receive mailings from these companies, please check this box.

❑ You can quote me in future Nolo.com promotional materials. Daytime phone number _____

EVTEN 2.0

NOLO IN THE NEWS

"Nolo helps lay people perform legal tasks without the aid—or fees—of lawyers."
—USA TODAY

Nolo books are ..."written in plain language, free of legal mumbo jumbo, and spiced with witty personal observations."
—ASSOCIATED PRESS

"...Nolo publications...guide people simply through the how, when, where and why of law."
—WASHINGTON POST

"Increasingly, people who are not lawyers are performing tasks usually regarded as legal work... And consumers, using books like Nolo's, do routine legal work themselves."
—NEW YORK TIMES

"...All of [Nolo's] books are easy-to-understand, are updated regularly, provide pull-out forms...and are often quite moving in their sense of compassion for the struggles of the lay reader."
—SAN FRANCISCO CHRONICLE

fold here

- -

> **Place
> stamp here**

**nolo.com
950 Parker Street
Berkeley, CA 94710-9867**

Attn: | EVTEN 2.0 |